Death Notices from Steuben County New York Newspapers 1797-1884

Mary S. Jackson
and
Edward F. Jackson

HERITAGE BOOKS
2006

HERITAGE BOOKS
AN IMPRINT OF HERITAGE BOOKS, INC.

Books, CDs, and more—Worldwide

For our listing of thousands of titles see our website
at
www.HeritageBooks.com

Published 2006 by
HERITAGE BOOKS, INC.
Publishing Division
65 East Main Street
Westminster, Maryland 21157-5026

Copyright © 1998 Mary S. Jackson
and Edward F. Jackson

All rights reserved. No part of this book may be reproduced or transmitted in any form or by any means, electronic or mechanical, including photocopying, recording or by any information storage and retrieval system without written permission from the author, except for the inclusion of brief quotations in a review.

International Standard Book Number: 978-0-7884-0996-4

List of Newspapers

Addison Advertiser	1858 - 1884
Voice of the Nation (Addison, NY)	1855
Steuben American (Bath, NY)	1856 - 1857
Steuben Democrat (Bath, NY)	1843 - 1849
The Constitutionalist (Bath, NY)	1837 - 1842
Steuben Farmers Advocate (Bath, NY)	1831 - 1866
Steuben Courier (Bath, NY	1843 - 1884
Canisteo Times	1880 - 1884
Corning and Blossburg Advocate	1840 - 1843
Corning Democrat	1884
Corning Journal	1847 - 1872
Hammondsport Herald	1874 - 1884
Hornellsville Daily Times	1879 - 1881
Steuben Signal (Hornellsville, NY)	1883 - 1884
Painted Post Times	1870 - 1871
Prattsburgh News	1872 - 1884

Introduction

Newspapers are probably one of the most valuable and interesting sources for genealogy and are too often overlooked by researchers. Not only for the marriage and death notices that are published but many other articles are a valuable source of information. Some newspapers carry family histories of many of the local people. They also print sale of properties, notices of probate, advertising, personal items such as who is ill this week or who visited who, reunions, etc. They can be very entertaining as well as informative.

This volume contains nearly 7,000 death notices from Steuben County New York newspapers from 1797 to 1884 abstracted from microfilm copies available at the New York State Library. Other copies may be available elsewhere. Although these newspapers were published in Steuben County, they include notices for the surrounding counties and Pennsylvania. They also include many notices for those people who moved to other towns in New York or to other states.

Vital records were being recorded by the Town Clerks in New York State beginning in the 1880's. However, recording was not mandatory until 1906. Before 1880 one of the best sources for these vital records are local newspapers for that time period. Verification of the information contained in these newspapers should be made by using a primary source whenever possible. Sometimes mistakes were made in printing and these newspapers are very old and sometimes very difficult to read. It is still one of the best sources available.

Death Notices from Steuben County, NY Newspapers

1797 - 1885

Addison Advertiser

March 10, 1858 - December 25, 1884

WOMBOUGH Albert H. in his 17th yr son of Henry and Rachel Wombough in Addison, NY May 6, 1858

GILES Rulof S. in his 32nd yr in Addison, NY May 2, 1858

OTIS Sarah A. age 19y 5m dau of Galen Otis in Otisville, NY May 15, 1858

MARION Seth age 31y at Father's in Addison, NY June 29, 1858

SEARLES Henry age 27y in Addison, NY June 21, 1858

HIGLEY Helen M. in her 24th yr wife of H. M. Higley at Father's Abram **DUDLEY** in Addison, NY August 9, 1858

WILLAGE Sally age 86y widow of Rev. Elijah Willage of Rock Stream, NY January 1, 1859. Names dau Mrs. J. B. **PRATT** of Corning, NY

DICKERSON Eunice age 73y 11m in Corning, NY January 1, 1859

BROOKS Rev. R. D. Pastor of M. E. Church in Burlington, Pa. January 9, 1859

HOLLIS Oscar B. infant son of F. T. and L. G. Hollis formerly of Addison, NY in Woodhull, NY April 5, 1861

WEATHERBY George H. age 35y in Addison, NY April 29, 1861

SHEPARD Margaret infant dau of Orlando and Ruth Shepard in Hammondsport, NY May 30, 1861

TALERDAY Mary age 16m dau of John Talerday in Corning, NY June 11, 1861

RATHBONE Gen. Ransom age 81y in Rathbone, NY July 17, 1861. Born April 10, 1780 in Colechester, Ct. Father was officer in Revolution. Came to Rathbone 1806

WINCHELL _on T. (illegible) age 22y 14d adopted son of R. C. **TWOGOOD** in Jasper, NY July 17, 1861

NOBLE William of Co. E. 34th Reg. in Washington DC August 2, 1861

WHITTENHALL James age 27y son of late Otis Whittenhall in Belle Plain, Mn. August 27, 1861

PHILLIPS Mary age 26y wife of David Phillips in Addison, NY September 9, 1861

MITCHELL Fred S. age 9m died September 1, 1861 and Edward S. age 2y 9m died September 15, 1861 sons of Dr. J. and A. D. Mitchell in Addison, NY

MANNERS Gertrude B. age 6w 3d died September 28, 1861 and Clara Elsia age 2y 7m died September 29, 1861 daus of William H. and Sarah J. Manners in Addison, NY

LOOP Vivian age 22y 8m wife of Rev. D. C. Loop in Addison, NY December 20, 1861

PECK Esther age 2y 9m dau of John and Esther in Addison, NY December 15, 1861

HOFFMAN Charlotte A. died January 4, 1862 and Sarah E. age 12y died January 19, 1862 daus of Andries and Sarah Hoffman in Addison, NY

STEARNS John age 96y 3m 15d in Canisteo, NY November 25, 1861. Born 1765 in Worcester, Mass. Came to Canisteo in 1794, one of first settlers

ADSHEAD Samuel age 44y in Hornellsville, NY January 10, 1862

JAYNES Jesse age 72y in Caton, NY January 17, 1862

DOUD James M. age 10m son of John Doud and adopted son of Mrs. Sarah Jane **SEWARD** in Corning, NY (Newspaper date January 29, 1862)

HOFFMAN Lester A. age 10m 27d son of Andries D. and Sarah M. in Addison, NY February 12, 1862 and dau Mary J. age 10y 2m 26d died February 19, 1862

KINNEY Miss Kitt age 16y 11m dau of Benjamin J. and Julia Kinney in Addison, NY March 6, 1862

WEED Adelaide in her 22nd yr wife of Mason N. Weed and dau of Almon and Almira **BEEMAN** in Addison, NY March 7, 1862

TWOGOOD R. C. age 53y of Jasper, NY in Addison, NY March 25, 1862

BECHTOL William age 38y in Addison, NY March 28, 1862

FULFORD Sarah suicide in Corning, NY May 14, 1862

SMITH Martha age 15y dau of Richard Smith in Caton, NY October 29, 1862. His 5th child to die of diptheria in 15 days

GRIDLEY Viola age 9y dau of Lewis Gridley in Caton, NY October 31, 1862

BARNARD Frederick age 61y in Corning, NY October 15, 1862

GAYLORD Alonzo age 24y of Co. B. 75th Ill. Vol. son of Willis H. Gaylord of Hornby, NY in Perryville, Ky. October 14, 1862

WHEAT Benjamin P. age 53y formerly of Addison, NY son of Rev. Thomas Wheat in Tonica, Ill. September 30, 1862

BADGER Theodore P. age 39y died November 4, 1862

HEMMENWAY Freddie H. age 8m 7d son of Freeman and Jane Hemmenway in Cameron, NY October 31, 1862

COOPER Lieut. Thomas W. in his 26th yr son of John Cooper Jr. of Coopers Plains, NY in St. Louis, Mo. October 31, 1862

STURDEVANT Edward M. age 31y in Hornellsville, NY November 17, 1862

GRIDLEY Henrietta V. age 7y dau of Lewis Gridley in Caton, NY November 11, 1862. His 4th child to die of diptheria in 18 days

BEACH William R. age 64y in Bath, NY November 18, 1862

STEBBINS Fannie Belle age 6y 5m 20d dau of J. E. and M. M. Stebbins in Owego, NY (Newspaper date December 17, 1862)

HENDERSON Clara Mabel age 13y dau of Charles H. and Harriet E. Henderson in Addison, NY December 25, 1862

ROBBINS John of the 31st Reg. NYV at camp February 12, 1863

WAGNER F. W. of the 107th Reg. buried in Addison, NY February 17, 1863

JONES Nancy E. age 2y 2m 23d dau of Henry S. and Maria Jones in Addison, NY February 23, 1863

JAYNES Albert of the 107th Reg. son of Edwin Jaynes of Hornby, NY at Hospital in Frederick City, Md. last week (Newspaper date March 4, 1863)

BAXTER H. M. in his 9th yr in Woodhull, NY February 8, 1863

SPICER Mary in her 6th yr dau of Michael and Hulda Spicer in Tuscarora, NY March 17, 1863

VAN VALKENBURGH Catherine F. age 40y wife of R. B. in Bath, NY April 27, 1863

ORR Adelbert son of Phillip W. Orr in Addison, NY last week (Newspaper date May 27, 1863)

DEATH NOTICES

BALDWIN Capt. Henry late of 34th Reg. NYV in Addison, NY September 22, 1863

SHERWOOD Catherine age 70y of Woodhull, NY in Bath, NY September 23, 1863. Mother of Hon. Henry Sherwood of Corning, NY

KATHAN Thomas A. age 46y formerly of Addison, NY in E. Greene, NY November 10, 1863

BROWN Cornelia M. age 25y wife of F. B. Brown Editor of the Corning Democrat December 2, 1863

VAN ORSDALE Mellie J. age 3w son of J. C. and Emma A. Van Orsdale in Jasper, NY January 11, 1864

LYNCH Albert Franklin age 22y 10m of Co. E. 141st Reg. NYV January 1, 1864

BATES Edward F. age 23y Surgeon US Vol. son of Mrs. L. D. **COBURN** of Addison, NY in Washington DC March 6, 1864

HORN Katie Dee age 5y 20d dau of Oliver and Kate in Addison, NY March 28, 1864

DUNN Lieut. M. S. of Addison, NY in Co. G. 2nd Vet. NY Cav. (Newspaper date April 27, 1864)

MANDEVILLE James age 19y son of Homer in Tuscarora, NY March 4, 1864

WINSOR Marian age 21y 1m 17d dau of Rev. Ira **BROWN** in Corning, NY May 24, 1864

HOLLIS Georgie age 1y 8m 19d son of Eugene T. and Loretta Hollis in Hornellsville, NY June 28, 1864

BALDWIN Mrs. James age 64y in Addison, NY May 22, 1864

TAGGART George L. age 42y Quartermaster 64th Reg. NYV in Addison, NY May 27, 1864

GRISWOLD Julius killed by cars in Corning, NY July 14, 1864

SHEPARD Georgie age 6y 5m 3d son of George S. and Eliza Shepard in Addison, NY July 17, 1864

HARFORD Tommie P. age 1y 3m son of Fred and Ann Harford of Lincoln, Cal. in Addison, NY July 17, 1864

COLWELL Sally M. age 33y 5m 15d wife of Benjamin in Addison, NY August 5, 1864

PHINNEY Capt. John of Co. K. 86th Reg. NYV at Father-in-law's William **CURTIS** in Addison, NY August 9, 1864 of wounds received at Battle of the Wilderness May 10, 1864. Born June 2, 1836 in Athens, Pa.

ST JOHN Catherine age 69y wife of John T. in Addison, NY August 24, 1864

ROOT Oscar of Co. F. 107th Reg. NYV at Hospital in Louisville, Ky. (Newspaper date September 7, 1864)

KEYES Elijah age 68y in Addison, NY September 16, 1864

COOK Samuel age 85y 7m 8d in Campbell, NY September 8, 1864

LYNCH Sylvester age 16y of Co. G. 21st NY Cav. at Hospital in Natchez, Miss. (Newspaper date September 28, 1864)

MC KENZIE Edward age 67/68y of Orange, NY in Corning, NY November 12, 1864

BALDWIN Pamela age 65y in Pontiac, Mi. November 20, 1864. Came to Addison, NY with Father William **WOMBOUGH** in 1802, married Rufus Baldwin who died 1843 and 2 sons died soon after. Her dau Parmelia W. **STOUT** age 25y wife of Hon. Bryon G. Stout of Pontiac, Mi. died October 28, 1864.

ROBINSON Harriet M. age 32y wife of Charles W. in Tuscarora, NY October 9, 1864

RICE Capt. Burrage of the 2nd Brigade 1st. Div. 5th A. C. January 11, 1865

SHEPARD Marcia M. age 21y 4m 29d dau of J. K. in Addison, NY March 25, 1866

TUTTON James age 31y formerly of Addison, NY in Lacrosse, Wis. March 18, 1866

PHILLIPS Julia age 4y 4m dau of Ransom R. and Susannah Phillips in Addison, NY August 6, 1866

LOGAN Sarah M. age 41y dau of Moses and Melissa **STEVENS** in Hornellsville, NY July 25, 1866

CRAFT Lizzie age 1y 1m 14d dau of Isaac and Cecelia Craft in Addison, NY August 14, 1866

NICHOLSON Sarah E. age 18y 5m 16d dau of J. B. and M. A. **SHURBIN** of Avoca, NY in Hornellsville, NY August 8, 1866

BROOKS Mary E. age 22y 2m 21d dau of William Brooks in Bath, NY August 2, 1866

WHITTENHALL Eliza A. wife of Elihu Whittenhall formerly of Oxford, NY and Mother of Capt. D. S. of St. Louis, Mo. in Albany, Ks. August 23, 1866

KNAPP Duran age 27y in Cameron, NY August 27, 1866

NEWHALL George B. age 4m son of William J. and Jennie E. Newhall in Addison, NY September 29, 1866

SMITH Mrs. David in her 69th yr in Addison, NY November 30, 1866

DEATH NOTICES

BROWN Cora Agnes age 2m 13d dau of Charles C. and Roby Brown in Addison, NY November 25, 1866

CARR Sgt. Amos Jr. age 23y of 2nd NY Vet. Cav. in Tuscarora, NY October 10, 1866

REYNOLDS Thomas J. age 66y in Hornellsville, NY April 30, 1867

WILLIAMS Anna M. age 54y wife of Ira C. Williams in Avoca, NY April 30, 1867. Leaves son Francis A. Williams of Corning, NY

SMITH Darius age 85y Father of Justin M. Smith of Corning, NY in Masonville, NY May 3, 1867

MURRAY Thomas abt 60y formerly of Corning, NY in Somerville, Pa. June 8, 1867

LANE David abt 60y in Corning, NY June 7, 1867

WELLS Adell age 34y 8m 23d wife of S. H. Wells in Penn Yan, NY June 6, 1867

AUSTIN Charles H. age 22y formerly of Co. E. 141st Reg. NYV son of Richard Austin in Corning, NY June 15, 1867

ORR Rosabell infant dau of William H. and Mary J. Orr in Addison, NY July 12, 1867

RUTHERFORD William D. age 48y 2m 25d in Knoxville, Pa. July 18, 1867

MATTESON Le Blanche age 1y 2m 22d dau of Dr. G. W. and A. A. Matteson late of Knoxville in Middleville, Mi. July 8, 1867

WILLARD Enos G. crushed by cars July 29, 1867

SMITH Martha H. age 34y wife of Rollin R. Smith in Addison, NY August 20, 1867

SHARP Mrs. Peggy age 56y in Bath, NY August 23, 1867

SHULTS Bertha age 6m in Bath, NY August 27, 1867

WEBSTER Emma age 15m in Bath, NY August 29, 1867

COSS Charlotte age 48y wife of D. M. Coss in Bath, NY September 3, 1867 and dau Minnie age 6y died September 2, 1867

HOWELL John Magee age 14m son of A. S. and Mary in Bath, NY September 5, 1867

WILLIAMSON Rose age 4y in Bath, NY September 5, 1867

SIMMONS Elizabeth age 19y in Bath, NY September 8, 1867

DECK Urial age 68y in Jasper, NY Friday last (Newspaper date September 25, 1867). Native of Montgomery Co. NY and came to Jasper in 1823

WHITTENHALL Louise L. wife of Henry Whittenhall formerly of Addison, NY in Lincoln, Cal. September 13, 1867

PRATT Cerinthia W. age 73y wife of Joel B. Pratt and Mother of the Editor of Corning Journal at res. of son Claudius B. Pratt in Binghamton, NY October 10, 1867

TRUE Anna age 21y of Addison, NY in Whitesville, NY October 15, 1867

TURK David in Addison, NY Monday last (Newspaper date November 13, 1867)

SCHUE Lizzie age 6y 9m 21d dau of Jacob and Lizzie Schue in Hornellsville, NY November 8, 1867

BEMIS Caroline S. age 43y wife of Horace in Hornellsville, NY November 9, 1867

LAMPHEARE Jabish age 74y in Arkport, NY November 25, 1867

HILL Noah in his 25th yr in Pulteney, NY December 1, 1867

BROWN Elizabeth in her 75th yr in Addison, NY December 30, 1867

ANDREWS Harvey in his 67th yr in Nelson, Pa. January 5, 1868

BOSTWICK E. Dewitt in his 22nd yr formerly of Addison, NY in Janesville, Wis. December 1, 1867

BARREN William in his 78th yr in Rathbone, NY February 28, 1868

MEWYER Mrs. Isaac in Rathbone, NY March 2, 1868

MAGEE John age 73y 7m in Watkins, NY April 5, 1868. Born nr Easton, Pa., lived Livingston Co. NY then Mi., back to Bath and later to Watkins

AMES Ebenezer age 89y of Addison, NY at son-in-law's George **BLISS** in Hornellsville, NY May 21, 1868

FAIRBANKS Lorenzo age 58y formerly of Addison, NY in Osceola, Ill. May 16, 1868

CONGDON Rev. S. L. in Corning, NY May 27, 1868

COLVIN Mary age 29y wife of Stephen Colvin Jr. in Woodhull, NY July 2, 1868

ELDRIDGE Walter Worth age 5m 7d son of Hiram and Jane Elizabeth Eldridge in Addison, NY August 9, 1868

RIDDLE Lemuel C. of Canisteo, NY in Addison, NY August 23, 1868, buried Canisteo

WOMBOUGH Carlotta M. age 1y 2m 13d dau of Addison and E. Velnette Wombough in Addison, NY August 20, 1868

DEATH NOTICES

PRITCHARD Hiram Mc Carty age 1y 1m 14d son of Truman S. Pritchard in Corning, NY August 21, 1868

COBURN Harvey age 74y in Addison, NY August 22, 1868

WILBER Charles H. age 20y son of Martin Wilber in Addison, NY August 28, 1868

WADDELL Samuel of Addison, NY mem. of the 106th Reg. jumped a train in Corning to join Reg. caught and dragged October 16, 1868. Leaves wife and 5 children

WESTCOTT Daniel P. age 45y formerly of Addison, NY son of Arthur Westcott late of Caton, NY in Jamestown, NY October 1, 1868

PARK Estella age 7m 22d dau of James H. and Adelaide Park in Patterson, NJ October 16, 1868

PROTZMAN Nicolas abt 56y in Jasper, NY (Newspaper date December 16, 1868) Born 1812 in Jasper son of Nicolas one of first settlers

SHERWOOD Margaret (**FASSETT**) wife of James in Corning, NY December 10, 1868

MILLER George W. age 5y 10m son of Valentine Miller of Elmira, NY in Corning, NY December 6, 1868

WHEELOCK Olive (**ROCKWELL**) age 50y wife of Marcus M. Wheelock formerly of Corning, NY in Washington DC December 7, 1868

BACHMAN Albert Morgan age 1y 11m 21d son of Maj. M. V. Backman of Horseheads, NY and nephew of Maj. S. M. **MORGAN** of Lindley, NY in Lindley January 3, 1869

NORTHRUP Lusilla age 47y wife of George Northrup of Rathbone, NY at brother-in-law's J. H. **DRAKE** in Elmira, NY January 4, 1869

ADAMS Laura age 8y dau of John Adams in Corning, NY December 30, 1868

GRIFFITHS Mary C. age 26y wife of William E. Griffiths in Addison, NY January 17, 1869 and son Georgie S. age 2w 2d died January 12, 1869

ELDRIDGE James in his 40th yr in Addison, NY February 2, 1869

LANSING James age 70y formerly of Albany, NY at son's Gen. J. H. Lansing in Corning, NY February 15, 1869

CLINTON Harmon in his 67th yr in Erwin Center, NY February 19, 1869

ATWOOD Sarah H. in her 39th yr wife of Urial Atwood and dau of Luke **DARLING** of Colesburgh, Pa. in Woodhull, NY May 4, 1869. Born 1830 in Sullivan, Pa. Leaves husband and 3 children

BIRDSALL Rizpah age 77y widow of James formerly of Addison, NY, Mother of H. H. of Erwin, NY at son-in-law's W. M. **FENTON** in Flint, Mi. May 10, 1869

LYON Julia age 57y at son's David Lyon in Addison, NY (Newspaper date June 2, 1869)

FISHER Miss Fidelia E. age 19y 3m in Fremont, NY May 28, 1869

LORD Daniel in his 70th yr in Corning, NY May 27, 1869

FARWELL Harriet K. age 26y wife of J. K. Farwell and dau of James **ROSE** of Painted Post, NY in Chicago, Ill. May 27, 1869

SERGEANT John age 47y in Knoxville town of Corning, NY June 7, 1869

WOMBOUGH Henry age 69y in Addison, NY June 13, 1869. Born May 26, 1800 in Delaware Co. NY and came to Addison in 1804

GREEN Rachel age 22y dau of J. B. Green in Prattsburgh, NY June 27, 1869

SLY John age 79y in Knoxville/Corning, NY July 5, 1869

GILLETT Elizabeth B. age 75y 6m wife of John in Caton, NY July 18, 1869

ROGERS Lovisa A. age 52y wife of Ephraim P. in Corning, NY July 15, 1869

FLYNN Miss Rhoda age 31y in Bath, NY July 7, 1869

RUTHERFORD William T. age 26y formerly of Addison, NY in Coopers Plains, NY August 4, 1869

OSBORNE Maria age 28y dau of Charles E. Osborne in Corning, NY August 2, 1869

BISHOP John age 62y in Knoxville, NY July 22, 1869

CUTLER Emma age 14m dau of Milton and Mary in Knoxville, NY August 2, 1869

RICE Nathaniel age 69y 2m 26d in Pulteney, NY July 23, 1869

WOOD Sarah age 77y 2m wife of Samuel L. Wood at son-in-law's W. H. **MANNERS** in Addison, NY August 6, 1869

SHARP Isaac E. age 42y in Hornellsville, NY August 5, 1869

WEBB Mrs. Hannah T. age 70y in Hornellsville, NY August 4, 1869

MC GOWAN Edwin age 3m son of James and Maria Mc Gowan in Hornellsville, NY August 7, 1869

BISHOP Lewis infant son of John and Elizabeth in Knoxville, NY August 5, 1869

DEATH NOTICES

MC CANN Sorena age 30y 7m 2d wife of Jackson in Corning, NY August 8, 1869

GREGORY Charles abt 35y in Caton, NY August 9, 1869

FRYMIRE Charles C. age 3y 7m 19d son of Samuel in Knoxville, NY August 3, 1869

PARKS Daniel age 76y in Big Flats, NY July 29, 1869

TOWNSEND Fanny J. age 20y dau of Edward E. in Erwin, NY August 7, 1869

BABCOCK Theodosia age 2y dau of Ezekiel and Mary Babcock in Knoxville, NY August 13, 1869

FIELD Grace age 8m dau of Thomas B. Field in Corning, NY August 5, 1869

HAMILTON Mary E. age 48y wife of Lewis Hamilton and dau of Lyman **BALCOM** of Painted Post, NY in Cedar Rapids, Iowa (Newspaper date August 25, 1869)

ARLINGTON Mary J. age 35y 8d wife of Jonathan Arlington and dau of Albert **LYNCH** in Addison, NY September 22, 1869

WILSON Elizabeth age 37y wife of Alanson in Woodhull, NY October 28, 1869

VAN BINDER Hattie E. age 19y 3m in Canisteo, NY November 18, 1869

FARNHAM Julia J. age 47y wife of Col. George Farnham of Addison, NY at Elmira Water Cure December 27, 1869

SMITH Mrs. Sybil age 69y in Addison, NY December 27, 1869

EATON Elizabeth B. age 39y in Addison, NY November 17, 1869

SMITH Mrs. Josephine dau of William **WESTCOTT** of Addison, NY in Binghamton, NY January 16, 1870

PECK Frankie age 6m 16d son of John and Almyra in Addison, NY February 8, 1870

CONNELLY Patsy of Corning, NY in RR accident at Avon, NY last week (Newspaper date March 16, 1870)

BEARDSLEY Gertrude age 17y 10m dau of Eugene and Helen M. **(WADE)** Beardsley in Addison, NY March 19, 1870

COWLEY Dwight R. in his 38th yr of Woodhull, NY in Addison, NY March 27, 1870

WILCOX Calvin age 53y in Addison, NY April 12, 1870

DURAND Daniel D. age 40y in Addison, NY April 16, 1870

SEXTON Harriet age 48y wife of A. G. Sexton in Addison, NY April 15, 1870

MILLARD Lura Ellen age 13y 8m in Corning, NY April 23, 1870

PURSONS Edula L. age 2y dau of Nathaniel and Martha in Hornby, NY April 20, 1870

GORTON Mary E. age 24y dau of Thomas and Anna **SMITH** in Corning, NY April 30, 1870

DRAKE George W. age 50y 3m in Cohocton, NY April 27, 1870

HIGGINS William C. age 42y formerly of Bath, NY in Rocktown, Pa. May 2, 1870

EASON Hart age 60y in Canisteo, NY March 22, 1870

THURBER Benjamin H. in his 51st yr in Corning, NY April 30, 1870

VAN ETTEN Martha age 24y wife of Andrew Van Etten in Gibson, NY May 1. 1870

HANDEE Lucina C. in her 20th yr wife of Myron in Hartsville, NY April 27, 1870

CLARK Ella age 14y dau of Sawyer and Eydia in Canisteo, NY April 30, 1870

DAVIDSON Susan J. age 5y 9m died February 4, 1869, Mary Estelle age 3y 3m 12d died May 27, 1870 and Clara Bell age 1y 4m (no date) all children of George W. and Alice Davidson of Addison, NY

WILEY Sarah A. in Bath, NY May 22, 1870

HARRIS Esther A. age 24y in Hornellsville, NY May 14, 1870

BULLOCK Arthur La Grand age 1y 8m died May 28, 1870 and Martha L. in her 3rd yr died June 2, 1870 in Tuscarora, NY

GRISWOLD Franklin N. in his 27th yr son of Chester N. and Sophronia Griswold natives of Addison, NY in Woodhull, NY June 18, 1870, formerly of 21st Vet. Cav.

KINNE Jennie E. age 2y 4m dau of George P. and Catherine E. Kinne in Addison, NY June 28, 1870

KINNE Letitia age 33y dau of Alfred and Harriet Kinne in Addison, NY July 9, 1870

DELAMATER Abram age 60y formerly of Addison, NY in Woodhull, NY July 7, 1870

MC CAIG Richard age 20y 6m 26d in Woodhull, NY August 13, 1870

WALTON Margaret age 74y wife of Edward Walton in Cameron, NY August 24, 1870

KELLOGG Josie H. age 7m dau of George and Mary in Addison, NY August 26, 1870

JONES Anna age 72y wife of Samuel Jones in Howard, NY September 7, 1870

DEATH NOTICES

GRAY Lida age 16y 10m dau of Andrew Gray in Painted Post, NY August 28, 1870

WELLMAN Lucy age 76 wife of Lemuel Wellman in Corning, NY August 25, 1870

CARR Amos age 71y in S. Addison, NY September 25, 1870

KNAPP Lily age 9y dau of George W. Knapp in Corning, NY September 21, 1870

BUMP Sarah D. age 36y 4m wife of Benoni F. Bump in Corning, NY September 19, 1870. Buried Livonia, NY

DAVIS Sarah age 30y wife of Darius Davis at res of John N. Davis in Corning, NY October 1, 1870

WOLCOTT Pantha age 21y dau of Frederick W. Wolcott of Corning, NY in Winchester, Ohio October 11, 1870

WILLIAMS John A. in his 80th yr in Woodhull, NY October 10, 1870

BOYD Henry age 8y son of John Boyd in Prattsburgh, NY October 9, 1870

HARFORD Rolla age 5y 11d only son of Frederick and Ann A. Harford in Lincoln, Cal. September 23, 1870

HORN Kate E. in her 29th yr wife of O. A. Horn in Addison, NY October 28, 1870

DATES George age 37y in Corning, NY October 31, 1870

HILL Harriet age 40y 6m 7d wife of I. E. Hill in Caton, NY October 29, 1870

JOSLIN Sylvester in his 88th yr in Oswego, NY October 31, 1870

MONTANYA Mary N. age 38y in Hornellsville, NY October 30, 1870

HELLER Addie age 16y 5m in Hornellsville, NY October 30, 1870

BARRETT Mary age 17y in Hornellsville, NY October 29, 1870

JONES Fred age 1y 2m son of H. S. and Maria R. in Addison, NY December 5, 1870

HOLMES William age 16y in Addison, NY November 24, 1870

STICKNEY Isaac M. age 31y in Morris Run, Pa. November 30, 1870. Leaves wife and 2 children

COOLEY Jesse H. age 44y in Bath, NY November 30, 1870

MINER Laura A. age 21y in Hornellsville, NY December 10, 1870

HEMINGWAY Mark A. age 38y in Hornellsville, NY December 7, 1870

WIXOM Norman age 33y in W. Urbana, NY January 4, 1871

NORRIS Lewis in his 6th yr son of James and Cordelia Norris January 8, 1871

SHEPARD Jesse K. in his 52nd yr in Addison, NY January 19, 1871

LOPER John H. age 78y in Rathbone, NY February 3, 1871

FARRINGTON Phebe Jane age 2m 22d dau of Peter and Eliza S. Farrington in Corning, NY January 25, 1871

GIBSON Nancy age 54y wife of John W. Gibson in Erwin, NY April 16, 1871

DENNIS David in his 71st yr in S. Bradford, NY April 7, 1871

GRAHAM Merlin age 1y 27d son of Miles G. and Sarah J. in Bath, NY May 1, 1871

HAVENS Nathaniel age 79y at son-in-law's J. J. TEFFT in Big Flats, NY April 30, 1871

CRANE Mrs. ___ wife of Rev. E. F. Crane former Pastor Baptist Church at Elmira, NY in Dansville, NY April 29, 1871

FINCH Eliza age 45y wife of Hiram R. Finch in Campbell, NY June 25, 1871

PLATT Andrew nr 25y in Merchantville, NY May 29, 1871

RICE Samuel B. age 42y in Troupsburg, NY July 14, 1871

HOBER J. age 60y in Troupsburg, NY July 15, 1871

JONES Llewellyn age 78y 8m in Addison, NY last wk (Newspaper date August 8, 1871) Res of Addison 60 yrs

HAWKINS Emma F. age 10m 20d dau of Rev. L. T. in Wayland, NY August 6, 1871

PEEK Adam age 78y in Avoca, NY August 5, 1871

ADAMS Rosa age 2y dau of William Adams in Hornellsville, NY August 7, 1871

WALDON John age 80/86y in Caton, NY September 20, 1871

PAYNE Annette age 16y dau of Sylvester Payne in Cameron, NY September 26, 1871

LOZIER Hattie A. age 26y dau of John G. in Troupsburgh, NY September 30, 1871

MILLS Thomas age 90y in Cohocton, NY October 2, 1871

MALLORY Mrs. Harriet abt 40y in Corning, NY October 12, 1871

DEATH NOTICES

MC COLLOUGH Mary age 11y in Wayne, NY October 8, 1871

HUNGERFORD Mary W. wife of John W. Hungerford and dau of Ten Eyck **GANSEVOORT** of Bath, NY in Corning, NY October 24, 1871

HARRISON Emeline age 69y 2m at res of J. E. **WESTLAKE** November 8, 1871

SHERWOOD Mrs. Henry in Corning, NY November 13, 1871

YOUNG Martha age 68y wife of Martin B. Young in Rathbone, NY December 3, 1871

HALLETT William age 52y in Adrian, NY December 1, 1871

DANIELS Mrs. Sophia S. age 26y in Caton, NY December 1, 1871

BEERS Lama age 3y dau of Mrs. Mary J. Beers in Cameron, NY December 16, 1871

ANNABEL Nettie R. dau of Andrew and Amanda in Cameron, NY December 17, 1871

EVERSON William T. age 32 in Bath, NY December 20, 1871

MC KENZIE Hannah M. age 45y 8m 4d wife of Amos Mc Kenzie in Cameron, NY December 24, 1871

HECKMAN Andrew age 21y son of Robert H. Heckman crushed by logs in Thurston, NY January 4, 1872 (Bath paper gives date as December 28, 1871)

PURDY J. age 54y in Jasper, NY February 8, 1872

STRAIT Julia R. age 44y wife of Luke Strait in Tuscarora, NY (Newspaper date February 21, 1872)

BORDEN Maryette age 53y wife of S. B. Borden in Addison, NY February 19, 1872

BARSE Mrs. B. B. in Tuscarora, NY February 18, 1872

HUSTED Gilbert age 16y in Woodhull, NY March 3, 1872

MILLER Parley B. age 66y in Woodhull, NY March 3, 1872

MC CAIG Margaret age 58y wife of John Mc Caig in Rathbone, NY March 9, 1872. Born Scotland

HUSTED Amy age 70y wife of Abram Husted in Woodhull, NY March 16, 1872

BRADY Joey S. age 3y 5m 5d son of J. N. and Hattie Brady in Hornellsville, NY March 31, 1872

JONES Mrs. Edward abt 30y dau of John **COWEN** of Corning, NY in Erwin, NY April 14, 1872

WESTLAKE Henry E. age 4m 8d son of C. D. and Louisa Westlake at res of John Westlake in Addison, NY April 19, 1872

ROGERS Ama age 61y wife of Mathew Rogers in Troupsburgh, NY April 15, 1872

ROBERTSON Lavonia age 26y wife of Almon T. Robertson and dau of James and Anna **SHEPARD** in Corning, NY May 9, 1872

WILCOX William age 82y in Corning, NY April 16, 1872

WARD William F. age 39y in Hornellsville, NY May 2, 1872

TUBBS Mrs. John in Osceola, Pa. June 3, 1872

HATHAWAY Edgar L. in Addison, NY June 14, 1872

ORVIS Enos S. age 13y 6m son of H. Orvis in Addison, NY July 3, 1872

STEVENS Willie A. age 3y 3m son of Isaac and Martha Stevens formerly of Addison, NY in Wellsville, NY July 4, 1872

EDMINSTER Martha E. in her 40th yr dau of Samuel **HATCH** formerly of Addison, NY in Tuscalwa, Ill March 9, 1872

BONNETT Hulda A. age 15y dau of J. D. in Troupsburgh, NY August 16, 1872

HATCH Samuel age 80y formerly of Addison, NY while visiting dau in Humbolt, Cal. August 8, 1872

TOWNSEND Addie age 19y wife of C. Townsend in Troupsburgh, NY August 27, 1872

JAYNES Fanny in her 54th yr wife of A. S. Jaynes in Sonora, NY August 13, 1872

OWEN Hannah on her 71st birthday widow of Lyman in Wayland, NY August 19, 1872

DANFORTH Halsey Jr. age 14m son of H. J. and Harriet M. Danforth in Hornellsville, NY August 26, 1872

HUMPHREYS Amanda age 61y wife of P. D. in Hornellsville, NY August 24, 1872

BAILEY David in his 68th yr in Hammondsport, NY August 20, 1872. Leaves dau Mrs. J. E. **ORDWAY** of Hornellsville, NY

WESTLAKE Ida S. age 11m 15d dau of John A. and Kate Westlake in Addison, NY September 15, 1872

DICKINSON Fanny B. age 8y dau of A. B. C. and Anna Dickinson in Addison, NY September 16, 1872

TURNER Ernest age 5y 2m son of Mrs. J. F. Turner in Addison, NY October 7, 1872

DEATH NOTICES

JONES Reuben age 2y 6m son of James E. and Betsey in Addison, NY October 7, 1872

BARBER Amanda age 11y 8m 19d dau of Washington and Elizabeth Barber in Addison, NY October 4, 1872

MILLER Frank H. age 11y 8m 16d in Addison, NY September 21, 1872

CARR Charles age 16y in Addison, NY October 22, 1872

CURTIS Arthur age 1y 6m son of Eugene and Helen in Addison, NY October 26, 1872

BALDWIN Walter G. age 21y of Glen's Falls, NY in Addison, NY November 6, 1872

SMITH Marietta age 41y wife of William A. Smith in Addison, NY November 5, 1872

ALLEN Ebenezer age 74y in Addison, NY November 6, 1872

FERROW Annie S. age 30y 10m formerly of Addison, NY in Correy, Pa. January 5, 1873, buried Addison. Leaves husband and 2 children

JONES Ellen C. age 62y in Addison, NY January 11, 1873

MANLEY George age 78y in Tuscarora, NY January 19, 1873. Leaves wife and 2 children

ANGELL Mrs. Martha sister of A. **DUDLEY** of Addison, NY in Odell, Ill. January 15, 1873

SCHOTTS John age 77y in Elkland, Pa. February 18, 1873

GUINNIP Thomas H. age 35y of Addison, NY in Rochester, NY February 23, 1873

RUSSELL Mrs. Orrin age 70y in Addison, NY February 21, 1873

WAKELEY May age 6y dau of Mortimer and Anna Wakeley in Brookfield, Pa. February 24, 1873

DREW Asa B. age 64y in Tuscarora, NY March 11, 1873

LUGG Mary A. age 75y wife of Charles Lugg in Farmington, Pa. March 12, 1873

PURDY Nehemiah age 76y in Woodhull, NY March 20, 1873

BIERLY Florence H. age 21y 10m 9d wife of W. R. Bierly in Williamsport, Pa. March 20, 1873

SANBORN Mrs. A. age 66y in Lawrenceville, Pa. March 24, 1873

WILSON Ambrose age 23y in Addison, NY April 14, 1873

DE GRAW William age 82y in Addison, NY April 13, 1873. Native of Orange Co. NY, served in War of 1812

PENCE Mrs. Jacob age 19y 8m in Lock Haven, Pa. May 5, 1873

REYNOLDS James age 61y in Jasper, NY May 5, 1873

MILLER Isaac age 29y in Addison, NY May 11, 1873

SEXTON Thomas G. age 59y in E. Woodhull, NY May 10, 1873

COON Alice age 17y wife of Albert Coon formerly of Tuscarora, NY in Midland, Mi. May 11, 1873

STEWARD Madison age 53 in Woodhull, NY May 24, 1873 (Bath papers please copy)

WESTLAKE Jessie S. age 3y 4m dau of John A. and Kate in Addison, NY July 2, 1873

GUINNIP Lock Winchester age 4m 9d son of W. J. and L. W. Guinnip in Canaseraga, NY August 5, 1873

POTTER Mrs. Lucretia P. age 25y in Troupsburgh, NY August 25, 1873

COLVIN Stephen age 75y in Woodhull, NY September 19, 1873

BELYEA Peter H. age 41y 6m formerly of Addison, NY in Conneaut, Ohio September 16, 1873

BROWN Byron G. age 33y in Corning, NY October 30, 1873

SEARLES Mary H. age 16y in Addison, NY November 2, 1873

ALLINGTON Alice May age 19y 5d in Addison, NY November 12, 1873

SIZER Samuel age 25y in Rathbone, NY January 12, 1874

SMITH Willard O. in his 20th yr in Addison, NY January 27, 1874

WILHELM Harriet E. age 42y wife of John in Addison, NY February 13, 1874

SMITH Sarah Dickson in her 36th yr relict of late Rodney Smith and dau of D. D. MC GEORGE of Oxford, NY in Oxford March 8, 1874

MANNERS Kate L. dau of William H. and Sarah in Addison, NY March 14, 1874

BONIFIELD infant dau of Capt. Samuel and Frances L. Bonifield of San Francisco, Cal. in Addison, NY March 8, 1874

GREEK Isabella age 11y dau of Thomas and Sarah in Erwin, NY March 14, 1874

DEATH NOTICES

ALLEN Eliza J. age 22y 5m 17d wife of Isaac in Annin Creek, Pa. March 17, 1874

STORY Samuel Jr. in Addison, NY March 25, 1874 from chloroform at dentists

PRICE Edith L. age 11y 21d dau of Lewis S. and Lois E. Price in Addison, NY March 12, 1874

WESTLAKE Elizabeth age 79y 1m 14d wife of John E. Westlake April 16, 1874

GREEK Frederick age 6y 7m in Erwin, NY April 13, 1874

LANE Stephen age 61y 1m in Brookfield, Pa. March 31, 1874

THOMPSON Robert in his 30th yr in Addison, NY May 20, 1874

CHASE Clara A. age 21y wife of C. W. Chase in Cameron, NY (Newspaper date June 11, 1874)

GRISWOLD Frederic Leon age 7y in Hornellsville, NY May 28, 1874

HUNT Martha age 77y 6m in Corning, NY May 26, 1874

MALLORY Lemira age 56y wife of John Mallory in Corning, NY May 29, 1874

SEYMOUR Florence age 6y dau of George W. and Martha Seymour in Hornellsville, NY June 1, 1874

SMITH Abigail age 70y wife of George Smith in Corning, NY May 29, 1874

THOMPSON Shadrack age 83y 3m in Coopers Plains, NY May 29, 1874

CRAM Mrs. Lewis age 74y at son-in-law's Isaac **JUNE** in Addison, NY July 21, 1874

ELMER Bertie age 10m son of Sanford and Matilda in Addison, NY July 6, 1874

LAKE Winnie age 3m 1d dau of F. C. and Dema Lake in Addison, NY July 21, 1874

HEMLEY Mary M. age 42y wife of R. C. Hemley in Addison, NY July 24, 1874

WALKER Elizabeth relict of late J. R. Walker and dau of J. T. **BENEDICT** in Woodhull, NY June 27, 1874

LINNELL Minnie age 1y 1m 14d dau of Charles H. and Mary Linnell in Addison, NY July 30, 1874

MASTEN Ella Case age 21m dau of J. H. Masten in Rathbone, NY August 31, 1874

LYON Mary age 58y wife of J. Smith Lyon in Addison, NY September 8, 1874

RICKEY Charlie B. age 4m 15d son of John V. and Frances Rickey in Addison, NY

September 11, 1874

MC MURRAY Nellie age 5m dau of J. H. in Hornellsville, NY January 18, 1875

MURRAY Mrs.Phebe age 85y at res of G. S. **BONHAM** in Osceola, Pa. January 18, 1875

WATKINS Mrs. Evelyn age 86y in Brookfield, Pa. January 22, 1875

DOW Henry S. abt 34y former Editor of this paper in Bay City, Mi. last week (Newspaper date February 18, 1875)

MILLER Sarah H. C. age 35y wife of William G. Miller in Addison, NY March 14, 1875, buried Lawrenceville, Pa.

COLBURN Freddie age 5m 14d son of Oliver and Abbie E. Colburn in Addison, NY March 13, 1875

JONES John R. age 71y in Rathbone, NY March 24, 1875. Funeral at dau Mrs. M. **VAN TUYL**

HORN Jane E. age 27y wife of Oliver A. Horn in Addison, NY March 26, 1875

BROTZMAN George age 57y in Jasper, NY April 8, 1875

SAXTON Gertrude E. age 7m 16d dau of John B. and Mary Saxton in St. Louis, Mo. April 11, 1875

OLMSTEAD Lizzie A. age 5m 16d dau of Samuel and Sarah E. Olmstead in Hedgesville, NY May 22, 1875

SIMMONS Alonzo age 77y Veteran of War of 1812 in Reading, NY (Newspaper date June 17, 1875)

HENDERSON Charles H. age 53y in Addison, NY July 15, 1875

NORTHRUP Peter in Hedgesville, NY July 19, 1875. Born October 10, 1823 in Sussex Co. NJ

SHERWOOD Henry abt 52y of Addison, NY in Avon Springs, NY July 23, 1875 buried Corning, NY. Wife died 4 yrs ago. Leaves brothers and sisters William M. of Woodhull, NY, Hiram of Jasper, NY, Mrs. **EDWARDS** of Bath, NY and Mrs. **DE HUNTER** of Addison, NY

BEARD James at son-in-law's E. K. **POWELL** in Hartsville, NY last Thursday (Newspaper date August 12, 1875) Born Mass.

BROWN Simon age 84y 7m in Addison, NY last Monday (Newspaper date August 12, 1875) Married 62 yrs ago Betsey **BLISS** who died several yrs ago, 6 children, 2 daus live in Addison, Mrs. E. J. **HORN** and Mrs. J. E. **STEBBINS**

DEATH NOTICES

HILL Minnie age 78y wife of Arthur P. Hill in Addison, NY August 12, 1875

COUNTRYMAN Solomon of Jasper, NY at Ft. Plain, NY September 21, 1875

CHATFIELD Judge Andrew Gould formerly of Addison, NY at Belle Plaine, Mn. August 31, 1875. Born January 27, 1810 in Butternuts, NY son of Enos native of Conn. Maternal Grandfather Jonathan **STARR** of Rev. War and maternal Grandmother was a **RUGGLES**. 2 brothers Andrew G. and Levi S. Married June 27, 1836 Eunice E. **BEEMAN** of Addison. Leaves wife and dau Mrs. Robert A. **IRWIN**

CURTIS James in Addison, NY September 28, 1875. Born 1827 in Addison

ROLLS Benjamin in his 37th yr in Addison, NY December 9, 1875

TOWNSEND Orphis age 9y 1m dau of Walter and Mary Townsend in Addison, NY February 9, 1876

GIBSON Florence Estellie age 5y 10m dau of Mason J. and Marie E. (**TINSLEY**) in Palopinto, Tx. February 22, 1876

CRANE Mary E. age 26y wife of George Crane in Addison, NY April 4, 1876

MC CONNELL Eva Bell age 20y dau of B. H. of Horseheads, NY April 5, 1876

SHUMWAY Oliver age 86y 2m 18d in Addison, NY April 11, 1876. Res 48 yrs

BURNSIDE Edward age 30y 1m 17d in Tuscarora, NY April 22, 1876

DOLPH Mrs. Lucy age 87y 6m 7d at res of Erastus **BROOKS** in Addison, NY June 4, 1876

COSO John B. age 38y 11m 25d in Hedgesville, NY June 5, 1876

TOBINS Patrick age 48y in Addison, NY July 29, 1876

CLARK George Stanley age 3m 27d son of John W. and Mary Clark in Addison, NY August 16, 1876

BORDEN Victoria age 1y 7m dau of S. B. and Lizzie in Addison, NY August 21, 1876

WHITEHEAD Willie age 4m 7d son of Leroy and Kate Whitehead in Addison, NY August 22, 1876

ROWLEY Huldah L. in her 47th yr wife of J. W. in Pulaski, Ill, August 19, 1876

BABCOCK Mrs. Catherine M. in her 27th yr in Greenwood, NY August 23, 1876

CARPENTER Willis in his 50th yr in Woodhull, NY August 17, 1876

HAIRE Nora age 19y 2m 18d in Addison, NY August 28, 1876

MC CHESNEY William H. of Addison, NY in Binghamton, NY August 27, 1876. Married 2 yrs ago dau of John **LOPER** of Addison. Buried Rathbone, NY

TEED Mabel E. age 7m dau of Rodney A. and Carrie T. Teed in Elmira, NY September 15, 1876

HARDER Addie G. age 18y 3m 3d dau of J. F. and Annetta Harder in Addison, NY October 9, 1876

DAWSON Mary A. A. age 50y 6m in Addison, NY October 15, 1876, buried Cazenovia, NY

PIERCE Stephen A. age 69y in Addison, NY December 3, 1876

CRANE Dr. John M. in Addison, NY December 27, 1876. Born December 19, 1812 in Wilberham, Mass. moved to Cortland Co. NY age 4 yrs. Married 1836 Lorenda **HUTCHINSON** 8 children all living

STROCK Jesse K. in Woodhull, NY January 12, 1877. Leaves wife and 3 children

JONES Janie N. age 7m 12d dau of Llewelyn M. and Mary E. Jones in Painted Post, NY February 1, 1877

BOSARD Andrew K. in Osceola, Pa. February 12, 1877

ALLEN George age 58y in Cameron, NY March 5, 1877. Born 1819 in Sussex Co. NJ and came to Cameron age 8 yrs

STRYKER Peter in his 68th yr in Woodhull, NY March 2, 1877

MARTIN Ira age 78y 5d in Addison, NY March 21, 1877

HUNTLY Abner age 109y in Scio, NY Saturday March 19, 1877. Born August 4, 1767 in Norwich, Ct. Moved to Cuba, NY 1822. Married Mary **MC CARTY** of Herkimer Co. NY who died age 84y. 1 son and 3 daus, son living

SHIPMAN Mrs. Dorethea age 85y in Addison, NY May 15, 1877

VAN ORSDALE Emily age 19y wife of Lieut. J. T. Van Orsdale at Ft. Shaw Montana Terr. May 10, 1877

DAVIDSON George W. in Addison, NY June 27, 1877. Born May 16, 1839 in Bainbridge, NY. Moved to Potter Co. Pa. age 17y. Married spring of 1862 only dau of Gardner **OLMSTEAD**. Injured January 16, 1864 at Petersburg. Wife died while he was in service. Married fall of 1865 eldest dau of George S. **OLMSTEAD** and removed to Addison. Spring of 1869 his dau Jennie by 1st wife died. In May of 1870 2 daus by 2nd marriage died and in 1873 adopted dau age 7y and another dau died same year. Son born 1875. Leaves wife, 2 daus Nellie and Carrie and son George.

HINCKLEY Maria C. (**GORTON**) age 57y wife of Joseph Hinckley in Cowlesville, NY

DEATH NOTICES

August 2, 1877

TURNER Walter A. age 7y 6m son of Mrs. Harriet A. Turner in Addison, NY July 8, 1877

POTTER Elizabeth age 55y wife of Allen Potter in Troupsburgh, NY August 18, 1877

HOLLIS William while visiting in Addison, NY August 26, 1877, buried Nelson, Pa. Born March 28, 1809 in Boyleston, Derbyshire, Eng. Came to U. S. in 1821. Married 1829 Maria **STRONGATHRAM** who died 1872. 6 brothers and sisters Thomas, Denzil, Maria, Elizabeth, George M. and Emma, 2 living, Mrs. Maria **OAKDEN** wife of Joseph of Nelson, Pa. and George M. of Butternuts. 7 children, 2 died infancy, 5 living Louisa at home, Thomas James of Erie, Pa., Mrs. Sarah S. **BOGART** of Nelson, Pa., George H. of Addison, NY and Mrs. Maria E. **RYAN** of Tuscarora, NY

BIXBY Mrs. Tamar age 64y 3m at dau Mrs. Mary A. **BELDEN** in Castile, NY September 13, 1877

MC PHEE Jessie Nina age 2y 6m dau of John W. and Frank O. Mc Phee in Woodhull, NY September 25, 1877

COWLEY Axtell of Addison, NY at Warsaw, NY October 2, 1877, buried Lawrenceville, Pa.

WAGNER Catherine in her 66th yr wife of Dr. Frederick E. Wagner in Addison, NY October 30, 1877. Born December 25, 1811 in Bainbridge, NY dau of Benjamin S. **CARPENTER** 6th of 7 daus, 1 living Mrs. D. **CARPENTER** of Addison. Mother died when she was young and she lived with sister Mrs. **LANDERS** until 1829. Came to Addison, NY, lived with sister Mrs. L. B. **SEARLES**. Married October 14, 1834, 2 children, 1 dau living, son died in army in 1863

GRENELL Caroline in her 46th yr wife of Zelotus Grenell in Monistique, Mi. November 15, 1877

PHELPS Milo age 80y 1m 2d in Addison, NY November 21, 1877

HOLLIS Loretta age 37y wife of Eugene T. in Woodhull, NY December 16, 1877

ATWOOD Jesse eldest son of Calvin Atwood in Troupsburgh, NY December 27, 1877

HOFFMAN Addie E. age 23y 5m 6d in Addison, NY December 26, 1877

WHITING Mrs. Hattie A. age 25y of Addison, NY in Concordia, Ks. December 30, 1877

FINNICAN Michael (Newspaper date January 31, 1877). Born November 7, 1846 in Tarbut Co. Kerry, Ireland

BURNHAM Mrs. Julia J. in her 48th yr formerly of Addison, NY in Elmira, NY January 26, 1878

WASS Lizzie age 3y dau of Robert and Parmelia G. in Osceola, Pa. January 26, 1878

KNAPP Cora B. age 16y in S. Addison, NY March 4, 1878

WESTLAKE Annie age 2y 6m dau of Dr. John A. and Kate Westlake in Cooperstown, NY March 8, 1878

PERKINS Samuel R. age 9y 8m 22d son of P. W. in Tuscarora, NY June 2, 1878

MC KAY Prudence wife of H. C. Mc Kay in Addison, NY June 1, 1878. Born April 18, 1815 in Pompey, NY dau of Allen S. **MURRAY**. Married September 5, 1837 and moved to Addison 1851 from Truxton, NY

VERMILYEA Horace Clark in Wellsboro, Pa. June 4, 1878. Born April 10, 1815 in Otego, NY, moved to Tioga, NY 1846 and in 1855 to Gaines, Pa. Leaves wife, 2 sons and 2 daus.

SMITH Col. A. C. age 85y July 10, 1878. Born 1793 in Bristol, Ct. and moved to Meredith, NY 1810 and then Erwin and Lindley, NY

FULKERSON Julia in Addison, NY May 16, 1878

HILL Eliza J. age 57y wife of Charles Hill in Addison, NY September 2, 1878

POWERS Patrick in his 65th yr in Rathbone, NY October 11, 1878

JOHNSON Josiah R. age 23y 4m 7d son of William E. and Caroline Johnson of Risingville, NY formerly of Addison, NY in Woodhull, NY October 6, 1878

DAVENPORT Col. Lemuel 1 week ago last Thursday (Newspaper date Tuesday November 7, 1878) at daus in Elkland, Pa. Born 1792 in Vermont and came here 1814. Married (1) dau of Israel **BUCKLEY** and (2) Polly **BROWN** widow of D. Brown of Deerfield, Pa. still living

SMITH Mary relict of Nathaniel at son's Henry M. in Addison, NY October 28, 1878

CASS Maj. Charles in his 53rd yr in Campbell, NY November 1, 1878. Born December 7, 1825 in St. Thomas, Canada. Moved to Broome Co. NY with father and then moved to Campbell and lived with aunt Mrs. Solomon **CAMPBELL**. Married July 15, 1850 Mary **STEWART**.

ROUSE Chauncey age 5y 5m 2d son of Frank and Ann J. Rouse in Addison, NY November 14, 1878

CORNWELL Mrs. Lucilla in her 64th yr in Tuscarora, NY January 4, 1879. Born June 11, 1815 in Dutchess Co. NY nee **GOULD**. Married 1832 Eliah Cornwell who died 1872, 3 children Baldwin Cornwell, Mrs. **PAUL** and Rose Cornwell

BOSTWICK Mrs. Charlotte M. age 63y 10m 2d in Chicago, Ill. December 21, 1878

DEATH NOTICES

HELMER Georgia A. age 2y 5m 4d son of Andrew and Emma Helmer in Addison, NY January 4, 1879 and son Arthur A. age 9m 21d died February 1, 1879

GRIFFITHS Erastus age 3w son of William E. and R. A. Griffiths in Addison, NY January 31, 1879

COON Sally wife of Stephen Coon in Addison, NY February 16, 1879. Born March 20, 1812 in Oxford, NY one of 9 children, none living. Married October 1852

SPRAGUE Vinnie age 7m dau of Cyrus and Lucinda Sprague funeral February 20, 1879

FAIRMAN Mrs. Charles G. in Elmira, NY February 17, 1879

HOGENCAMP Mrs. Ann age 46y in Knoxville, NY/Pa.? February 24, 1879

GRAHAM Joseph in his 54th yr in Caton, NY March 8, 1879. Born 1825 in Ithaca, NY. Married dau of Evan **BECHTOL**. Leaves widow and 8 living children. 3 brothers, and 1 sister Mrs. Seymour **INGALLS** still living

MARLATT Elizabeth in Jasper, NY February 12, 1879. Born April 5, 1798 in Monmouth Co. NJ dau of Jonathan C. **PEASE** 5th child of 12. Father a Rev. Soldier who died 1840 and his wife died 1841. Married Joseph V. Marlatt in NJ moved to this area in 1820. Husband in War of 1812 and died 1857 in Troupsburgh, NY. 5 sons and 4 daus. 3 sons in Civil War.

BALDWIN Mrs. Penelope in her 53rd yr in Woodhull, NY April 21, 1879

STRAIT Almira age 65y relict of Jonathan Strait in Woodhull, NY May 15, 1879

BRYANT Mrs. Clara Ann age 70y in Rathbone, NY June 15, 1879

CROFT Leon L. age 3m 22d son of Gettie and M. A. in Farmington, Pa. July 1, 1879

LA BAR Mrs. Frances age 82y in Westfield, Pa. July 30, 1879

RICHARDS Mrs. Ann age 65y in Addison, NY August 23, 1879

MANLEY Nehemiah in Addison, NY September 2, 1879. Born January 1800 in Otsego Co. NY, came to Addison 1826. Leaves wife and 1 son Lucius N. of Long Island City

BARBER Mrs. Abigail M. C. age 80y 7m 18d in Candor, NY August 18, 1879. A widow for 30 yrs. 17 children

MOURHESS Sally in her 67th yr widow of John Mourhess of Tuscarora, NY at son's James in Arnot, Pa. August 22, 1879

DICKINSON Julia Ann age 79y in Addison, NY August 16, 1879. Married 59 yrs, husband survives

DUNHAM William age 80y in Knoxville, NY/Pa.? October 6, 1879. Leaves wife and

5 children

RIDER Frank of Hornellsville, NY crushed by cars October 14, 1879. Leaves wife and 3 children

KIMBALL Dr. Minor abt 30y in Woodhull, NY October 18, 1879

BOOM Menzo age 32y in Danville, Pa. Hospital October 10, 1879

CLARK Chad B. age 75y in Chatham, Pa. October 18, 1879

OAKDEN Maria wife of Joseph Oakden formerly of Tuscarora, NY in Nelson, Pa. October 14, 1879. Born Feruary 22, 1811 in Boyleston, Derbyshire, Eng. dau of Humphrey and Elizabeth **HOLLIS**. Married February 22, 1833

COLBERT Thomas age 69y in Addison, NY December 13, 1879. Born Waterford Co. Ire.

CARPENTER Mercy S. age 29y 6m in Deerfield, Pa. August 13, 1876 (possible misprint and should be 1879?)

KELLEY Michael age 12y 2m 28d son of Phillip in Erwin, NY December 31, 1879

SIMMONS William in his 76th yr in Brookfield, Pa. January 17, 1880. Born April 7, 1804 in Chemung Co. NY. Married Mary A. **BROWN**

DUNN Mary Ann in her 64th yr widow of Edward Dunn who died 1857 in Troupsburgh, NY January 28, 1880. Born Co. Antrim, Ire. Married 1844, 7 children

PIER Jane wife of Capt. John Pier in Corning, NY March 20, 1880

GOSS Allen conductor Erie RR for 28y in Cameron Mills, NY April 1, 1880

PRATT Mrs. George W. in Corning, NY April 4, 1880

HORN John abt 36y son of E. J. Horn and brother of Oliver, suicide in Addison, NY April 13, 1880

DRISCOLL ___ age 2y dau of Cornelius of Tuscarora, NY burned by brush fire May 7, 1880, buried Southport, NY

GILLETT John age 98y of Caton, NY April 12, 1880

MARK Aaron one of Erie RR oldest Engineers in Dunkirk, NY May 30, 1880. Brother Alfred Mark of Hornellsville, NY

KNIGHT Warren age 24y killed by falling tree in Caton, NY May 31, 1880

DAVIS John William in his 40th yr in Caton, NY June 19, 1880. Born August 26, 1840 in Germany and served 3 yrs in Civil War.

DEATH NOTICES

LINZA Alfred killed by fallen tree in Troupsburgh, NY June 24, 1880

BLY Albert J. in his 29th yr in Chicago, Ill. June 29, 1880

BROWN Rev. J. W. in his 69th yr at Mine Creek, NY April 29, 1880. Born December 14, 1810 at Mt. Desert Island, Me.

COBURN Ellsworth M. age 29y last October son of L. S. Coburn of Addison, NY killed on tugboat on Lake Erie July 16, 1880. Leaves wife and 2 children, parents and sister Mrs. Rodney **TEED** of Elmira, NY

WESTCOTT Miss Ruth A. age 41y dau of James Westcott Editor of Dundee Record in Dundee, NY July 16, 1880.

WILLOUGHBY D. Lawrence age 1y 5d son of C. B. and Emma C. Willoughby in Woodhull, NY July 27, 1880

JENNINGS Jane E. age 71y 6m 1d in Addison, NY August 9, 1880

GORMAN John age 56y killed by cars in Cameron, NY August 23, 1880

CURTIS Coe J. age 4m 13d son of Monroe Curtis in Addison, NY August 23, 1880

THOMAS Mrs. Mary in her 83rd yr in Lawrenceville, Pa. August 23, 1880

GRAHAM Sarah J. wife of Curtis S. Graham formerly of Big Flats, NY in Addison, NY September 15, 1880

JONES William S. in his 70th yr in Addison, NY October 28, 1880

FULTZ Guy age 6y 9m 22d son of Moses and Rosanna Fults in Woodhull, NY November 6, 1880

WAGNER Dr. Frederick R. in his 67th yr in Addison, NY November 30, 1880. Born April 16, 1805 in Lyden, Mass. Married October 14, 1833, wife died October 31, 1877. Leaves 1 dau Sarah

PARKE Theodosia wife of Rev. Robert N. Parke December 2, 1880

JONES Betsey age 57y wife of L. A. Jones in Addison, NY December 4, 1880

SAXBURY Katie age 4y 11m dau of C. W. and Ida Saxbury in Addison, NY December 7, 1880

DINGMAN William from accident in sawmill in Nelson, Pa. January 26, 1880

SEAMAN Alfred F. age 78y in Addison, NY January 29, 1881

COOK Phebe age 88y at dau Mrs. A. M. **PIERSON** in Elmira, NY February 5, 1881. Other children Mrs. Lydia **NICKERSON**, Mrs. Mary **PIERCE** of Grand Rapids, Mi.,

John of St. Lawrence Co. NY, F. F. of Addison, NY and George of Elmira, NY

SMITH Alonzo age 27y in Tuscarora, NY November 19, 1880

BREWSTER Alsop age 83y in Wolcott, NY January 30, 1881

EVERT Walter J. son of J. J. Evert in Elmira, NY February 14, 1881

JONES Jane M. wife of Etsell L. Jones in Addison, NY March 12, 1881. Born July 28, 1818 nee **SWARTWOOD**. Married age 18y

CHAPMAN Mrs. Frances age 47y dau of Galen **OTTS** in Addison, NY February 28, 1881, buried Otisville, NY

MANLEY Florence age 1y 7m 15d dau of Lucius and Olive Manley at Long Island City, NY March 21, 1881, buried Addison, NY

MALLORY Edward H. formerly of Corning, NY in Des Moines, Iowa recently (Newspaper date April 7, 1881) buried Corning

EVERTS Hannah age 62y wife of Abel Everts in Tuscarora, NY April 10, 1881

SMITH Florence Alden in her 7th yr in Addison, NY April 8, 1881

BUCK Amanda M. age 41y wife of Lester Buck April 9, 1881

HOAGUE Winiford age 74y in Addison, NY April 16, 1881. Son Patrick J. Jr.

MOSER Mrs. Allen age 17y shot herself in Addison, NY May 2, 1881

WOOSTER Rev. Edson G. age 31y son of J. G. in Addison, NY May 10, 1881

MILLER Jane in her 74th yr relict of William B. Miller in Woodhull, NY May 21, 1881. Dau Mrs. G. W. **WILDRICK** of Addison, NY

CORNELL Judge Francis E. formerly of Addison, NY, native of Coventry, NY in Minneapolis, Mn. May 24, 1881

BREES Nathan of Gibson, NY from accident in sawmill in Caton, NY June 8, 1881

WALRATH Howard abt 22y hit by lightning in Rathbone, NY July 25, 1881

REYNOLDS Thomas S. age 63y in Addison, NY July 21, 1881. Born December 8, 1818 in Smithfield Flats, NY, came to Addison in 1846. Leaves wife and 4 children

SILSBY ___ age 10m dau of Elias Silsby in Canisteo, NY July 13, 1881

GIBBONS Alphonso age 7y son of William G. Gibbons in Corning, NY July 24, 1881

HALL Cornelia age 52y wife of William Hall and sister of Mrs. James **JOHNSON** of

DEATH NOTICES

Corning, NY in Corning July 25, 1881

NEWMAN R. T. age 76y fell from load of hay in Woodhull, NY August 4, 1881

GOODWIN Henry age 20-25y of Hardscrapple Hill found drowned in Tuscarora Creek August 11, 1881

KLINE Peter age 79y in Hornellsville, NY August 4, 1881

HICKOK Mrs. N. E. age 47y in Avoca, NY July 27, 1881

DAWSON ____ inf dau of Thomas N. W. Dawson in Canisteo, NY July 21, 1881

CRAWFORD Louis abt 80y in Cameron Mills, NY August 18, 1881

HAYNES Amasa age 12y 5m 2d son of Thomas and Winifred Haynes July 11, 1881

HOFFMAN George A. age 2m 16d son of Josiah and Kate Hoffman in Addison, NY August 29, 1881

MANNING Marcus age 51y in Addison, NY August 30, 1881

COLVIN Archie age 4m 4d son of D. and Mary in Woodhull, NY August 20, 1881

RAGAN Catherine age 75y at son-in-law's David **O'BRIEN** in Elmira, NY August 31, 1881

JUNE Mary A. age 45y wife of Isaac June and dau of Lewis **CRAM** in Addison, NY September 11, 1881

MATHEWS Manley T. age 41y son of David and Cynthia Mathews of Reading Center, NY and brother of Mrs. David **DARRIN** of Addison, NY in Little Rock, Ark. September 11, 1881. Married abt 1863 Sarah **OSTRANDER** of Kanona, NY, buried Kanona

MILLER F. D. in his 33rd yr in Savona, NY September 14, 1881

HAIRE Mrs. Phebe age 62y at dau Mrs. J. A. **HOFFMAN** in Hornellsville, NY (Newspaper date October 6, 1881)

WHITTENHALL Elenor age 62y 7m 1d in Addison, NY September 29, 1881

WOLCOTT Sidney in his 71st yr in Addison, NY October 8, 1881

GREEK Frank age 23y son of Thomas and Sarah Greek in Elmira, NY October 4, 1881

WHITMORE Emma age 33y in Addison, NY October 14, 1881

CURTIS Albert A. age 3m son of Monroe and Celia A. Curtis in Addison, NY October 18, 1881

BESSEE Belle age 15y dau of H. W. Bessie in Addison, NY October 25, 1881

BOWEN Nathan age 51y in Jasper, NY October 14, 1881

LE MUNYAN Imogene age 11m 11d dau of E. M. and L. R. Le Munyan in Hornellsville, NY October 25, 1881

VAN GORDON Nellie May age 17m dau of George E. and Frances E. Van Gordon in Addison, NY November 2, 1881

SCHOONOVER Mrs. Frederick age 86y in Troupsburgh, NY October 17, 1881

SEVERANCE Lutyer age 64y in Thurston, NY November 26, 1881

EDGETT Clinton abt 20y in Troupsburgh, NY November 25, 1881

WHITTENHALL Elihu age 73 6m 7d in Sabitha, Ks. December 1, 1881

WOMBOUGH Maggie age 29y wife of Charles H. of Addison, NY and dau of John and Mary **GREENHOW** of Hornellsville, NY in Hornellsville December 11, 1881

EMERSON Mrs. Delbert age 20y dau of C. J. **VAN GORDON** in Addison, NY December 26, 1881

VAN GORDON Grant son of C. J. Van Gordon in Addison, NY December 28, 1881

HOFFMAN Willie R. in Addison, NY December 24, 1881

BAKER John age 60y in Canisteo, NY January 31, 1882

CLEMMONS Willie F. age 20y in Addison, NY February 19, 1882

WESTCOTT Edward bro of William Westcott formerly of Addison, NY in Westfield, Pa. March 8, 1882

BRACE Maria D. age 84y in Dansville, NY February 23, 1882

FISK Esther **(POLMITER)** age 69y wife of E. G. in Alfred, NY February 24, 1882

BRONSON Carrie dau of I. Bronson in Hornellsville, NY March 2, 1882

COVELL Mrs. C. age 85 in Cameron, NY last week (Newspaper date March 9, 1882)

WILHELM Eugene age 27y in Littleton, Col. February 27, 1882. Born Woodhull, NY

ORSER David H. age 63y in Addison, NY March 23, 1882. Born Binghamton, NY, served Civil War

MILLER Melissa age 34y wife of Josiah B. Miller in Jasper, NY March 23, 1882

DEATH NOTICES

CRANCE Mrs. Catherine age 79y in Woodhull, NY March 8, 1882

CORKINS Clara age 23y wife of Daniel Corkins in Woodhull, NY March 10, 1882

PUNCHES James in Canisteo, NY March 7, 1882

CRANDALL Truman in his 86th yr in Nelson, Pa. March 23, 1882

MATHER Mrs. Charles age 20 at Addison Hill, NY April 2, 1882

NORTHRUP Cornelius age 27y (known as Lynn) son of Peter and Alice Northrup February 27, 1882

DUNN Mrs. Syrena age 73y in Addison, NY April 14, 1882

SPRAGUE Amos age 81y in Woodhull, NY April 14, 1882

LYNCH John on the Goodhue April 18, 1882

SAVAGE Charles age 52y in Troupsburgh, NY April 19, 1882

CASSON Mordedai age 79y in Tuscarora, NY May 2, 1882

TOBEY C. Elizabeth age 34y in Addison, NY May 12, 1882

JONES Sallie age 6y 6m 24d dau of H. S. Jones in Addison, NY June 16, 1882

HARDEN Mary Ann wife of C. L. Harden August 18, 1882

COOLEY Frances in her 33rd yr wife of D. D. Cooley and dau of Charles and Maria K. **AMES** of Addison, NY in Ashland, Neb. August 11, 1882

MEAD Stephen age 84y in Rathbone, NY September 4, 1882

MILES James H. age 76y in Addison, NY September 21, 1882

PHILLIPS Betsey M. in her 77th yr at son's in Addison, NY October 16, 1882. Mother of Elisha B. **MURRAY**

BROWN Robert E. in his 73rd yr in Cameron, NY September 5, 1882. 6 children

FORD Charles H. L. age 75y in Lawrenceville, Pa. October 8, 1882

ROBERTSON Mrs. Samuel C. jumped from bridge in Corning, NY October 15, 1882

ALDRICH Esther wife of Ethan Aldrich at son's Oscar E. in Elmira, NY October 26, 1882. 6 children Ethan A., Vanderlyn V., Loren, Charles D., Oscar E. and Mrs. Ann H. **ORR**

CLUTE Isaac M. Sr. in his 66th yr in Corning, NY November 7, 1882, one of the earliest settlers. Dau Mrs. Sanford **ELMER** of Addison, NY

TITUS Mrs. Charles W. in her 35th yr in Rathbone, NY November 22, 1882

HERRINGTON ___ child of Cornelius in Addison, NY November 22, 1882

TOBEY Miss Frankie age 25y in Addison, NY December 2, 1882

NORTHRUP Sarah A. in her 35th yr dau of James and Eliza Northrup in Rathbone, NY December 4, 1882

CHRISTIAN Levantia age 69y wife of Daniel Christian in Addison, NY November 27, 1882. Children Mrs. Loren **ALDRICH**, S. B. **HOUGHTALING** and Mrs. J. P. **RICKEY**

HULL Phillip Duncan age 1y 2m 27d son of Phillip M. and Amanda S. Hull in Addison, NY December 2, 1882

CASTLE Gertie May age 7y 9d dau of C. S. in Woodhull, NY December 14, 1882

CARPENTER James age 82y 9m in Troupsburgh, NY January 14, 1883

VAN GORDON Lizzie wife of Dewitt Van Gordon February 16, 1883. Leaves husband and 5 children, youngest 10 days old

WORMLEY Frank son of Fred Wormley in Rathbone, NY March 1, 1883

WARNER ___ age 1m 21d son of Frank and Maria Warner in Canisteo, NY February 13, 1883

MACK Clayton age 4y son of Ed and Aggie Mack in Addison, NY March 15, 1883

COHN Myer age 54y in Addison, NY March 22, 1883

MILLARD Eliza Ann age 66y wife of Philo Millard in Woodhull, NY March 10, 1883

ACKLEY Ann age 16y dau of Samuel Ackley in Troupsburgh, NY March 10, 1883

LEWIS Susan age 65y wife of Sterling Lewis in Troupsburgh, NY March 9, 1883

BURDICK Tiney age 27y wife of Uriah Burdick in Osceola, Pa. March 20, 1883

BRADY Sarah Ann age 58y wife of James Brady in Woodhull, NY March 20, 1883

BARNEY Ira P. in Wheeler, NY March 23, 1883

ENSIGN Mary A. age 45y 6m in Keeneyville, Pa. April 9, 1883. Married age 16y James **SMITH** who died 37 yrs ago, 5 children John and Cornelius of Keeneyville, Mrs. James **STEVENS** of Tioga, Pa., Mrs. S. D. **CLINTON** and Mrs. Andrew **BOOTH**. After 14 yrs married Mr. **BALCH** of Westfield, Pa. who died after 2 yrs. Later married

DEATH NOTICES

William Ensign who died 7 yrs later. 1 brother H. A. **SEAMAN**

DILLAYE Henry Augustus in Addison, NY April 25, 1883. Grand son of Henri a French Royalist who returned to France leaving a son Rene Duguessut Dillaye a child age 6 yrs who later married Clarissa **NORTON**. Their son Henry A. born 1813 in Plymouth, Chenango Co. NY married age 25y Sarah J. **BIRDSALL** dau of James of Norwich, NY. Leaves wife and 2 children Henry D. and Mrs. Florence D. **VANN**

SWAN Raymon son of Ephram in Tuscarora, NY May 7, 1883

PLANK Isaac of Westfield, Pa. in Addison, NY May 10, 1883. Leaves 3 sons 2 dau

ALBEE Olney in Tuscarora, NY May 12, 1883

ALLEN Wallace age 6y son of Edward Allen when struck in head with hay rack in Canisteo, NY May 16, 1883

SMITH Mrs. Charles O. abt 63y in Tuscarora, NY May 21, 1883. Born Greene, NY

HATHAWAY Mrs. Lola in her 72nd yr in Van Mater, Iowa June 28, 1883

NICHOLS W. M. in his 61st yr in Bath, NY July 12, 1883

WATSON Mrs. Leroy in Lindley, NY July 18, 1883

GENUNG Clinton struck by train in Addison, NY August 11, 1883

CRAWFORD John age 70y in Rathbone, NY September 1, 1883

NEWSOM Benjamin age 50y at Beaman Creek, NY September 3, 1883. Born 1833 in Geneseo, NY. Moved to Wisconsin and married Sarah Melissa **EATON**, moved back to Addison, NY

ARNOLD Carrie M. widow of George H. Arnold of Cortland, NY (who died July 14, 1883) at brother's Dr. H. R. **AINSWORTH** in Addison, NY October 14, 1883, buried Cortland

WALKER Henry age 68y in Lindley, NY October 23, 1883. Children Robert of Buffalo, NY, Henry, James, Mrs. Henry **MARTIN**, Mrs. John **HUGGINS** of Lindley

MULFORD John Jr. age 19y in Lindley, NY November 6, 1883, brother Cameron died March 23, 1883

UPDYKE Jonathan age 93y vet. War of 1812 in Jasper, NY December 7, 1883

TOBEY Miss Kate age 30y in Addison, NY December 9, 1883

HEYSHAM Jessie age 21y 8m in Nelson, Pa. December 8, 1883

HEAD Mrs. Julia age 28y 9m 12d sister of Mrs. Samuel **BURNSIDE** of Addison, NY in Lawrencville, Pa. December 15, 1883

GARRETT Cyrenus age 78y in Westfield, Pa. December 20, 1883

WHITMORE Keyes in Rathbone, NY December 26, 1883. Born April 4, 1814 in Vt. and moved to Madison Co. and Chenango Co. NY. Later came to Rathbone with 2 brothers Orman and Seth. Unmarried

LYON Mrs. James dau of Reuben **ROBIE** of Bath, NY in Bath December 30, 1883

REYNOLDS Mrs. Ann age 61y in Northrup Settlement, NY January 12, 1884

SEVERANCE Mrs. M. age 35y in Cameron Mills, NY January 13, 1884

HORN E. J. age 71y in Addison, NY January 19, 1884. Born December 1812 in Scranton, Pa. Leaves wife and 5 children by former wife.

COLE Henry age 76y in Rathbone, NY January 4, 1884

LOPER Catherine age 90y widow of John Loper in Rathbone, NY January 26, 1884. Born April 1794 near Geneva, NY. Parents emigrated from Germany. Married January 29, 1813. Husband died 13 yrs ago, large family 6 living

FERENBAUGH Mary (**GIBBS**) age 71y widow of Valentine Ferenbaugh in Painted Post, NY February 4, 1884. Married (1) George **WHEAT** who died 1840

EARLY Catherine widow of Daniel Early from a fall down stairs in Addison, NY February 9, 1884

ORR Ann H. age 41y wife of Levi J. Orr formerly of Addison, NY in Elmira, NY February 13, 1884 Sister of Loren **ALDRICH** of Addison

NORTHRUP Eliza B. wife of James E. Northrup in Northrup Settlement, NY February 24, 1884. Moved to Jasper from Montour Co. Pa. at age 6y. Had 2 sons 3 daus, 1 son and 1 dau deceased

HARVEY William age 52y in Thurston, NY April 25, 1884. Born July 1832 in Yates Co. NY. Married September 14, 1852 Mary E. **BARKER** and had 2 sons and 2 daus. 1 son died a few months ago

CRANE Jane age 37y wife of Harrison Crane and dau of Isaac **HALLETT** of Cameron, NY in Canisteo, NY April 23, 1884. 4 children 1 child born 11 days ago

BARRY Mrs. Charles age 47y fell from window in Corning, NY June 20, 1884

JACOBS Jessie age 63y in Corning, NY August 10, 1884

ALBEE Mrs. Maria age 69y in Tuscarora, NY July 17, 1884

GRAVES Dr. J. B. in his 78th yr in Corning, NY September 2, 1884. Born Vermont, married 3 times

HILL Hattie U. age 3m 6d dau of William H. and late Cinthy M. Hill in Tuscarora, NY September 6, 1884

BLAKESLEE Dr. Bradley B. in Addison, NY October 13, 1884. Born October 16, 1794 in Brattleboro, Vt. and came to Addison in 1840. Married 1823 Phebe **BLAKESLEE** a cousin who survives and will be 90 on December 5 this year. 1 adopted dau Mrs. Miles **STEVENS**

MOLSON Louisa wife of John Molson in Addison, NY November 14, 1884. Would have celebrated their 48th anniversary on November 20 this year.

Voice of the Nation

January 10, 1855 - December 19, 1855

HARTSHORN Jerusha in her 76th yr wife of Jacob Hartshorn in Hornellsville, NY January 9, 1855

DENNIS S. B. formerly of Corning, NY in Susquehanna, Pa. January 8, 1855

EGBERT Ralph in his 4th yr son of B. Egbert in Corning, NY January 7, 1855

WALLACE Marinda age 44y 5m wife of Joseph in Hornellsville, NY January 14, 1855

CHURCH Catherine A. wife of Edwin F. Church in Bath, NY January 10, 1855

FONDA Harriet M. age 7m dau of Henry J. and Marion E. Fonda in Addison, NY January 24, 1855

PERRY John M. age 21y son of Nelson Perry of Woodhull, NY in Hornby, NY February 3, 1855

MINARD Joel age 22y died January 20, 1855, William age 26y died January 25, 1855, Michael age 17y died January 31, 1855 sons of Joseph Minard nr Monterey, NY

DONAHE William Hamilton age 10m 12d son of Horace G. and Mary F. Donahe in Bath, NY February 7, 1855

RUTHERFORD Edward Sr. in his 89th yr in Addison, NY February 12, 1855. Born 1766 in Northumberland Co. Eng. Came to US 1819

MAXWELL Dugald Cameron abt 30y in Elmira, NY March 6, 1855

BROWN Millicent in her 40th yr in Caton, NY March 7, 1855

DUDLEY Ann Eliza in her 19th yr dau of Abram in Addison, NY March 20, 1855

GOBLE Myranda age 55y in Bath, NY March 21, 1855

BLAKESLEE Bradley 2nd age 31y in Addison, NY April 3, 1855

ADAMS Theodora age 75y in Addison, NY April 22, 1855. Dau Mrs. William R. **SMITH**

BURKE Mrs. Toby and infant drowned in Addison, NY April 21, 1855

WATROUS Phebe age 42y wife of Riggs Watrous in Elmira, NY May 7, 1855

HIGGINS John D. Md. in Bath, NY May 9, 1855

JOHNSON Anna Melissa inf dau of Thomas H. and Melissa D. Johnson in Knoxville, Pa. May 16, 1855 (Philadelphia papers please copy)

WARD Hamilton age 21y in Painted Post, NY May 29, 1855

HOYT Henry J. age 37y of Cameron, NY in Columbia, Pa. May 23, 1855. Native of New England and res of Cameron 15y. Leaves wife of 1 child

BALDWIN James in his 74th yr in Addison, NY June 16, 1855

MULLEN Ella age 3y dau of Seth Mullen in Addison, NY June 26, 1855

RHODES Wallace age 21y in Caton, NY June 15, 1855

WRIGHT William age 35y in Addison, NY September 19, 1855

ROWLEY Mrs. Robert age 65y in Addison, NY October 3, 1855

STEPHENS William age 78y in Canisteo, NY November 5, 1855. Lived on same farm since 1799

Bath Gazette and Genessee Advertiser

January 1, 1797 - April 12, 1898

SYTEZ Capt. George in Detroit, Mi. October 3, 1797

DEATH NOTICES

Steuben American (Bath, NY)

January 2, 1856 - May 6, 1857

LOCKWOOD Mrs. C. M. in her 45th yr of Wheeler, NY in Bath, NY January 21, 1856

POTTER E. K. age 30y native of Vt. in Bath, NY (Newspaper date February 20, 1856)

TOWLE ____ infant child of Richard in Towlesville, NY last week (Newspaper date March 12, 1856)

HOTCHKIN Rebecca age 78y widow of Rev. J. H. Hotchkin in Prattsburg, NY March 12, 1856

SMITH George age 25y in Addison, NY March 15, 1856

ERWIN Sophia age 49y wife of Gen. Francis E. Erwin and dau of Ansel **MC CALL** of Painted Post, NY in Painted Post May 16, 1856

GANSEVOORT John R. age 58y in Bath, NY May 19, 1856. Came from Albany, NY in 1817

MASON Charles a suicide in Addison, NY May 16, 1856

GANSEVOORT Peter C. age 29y accidental drowning in Cincinnati, Oh. May 31, 1856

SIBLEY Abijah in his 66th yr Father of Dr. J. C. Sibley of Bath, NY in Erie Co. NY June 3, 1856

VAN LOON James H. age 24y of Steuben Co. NY in Livingston, Mi. July 4, 1856

FAY Lydia M. in her 33rd yr wife of Sheriff Lewis D. Fay in Bath, NY August 3, 1856

HESS Mary Lizzie dau of Hiram R. Hess in Bath, NY August 21, 1856

CONNOR W. Franklin age 8m son of J. H. and A. J. Connor in Corning, NY (Newspaper date September 3, 1856)

HOTCHKIN Mrs. Janes H. age 47y of Prattsburgh, NY August 28, 1856

HOTCHKIN James J. age 25y in Prattsburgh, NY October 7, 1856

LENHART Mary Louise age 11m died September 30, 1856 and Osa Kate age 3y 9m died October 22, 1856, daus of Charles and Elizabeth Lenhart in Bath, NY

BARTON Frances M. wife of E. P. Barton in Bath, NY February 20, 1857

BROWN Margaret C. age 15y 6m dau of late John Brown in Bath, NY March 27, 1856

DONAHE Betsey Ann dau of John and Lucy Donahe in Avoca, NY March 25, 1857

GARDNER Daniel in his 79th yr at son's Rev. C. M. Gardner in Bath, NY March 30, 1857. Born New York City

STANIFORD A. Eugene age 21y 10m in Bath, NY April 1, 1857

MILLS Almon T. age 4y 4m son of Daniel A. and Esther E. Mills in Bath, NY April 13, 1857

Steuben Democrat (Bath, NY)

November 15, 1843 - May 22, 1844

COOK John M. age 16y son of Constant of Bath, NY January 11, 1844

SMITH John abt 8y son of James Smith in Bath, NY January 25, 1844

HARRISON Robert age 90y a Revolutionay Soldier in Urbana, NY (Newspaper date February 14, 1844)

EDWARDS Mason in his 19th yr son of George C. Edwards Sunday last (Newspaper date April 10, 1844)

NEWCOMB George age 61y of Bath, NY in New York City at brother's April 29, 1844

TRIMBLE Elizabeth age 22y dau of John Trimble of Mud Creek, NY, body found in Niagara River April 18, 1844

DOTY Lydia age 26y dau of Christopher and Lucinda in Hornellsville, NY May 2, 1844

BARTON Mrs. Polly abt 28y in Bath, NY May 2, 1844

Steuben Democrat (Bath, NY)

June 14, 1848 = June 13, 1849

SHANNON James age 38y in Bath, NY June 7, 1848

PERSOS Louise Marie age 22y dau of David Persos of Howard, NY in Waterloo, NY June 10, 1848

DYGERT Sylvanus age 88y a Revolutionary Soldier in Wheeler, NY June 20, 1848

WYLLYS Harry age 45y in Bath, NY June 23, 1848

DEATH NOTICES

ABBOTT Martha Matilda age 16y 2m 6d dau of Moses and Caroline Abbott in Urbana, NY February 8, 1848

RANDLE Hannah R. age 29y 1m 20d wife of William in Urbana, NY April 29, 1848

MESSENGER Rosanna Mary Theresa age 20y wife of George Messenger in Corning, NY July 20, 1848

ROBIE Lydia age 20y dau of Reuben Robie in Bath, NY August 9, 1848

SMALL Joseph abt 5y son of Hiram Small in Bath, NY Monday last (Newspaper date August 16, 1848)

FAULKNER Catherine age 88y in Urbana, NY August 11, 1848. Leaves sons John and Richard Faulkner

DANIELS T. W. age 52y in Wheeler, NY August 25, 1848

BEAN Isaac abt 74y in Bath, NY August 29, 1848

BLOOD Charles B. age 18m son of Charles Blood in Bath, NY September 2, 1848

BLOOD Charles age 28y in Bath, NY September 12, 1848

MAGEE Arabella abt 7y dau of John Magee in Bath, NY September 3, 1848

PURDY ____ a son of Charles Purdy in Bath, NY September 2, 1848

RUMSEY David Jr. in Bath, NY Monday last (Newspaper date September 27, 1848)

HARKINSON Joseph age 45y in Wheeler, NY August 29, 1848

BROWN Philander age 19y son of William Brown in Thurston, NY August 23, 1848

GILLETT Joseph age 80y a Lieut. in War of 1812 in Caton, NY September 29, 1848

HOPKINS Charlotte wife of Norman Hopkins in Bath, NY October 18, 1848. Brothers Edward and William **HOWELL**

HELMER Daniel age 33y in Addison, NY July 7, 1848

HELMER Charlotte age 60y wife of Andrew Helmer in Addison, NY October 8, 1848

BAKER Miss ____ age 19y dau of Noah Baker in Canisteo, NY October 19, 1848

BONHAM Robert T. age 69y in Campbell, NY October 22, 1848

VAN SICKLE Andrew in his 56th yr in Greenwood, NY November 6, 1848

RICE Caroline L. age 29y wife of Joel H. Rice in Bath, NY November 6, 1848

PETERS Elizabeth age 26y wife of Charles Peters in Bath, NY November 18, 1848

EVANS Elijah age 68y in Bath, NY November 2, 1848

GRAVES Charles age 61y in Howard, NY November 4, 1848

KNOX Mrs. ___ age 73y wife of Jno. Knox in Campbell, NY November 5, 1848

MADOLE John age 43y in Howard, NY November 20, 1848

VAN SICKLE Andrew in his 56th yr in Greenwood, NY November 6, 1848

STEVENS Olive in her 83rd yr relict of Col. John Stevens (who died March 19, 1837 age 70y) and dau of Russell **FRANKLIN** in Greenwood, NY November 6, 1848.

LOOMIS Julina F. age 28y wife of Henry Loomis in Bath, NY November 26, 1848

VAN NESS Lucy (**HART**) age 21y wife of Peter in Mud Creek, NY December 1, 1848

BARRETT Harriet abt 28y wife of Cornelius in Bath, NY December 8, 1848

PERINE Rachel Elizabeth age 21y wife of P. S. Perine and dau of late John **BROWN** of Bath, NY in Bath January 4, 1849

SKINNER Eliza age 15y dau of Col. D. G. Skinner of Bath, NY in Avoca, NY January 15, 1849

YOST Jacob S. age 39y in Cameron, NY February 26, 1849

MERRILL George H. in his 18th yr in Howard, NY March 3, 1849

HUNT Ezekiel age 77y in Bath, NY March 10, 1849

PERRY Alanson age 67y in Troupsburgh, NY March 14, 1849

OLMSTEAD Melvina age 5y dau of John and Amanda Olmstead in Avoca, NY March 24, 1849

ALDEN Lewis age 18y son of Benjamin Alden in Howard, NY April 14, 1849

CLIZBE Phebe age 30y wife of Joseph Clizbe in Avoca, NY March 29, 1849

COTTON William Henry age 3y 5m son of Edward and Phebe Cotton in Wayland, NY March 23, 1849

KNOX Ada Zilla age 48y wife of Levi Knox in Wayne, NY March 12, 1849

JOHNSON Sophia L. age 22y dau of Samuel A. in Prattsburgh, NY March 25, 1849

LOOMIS Nathaniel S. of Durhamville, NY in Bath, NY April 2, 1849

DEATH NOTICES

BIDWELL Harriet age 59y wife of Capt. E. Bidwell of Bath, NY in Rochester, NY April 3, 1849, buried in Bath

ERWAY Peter Henry age 2y 9m 6d son of Ira Erway in Bath, NY May 3, 1849

CHAMBERLAIN Joshua age 76y in Orange, NY April 25, 1849

GRACE William P. age 28y native of Boston, Mass in Bath, NY May 29, 1849

STEVENS Elizabeth age 85y wife of Uriah Stevens in Canisteo, NY March 30, 1849

STEVENS Rachel Celestia age 10y dau of Franklin D. and Sophrona Stevens in Canisteo, NY May 16, 1849

The Constitutionalist

August 23, 1837 - February 16, 1842

WARREN Danford age 31y son of Phineas Warren in Bath, NY August 23, 1837

COOK Edwin age 22y in Cohocton, NY October 11, 1837

TOWNSEND Henry A. age 68y in Urbana, NY October 23, 1837

MOORE Eunice age 25y in Mud Creek, NY October 18, 1837

WHITNEY William Wallace in his 27th yr in Bath, NY October 12, 1837. Born 1810 in Broome Co. NY son of Gen. Joshua Whitney of Binghamton, NY. Leaves wife and 2 children

COMSTOCK S. E. age 28y wife of Dr. A. L. Comstock in Bath, NY November 12, 1837

EDWARDS Hon. George C. 1st Judge of Steuben Co. in Bath, November 18, 1837. Born September 29, 1787 in Stockbridge, Mass.

THOMAS James in Erwin, NY (Newspaper date December 27, 1837)

CONTARANAN Samuel suicide in Howard, NY Monday last (Newspaper date January 10, 1838)

WILKES James age 2y son of B. Wilkes in Bath, NY January 20, 1838

DICKINSON Charles Wesley in his 9th yr son of Samuel Dickinson in Cameron, NY March 23, 1838

HARDING Oliver age 83y a Revolutionary Soldier in Hornellsville, NY April 8, 1838.

One of the first settlers in this section

PRATT Joel in his 59th yr formerly of Prattsburgh, NY in Hopewell, NY May 18, 1838

WALKER Sarah Maria age 14y dau of James Walker in Bath, NY May 20, 1838

COLE Caleb age 50y formerly of the eastern states at res. of Amos **PRESTON** in Dansville, NY May 7, 1838

MITCHELL Thomas son of J. B. Mitchell of Wayne, NY in Randolph, Ohio April 20, 1838, buried in Wayne

SHELDON Wealthy in her 54th yr wife of Col. Daniel Sheldon in Pulteney, NY May 10, 1838

KELLY Elizabeth age 31y wife of Dr. Manning Kelly in Hornellsville, NY August 4, 1838

HASTINGS Edward age 16m son of William in Hammondsport, NY August 23, 1838

STOCKING John A. abt 60y of Bath, NY at Ann Arbor Mi. (Newspaper date September 5, 1838)

GLASS Franklin abt 36y in Bath, NY September 17, 1838

MAY Charles age 28y on Steamboat on Mississippi River formerly of Bath, NY (Newspaper date October 31, 1838) buried Paducah, Ky.

BLOOD Allen age 38y in Bath, NY October 31, 1838

DUDLEY Jeremiah age 85y in Bath, NY November 10, 1838

WHITE Emily age 27y wife of Isachar White in Wayne, NY December 5, 1838

HUNTER Mrs. Eleanor age 30y wife of Dr. William Hunter in Jasper, NY November 27, 1838

CALKINS Ripley age 54y in Howard, NY December 22, 1838

DUDLEY Jennette age 2y dau of T. J. Dudley in Buffalo, NY (Newspaper date January 16, 1839)

DAVIS ____ age 2y son of Cornelius Davis in Bath, NY January 14, 1839

LINDSLEY Levinia wife of Abial Lindsley in Prattsburgh, NY December 21, 1838

KINNEY Mrs. Catherine abt 24y in Jasper, NY March 6, 1839

GOULD Mary age 5y 3m dau of A. R. Gould in Bath, NY April 13, 1839

DEATH NOTICES

BARNEY Clarence S. age 1y 3m son of Nathan in Wheeler, NY April 17, 1839

BOYD Joseph in his 65th yr in Jasper, NY April 29, 1839

RYERSS John P. in his 64th yr of Lindley, NY in Campbell, NY April 24, 1839

WEST X. abt 55y in Bath, NY May 12, 1839

MC CLURE Charles H. abt 26y formerly of Bath, NY son of Finla Mc Clure of Bath in Clinton, Mi. May 23, 1839

DYKEMAN Mrs. Oliver late of Broome Co, NY in Bath, NY June 5, 1839

PHELPS Charlotte age 41y wife of Milo Phelps in Jasper, NY May 28, 1839

ROBINSON Daniel age 67y in Howard, NY July 22, 1839

LEWIS Eliza (**FORBES**) age 34y wife of James Lewis in Bath, NY August 17, 1839

NEALLY Harriet age 34y wife of Samuel Neally in Bath, NY August 8, 1839

LUDLOW Jehiel Sheriff of Tompkins Co. NY in Ithaca, NY August 11, 1839

HENRY David age 50y in Bath, NY August 29, 1839

REASON ____ age 7m child of S. Reason in Bath, NY August 29, 1839

ERWIN Francis age 59y 6m formerly of Easton, Pa. in Erwin, NY September 6, 1839

FLEET Daniel age 17y son of Abram Fleet in Tyrone, NY September 1, 1839

NILES Mary in her 21st yr dau of Doah in Prattsburgh, NY September 2, 1839

SCHERMERHORN Robert Campbell age 17y son of Mathew Schermerhorn in Bath, NY Sunday (Newspaper date October 2, 1839)

BRUNDAGE James age 74y in Urbana, NY September 27, 1839

HANKS Brigham formerly of Bath, NY in Ill. (Newspaper date October 9, 1839)

JAMIESON Mary wife of Capt. Jamieson and dau of Gen. George **MC CLURE** formerly of Bath, NY in Texas (Newspaper date October 9, 1839)

LAWRENCE Mary Ann age 33y wife of Maj. James Lawrence in Cameron, NY October 24, 1839. Leaves husband and 6 children

TAYLOR Clarissa age 30y wife of Dugald Taylor and dau of Caleb **FARNHAM** in Bath, NY September 26, 1839

BURGHER Benjamin abt 50y in Dansville, NY December 10, 1839

SHUMWAY Olive age 58y wife of Daniel in Addison, NY December 21, 1839

BRINKERHOFF Caroline C. age 25y wife of Jacob Brinkerhoff Atty. of Mansfield, Ohio formerly of Bath, NY in Lodi, NY November 18, 1839

STARR Ann wife of William Starr in Howard, NY January 17, 1840

BURNSIDE James F. age 25y in Bath, NY February 10, 1840

ROOT Charles Andrew age 23y son of Adam L. **PEEK** in Avoca, NY February 8, 1839

STEPHENS Sarah Elizabeth dau of Sylvanus Stephens in Bath, NY February 3, 1840

SWEZEY Nancy Maria age 11m dau of Walter F. Swezey in Bath, NY February 5, 1840

LEWIS James age 34y in Bath, NY March 4, 1840

VAN VALKENBURGH George Rudd infant son of J. Van Valkenburgh in Prattsburgh, NY March 10, 1840

KATNER Harlow P. age 24y in Wheeler, NY March 12, 1840

BUSH Gideon D. age 26y in Urbana, NY (Newspaper date March 18, 1840)

HENSLEY Col. John in his 83rd yr in Elmira, NY (Newspaper date March 25, 1840)

GRAHAM George P. age 18y in Bath, NY April 3, 1840

MALLORY Minerva age 36y wife of John Mallory in Painted Post, NY March 24, 1840. Leaves husband and 5 children

SMITH Phidelia age 21y dau of Edward Smith in Bath, NY May 10, 1840

COLE Sophrona relict of late Hezekiah M. Cole in Howard, NY May 11, 1840

FLUENT John age 39y in Cameron, NY May 22, 1840

BIRDSALL Maria D. in her 27th yr wife of Ransom in Elmira, NY May 23, 1840

CROUCH Mary age 96y Mother of Richard and Caleb Crouch in Cohocton, NY August 18, 1840

BISHOP Lucietta age 32y dau of Robert H. Bishop in Bath, NY September 11, 1840

FLUENT Boanerges abt 74y formerly of Cameron, NY in Elgin, Ill. August __, 1840. Originally from the state of Maine

SHAUT Clarinda in her 34th yr wife of Joseph Shaut in Bath, NY September 24, 1840

DEATH NOTICES

HALL Maria age 17y in Kennedyville, NY October 4, 1840

PRENTISS John in his 50th yr native of Lancaster, Mass. in Pulteney, NY November 1, 1840

MAY Mrs. Hannah in her 71st yr in Bath, NY December 9, 1840

GRAHAM Henry A. age 77y 7m in Bath, NY January 3, 1841

ROWE William age 55y formerly of Bath, NY in Parkhurst, Io. December 30, 1840

HEMPSTED Mrs. Mary age 75y formerly of Hartford, Ct. in Erwin, NY February 13, 1841

ROBBINS Edwin in his 75th yr formerly of Guilford, NY in Caton, NY January 25, 1841

AULLS Miss Sophia age 23y in Hammondsport, NY February 18, 1841

MAGEE Charles age 7y son of John Magee in Bath, NY February 26, 1841

CAMERON Jane age 65y wife of Charles Cameron in Greene, NY January 31, 1841

STONE Charles V. in his 35th yr in Prattsburgh, NY March 10, 1841

MAGEE John son of John Magee in Bath, NY March 13, 1841

LITTLE James abt 40y in Bath, NY March 8, 1841

PRATT Joel in his 20th yr son of Elisha Pratt in Prattsburgh, NY March 14, 1841

HARROWER Mrs. Rev. David Harrower age 71y in Lindley, NY March 11, 1841

DICKINSON Angeline abt 4y dau of David Dickinson in Cameron, NY March 28, 1841

BACON Ruth Amy age 15y dau of Noah B. Bacon in Bath, NY April 10, 1841

RICE Burrage in his 59th yr in Prattsburgh, NY April 3, 1841. Born September 14, 1782 son of Samuel Rice formerly of Wallingford, Conn. Married 1806 dau of Joel **PRATT** of Prattsburgh

HALLIDAY Eliza in her 41st yr consort of Harvey in Cameron, NY April 12, 1841

HOPKINS Horatio in his 52nd yr in Prattsburgh, NY April 11, 1841

SWEET Jonathan in his 93rd yr a Revolutionary Soldier in Prattsburgh, NY April 4, 1841

LELAND Charles in his 3rd yr son of Z. A. Leland April 22, 1841

HAVERLING Elizabeth age 62y consort of Adam Haverling in Bath, NY June 13, 1841

UNDERHILL Punderson B. in his 56th yr in Orleans, NY June 14, 1841

AINSWORTH Willard in his 24th yr in Prattsburgh, NY June 21, 1841

NEALLY William age 6y son of Samuel Neally August 23, 1841

MC BEATH Sarah age 16m dau of James Mc Beath in Bath, NY August 31, 1841

ROSENCRANS Dr. Simeon in his 67th yr formerly of Sussex Co. NJ in Cohocton, NY August 22, 1841

WILLIAMS Zopher age 25y in Urbana, NY September 8, 1841

HAYES Samuel age 72y 6m in Prattsburgh, NY August 28, 1841

LOOMIS Ellen in her 25th yr wife of Theron Loomis of Prattsburgh, NY and dau of late Brigham HANKS of Bath, NY on Steamboat on Lake Erie October 10, 1841

TOLLIVER William abt 70y in Bath, NY October 15, 1841

SHIPMAN Sarah wife of Dr. D. M. Shipman formerly of Bath, NY in Rochester, NY October 29, 1841

BATCHELDER Demaris in her 48th yr wife of Joseph Batchelder formerly of NH in Jasper, NY November 13, 1841

ELLIS Doctor John in his 13th yr in Bath, NY December 15, 1841 and George Ellis age 23y died December 17, 1841

MATHEWS Mary dau of Gen. Vincent Mathews in Rochester, NY December 9, 1841

VEDDER Jemima age 36y wife of William in Prattsburgh, NY December 13, 1841

WARREN Rachel Amelia infant dau of late Stewart K. Warren in Bath, NY January 18, 1842

Steuben Farmers Advocate (Bath, NY)
Wednesday
January 5, 1831 - November 14, 1866

ROCHESTER Amanda consort of William B. in Buffalo, NY January 16, 1831

JOHNSON Eunice age 22y dau of James Johnson in Bath, NY Saturday last (Newsaper date February 2, 1831)

DEATH NOTICES

AMES Erastus Jr. age 23y hit by falling tree in Cohocton, NY Thursday last (Newspaper date February 2, 1831)

KNICKERBOCKER Solomon abt 46y in Cameron, NY February 11, 1831

MITCHELL James age 70y fell into fire in Southport, NY February 19, 1831

LANSING Laura age 37y wife of Rev. D. C. Lansing and dau of late Rev. Caleb **ALEXANDER** in Utica, NY March 6, 1831

DAGGETT Betsey abt 4y dau of Levi Daggett in Bath, NY March 22, 1831

MARTHER Ebenezer age 36y formerly of Bath, NY in Mi. Terr. February 19, 1831

MC HENRY Mary M. age 30y wife of Daniel Mc Henry in Angelica, NY Friday last (Newspaper date March 30, 1831)

LIVERMORE Samuel age 56y in Independence, NY April 5, 1831. Born Mass. Married Vt.

THOMAS Isaiah age 82y in Worcester, Mass. April 4, 1841

GRINOLDS Mrs. Levi age 23 dau of William **CHILDON** in Troupsburgh, NY April 14, 1831

MORRISON Jane T. age 34y consort of James Morrison formerly of Bath, NY in Indianapolis, Ind. March 29, 1831

LOGAN Robert age 53y in Bath, NY May 9, 1831

CHILDS Daniel age 51 who was shot by Augustus **HALL** abt 1 yr ago died in Tyrone, NY May 4, 1831

HERRICK Arthur Atty. of Angelica, NY in New York City May 9, 1831

GLEN John D. in his 56th yr formerly US Army in Schenectady, NY June 19, 1831

WOODS James Lyon age 15y son of William Woods in Bath, NY July 5, 1831

NUTE Elias age 22y in Campbell, NY July 24, 1831

GREGORY Simeon age 18m son of Stephen in Mud Creek, NY August 19, 1831

COFFMAN Abraham age 8m son of Norris Coffman in Bath, NY August 23, 1831

CRAWFORD David abt 21y in Cohocton, NY August 21, 1831

ELDRED Mrs. Cooper abt 35y in Cohocton, NY August 21, 1831

HEMPSTED Charles S. age 1y son of Elisha in Bath, NY September 1, 1831

HUBBELL infant child of William S. Hubbell September 2, 1831

ELLAS Joshua Young abt 18m in Bath, NY September 9, 1831

STONE infant son of Jason H. Stone in Kennedyville, NY September 8, 1831

MITCHELL Dr. Samuel R. abt 70y in New York City September 9, 1831

WARREN Capt. William age 80y a Revolutionary Patriot of Worcester, Mass. nephew of Gen. Joseph Warren and Father of Oliver W. L. Warren of Bath, NY (Newspaper date September 14, 1831)

HOPKINS Abigail age 71y wife of Elias Hopkins in Bath, NY September 19, 1831

LINDSLEY Catherine age 10m dau of James Lindsley in Bath, NY September 17, 1831

OSBORN John H. age 42y at Head of Seneca Lake September 12, 1831

STRONG John age 33y in Bath, NY October 12, 1831

FRENCH Joseph age 33y died October 16, 1831

HULBURT John W. in Auburn, NY (Newspaper date November 2, 1831)

CRUGER Hannah age 40y consort of Daniel Cruger formerly of Bath, NY in Syracuse, NY December 7, 1831

BECKWITH Arilla Jane age 11y dau of Amasa Beckwith of Bath, NY in Prattsburgh, NY December 6, 1831

GRAVES Randall late member of assembly in Howard, NY December 21, 1831

DOOLITTLE Jesse age 38y in Painted Post, NY December 21, 1831

SEDGEWICK Henry D. age 46y in Stockbridge, Mass. December 16, 1831

PUTNAM Rev. Aaron age 45y in Owego, NY December 28, 1831

EDWARDS infant son of Hon. George C. Edwards in Bath, NY January 8, 1832

SWARTHOUT Lydia age 64y wife of Aaron in Barrington, NY January 11, 1832

TROUP Col. Robert in his 75th yr in New York City January 14, 1832

WALKER Hon. John age 63y member of Assembly from Clinton Co. NY in Albany, NY January 14, 1832

MARSHALL Mrs. ____ wife of Chief Justice Marshall December 25, 1832

HOWE infant son of John Howe in Bath, NY January 19, 1832

DEATH NOTICES

COTTON Maria age 28y wife of Henry G. Cotton and dau of Thomas **MC BURNEY** in Painted Post, NY January 29, 1832

SALISBURY Smith H. Editor of Rochester Advertiser in Rochester, NY (Newspaper date February 8, 1832)

MC BURNEY Lucretia in her 51st yr wife of Col. James Mc Burney in Hornellsville, NY February 8, 1832

TOWLE Hester Ann age 19y in Howard, NY February 11, 1832. Her husband John Towle age 21y died February 16, 1832 leaving infant son of 15m

BULL Susan infant dau of Col. William H. Bull in Bath, NY February 17, 1832

HOWELL Charles age 35y February 19, 1832

ROSE Ruth age 50y wife of Nathan Rose in Wheeler, NY February 12, 1832

HOYT Sarah Ann **(HARRISON)** age 23y wife of Dr. Hoyt in Painted Post, NY February 28, 1832

HANNA Jane age 75y native of Scotland widow of Capt. William Hanna of Unadilla, NY in Bath, NY February 24, 1832

WEST Mary age 1y 10m dau of Xenocrates West in Bath, NY March 12, 1832

CLARK Mrs. Calvin in Bath, NY March 14, 1832

JACKSON Franklin age 4y son of widow Jackson in Bath, NY March 14, 1832

SMITH Waterman age 2y son of Orrin Smith March 15, 1832

LEMM Mrs. Rouse of Cameron, NY March 16, 1832

WOODS ____ age 9m son of William Woods in Bath, NY March 17, 1832

HERRICK Daniel D. of Erwin, NY and B. **ROWLEY** of Painted Post, NY drowned in Tioga River March 12, 1832

CAMERON Ewen Father of late Gershom Cameron of Bath, NY in Prattsburgh, NY April 21, 1832

WOLCOTT Rhoda age 38y wife of Caleb Wolcott in Bath, NY April 27, 1832

RUMSEY Lydia age 21y wife of Martin S. Rumsey in Bath, NY May 10, 1832

HUNT Mr. ____ a pauper of Cohocton, NY in Bath, NY May 12, 1832

GOFF Alma a widow age 89y in Howard, NY May 11, 1832

GREGORY William S. suicide in Bethany, NY May 11, 1832

MONTGOMERY Mary age 53y wife of Reuben in Wheeler, NY June 20, 1832

GANSEVOORT Susan age 4y dau of Capt. John R. in Bath, NY July 1, 1832

CAMERON Charles age 22y son of late Dugald Cameron in Hornellsville, NY August 8, 1832, buried Bath, NY

CLARK Samuel W. age 53 former Editor of the Bee in Hudson, NY August 16, 1832

BECKWITH Amasa age 51y in Windham Co. Conn. August 14, 1832

EDDY Elizabeth age 45y in Bath, NY September 4, 1832

KENNEDY William abt 32y in Bath, NY October 2, 1832

KENNEDY Maj. John age 42y in Dansville, NY October 8, 1832

CLISBE Addison age 26y in Bath, NY November 9, 1832

BLAIR Dr. A. E. age 22y in Kennedyville, NY November 12, 1832

BACHMAN Henry age 23y in Pulteney, NY November 21, 1832

SILSBEE Enos age 69y in Wayne, NY December 12, 1834

TOLBERT John age 45y in Mud Creek, NY December 26, 1834

RICHARDSON William L. age 18, son of John in Urbana, NY December 27, 1834

BRYAN David age 25y formerly of Bath, NY in Renssalaer, NY December 9, 1834

LYON William B. age 18y son of Capt. Moses H. Lyon of Bath, NY in Litchfield, Ct. January 1, 1835

HAVERLING Henry age 19y in Bath, NY January 15, 1835

ROSE Samuel age 90y a Revolutionary Soldier in Wheeler, NY February 2, 1835

RUTHERFORD Thomas age 22y son of William in Bath, NY February 9, 1835

PRENTICE Henry age 73y in Jasper, NY February 3, 1835

JONES Jane E. age 22y eldest dau of Isaiah J. Jones of Erwin, NY while crossing Canisteo River in sleigh and ice broke in Addison, NY February 14, 1835

SMEAD David age 74y brother of the Editor of this paper in Greenfield, Mass. January 8, 1835

DEATH NOTICES

HAMPTON Gen. Wade in Columbia, SC February 4, 1835

MC NORTON Mrs. ____ age 92y in Howard, NY February 24, 1835

WENTWORTH Renning age 50y in Kennedyville, NY February 9, 1835

BUTLER William uncle to US Atty. a temporary res. of Bath, NY in Deposit, NY March 3, 1835

MORGAN Wakeman age 39y in Bath, NY March 16, 1835

BEAMAN Mary age 7y in Bath, NY March 20, 1835

ELLAS Mary age 36y wife of Henry Ellas in Kennedyville, NY April 18, 1835

SMITH Reuben age 56y in Bath, NY April 14, 1835

GLASS Lydia abt 53y wife of Erastus Glass in Bath, NY May 1, 1835

HEMMENWAY Elizabeth age 37y wife of Aaron in Bath, NY May 9, 1835

HUBBELL Nehemiah age 71y in Painted Post, NY June 21, 1835. Leaves son William of Bath, NY

HOLLADAY Lazarus Hammond age 2y son of E. G. Holladay in Hammondsport, NY July 22, 1835

BAKER Armenia age 27y consort of Andrew Baker Jr. in Howard, NY August 30, 1835

THURBER Mrs. Abner in Erwin, NY September 6, 1835

ELLAS Henry age 36y of Bath, NY in Huron, Ohio September 5, 1835

PORTER Roxanna age 71y consort of Robert in Prattsburgh, NY October 24, 1835

BRIDGEMAN Louisa H. age 21y wife of Lewis H. in Coventry, NY October 23, 1835

BILLINGS Rosette age 36y wife of Silas Billings in Knoxville, NY December 25, 1835

PURDY Hannah wife of Erastus Purdy in Bath, NY January 14, 1836

CORNELL Zopher of Howard, NY in Bath, NY January 18, 1836

BENNETT Miss Esther age 37y in Starkey, NY January 10, 1836

SWITZER Peter Muhlenburg in his 19th yr in Jersey, NY February 5, 1836

TOWNSEND Mrs. Abraham in Tyrone, NY March 6, 1836

HANKS Betsey dau of Elisha Hanks in Bath, NY March 3, 1836

BENNETT Isaac B. age 46y in Howard, NY March 26, 1836

HALL Mary consort of David Hall in Wayne, NY April 15, 1836

READ William age 76y one of 1st settlers of Co. in Urbana, NY April 21, 1836

LIVINGSTON Edward age 72y in Red Hook, NY May 23, 1836

MATHEWS Thomas age 40y formerly of Bath, NY in Elmira, NY June 16, 1836

FAULKNER Mary age 42y dau of late John Faulkner in Urbana, NY July 22, 1836

MC BURNEY Col. James abt 70y in Hornellsville, NY July 25, 1836

CHAPIN Loisa Maria age 10m dau of Vestus Chapin in Kennedyville, NY July 29, 1836

RIPLEY Laura in her 17th yr dau of Hezekiah and Laura Ripley in Hammondsport, NY (Newspaper date September 7, 1836)

WAKEMAN ___ age 18y son of Elisha and Maria Wakeman of Covert, NY in Prattsburgh, NY September 10, 1836

BURR Col. Aaron former Vice President of US in his 81st year at Staten Island September 13, 1836

KENNEDY Hiers age 40y in Kennedyville, NY September 21, 1836

BUTLER Juba a native African age 125y in Bath, NY October 12, 1836

MASTEN Dr. John age 66y formerly of Red Hook, NY in Bath, NY October 27, 1836

STRICKLAND Daniel age 70y in Wheeler, NY October 26, 1836

ERWIN Samuel age 67y in Erwin, NY November 10, 1836

SEARLES Lemuel B. age 36y in Addison, NY January 13, 1837

EMERSON George W. abt 30y in Cameron, NY January 12, 1837

LEWIS Mrs. Rufus M. in Bradford, NY January 11, 1837

SMITH Ferman age 13m son of Charles Smith in Tyrone, NY January 11, 1837

SMITH Benjamin age 72y in Tyrone, NY January 12, 1837

GERMAN ___ infant son of Andrew T. German in Tyrone, NY January 13, 1837

BUSH Alpheus age 82y a Revolutionary Soldier and wife Sarah age 74y in Tyrone, NY January 14, 1837

DEATH NOTICES

STEEL B. G. age 60y in Tyrone, NY January 14, 1837

RYNOE Samuel age 15y son of Henry Rynoe in Tyrone, NY January 14, 1837

MILLARD Abigail in her 86th yr in Cameron, NY January 13, 1837. Son Stephen

GILMORE Peres in Bath, NY January 18, 1837

DIVINE Samuel N. age 50 on way to Neversink with Mother January 18, 1837

WILCOX Mrs. Jane age 74y in Tyrone, NY January 25, 1837

PRATT Mrs. A. E. age 21y in Bradford, NY January 26, 1837

PURDY Erastus age 41y in Bath, NY March 16, 1837

STEPHENS Col. John age 71y in Greenwood, NY March 19, 1837

GOULD Lucy age 31y wife of A. R. Gould in Bath, NY April 9, 1837

WEST Capt. Amos C. age 80y a Revolutionary Soldier in Milo, NY April 14, 1837

BLOOD Catherine age 44y wife of Calvin Blood in Cohocton, NY June 29, 1837

TILTON Jonathan age 75y in Bath, NY July 3, 1837

STEWART Livia M. age 37y wife of R. B. Stewart late of Bath, NY in Ovid, NY (Newspaper date July 19, 1837)

RANNEY George a Revolutionary Soldier in Bath, NY July 20, 1837

DELEVAN Emily age 24y wife of George E. Delevan and dau of James **WILTSIE** of Fishkill Landing, NY in Hammondsport, NY August 3, 1837

COLLYER Fletcher W. in his 25th yr formerly of Cohocton, NY in Dearborn. Mi. September 3, 1837

DEY Benjamin F. age 21y formerly of Penn Yan, NY in Harrisburgh, Tx. July 24, 1837

CURTIS Joseph age 5y in Mud Creek, NY September 9, 1837

WILCOX Martha age 2y 3m adopted dau of George in Bath, NY September 14, 1837

MAGEE Ann Eloise age 17m 2w dau of John Magee in Bath, NY September 12, 1837

GILMORE Nelson G. age 18m son of Peres Gilmore in Bath, NY September 11, 1837

SMITH Andrew age 76y in Bath, NY September 18, 1837. Born Scotland and came to this Co. in 1793

STEUBEN COUNTY NEWSPAPERS 53

SWART Mary B. nr 4m dau of Peter Swart in Bath, NY September 28, 1837

METCALF Franklin age 26y in Bath, NY October 24, 1837

BLACK John in his 43rd yr in Wayne, NY October 14, 1837

METCALF Osey age 45y widow of John Metcalf in Bath, NY December 13, 1837

PALMER Andrew age 16y in Mud Creek, NY November 30, 1837

FOWLER William Mc Kay infant son of John W. Fowler in Bath, NY February 1, 1838

ROBINSON Mary age 40y wife of Dr. Jedediah Robinson in Howard, NY February 20, 1838. Leaves Husband and 8 children

PORTER Robert L. age 27y son of Judge Porter in Prattsburgh, NY May 29, 1838

KENT Abigail in her 57th yr wife of John Kent in Woodhull, NY June 16, 1838

WILBER Elmira age 27y wife of Hoxy H. Wilber in Bath, NY July 26, 1838

LOGHRY James age 76y in Howard, NY August 3, 1838

FRANKLIN Walter S. in Lancaster, Pa. September 20, 1838

WASS Adam age 70y in Jasper, NY September 29, 1838

SMITH Miss Cassandra abt 28y in Kennedyville, NY October 15, 1838

BABCOCK William abt 50y in Penn Yan, NY October 20, 1838

SMITH Miss Electa age 20y in Kennedyville, NY October 27, 1838

TOWNSEND Abraham crushed by fallen log in Tyrone, NY November 29, 1838

SOUTHERLAND Isaac age 65y in Batavia, NY November 19, 1838

HAUSE Joseph age 51y in Tyrone, NY December 3, 1838

DARRIN Daniel age 92y Revolutionary Soldier in Troupsburgh, NY November 4, 1838

PEAK Charles abt 22y in Avoca, NY February 8, 1840

BURNSIDE James abt 24y in Kennedyville, NY February 8, 1840

LEWIS James age 33y in Bath, NY March 4, 1840

AINSWORTH Isaac in his 54th yr in Prattsburgh, NY March 8, 1840

DEATH NOTICES

EDWARDS Samuel T. age 24y in Bath, NY March 24 or 31, 1840

RICHARDSON Miss Nancy age 29y in Mt. Washington, NY April 6, 1840

CHAMBERLAIN Angeline age 25y wife of W. W. Chamberlain late of Bath, NY in Livonia, NY April 14, 1840

PLATT Benjamin Jr. age 21y in Bradford, NY April 22, 1840

SNOOK Mrs. Mathias abt 45y in Campbell, NY May 11, 1840

HIGGINS James G. age 49y formerly of Bath, NY on Ottawa, Ill. April 24, 1840. Leaves widow and 7 children

STEVENSON Miss Margaret age 29y dau of John in Howard, NY May 26, 1840

BIDWELL Adoplhus age 84y Father of Eli Bidwell of Bath, NY in E. Hartford, Ct. May 29, 1840

NILES Dr. Noah age 61y in Prattsburgh, NY June 3, 1840. Native of Colechester, Ct. and came to Prattsburgh in 1809

LIVINGSTON Edward Atty. in Albany, NY (Newspaper date June 24, 1840)

SWARTHOUT Robert age 61y in Hector, NY June 14, 1840

ANDREWS Ichabod in his 74th yr in N. Reading, NY July 18, 1840

SANTEE Nancy age 46 wife of Isaac Santee in Cameron, NY July 15, 1840

CLARK Ira C. in his 47th yr in Prattsburgh, NY August 1, 1840. Native of N. Salem, NY and came to Prattsburgh in 1824 from Manlius, NY

MEDBURY Mary age 49y wife of Orson Medbury both formerly of Otsego Co. NY in Tyrone, NY July 19, 1840

CHAMBERLAIN Angeline age 4m 2w dau of Henry W. and Angeline Chamberlain in Howard, NY August 21, 1840

YOUNG Mrs. Julia age 33y formerly of Bath, NY in Benton Center, NY August 20, 1840

SHERWOOD Miss Janet at sister's Mrs. Mary **WIGHTMAN** both formerly of Wayne, NY in Texas July 5, 1840

HALL Maria age 17y in Kennedyville, NY October 4, 1840

PATTERSON Robert in his 79th yr a Revolutionary Soldier in Lindley, NY October 2, 1840

SMITH Joseph G. age 26y in Bath, NY October 8, 1840

MAY Dr. Joseph Adams age 24y son of James May of Bath, NY in Red River Landing, La. October 22, 1840

TOMPSON Samuel age 73y a Revolutionary Soldier in Bath, NY November 3, 1840

GUNSOLUS Rena M. age 30y wife of Lombert V. Gunsolus formerly of Bath, NY in Portage, NY (Newspaper date January 6, 1841)

ANNABEL Phebe age 25y wife of Caleb Annabel in Milo, NY January 3, 1841

DUDLEY Edward infant son of Moses Dudley in Bath, NY January 31, 1841

WOODARD William infant son of William Woodard in Bath, NY February 1, 1841

JOHNSON Anna age 58y wife of John Johnson formerly of Bath, NY in Jasper, NY February 4, 1841

HAMMOND ___ infant son of Samuel H. Hammond in Bath, NY February 5, 1841

HEMPSTED Mrs. Mary age 75y in Erwin, NY February 13, 1841

ROBBINS Edward age 75y of Guilford, NY in Caton, NY January 25, 1841

CAMERON Jane age 65y wife of Charles in Greenwood, NY January 31, 1841

TIFFANY Norman age 18y son of W. N. Tiffany of Bath, NY in New Lebanan, NY February 17, 1841

HAMMOND James R. L. age 7y son of Samuel H. Hammond in Bath, NY February 25, 1841

DANIELS Catherine age 2y 6m dau of Norman Daniels February 27, 1841

GARROW Nathaniel in Auburn, NY March 3, 1841

MESSENGER Eland age 32y formerly of Cleveland, Ohio in Orange, NY February 27, 1841

LANE Charles age 3y son of David Lane March 14, 1841

NEALLY Mrs. Elizabeth age 84y in Bath, NY March 20, 1841

GLASS Erastus age 60y in Bath, NY April 2, 1841

FOWLER John age 2y son of John Fowler in Bath, NY April 19, 1841

ERWIN John A. infant son of Gen. F. E. Erwin in Painted Post, NY April 13, 1841

DEATH NOTICES

GAY Joseph age 2y son of William Gay in Howard, NY April 12, 1841

COMPTON Hannah Louisa in her 16th yr dau of Peter Compton in Orange, NY April 19, 1841

MINOR Mrs. Maria age 43y in Campbell, NY April 24, 1841

LELAND Charles Edward age 2y son of Judge Leland in Bath, NY April 22, 1841

COMPTON Mrs. Hannah in her 65th yr in Orange, NY April 25, 1841

MACOMBS Michael Josiah age 3y son of John in S. Dansville, NY May 3, 1841

SMITH Hannah age 64y wife of Joseph Smith in Bath, NY May 10, 1841

BARTON Andrew G. in his 16th yr in Bath, NY May 22, 1841

ROWE Rachel age 40y consort of John Rowe formerly of Bath, NY in Portland, Ill. May 1, 1841

LORIN Anna A. age 64y wife of William Lorin in Cameron, NY May 30, 1841

WARREN Steward K. age 26y in Bath, NY May 31, 1841

STEWART George in his 55th yr in Howard, NY June 5, 1841. Native of Ireland, leaves large family

WILLYS Mr. ____ late keeper of Hotel in Bennetts Flats in Howard, NY June 4, 1841

COOK Bates in Lewiston, NY May 30, 1841

MC HENRY James in his 53rd yr in Almond, NY May 16, 1841

BORDEN George Isaac abt 12y son of Isasc and Eliza C. Borden in Hornellsville, NY May 16, 1841

SMEAD Cornelia M. age 11m 17d dau of T. H. and M. E. in Ohio City July 28, 1841

WALKER Helen Amelia abt 3y dau of Hiram and Nancy Walker in Bath, NY August 21, 1841

GOODSELL Isaac age 51y Postmaster of Hornby, NY in Port Jefferson, NY August 25, 1841

NEALLY William age 6y son of Samuel Neally in Bath, NY August 23, 1841

BRADLEY Mary Ann age 32y wife of Zera A. Bradley and dau of George **WHEELER** in Bath, NY September 13, 1841

CONNOR Alexander abt 22y at res. of Mrs. Lewis **BILES** in Bath, NY September 11,

1841

SHOCKEY John age 72y in Elmira, NY September 12, 1841

GREGG John age 63y in Bath, NY August 28, 1841

WIXOM Elizbeth age 22y wife of William in Prattsburgh, NY September 16, 1841

WARREN Lucretia age 4y dau of J. W. and Sarah in Bath, NY September 20, 1841

NEALLY Mathew age 86y 11m Revolutionary Soldier in Bath, NY September 22, 1841

BELLOWS William H. age 3y 29d son of Isaac in Prattsburgh, NY September 18, 1841

BENTON Alonzo age 19y in Urbana, NY September 28, 1841

WARDEN John age 78y one of earliest settlers in Bath, NY September 30, 1841

SILSBEE Edward Clark age 4y 4m 18d son of Alfred and Jane Silsbee in Avoca, NY October 3, 1841

MC MASTER Adeline A. in her 35th yr wife of David Mc Master and only child of Mrs. A. **HUMPHREYS** in Bath, NY October 7, 1841

BRACE Elizabeth age 37y wife of Charles Brace in Bath, NY October 8, 1841

SOBER Martin age 19y in Bath, NY October 9, 1841

BABCOCK Mrs. Sarah age 63y in Caton, NY (Newspaper date October 13, 1841)

HATHAWAY Sally age 21y in Addison, NY (Newspaper date October 13, 1841)

POTTER Gifford age 42y in Wheeler, NY October 25, 1841

PORTER Robert H. age 3y 11m son of William L. and Olive L. Porter in Prattsburgh, NY November 4/5, 1841

TAYLOR Christina age 48y consort of George W. Taylor in Wheeler, NY November 12, 1841

BLACK William G. age 9y son of Jeremiah Black in Bath, NY November 21, 1841

DABOLL Mary wife of Anson Daboll in Prattsburgh, NY December 21, 1841. Native of Litchfield, Ct. and came to Prattsburgh in 1822

RAYMOND Lucy age 86y wife of Daniel in Cohocton, NY December 31, 1841

GOODRICH James age 72y in Columbia, Pa. January 21, 1842. Married Miss **BELL** of this area abt 2 yrs ago

DEATH NOTICES

ROWE Cornelia age 24y wife of Anson Rowe and dau of late Erastus **GLASS** in Bath, NY January 21, 1841

SANFORD James who fell from horse last week in Wayne, NY January 31, 1842

WILLOUR Hannah M. age 5y dau of Jacob and Rachael in Bath, NY February 9, 1842

SMITH Egbert age 17m son of Orren Smith in Bath, NY February 28, 1842

KNOWLTON Sarah in her 46th yr wife of Chester in Hornby, NY October 25, 1841

WARREN Phineas age 65y in Bath, NY March 4, 1842

LAWTON Permelia in her 25th yr consort of Rev. D. B. Lawton in Bath, NY March 17, 1842

EDWARDS Sarah in her 12th yr dau of late George C. in Bath, NY March 18, 1842

DAVENPORT Lydia age 41y wife of Ira Davenport and dau of late Dugald **CAMERON** in Hornellsville, NY March 20, 1842

LELAND Belinda P. age 39y consort of Z. A. Leland and dau of Robert **PORTER** of Prattsburgh, NY in Bath, NY March 26, 1842

CAMPBELL Robert age 1m son of John Campbell in Bath, NY March 26, 1842

PURDY Mary Lurany age 3y 10m dau of Charles and Harriet L. Purdy in Bath, NY April 2, 1842

BARNEY Caroline age 10m dau of Nelson Barney April 2, 1842

SEARS Rev. Rufus age 25y in Bath, NY April 9, 1842

RICE Sarah H. age 20y dau of Ebenezer of Prattsburgh, NY in Bath, NY April 9, 1842

HUNTER Sarah F. age 14y dau of Peter Hunter in Bath, NY April 9, 1842

COLCORD Phineas age 19y son of Joseph Colcord in Cameron, NY April 14, 1842

BERTINE Louisa age 13y in Bath, NY April 16, 1842

RUTHERFORD James M. abt 38y in Bath, NY April 22, 1842

MARKHAM Henry formerly of Bath, NY in Houston, Tx. March 30, 1842

BROWN Charles Leslie age 3m son of George Brown in Bath, NY April 29, 1842

ROSE Mrs. Lydia in her 72nd yr in Wheeler, NY May 1, 1842

SWICK Benjamin age 78y in Urbana, NY May 6, 1842

CLEVELAND Marcia in her 45th yr in Hammondsport, NY May 5, 1842

SHERWOOD Micajah in Woodhull, NY May 6, 1842

SMITH David age 3y son of Orren Smith in Bath, NY May 17, 1842

PHALING Capt. Phillip age 77y 3m a Revolutionary Soldier in Jasper, NY May 16, 1842

KELLOGG Charles in his 69th yr formerly of Kelloggsville, NY in Ann Arbor, Mi. May 11, 1842

WARREN Maria L. age 21y relict of Stewart K. Warren in Bath, NY May 13, 1842

WILLIAMS Henry S. in his 47th yr in Tyrone, NY May 27, 1842. Leaves wife and 6 children

HUBBELL Jemima age 78y relict of Nehemiah Hubbell of Painted Post, NY in Bath, NY May 27, 1842. Buried Painted Post

DAY Margaret Maria age 23y wife of Jackson J. Day in Howard, NY May 21, 1842

CLARK George W. abt 30y formerly of Bath, NY son of Jonas Clark in Naples, NY May 31, 1842

WAGGONER Harriet age 4m dau of James Waggoner in Bath, NY June 3, 1842

RUTHERFORD Elizabeth age 73y wife of Edward Rutherford in Bath, NY June 13, 1842

ZIELIE Mrs. Sally age 60y in Oil City, Pa. May 18, 1842

JOHNSON James age 90y a Revolutionary pensioner in Bath, NY June 27, 1842

SQUIRES George W. age 6y 5m eldest son of Nathaniel and Eliza Ann Squires in Davenport, Io. June 2, 1842

KINNEY Daniel age 72y in Bath, NY June 29, 1842

BARNUM Lucy age 63y consort of Isaac Barnum in Prattsburgh, NY June 29, 1842

HIGGINS Rev. David formerly of Bath, NY in Norwalk, Oh. (Newspaper date July 13, 1842)

HADLEY Rhoda age 80y widow of James in Canisteo, NY July 9, 1842. Res 52 yrs

BLOOD Isaac age 82y in Cohocton, NY July 18, 1842. Leaves son Capt. Asa Blood of Bath, NY

DORSEY Cecelia M. age 24y dau of Dr. John D. **HIGGINS** in Bath, NY August 8,

DEATH NOTICES

1842. Son age 6m died July 22, 1842

HALL Adeline age 17m dau of Austin Hall in Bath, NY July 23, 1842. Rhoda H. wife of Austin and dau of Elisha **HANKS** died August 9, 1842

FARNHAM Adelaide age 22y dau of Caleb Farnham in Bath, NY August 14, 1842

CROUCH Caleb in his 55th yr in Cohocton, NY August 21, 1842

COLE James B. age 29y formerly of Bath, NY in Jackson, Mi. (Newspaper date August 31, 1842)

HOWELL ____ inf child of William Howell in Bath, NY August 28, 1842

TERRELL ____ inf child of Miles Terrell in Bath, NY August 28, 1842

TICKNER Jane age 62y wife of Roswell Tickner in Bath, NY September 12, 1842

READ James age 17m son of L. H. Read in Bath, NY September 11, 1842

JONES Margaret age 46y wife of Bidear Jones in Bath, NY September 9, 1842

GANSEVOORT Dr. Ten Eyck age 39y in Bath, NY September 24, 1842

GILBERT Andrew J. age 6y son of Franklin Gilbert drowned while trying to cross river on a log in Cohocton, NY September 23, 1842

MC KIBBEN ____ only son of James Mc Kibben in Howard, NY September 26, 1842 and only dau died September 2, 1842. Recently lost 5 children

PERRY Rachel age 57y wife of Alanson Perry in Troupsburgh, NY October 6, 1842

OGLEY Mary S. H. age 10w dau of W. H. Ogley in Buffalo, NY September 29, 1842

PULLING Abel in his 83rd yr formerly of Galway, NY at son's Dr. E. B. Pulling in Hammondsport, NY October 14, 1842. One of early setlers

CAMPBELL Permillia age 20y dau of John Campbell in Bath, NY October 10, 1842

LEGRO Betsey age 52y wife of Samuel Legro in Bath, NY October 20, 1842

IRWIN M. Robert age 79y in Bath, NY October 26, 1842

SHATTUCK John Tyler age 20y 8m son of Lucius Shattuck in Cohocton, NY November 5, 1842

MC KIBBEN Dorothy M. wife of James in Howard, NY November 28, 1842

GUYON Samuel H. age 18y son of Elijah Guyon of Green, NY at uncle's Daniel **JAMISON** in Canisteo, NY (Newspaper date December 7, 1842)

BARTHOLOMEW Daniel age 84y a Revolutionary Soldier in Bradford, NY November 22, 1842

HALL Lucinda age 51y wife of Timothy Hall in Troy, NY/Pa.? November 28, 1842

missing issues

GLENN Pierce in his 30th yr in Dansville, NY December 22, 1844

ROSE Silas W. abt 40y formerly of Bath, NY in Ingham Co. Mi. November 25, 1844

CHADWICK Sarah in her 67th yr wife of Jabez in Bath, NY January 15, 1845

DECKER Mrs. Betsy abt 45y in Bath, NY January 27, 1845

COOK Comfort age 88y formerly of Hartwick, NY in Bath, NY January 29, 1845

LUCAS Harry age 76y in Bath, NY February 7, 1845, freed from slavery abt 28 yrs ago

CAMPBELL John age 65y in Bath, NY February 15, 1845

PULLING Mary Frances E. age 2y 6m dau of Dr. E. B. and Mary Pulling in Bath, NY January 27, 1845

FRANCIS Richard age 83y 10m in Prattsburgh, NY February 12, 1845

CHAMBERLAIN Rhoda Amanda in her 13th yr in Bath, NY February 11, 1845

CHAMBERLAIN Betsy age 50y consort of Sen. Calvin T. Chamberlain at Cuba, NY February 27, 1845

VAN GELDER Mrs. Polly age 44y in Bath, NY March 15, 1845

WALKER Lydia wife of John Walker in Bath, NY March 23, 1845

HANKS Lydia wife of John Hanks in Bath, NY March 24, 1845. Infant son died March 26, 1845

HERKIMER Abner M. in Washington, Ark. February 10, 1845

DAWSON Mrs. Jane age 48y in Bath, NY April 25, 1845

LEGGETT Isaac Whitmore age 22y son of Allen Leggett in Cohocton, NY May 6, 1845

HARTWELL Sophrona age 28y wife of Elijah Hartwell and dau of Thomas and Percy **FREEMAN** of Manchester, Mi. in N. Cohocton, NY May 12, 1845

BURLEY Hannah age 26y wife of Daniel Burley in Bath, NY May 13, 1845

HAMILTON John found dead nr home in Howard, NY June 17, 1845

DEATH NOTICES

GLENN John age 63y formerly of Urbana, NY in Dansville, NY June 1, 1845

KING Fanny A. age 23y wife of Horace King of Ithaca, NY June 6, 1845

CAMPBELL John age 76y in Thurston, NY June 12, 1845

WHITAKER Hester D. age 38y wife of John in Mud Creek, NY June 12, 1845

MC CAY Orange W. age 41y in N. Almond, NY June 13, 1845

READ Elizabeth abt 1y dau of Lazarus Read in Bath, NY July 21, 1845

RIDDLE George age 49y in Canisteo, NY July 26, 1845

SIMPSON Andrew age 84y 1m 28d a Revolutionary Soldier in Jasper, NY August 11, 1845

CHAMBERLAIN Eslhon age 51y widow of Joseph in Bath, NY August 22, 1845

WALKER Nancy age 31y wife of Hiram Walker in Bath, NY August 31, 1845

BURKET Mary abt 50y wife of William Burket in Bath, NY September 8/15, 1845

WATTLES Irving age 12y 3m 5d son of Lorenzo and Phebe Wattles in Corning, NY September 7, 1845

STEPHENS Alfred age 58y formerly of Tompkins Co. NY in Cameron, NY September 29, 1845

SWART Clarinda Maria inf dau of Peter Swart in Bath, NY October 13, 1845

BRINK Amanda age 15y in Urbana, NY October 27, 1845

HUNTER George age 57y in Wayne, NY October 21, 1845. Leaves large family

CARTER John age 86y a Revolutionary Soldier in Seneca Falls, NY October 24, 1845. Leaves grandson Capt. E. R. **BIDWELL** of Bath, NY

DOBBS Mrs. Anna age 82y in Thurston, NY December 20, 1845

GILSTON Mrs. Sally age 32y formerly of Bath, NY in Salina, NY November 14, 1845

WOODRUFF Oliver age 90y a Revolutionary Soldier in Lavonia, NY December 24, 1845

SMITH Fidelia age 6m dau of Daniel C. Smith in Bath, NY January 2, 1846 and Daniel age 26y died January 8, 1846

HOVEY Betsey age 8y in Bath, NY February 11, 1846

WOODWARD Moses Lyon age 3y 1m son of William A. and Sally Woodward in Bath, NY February 22, 1846

COOPER Thomas age 67y in Bath, NY February 26, 1846

SWITZER Henry age 78y late of Bradford, NY in Ill. December 20, 1845 and wife Elizabeth age 72y died February 6, 1846

METCALFE Nancy age 58y consort of Thomas Metcalfe in Bath, NY March 4, 1846

ROBARDS Ann age 21y 3m dau of John L. Robards of Avoca, NY in Howard, NY April 27, 1846

BELL Elizabeth in her 63rd yr wife of William Bell in Orange, NY April 17, 1846

HARROWER Susan age 28y consort of G. T. Harrower and dau of Alva **THURBER** in Lindley, NY April 20, 1846

WENTWORTH Chester abt 35y in Bath, NY May 13, 1846

STEWART Charlotte age 26y wife of Richard B. Stewart and dau of Thomas and Nancy **METCALFE** in Bath, NY August 5, 1846

CLARK Mary A. **(MILLS)** age 20y wife of Jonathan in Bath, NY August 30, 1846

JACOBS Rev. Joseph age 70y in Howard, NY September 5, 1846

GOODRICH Dr. Levi S. age 53y in Almond, NY September 16, 1846

MATHEWS Vincent age 80y formerly of Bath, NY in Rochester, NY (Newspaper date September 30, 1846)

OSBORN Sheldon age 56y formerly of Alfred, NY in Wis. September 19, 1846

POWELL Lurany in her 79th yr widow of Stephen Powell of Dansville, NY at res of C. **PURDY** in Bath, NY November 14, 1846

SHEPARD Morris P. in Penn Yan, NY November 18, 1846

WILBUR John age 86y in Troy, Pa. November 9, 1846. Son Samuel of Bath, NY

WATSON Mrs. Margaret a widow in Bath, NY December 6, 1846

MORRIS John inf son of Israel Morris in Bath, NY December 13, 1846

RICE Anna Mariah age 27y in Avoca, NY on birthday January 1, 1847

CARUTHERS Katurah D. age 22y wife of Cameron Caruthers and dau of James **BOWLBY** in Bath, NY December 8, 1846

DEATH NOTICES

EMERSON Marilla age 46y wife of Joseph in Bath, NY January 18, 1847

BIDWELL Rebecca G. age 8y dau of Capt. Edwin R. in Bath, NY January 26, 1847

MEGRADY Benjamin age 23y in Prattsburgh, NY January 29, 1847

CLEVELAND Henry age 21y in Prattsburgh, NY February 4, 1847

JOHNSON Elmira age 47y wife of S. A. Johnson and dau of William **CURTIS** died February 1, 1847, son James C. died February 10, 1847 and dau Helen age 21y died February 2, 1847, buried Prattsburgh, NY

LEMON Michael age 70y formerly of Howard, NY in Napoleon, Mi. February 24, 1847

WEBSTER Fanny Delphine age 9m dau of James and Caroline Webster in Bath, NY March 24, 1847

FISHER John in his 70th yr at son-in-laws Gen. R. **RATHBONE** in Rathbone, NY March 15, 1847

GLOAD Charles W. age 6y son of John Gload in Pulteney, NY April 2, 1847

GLASS Lydia Ann age 17y only dau of late Franklin Glass in Kennedyville, NY March 30, 1847

NICHOLSON James age 27y in Elmira, NY May 6, 1847

RUTHERFORD Turzah E. age 12y dau of Edward in Thurston, NY June 16, 1847

EATON Benjamin age 84y 10m a Revolutionary Soldier at bro in Urbana, NY May 28, 1847. Native of Mass. and res of Steuben Co. 60 yrs.

PATTENT Alexander age 64y in Wayne, NY July 2, 1847

FRINK R. Robie age 19y at Father's in Bath, NY July 16, 1847

COLLINS Martin abt 55y in Bath, NY July 30, 1847

COOPER Daniel abt 80y in Bath, NY July 30, 1847

FORD Maria consort of James Ford and dau of late Judge **LINDSLEY** in Lawrenceville, Pa. July 26, 1847

ROBERTS Catherine abt 70y relict of Joseph Roberts in Bath, NY August 12, 1847

LITTLE Catherine age 17m dau of William Little in Bath, NY August 1, 1847

EASON Mary age 16m dau of Hart Eason in Canisteo, NY August 17, 1847

KENNEDY Anna in her 78th yr widow of Henry Kennedy in Kennedyville, NY September 6, 1847

EATON Mary abt 45y wife of Benjamin Eaton in Bath, NY September 7, 1847

DORR Louisa M. age 23y wife of Dr. James D. Dorr in Bath, NY September 11, 1847

FLUENT Fanny E. age 22y dau of Joseph and Fanny in Addison, NY August 27, 1847

STRAIGHT Elijah age 71y in Avoca, NY September 12, 1847

WOODARD Joseph age 79y in Avoca, NY September 14, 1847

HAYT Samuel age 31y in Corning, NY September 7, 1847

ROBIE Jonathan in his 76th yr in Corinth, Vt. October 3, 1847

PAWLING Henry age 59y in Avoca, NY October 17, 1847

STEWART James age 32y in Howard, NY October 18, 1847

HOFFMAN Chauncey Md. age 52y formerly of Chenango Co. NY recently of Bath, NY in Ill. September 27, 1847

GOULD Ralph F. age 14m son of Azel R. Gould in Bath, NY September 22, 1847

PAGE Adelaide R. age 3y dau of John Page in Bath, NY September 22, 1847

MC CLURE Finla abt 47y son of Gen. George Mc Clure formerly of Bath, NY in Canisteo, NY October 28, 1847

BROOKS Henry age 26y son of Birdsey Brooks of Oakland Co. Mi. in Fairport, NY October 25, 1847

HARRIS William D. age 27y thrown from wagon and dragged nr Tyrone, NY November 17, 1847

HUNTER Miss Hannah age 56y in Bath, NY November 17, 1847

missing issues

ANTHONY Charles F. age 23y in Bath, NY December 8, 1848

BRECK Marcia Ann in her 29th yr wife of George W. in Bath, NY December 13, 1848

ALLIS Josiah in his 70th yr in Prattsburgh, NY November 27, 1848

PERKINS James H. age 24y son of Capt. John Perkins in Pulteney, NY December 11, 1848

JONES Col. Drayton fell through scaffolding in loft of barn in Wayne, NY December 26, 1848

GRAVES Mrs. Charles abt 65y in Howard, NY January 20, 1849

WILBER Miss Abigail age 32y in Bath, NY January 23, 1849

COOPER Hannah R. age 26y in Bath, NY January 26, 1849

MULHOLLEN Jane age 65y 5m consort of William S. in Bath, NY February 6, 1849

EMERSON Joseph age 60y in Bath, NY February 7, 1849

ADAMS Samuel H. age 28y 2m at Father's in Painted Post, NY February 27, 1849

MERRILL George H. age 18y at Father's in Howard, NY March 3, 1849

DOLLY Christopher age 73y in Howard, NY March 1, 1849

FORD Eliza age 16y dau of Eli of Howard, NY at Alfred Academy March 2, 1849

COTTON William Henry age 3y son of E. Cotton in Patchinsville, NY March 23, 1849

CLIZBE Phebe in her 39th yr wife of Joseph Clizbe in Avoca, NY March 29, 1849

HUNTER Fanny age 5y dau of James and Catherine in Bath, NY March 19, 1849

FRANKLIN Mrs. ____ at advanced age in Bath, NY May 28, 1849

AMIDON Lucy age 31y 10m wife of Shepherd in Greenwood, NY June 18, 1849

SPORE John abt 89y in Italy, NY July 12, 1849

HAMILTON Keziah age 87y widow of Daniel Hamilton a Revolutionary Soldier in Bath, NY August 11, 1849

MC QUAHAE John in his 34th yr in Danville, Pa. August 12, 1849

BOSTWICK Miss Mercy in her 62nd yr sis of H. W. Bostwick in Corning, NY August 24, 1849

DECKER Sidney S. in Havana, NY August 25, 1849

VANDERHOVEN Elizabeth age 10m 25d dau of Jesse and Annis Vanderhoven in Bath, NY August 29, 1849

ELLIS Eugene age 10m son of Ella and Jane Ellis in Bath, NY September 3, 1849

DODGE Warren age 33y in Wayne, NY August 24, 1849

VAN CAMPEN Maj. Moses age 92y 9m in Angelica, NY October 15, 1849. Born January 21, 1757 in Hunterdon Co. NJ a brave officer in Revolutionary War

CHAPMAN Roswell R. age 72y in Bath, NY November 16, 1849

BLOOD Indianna in her 57th yr widow of Capt. Asa Blood of Bath, NY at res of T. C. **THOMPSON** in Ithaca, NY November 24, 1849

BODINE John C. age 54y early settler in Tyrone, NY (Newspaper date January 2, 1850)

RUTHERFORD Mrs. Nancy dau of Henry **MC ELWEE** in Bath, NY January 12, 1850

STEWART Elizabeth in her 34th yr wife of Samuel Stewart 3rd and dau of John and Elizabeth **MC ELWAIN** in Howard, NY January 8, 1850

BAILEY Richard age 11m son of Thomas and Lorinda in Bath, NY February 5, 1850

SALISBURY Charles Andrew age 6y 1m son of Tobias and Mary Salisbury in Urbana, NY February 26, 1850

METCALFE Miss Nancy age 82y in Bath, NY March 6, 1850

FROST Nancy age 15y dau of Jacob Frost in Orange, NY February 26, 1850

HARTSHORN Jacob age 72y 3m 8d one of 1st settlers of Madison Co. NY in Lebanon, NY January 30, 1850

HARROWER Mary widow of Levi B. Harrower in Big Flats, NY March 20, 1850

WILLOUR Rachel wife of Jacob Willour in Bath, NY March 25, 1850

MYRTLE Phillip age 75y in Wheeler, NY March 28, 1850

SWICK Hily Ann age 44y wife of Rev. B. R. Swick in Bath, NY April 2, 1850

CLARKE Theodore F. age 19y 10m son of late James C. and Eliza A. Clarke of Newburgh, NY in Poughkeepsie, NY April 3, 1850

PERKINS John age 66y in Pulteney, NY March 27, 1850, res for 40 yrs

FRANKLIN Charles age 35y in Bradford, NY April 9, 1850

DAVIDSON David age 71y in Monterey, NY April 1, 1850

JOHNSON Joel age 81y in Monterey, NY April 2, 1850

SPRAGUE Stephen age 16y son of John S. Sprague in Bradford, NY April 6, 1850

DICKINSON Walter age 58y nr Jefferson, NY April 10, 1850

ROBERTS Charles age 30y late of Reading, NY in Cal. rec (Newspaper date May 1, 1850)

LYNCH Henry C. in his 16th yr son of Albert and Mary C. Lynch in Orange, NY April 16, 1850

DRAKE Ruhamah age 59y 1m 14d wife of Deacon Drake in Jasper, NY April 30, 1850

SMITH Isaac in his 51st yr in Bath, NY June 18, 1850

WILLOUR Nancy Adeline age 21y wife of Alonzo Willour in Bath, NY June 10, 1850

WEBSTER Ithamer in his 26th yr in Bath, NY June 23, 1850

MARTIN Elisha abt 65y in Bath, NY July 5, 1850

WOODWARD Thomas age 22y in Bath, NY July 12, 1850

CROCKER Wickham R. age 11m son of Dr. Wickham R. and Jane R. Crocker in Cameron, NY July 24, 1850

BLOOD Charles age 1y 6m son of Mrs. Ellen Blood in Bath, NY July 28, 1850

WATKINS Samuel (colored) in his 65th yr in Bath, NY August 22, 1850. Born a slave in Va. and came to Steuben Co. with master Capt. **HELM** more than 40 yrs ago

SMITH Mrs. Elizabeth in her 54th yr Mother of Frederick **WARD** of Bath, NY in Owego, NY August 28, 1850

GOODRICH Rhoda in her 74th yr in Bath, NY September 12, 1850

LOOMIS Gelina F. dau of Henry Loomis in Bath, NY September 28, 1850

MASON Jemima age 44y wife of Elliott Mason in Hornellsville, NY November 5, 1850

MAGEE Jane age 43y wife of Thomas Magee in Hornellsville, NY November 25, 1850

SIMMONS Calvin age 60y in Bath, NY November 29, 1850

WHEELER Mary in her 90th yr consort of Jeremiah in Bath, NY November 28, 1850

COLLIER Richard in his 91st yr formerly of Green Co. NY in Avoca, NY December 21, 1850

UNDERHILL Porcia Maria in her 44th yr wife of Charles Underhill in Horseheads, NY December 22, 1850

WATROUS Eleanor in her 46th yr wife of John Watrous and dau of Robert **DOWNEY** of Yates Co. NY in Pulteney, NY January 7, 1851

STEUBEN COUNTY NEWSPAPERS 69

FERRIS Lewis G. age 36y 9m in Mt. Morris, NY January 10, 1851

RHODES Helen wife of B. K. Rhodes and dau of late David **PETRIKIN** in Danville, Pa. January 9, 1851

WHITING Abram age 18y son of John W. Whiting in Howard, NY February 15, 1851

BURNHAM George W. age 43y in Avoca, NY April 6, 1851

FISK Mary Ellen age 1y 3m dau of F. A. and Mary S. Fisk in Bath, NY June 5, 1851

CAMPBELL Fowler age 6y 3m 22d son of Robert Campbell in Bath, NY July 9, 1851

MESICK Henry in his 62nd yr in Kennedyville, NY September 20, 1851

WEBSTER James age 30y formerly of Owego, NY in Bath, NY October 1, 1851

EVANS Elisha H. in Kennedyville, NY October 12, 1851

WILHELM Sarah age 50y 8m 28d wife of Joseph in Bath, NY November 25, 1851

HOWELL Frances Minerva age 15w dau of Edward and Mary Howell in Bath, NY December 7, 1851

BARNEY Col. Jonathan age 74y in Wheeler, NY December 4, 1851

CHAPIN Ezra age 66y in Prattsburgh, NY December 10, 1851

GARDNER Caleb Lewis age 45y in Elmira, NY December 8, 1851

RHODES John age 65y 5m 14d Father of the Editor of this paper W. C. Rhodes in Danville, Pa. January 7, 1852

ALDERMAN Emma age 10m 28d dau of O. P. in Thurston, NY January 21, 1852

NYCE Simeon R. in his 27th yr formerly of Hammondsport, NY at Father's in Sugar Creek, Wis. December 29, 1851

LITTLE William Graham age 25y 10m 4d in Bath, NY January 26, 1852

WHEELER Grattan H. age 68y 6m in Wheeler, NY March 10, 1852, One of the 1st settlers, res for 50 yrs

BENJAMIN Samuel abt 65y formerly of New York City in Bath, NY March 18, 1852

ROWLAND Mrs. ____ of Avoca, NY in Steuben Co. jail March 21, 1852. Accused of poisoning her husband, subsequently found innocent

RICHARDSON Nancy age 61y in Genessee Grove, Ill. March 22, 1852

DEATH NOTICES

BARTON Amanda age 11y 10m dau of Thomas and Sarah Barton April 11, 1852

MC CLARY Nancy J. age 17y 1m 4d in Avoca, NY March 22, 1852

HOPPER Martha wife of Mansfield Hopper in Towlesville, NY April 11, 1852. Leaves husband and 2 daus

HALLOCK John D. age 15y 4m 19d son of Benjamin and Abby Hallock of Bath, NY in Hornellsville, NY May 29, 1852

RATHBONE Nancy in her 68th yr wife of Hubbard W. in Howard, NY June 6, 1852

MC CALL Rebecca M. age 29y wife of Dr. William Mc Call and dau of A. C. **SMITH** of Erwin Ctr., NY in Rushford, NY June 10, 1852

ROSE Rev. Levi abt 40y in Howard, NY June 4, 1852

NIXON Eleanor age 66y 8m 4d in Bath, NY June 9, 1852

BESLEY Samuel age 70y in Campbell, NY July 2, 1852. His wife Mary died December 29, 1851 in her 68th yr

COOPER Harriet age 75y in Bath, NY June 28, 1852

DOLBY Rhoda abt 90y relict of Pardon Dolby a Rev. Soldier in Howard, NY July 19, 1852. Came to Howard with husband 34 yrs ago

RICHARDSON George W. in Memphis, Tn. July 9, 1852

DAWSON Lancelot age 49y native of Ireland in Howard, NY September 24, 1852

WIXOM Ann age 17y in Prattsburgh, NY September 17, 1852

CHAMBERLAIN William W. age 22y formerly of Bath, NY in Plymouth, Wis. September 4, 1852

ROW John S. age 53y formerly of Bath, NY in Whiteside, Ill. December 9, 1852

MC ELWEE Sarah in her 79th yr wife of Henry in Bath, NY January 9, 1853

WHITING John age 70y in Bath, NY January 14, 1853. One of early settlers

BENTON Daniel age 88y 6m 10d at son's Jared D. Benton in Pulteney, NY February 12, 1853. Born September 2, 1772 in Guilford, Ct. and came to NY in 1828. 12 children, 9 living Rev. Joseph A. of Sacramento, Cal. and Rev. John Elliott in Yreka, Cal. 1 son of Wis. 1 son in Mi. and 2 in Pulteney, 1 dau in Cattaraugus Co. NY and 1 dau in Pulteney

CHAMBERLAIN Harlow M. age 8y son of H. W. Chamberlain of Sheboygan, Wis. at Grandfather's Stephen **WEBB** in Hornellsville, NY February 6, 1853

DE WITT John in his 71st yr in Bath, NY February 8, 1853. Born December 19, 1782 in Sussex Co. NJ. Age 36y married Sally **CARPENTER** while living in Starkey, NY

ROBINSON Richard Sheffield age 3y 10m in S. Addison, NY February 21, 1853

HILL Samuel age 3y 8m 15d in S. Addison, NY February 27, 1853

ROBIE Samuel age 59y in Fairfield, Vt. March 6, 1853

SCOVEL Harriet A. in her 20th yr dau of Christopher and Harriet Scovel in Avoca, NY April 9, 1853

HALLOCK Joshua age 83y in Bath, NY May 22, 1853 (Poughkeepsie, NY papers please copy)

TOLLIVER Nancy abt 62y widow of William Tollover in Bath, NY June 13, 1853. Brought as slave 42 yrs ago from Prince William Co. Va. by John **FITZHUGH** son-in-law of William **HELM**

FAULKNER Miss Catherine age 50y at bro John's in Urbana, NY June 25, 1853

PIER Miss Mary B. in her 30th yr in Hyde Park, Pa. June 20, 1853

COOK Clarissa in her 81st yr in Auburn, NY July 2, 1853

COSS William in his 69th yr in Bath, NY July 13, 1853. One of early settlers

METCALFE Joseph age 41y in Bath, NY August 9, 1853

ROSENCRANS John age 58y 4m 14d in Independence, Mi. August 2, 1853

HODGE Andrew E. age 14y 8m 18d in Bath, NY August 7, 1853 and Ellen age 17y 6d died August 20, 1853 children of Jacob E. and Nancy

WISNER Francis G. age 21y son of R. P. Wisner in Bath, NY August 19, 1853

HANKS Elijah age 74y in Bath, NY September 26, 1853

KINGKADE Crownage in his 75th yr in Avoca, NY September 21, 1853. Born Palatine, NY and came to Avoca April 1841

ROWE Edward Moore age 4y 6m 11d son of Van Rensalaer and Helen E. Rowe in Rochester, NY October 2, 1853

ROWLEY Mary P. age 82y in Dansville, NY October 13, 1853. Her husband died 20 yrs ago

PATTERSON William M. age 52y formerly of Binghamton, NY in Kingston, Wis. October 10, 1853

DEATH NOTICES

FAULKNER Richard in his 48th yr in Bath, NY November 12, 1853

VAN DUSEN Christopher age 62y 3m 28d in Dansville, NY December 10, 1853

HAYES Harriet Ann age 24y dau of Casson Hayes December 20, 1853

BALDWIN Maj. Rufus age 58y in Addison, NY January 10, 1854

BEGOLE Thomas age 78y in Wayland, NY January 18, 1854

DILDINE Levi R. age 38y in Wayland, NY January 21, 1854

HARING Garrett in his 73rd yr in Orange, NY February 7, 1854

CHICHESTER Mary F. age 18y 7m dau of Henry and Eliza Chichester in Wheeler, NY January 29, 1854

BAILEY Nancy F. age 25y 1m 12d in Urbana, NY January 28, 1854

POTTER Martha S. age 71y Mother of Capt. E. R. **BIDWELL** of Bath, NY in Prattsburgh, NY February 11, 1854. Came from Onieda Co. NY 47 yrs ago

READ Capt. James age 70y 8m 24d in Bath, NY March 8, 1854. Came to Urbana, NY from RI in 1796, later to Bath

MULHOLLEN William S. age 73y late of Bath, NY at brother's in Jasper, NY March 9, 1854. Came to Painted Post, NY from Pa. abt 1800 and later to Bath

missing issues

ALLEN William age 65y in Avoca, NY April 28, 1855, res over 40 yrs

HOYT Henry J. in Columbia, Pa. May 23, 1855

DAWSON Richard age 19y 2m 2d in Bath, NY May 29, 1855

THOMPSON Daniel in his 81st yr in Wheeler, NY June 15, 1855

VAIL Anna Maria wife of C. C. Vail and dau of Benjamin **HALLOCK** in Bath, NY July 7, 1855 (Albany and Poughkeepsie papers please copy)

CHAPMAN George S. in his 28th yr son of R. L. Chapman formerly of N. Urbana, NY in Chicago, Ill. August 13, 1855

DORR Dr. James D. age 43y formerly of Washington Co. NY in Bath, NY September 6, 1855

MC COLLOUGH Mary inf dau of Alex Mc Collough in Bath, NY September 9, 1855

HERRICK Fanny age 2y 1m dau of Frank and Amelia Herrick September 9, 1855

CRANDALL Joseph age 89y 10m in Prattsburgh, NY September 13, 1855. Born abt 1765 in Westerly, RI. At age 16 enlisted in Revolutionary War. Res of Rensalaer Co. NY until 1848 when he came to Prattsburgh to live with dau

WALKER Hellena age 1y 7m dau of Hiram and Sarah in Bath, NY September 30, 1855

PERINE John W. age 18y in Bath, NY October 8, 1855

SILSBE Josh a comedian in San Francisco, Cal. December 22, 1855. Believed born in Steuben Co. has relatives in Wayne, NY

NILES Moses abt 65y in Prattsburgh, NY February 6, 1856

TOWLE Moses E. age 32y formerly of Bath, NY in New York City March 22, 1856

TOOKER Enoch formerly of Bath, NY in Elmira, NY March 21, 1856

missing Issues

PRATT Aden J. age 72y in Campbell, Ny January 30, 1865

EDSALL Charlotte age 49y wife of Thomas D. Edsall in Thurston, NY July 3, 1865

WHITMAN Augustus in Wayland, NY October 1, 1865

GARDNER Alice P. age 22y 11m wife of D. F. Gardner and dau of Dr. E. H. **MASON** in Towanda, Pa. October 7, 1865

ADSIT Henry a cadet in Pa. Military Academy, son of Martin Adsit of Hornellsville, NY November 3, 1865

SHARP Webster son of Lawrence Sharp in Howard, NY November 6, 1865

STONE Clarence age 17y son of J. H. Stone nr Kanona, NY Decembr 7, 1865

BENJAMIN Marion Francelia age 7y 11m dau of Silas and Abigail Benjamin in Fremont, NY December 19, 1865

WINSOR William age 87y in Campbell, NY January 12, 1866. Native of Worcester Co. Mass.

READ Arnold D. in his 73rd yr in Bath, NY February 20, 1866. Born eastern NY

BABCOCK Elias P. over 80y in Caton, NY March 3, 1866

TOWNSEND Annette F. in her 39th yr wife of Calvin in Thurston, NY March 16, 1866

GAYLORD Carrie age 23y wife of Leroy Gaylord and dau of James **MC ELWEE** of Savona, NY in Orange, NY April 24, 1866

DEATH NOTICES

BROWN Col. J. Smith native of Steuben Co. NY late of the 126th Reg. NYV in Penn Yan, NY April 27, 1866

HUBBARD Frances Gertrude age 23y dau of E. A. and L. C. Hubbard in Prattsburgh, NY May 2, 1866

GILES Richard age 55y of Pulteney, NY found dead nr home June 1, 1866

SCOTT William in his 73rd yr in Prattsburgh, NY August 16, 1866, native of Inverness, Scotland

VAN GELDER John age 94y of Wheeler, NY in Co. Home May 27, 1866

DRAKE Anna age 41y of Wheeler, NY in Co. Home June 1, 1866

VAN SKIVER James age 28y in Co. Home June 16, 1866

LAWRENCE Col. John I. in Havana, NY July 30, 1866

CLARK Gains age 80y formerly of Geneva, NY in Prattsburgh, NY August 20, 1866

FRENCH James F. old res of Bath, NY hit by train nr Painted Post, NY September 12, 1866

ELLAS George S. age 50y in Bath, NY September 21, 1866

Steuben Courier (Bath, NY)

September 20, 1843 - December 26, 1884

RICHARDSON James age 23y in Bath, NY September 17, 1843

WHITING Harriet age 4y 6m dau of Maj. Timothy Whiting in Bath, NY September 19, 1843

HIGGINS Eunice in her 82nd yr widow of Rev. David Higgins formerly of Bath, NY in Norwalk, Ohio October 2, 1843

PLATT Joseph Sloan age 18y son of Rev. Isaac W. Platt in Bath, NY October 18, 1843

LILLY Benjamin D. age 26y son of Col. William Lilly late of Howard, NY now of Parryville, Pa. in Bath, NY October 19, 1843

VROOMAN Mrs. Catherine formerly of Ithaca, NY in Cohocton, NY November 7, 1843

KENNEDY James age 32y formerly of Bath, NY in Portland Ky. October 25, 1843

MILES Isaac age 80y a Revolutionary Soldier in Addison, NY November 22, 1843

STEPHENS Joseph age 71y 11m 27d in Campbell, NY December 1, 1843. Leaves wife and 11 children

RUSSELL Lucretia age 16y in Reading, NY February 23, 1844

THOMAS John in state of beastly intoxication in Bath, NY March 4, 1844

ARNOLD Alexander age 89y a Revolutionary Soldier in Avoca, NY March 22, 1844

HOPKINS John age 80y in Prattsburgh, NY March 19, 1844

MONELL Charles R. in his 23rd yr son of Judge Monell of Greene, NY in Angelica, NY April 1, 1844

EDWARDS Mason age 18y son of late George C. Edwards in Bath, NY April 7, 1844

LYON Thomas Hammond age 7y son of Abner P. and Helen H. Lyon in Prattsburgh, NY April 7. 1844

WALDO Jesse in his 54th yr in Prattsburgh, NY April 2, 1844

WILLIAMS Miss Sarah age 21y in Cameron, NY April 11, 1844

BOYD Mrs. Adeline P. age 31y in Addison, NY May 7, 1844

MILLER Mark in his 29th yr formerly of Bath, NY in Pensicola, Fl. April 29, 1844

GOODWIN George age 87y in Hartford, Ct. May 13, 1844

SMITH Mary E. age 19y wife of Thomas Smith and dau of Frederick and Lucy **BARNARD** at Grandfather's Gershom **WILCOX** in Corning, NY April 28, 1844

BRUCE Peter age 23y in Geneva, NY June 9, 1844

MC HENRY Miss Margaret abt 44y in Bath, NY June 27, 1844

MITCAELL John B. in his 73rd yr in Wayne, NY July 9, 1844

LINDLEY William age 55y grandson of Col. Lindley who purchased town of Lindley from Phelps and Gorham in Lindley, NY June 24, 1844

HASTINGS Sarah Elizabeth wife of Rev. G. H. Hastings formerly of Bath, NY in Greensburg, Pa. July 2, 1844

OSBORN Alexander C. age 2y son of Charles E. and Margaret Osborn in Corning, NY July 17, 1844

THOMPSON Jane age 25y wife of A. D. Thompson in Hartsville, NY July 16, 1844

DEATH NOTICES

WHITNEY William age 2y 1m son of Birdsall N. and Pamela W. Whitney in Painted Post, NY August 6, 1844

ROBINSON Mary D. Ette infant dau of Lemuel H. and Chloe Robinson in Painted Post, NY August 6, 1844

WOOD John age 5y 9m son of Israel R. Wood in Wayne, NY August 9, 1844

DUDLEY Caroline consort of Thomas J. Dudley and dau of late Howell **BULL** formerly of Bath, NY in Buffalo, NY August 17, 1844

JONES Ezekiel in his 83rd yr a Revolutionary Patriot in Thurston, NY September 1, 1844

BARDEN Eunice age 49y wife of Stephen H. Barden and dau of Nicholas **ROOT** formerly of Bath, NY in Herrick, Pa. August 26, 1844

HOWARD C. W. C. Md. formerly of Avoca, NY in Oxford, Ohio August 5, 1844

PULLING Ezekiel B. Md. age 46y 10m in Bath, NY September 18, 1844

SMITH Harriet Frances age 18m dau of D. C. and Eby Smith in Bath, NY September 17, 1844

WHIPPLE Rev. Phineas L. in his 53rd yr in Bath, NY October 5, 1844

PULLING Smith B. age 13m 16d son of D. P. and Mary E. Pulling in Bath, NY October 4, 1844

BOWEN Martha in her 66th yr wife of Peter Bowen and dau of Capt. Aaron **NORTON** who removed from Goshen, Ct. abt 50 yrs ago and settled in Bloomfield, NY in Bath, NY October 24, 1844

SMITH Martha B. age 26y wife of Justin M. Smith in Erwin, NY October 25, 1844

WOOD Sarah G. age 22y dau of Benjamin H. Wood in Bath, NY October 26, 1844

DUDLEY Sally age 45y wife of Capt. Ward Dudley in Corning, NY October 30, 1844

DUNNING Moses in his 57th yr in Wayne, NY December 2, 1844. Res 2 yrs

CHAPIN Timothy age 85y formerly of Springfield, Mass. in Howard, NY December 11, 1844

BULL Aaron age 63y 6m 23d in Prattsburgh, NY December 10, 1844

HALSEY Orpha age 35y wife of Job Halsey and dau of A. and L. **FORD** in Howard, NY December 12, 1844

TICHENOR Julia Maria age 23y wife of James H. Tichenor in Avoca, NY January 9,

1845

HOTCHKIN Beriah age 61y youngest son of late Rev. Beriah Hotchkin in Prattsburgh, NY January 23, 1845

WALDO Mary age 34y wife of Henry H. Waldo in Prattsburgh, NY January 27, 1845

BRIDGES Benjamin age 59y in Prattsburgh, NY (Newspaper date February 5, 1845)

BACHMAN Catherine age 86y relict of Jacob at son's John Bachman in Pulteney, NY January 5, 1845

GRAHAM John age 65y in Bath, NY February 6, 1845

HOTCHKIN Eveline S. in her 28th yr wife of John D. Hotchkin in Prattsburgh, NY February 4, 1845

WHEELOCK Julia Ann age 26y dau of Paris and Diana Wheelock in Corning, NY February 5, 1845

WILEY Emma Clementine age 16y dau of Joseph and Delilah Wiley in Woodhull, NY February 8, 1845

SIMONS Adeline age 14y 9m dau of Benjamin and Abigail Simons in Bath, NY February 24, 1845

CORNELL Amos age 72y 7m in Barre, NY January 31, 1845 and wife Lucy age 75y 25d died February 6, 1845

NILES Martha age 30y wife of Dr. Addison Niles in Bath, NY March 14, 1845

BENTON David in his 83rd yr formerly of Ontario Co. NY in Brownstone, Ind. March 7, 1845. Native of Ct. and settled Ontario Co. in 1790

PINCH Selina age 24y wife of Owens Pinch in Cohocton, NY April 5, 1845

LANG Robert in his 70th yr brother of late John Lang former Editor of New York Gazette in Tyrone, NY April 8, 1845

ROSE Eliza **(STRATTON)** age 30y 6m wife of Rev. L. Rose on the day of their 3rd wedding anniversary in Howard, NY April 7, 1845

STEWART Charles H. age 43y in Bath, NY April 19, 1845

BEECHER Welthy in her 29th yr wife of Randal F. Beecher and dau of John **DONAHE** in Howard, NY April 23, 1845

ADAMS Ann Eliza in her 22nd yr in Bath, NY April 30, 1845

HOYT William H. age 26y son of Dr. R. H. Hoyt of Painted Post, NY in New York

DEATH NOTICES

City May 6, 1845

BONHAM Olive age 11y 10m dau of Enos and Elizabeth Bonham in Caton, NY May 3, 1845

MILLS Charles R. in his 43rd yr native of Fairfield Ct. and graduate of Yale in 1824 in Corning, NY May 26, 1845

RICHARDSON Amanda R. age 26y wife of Thomas J. Richardson in Bath, NY May 28, 1845

WHEELOCK Sally Ann age 30y 10m wife of Marcus M. Wheelock in Corning, NY June 9, 1845. Their dau Sally Ann age 2m 11d died July 22, 1845

KERR Margaret age 38y consort of William Kerr in New York City June 11, 1845

METCALFE Thomas J. in his 21st yr son of Thomas and Nancy Metcalfe in Bath, NY June 23, 1845

PERINE Lucy B. age 23y 5m wife of P. S. Perine and dau of Whittington **SAYRE** formerly of Southport, NY in Bath, NY July 2, 1845

RUMSEY Lydia age 54y wife of David Rumsey Sr. in Bath, NY July 28, 1845

HURLBUT Martha L. age 16y 5d dau of late John and Piscilla Hurlbut in Arkport, NY July 20, 1845

ROSE Mary Eliza age 10m 19d only surviving child of Rev. L. Rose in Howard, NY July 30, 1845

MOORE Amanda age 31y wife of James Moore in Mud Creek, NY July 25, 1845

CLARK George W. age 4m 10d son of Charles and Prudence Clark in Corning, NY August 8, 1845

SEYMOUR Irving Wattles age 12y 3m 5d son of Lorenzo and Phebe Ann Seymour in Corning, NY September 7, 1845

DUDLEY William age 23y son of John Dudley in Bath, NY September 25, 1845

CHENEY Sarah Louisa age 21y wife of Dr. W. D. Cheney and dau of late Isaac **AINSWORTH** in Prattsburgh, NY October 10, 1845. Leaves husband and 2 children

MURRAY William in his 45th yr formerly in Bath, NY in Joliet, Ill. September 28, 1845. Leaves wife and 5 children

HARROWER Margaret Eliza in her 39th yr dau of Rev. David Harrower in Lindley, NY October 3, 1845

CARTER Jabez age 86y 6m 13d a Revolutionary Soldier Grandfather of Capt. E. R.

STEUBEN COUNTY NEWSPAPERS

BIDWELL of Bath, NY in Seneca Falls, NY October 23, 1845

BOSTWICK Rev. W. W. age 48y in Joliet, Ill. October 6, 1845. His wife age 36y died September 28, 1845

ALLEN Sarah Emily age 13y 29d dau of Hiram D. Allen and Jerusha Lee in Bath, NY November 5, 1845

DUDLEY Harriet Eliza in her 18th yr in Corning, NY November 11, 1845

MATTISON ____ abt 2y burned to death in Bath, NY last week (Newspaper date December 3, 1845)

GORDON Sarah Isabella age 5y 5m dau of William W. Gordon in Hammondsport, NY November 26, 1845

CLARK Naomi (widow) age 90y 11m formerly of Northampton, Mass. in Wheeler, NY November 23, 1845

BILES William A. age 25y in Bath, NY December 27, 1845 and dau Delaney Eliza died January 6, 1846

GAMBLE Robert Alexander age 23y son of William in Bath, NY December 21, 1845

HOTCHKIN William R. age 25y son of Rev. J. H. Hotchkin in Pulteney, NY January 9, 1846

GONSOLUS Emanuel age 63y in Wheeler, NY January 12, 1846

HESS Hannah Elizabeth age 2y 3m 25d dau of Alexander and Martha Hess in Bath, NY January 27, 1846

VAN HOUSEN E. Benedict age 20y 11m 17d in Howard, NY January 27, 1846

DENNIS Moses age 93y 6m 21d a Revolutionary Soldier in Hancock, NH December 18, 1845

SWITZER Henry age 78y late of Bradford, NY in Illinois December 20, 1845. Wife Elizabeth abt 72y died in Bradford February 6, 1846

WOOD Benjamin abt 50y formerly of Bath, NY in Washington DC February 28, 1846

SHERMAN Francis age 45y 10m 3d in Urbana, NY March 7, 1846

HALLIDAY William H. former teacher in Bath and Cameron, NY in Mechlinburgh, NY March 9, 1846

HARROWER Susan age 28y consort of Col. G. T. Harrower and dau of Abner **THURBER** in Lindley, NY April 20, 1846

DEATH NOTICES

VAN HOUSEN Adeline Rebecca age 33y wife of John Van Housen and dau of late Beriah **HOTCHKIN** in Prattsburgh, NY May 13, 1846

COVERT Luke in his 89th yr a Revolutionary Soldier in Bradford, NY May 15, 1846. One of first settlers in Seneca Co. NY moved from Ovid, NY to Bradford 17 yrs ago

BIXBY William H. age 32y in Bath, NY May 28, 1846. Leaves wife in Bath and parents in Otsego Co. NY

SPENCER Roxana I. age 3m 17d dau of George T. in Corning, NY July 1, 1846

CHAPIN Col. Pulaski in his 32nd yr son of Ezra in Prattsburgh, NY July 4, 1846

COOK Phillip in his 83rd yr in Avoca, NY July 16, 1846. Res for 26 yrs.

BURKE Thomas and wife Sarah E. in Corning, NY July 22, 1846, buried in one grave

PAWLING Henry Jr. age 33y at Father's in Avoca, NY July 9, 1846

WILCOX Samantha age 27y wife of T. A. Wilcox in Bath, NY August 13, 1846

MC CLURE Miss Sarah age 44y dau of Gen. George Mc Clure of Dundee, Ill. formerly of Bath, NY at res. of George W. **GIBBS** in Chicagio, Ill. August 1, 1846

JOHNSON Lyman age 38y n Orange, NY August 27, 1846

COVELL Stephen I. age 30y at Father's in Elmira, NY (Newspaper date September 2, 1846)

LOZIER Hannah in her 47th yr wife of John P. Lozier and dau of John I. **GUEST** of Albany, NY in Tyrone, NY September 7, 1846

GARDNER Welthey age 67y widow of Col. P. Gardner of W. Bloomfield, NY and Mother of Mrs. Rev. L. W. **RUSS** of Bath, NY in Bath September 12, 1846

RICE Grover Emery age 1y 1d son of Joel H. and Caroline L. Rice in Bath, NY September 15, 1846

MALLORY P. J. age 31y at Father's in Corning, NY September 23, 1846

DENTON Diantha age 19y 3m dau of S. B. Denton formerly of Bath, NY in Jefferson, NY September 28, 1846

CHAPIN Dorcas D. age 36y dau of E. Chapin in Prattsburgh, NY November 5, 1846

PRITCHARD Calvin age 70y in Lawrenceville, Pa. November 16, 1846

HIGGINS Cecelia age 53y wife of David Higgins late of Norwalk, Ohio formerly of Bath, NY in Washington DC November 23, 1846

STEUBEN COUNTY NEWSPAPERS 81

GRIFFITH John in his 81st yr in Bath, NY December 29, 1846

BABCOCK Eunice age 51y wife of Elias P. Babcock in Caton, NY January 1, 1847

JOHNSON James C. age 23y son of Samuel A. in Prattsburgh, NY January 7, 1847

ROBBINS Peter age 97y a Revolutionary Soldier in Wheeler, NY January 9, 1847

GANSEVOORT Rebecca age 8y 4m dau of Capt. E. R. Gansevoort and Harriet (**BIDWELL**) in Bath, NY January 26, 1847

THOMAS Sarah in her 27th yr wife of C. D. Thomas and dau of Gamaliel and Elizabeth **DICKINSON** of Seneca Co. NY in Hornby, NY January 8, 1847

HOTCHKIN Mary Rebecca age 6y dau of John N. in Prattsburgh, NY January 29, 1847

HAMILTON Lester age 16y son of late John in Howard, NY February 8, 1847

STEVENSON Catherine age 70y wife of John Stevenson formerly of Salem, NY in Howard, NY February 23, 1847

MERRIMAN Henry B. age 7m 8d son of Hiram in Bradford, NY March 14, 1847

CALKINS John K. late of Painted Post, NY now of Hornellsville, NY in Bath, NY March 21, 1847

AINSWORTH Dewitt C. age 21y in Prattsburgh, NY March 17, 1847

HOTCHKIN John H. age 33y son of Rev. James H. Hotchkin in Prattsburgh, NY March 23, 1847

POWERS Charles H. age 33y in Corning, NY March 24, 1847. Leaves wife and 2 children

COOK Mary Elizabeth age 17y dau of late John and Sarah Cook in Prattsburgh, NY March 26, 1847

CORNELL Amos age 17y of Mud Creek, NY and James H. **O'DELL** age 23y both killed by train in Corning, NY April 14, 1847. Mr. O'dell married just 10 days

BOSTWICK Elizabeth W. age 34y wife of H. N. Bostwick in Corning, NY April 20, 1847

GILCHRIST Mrs. A. G. in her 44th yr in Howard, NY April 21, 1847

COOK Adeline age 21y 6m former teacher Bath, NY in New Berlin, NY April 21, 1847

PEARSALL Jane Eliza age 17y 6m dau of William T. and Eliza Pearsall in Owego, NY May 1, 1847

DEATH NOTICES

STEVENS Anna in her 70th yr consort of Col. William Stevens in Canisteo, NY May 5, 1847

BENJAMIN Maria age 23y 3w 6d dau of Samuel Benjamin formerly of NJ in Bath, NY May 14, 1847

WHITING Mariana age 2y 15d in Bath, NY May 25, 1847

DRAKE Amanda P. age 86y wife of Allen Drake in Jasper, NY May 29, 1847

NOBLE Mrs. Mary W. age 36y in Bath, NY June 12, 1847

WHITING Pamelia age 21y wife of Levi Whiting and dau of William **WOODS** in Bath, NY July 29, 1847

SHATTUCK Hittie in her 53rd yr wife of Lucius in Cohocton, NY July 12, 1847

RAYMOND Eleanor Maria age 22y 6d dau of Alva and Phebe Raymond in Bath, NY July 23, 1847

KENNEDY Lucy age 41y consort of James Kennedy in Wheeler, NY August 16, 1847

TUTHILL Mandeville in his 30th yr in Prattsburgh, NY October 16, 1847

MC BEATH Charlotte age 45y wife of James in Bath, NY November 15, 1847

BRIDGES Elam in his 64th yr of Prattsburgh, NY in Utica Asylum November 6, 1847

BROTHER Anna Rice age 9m 13 dau of Henry Brother in Bath, NY February 29, 1848

MILLER James age 4m 12d son of Joel B. and Caroline (**RICE**) in Bath, NY February 12, 1848

BROTHER Mrs. Margaret in her 72nd yr in Seneca, NY February 27, 1848

missing issues

MAPES Mrs. Leonora age 19y in Orange, NY May 5, 1849

SHANNON Samuel formerly of Bath, NY in Dansville, NY May 30, 1849

STEPHENS Elizabeth age 85y wife of Uriah Stephens in Canisteo, NY March 30, 1849

WARREN Miss Sarah age 67y in Bath, NY June 9, 1849

MC KENSIE Daniel age 87y in S. Dansville, NY June 8, 1849. Native of Scotland, came to US in 1794

KNIGHT John in his 83rd yr in Bath, NY July 13, 1849

PATTERSON Mrs. Sarah in her 87th yr of Bath, NY while visiting son at res of Mr. Patterson in Erwin, NY July 6, 1849

PORTER William G. in his 33rd yr in Woodhull, NY August 5, 1849. Leaves wife and 3 children

WALDO Mary F. widow of Jesse Waldo of Prattsburgh, NY in Poughkeepsie, NY August 7, 1849

BLOOD Capt. Asa age 63y in Bath, NY September 1, 1849

FRENCH John F. in his 49th yr in S. Cameron, NY August 20, 1849

HENDRYX George Washington son of Thomas and Harriet Hendryx in Cohocton, NY September 2, 1849. Born February 22, 1849

CHASE Harriet O. wife of Charles Chase and dau of Nathaniel **BUNDY** in Cameron, NY September 5, 1849

BAILEY William abt 50y of Orange, NY on Lake Erie September 1, 1849

WYGANT William age 31y in Thurston, NY August 20, 1849. Leaves wife and 1 child

MINER William B. son of Whitman R. and S. M. in Harding, Ill. August 16, 1849

BRADLEY Sturges in his 86th yr at son's in Bath, NY October 22, 1849

FOSS Mrs. Meribah in her 54th yr October 21, 1849

CLARK Anna S. age 66y wife of John Clark in Wheeler, NY November 13, 1849 (Northampton, Mass. papers please copy)

BIDWELL Eli Sr. in his 62nd yr in Bath, NY November 22, 1849. Born September 20, 1788 in E. Hartford, Ct. At age 17y settled in Prattsburgh with older brother, lived in Bath 36 yrs.

SEAMAN Franklin age 19m son of John and Polly in Bath, NY November 16, 1849

ROCKWELL Joseph G. age 26y teacher at Haverling School in Bath, NY November 10, 1849

WATKINS Mrs. Harriet age 57y 8m former teacher, wife of Simon Watkins in Penn Yan, NY in Bath, NY December 20, 1849

SALMON Miss Mary Ann age 25y in Avoca, NY January 8, 1850

GANSEVOORT Elizabeth in her 82nd yr relict of Conradt Gansevoort of Albany, NY Mother of John R. Gansevoort of Bath, NY at son-in-law's Dr. Robert W. **COOK** in Hollindell, NJ January 11, 1850

DEATH NOTICES

VAN HOUSEN Henry in his 75th yr formerly of Howard, NY in Prattsburgh, NY February 2, 1850

ABER Anna in her 54th yr wife of Nathaniel Aber in Bath, NY February 13, 1850

CHAPIN Mrs. Lucy in her 86th yr in Bath, NY February 11, 1850

FRACE Calvin age 22y in Canisteo, NY January 28, 1850

STEPHENS Rachel age 67y wife of Capt. Nathan Stephens in Canisteo, NY February 8, 1850

HARROWER Levi B. son of B. Harrower of Lindley, NY in Jacksonville, Fl. January 20, 1850

MC CALLA Miss Nancy age 69y in Bath, NY March 23, 1850

YOUMANS Jonas age 92y 10m 11d a Revolutionary Soldier in Thurston, NY March 28, 1850

JOHNSON Rhoda age 64y 7m wife of Benoni Johnson in Caton, NY March 29, 1850

HARROWER Mary D. W. age 22y in Big Flats, NY March 19, 1850 just 2 mo. after husband died. Married a little more than 2 yrs

WILLOUR Rachel in her 53rd yr wife of Jacob Willour March 25, 1850

GRAVES Elizabeth age 51y widow of Randall Graves of Howard, NY in Liberty, NY April 8, 1850

ELLAS John M. in his 25th yr in Sacramento, Cal. January 29, 1850

BAIN Nathan age 23y in Bath, NY February 16, 1850

TUTHILL Harriet Malvina age 3y 6m dau of Mrs. Esther Tuthill in Tyrone, NY June 8, 1850

STARKWEATHER Sarah age 23y stepdau of Julius **BARTLETT** of Prattsburgh, NY June 6, 1850

BRECK Elizabeth in her 68th yr wife of Joseph Breck of Bath, NY June 28, 1850. Leaves husband and 8 children

ADSIT Caroline B. dau of M. J. Adsit of Hammondsport, NY in Middletown, Ct. July 2, 1850

TAYLOR Eliza M. age 36y wife of G. W. Taylor in Bath, NY July 5, 1850

SPRING Mrs. Olive in Milltown, Pa. July 20, 1850

FOWLER Hannah age 9y 4m 17d dau of John W. Fowler in Bath, NY August 3, 1850

MC MASTER Adeline in her 7th yr dau of D. Mc Master in Bath, NY August 15, 1850

SMITH Augustus age 21m son of Jared Smith in Bath, NY August 25, 1850

YOUMANS Mary Jane Elizabeth age 14y 4m 6d in Bath, NY August 19, 1850

COOPER Lois age 30y 11d wife of Hinman Cooper and dau of Enos **CALKINS** in Painted Post, NY July 31, 1850

NOBLE Sophia in her 19th yr dau of Harvey Noble in White Deer Mills, Pa. August 15, 1850

WARREN Sarah in her 39th yr wife of Jonathan Warren and dau of J. T. and Lucretia **JOHNSON** in Bath, NY August 25, 1850

HESS Mary age 4m 12d dau of Alexander and Martha T. Hess September 7, 1850

READ James H. Md. age 27y son of Capt. James Read of Bath, NY in Coloma, Cal. July 15, 1850

MILLER Miles Fowler age 1y 13d in Bath, NY September 11, 1850

DUDLEY Benjamin F. age 47 in Cal. July 30, 1850. Left Bath, NY during gold rush in March 1849

DRYER Otis age 10m son of A. C. and Mary in Palmyra, NY September 20, 1850

ROGERS Sarah S. in her 84th yr relict of Samuel Rogers formerly of Unadilla, NY at dau Mrs. **MILLS** October 2, 1850. Mother of Dr. D. A. Rogers of Bath, NY

BARNEY Philance T. age 35y wife of Nelson Barney in Bath, NY October 5, 1850

WHITTEMORE Herman Fuller in his 7th yr son of M. F. and Sarah Whittemore in Jasper, NY October 3, 1850

VAN BUSKIRK Richard age 62y in Avoca, NY October 22, 1850

WALKER Gideon age 80y formerly of Hartford Co. Ct. in Bath, NY October 25, 1850

FULLER Thomas F. age 36y at res. of Richard **FAULKNER** in Bath, NY November 11, 1850

ROGERS Robert C. age 22y 7m son of G. A. Rogers of Bath, NY in Sacramento, Cal. October 17, 1850

SILSBE Sarah Jane age 2y 4m dau of A. H. Silsbe in Bath, NY November 17, 1850

BRUSS John M. age 25y brother of Rev. L. W. Bruss formerly of Bath, NY in Romeo,

Mi. November 17, 1850. Graduated from Hamilton College last July

COATS Nancy Whiting in her 28th yr wife of L. Coats and dau of Col. Stephen **GRANT** in Bath, NY December 12, 1850

MANSON Harriet Eliza in her 27th yr wife of Edgar Manson at Father's J. **TALLMADGE** on Allens Hill, Ontario Co. NY November 24, 1850

BORDEN Stephen abt 7y son of Stephen H. and Eunice Borden in Southport, NY February 11, 1851

HAYES Drayton age 46y in Prattsburgh, NY February 21, 1851

CROCKER Jane R. in her 27th yr wife of Dr. Wickham R. Crocker in Cameron, NY February 19, 1851

EDWARDS William in his 72nd yr in Bath, NY March 8, 1851. Born Easton, Pa. and came to Bath in 1801

WHITTAKER Amanda age 14y in Savona, NY March 7, 1851

HOAGLAND Eunice A. age 25y dau of Abraham Hoagland of Howard, NY at Alfred Institute March 19, 1851

BOWLBY William T. in his 24th yr son of John and Catherine Bowlby formerly of Bethlehem, NJ in Greenwood, NY February 4, 1851

STEELE William in his 90th yr a Revolutionary Soldier native of New York City, life long res. of Painted Post, NY in Bath, NY April 4, 1851

ROBIE James W. in his 13th yr son of Reuben Robie in Bath, NY April 21, 1851

THOMPSON Lydia age 80y 7m widow of Samuel in Bath, NY March 28, 1851

ROWE Lucy Jane age 28y 4m 12d wife of Anson Rowe in Bath, NY April 17, 1851

SMITH Anna in her 58th yr wife of Henry Smith in Avoca, NY June 1, 1851

BEULL Rev. Parker age 67y in Wayland, NY May 30, 1851

HODGEMAN Mary J. dau of Leonard and Jennet in Stillwater, NY May 21, 1851

WOLCOTT Elizabeth age 89y wife of Charles Wolcott nr Corning, NY June 25, 1851

DUDLEY Miss Lois age 58y in Bath, NY July 2, 1851

STEWART Mrs. Ruth age 79y 6m in Campbell, NY July 11, 1851

WYGANT James age 11m 3d son of Benjamin and Ann Wygant in Wheeler, NY August 13, 1851

BELDEN Comfort E. Md. in his 46th yr in Hornellsville, NY September 11, 1851

HOTCHKIN James H. age 70y in Prattsburgh, NY September 21, 1851

PAWLING Catherine age 63y relict of Henry in Avoca, NY September 23, 1851

DOLPH Mrs. Elizabeth age 77y at nephew's George T. **BONHAM** in Addison, NY November 5, 1851

PARSON Sophia M. age 18y 6m December 21, 1851

NORTON Sarah E. age 32y wife of Dr. George Norton in E. Pembroke, NY November 23, 1851

BARTO James G. age 67y in Avoca, NY December 13, 1851

CHURCH Dr. ___ age 42y in Hammondsport, NY December 18, 1851

STANTON Mary Ann age 27y wife of George W. Stanton and dau of Benjamin **HARROWER** and Grand dau of Rev. David Harrower in Lindley, NY January 13, 1852

FRENCH Ruth M. age 24y dau of late John F. and Almira French in Cameron, NY January 4, 1852

PALMER Capt. R. W. in his 36th yr formerly of Otsego Co. NY in Lindley, NY January 29, 1852

PRATT Hester A. age 29y wife of William H. in Prattsburgh, NY February 19, 1852

HESS Martha P. in her 35th yr wife of Hiram Hess in Bath, NY March 8, 1852

MC KENSIE Elizabeth in her 88th yr widow of Daniel Mc Kensie in S. Dansville, NY March 7, 1852. Emigrated from Scotland 53 yrs ago

MATHER Dortha in her 81st yr at son's in Bath, NY March 18, 1852

WOODWARD David age 65y in Jasper, NY March 15, 1852. Native of Linesborough, NH and pioneer of Jasper

RICE Juliett E. age 15y 7m dau of W. B. Rice in Howard, NY March 23, 1852

STEWART Thadlens age 35y in Thurston, NY March 28, 1852

BULLARD Angeline Augusta age 28y wife of Otis A. Bullard and dau of Augustus A. **OLMSTEAD** in Howard, NY April 4, 1852

KYSER Mrs. Henry age 61y in Avoca, NY April 16, 1852

TOWLE Richard in his 69th yr in Howard, NY April 10, 1852, removed from Canadia, NH in 1814 (Manchester NH papers please copy)

DEATH NOTICES

SAYLES Simeon in his 75th yr in Bath, NY May 2, 1852. Father of Alexander Sayles of Painted Post, NY and Mrs. Jesse P. **BRACE** of Bath

TURNER Samuel age 71y native of Ireland and one of early settlers of Steuben Co. in Wayne, NY May 8, 1852

CAMPBELL Harriet age 27y wife of Charles W. Campbell and dau of Robert H. **HOYT** formerly of Painted Post, NY and niece of William S. and P. P. **HUBBELL** of Bath, NY in Bath June 7, 1852

HOYT Sarah L. age 4y 4m dau of Henry J. and Lydia in Cameron, NY June 12, 1852

MACK Elisha hit by lightning near Kennedyville, NY June 21, 1852

KENNARD Mary age 38y wife of Rev. John Kennard and dau of John **WHITING** of Bath, NY in Otto, NY June 15, 1852

WHITING Nancy age 70y wife of Col. John Whiting in Bath, NY May 14, 1852

COTTON Elizabeth age 84y widow of Silas Cotton in S. Dansville, NY June 20, 1852

BIDWELL Mary Elizabeth age 32y 8m 23d wife of George H. Bidwell of Bath, NY at Elmira Water Cure August 17, 1852, formerly of Hartford, Ct.

BRONSON Ira A. age 24y in Howard, NY August 2, 1852

LA FORGE Martin age 32y thrown from wagon near Hammondsport, NY September 10, 1852. (Warsaw and Leroy NY papers please copy)

MAY Adeline age 22y wife of Henry R. May in Cohocton, NY October 14, 1852

MC CAY Mary age 66y 1m 2d sister of William W. Mc Cay in Bath, NY October 8, 1852

CROSBY Sarah Emily age 11y 8m 22d dau of William and Elizabeth Crosby in Bath, NY October 17, 1852

TOPPING Elizabeth age 28y wife of Perry Topping and dau of Nathaniel **BUNDY** of Cameron, NY in Bath, NY October 31, 1852

MC CLARY Miss Fanny age 25y in Avoca, NY August 7, 1852

SHANNON John age 20m son of Thomas and Martha Jane Shannon in Monterey, NY November 9, 1852

STEWART William age 2y 2m 6d son of John W. R. and Emeline Stewart in Orange, NY October 28, 1852

LEWIS Jane F. age 27y wife of Daniel D. Lewis and dau of John **WHEELER** in Wheeler, NY October 12, 1852

MC CAY William native of Orange Co. NY in Bath, NY November 28, 1852

DAVIS James C. suicide by hanging in Corning, NY last week (Newspaper date January 19, 1853)

HOWELL Edward Jr. in his 33rd yr in Bath, NY March 4, 1853

GUSTIN Alonzo age 20y suicide by hanging in Bath, NY March 8, 1853

BULL Sarah in her 48th yr wife of Col. William H. Bull in Bath, NY March 14, 1853

DAVENPORT Dugald Cameron in his 28th yr eldest son of Ira Davenport of Bath, NY at Island of St. Thomas February 10, 1853

HUBBELL Maria age 52y 2m wife of William S. Hubbell and dau of Ansel **MC CALL** of Painted Post, NY in Bath, NY March 18, 1853

SHULTS Michael age 60y in Avoca, NY March 14, 1853. Born Palatine, NY and came to Avoca in 1848

TAYLOR Mrs. Sarah in Bath, NY (Newspaper date March 16, 1853)

RUTHERFORD Alice age 52y 3m 27d wife of Edward Rutherford in Thurston, NY February 18, 1853

OLMSTEAD Miss Huldah L. age 19y in Troupsburgh, NY March 10, 1853

LARROWE Jeanette in her 78th yr consort of Albertus and mother of Judge Larrowe of Bath, NY in Wheeler, NY April 9, 1853. Born 1776 in Lancaster, Pa. nee **AULLS**. Married age 22, had 12 children

COOPER Harriet A. in her 20th yr dau of Christopher and Harriet Cooper in Avoca, NY April 9, 1853

NOBLE Lyman F. in his 37th yr in Wayne, NY April 4, 1853

LOZIER Ashman age 4m 9d son of William T. and Mary Ann Lozier in Weston, NY April 16, 1853

COLLIER John M. in his 20th yr son of Jacob H. Collier in Avoca, NY May 15, 1853

SHULTS William H. age 24y son of late Michael Shults in Avoca, NY May 18, 1853

ROSENCRANS Sarah age 73y widow of Dr. Simeon Rosencrans of Liberty, NY at son-in-law's A. W. **MOORE** in Bath, NY May 25, 1853

WOMBOUGH William in his 83rd yr in Addison, NY May 21, 1853. Born in Auriel, Huntington Co. NJ and came to Addison 1803

PECK Matilda age 53y wife of William Peck in Avoca, NY May 24, 1853

DEATH NOTICES

DARROW Ezra of Prattsburgh, NY June 4, 1853

HUNTER Augusta A. wife of S. Hunter and dau of P. L. **WHIPPLE** June 13, 1853

LEWIS Francis age 8m 15d son of D. D. Lewis in Wheeler, NY June 6, 1853

SIMERSON Mrs. ____ killed by husband with axe in Pulteney, NY July 5, 1853

LYON Mary Elizabeth age 21y dau of Abner P. Lyon of Prattsburgh, NY in Bath, NY July 12, 1853

CLEMENT Theodore age 1y 6m son of Prof. S. B. and Ann Eliza **COLE** in Prattsburgh, NY June 30, 1853

DAWSON Mary age 15y oldest dau of Bonham Dawson in Bath, NY July 12, 1853

MC CLURE Finla in his 80th yr in Elgin, Ill. May 24, 1853. Born 1773 in Londonderry, Ire., came to US age 20y and one of first settlers of Bath, NY. Went to Elgin 1846

HESS Samuel Seely infant son of Alexander and Martha T. Hess July 23, 1853

ROBINSON M. age 22y son of Deacon L. Robinson in Corning, NY July 24, 1853

GUSTIN Jerusha age 42y wife of George W. Gustin and dau of David and Lovina **FOWLER** in Thurston, NY July 17, 1853

MEEKS Mary Jane in her 23rd yr wife of Christopher Meeks and dau of William and Phebe **ALLEN** in Avoca, NY July 23, 1853. Married less than 1 yr.

DUTCHER Col. William S. age 44y in Chicago, Ill. August 10, 1853

DANIELS Kendrick Phineas age 11m son of Kendrick and Sarah Daniels in Bath, NY July 27, 1853

OGDEN Henry A. in his 38th yr of Cincinnati, Ohio in Bath, NY August 30, 1853

DRAKE William B. formerly of Savona, NY in New Orleans, La. (Newspaper date August 24, 1853)

MAGEE Leland Whipple age 5m son of Thomas J. and Ellen P. Magee in Hornellsville, NY September 8, 1853

LOOMIS Ann E. age 22y 6m in Bath, NY September 22, 1853

GOODSELL Abby in her 65th yr consort of Jared in Bath, NY October 29, 1853

BULL Sybil age 73y 5m 10d wife of Epaphras Bull and dau of Stephen **IVES** of Northampton, Mass. in Bath, NY December 1, 1853

HARROWER Rev. David in his 87th yr in Lawrenceville, Pa. December 20, 1853, born Scotland

STEERE Mrs. Naomi in her 78th yr at son-in-law's L. V. **CHURCH** in Bath, NY December 29, 1853. Early settler of Otsego Co, NY from RI

GARDNER Mary age 30y wife of George Gardner of Prattsburgh, NY while visiting brother Sheriff **ALLEN** in Columbia Co. NY December 16, 1853

DABOLL Frances Jane age 26y dau of Auren in Prattsburgh, NY December 17, 1853

GRAVES Joshua David in his 19th yr eldest son of Dr. J. B. Graves of Bath, NY in Danby, NY February 5, 1854

SPENCER Rev. H. S. formerly of Bath, NY suicide at Utica Asylum February 19, 1854

KNIGHT Royal age 84y in Bath, NY February 15, 1854

HOYT Mary Jane abt 33y dau of Dr. R. H. Hoyt of Bath, NY in Philadelphia, Pa. February 18, 1854

CLAWSON Garret cut his throat after being accused of forgery March 1, 1854. Owned 300 acres one of the best farms in Hector, NY area. Leaves wife and 6 children

WARDEN Dr. James in his 62nd yr in Orange, NY March 27, 1854. Born Pa. graduated Herkimer Co. NY and practiced in Bath, NY

CLEMENT Alvah age 49y of Kittle Creek, Pa. in Northumberland, Pa. March 26, 1854

KNOX John age 84y in Corning, NY last week (Newspaper date April 19, 1854)

PATCHIN Walter age 90y a Revolutionary Soldier in Wayland, NY March 20, 1854. Born Ct. son of Jabez Patchin. After war settled Onondaga Co. NY and came to Cohocton, NY in 1814

MC WHORTER Ann age 76y 6m wife of James in Avoca, NY April 25, 1854

WOOD Ann Fleet age 10y 3m only dau of late Abraham Fleet Wood and Mrs. A. G. **GILCHRIST** in Howard, NY April 6, 1854

READ Ira age 48y 1m in Urbana, NY April 26, 1854

LYON Sarah Ann age 26y 11m 14d wife of Dr. A. P. Lyon in Bath, NY June 10, 1854

SMITH Sarah Jane age 17y dau of Rev. B. C. Smith in Prattsburgh, NY June 29, 1854

STODDARD Sarah Jane in her 23rd yr wife of P. Stoddard Md. in Prattsburgh, NY July 4, 1854

GOODSELL Amanda A. age 19y 6m dau of Reuben and Mary Goodsell in Bath, NY

DEATH NOTICES

July 14, 1854

HUY John crushed by cars in Corning, NY September 1, 1854

LAKE T. C. S. age 33y formerly of Bath, NY in Princeton, Ill. September 5, 1854

RICHARDSON Florence Marion age 4y 8m dau of Thomas J. and Amanda Richardson August 30, 1854

HESS Charles Miller age 4m 1d son of Alexander and Martha Hess December 12, 1854

CHURCH Catherine wife of Edwin F. Church in Bath, NY January 10, 1855. Born April 10, 1825 in Ithaca, NY dau of William and Catherine **ANDRUS**. Married in Ithaca December 26, 1849, 2 children

RICHARDSON John Sr. in his 78th yr at Mt. Washington, NY January 9, 1855. Born 1777 in Franklin Co. Pa. and came to Steuben Co. 1800

REDFIELD Alva abt 54y of Tunckhannock, Pa. found dead in Corning, NY February 1, 1855

PRATT Susan in her 58th yr wife of Rev. B. Foster Pratt in Campbell, NY January 14, 1855

RUTHERFORD Edward Sr. in his 89th yr in Bath, NY February 12, 1855. Born 1766 in Northumberland Co. Eng. and came to Steuben Co. 1819

LELAND Abay wife of Ziba A. and dau of late Dr. Elijah **PORTER** of Waterford, NY in Halfmoon, NY February 1, 1855

GOULD Myranda age 55y in Bath, NY March 21, 1855

ANGELL Mary (**METCALFE**) age 38y wife of William P. Angell in Ellicottville, NY March 25, 1855

ABLE Eleanor age 43y consort of John Able in Bath, NY March 30, 1855

HARROWER Antoinette in her 41st yr wife of Sheriff G. T. Harrower and dau of Ambrose **KASSON** of Utica, NY in Bath, NY May 10, 1855

BOGARDUS Margaret wife of Cornelius in Bath, NY May 2, 1855. Res. Bath 50 yrs

CORBITT J. L. age 20y son of Thomas of Savona, NY in St. Louis, Mo. May 6, 1855

WARD Esther A. in her 24th yr wife of W. A. Ward in Wilkesbarre, Pa. May 10, 1855

COLE Lydia M. age 34y formerly of Steuben Co. NY wife of John Cole of Elkhart, Ind. formerly of Lisle, NY near Goshen, Ind. May 23, 1855

OLMSTEAD Charles age 31y 14d formerly of Monterey, NY in St. Louis, Mo. July

21, 1855

DANIELS Francis Eugene age 1y 5m son of Kendrick and Sarah Daniels in Bath, NY August 12, 1855

WILLISTON Horace age 72y in Athens, Pa. August 14, 1855. Native of Ct.

CAVENER James age 7m 15d son of James and Mary Cavener in Bath, NY September 3, 1855

HIGGINS Eliza in her 56th yr relict of Dr. John D. Higgins in Bath, NY September 5, 1855

MAY Sarah M. age 22y wife of Henry R. May and dau of David **ABBEY** of Akron, Ohio in Bath, NY September 7. 1855

LEIGHTON Mrs. Ellen in her 26th yr in Bath, NY September 25, 1855

VAN BUSKIRK Alida in her 54th yr relict of Richard Van Buskirk October 3, 1855

HIGGINS Miss Annie M. age 19y 3m in Bath, NY November 29, 1855

DE FOREST Capt. Abel age 94y 8m a Revolutionary Soldier in Binghamton, NY December 24, 1855

WILLISTON Hannah widow of Horace Williston in Athens, Pa. December 31, 1855

POTTER George E. age 1y 7m son of Edward K. and Orilla L. Potter in Bath, NY February 2, 1856

POTTER Edward K. age 30y in Bath, NY February 19, 1856. Native of Vt.

LOUNSBERRY Phineas found dead in shed nr his barn (Newspaper date February 27, 1856)

SHANNON Thomas Edwin age 1y 9m 24d son of Thomas and Martha Jane Shannon in Monterey, NY February 27, 1856

TULLEY William W. in his 24th yr in Lafayette Co. Ill. April 5, 1856

ERWIN Sophia age 49y wife of Gen. Francis Erwin and dau of late Ansel **MC CALL** of Painted Post, NY in Painted Post May 16, 1856

WALLING D. W. C. in his 34th yr formerly of Dundee, NY son of J. Walling of Cohocton, NY in Rockford, Ill. May 10, 1856

CHURCH Robert W. in his 56th yr in Bath, NY May 28, 1856

PALMER Louisa in her 14th yr in Bath, NY May 30, 1856

DUNN Lida age 5y 10m dau of James Dunn in Elmira, NY June 4, 1856

BAYMAN Philander W. age 20y son of Thomas and Mary Bayman at stepfather's David **CARTER** in Corning, NY June 20, 1856

BENTLEY Lucinda age 54y wife of George C. Bentley in Dansville, NY July 14, 1856

WAUGH Letta age 21y dau of Elder A. Waugh in Cohocton, NY July 15, 1856

FAY Lydia Jane in her 22nd yr wife of Franklin Fay and dau of Henry and Margaret **VAN HOUSEN** in Prattsburgh, NY August 23, 1856

HOTCHKIN N. E. age 47y wife of James H. in Prattsburgh, NY August 28, 1856

HANFORD Stephen W. age 46y in Elmira, NY September 4, 1856

HASTINGS Mrs. H. age 53y in Howard, NY August 27, 1856

FAULKNER William in his 26th yr of Bath, NY in Chicago, Ill. September 15, 1856

PERRIGE Charles age 86y in Addison, NY December 9, 1856

JOHNSON Lucretia age 70y wife of James Johnson in Bath, NY December 12, 1856

CONWAY Patrick of Harrisburgh Hollow Monday last (Newspaper date January 14, 1857)

HAVENS Mrs. ____ age 33y wife of Rev. E. H. Havens in fire at Dudley Settlement, NY January 21, 1857 and child age 2y died January 22, 1857

SQUIRES Eliza Ann wife of Nathaniel Squires and dau of late Robert **LOGAN** in Davenport, Iowa February 2, 1857

BARTON Frances M. age 24y wife of W. P. Barton of Bath, NY and dau of Col. E. G. **PETTIBONE** of Elba, NY February 20, 1857, buried in Elba

PRENTISS Martha B. in her 89th yr relict of John Prentiss in Pulteney, NY March 2, 1857. Native of E. Sudbury, Mass. and dau of Rev. Josiah **BRIDGES**. Came to Pulteney in 1813

WIXOM Ella age 7m 2d dau of Charles N. and Cornelia E. in New York City March 1, 1857, buried in Pulteney, NY next to Great Grandmother who died March 2, 1857

BROWN Margaret C. age 15y 6m dau of late John Brown in Bath, NY March 27, 1857

LYON Dr. Abraham T. age 30y at Father's Samuel Lyon in Bath, NY March 16, 1857

PRENTICE Permilia D. in her 51st yr wife of Dr. William H. Prentice formerly of Hancock, NH in Jasper, NY March 22, 1857

STEUBEN COUNTY NEWSPAPERS 95

RICE H. D. of Owego, NY in Corning, NY April 2, 1857

WELLES J. Nelson in his 35th yr son of Benjamin F. and Rebecca Welles in Pulteney, NY April 18, 1857

GOODSELL Mary Ann age 21y wife of John R. Goodsell in Bath, NY April 19, 1857

CORBITT A. Judson age 23y son of Thomas and Nancy in Savona, NY April 23, 1857

SHANNON Elizabeth age 86y at son-in-law's John **FAWCETT** in Bath, NY May 1, 1857. Native of Co. Sligo, Ireland. Leaves 5 children

CASE Henry Seymour age 13y son of Jarvis P. Case from accidental discharge of gun in Arkport, NY April 18, 1857

HOYT Willard Gilmore age 7y 7m son of William C. and Emeline S. Hoyt in Bath, NY May 11, 1857

ELLIS Mrs. Isabel age 78y in Pulteney, NY May 15, 1857, native of Paisley, Scotland

HOLMES Simeon age 62y formerly of Avoca, NY in Mt. Morris, NY May 22, 1857

WARNER Amy Ann age 1y 11m 18d dau of Ira and Cornelia Warner in Rathbone, NY July 2, 1857

WILBUR Lucinda age 45y wife of Samuel K. Wilbur in Thurston, NY July 14, 1857

PORTER Edward R. age 50y of Prattsburgh, NY in Darien, NY August 1, 1857

SMITH Mary Ann wife of Edward Smith formerly of Bath, NY in W. Otis, Mass. August 1, 1857

NOBLE Abigail age 85y at son's Lay Noble in Bath, NY August 22, 1857

MITCHELL John abt 50y of Johnson Settlement, NY from accidental discharge of gun September 3, 1857

COMSTOCK Lucinda M. age 40y wife of Augustus in Bath, NY September 7, 1857

CURTIS Amos age 78y Father of Mrs. Egar **MUNSON** of Bradford, NY in Meriden, Ct. September 25, 1857

TAYLOR George W. in his 74th yr in Canisteo, NY November 3, 1857. Came to Canisteo in 1797

RICHARDSON Hattie age 9m dau of George B. and Eliza R. November 7, 1857

POTTER Miss Mary Ann age 37y in Bath, NY December 7, 1857

MC CALL Sarah age 4m dau of A. J. and M. A. in Bath, NY December 17, 1857

DEATH NOTICES

DANIELS Mortimer in his 12th yr son of P. J. Daniels in Bath, NY December 15, 1857

STANLEY Col. Salma age 78y in Geneva, NY February 1, 1858. In battle of Queenston on October 13, 1812 where he received slight wounds

MC ELWEE Henry in his 88th yr in Savona, NY February 5, 1858. Came to Bath, NY 63 yrs ago, farm occupied by son Henry Jr.

MARSELL John Powers age 24y at Grandfather's John **POWERS** in Avoca, NY January 30, 1858

WHITEHORN Fidelia A. age 22y of Penn Yan, NY in Prattsburgh, NY February 7, 1858

AYERS Agnes age 9y 10m dau of late Nathan **STEVENS** in Bath, NY February 6, 1858

CROSBY David age 68y 2d in Cohocton, NY (Newspaper date February 24, 1858)

PLATT Rev. Isaac W. former Pastor 1st Pres. Church of Bath, NY in West Farms, NY February 9, 1858. Born October 1788 in Huntington, Long Is.

CURTIS John B. age 27y son of Daniel Curtis of Campbell, NY in Angus, Canada W. February 26, 1858

TAYLOR Osman age 14y son of Henry Taylor in Bradford, NY March 2, 1858

DAILEY John H. abt 30y kicked by horse in Pulteney, NY March 29, 1858. Leaves wife and 3 children

WIXOM Fanny Augusta age 6w 2d dau of Charles N. and Cornelia E. Wixom in Pulteney, NY March 25, 1858

MARSHALL Dolly Nelly age 69y wife of Gen. O. F. Marshall in Wheeler, NY March 24, 1858

CROCKER Helen M. age 28y wife of Dr. Wickham R. Crocker in Cameron, NY April 5, 1858

WELLES Charlotte age 19y wife of Charles D. Welles of Wayne, NY in Horseheads, NY April 18, 1858

BROWN Rev. Charles in his 41st yr colored Baptist Minister from Canada West in Bath, NY April 29, 1858

BROWN William Marcus age 4m son of Rev. Charles and Eliza (**COOPER**) Brown April 15, 1858

RICHARDSON Catherine age 75y widow of John Richardson in Mt. Washington, NY April 21, 1858. Native of Hagerstown, Md. Came to Bath, NY over 50 yrs ago

BILLINGTON John in his 40th yr near Bath, NY May 10, 1858, born Montgomery Co.

PRATT Dexter age 63y formerly of Howard, NY and pioneer settler of Bath, NY at Castile Water Cure June 24, 1858

HOPKINS Elizabeth in his 91st yr widow of John in Prattsburgh, NY July 31, 1858

PURDY Dr. Jotham age 59y of Elmira, NY near Southport, NY August 11, 1858

VAN AUKEN Kate Wise age 2y 8m 10d dau of Jacob and Mary Ann Van Auken in Hammondsport, NY August 17, 1858

DRAKE Freddie Luce age 2m 4d son of Theodore M. and Maria L. Drake in Bath, NY September 3, 1858

ATWATER Lewis Curtis age 9m son of Dwight in Corning, NY September 5, 1858

MANTOR Eunice abt 65y Mother of Mrs. L. D. **DODGE** in Corning, NY September 6, 1858

BARNES Louisa age 40y wife of Washington Barnes and sister of Mrs. T. A. **JOHNSON** of Corning, NY in Painted Post, NY September 5, 1858

BONHAM William abt 70y in Knoxville, Pa. September 5, 1858

VEITH Evangelina age 4m 15d dau of Frank Veith in Corning, NY September 7, 1858

MURRAY James C. age 46y in Corning, NY September 9, 1858

BACHMAN Sarah in her 77th yr wife of Jacob in Pulteney, NY September 7, 1858

MOREY Mc Clelland age 22y in Painted Post, NY September 14, 1858

RICHARDSON George C. age 21y son of H. S. Richardson formerly of Bath, NY hit by falling tree in Friendship, NY September 13, 1858

HILTON Henry of Hornby, NY drowned October 17, 1858

BRYANT Joseph in his 63rd yr in Bath, NY October 26, 1858

SEELEY Hiram of Ovid, NY October 19, 1858

QUICK Milo of intoxication in Jasper, NY Election night (Newspaper date November 17, 1858)

VAN HOUSEN Joseph H. in his 30th yr in Prattsburgh, NY December 9, 1858

HAYES Emma Jane age 16y dau of Samuel Hayes in Prattsburgh, NY January 7, 1859

SMITH William age 26y at Father's Charles A. Smith in Bath, NY February 10, 1859

DEATH NOTICES

BAILEY Jarvis suicide in Tyrone, NY February 18, 1859

WILLIAMS Charles suicide in Tyrone, NY February 19, 1859

HAVERLING Adam age 85y 5m in Bath, NY March 6, 1859

PERINE Abigail age 59y wife of William Perine and dau of late Col. John **WHITING** in Dansville, NY February 11, 1859

STARR Miss Rebecca abt 80y sister of Mrs. Charlotte **HAYT** of Ithaca, NY recently from Patterson, NJ (Newspaper date March 16, 1859)

BURROWS Periam D. age 19y at Father's in Andover, NY April 8, 1859

RANDALL Arlington age 4m 6d son of John and Eugenia E. Randall in Bath, NY April 24, 1859

BONHAM Delphine age 15y dau of Mrs. Mary Bonham and adopted dau of Dr. N. D. **GARDNER** of Elmira, NY in Campbell, NY May 12, 1859

WHITWOOD Miss Fanny age 72y in Howard, NY June 13, 1859

REYNOLDS John N. age 66y in Pulteney, NY July 11, 1859

SHOEMAKER John age 90y a pioneer of Yates Co. in Barrington, NY July 11, 1859

STOCKING George O. age 7y 10m 21d son of Henry and Martha Stocking in Avoca, NY August 24, 1859

HOWARD Loren Joseph age 1m 19d son of Rev. O. R. and Emily M. Howard in Bath, NY August 26, 1859

EDWARDS Mrs. Mary age 78y in Bath, NY August 2, 1859

TIFFANY Willis N. age 65y in Kanona, NY August 3, 1859

AINSWORTH Willard Smith age 4y son of R. R. and M. E. Ainsworth in Prattsburgh, NY August 28, 1859

SHEFFIELD Sarah age 79y 11m 11d wife of R. H. Sheffield in Jasper, NY September 9, 1859

OGDEN Henry L. in his 18th yr mem of US army and son of late E. A. Ogden in Bath, NY September 28, 1859

WATSON William in his 83rd yr in Bath, NY October 9, 1859

LAYTON Abigail in her 53rd yr wife of Jesse S. in Savona, NY September 23, 1859

ANDERSON John age 49y 10m funeral at Prattsburgh, NY November 28, 1859

OWEN Eleazor age 80y in Big Flats, NY last week (Newspaper date December 28, 1859). One of first settlers this region, came here 70 yrs ago

LEE Phebe in her 68th yr consort of William Lee and dau of Samuel and Caroline **ORVIS** in Prattsburgh, NY December 27, 1859

CHARLESWORTH Clark L. suicide in Avoca, NY January 7, 1860

FERRIS Reuben age 78y Father of A. P. Ferris of Bath, NY in Howard, NY January 8, 1860

ORTON William age 71 at son's Andrew J. Orton in Woodhull, NY January 25, 1860

WHITNEY Hannah in her 94th yr wife of Nathan in Bath, NY February 7, 1860

BAKER Catherine in her 60th yr widow of Samuel Baker Jr. in Hammondsport, NY January 26, 1860

SWARTHOUT Miss Elizabeth J. age 23y 1m in Bath, NY February 18, 1860

ALDRICH Watson age 4m son of Rev. S. H. and Harriet A. P. Aldrich in Troupsburgh, NY March 23, 1860

FRY William H. in his 22nd yr in Campbell, NY March 26, 1860

LEWIS James S. age 28y in Prattsburgh, NY March 29, 1860. Graduated from Poughkeepsie Law School in 1857

WILBER Samuel in his 79th yr in Bath, NY May 2, 1860

RUMSEY Mary in her 17th yr dau of D. Rumsey in Bath, NY May 22, 1860

HERRON Mrs. Elizabeth age 73y formerly of Middleburgh, NY in Bath, NY June 2, 1860

DAVIS Samuel Jr. age 27y in Avoca, NY May 22, 1860

WHITNEY Nathan in his 96th yr in Bath, NY June 7, 1860. Born Danbury, Ct. Married age 23y Hannah **TAYLOR** of Danbury, married 73 yrs. Wife died 4 mos ago

WOLCOTT Nelson an old res. of Caton, NY suicide June 24, 1860

BRECK Roxana E. age 44y wife of George W. Breck in Bath, NY June 29, 1860

WOODARD Sarah age 52y wife of W. A. Woodard formerly of Bath, NY in Omro, Wis. June 14, 1860

HUNTER Peter in his 60th yr in Bath, NY July 8, 1860

WARREN Phineas in his 58th yr in Bath, NY June 28, 1860

GREGG Sarah Ann in her 31st yr wife of William M. Gregg and dau of late Judge John W. **WISNER** in Elmira, NY July 16, 1860

MILES Rev. H. G. age 47y formerly of Bath, NY in Corning, NY July 21, 1860

TRIMBLE John in his 87th yr in Savona, NY August 28, 1860. Wife Mary Trimble in her 70th yr died July 1, 1860

WELLS Helen Cordelia age 25y 8m 10d dau of B. F. in Pulteney, NY August 26, 1860

GORDON ___ age 23y son of Rufus burned to death in house September 19, 1860

LEWIS Mrs. Margaret age 62y in Wheeler, NY August 19, 1860. Born and married in Renssalaer Co. NY

COLLIER Addison Niles age 10y 6m son of J. H. and Charlotte Collier in Avoca, NY October 15, 1860

PETERS Mrs. Jane in her 74th yr at res. of Thomas **RICHARDSON** in Bath, NY October 14, 1860

WALLACE James age 76y in Cohocton, NY October 9, 1860

ABEL Peter in his 25th yr son of John Abel in Bath, NY (Newspaper date November 7, 1860)

SWITZER John age 74y in Bradford, NY December 18, 1860

BLACK David S. age 24y son of Jeremiah and Eliza in Bath, NY December 19, 1860

SPALDING Ellen Frances age 17y dau of Philo Spalding January 21, 1861

WALDO Mary age 22y wife of D. D. Waldo in Prattsburgh, NY January 17, 1861

ROYER Isabella in her 72nd yr in Bath, NY January 24, 1861

MILLS Anna Kate age 8m dau of D. A. and E. E. Mills in Bath, NY February 23, 1861

HIGGINS Emily B. age 25y dau of late Dr. John D. Higgins in Bath, NY March 5, 1861

LYON Mary Ann in her 56th yr wife of Samuel at son's John Lyon March 17, 1861

COLLIER Jacob H. Jr. age 25y in Avoca, NY March 7, 1861

BRONSON Helen D. age 9y died March 30, 1861 and Laura Etta age 12y died March 31, 1861 daus of Rev. Mr. Bronson in Canisteo, NY from explosion of kerosene lamp on March 29

WILBER Elizabeth in her 80th yr wife of Samuel Wilber in Bath, NY April 1, 1861

HICKS Solomon A. abt 30y crushed by rolling log in Hornby, NY April 6, 1861

WHITING Col. Levi Carter in his 47th yr in Bath, NY April 9, 1861. Born 1814 in Maine

HULETT ____ age 6y son of Emory Hulett crushed by rolling log in Savona, NY last week (Newspaper date May 1, 1861)

BIDWELL Andrew in his 26th yr formerly of Bath, NY in Omaha, Neb. May 6, 1861

BLOOD Phebe age 72y wife of Calvin Blood formerly of Cohocton, NY in Painted Post, NY May 14, 1861

CHURCH Edwin F. age 36y in Bath, NY May 28, 1861

NICHOLS Miss Edith E. in her 21st yr dau of A. H. and Emeline Nichols in Burlington, Iowa May 29, 1861

WILLIAMS Fannie T. **(TAYLOR)** age 27y wife of W. A. in Tacusa, Ill. May 6, 1861

HARROWER Benjamin in his 70th yr in Lindley, NY May 18, 1861. Born Walton, NY son of Rev. David Harrower and res of Steuben Co. 40 yrs

SHEPARD Margaret infant dau of Orlando and Ruth Shepard in Hammondsport, NY May 30, 1861

LINDSAY Catherine Jane in her 27th yr dau of James and Maria Lindsay in Bath, NY June 17, 1861

ELMENDORPH Phebe in her 57th yr wife of Dr. Stephen Elmendorph and dau of late Salmon **TOUCEY** in Bath, NY June 24, 1861. Born Fairfield Co. Ct.

FRY Hopey Sophia age 3y 11m dau of William H. and Ellen in Bath, NY July 7, 1861

WELLES Julia eldest dau of B. F. Welles in Pulteney, NY June 9, 1861

BRYAN Jacob age 77y in Sonora, NY June 30, 1861

SEAGER Moses age 63y in Sonora, NY July 2, 1861

BRYAN Aryann age 13y dau of Joshua W. Bryan on Oak Hill, NY July 3, 1861

CHICHESTER William W. son of Henry and Eliza in Wheeler, NY July 9, 1861

BROWNELL Emmagene in her 9th yr dau of Martin and Cornelia Brownell in Bath, NY July 21, 1861

SECOR David in his 24th yr son of Worthington and Lusilvia Secor in Bath, NY July 30, 1861

DEATH NOTICES

SLINEY Lily Grace age 8y 10m dau of Thomas and Hannah in Bath, NY July 23, 1861

SHERWOOD Alfred age 23y in circular saw accident in Bath, NY August 21, 1861

BACHMAN Jacob in his 86th yr in Pulteney, NY August 19, 1861. Res. abt 40 yrs

YOUNG Jane T. in her 67th yr wife of William Young in Bath, NY September 3, 1861, buried Geneva, NY

WELCH Henry H. age 7y died September 13, 1861 and Hannah C. age 3m died September 19, 1861 children of Warren H. and Merab Welch in Elmira, NY

CUMMINGS James a Vol. in Capt. King's Co. 34th Reg. of Pulteney, NY at Camp Jackson, Md. September 8, 1861

BRUNDAGE Benjamin S. age 67y in Greenwood, NY October 4, 1861

DOUGHTY Mr. ___ hit by train in Wayland, NY last wk (Newspaper date October 23, 1861)

SMITH Rev. Benajmin Coleman age 61y in Prattsburgh, NY October 10, 1861. Born 1800 in Windsor, Vt.

BIDWELL Lieut. Solomon age 33y a native of Bath, NY of the 6th Ohio Reg. accidently shot by soldiers of Ind. 17th Reg. October 4, 1861

CLARK John age 81y in Wheeler, NY October 29, 1861. Settled in Wheeler in 1808

PAULDING Mary in her 21st yr dau of Thomas in Bath, NY November 6, 1861

GRAHAM John age 77y native of Scotland in Bath, NY October 28, 1861

TYLER Col. William of remarkable age at Co. House November 18, 1861

LOZIER Byron in his 19th yr a Vol. in Reg. of Steuben Co. Rangers in Elmira, NY November 20, 1861

SHULTS Herkimer of Kanona, NY in Hospital in Washington DC December 18, 1861

DUDLEY John James age 3y son of Charles and Mary C. Dudley in Bath, NY December 29, 1861

KELLOGG Sarah age 38y in Savona, NY December 24, 1861

STEWART Arthur age 21y hit by falling limb February 3, 1862

CHASE Mary E. age 22y formerly of Bath, NY in Lancaster, Pa. January 29, 1862

RISING William age 38y hit by falling tree in Thurston, NY February 8, 1862

OTIS Mary Carr age 2y 1m 20d dau of J. T. and R. W. Otis in Kanona, NY February 12, 1862

SHEPARD Orlando in Hammondsport, NY February 14, 1862

ARNOLD Rufus age 63y in Corning, NY February 24, 1862

WILLIAMS Susan B. in her 23rd yr dau of William in Bath, NY January 27, 1862

SHANNON Henry age 4y 10m son of Thomas and Martha J. Shannon in Monterey, NY February 19, 1862

WALLING Jacob age 65y in N. Cohocton, NY March 30, 1862

SWITZER Peter age 62y in Bradford, NY April 4, 1862

BARNEY Charles E. age 26y son of Nelson Barney of Bath, NY in Stillwater, Mn. April 4, 1862

HESS Alexander age 57y in Bath, NY April 11, 1862. Born Easton, Pa. and came to western NY 1828

SMEAD Ella E. age 15y 6m in Bath, NY April 20, 1862

FAULKNER Amelia age 30y eldest dau of Richard in Bath, NY April 16, 1862

WALDO Capt. Edward abt 28y of the 14th Wis. Reg. (where he lived for 2 yrs.) son of A. G. Waldo of Prattsburgh, NY at the battle of Pittsburgh Landing (Newspaper date April 30, 1862)

STEWART Col. Warren of Campbell, NY wounded and died at Pittsburgh Landing. (Newspaper date May 7, 1862)

CARPENTER Thomas S. in his 22nd yr of Troupsburgh, NY in Co. H. 86th Reg. NYV at Washington DC April 11, 1862

GOULD Thomas abt 15y son of Caton Gould from accidental discharge of gun at Mt. Washington, NY April 15, 1862

BURTON Fanny age 57y wife of G. E. Burton in Corning, NY April 11, 1862. Born April 14, 1805 in Paris, NY dau of John **HOPKINS**

ADAMS Alexander age 25y son of Daniel Adams of Bath, NY near Williamsburg, Va. member of Capt. Wheeler's Battery (Newspaper date May 21, 1862)

READ Martin son of Arnold D. Read of Bath, NY in Hospital at Washington DC April 20, 1862

MARCH William member of Capt. Schlick's Co. 23rd Reg. at Fredericksburg, Va. Notice from Headquarters on May 26, 1862

LOUCKS Andrew K. age 27y 12d in Quincy, Ill. May 19, 1862

BAILEY Col. G. D. and Maj. D. H. **VAN VALKENBURGH** of the 1st NY Artillery. (Telegram received June 2, 1862)

CRANDALL ____ age 4/5y son of S. W. by falling tree in Fremont, NY June 7, 1862

BRYANT James of Bath, NY member of Capt. Wheeler's Battery hit by lightning June 3, 1862

CLARK Solomon S. son of Mathias Clark of Urbana, NY in Co. I, 34th Reg. NYV this week (Newspaper date June 11, 1862)

JACOBUS Jesse member of Capt. Kings Co. of Hammondsport, NY of wounds at Fair Oaks (Newspaper date June 25, 1862)

DONAHE Horace G. in his 41st yr in Bath, NY June 22, 1862

SMITH Heywood in his 5th yr son of H. B. and Mary S. in Avoca, NY June 13, 1862

LYNCH James from accident in saw mill at Campbell, NY last week (Newspaper date July 2, 1862)

BRECK George son of George W. Breck of Bath, NY member of Capt. Wheeler's Co. June 7, 1862

PELTON Wesley M. in his 21st yr of Pulteney, NY at camp nr Harrison's Landing July 22, 1862. Mem of Co. I 34th Reg. NYV

ELLAS Jane age 35y wife of Ella in Bath, NY August 8, 1862

CRANE Estella in her 5th yr dau of John and Elizabeth Crane in Wayne, NY July 17, 1862 and son George W. Crane died July 30, 1862

LOVELESS Frank A. age 8y 7m 22d at Grandfather's John **GUSTIN** September 6, 1862

PAWLING Ten Eyck Gansevoort in his 24th yr son of Thomas Pawling at Battle of Bull Run August 29, 1862

BOWLBY James age 83y in Bath, NY September 14, 1862

STOCUM Cora Langdon age 1y 6m 4d dau of John and Susan Stocum in Bath, NY September 8, 1862

WILLIAMS Seabury and David **FARRON** members of Co. A. 23rd Reg. killed in late battles in Maryland (Newspaper date October 1, 1862)

SILVERNAIL Miss Silva Ann age 49y 9m 11d dau of Benjamin Silvernail in Bradford, NY September 21, 1862

MARIM Cornelius Comeges age 30y late of Bath, NY a marine of US Brig. St. Lawrence at Key West of yellow fever September 12, 1862

SNELL Marcellus K. age 26y son of Peter Snell of Bath, NY at battle in Corinth, Miss. October 3, 1862

BORDEN Albert V. of Bath, NY member of Capt. Laman's Co. 107th Reg. funeral in Bath November 2, 1862

SEXTON Capt. John A. of Bath, NY member of 34th Ind. Vol. from wounds in battle at Perryville, Ky. Funeral in Bath November 16, 1862

HOWELL Hannah age 5m dau of James F. and Lydia S. Howell in Bath, NY November 10, 1862

PALMER Ezekiel age 76y in Bath, NY November 16, 1862

FRENCH Luella Suzy age 4y 8m dau of F. L. and Eva L. French in Chittenango, NY November 7, 1862

SEELEY Lennie L. age 3y 6m dau of R. L. and Susey J. Seeley in Hammondsport, NY November 7, 1862

SPAFFORD George F. age 21y formerly of Bath, NY member of the 101st Ohio Reg. at hospital in New Albany, Ind. October 28, 1862

DURHAM Squire M. age 25y 5m 20d member Co. F. 121st Reg. in Elmira, NY November 28, 1862

ERWIN Albert age 16y 16d son of William and Mary E. Erwin fell from horse on RR track in Painted Post, NY November 26, 1862

YOUMANS Nehemiah age 14 of Eagle Valley, NY of typhoid fever contracted in Camp in Elmira, NY November 21, 1862. Member of Capt. Bile's Co. 161st Reg. NYV

CALKINS Levi age 23y son of Ira M. Calkins Vol. in 161st Reg. at Camp Smith Elmira, NY in Bath, NY December 9, 1862

SANFORD George would be 42y next week in Sonora, NY December 27, 1862. Leaves wife and 5 children

WHITTEMORE Abijah Webster in his 16th yr son of Moses F. and Sarah Whittemore at New York City hospital December 26, 1862. Member of Capt. W. E. Craig's Co. 161st Reg. NYV

COOPER Miss Lydia M. in her 47th yr in Bath, NY December 31, 1862

HURLEY Cpl. John W. of Capt. King's Co. I, 34th Reg. NYV at battle of Fredericksburg December 15, 1862

DEATH NOTICES

KNAPP Jacob in his 41st yr in Bath, NY January 29, 1863

SILSBEE George B. age 32y formerly of Avoca, NY in San Francisco, Cal. November 14, 1862

DENNISTON Abraham funeral at Prattsburgh, NY February 19, 1863

WOODRUFF James W. son of B. W. Woodruff of Dansville, NY in Co. B. 130th Reg. NYV near Blackwater (Newspaper date February 18, 1863)

MOORE ____ abt 8y son of Jefferson drowned in Savona, NY February 23, 1863

MILES Frank in his 10th yr son of William and Nancy A. in Bath, NY March 1, 1863

POWERS John age 75y in Avoca, NY March 5, 1863

COOK Quartus in his 68th yr in Prattsburgh, NY January 24, 1863. Born Northampton, Mass. son of Aaron and Miriam Cook. Father died age 83y and Mother died at age 84y

FOWLER Catherine age 30y dau of William and Fanny **PRENTISS** in Pulteney, NY March 14, 1863

WILLIAMS David in his 48th yr formerly of Bath, NY in Mazo Maine, Wis. January 2, 1863

SMEAD Henry D. in his 56th yr formerly of Bath, NY in Cincinnati, Ohio March 24, 1863

ROBIE Eben age 58y in Jeffersonville, Vt. March 21, 1863

LOUCKS Maggie age 13y in Bristol Station, Ill. March 24, 1863

DOUBLEDAY Elisha age 67y in Italy Hill, NY April 2, 1863

GRAVES Frederick A. age 24y son of Rev. F. Graves of Avoca, NY at hospital near Falmouth February 26, 1863. Body removed and sent north for burial by mistake with other parents. Not known where buried, probably near Syracuse, NY. Member of Co. K. 140th Reg.

UPTHEGROVE Charles age 22y 10m 12d son of Thomas and Samantha Upthegrove in Wheeler, November 28, 1862. Private in Capt. Van Tuyl's Co. 161st Reg.

MERRITT Sidney D. age 15y 5m 17d son of Jesse and Lydia B. Merritt in Wheeler, NY December 21, 1862. 3rd death in family within 23 days

UPTHEGROVE Thomas in his 46th yr in Wheeler, NY December 15, 1862

UPTHEGROVE Phebe Eveline age 19y 10m 13d in Wheeler, NY December 28, 1862

TOWNSEND Josiah S. in his 62nd yr in Southport, NY April 12, 1863

BULL Hulda in her 60th yr wife of Frederick Bull in Bath, NY April 22, 1863

DAVISON Charlie F. age 3m 6d son of Thomas and Elizabeth Davison in Bath, NY April 27, 1863

MILLER Ida age 14y 1m dau of Charles and Gabriella in Watkins, NY April 16, 1863

SALT John D. son of William Salt of Bath, NY member of 133rd Reg. in engagement at New Orleans, La. (Newspaper date May 6, 1863)

HAYES Simeon in his 63rd yr in Prattsburgh, NY May 11, 1863

RICHARDSON George W. age 14m 13d son of George B. and Eliza R. Richardson in Bath, NY May 8, 1863

RICHARDSON Thomas J. age 28y son of Henry S. and Eunice Richardson at Father's in Belfast, NY May 10, 1863. Member Co. F. 85th Reg.

COVENHOVEN Sarah M. age 63y wife of Peter in Hornby, NY May 18, 1863. Born Northumberland, NY dau of Daniel and Prudence **ROOKS**. Married 32 yrs.

TURNER Sgt. Samuel of Co. A. 161st Reg. NYV of Prattsburgh, NY in hospital at Baton Rouge, La. May 12, 1863

ROSE Mortimer W. age 23y son of John Rose in Coopers Plains, NY June 1, 1863

TOWNSEND Henry abt 58y late of Bath, NY at Middletown Staten Is. June 25, 1863

EVANS Cassandra age 48y dau of John Evans of Allentown, Pa. in Painted Post, NY June 26, 1863

ROWE Mary Ann wife of James Rowe formerly of Cameron, NY in Springhill, Ill. July 2, 1863

PRATT Harriet in her 54th yr wife of Joel D. Pratt in Bath, NY April 19, 1863. Born Ct. and came to Steuben Co. 36 yrs ago.

HAGADORN Dr. Stephen age 51y in Bath, NY August 1, 1863, was imprisoned at Richmond in July 1861

LOSEY Sgt. Dennis abt 26y of Co. D. 161st Reg. NYV in hospital at Baton Rouge, La. July 19, 1863

TOWLE Capt. Richard in his 39th yr of Co. H. 141st Reg. NY militia near Warrentown Junction August 2, 1863. Wife lives in Bath, NY

SEXTON Henry in his 26th yr son of Michael Sexton killed at battle of Hover's Gap June 24, 1863, second son lost in war

BURCH Margaret age 17 hit by lightning at home of Ambrose **SMITH** in Bath, NY

DEATH NOTICES

August 24, 1863

HUGHES Charles E. age 24y son of Thomas P. and Mary of Savona, NY. Mem of 141st Reg. at hospital in Washington DC (Newspaper date August 26, 1863)

GARDNER George age 45y formerly of Avoca, NY in Chicago, Ill. May 30, 1863

STRONG Willie B. age 1y 7m son of J. Harvey and Ellen G. Strong in Clarksville, NY August 26, 1863

FLEMING Dr. J. B. age 48y formerly of Bath, NY in Johnstown Center, (Newspaper date September 2, 1863)

VAN GELDER Levi W. abt 36y of Wheeler, NY murdered September 10, 1863, Seaman **SIMONS** suspected

WOOD Henry S. age 30y of Wayne, NY member of Co. B. 141st Reg. at Camp Hospital near Warrenton Junction August 16, 1863

BABCOCK John R. age 21y adopted son of William N. **DEAN** a Private in Co. A. 161st Reg. in Pulteney, NY December 20, 1862

REYNOLDS Carrie Louella age 3y 2m 3d dau of James J. and Lucie A. Reynolds in Pulteney, NY August 20, 1863

MC ANDREW William age 6y died October 17, 1863 and Maria age 4y died October 18, 1863 children of John Mc Andrew of Bath, NY

SEXTON Mary age 30y in Bath, NY November 3, 1863

FAULKNER Sarah M. age 6y dau of John Faulkner in Bath, NY November 20, 1863

MERRITT Franklin E. age 18y 5m 15d son of Jesse and Lydia B. Merritt in Wheeler, NY November 21, 1863

SPALDING Jacob in his 86th yr in Bath, NY November 20, 1863. Born Plainfield, Ct.

BROWN Cornelia M. wife of Frank B. Brown Editor of Corning Democrat in Corning, NY December 2, 1863

MAGEE Hugh age 67y 5m 15d in Watkins, NY November 26, 1863. Born June 11, 1796

HALSEY George age 62y at Riverhead, Long Island December 12, 1863

BACHMAN Willie age 7y son of William and Anna D. Bachman in Pulteney, NY November 20, 1863

YEISLEY Mary Allena age 2y dau of George and Elizabeth Yeisley in Avoca, NY November 13, 1863

HEES Ella P. age 12y dau of James and Belinda in Avoca, NY November 20, 1863

PARTRIDGE Stephen at Cattlet Sta. Va. November 5, 1863

HENRY Polly Hogan age 69y 3m in Bath, NY December 18, 1863

WHEELER Barton F. age 6y 7m died December 5, 1863 and Ida age 15m died November 6, 1863 children of Jonas and Mary Ann Wheeler in Urbana, NY

MC CAY S. N. in her 64th yr relict of W. W. Mc Cay of Bath, NY at son-in-law's M. **BIXBY** in New York City January 1, 1864

KELLOGG Russ in his 70th yr in Kanona, NY January 4, 1864

VAN HOUSEN Charlotte A. wife of J. H. Van Housen of Bath, NY at Uncles in St. Albens Bay, Vt. November 26, 1863

WOOD Jonathan in his 8th yr died November 25, 1863 and Laura M. age 6y died December 5, 1863 children of Israel and Orilla Wood in N. Urbana, NY

SAYRE Owen R. age 16y 4m 20d son of William and Harriet Sayre formerly of Thurston, NY in Washington, DC November 17, 1863

WHITE Mrs. Jane age 61y 8m 28d in Bath, NY January 26, 1864

WHITEHEAD Theodore B. age 2m 22d son of William and Emily Whitehead in Bath, NY January 4, 1864

WOHLGEMUTH Mary A. in her 35th yr wife of Rev. William Wohlgemuth in Bath, NY January 19, 1864. Born England

GULWITE Jennie in her 32nd yr wife of Francis H. in Avoca, NY January 16, 1864

BENJAMIN Phebe in her 67th yr in Bath, NY January 28, 1864

DENSE Mary Elizabeth age 24y 5m wife of Theodore in Flint, Mi. January 16, 1864

ABEL William age 36y hit by falling tree in Savona, NY January 28, 1864. Leaves wife and 1 child

COMSTOCK Sgt. George S. F. age 31y of Co. D. 16th Reg. NY Heavy Artillery at General Hospital in Elmira, NY February 3, 1864

WILLIAMS George age 79y 5m 13d in Troupsburgh, NY February 3, 1864

COOK James Jr. in his 36th yr of Bath, NY member of 141st Reg. at Murpheesboro, Tn. December 16, 1863

Members of Co. D. 161st Reg. taken prisoner at Sabine Pass between Union Gunboat and rebel fort on September 8, 1863. Killed on board Anthony **COMPTON** of

Bradford, NY. Died at Sabine village same night Patrick **HART** of Bath, NY, Adam H. **WILCOX** of Bath, NY and Gary **DODGE** of Bradford, NY. Died at Beaumont next day Abram **BLAKESLEE** of Bath, NY. Died 5 days later at Beaumont James M. **SNYDER** of Cameron, NY and George T. **BRANNON** of Bradford, NY (taken from a letter from Lieut. Lindsay)

LENHART Godfrey in his 50th yr in Bath, NY February 16, 1864. Volunteer in Mexican War and Civil War

SIMONS Seaman who was to be executed for the murder of Levi **VAN GELDER** on March 11, 1863 committed suicide by hanging in jail February 24, 1864

CAMPBELL James L. formerly of Bath, NY in Washington DC February 17, 1864

FORD Carrie A. age 20y in Howard, NY February 25, 1864

CLARK Phebe A. age 18y 6m dau of Stephen in Prattsburgh, NY February 28, 1864

CALKINS Estella age 3y 8m dau of A. C. and Annis in Bath, NY February 19, 1864

RUNYAN S. L. wife of Prof. W. W. Runyan in Sonora, NY March 19, 1864

PALMER William age 45y in Kanona, NY March 14, 1864

GILBERT Ann age 48y wife of Samuel Gilbert in Avoca, NY March 18, 1864

MILLS Minnie May age 1y 10m 6d dau of D. A. and E. E. Mills in Bath, NY March 18, 1864

NEAR Richard in his 59th yr in Kanona, NY March 31, 1864 (Watertown, NY papers please copy)

HOPKINS Norman age 75y in Bath, NY March 29, 1864

COLLIER Mahlon in his 18th yr son of I. H. and Charlotte Collier in Avoca, NY April 14, 1864

MILES Horace G. age 18y son of William and Nancy A. in Sonora, NY April 25, 1864

HOYT Elmer age 1y 11m son of William C. and E. S. Hoyt in Bath, NY April 20, 1864

FAUCETT George age 73y 5m in Bath, NY April 20, 1864

WISWALL Lucretia wife of Henry T. Wiswall and dau of late Dr. Asa **PERKINS** of Dover, NH in Dover April 21, 1864

WAIT Lyman S. of Bath, NY member of 97th Reg. NYV in late battle of Va. from a letter of a soldier in Army of Potomac (Newspaper date May 18, 1864)

RICHARDSON William H. age 28y in Bath, NY April 29, 1864

SPRAGUE John L. age 28y of Bath, NY in Co. F. 161st Reg. at battle at Sabine Crossroads, La. April 8, 1864

REDINGTON Thomas age 45y hit by train near Cameron, NY May 29, 1864

NEWTON Jerome B. of Avoca, NY member Co. K. 107th Reg. NYV at Resaca, Ga. May 15, 1864. Leaves wife and 5 children

GRANT Col. Stephen in his 75th yr near Bath, NY March 29, 1864. Born 1789 in Bangor, Me. and came to Bath, 1813. Wife died April 18, 1864, 6 children

Members of Co. G. 107th Reg. killed near Dallas, Ga. May 25, 1864 Cpl. Adam **TOMER**, David B. **SANFORD** and Theron **ALDERMAN**

FRENCH Mrs. Mary age 84y 7m in Bath, NY June 9, 1864

SMITH Lucy L. age 22y 4m wife of E. A. Smith in Prattsburgh, NY May 26, 1864

SHOEMAKER Phebe age 12y dau of Daniel and Elizabeth in Bath, NY June 10, 1864

CONDERMAN Orrin age 26y of Howard, NY of Co. F. 141st Reg. in Dallas, Ga. May 25, 1864. Married dau of Mr. **BRASTED**. Leaves wife and 1 child

LAYTON Lieut. Daniel of Co. G. 22nd NY Cav. of Hammondsport, NY June 15, 1864. Leaves wife and 2 children

HILL Jennie E. age 2y 3m dau of Josephus and Amelia A. in Watkins, NY June 8, 1864

MC DOWELL Spencer K. son of George W. and Mary E. Mc Dowell in Leavenworth, Ks. June 1, 1864

BENHAM Emily J. age 20y dau of Henry Benham in Hammondsport, NY July 20, 1864

BROWN Capt. Morris Jr. of Penn Yan, NY native of Steuben Co. in 126th Reg. NYV near Petersburg (Newspaper date July 27, 1864)

ALLEN Sarah age 79y of Howard, NY one of earliest settlers at son's Israel B. Allen in Bath, NY (Newspaper date August 10, 1864). Lived on same farm 50 yrs

READ Dr. John H. age 43y in Bath, NY August 14, 1864

MARCY Oscar W. abt 30y of Avoca, NY mem of 107th Reg. at hospital in Chattanooga July 26, 1864 from wounds in battle near Dallas Ga. rec. May 25, 1864

HOTCHKIN 6 of the 8 children of Joseph B. Hotchkin died of diptheria, Lucius H. age 17y died June 23, 1864, Joseph Allen age 2y died August 2, 1864, Charles D. age 7y died August 2, 1864, Fannie D. age 4y died August 7, 1864, Maria L. age 15y died August 15, 1864 and Agnes age 9y died August 15, 1864

HOLLETT Mrs. Margaret C. age 39y formerly of Geneva, NY in Sonora, NY August

DEATH NOTICES

23, 1864

EMERSON Amos age 39y of Co F. 161st Reg. in New Orleans, La. July 8, 1864. Leaves wife and 1 child

PARMETHER Edwin abt 18y in Cohocton, NY September 1, 1864

COOK Samuel age 85y in Campbell, NY rec (Newspaper date September 21, 1864)

JEWETT George Winthrop age 5y son of William and R. A. **(ATWILL)** in Bradford, NY September 5, 1864

KNIGHT George H. age 53y in Bath, NY September 18, 1864

FISK Ebenezer age 71y 10m in Bath, NY September 16, 1864. Born Southington, Ct. was Lieut. in War of 1812

VAN GELDER Abigail age 86y Mother of Jonathan in Bath, NY September 18, 1864

TOWNSEND Skiley age 3m 3w 4d died September 13, 1864 and twin sister Sarah age 4m 2d died September 21, 1864 children of John and Susan in Bath, NY

LOUNSBERRY William age 23y of Co. F. 179th Reg. in Pulteney, NY September 15, 1864

HAHN William from a blow to head from Wendell **LAUDERBEAU** in Perkinsville, NY September 8, 1864

WHITE George Thomas age 22y formerly of Albany, NY from wounds rec'd at Atlanta, Ga. August 28, 1864

FLETCHER Myron H. age 42y in Bath, NY October 6, 1864. Born Salsbury, Ct.

STODDARD Lena age 2y 3m dau of Leonard and Mary Stoddard formerly of Bath, NY in Jeffersonville, Ind. October 2, 1864

BOGARDUS Cornelius in his 85th yr of Bath nr Avoca, NY in Co. A. 161st Reg. at New Orleans, La. August 15, 1864. Came here from New York City 60 yrs ago

TAYLOR Sylvanus P. age 16y 1m 15d of Co. A. 161st Reg. in New Orleans, La. August 15, 1864

CARPENTER Sarah E. age 26y wife of Lt. Otis A. Carpenteer of the 2nd colored Reg. Co. D. in Troupsburgh, NY October 2, 1864

DURFY George S. in his 21st yr son of John and Abigail Durfy of Exeter, NY bro of E. G. in Hornellsville, NY October 3, 1864, buried Exeter

SMITH Lemuel H. age 28y 7m 19d of Co. D. 16th NY Heavy Art. at Post Hospital, Va. (Newspaper date November 23, 1864)

BROADHEAD Catherine L. age 9y 2m 21d dau of Benjamin and Mary Broadhead in fire at school in Bath, NY December 1, 1864

WILCOX Charles R. age 6y son of Elijah and Sally in Bath, NY December 2, 1864

MC KENZIE Edward age 67/70 of Orange, NY in Knoxville December 9, 1864. Leaves wife and child in Orange

CHAMBERLAIN Henry W. age 49y of Bath, NY in Chicago, Ill. November 2, 1864

MILLS Daniel age 45y in Bath, NY December 2, 1864

ROBINSON Charles age 18y 10m son of Mrs. Maria Robinson of Bath, NY with Co. F. 161st Reg. in Memphis, Tn. December 13, 1864

SALTSMAN William C. age 21y of Avoca, NY with 1st NY Ind. Vet. Battery in Hospital November 21, 1864

SANDERS Rowland age 74y 6m in Rathbone, NY December 25, 1864

AUSTIN Albert son of E. A. and L. C. **HUBBARD** in Prattsburgh, NY January 1, 1865

PERKINS William A. abt 60y only son of late Dr. Asa Perkins of Dover, NH in Dover January 1, 1865

SEAMANS S. C. age 65y consort of Parley Seamans in Savona, NY January 8, 1865

SHEPARD Clara G. age 4y 3m dau of Otis and Lydia A. Shepard in Wheeler, NY January 5, 1865

BROWN Phebe age 94y 10m at son's Joseph M. Brown in Bath, NY December 20, 1864. Born February 10, 1770 in Morristown, NJ. She was widow 34 yrs and had 11 children 7 living, 61 grandchildren 42 living, 88 great grandchildren 73 living

MOORE William W. age 65y 8m in Kanona, NY December 20, 1864

WOODWARD Phebe in her 47th yr wife of D. F. in Jasper, NY February 9, 1865

KINNER Alanson age 61y in Woodhull, NY February 11, 1865

CHENEY Candace (**CONE**) wife of Allen Cheney and dau of late David **RUMSEY** in Bath, NY February 28, 1865

CURTIS Edwin age 6y 3m son of Edgar and Lucy Maria Curtis in Bradford, NY February 9, 1865

FRASHER Ella age 3y only dau of Uri and Caroline in Avoca, NY March 11, 1865

WILBER Griffin age 42y 10m in Thurston, NY March 14, 1865

DEATH NOTICES

STORY Rev. James Cyrus age 91y 4m 11d of E. Genessee Conference at res of David **DICKINSON** in Thurston, NY March 15, 1865

BROWN Rev. Eli H. nr Hammondsport, NY March 21, 1865

WEBB Joseph J. age 104y in Co. Home November 28, 1864

SICKELS John age 90y in Co. Home February 25, 1865

HOSFORD Mariett age 21y in Co. Home March 3, 1865

GILMORE Ellen M. age 27y dau of Perez Gilmore in Bath, NY March 23, 1865

BULL Henry G. in his 21st yr son of Harvey and Lucinda Bull with Co. C. 189th Reg. NYV at City Point, Va. January 13, 1865

SKINNER Israel age 78y in Prattsburgh, NY March 22, 1865, res 55 yrs

HARRIS Minerva in her 45th yr wife of Nelson Harris and dau of Charles **KNAPP** April 5, 1865

WISE Sgt. Chester M. in his 29th yr in General Hospital in Savannah, Ga. January 27, 1865, buried Laurel Grove cem in Savannah

WELLES John P. age 47y son of S. F. Welles of Pulteney, NY with Co. I 85th Reg. NYV in hospital in Wilmington, Del. March 12, 1865

HICKOK Nellie age 87y 1m 13d at res of Samuel Hickok in Bath, NY (Newspaper date April 26, 1865)

SNOOK Tunis age 80y in Canada March 29, 1865

SMITH Lt. Seymour M. in his 24th yr of Prattsburgh, NY with Co. B. 20th Ct. S. V. at Silver Creek nr Ayersboro, NC March 16, 1865

JACKSON George M. in his 28th yr in Prattsburgh, NY April 25, 1865

TOWNSEND Estella in her 22nd yr in Bath, NY May 14, 1865

AVERILL William age 1y 6m 26d son of Oscar and Helen C. Averill (Newspaper date June 7, 1865)

MITCHELL Thomas in his 25th yr son of John B. Mitchell of Wayne, NY with Co. G. 22nd NY Cav. in hospital at Wilmington, Del. March 5, 1865

ROSENCRANS Henry in his 23rd yr son of Simeon in Avoca, NY May 21, 1865

HULL Harriet in her 76th yr in Bath, NY June 14, 1865

WHEELER N. J. age 40y of Liberty, NY in Bath, NY June 16, 1865

HICKOK James Henry age 25y late of 1st NY Light Art. at res of C. W. **MASON** June 11, 1865

COOK Paul C. in his 73rd yr in Bath, NY July 11, 1865. Born Saratoga Co. NY and came to Cohocton 1819

COURTNEY ___ child of Michael of Cohocton, NY drowned July 14, 1865

YOUNGS Kate S. dau of Dr. William and Harriet **SAYER** of Merchantville, NY while visiting husband in Richmond, Va. June 28, 1865 (Penn Yan papers please copy)

CONKLIN Sarah age 57y wife of Joseph Conklin in Bath, NY July 15, 1865

SWART Winfred T. age 4m 16d dau of Ten Eyck and Ellen in Bath, NY July 29, 1865

WHITNEY Maria age 7m 13d dau of Edwin C. and Addie (**COOK**) in Bath, NY July 28, 1865

STRONG Hubbard in his 25th yr son of Truman in Prattsburgh, NY July 21, 1865

SKINNER Reuben age 22y late of Battery I 3rd NY Art. at Father's in Troupsburgh, NY August 3, 1865

COLLIER Frederick W. in his 35th yr member of 22nd NY Cav. in Avoca, NY August 6, 1865

VAN GELDER Robert with 14th NY Heavy Art. in Thurston, NY July 31, 1865

ELLAS Francis S. Jr. age 26y in Bath, NY August 18, 1865

WRIGHT Henry William age 2y 4m 6d son of H. W. and C. S. Wright in Bath, NY August 28, 1865

TALLMADGE Jonathan age 67y in Bradford, NY September 10, 1865

DENNISTON Fanny age 62y wife of G. Denniston in Prattsburgh, NY September 9, 1865

ELLAS Sarah H. age 18y dau of Francis S. Ellas in Bath, NY September 11, 1865

FAULKNER Sarah H. widow of William Faulkner in New York City Septembr 9, 1865

TYLER Lottie M. in her 4th yr in Savona, NY September 1, 1865

TYLER William L. G. in his 21st yr son of James and Charlotte Tyler in Savona, NY September 12, 1865

ALLERTON Mary L. age 17m dau of Delanson and Jane Allerton in Savona, NY September 22, 1865

DEATH NOTICES

BELL Jennie age 2y 1m 2d in New York City September 26, 1865, funeral in Bath, NY

BROTHER Charles Hobart age 2y 2d son of James and E. M. **(YOUNG)** in Bath, NY October 1, 1865

NELLIS Josiah in his 56th yr in Kanona, NY October 8, 1865

NELLIS Ferdinand in his 27th yr in Cahawba Ala. March 28,1865

FRENCH Marie age 4y 6m 10d dau of Wright and Emeline French formerly of Bath, NY in Defiance, Oh. October 9, 1865

SEYMOUR Theodosia in her 12th yr dau of William and Elizabeth Seymour in Savona, NY October 8, 1865

SMITH Orren in Bath, NY November 7, 1865

BOUTEN Gilbert hit by falling tree in Avoca, NY November 9, 1865

SMALLIDGE Sarah P. age 1y 7m dau of Jerome B. and Mary Smallidge in Bath, NY October 4, 1865

SNELL William age 65y suicide by hanging nr Kanona, NY November 20, 1865

THURBER Abner in his 84th yr in Lindley, NY November 21, 1865. Born in east and came to Painted Post, NY abt 1793

MURPHY Mrs. ____ accidently shot by son Lewis in Pulteney, NY November 21, 1865

OSTRANDER John of Kanona, NY November 26, 1865

YOUNG William age 71y at son's in Ontario, NY December 7, 1865

DICKEY William abt 40y unm. murdered in Cameron, NY December 17, 1865

RICE William and wife drowned crossing the "Pond" in Howard, NY January 1, 1866

BOND Phebe of Campbell, NY in Co. Home December 5, 1865

MERRITT Felix age 65y in Greenwood, NY December 11, 1865

JOHNSON Mrs. Abigail (colored) burned to death in Bath, NY January 15, 1866

FINCH Nathaniel in Hornellsville, NY January 17, 1866

BUTLER James age 19y 9m 17d in Bath, NY December 12, 1865. Enl. August 1862 in Co. F. 161st Reg. NYV

SHULTS Conrad suicide by hanging February 6, 1866

EDWARDS Jesse formerly of Bath, NY in Plover, Wis. February 7, 1866

INGERSOLL William K. age 22y son of Gilbert and Nancy February 16, 1866

WADSWORTH Gratton age 4m 12d son of George and Henrietta **(LOUCKS)** in Aurora, Ill. January 29, 1866

DE CAY Helen age 68y 6m widow of John W. **FOWLER** in Bath, NY March 11, 1866

HATTER Peter age 83y of Corning, NY in Co. Home March 8, 1866

CHAMPLIN Eli age 63y of Mt. Washington, NY in Co. Home March 12, 1866

MONELL Mrs. ___ abt 70y of Bath, NY hit by train April 20, 1866

MILLER Cynthia age 32y wife of Charles Miller and dau of late Stephen **GRANT** in Bath, NY April 19, 1866

TALLMADGE Helen Adelaide age 1y 11m 7d dau of John E. and Emily S. Tallmadge in Bath, NY May 7, 1866

CARRINGTON Martha in her 47th yr wife of Joel in Avoca, NY April 28, 1866

BAILEY Col. B. P. in his 67th yr formerly of Corning, NY in Corydon, Pa. rec. (Newspaper date May 23, 1866)

MORSE infant twin dau of Mary Morse of Savona, NY in Co. Home April 12, 1866

BUTLER infant twin dau of Caroline of Canisteo, NY in Co. Home April 16, 1866

CRONAN John of Corning, NY in the Co. Home May 15, 1866

SCHANK John age 85y of Bath, NY in the Co. Home May 17, 1866

BRINK Samuel age 103y in the Co. Home May 21, 1866

VAN PELT___ two boys age 13y and 9y drowned in Canisteo River at Erwin, NY May 29, 1866

JACOBUS Franklin W. age 14y son of Isaac of Bath, NY June 18, 1866. Hit by chain in upper leg cutting artery

DURFY E. G. age 38/40y in Hornellsville, NY last week (Newspaper date July 4, 1866

RICE Clark age 65y of Jasper, NY in the Co. Home June 18, 1866

SPENCE Dr. Henry age 68y in Starkey, NY July 2, 1866

BROOKS Mary E. age 22y 2m 21d dau of William Brooks in Bath, NY August 2, 1866

DEATH NOTICES

CALKINS Josephine age 26y at stepfather's H. D. **JOHNSON** in Minneapolis, Mn. July 30, 1866

ALLEN Hattie age 19y died August 3, 1866 and Valencourt age 23y died August 17, 1866 in Oregon, Mo. children of Benjamin and Ann Allen

PULLING Mrs. Mary age 67y in Bath, NY August 30, 1866

KINGSLEY Minerva age 60y wife of F. J. in Hammondsport, NY August 31, 1866

WALLACE Delos age 21y son of Edward drowned nr Pine Pt. September 6, 1866

WARREN Mary L. age 15y 10m dau of George and Julia A. E. Warren in Wayne, NY August 29, 1866

ANDREWS William age 62y at res of James **POOLE** in Bath, NY September 11, 1866. Born Failmill, Ayreshire, Scotland and came to US in 1837

ROSENCRANS Louise age 27y only dau of Simson and Mary Rosencrans of Avoca, NY at bro in Cohocton, NY August 29, 1866

RUMSEY Mrs. Huldah in her 64th yr in Painted Post, NY September 15, 1866

MORSE Harriet M. wife of Samuel W. Morse in Levanna, NY September 23, 1866

DAVISON Maggie age 23y 2m 11d in Bath, NY October 2, 1866

ALDERMAN Melvin son of Rev. A. P. Alderman of Merchantville, NY accidenly shot himself October 11, 1866

PRATT ___ age 12y dau of Joseph Pratt burned to death from exploding kerosens lamp October 13, 1866

BLYN Nye of Woodhull, NY hit by tree limb October 19, 1866

MC NEIL Margaret A. age 37y wife of Gillis Mc Neil in Bath, NY October 15, 1866 (Washington Co. papers please copy)

FLYNN Allen age 28y October 17, 1866

YOST Dennison abt 30y son of John D. Yost hit by train November 5, 1866

HENRY Josiah age 90y formerly of Bath, NY in Elmira, NY November 2, 1866

DAWSON Richard age 74y at Ira P. **EDWARDS** October 27, 1866

MATHEWSON Orline wife of Lemuel Mathewson and dau of John and Ann **FINCH** formerly of Avoca, NY in Tecumseh, Mi. (Newspaper date November 14, 1866)

ROLFE Eliza age 64y 4m 3d wife of Joseph Rolfe November 16, 1866

RICHARDSON Ammorette age 20y dau of Henry S. and Eunice Richardson August 1, 1866

HODGEMAN Henry D. age 17m son of L. D. and A. C. Hodgeman in Bath, NY November 28, 1866

SPAULDING Naomi age 82y widow of Jared in Bath, NY November 20, 1866

SHURBIN Elma M. age 16y 4m dau of J. B. and A. M. Shurbin in Avoca, NY December 26, 1866

MUNSON Rufus in Bradford, NY January 5, 1867. Born November 16, 1813 in Greenfield, NY and res here 30 yrs

GUSTIN Miss Abigail age 24y in Bath, NY January 6, 1867

WILBER Reuben in his 45th yr in Bath, NY December 16, 1866

ROSEBOOM Abraham in his 90th yr in Roseboom, NY January 5, 1867

TIFFANY Martha H. age 70y in Bath, NY January 23, 1867

HOWELL Hannah wife of E. Howell in Bath, NY January 21, 1867

GOODSELL Jared in his 86th yr in Bath, NY January 6, 1867

GREEN Lumira age 70y Mother of Dr. W. S. **CHENEY** in Prattsburgh, NY January 6, 1867 (Livingston Co. papers please copy)

MILLS Rachel age 77y wife of Thomas Mills in Liberty, NY January 16, 1867

LYKE Mrs. Lucinda age 48y suicide by hanging in Bath, NY January 31, 1867

NOBLE Lucinda age 63y wife of Lay Noble in Bath, NY February 1, 1867

WELLES Elihu S. age 68y in Wayne, NY February 8, 1867

WARREN Miss Lydia age 54y formerly of Cameron, NY in Spring Hill, Ill. January 27, 1867

BURGESS Moses in Co. Home January 31, 1867

BEEMAN Daniel in Co. Home February 23, 1867

BAKER Miss Caroline age 40y in Bath, NY March 3, 1867

CLARK John age 2y son of Thomas and Catherine Clark in Savona, NY March 5, 1867

DUDLEY John age 72y in Bath, NY March 6, 1867

DEATH NOTICES

HILL Mrs. Eunice P. age 66y at bro Harvey **BUSHNELL** in Bath, NY March 30, 1867

SILVERNAIL Azuba age 64y 1m 13d wife of Benjamin Silvernail in S. Bradford, NY April 10, 1867

BATES Augustus suicide by arsenic after attempting to kill his wife in Benton Ctr., NY April 30, 1867

GRANT H. L. age 31y at res of Levi **KEYSER** in Avoca, NY May 22, 1867

GUILE ____ 2 sons of C. C. Guile ages 6y and 8y drowned in Lindley, NY June 6, 1867

HALSEY Susie M. in her 25th yr wife of William L. Halsey and dau of late Alonzo A. **ALVORD** June 5, 1867

DENTON Maj. S. B. former Post Master of Corning, NY in Elmira, NY July 3, 1867

FAY Frank G. age 20y son of George of Bath, NY nr Bunker Hill Sta. July 8, 1867

MC BURNEY John age 65/70 in Corning, NY August 10, 1867

FINCH Mrs. Samuel suicide by hanging in Orange, NY August 5, 1867

GOODSELL Freddie M. age 3m son of John R. and H. L. in Bath, NY July 27, 1867

BULL Eunice age 96y 1m 2d relict of Howell Bull and Mother of Col. William H. of Bath, NY in Buffalo, NY August 20, 1867. Came to Painted Post, NY in 1796 and to Bath, NY in 1804. Husband died over 30 yrs ago, lived with children in Buffalo since

TERRY Anna age 62y wife of Dr. M. Terry in Painted Post, NY August 21, 1867

GRAVES Frank in his 21st yr son of C. C. Graves in Howard, NY August 23, 1867

SMEAD David H. age 14y 4d son of Edwin and Maria in Bath, NY September 1, 1867

ROBIE Jessie age 13m dau of Levi and Annie P. Robie in Bath, NY August 27, 1867

HUNTER Caroline in her 41st yr wife of S. D. Hunter in Bath, NY September 2, 1867

PERKINS Carrie Bell age 3y 7m 3d dau of E. B. and Margaret Perkins in Bath, NY August 30, 1867

MAY Mary Montford dau of Charles and Eloise May in Bath, NY September 19, 1867

BILES Delana age 72y wife of Lewis in Bath, NY September 24, 1867, res 45 yrs

ELLAS Dr. Simpson age 83y 2m 9d in Bath, NY October 4, 1867

CORNELL Thomas of Tuscarora, NY at Co. Home September 25, 1867

LINDLEY Thomas of Lindley, NY in Co. Home October 5, 1867

GANSEVOORT Ten Eyck age 25y in Watkins, NY October 8, 1867

WILLIAMS Carrie Susan age 5y 8m 23d dau of William and Susan B. Williams October 13, 1867

LORD Charles age 17y son of George P. Lord in Wayne, NY December 19, 1867

WIXOM Ida age 21y dau of Joel and Lydia Wixom in Wayne, NY January 4, 1868

MASON Elias age 75y in Cameron, NY December 17, 1867

CURRAN ____ age 10y late of Campbell, NY drowned in Mitchellville, NY last week (Newspaper date January 29, 1868)

MC ELWEE James age 62y in Savona, NY January 24, 1868

OSBORNE David A. age 62y in Pulteney, NY (Newspaper date March 18, 1868)

BLACK Jeremiah age 72y in Bath, NY March 14, 1868

HALLOCK Mrs. Sarah in her 84th yr Mother of William H. **DOUGHTY** of Wayne, NY in Wayne March 10, 1868

SUTTON Alexander age 42y in Thurston, NY March 21, 1868

JONES Susan E. age 37y in Rathbone, NY March 15, 1868

DE PUY Jane age 82y wife of James De Puy in Bath, NY March 20, 1868

WHITMATH Mary Ann age 11y 1m 14d formerly of Geneseo, NY in Female Orphan Institute Davenport, Io. March 17, 1868

TALLMADGE Abigail **(BEERS)** age 70y in Bradford, NY March 18, 1868

LAFFERTY Albert murdered in Greenwood, NY last wk (Newspaper date April 1, 1868)

HADDEN Mrs. ____ in her 39th yr wife of A. in Hammondsport, NY March 16, 1868

MC GONNEGAL Horace age 67y in Howard, NY April 25, 1868

DAVENPORT Col. Ira in his 73rd yr in Bath, NY May 2, 1868. Born Spencertown, NY son of Noah who came to Hornellsville, NY 1815 and to Bath 1847. Leaves 2 sons and 3 daus, 3 grandchildren, children of dec dau Mrs. **WATERMAN**

BROWN Mrs. Mary of Cameron, NY in Co. Home February 26, 1868

MERIARD Mrs. Frances of Thurston, NY in Co. Home March 26, 1868

DEATH NOTICES

ARMSTRONG Jesse of Urbana, NY in Co. Home April 1, 1868

SAMPLE Hugh of Bath, NY in Co. Home April 15, 1868

HUNT Joseph of Howard, NY in Co. Home May 6, 1868

SEELEY Charles Benjamin age 2y 1m 8d son of Edwin and Lucy T. Seeley in Pulteney, NY May 14, 1868

STODDARD Mary Jane age 1y 11m 7d dau of William in Bath, NY May 27, 1868

WILLIAMS Capt. E. C. of Rochester, NY in Bath, NY May 31, 1868

KNIGHT Mary E. in her 39th yr widow of George H. in Bath, NY June 8, 1868

RICE Lyman A. age 4y 2m 26d son of Horace A. and Sarah M. Rice in Avoca, NY May 16, 1868

FRY Mrs. Roxanna in her 81st yr in Cohocton, NY July 6, 1868

SWART Ellen T. age 30y wife of Ten Eyck G. Swart in Bath, NY August 3, 1868

BAKER Isaac over 60y of Osceola, Pa. in Elmira, NY last wk. (Newspaper date August 5, 1868). Leaves son John K. of Bath. Buried Bath

BALDWIN Israel age 86y one of 1st settlers of Howard, NY in Avoca, NY July 30, 1868

CLARK Mathias M. age 38y in Hammondsport, NY August 15, 1868

HOLDEN Amaza age 93y in Penn Yan, NY August 10, 1868

PORTER Mrs. L. C. age 58y in Prattsburgh, NY August 23, 1868

ROBIE Annie P. age 35y wife of Levi Robie in Bath, NY September 3, 1868 (Dover, NH papers please copy)

WHITTEMORE Sarah in her 55th yr wife of M. F. Whittemore in Jasper, NY August 24, 1868

SWART William Ten Eyck age 1m 14d son of Ten Eyck and Ellen Swart in Bath, NY September 14, 1868

EARLY Jackson age 83y in Prattsburgh, NY September 7, 1868

FAULKNER Kate age 29y in Bath, NY September 8, 1868

WESTCOTT William B. brother of the Editor of Dundee Record in Rochester, NY August 24, 1868

WHITTEMORE Maria age 41y wife of M. Seth Whittemore in Rathbone, NY August 29, 1868

WHEATON Mary A. in her 52nd yr wife of Henry in Bath, NY August 30, 1868

HESS William A. age 22y son of late Alexander Hess in Bath, NY September 16, 1868

STEWART Luther age 26y of Howard, NY in Crystal Springs Hotel September 10, 1868

SEDGEWICK Mary Ann wife of L. E. Sedgewick and Mother of W. W. in Warrensburgh, Mo. September 27, 1868 (Ithaca and Trumansburgh papers please copy)

HUMPHREYS Abby R. in her 85th yr relict of Guy Humphreys formerly of Marcellus, NY at grandson's Guy H. MC MASTER in Bath, NY October 3, 1868

CARPENTER Richard E. age 62y murdered in bed at W. Almond, NY September 25, 1868

KELLY Susan abt 38y in Co. Home September 17, 1868

CRAIKS Frances of Campbell, NY in Co. Home September 19, 1868

VAN HOUTEN Jennie H. age 20y 22d in Dakota City, Io. October 1, 1868

CURTIS Daniel age 68y formerly of Campbell, NY in Bridgeport, Ct. October 27, 1868

WOOD Israel L. in his 78th yr formerly of Urbana, NY in Wayne, NY November 9, 1868

MITCHELL George D. age 62y at res of Mrs. A. E. **HALLETT** in Wayne, NY November 26, 1868

HARDENBROOK Catherine dau of George H. and Mollie Hardenbrook in Bath, NY November 15, 1868

BRUNDAGE George W. age 6m 15d son of Morris and Maria November 27, 1868

SEAMANS Alva P. age 5m 13d son of A. N. and H. D. Seamans in Savona, NY November 13, 1868

BOZZARD Simon a widower hung himself in Sullivanville, NY December 9, 1868

SPICER John age 78y formerly of Barrington, NY in Ks. rec (Newspaper date December 16, 1868)

SMITH Enos age 65y in Big Flats, NY December 12, 1868. Res of Caton, NY 40 yrs

CROOKSTON Sarah age 70y wife of Moses in Wayne, NY November 15, 1868

DEATH NOTICES

DILLENBACK Anna in her 67th yr wife of Isaac in Avoca, NY December 29, 1868

WEAVER Sarah (**COBURN**) age 27y in Troy (NY or Pa.?) January 5, 1869

QUIMBY ___ age 7y on sleigh load of wood in Campbell, NY January 26, 1869

BRINK Judson A. age 26y at father-in-law's Russell R. **FARGO** in Pulteney, NY January 11, 1869

WHITEHEAD Clarissa age 58y wife of Aaron in Prattsburgh, NY January 23, 1869

UNDERHILL Robert Campbell inf son of E. H. and L. Underhill in Syracuse, NY February 7, 1869

WHITTAKER Nancy Maria age 41y 11m 7d wife of James L. Whittaker and dau of Amos N. and Sally **MALLORY** in Troupsburgh, NY January 21, 1869

BAILEY Lewis age 40y in Urbana, NY February 22, 1869

ALBRO Samuel C. age 77y 11m 11d veteran of War of 1812 at res of Simeon **COLE** in Benton, NY February 12, 1869

GORDON Peter of Scio, NY killed by cars between Corning and Painted Post, NY February 16, 1869

MORRIS Rosalia abt 19y suicide with pistol in Hornellsville, NY February 23, 1869

MORGAN Lewis Fraser age 10y 7m son of late William in Bath, NY February 12, 1869

PRATT Joel B. Editor of Corning Journal in Corning, NY February 21, 1869. Born Colechester, Ct. came to Yates Co. in 1819 to Corning 1834, buried Hope cemetery

PRATT Hannah age 68y 6m relict of A. J. in Campbell, NY February 5, 1869

MC DOWELL Lucey A. age 52y wife of C. J. Mc Dowell in Cohocton, NY March 6, 1869. Leaves 1 dau Mrs. J. H. **BUTLER** of Cohocton and 1 son in Mi.

RICHARDSON James age 25y son of John Richardson in Bath, NY March 13, 1869

BECKWITH Nettie age 5y died February 19, 1869 and Lizzie age 2y 10m died March 10, 1869 daus of John and Jane Beckwith

SLAIGHT John W. age 2y son of Jeremiah and Almeda Sleight March 9, 1869

SCOTT Agnes age 23y March 12, 1869

RILEY Owen age 90y at son's Owen Jr. in Pulteney, NY March 20, 1869

GRIFFITH Almira in her 59th yr wife of John Griffith in Bath, NY March 6, 1869

HOWELL ___ infant child of A. S. Howell in Bath, NY March 29, 1869

SMITH Ephraim T. age 90y funeral in Bath, NY March 29, 1869

RAPLEE Belden age 69y in Avoca, NY March 3, 1869 (Yates Co. papers please copy)

HILL Harlan age 22y son of William P. Hill of Caton, NY drowned in Iowa River nr Iowa Falls, Io. April 2, 1869

STEWART David in his 86th yr at son's Dr. W. A. Stewart in Avoca, NY March 27, 1869

WYGANT Mary age 81y at res of Richard **MITCHELL** in Urbana, NY March 29, 1869. Born Dutchess Co. NY and res of Wheeler, NY 40 yrs

EARNEST Isabel in her 74th yr wife of John in Wayne, NY March 21, 1869, res 50 yrs

CARPENTER David H. age 63y hung for murdering his brother in Angelica, NY April 16, 1869

ROWE ___ age 20y son of Lewis killed on hand car in Kanona, NY April 18, 1869

OLMSTEAD William R. Henry age 3y 5m 22d son of Samuel and Sarah E. Olmstead in Hedgesville, NY March 18, 1869.

ROSE Mrs. H. S. abt 55y of Corning, NY formerly of Bath, NY in Avoca, NY April 20, 1869

BUTLER Allen age 85y in Bath, NY May 4, 1869

CLARK Hiram L. in S. Pulteney, NY May 9, 1869

CHAPIN Edward R. age 44y eldest son of Vestur and Anna Chapin of Bath, NY in San Francisco, Cal. April 19, 1869

CARRINGTON Capt. ___ abt 97y in S. Dansville, NY May 5, 1869

FREEMAN ___ age 2y son of Richard Freeman scalded nr Savona, NY last week (Newspaper date May 19, 1869)

RICE Henry age 56y in Bath, NY May 25, 1869

WILLIS Orson age 68y in Towlesville, NY May 30, 1869

ALLEN Elijah age 78y father of Mrs. Fanny **FLYNN** of Bath, NY in Urbana, NY May 29, 1869

RICE William age 62y in Mitchellville, NY June 13, 1869

TUBBS Sandford H. age 25y in Bath, NY June 21, 1869

DEATH NOTICES

SHUART Andrew Jackson age 24y at res of Mrs. Elizabeth Shuart in Pulteney, NY June 23, 1869. Parents live in Cattaraugus Co. NY

WOODRUFF Benjamin in his 73rd yr in Delaware July 19, 1869. Res. of Urbana, NY 50 yrs

GUINNIP George B. age 75y in Watkins, NY July 20, 1869

CHAPIN Vestus age 72y 8m in Bath, NY July 27, 1869

COLGAN Benjamin age 80y Father of Rev. P. Colgan of Corning, NY funeral in Dunkirk, NY August 20, 1869

BUSHNELL Harvey age 66y funeral in Bath, NY September 8, 1869, buried W. Bloomfield, NY

SKINNER Dr. D. G. age 73y 7m 5d in Prattsburgh, NY August __, 1869

HARROWER D. age 76y widow of Benjamin Harrower of Lindley, NY, Mother of Gabriel T. in Wilkesboro, Pa. August 28, 1869

HOPKINS Horace age 70y bro of L. R. Hopkins of Prattsburgh, NY at home in Whitesville, NY (Newspaper date September 15, 1869)

PORTER Sarah M. age 22y wife of E. P. Porter formerly of Prattsburgh, NY and dau of E. T. **WATKINS** of Prattsburgh at Plum Point, NY September 4, 1869

KNIGHT Daniel age 61y in Bath, NY September 10, 1869

MARSH Henrietta P. wife of A. T. late of Bath, NY in Elmira, NY September 20, 1869

BRIGHAM Abigail age 78y 6m in Bath, NY September 8, 1869. Born Danbury, Ct.

JOHNSON Clara age 50y wife of William Johnson in Bath, NY September 23, 1869. Born 1819 in Madison Co. NY nee **WILDER**

ABER Milon E. age 3y 29d in Urbana, NY October 9, 1869

DUNTON Nellie M. in her 3rd yr dau of J. C. and Phylinda November 3, 1869

CONNER John age 67y formerly of Avoca, NY at son's Edward Conner in Elgin, Ill. October 19, 1869

RICE Merton age 18y 8m son of S. H. and Gratia Rice in Towlesville, NY November 6, 1869

CAMERON Dugald Sr. age 76y in Hornellsville, NY November 28, 1869 res 52 yrs

PAWLING Thomas age 76y in Bath, NY November 7, 1869. Born August 1793 in Dutchess Co. NY and came to Bath 1807

GRIFFITH Jennie K. age 42y wife of Charles Griffith and dau of late Russell **KELLOGG** of Kanona, NY in New York City December 17, 1869

MEADE Dr. Andrew murdered in Allegany, NY December 18, 1869

CHENEY Louisa age 49y wife of Dr. Walter S. Cheney in Prattsburgh, NY December 23, 1869. Born February 17, 1820 in New Windsor, NY nee **FALLS**

COOPER William hit by falling limb nr Caton, NY December 20, 1869

GREEN Frank J. abt 30y res of Middlesex, NY suicide by hanging January 1, 1870

STANIFORD Horatio C. age 50y formerly of Bath, NY in E. Saginaw, Mi. January 7, 1870, buried Grove Cemetery in Bath

CRAWFORD Daniel abt 73y in Caton, NY rec. (Newspaper date January 12, 1870)

REYNOLDS Robert son of P. Bates and Lizzie May Reynolds in Prophetstown, Ill. December 31, 1869

WILKES Mrs. Ann age 67y in Bath, NY January 11, 1870

SPENCER William abt 60y in Corning, NY February 1, 1870

YOUNG Aaron age 79y in Geneva, NY January 25, 1870

REZNOR John age 67y of Hornellsville, NY nr Arkport, NY February 5, 1870

SHELDON O. abt 60y suicide by hanging in Hornellsville, NY February 11, 1870

PETERSON Elizabeth in her 72nd yr wife of John in Bath, NY February 17, 1870

FLETCHER Rispah age 81y 5m 26d Mother of late Myron Fletcher in Tyrone, NY December 11, 1869

ABER Mrs. Susan died March 5, 1870

ROYCE Mathew would be 98y on March 10 in Starkey, NY died March 5, 1870. Settled in Reading, NY age 18 yrs

MC CALLA John at nephew's John Mc Calla **CAMPBELL** in Bath, NY March 13, 1870. Born November 21, 1785 of Quaker parents in Bucks Co. Pa. youngest of 11 children, came to Bath in 1807

ADSIT Arunah M. formerly of Steuben Co. NY in Glens Falls, NY March 21, 1870. Born Columbia Co. NY and came to Hammondsport, NY in 1831. Married 1836 Miss **ROSENCRANS** and moved to Potsdam, NY 1851. Leaves wife, 1 son, Mother and 3 bro James M. of Chicago, Ill., Martin of Hornellsville, NY and 1 bro in western NY

TILTON Daniel nr 73y in Avoca, NY March 26, 1870

DEATH NOTICES

PIATT James A. in his 27th yr in Avoca, NY April 13, 1870. Enlisted in Co. B. 104th Reg. NYV wounded at Gettysburg (Livingston Co. papers please copy)

SEELEY Edwin L. age 43y 6m 4d in Pulteney, Ny April 16, 1870

RETAN John age 60y of Pulteney, NY suicide by hanging April 29, 1870

SEELEY Lucy age 18d dau of Edwin L. and Lucy T. in Pulteney, NY April 27, 1870

TAYLOR Nathaniel C. age 53y in Canisteo, NY May 10, 1870

MC BURNEY Thomas age 56y formerly of Corning, NY in Elmira, NY June 7, 1870

KIMBALL Carl abt 15y fell on circular saw at Wallace Station, NY June 21, 1870

WALDO Otis age 75y in Prattsburgh, NY July 15, 1870

HOWLETT Mary Ann nr 61y wife of Rev. James Howlett in Bath, NY July 18, 1870

LOOK Hattie Frances age 2y 5m dau of Isaiah and Polly in Bath, NY July 31, 1870

VEITH Nicolas age 41y a German citizen of Corning, NY July 26, 1870

HOYT Lillie age 4y dau of William C. Hoyt in Bath, NY August 21, 1870

BUSHNELL Alice inf dau of Watts Bushnell in Bath, NY last week (Newspaper date August 31, 1870)

THOMPSON Mrs. Judy (colored) nr Bath, NY September 3, 1870

TAYLOR Francis M. age 28y son of Francis and Lucy Taylor of Wayne, NY at Cameron Station, Pa. August 24, 1870

MINDRINK John age 47y suicide by hanging in Hornellsville, NY August 31, 1870

SMITH William C. age 36y in Bath, NY August 31, 1870. Married previous Sunday to Susan **DAVIS**

VAN GELDER Jonathan age 71y of Bath, NY on train at Cleveland, Oh. September 11, 1870

FAY Sylvester G. age 47y formerly of Bath, NY in Avon, NY September 26, 1870

TOWLE ____ abt 18y dau of P. S. Towle of Clinton, Io. in Bath, NY last week (Newspaper date September 28, 1870)

CHASE Horace A. Jr. age 36y only son of H. A. Chase in Bath, NY September 24, 1870, buried Grove cem

SEYMOUR Mrs. S. M. while visiting husband at Washington, Io. September 30, 1870, buried Bath, NY

MARSHALL Peter age 80y buried Hammondsport, NY October 2, 1870

WHEELER N. S. age 51y in Avoca, NY September 24, 1870

WATKINS Mrs. Julia nr 80 yrs (colored) buried Bath, NY October 9, 1870

JONES Nancy age 78y at son-in-law's H. A. **COMPTON** in Bath, NY October 11, 1870

HILL Jeannie formerly of Bath, NY dau of Ebenezer and Abigail **JENNINGS** of Chicago, Ill at Brooklyn, NY October 14, 1870

BROWER Richard in Hornellsville, NY October 24, 1870

CULVER Charles age 20/30 of Avoca, NY killed by cars at Spaulding's Crossing nr Bath, NY October 19, 1870

KING Capt. William H. at beginning of Rebellion was a res of Hammondsport, NY and enlisted Co. I 34th Reg. NYV died August 23, 1870. Leaves widow, 1 son age 9y and sis Mrs. Gratton H. **WHEELER** of Hammondsport

DICKEY Samuel age 55y 5m 8d in Cameron, NY November 4, 1870

TURN Ryfus age 43y wife of S. S. Turn in Cohocton, NY November 9, 1870

SMITH Loretta age 41y wife of Harlow Smith formerly of Bath, NY in Mo. November 6, 1870

WALKER James age 55y 8m in Canisteo, NY November 1, 1870

ANDREWS Jonas age 59y in Bradford, NY November 24, 1870

PHILLIPS Estella age 1y in Bradford, NY November 24, 1870

EMERSON Amancy in her 69th yr wife of John Emerson in Bath, NY December 15, 1870. Came from Springfield, Mass at early age. Married June 1832

AINSWORTH Minnie age 14y dau of G. R. B. and Mary E. Ainsworth in Prattsburgh, NY December 22, 1870

HODGEMAN Jenette in her 79th yr Mother of L. D. Hodgeman of Bath, NY in Stillwater, NY December 25, 1870

TAYLOR Ann S. wife of James W. Taylor in Towanda, Pa. November 17, 1870

BRUNDAGE Israel M. in Green, NY rec (Newspaper date January 11, 1870). Bron Bath, NY. Leaves wife and 4 children

DEATH NOTICES

RETAN Nellie age 3y dau of Nelson and Esther in Bluff Point, NY January 2, 1871

MORRIS Adelbert age 15y son of Shadrack and Elvira in Bluff Pt., NY January 6, 1871

WIXOM Mrs. Norman age 33y in W. Urbana, NY January 4, 1871

ARMSTRONG Levina age 70y wife of Hugh in Pulteney, NY January 6, 1871

GARRISON Alida Bell age 5y 2m 9d died December 17, 1870 and Lily Frances age 3y 11m 5d died January 21, 1871 in Avoca, NY daus of E. and E. S. Garrison of Kanona, NY and grand daus of Francis and Alida **OTIS**

HOGOBOOM Peter L. of Titusville, Pa. cut his throat in hotel in Rochester, NY February 5, 1871

STEVENS John age 92 oldest man in Hornellsville, NY January 27, 1871

WHIPPLE Marshall age 80y of Union Springs, NY found dead nr Auburn, NY February 10, 1871

ROWE James age 68y formerly of Bath, NY in Spring Hills, Ill. March 2, 1871

WHEELER Sarah age 71y widow of Jeremiah at son's Carlton J. Wheeler in Kanona, NY February 17, 1871

HAWKINS Emma L. in her 50th yr wife of Rev. L. T. Hawkins in Wayland, NY March 15, 1871

WAGNER Susan in her 32nd yr dau of Simeon and Eunice Wagner in Wheeler, NY March 9, 1871

CHASE Horace A. age 61y in Bath, NY March 26, 1871

DIMMICK Elizabeth age 52y wife of Dr. M. D. Dimmick of Burns, NY and sister of Mrs. A. R. **GOULD** of Bath, NY in Burns March 27, 1871

BADEAU Eda R. age 2m 11d died January 10, 1871 and Albert S. age 11y 1m 15d died April 2, 1871 children of Peter and Nancy Badeau in Howard, NY

RICHARDSON J. Willis age 2y 3m only child of Mrs. J. S. Richardson and grandson of D. F. **POMEROY** in Troy, Pa. April 4, 1871

CROSBY Rachel (**DEUEL**) wife of Edward Crosby Md. in Mahopac Falls, NY April 7. 1871

FAULKNER Elizabeth C. age 24y dau of Richard and Caroline April 2, 1871

COLLIER Charles E. age 27y 5m in Avoca, NY April 15, 1871

ROSE Eliza Ann M. age 56y widow of M. H. Rose in New York City May 5, 1871

THAYER Joseph in his 63rd yr undersheriff of Yates Co. NY in Penn Yan, NY May 2, 1871

BARKER Nelson age 56y in Bath, NY May 5, 1871

SULLIVAN John age 96y in Pulteney, NY March 22, 1871

BALL Nathaniel in his 83rd yr formerly of Pulteney, NY, father of S. S. Ball now of Penn Yan, NY at his home in Auburn, NY April 24, 1871, buried Pulteney

CRANE Mrs. Rev. E. F. age 58y formerly of Bath, NY in Dansville, NY April 29, 1871

HESS Minnie A. age 7y 10m 3d only dau of L. L. and Florence A. Hess in Pulteney, NY April 10, 1871

STEWART Finetta age 50y wife of R. Stewart in Bath, NY May 4, 1871

RHINEVAULT Charles A. age 20y 22d son of Rev. S. G. Rhinevault in Mainesburg, NY May 16, 1871. Born Alfred, NY

DAVIS Fannie age 86y wife of Orlando Davis at son's Charles D. in Milo, NY April 28, 1871. Born Columbia Co. NY sister of Col. Ira D. **DAVENPORT**. Married (1) Leonard **ADSIT** who died leaving 4 sons and 1 dau. Married (2) Orlando, 3 sons John W. of Hammondsport, NY, Charles D. and George died young

HYATT Thomas age 38y in Pulteney, NY May 21, 1871

MUNSON Sophia age 80y wife of Jesse Munson in Bradford, NY May 10, 1871

ABEL Joseph age 71y formerly of Wheeler, NY in Pinckney, Mi. April 25, 1871

VAN VALKENBURGH Mary B. H. in her 78th yr of White Lake, Mi. wife of Jacob formerly of Prattsburgh, NY at son-in-law's Charles **DELEVAN** in Racine, Wis. May 10, 1871

READ Hannah age 75y widow of James Read in Bath, NY May 20, 1871. Born Newtown, NY

SLATER Delia from affects of abortion last week (Newspaper date June 7, 1871)

DYKE V. R. age 26y in Bradford, NY May 24, 1871

ARNOLD Mrs. ___ age 100y 9m in Ulysses, NY June 9, 1871

WHITING John W. abt 86y in Howard, NY June 15, 1871

WALKER Gilbert of Lindley hit by falling tree limb rec. (Newspaper date June 28, 1871) formerly in Co. I 50th Reg. NYV

DEATH NOTICES

BOYD Mary C. age 31y 22d wife of David M. Boyd in Woodhull, NY June 6, 1871. Dau of Russell E. **FARGO** of Pulteney, NY

DUDLEY Moses in Bath, NY July 5, 1871. Born Bangor, Me. son of Jeremiah Dudley 1 of 8 children. Came to Bath, in 1819. Married 52 yrs ago Mary **ATWOOD** also from Me., 10 children 8 living, Mrs. D. **ALLERTON** of Savona, NY, Lydia the youngest teacher at Haverling School, Joseph and Henry at home, Dr. John, Moses Jr. and Benjamin in Cal. and Guilford in Kanona, NY

BYNDERS Llewelyn J. age 16y son of Hiram Bynders of Cohocton, NY from accidental discharge of canon at Loon Lake, NY July 14, 1871

WILBUR Enoch age 80y res of Reading, NY for 40 yrs in Watkins, NY August 11, 1871

DANNALS Capt. Philander J. age 59y in Bath, NY August 20, 1871

GARLINGHOUSE Julia age 7y dau of Daniel B. in N. Urbana, NY August 15, 1871

PRATT Ezilom in his 71st yr bro of Joel D. Pratt of Bath, NY in Winnebago City, Mn. August 9, 1871. Came from Cortland Co. NY to Bath in 1815. Wife and 2 daus

WAY James S. in his 67th yr in Pulteney, NY August 12, 1871

OLNEY Philetus former Pastor in Barrington Baptist Church in Mi. July 25, 1871

MAY Robert Harris age 1m son of Charles A. and Anna L. May in Bath, NY August 30, 1871

STITSON Lyman age 36y of Elmira, NY at Father's in W. Meridith, NY September 5, 1871

BLAKE William age 65y overdose of Laudanum in Dundee, NY September 6, 1871

GRAVES Charles M. age 3y son of Dr. J. B. in Corning, NY September 9, 1871

ANDREWS Charles age 20y accident by thrashing machine in Reading, NY September 11, 1871

TEACHMAN Abram age 98y 8m at res of Ritchell **LYONS** in Rathbone, NY September 18, 1871. Lived with son-in-law Samuel Lyons nr Bath, NY several years

JONES Adelbert age 19y 6m son of David D. A. Jones of Cohocton, NY in Rochester, NY September 27, 1871

MACKEY Robert age 84y of Bath, NY September 20, 1871

SUTHERLAND Elizabeth age 50y wife of James Sutherland in Bath, NY October 2, 1871. Native of London, Eng. Came to Bath with husband in 1849, 4 sons and 1 dau

COTTON Silas age 71y at son's Thomas Cotton in Avoca, NY October 20, 1871

SUTTON Mary A. age 37y 11m wife of John D. Sutton in Prattsburgh, NY October 9, 1871. Born Starkey, NY. Married May 5, 1854

YOST Mary (**WAIT**) age 24y wife of Byron Yost in Bath, NY October 27, 1871

LOOK Almira age 33y wife of E. V. Look in Bath, NY November 11, 1871

MARGESON Mrs. Elizabeth age 75y 10m in Cameron, NY November 11, 1871

OTIS David Day age 28y 9m son of James Otis formerly of Kanona, NY at Willard Asylum November 1, 1871

TILTON David age 72y formerly of Avoca, NY in Starkey, NY December 2, 1871

WHITE Helen A. wife of George White late of Albany, NY and dau of G. W. **TAYLOR** an early settler of Steuben Co. in Assumption, Ill. November 24, 1871

SMITH Melinda wife of E. Smith formerly of Hammondsport, NY in Monterey, NY December 2, 1871

BRIGHAM Col. Bela R. age 87y formerly of Bath, NY at dau in Detroit, Mi. December 5, 1871. Served in War of 1812

JOHNSON Mrs. Jane age 64y in Cameron, NY December 21, 1871

CLARK Lewis age 66y in Wayne, NY December 1, 1871. Native of Warwick, NY, lived Romulus, NY and moved to Barrington, NY 1826. Lived Wayne 8 yrs. Married spring of 1826 Miss **MC DANIELS** who died 1829 married (2) 1830 Miss **HOLLENBECK** who survives

HECKMAN Andrew age 21y son of Robert H. Heckman brushed by load of logs in Thurston, NY December 28, 1871

BARDEN Dr. Henry of Penn Yan, NY December 19, 1871

MOREHOUSE Henry age 75y in Wayland, NY December 31, 1871. Came from Saratoga Co. NY to Cohocton, NY 1825

SINCLAIR Celinda age 42y wife of Adolphus Sinclair in Bath, NY January 7, 1872

FREEMAN Deacon W. age 80y a Revolutionary Soldier in Bath, NY January 12, 1872

ALLEN Miss Polly age 52y in Wheeler, NY January 16, 1872

ROBIE Reuben in Bath, NY January 22, 1872. Born July 15, 1799 in E. Corinth, Vt. and came to Bath 1820. Married 1824 dau of Col. John **WHITING**, 12 children 8 living. All but 1 Mrs. David **WOODS** live in Bath

DEATH NOTICES

POTTER Hiram in Coopers Plains January 26, 1872. Born January 1800 in Galway, NY, and came to Corning, NY abt 40 yrs ago. Leaves wife 3 sons and 2 daus

WARREN Herman L. age 19y only remaining son of George Warren in Wayne, NY January 22, 1872

PRATT Theodore W. age 21y 6m son of Dr. George W. Pratt of Corning, NY in Riverside, Cal. February 3, 1872

MASSON Joseph D. age 42y in Hammondsport, NY February 13, 1872. Leaves wife and 4 children

CHASE Deborah in her 56th yr wife of N. B. Chase in Avoca, NY February 7, 1872. Born Pompey, NY lived here 20 yrs.

MC MULLEN Rev. Father Charles D. in Greenwood, NY February 9, 1872

ALLEN May age 20m dau of Eugene and Rachel Allen in Bath, NY February 15, 1872

GRAHAM Merlin age 64y in Bath, NY February 14, 1872. Leaves wife and 1 son

PATCHIN Dr. Warren age 89y in Wayland, NY February 13, 1872, res over 50 yrs

SHAVER Abram age 73y of Avoca, NY suddenly in Rumsey's law office where he went with son-in-law Samuel O. **ALLEN** (Newspaper date February 28, 1872). Leaves wife and several adult children. Brother-in-law of James **HEES**, Isaac **BASSETT** and late Josiah **NELLIS** of Avoca

DECKER Benjamin age 76y in Hammondsport, NY March 5, 1872, served War of 1812

WARREN Herman L. age 19y 6m only remaining child of George and Julia E. Warren in Wayne, NY January 22, 1872

STEVENSON John Goff in Bath, NY February 28, 1872, buried in Howard, NY

ALDEN Abbie **(CROSS)** age 70y in Howard, NY February 26, 1872

HESS Jacob age 64y 8m 12d in Pulteney, NY February 17, 1872

SHANNON Lucy in her 55th yr widow of James Shannon of Bath, NY in Cherry Valley, NY February 25, 1872. Dau of late Abraham **ROSEBOOM** of Cherry Valley

NOBLE Adelia Lydia age 2y 10m 13d dau of M. W. Noble in Bath, NY March 5, 1872

MACKEY Ruth age 80y widow of Robert Mackey in Bath, NY March 1, 1872

WILCOX Maud Eddena age 13m 19d dau of Thomas and Flora Wilcox in Wayland, NY February 29, 1872

BUTLER Mrs. William A. middle aged in Bath, NY March 12, 1872

MILLER Parley B. age 66y in E. Troupsburgh, NY March 3, 1872

PERINE Fred age 20y in Avoca, NY March 6, 1872

DUDLEY Nancy in her 65th yr wife of B. F. Dudley in Bath, NY March 11, 1872. Born February 28, 1808 in Bangor, Me. and res here nr 60 yrs.

BARTON Otto Myrtle age 1y 9m 12d child of A. J. and Lucy Barton in Bath, NY March 11, 1872

MACKIE Elizabeth in her 92nd yr in Howard, NY March 11, 1872, widow of William Mackie who died December 21, 1871 in his 90th yr. Born 1781 in Scotland, came to US from Glasgow in 1820 and settled Avoca, NY 1824

STRYKER John abt 30y in saw mill accident in Rathbone, NY March 22, 1872. Leaves wife and 1 child

BIRDSEYE John B. age 76y in Wayne, NY March 25, 1872. Native of Ct. here 30 yrs

LOOMIS Col. ___ age 83y Father of Mrs. James **GANSEVOORT** of Bath, NY in Stratford, Ct. March 5, 1872

SHAVER Mrs. ___ widow of Abram Shaver in Avoca, NY March 30, 1872

KNOWLES Andrew suicide by hanging in Mechantville, NY March 27, 1872

BRADY Joey age 3y 5m 5d son of J. N. and Hattie Brady in Hornellsville, NY March 31, 1872

BRUNDAGE Elizabeth in her 70th yr wife of Abram in Urbana, NY April 10, 1872

FAUCETT George L. age 28y eldest son of Richard in Bath, NY April 12, 1872

POMEROY Daniel F. father of Mrs. James S. **RICHARDSON** in Troy, Pa. April 9, 1872. Born February 1816 in Geneva, NY

BLACK Mrs. Benjamin in Bath, NY April 13, 1872

OAKLEY Timothy in Addison, NY April 10, 1872

EMERSON Benjamin age 74y in Bath, NY April 26, 1872

CARTER Joseph L. age 8y 9m 18d son of Oren L. and Lydia M. Carter in Corning, NY April 22, 1872

MILLS Lottie age 10m 16d dau of H. J. and Mary in Campbell, NY April 20, 1872

HEES D. H. C. age 40y formerly of Steuben Co. NY in Lincoln, Mi. rec. (Newspaper date May 1, 1872)

DEATH NOTICES

FULSOM Emma age 13m dau of Fred L. and Martha in N. Urbana, NY April 26, 1872

RICHARDSON John J. age 21d in Bath, NY May 1, 1872

DORSEY Mrs. Sally (colored) in Bath, NY May 3, 1872

JONES Benjamin E. in his 86th yr in Rock Stream, NY April 26, 1872. Came to Yates Co. in 1816

SMITH E. H. formerly of Bath, NY in Towanda, Pa. May 2, 1872

SHULTS Nellie age 15y dau of T. A. Shults funeral in Avoca, NY May 18, 1872

ACKERSON ____ son of Charles N. Ackerson in Bath, NY June 1, 1872

TOWNSEND William age 28y of Bluff Pt., NY drowned in Keuka Lake May 26, 1872

WILSON Mary Louisa age 31y 9m wife of J. R. Wilson of Buffalo, NY in Prattsburgh, NY May 24, 1872. Born August 24, 1840 in Prattsburgh dau of Addison and Julia **AINSWORTH**. Lived Minnesota Falls until August 24, 1861 and moved to Buffalo

THARP James N. age 25y son of J. R. and Angeline in Bath, NY June 12, 1872

RATHBONE Capt. John B. abt 35y in Caton, NY June 16, 1872

SWENSON August age 23y native of Sweden, raised by Dr. **CHENEY** of Prattsburgh in Auburn, NY June 24/25, 1872, buried Prattsburgh, NY

ELLIS Joseph H. in his 29th yr in Harford, NY (Newspaper date June 26, 1872, Utica and Elmira papers please copy)

BRUNDAGE ____ 2 children 1 age 10y and 1 younger buried in Wayne, NY June 20, 1872, dau died June 18, and son died June 19, 1872

MORROW Elizabeth age 48y wife of Robert Morrow in Avoca, NY June 22, 1872

O'NEIL Mrs. James in Bath, NY July 7, 1872

WOODS Olive age 41y 7m 21d wife of David Woods of New York City and dau of late Reuben **ROBIE** of Bath, NY in Bath July 15, 1872

BRINK John age 70y in Savona, NY July 22, 1872. Born November 10, 1803 in Sandyston, NJ son of Derrick and Catherine Brink

BROOKS John of Bath, NY drowned possible suicide in Lake Salubria July 16, 1872

TREMAIN Willie age 4y 10m 21d son of William B. and Emma C. Tremain in Lake Keuka, NY July 21, 1872, buried New York City

GREGG Lucinda abt 33y wife of T. W. Gregg in Bath, NY July 22, 1872

RICHARDSON E. Augusta age 30y wife of Edward M. in Bath, NY July 24, 1872

BUSHNELL Amelia 2m 2w twin dau of Watts Bushnell in Bath, NY August 3, 1872

EMERY Lena age 5m dau of A. W. Emery of Syracuse, NY and grand dau of Rev. I. W. Emery in Bath, NY August 5, 1872

BERNS Samuel age 5m 11d son of J. H. and Mary E. in Bath, NY August 23, 1872

AULLS Menzo age 1y 7m son of Lyman and Louise in N. Urbana, NY August 17, 1872

WELD Charles Edward age 9y 4m 23d son of Albert H. and Larissa Weld in Cohocton, NY August 25, 1872

SEYMOUR Carrie Eugene age 11y only dau of S. M. in Bath, NY August 21, 1872

SINCLAIR Mertie age 8m dau of Adolphus Sinclair in Bath, NY September 2, 1872

FAIRCHILD Morse Benham age 1y 2m son of Capt. F. S. and Hattie Fairchild in Hammondsport, NY September 4, 1872

GERRY Olive age 22y wife of Edward Gerry in Bath, NY September 14, 1872. Leaves husband and infant child

AULLS Minnie age 1y 7m 17d dau of Lyman and Louise Aulls in N. Urbana, NY September 10, 1872

LAMSON Sylvester abt 53y in Jasper, NY September 20, 1872

REYNOLDS Martha T. in her 24th yr wife of S. S. Reynolds and dau of Capt. A. **WOOD** in Bath, NY September 20, 1872

ELLIS Sarah age 12y 4m dau of Jerome and Caroline Ellis in Avoca, NY September 30, 1872

WILBER Samuel K. age 66y in Thurston, NY October 5, 1872

EMERSON Sophronia age 16y in Bath, NY October 22, 1872

SHULTS John I. in his 90th yr at son's Lyman Shults in Avoca, NY October 10, 1872. Leaves widow age 71y

OLMSTEAD Eliza age 56y wife of Abijah Olmstead October 4, 1872

UPSON Dr. Hiram age 69y at son-in-law's Rev. James M. **PLATT** in Bath, NY November 17, 1872. Born Columbia Co. NY, spent boyhood in Goshen, Ct. moved to Warwick, NY 1848. Married dau of Rev. Cyrus **GILDERSLEEVE** of Bloomfield, NJ who died 1849. Lived with only dau who married 1854

SCUTT Matilda age 56y wife of Jonas Scutt and dau of Late Mrs. Eunice **OSMUN** of

DEATH NOTICES

Rock Stream, NY in Cameron, NY November 26, 1872

DUDLEY James G. of Buffalo, NY son of Thomas formerly of Steuben Co. NY in Geneva, NY November 25, 1872

BELL Mrs. Frances (colored) 1 of oldest res of Bath, NY December 17, 1872

WATKINS Willis age 42y in Bath, NY December 15, 1872. Born Bath

SHULTS Sarah widow of A. J. Shults who dropped dead in road September 1871 and dau of Col. **BARNEY** in Wheeler, NY December 11, 1872

RICHARDSON John age 65y in Mt Washington, NY December 19, 1872

FREEMAN Howard age 1y 4m son of Baskin and Elizabeth Freeman in Bath, NY December 18, 1872

BATY Mrs. John an Irish citizen of Bath, NY December 29, 1872

ALDRICH ___ in her 51st yr wife of Dr. Thomas Aldrich in Thurston, NY December 29, 1872

CHENEY Dr. Walter S. age 52y in Bath, NY January 12, 1873. Leaves wife and 2 daus Mrs. B. F. **VAN TUYLE** of Petrolia, Ontario Canada and Mrs. Dr. **HUDSON** of Auburn, NY, buried Prattsburgh, NY

O'BRIEN Edward atty of Dansville, NY formerly of Howard, NY in Fremont, NY December 20, 1873, thrown from wagon when horses ran away

MITCHELL John B. age 70y 8m in Bath, NY January 14, 1873. Born May 14, 1802 of English parentage. Father moved to Utica, NY then Fredricksburg which embraced Bradford, Wayne, Tyrone and Barrington, NY. Youngest son died in Rebel Prison

CONDERMAN Jacob age 79y one of early settlers in Fremont, NY January 24, 1873. Served in War of 1812. Leaves wife age 82y

MOFFATT Sarah age 60y in Bradford, NY January 12, 1873

GRAHAM Lurah age 61y widow of Merlin Graham in Bath, NY January 23, 1873. Born Hamilton, NY, came to Bath with husband in 1838

PRINDLE George W. in his 27th yr of Rochelle, Ill. at uncle's James **BRUNDAGE** in N. Urbana, NY January 20, 1873, buried Rochelle

WOODARD Charlie age 7y drowned in Hornellsville, NY last week (Newspaper date January 29, 1873)

DOTY Col. Lockwood Lyon bro of M. A. W. **CROOKS** of Bath, NY in Jersey City, NJ February 1, 1873. Born May 15, 1827 in Groveland, NY

CHICHESTER Eliza age 65y wife of Henry Chichester and dau of late Aaron **OLMSTEAD** of Wayne, NY in Wheeler, NY February 4, 1873

JAMES John age 64y in Corning, NY February 4, 1873, buried Blossburg, NY

GRAY Catherine in her 29th yr wife of James Gray and dau of J. M. and E. H. **BROWN** of Bath, NY in Hornellsville, NY February 19, 1873

RYNIKER John killed by cars in Corning, NY February 20, 1873

SCHENCK Margaret age 62y wife of Christopher in Bath, NY February 23, 1873

WILCOX Mahala age 60y wife of Oren Wilcox in Howard, NY March 4, 1873

MAY James in his 82nd yr in Bath, NY March 5, 1873. Res here 50 yrs

BULL George B. age 62y in Buffalo, NY March 4, 1873. Born in Bath, NY bro of Col. William H. Bull of Bath and Mrs. Thomas J. **DUDLEY**

FARGO Polly age 96y 1m 13d Mother of R. R. Fargo of Pulteney, NY in Penn Yan, NY March 9, 1873

HESS Thomas age 72y bro of Hiram R. Hess in Bath, NY March 22, 1873

MORRELL Maria age 16y of Dansville, NY in Bath, NY February 16, 1873

SUTTON Herbert in his 4th yr son of E. W. and Huldah in Bath, NY March 20, 1873

GILLETT Johney age 33y formerly of Avoca, NY in Military Hospital Columbia, SC March 10, 1873

SMITH ___ infant son of Dr. Ira P. Smith in Bath, NY April 6, 1873

MAGEE John age 29y youngest son of John Magee and bro of Gen. George Magee and Mrs. Stewart S. **ELLSWORTH** of Penn Yan, NY in Watkins, NY April 29, 1873,

SEDGEWICK Louise age 1y 8m died April 24, 1873 and Elbert age 2y 10m died April 25, 1873 children of William P. Sedgewick of Bath, NY

PALMER Alice age 70y widow of Randall Palmer who died abt 15 yrs ago in Howard, NY April 30, 1873

DIVEN William age 84y in Reading, NY April 27, 1873. Born 1789 in Perry Co. Pa. and came to Steuben Co. 1809. Half bro Gen. A. S. Diven of Elmira, NY. Served War of 1812

GILMORE Susan age 70y wife of Perez Gilmore in Bath, NY May 3, 1873. Came to Bath 1809 with Father Thomas **TOWLE**

FELLOWS Joseph age 91y former agent of Pulteney Estate in Corning, NY April 29,

DEATH NOTICES
1873

OSMUN Daniel S. age 52y in Rock Stream, NY May 21, 1873

MINER Asa B. age 73y formerly of Prattsburgh, NY in Bath, NY May 23, 1873. Born Colbrook, Ct. Leaves wife and 10 children, 1 was adopted

DICKINSON A. B. age 72y in Leon, Nicaraugua April 21, 1873. Born 1801 in Trumansburgh, NY, later settled in Hornby, NY. Married twice, 5 children by 1st wife 4 living Mrs. Samuel **HALL**, Mrs. Isaac C. **HARRADAN** and Emma of Elmira, NY. Son O. B. of Chicago, Ill and son Mahlan killed by Indians in west when young. 2nd wife surviving and 2 children Hannah and Leon, unmarried

TERBELL Josephus age 68y formerly of Steuben Co. in Walden, NY May 29, 1873

LEWIS Joseph age 75y in Prattsburgh, NY May 22, 1873. res since 1819

NICHOLS John age 86y of Bath, NY while visiting dau in Cattaraugus Co. NY June 15, 1873

FOLSOM Otis W. in his 60th yr in Wayne, NY June 14, 1873. Born Washington Co. NY and left an orphan at age 5 yrs. 2 Sisters Mrs. James **BRUNDAGE** of Bath, NY and Mrs. Horace **MATHER** of Addison, NY and 1 bro Lewis of Mi.

SHEPARD Clarence age 2y 3m son of John F. and Pamelia W. Shepard in Bath, NY July 1, 1873

REEDER James M. age 62y in Starkey Station, NY June 29, 1873

HOUCK Lewis V. age 55y of Wayne, NY timber rolled on him at Keuka Landing, NY August 5, 1873

HOAGLAND Frank age 26y son of late Garrett Hoagland of Mt. Washington, NY August 10, 1873

CAMPBELL Charles abt 30y fell on circular saw in Mill at Merchantville, NY August 7, 1873. Leaves wife

FARR Erastus B. age 32y in Bath, NY August 9, 1873. Leaves wife and 3 children

GRAHAM Sarah J. age 38y wife of Miles G. in Hornellsville, NY August 27, 1873. Leaves husband and 4 children, eldest age 7 yrs

LITTLE Willie D. age 17y son of Charles C. and Susan in Bath, NY August 17, 1873

ST PETERS Josie age 7m 17d dau of Charles and Mary St Peters August 11, 1873

GILLETT J. S. age 52y of Penn Yan, NY hit by falling tree at Bluff Pt., NY September 8, 1873

FAY Samantha R. (**ROSENCRANS**) age 41y wife of Dr. H. G. Fay in Wayland, NY September 12, 1873

HOLMES Hannah abt 60y burned in home in Bath, NY September 20, 1873

CHASE Mary H. age 33y 10m wife of Thomas C. Chase and dau of James **HEES** formerly of Bath, NY in Avoca, NY October 13, 1873

BROWNELL James L. in Bath, NY October 14, 1873

DE WOLFE Dr. Alonzo age 64y in Bath, NY October 19, 1873. Born Virgil, NY

BRISCOE John Jr. son of John of Howard, NY in Chicago, Ill. October 26, 1873

BARNES Mrs. Jennett age 91y 11m at son's in Woodhull, NY October 19, 1873. Bro late W. W. **MC KAY** of Bath, NY

JONES Isaac Jr. age 44y in Canisteo, NY October 31, 1873. Married 1855 dau of Peter H. **DRAKE**

HUBBELL William S. in Bath, NY November 16, 1873. Born January 17,1801 in Painted Post, NY. Married 1822 Maria **MC CALL** sister of Ansel J. Mc Call of Bath, NY. She died 1852. Names son-in-law G. W. **HALLOCK**

YOUNG Helen A. nr 50y wife of Benjamin F. Young in Bath, NY November 17, 1873. Dau of Elisha **JOHNSON** pioneer of Rochester, NY. Married abt 30 yrs ago, 8 children 6 living

CHAMBERLAIN Levi J. age 56y son of late Joseph in Bath, NY September 8, 1873

BENNETT Sarah M. age 43y wife of Erastus in Bradford, NY November 27, 1873

LONGWELL Azariah age 38y son of Hosea in Bradford, NY December 2, 1873

MC CLURE Sarah E. age 86y widow of Gen. George Mc Clure in Wyoming, Io. November 10, 1873. Moved from Bath, NY to Elgin, Ill. 1835 and to Io. to live with son in 1860

HOUCK William age 64y in Wayne, NY December 30, 1873

TOWLE Miss Lydia age 58y at bro Jonathan Towle in Bath, NY January 4, 1874

COLLIER Miss Charlotte A. age 37y in Avoca, NY January 14, 1874

HAIGHT Silas age 62y in Elmira, NY January 25, 1874

BALDWIN Charles E. W. age 45y in Hornellsville, NY January 24, 1874. Leaves wife 5 sons and 2 daus

CAMPBELL Fannie Fowler age 14m dau of Robert J. and Virginia B. Campbell in

DEATH NOTICES

Chicago, Ill. February 2, 1874

WHIPPLE Lucy R. dau of late Dexter **PRATT** formerly of Howard, NY in Leoni, Mi. January 1, 1874

SMITH Reuben E. buried in Bath, NY February 6, 1874. Leaves wife and 5 daus

BIDWELL Mrs. ___ age 82y a widow buried in Bath, NY February 5, 1874

COMPTON Reuben age 35y in Bradford, NY February 9, 1874

BLACK Dr. J. W. in Bath, NY February 19, 1874

COOK Constant age 76y 3m 14d in Bath, NY February 24, 1874. Born November 10, 1797 in Warren, NY

BARNEY Floyd age 21y suddenly while ice fishing nr Avoca, NY March 5, 1874

CRAGAN Timothy age 14y in Bath, NY March 3, 1874

EMERSON John in his 78th yr in Bath, NY March 13, 1874. Born 1796 in Candia, NH and came to Bath 1818. Wife died abt 3 yrs ago

WARD Frederick L. son of late Dr. Ward in Hornellsville, NY March 6, 1874. Sister Mrs. Ebenezer **ELLIS** of Bath, NY

SLINEY Thomas formerly of Geneva, NY in Bath, NY March 18, 1874

RUNYAN ___ wife of Prof. W. W. Runyan in Sonora, NY March 19, 1874

COLLIER Charlotte age 69y 8m wife of J. H. Collier in Avoca, NY March 31, 1874

GAMBLE Col. William abt 80y at dau Mrs. Solomon **CAMPBELL** in Painted Post, NY April 3, 1874

LEGGETT Mrs. Allen age 53y in Cohocton, NY April 11, 1874

SMITH Enos in his 89th yr late of S. Canisteo, NY April 22, 1874. Born New Haven, Ct. and came to Bath, NY 1812, later to Greenwood, NY

WHITE Thomas age 46y in Cortland, Ill. April 20, 1874. Bro Josiah White of Chicago, Ill. and A. A. White of Hammondsport, NY

KEOUGH William rec pardoned from prison on account of health at Father's in Bath, NY April 26, 1874

EDMONDS Rosa age 18y died April 28, 1874

WILCOX Elijah of Bath, NY while visiting son in Ill. funeral in Bath May 10, 1874

PERINE William H. age 23y 4m 10d in Bath, NY May 10, 1874

STEWART Mahala age 44y wife of George Stewart in Howard, NY March 10, 1874

NORTHRUP Mrs. Priscilla in her 83rd yr at dau in Bath, NY May 16, 1874

KLOCK Katherine age 68y 6m 13d wife of Peter A. Klock in Bath, NY May 3, 1874

BRUNDAGE Maria age 68y wife of George S. Brundage in Urbana, NY May 5, 1874

BURKE Phillip funeral at Avoca, NY May 10, 1874

SMITH Azilla age 75y 1d widow of Charles Smith at son's Seneca Smith June 4, 1874. Born Cayuga Co. NY and res of Bath, NY 50 yrs.

GILBERT Stephen F. in Hornellsville, NY June 14, 1874. Born February 28, 1842 in Groveland, NY

NORTHRUP Benjamin D. age 86y in Rathbone, NY June 11, 1874. Came from Sussex Co. NJ December 1835. Leaves wife age 59y and 5 sons on farm

BECKWITH Amasa B. in Rathbone, NY June 11, 1874. Born 1807 in Ct. and res of Steuben Co. for 60 yrs

NEALLY Minnie E. age 17y 10m 21d dau of W. L. and L. A. Neally formerly of Steuben Co. and grand dau of Z. **BRADLEY** in Melvern, Ks. July 4, 1874

CRITTENDEN Mrs. Harriet age 76y formerly of Otsego Co. NY at son's July 29, 1874

ERWIN Capt. Samuel over 50y formerly of Painted Post, NY in Calvert Tx. August 4, 1871. Bro Charles H. Erwin

SHELDON Bert age 13y accidently shot himself in Bloods, NY August 25, 1874

EVERSON Eliza age 10m 21d dau of Sanford and Huldah in Bath, NY August 27, 1874

WHEELER Gratia age 91y widow of George Wheeler nr Kanona, NY September 1, 1874. Husband died abt 4 yrs ago. Came from New England 1810. 9 children 3 living A. J. and sister E. S. of Kanona and Mrs. Charlotte **JONES** of Danville, Ill.

DE PUY Dr. J. N. age 33y at Father-in-law's Rev. T. S. **HILL** in Wayne, NY (Newspaper date September 16, 1874). Leaves wife and 2 children

MILLER Jane age 2y 1m 4d dau of George M. and Harriet P. Miller and only grand child of Franklin and Jane **HOLDEN** in Pulteney, NY September 15, 1874

CAMERON Howard F. age 7m 13d son of Madison in Wayne, NY September 20, 1874

LOZIER Grace E. only dau of Charles and Mary in Bath, NY September 16, 1874

DEATH NOTICES

SMITH Dea. Porter age 68y in Cold Springs, NY September 16, 1874

DEMAREST Cornelius age 77y in Avoca, NY September 17, 1874. Born eastern NY State and came to Avoca 1830

BREWSTER John T. age 66y in Bath, NY October 1, 1874, res of Steuben Co. 36 yrs

CARR John S. age 2y 2m 3d only son of Charles D. and Adelaide Carr in Campbell, NY September 16, 1874

SEYMOUR Edwin B. age 22y only son of S. M. in Bath, NY November 3, 1874

FITCH David age 43y 11m 16d in Wayland, NY October 31, 1874

WALDO Otis H. atty age 52y in Milwaukee, Wis. October 30, 1874. Born Prattsburgh, NY. Married sister of Gen. R. B. **VAN VALKENBURGH**

STRONG Dolly C. age 29y dau of Ezra Strong suicide by hanging in Wheeler, NY November 12, 1874. Mother died September 1874

CARTER Joseph age 67y in Bath, NY November 16, 1874

ROBINSON Cornelia age 55y 9m wife of Amon Robinson in Bath, NY December 15, 1874. Born Palatine, NY and married there a Mr. **SMITH** abt 19 yrs ago, 2 sons 1 living, Cornelius and 1 dau

LONGWELL James C. of Penn Yan, NY December 6, 1874, leaves wife and 2 children

DAVIS Amasa age 15y 11m 25d in Avoca, NY December 14, 1874

SMITH Mrs. Edmond in Cosse's Corners, NY January 9, 1875

SMITH Ira son of Charles Smith suicide by hanging nr Kanona, NY January 7, 1875

BENTON Norman age 69y in Bath, NY January 13, 1875

BRUNDAGE David age 34y in Bath, NY December 29, 1874

SMITH Patience in her 56th yr January 9, 1875

DE PUY James in his 91st yr in Bath, NY February 23, 1875

SMITH William R. one of oldest Co. res. in Addison, NY February 16, 1875

BALDWIN Henry in Howard, NY March 3, 1875. Born Howard 1828

PLUMB Mrs. H. C. formerly Miss Sarah **GREGG** of Bath, NY in De Moines, Io. February 27, 1875

THOMAS Georgianna age 26y wife of Lemuel Thomas in Bath, NY March 30, 1875

PRENTISS Ella N. age 27y wife of J. Q. A. Prentiss and dau of Franklin and Matilda **CARPENTER** in Pulteney, NY April 17. 1875. 3 children, oldest child Frankie buried July 30, 1874

DAVISON Mrs. Sarah in her 92nd yr Mother of Thomas in Bath, NY April 13, 1875

SANDERSON Eliza (**LONGWELL**) age 29y in Pulteney, NY April 14, 1875

LITTLE Mrs. Catherine in her 77th yr nr Bath, NY April 14, 1875. Born Dumfries, Scotland and came to Bath 40 yrs ago. Husband died soon after, 6 children

DUDLEY Roswell Sedgewick abt 6y son of Albert D. Dudley of Corning, NY April 14, 1875, buried Bath, NY

MEDDICK Walter infant son of John Meddick of Bath, NY April 26, 1875. Sister Nancy died 3 yrs ago

BAUDER Susan age 41y wife of Dewitt Bauder formerly of Utica, NY in Pleasant Valley, NY April 28, 1875. Married 1858. Leaves husband and 3 children

SMITH Lewis H. from accident while trying to jump cars in Bath, NY May 5, 1875

WILBUR Luna Ann age 60y wife of John Wilbur in Bath, NY May 10, 1875. Leaves husband and 3 children

LANG Mrs. Charles nr Bath, NY May 15, 1875

KEOUGH Ellen age 18y dau of Patrick Keough of Bath, NY May 16, 1875

HANFORD Uriah age 76y in Jerusalem, NY May 9, 1875

ELLAS Mariah in her 77th yr widow of Alva Ellas at bro N. B. **MATHER** in Bath, NY May 20, 1875

WILCOX Betsey age 92y at son's Hiram Wilcox in Caton, NY May 7, 1875

DANIELS Orrin W. in his 68th yr native of Vt. in Bath, NY (Newspaper date June 9, 1875). Leaves wife and 5 children

WARD Henry father of B. C. Ward of Bath, NY in Painted Post, NY June 9, 1875. Born August 18, 1797 in Middleburgh, NY son of Abijah Ward a vet. of the Revolutionary War. Came to Steuben Co. in 1818

SMITH Mathew thrown from wagon when horses were scared by train nr Savona, NY June 22, 1875

EDWARDS Hannah age 84y widow of George C. Edwards June 19, 1875. Born June 1791 in Chester, NY dau of Jesse **CARPENTER**. At age 17 moved to Chemung Co. NY. Married 1812 and came to Bath, NY. Husband died 1837, oldest son George died March 1875

ALLEN Sarah Jane in her 38th yr wife of John in Cosse's Corners, NY June 25, 1875

DUDLEY Edward late of Bath, NY in Robertson Co. Tx. July 13, 1875

WILLISTON John Sedgewick Jr. age 27y in Athens, Pa. July 20, 1875

ROGERS Susanna age 72y widow of Dr. G. A. Rogers formerly of Bath, NY and only dau of Robert **CAMPBELL** 1 of early settlers, in Chicago, Ill. July 29, 1875. Leaves 4 sons and 5 daus, 3 with her in Chicago

DONAHE Lucy A. in her 83rd yr wife of John Donahe in Bath, NY August 15, 1875

DANIELS Sarah in her 59th yr wife of George T. Daniels in Bath, NY August 4, 1875

HAND Anna A. age 5y dau of E. P. and Mary A. Hand in Bath, NY January 14, 1876

MC GONEGAL Sarah D. age 64y 8m 4d wife of Oren Mc Gonegal in Avoca, NY January 16, 1876. Dau of Rosevald **TICKNER** from eastern NY State. Married May 4, 1835 and leaves 3 daus

ROBIE Nancy age 70y 1m 16d widow of Reuben Robie and dau of late Col. John **WHITING** in Bath, NY February 18, 1876 who came from Me. over 60 yrs ago with wife and 8 children. 7 children 6 living

JACOBS Benjamin age 58y formerly of Howard, NY in Cedar Falls, Io. February 3, 1876. Left Howard 1855

BARTON Harvey Bushnell age 21y son of A. J. Barton of Bath, NY March 11, 1876

BRINK Andrew age 73y nr Savona, NY March 18, 1876

FORD Mrs. Patrick formerly of Bath, NY in Kanona, NY March 28, 1876

MEEKS Joseph B. of Howard, NY from apoplexy in Croton Hotel in Bath, NY March 28, 1876

CALLANAN Ellen murdered by fiance John E. **MC NAMARA** in Corning, NY April 16, 1876

SHADER Adam age 40y in Wheeler, NY April 8, 1876

CUMMINGS John age 50y native of Ireland in Bath, NY April 24, 1876. Served 107th Reg. NYV

STEWART Ellen wife of William E. Stewart and dau of Samuel and Ann E. **HALLETT** in Wayne, April 16, 1876

ROBIE Levi age 50y in Bath, NY May 7, 1876. Born November 3, 1825 in Fairfield, Vt. In 1834 came to uncle's Reuben Robie in Bath, NY. Married (1) 1855 Anna **PERKINS** of NH. 7 children 2 died infancy. Married (2) Helen **CALKINS** of Bath,

NY, 1 son and 1 dau

NEWTON Silas A. run over by cars in Hornellsville, NY May 4, 1876

HOWELL Mrs. William in Bath, NY June 5, 1876

DEMAREST Mary age 81y at son-in-law's Eben **TOWLE** in Towlesville, NY May 12, 1876. Born Montgomery Co. NY came with husband to Avoca who died 18 months ago. Leaves 3 son and 1 dau

MARTIN Hattie age 22y dau of Mrs. John Martin in Bath, NY June 5, 1876

SMITH Willard H. age 26y 4m formerly of Prattsburgh, NY in Independence, Ks. May 30, 1876. Born New Canaan, Ct. 1 of 6 sons only 1 still living Oscar M. and sister Mrs. G. R. R. **AINSWORTH** of Prattsburgh

LEWIS Jesse son of William Lewis kicked by horse nr Bath, NY June 27, 1876. Leaves wife and small child, buried Sonora, NY

WARNER Edith age 7m dau of John S. and Clara (**WOODARD**) in Medina, Oh. July 3, 1876 (she has gone to meet her mother)

MOORE Abigail M. age 64y wife of Spence Moore in Avoca, NY July 12, 1876. Married 45 yrs

FAUCETT Mary age 80y in Bath, NY July 25, 1876. Funeral at sister's Mrs. Thomas **COLLINS**

WILCOX D. S. hit by train in Cohocton, NY July 26, 1876

TOWNER George W. age 41y 10m 10d in Avoca, NY July 22, 1876

HAND Addie age 4m dau of Edward P. and Mary E. Hand in Bath, NY (Newspaper date August 23, 1876)

WARREN Laurette age 36y wife of M. B. Warren August 17, 1876

WILLIAMS Barney in Pleasant Valley, NY August 25, 1876

LYON Sarah in her 86th yr in Bath, NY September 7, 1876. Born November 7, 1790 in Benton, NY. Married September 1814 and moved to Bath. Leaves 4 sons William, David, James and Robert the eldest died January 1, 1835

BAILEY Elizabeth A. age 78y at son's Cyrus Bailey in Hammondsport, NY September 16, 1876

CAMPBELL Hattie Hoyt dau of Charles W. Campbell formerly of Bath, NY October 20, 1876. Born April 8, 1852

BROWN Amy in her 83rd yr Mother of D. B. and George **WILLIAMS** in Ulysses, Pa.

November 19, 1876

HAVENS Matilda age 71y 9m consort of George in Bath, NY December 30, 1876

OVENSHIRE Miss Julia age 43y of Barrington, NY at bro H. C. Ovenshire at Mt. Washington, NY February 7, 1877

DAWSON Sarah age 63y widow of Bonham in Hornellsville, NY March 11, 1877

RICE Seth H. in his 58th yr in Towlesville, NY February 20, 1877. Born September 9, 1819 son of Jonas Rice who came from Mass. to Howard, NY 1811 and 1825 to Towlesville where Seth Jr. still resides. Leaves 2 sons and 1 dau

LOOK Benjamin in his 89th yr in Bath, NY March 21, 1877

MILLER Emma B. in her 77th yr formerly of Norwich, NY at son-in-law's E. Purdy **ALLEN** in Bath, NY (Newspaper date May 10, 1877)

LANE Mrs. Sarah age 50y dau of John **IRVING** formerly of Kanona, NY in Phelps, NY April 9, 1877

POTTER Fred D. age 2y 1m died May 2, 1877 and Willie J. age 3y 7m 11d died May 4, 1877 sons of J. T. and Emma Potter formerly of Bath, NY in Philadelphia, Pa.

BUTTS Delphine age 15y 9m dau of Joseph Butts in Wheeler, NY April 12, 1877

MAY Betsey in her 82nd yr widow of James May in Bath, NY May 22, 1877. Born Litchfield, Ct. and came to Bath 1823/24, Husband died 4 yrs ago

BROWN John in his 79th yr in Mitchellville, NY April 29, 1877. Born May 29, 1798 in Plattskill, NY and came to Steuben Co. November 1826. Leaves wife and 4 daus Mrs. O. C. **MATTESON**, Mrs. G. **HADDEN**, Mrs. Sarah **WILBER** and Mrs. Albert **WIXOM**, 2 sons Rev. J. W. Brown of Milo, NY and Joseph at home

HEMPSTED Eliza age 76y widow of Elisha Hempsted formerly of Bath, in Flushing, NY June 10, 1877, buried Litchfield, Ct. with husband who died 20 yrs ago

SAGAR William age 77y 5m formerly of Steuben Co. in Fairfax Court House, Va. July 5, 1877. Born February 5, 1800 in Rhinebeck, NY

YOST John D. age 70y in Thurston, NY July 25/31, 1877

SMALLIDGE Henry in Bath, NY July 28, 1877

HUNTINGTON Ann in her 83rd yr widow of George in Kanona, NY August 8, 1877

MERRILL Luretta age 27y wife of Jonas Merrill and dau of W. L. **KELLOGG** in Wayland, NY August 13, 1877

EGGLESTON Thomas an old res of Pulteney, NY August 20, 1877

FRINK Elam age 81y nr Bath, NY September 19, 1877. Came from New England over 50 yrs ago. Married dau of Samuel **TOWLE** who died 1 yr ago

THOMAS Abiel age 81y in Troupsburgh, NY October 1, 1877

DURHAM Anna L. dau of Ezra S. and Lucina R. in Bath, NY November 2, 1877

CORYELL Jacob age 81y in Pulteney, NY December 7, 1877

HOLLIS Mrs. E. T. in Woodhull, NY December 16, 1877. Leaves husband and dau, son died 10 mos ago

LITTLE James R. abt 40y in Babcock Settlement, NY November 22, 1877, youngest son of late James Little a native of Scotland. Leaves sister Mrs. A. F. **ELLAS** and Mrs. George **HUNTER** and bro John Little

HORTON G. P. in Orange, NY January 1, 1878

DAVISON James age 21y son of William Davison of Bath, NY in Willard Asylum January 1, 1878

TOPPING Cora (**ST JOHN**) age 19y 8m 21d wife of W. R. Topping in Rochester, NY February 8, 1878

KNICKERBOCKER C. A. age 28y of Cohocton, NY hit by train nr Wallace, NY February 24, 1878

FLYNN Lester age 32y nr Bath, NY March 2, 1878, youngest of 5 bro who served in Civil War

CLARK Anson age 81y 5m 20d at son's J. E. Clark in Prattsburgh, February 16, 1878

OLMSTEAD Ten Eyck G. age 45y formerly of Howard, NY in Manitowoc, Wis. February 26, 1878

PARSONS William formerly of Prattsburgh, NY in Woodhull, NY March 8/9, 1878, buried Prattsburgh. 4 children, 1 dau at home and Mrs. Joel **TOMER** of Prattsburgh

ABER Mary wife of George C. Aber in Bath, NY March 12, 1878, only remaining dau of Mrs. Charles **ELLAS**. Married last September

OSGOOD Christopher age 82y in Wayland, NY March 17, 1878

RICHARDSON Lula Beatrice age 9m 18d dau of Clinton W. and Delia D. Richardson in Elmira, NY March 16, 1878

RICHTMYER John age 73y 2m 17d in Thurston, NY March 15, 1878. Born Schoharie Co. NY and married Harriet **HEAD**, 7 children 3 daus 4 sons. Formerly resided in Enfield and Havana, NY

DEATH NOTICES

GOBLE Mary J. age 45y wife of J. M. Goble in Cameron Mills, NY March 29, 1878

STEPHENS Elias in Canisteo, NY April 12, 1878

MUDGE Libbie age 19y 11m 8d wife of Edgar E. Mudge and dau of William E. and Mary **MORRISON** in Pulteney, NY February 14, 1878

NILES Mary wife of Moses Niles in Bath, NY April 9, 1878

STANTON Col. Nathaniel B. drowned in well in Hornby, NY April 9, 1878

WILLISTON Horace of Athens, Pa. son of late Judge Horace Williston died April 13, 1878. Leaves sister Mrs. H. H. **HALL**, wife, 2 daus and 1 son

SMITH Rev. Jacob at son-in-law's Mr. **CHRISTIAN** on Addison Hill, NY April 6, 1878

FAUCETT Elizabeth age 82y wife of Robert Faucett in Bath, NY April 23, 1878

SMITH Chauncey B. in his 79th yr in Hornellsville, NY May 21, 1878

KNOX Mary G. age 72y widow of John P. Knox in Campbell, NY June 1, 1878

MOORE John in his 75th yr in Savona, NY May 31, 1878. Born July 25, 1803 in Bradford Hollow, NY. Married abt 48y ago Pelona **KINNEY**, 6 children 3 living

HAVERLING Ruby age 70y wife of George S. Haverling in Bath, NY June 9, 1878

RUGGLES Eva in her 21st yr dau of W. B. and Carrie in Bath, NY June 16, 1878

FAUCETT Robert S. age 88y in Bath, NY June 14, 1878

FAULKNER Mrs. Addie age 18y at Mother's Mrs. **GENUNG** in Bath, NY June 8, 1878

HUGHES Dr. Hiram age 67y in Savona, NY June 16, 1878. Wife died 3 yrs ago, leaves 3 daus

ORCUTT Rev. Asa age 82y in Sonora, NY June 17, 1878

BURNS James H. age 20y in Corning, NY June 25, 1878

FLYNN Mrs. James in Gibson, NY June 23, 1878

HILL Joseph H. age 60y formerly of Corning, NY nephew of late Joseph **FELLOWS** in New York City June 23, 1878

THURMAN Mrs. Joseph in Corning, NY June 22, 1878

GORTON Mrs. Orley Sr. abt 70y in Hornby, NY June 19, 1878

HENDERSCHOTT Samuel age 74y in Hornellsville, NY June 23, 1878

HOLLIDAY Mr. E. E. late of Hornellsville, NY in Canaseraga, NY June 21, 1878

SECOR Joseph H. age 72y in Wayland, NY June 30, 1878

BUSH Mrs. Wesley nr Cohocton, NY July 1, 1878. Leaves husband and 4 children

HOAR Mrs. David in Corning, NY July 9, 1878

HIGMAN Mrs. John in Corning, NY July 7, 1878

REYNOLDS Bertie son of Thomas T. Reynolds drowned in Addison, NY July 6, 1878

SMITH Daniel P. age 67y suicide by morphine nr Dundee, NY July 11, 1878. Leaves wife and 5 children. Made several previous attempts

ABRAMS Thomas nr Loon Lake, NY July 15, 1878. Leaves sons Dr. S. R. and Thomas Abrams of Cohocton, NY and A. J. Smith

SMITH E. D. in Hornellsville, NY July 27, 1878

LETTS Betsey M. in her 49th yr wife of Daniel A. in Woodhull, NY July 20, 1878

RICE Chester age 77y found dead in field in Neils Creek, NY July 22, 1878

EARNEST John age 85y at son's J. J. Earnest nr Wayne, NY July 13, 1878. Native of Herkimer Co. NY, moved to Seneca Co. NY after serving War of 1812 to Wayne 1817. Wife died abt 10 yrs ago leaving 8 children

BILLSON Cornelius age 79y in Avoca, NY July 23, 1878. Born Watervliet, NY and came to Steuben Co. age 25y. Wife died nr 4 yrs ago leaving 2 sons and 2 daus

MC CALL Ann in her 90th yr at son's A. J. Mc Call in Bath, NY July 26, 1878. Born December 1788 in Bucks Co. Pa. nee **SHANNON**. Mother married soon after Benjamin **PATTERSON** and moved to Painted Post, NY in 1797. Married 1809 Ansel Mc Call who died 1815, remaining widow for 63 yrs. Also leaves dau Mrs. Timothy **WHITING**

LOUNSBERRY Phineas in Pulteney, NY August 3, 1878

ALLEN Mrs. Joseph in Rathbone, NY July 28, 1878

HOPKINS Martha widow of William Hopkins formerly of Campbell, NY and dau of late Charles **BONHAM** of Campbell, NY in Bath, NY August 2, 1878. Husband died 2 yrs ago leaving 4 daus

BAKER Walter age 21y son of Philo Baker of Fremont, NY in Hornellsville, NY August 2, 1878

ALDRICH Adolphus in Cold Springs, NY August 2, 1878. Born 1812 in Berkshire Co.

DEATH NOTICES

Mass. and came to Hammondsport, NY 1834

HINES Gracie Sophia age 1y 2m dau of Anthony and Josephine Hines July 3, 1878

SHAUGER Ransom age 2m 5d son of William H. and Margarite Shauger in Thurston, NY August 10, 1878

EDDY Daniel in his 64th yr in Reynoldsville, NY July 29, 1878

HALLETT Jeremiah age 20y 9m son of A. S. and J. in Addison, NY August 8, 1878

BARNES Maggie wife of J. P. Barnes in Hammondsport, NY August 8, 1878

EDSON Mary M. dau of late Henry Edson of Corning, NY buried in Corning August 16, 1878

NEAR Alice G. age 34y wife of I. W. Near in Hornellsville, NY August 23, 1878

FRONK Mary in Cohocton, NY August 24, 1878

DARRIN Hattie wife of J. Wesley Darrin in Corning, NY August 26, 1878. Leaves infant child only 3 days old

LEE Mrs. Mary Ann age 71y in Pulteney, NY August 31, 1878

TRENCHARD Mrs. M. age 83y in Hornellsville, NY rec. (Newspaper date September 12, 1878)

LANNING Ferris age 20y at grandmother's Mrs. James **MOORE** in Rathbone, NY August 31, 1878

NIVER Emma L. in her 23rd yr in Caton, NY August 31, 1878

SOUTHARD John age 62y in Hornellsville, NY September 18, 1878

CURTIS Emma in her 47th yr wife of R. S. in Hornellsville, NY September 26, 1878

BOUGHTON Sarah E. age 35y in Hornellsville, NY September 18, 1878

BURDICK Jeremiah nr 100y found dead at son's home in Crosby Creek, NY September 26, 1878

COLE Lucy H. age 42y 1d wife of Joseph B. Cole in Wayne, NY September 22, 1878. Born W. Troy (NY or Pa.?)

BAKER Almira age 1y 7m 18d dau of Austin and Anabel in Bath, NY October 7, 1878

COOK ___ dau of L. A. Cook in Canisteo, NY September 29, 1878

FORRESTER Freelove age 85y 9m of Howard, NY at son's Charles in Scranton, Pa.

STEUBEN COUNTY NEWSPAPERS 153

September 17, 1878, formerly resided with dau Mrs. A. H. **BALDWIN** in Howard

HALLOCK Mrs. P. A. suicide in Eddytown, NY October 7, 1878

TOWNSEND Anna Maria age 66y 6m 6d wife of Robert in Bath, NY October 12, 1878, only sister of Franklin **HOLDEN** of Pulteney, NY

DECKER Van Rensalaer in Avoca, NY October 13, 1878

POWERS Patrick in his 65th yr in Rathbone, NY October 11, 1878

WOLF John J. age 64y in Wayland, NY October 14, 1878. Leaves wife and 4 children

HOTCHKIN Rev. Beriah of Philadelphia, Pa. bro of James Hotchkin of Prattsburgh, NY October 13, 1878

VAN HOUSEN Henry in his 81st yr in Bath, NY October 30, 1878. Born December 1797 in Montgomery Co. NY. Married 1818 Margaret **HOAGLAND**. Moved to Howard, NY 1832, to Prattsburgh, NY 1849 and 1858 to Bath, 10 children 4 living

PHELPS Mrs. Hannah age 77y formerly of Corning, NY in Scranton, Pa. October 22, 1878

GULLIVER Lemuel age 79y in Caton, NY October 31, 1878

ZIELLY Thomas age 56y in Avoca, NY October 26, 1878

WILLIAMSON Elizabeth in Cameron, NY October 13, 1878. Born December 31, 1805 in Renslerville, NY. Mother died when she was 2y. Married January 18, 1831 David Williamson his 2nd wife. Leaves 6 children

THARP Mary A. age 47y wife of Joseph Tharp November 18, 1878

HAMMOND Samuel H. formerly of Bath, NY in Watertown, NY November 27, 1878. Born March 8, 1809 in Bath

BRECK George W. in Bath, NY December 11, 1878. Native of Vt. born 1809

WOLCOTT Mrs. Elizabeth age 86y in Caton, NY December 15, 1878

WORMLEY Jacob age 70y in Corning, NY December 15, 1878

HASTINGS Mabel age 5y dau of E. H. and Mary C. in Bath, NY December 21, 1878

COOK Lyman A. in Canisteo, NY December 23, 1878

HOLLENBECK Rev. Joseph age 59y in Corning, NY December 20, 1878

GRANGER Roxana age 88y 9m in Hornellsville, NY December 21, 1878

DEATH NOTICES

LAMB Mary A. in her 58th yr wife of Francis in Wayne, NY December 26, 1878

KING Mary in her 69th yr at son-in-law's James **BOWLBY** in Bath, NY December 13, 1878

SAYRE Dr. William in his 67th yr in Washington DC January 6, 1879

MILLER James age 85y in Rogersville, NY December 24, 1878

MULHOLLEN William in Canisteo, NY January 1, 1879. Born April 1779 in Painted Post, NY. Res of Canisteo 70 yrs

FAIRBANKS Joel age 86y in Cameron, NY December 17, 1878, res for 60 yrs

PAUL John in Cohocton, NY December 30, 1878

CORNWELL Mrs. Lucelia age 64y in Tuscarora, NY January 4, 1879

WESTCOTT Horace age 77y in Caton, NY December 31, 1878

SILL Mrs. D. D. in N. Cohocton, NY January 9, 1879

QUILL Thomas age 15y son of Jerry Quill result of fall January 10, 1879

NORRIS Phebe wife of Levi Norris in S. Pulteney, NY January 5, 1879

MARGESON Bradley P. in Urbana, NY December 25, 1878

CORNELL Samuel age 86y in Campbell, NY January 2, 1879

SHEPPARD Mrs. Sally an old res of Cohocton, NY last wk (Newspaper date January 23, 1879)

LINDSAY John age 61y in Bath, NY January 19, 1879

BURRELL Samuel age 83y of Bath, NY January 20, 1879. Born Binghamton, NY, buried Greenwood, NY. Sons Alphonso and A. M. Burrell

PLATT Ebenezer age 56y in Elizabeth, NJ December 1, 1878. Oldest son of late Rev. Isaac Watts Platt and bro of Rev. James M. Platt of Pres. Church in Bath, NY

TAYLOR Dugald in Canisteo, NY January 22, 1879

BARNUM Mrs. Deborah at bro Dr. Bradley **BLAKESLEE** in Bath, NY January 26, 1879. Born September 17, 1799 in Brattleboro, Vt. In 1835 went to Ft. Snelling, Dak as missionary for 14 yrs. Married Russell Barnum who died 17 yrs ago, a cousin of P. T. Barnum. She is sister of Nathaniel Blakeslee of Hornellsville, NY

OXX Sarah J. age 25y 6m wife of Steuben C. Oxx and dau of Reuben and Anna **BAKER** in Haskinsville, NY January 2, 1879

STEUBEN COUNTY NEWSPAPERS 155

HUSTON George W. age 30y in Big Flats, NY January 18, 1879. Son-in-law of David **LONGWELL** of Bath, NY

ROOT William age 79y in Penn Yan, NY January 27, 1879

HENDERSON Dryden an old res of Hammondsport, NY January 29, 1879

DYGERT James S. age 67y in Kanona, NY January 29, 1879. Born 1812 in Montgomery Co. NY oldest of 6 children. Came to Kanona 1849, married Maria **SNELL** dau of late William. Leaves wife, 1 son Horace and Mother age 87y

WARD Emeline age 48y in Howard, NY February 4, 1879

HILL Mary H. age 48y wife of Willard A. in Rikers Hollow, NY February 1, 1879

BENNETT Martha in her 54th yr wife of James G. in Wayland, NY February 8, 1879

TERRELL William O. age 52y at Soldiers and Sailors, Home in Bath, NY February 14, 1879. Member of Co. I 32nd inf. Vol. Resided Ithaca, NY

CORY Orlando age 37y 3m in S. Dansville, NY January 27, 1879

SUTHERLAND Louisa C. age 27y wife of George R. Sutherland and dau of late Rev. David F. **CAMPBELL** and Mary B. **(JUDSON)** in Campbell, NY February 21, 1879. Born December 9, 1851 in Gaines, NY, moved to Seneca Ks. where her Father died, then moved to Prattsburgh, NY and married June 19, 1872. Leaves Mother Mrs. Dr. S. M. Campbell of Rochester, NY and sister Mrs. W. A. **WALDO** of Prattsburgh

YOST Wait age 10y died March 9, 1879

VAN VALKENBURGH Judge Jacob age 85y formerly of Bath, NY at son's R. B. in St. Nicolas, Fla. March 3, 1879. Born 1794 at Kinderhook, NY, came to Steuben Co. 1819 and married 1820 dau of David **HIGGINS** of Bath

CARLEY Clark of Pulteney, NY suicide at Avoca, NY March 8, 1879

MC COLLOUGH John age 85y in Bath, NY March 15, 1879

WHITE Ella F. age 26y wife of William W. White and dau of Justin M. **SMITH** in Corning, NY March 16, 1879

STEPHENS Christopher age 35y in Hornellsville, NY March 16, 1879

GRAVES Epahroditus age 80y at bro Luther in Prattsburgh, NY March 9, 1879

SCRAFFORD John age 62y in Bath, NY March 17, 1879. Came from Albany, NY 4 yrs ago

COLLINS Sarah Louise age 3y 3m 15d dau of Martin and Susan Collins in Bath, NY March 24, 1879

DEATH NOTICES

BUTLER Elnathan in Avoca, NY March 10, 1879. Born March 18, 1789 in Lime Ct. Married March 1829 Lydia **STORY** of Naples, NY, 3 sons, 4 daus, 4 living Harry and Mary at home, Mrs. Henry **WILLOUR** of Painted Post, NY and Henry on Pacific Slope

PATCHIN Warren in his 76th yr nr Loon Lake, NY March 13, 1879

BEYER Louie in his 5th yr son of C. H. and Elizabeth Beyer in Cohocton, NY March 17, 1879

WOODWORTH Mary L. in her 5th yr dau of S. F. and A. E. died March 17, 1879

SIDMAN Mrs. Susan age 59y in Haskinsville, NY March 16, 1879

RIDER Samuel in Haskinsville, NY March 3, 1879

MURPHY Patrick age 42y at Soldiers and Sailors Home in Bath, NY March 31, 1879. Member of Co. K. 47th Reg. NYV, resided Buffalo, NY

BODINE Sylvanus age 72y in Prattsburgh, NY March 23, 1879

LANDERS Thomas in Gang Mills, NY March 29, 1879. Leaves wife and several children

JENKS Simeon Sr. age 78y in Campbell, NY March 30, 1879

CAULKINS Mrs. Peter W. age 24y dau of William **CHRISTIAN** of Corning, NY in Gibson, NY April 1, 1879

MATHEWS Samuel age 78y in Arkport, NY April 10, 1879

SMITH Jay age 84y 7m in Prattsburgh, NY April 3, 1879. Came to Prattsburgh 1816

HILGERS John J. age 53y at Soldiers and Sailors Home in Bath, NY April 12, 1879. Native of Prussia and res of New York City. Mem of Co A. 46th Reg. NYV

CARTER Mrs. Joseph age 74y in Bath, NY April 15, 1879

VAN HEUSEN Margareth age 80y relict of Henry in Bath, NY April 20, 1879

BOWEN May age 9y 11m dau of William Henry and Juliza Bowen in Haskinsville, NY April 11, 1879

RINEHART Mrs. Anson in N. Urbana, NY April 22, 1879. Leaves husband and 4 children

GATES Sallie Ann age 64y in S. Dansville, NY April 17, 1879

JONES Sarah age 59y wife of W. B. in Bath, NY April 13, 1879. Born Barrington, NY

BELL Miss Joanna age 50y in Prattsburgh, NY April 29, 1879

SKINNER Aurelia widow of Erastus Skinner formerly of Prattsburgh, NY in Cincinnati, Oh. April 15, 1879, buried Prattsburgh

GRAHAM Edward at Soldiers and Sailors Home in Bath, NY April 17, 1879. Native of Ireland and member of Co. B. 5th NY Cav.

CHISSOM Ephraim age 84 yrs of Cameron, NY at son's Robert Chissom in Potter Brook, Pa. May 3, 1879

ARMSTRONG James age 67y in Wallace, NY or Cohocton, NY May 8, 1879

WINSHIP Sarah widow of Morey Winship in Cameron, NY May 9, 1879

BRYANT Ella in her 102nd yr in Fremont, NY May 7, 1879

WILLIAMS Josiah age 59y in Prattsburgh, NY May 2, 1879

STRAIT Elmira age 65y widow of Jonathan Strait in Woodhull, NY May 15, 1879

HOPPER Mary wife of Lawrence Hopper in Hartsville, NY May 25, 1879

SHULTS Ann Eliza wife of Casper Shults in Hornby, NY May 12, 1879

WHITE Mrs. Phidelia M. in Tyrone, NY May 27, 1879

CHAMPLIN J. J. age 56y in Jerusalem, NY May 23, 1879

SMITH Eliza age 41y wife of W. H. Smith in Cohocton, NY May 21, 1879

DRAPER James J. in Corning, NY May 26, 1879

MAYNARD Stephen age 71y in Stephens Mills, NY May 11, 1879

BROWN Betsey J. wife of Elnathan Grant Brown in Tuscarora, NY May 14, 1879

EDGER Hannah at son's Benjamin F. Edger in Gibson, NY May 24, 1879

AHERN Michael in Soldiers and Sailors Home in Bath, NY June 25, 1879, late Pvt. in Co. D. 12th NY Inf. and Co. F. 5th NY Inf.

HERRICK George W. in his 80th yr in Knoxville, NY June 29, 1879

FORTNER Mrs. Phebe age 73y at res of J. M. **SMITH** in Corning, NY June 25, 1879

BAXTER Charles age 57y funeral at Woodhull, NY July 3, 1879

BARTON Thomas abt 80y formerly of Bath, NY in Batavia, NY July 16, 1879, buried Bath

BARNEY Elijah in Soldiers and Sailors Home in Bath, NY July 15, 1879

DEATH NOTICES

COVERT Matt at Col. Bills Creek in Canisteo, NY July 13, 1879

CALLAHAN Michael age 24y in Corning, NY July 15, 1879

COOPER Mahala age 84y relict of Edmond Cooper in Painted Post, NY July 10, 1879

BAILEY May age 1y 2m 9d dau of John C. and Lucy A. in Wayne, NY July 14, 1879

HERRICK Isaac age 53y in Hornellsville, NY July 26, 1879

CARTER Mary age 63y wife of David Carter in Corning, NY July 28, 1879

ROSS Maria G. age 56y wife of A. J. Ross in E. Campbell, NY July 20, 1879

WINTERMUTE Nathaniel B. age 62y in Campbell, NY August 9, 1879

BESSIL Mrs. Henry age 43y in Addison, NY August 2, 1879. Leaves 5 children

TOWLE Mrs. Lucy A. formerly of Bath, NY in Grafton, Mass. August 17, 1879

LOOK Dr. Sylvester in his 79th yr in Bath, NY August 20, 1879. 2 sons and 5 daus by 1st wife who died 1870, 2 children by 2nd marriage

ROSE Mrs. Mahala age 70y in Kanona, NY August 7, 1879

EDGETT Bertha age 3m dau of George and Cora in Howard, NY August 16, 1879

WHEELER Eldrich age 70y formerly of Prattsburgh, NY in Bath, NY August 20, 1879

SEWARD Mary Louisa age 64y in Bath, NY August 28, 1879. Born New York City dau of John I. **MUMFORD**, married 1841 Benjamin J. Seward

LOVELESS Daniel age 63y in Corning, NY September 5, 1879

SHERWOOD Mrs. Wesley in Cameron, NY September 10, 1879

PIERCE Mary age 72y wife of Allen Pierce of Pulteney at dau Mrs. Daniel **FROST** in Wheeler, NY September 11, 1879. Married 51 yrs

MILLER Jane F. in her 38th yr wife of William Miller in Howard, NY September 16, 1879. Dau of Hiram **CLARK** of Campbell, NY

HULSE Benjamin age 78y in Jasper, NY September 21, 1879

GANTROP Mrs. Thomas age 45y in Corning, NY September 18, 1879 (paper gives date as October 18, 1879, date of issue October 9, 1879)

LEONARD Barnard a young man of Corning, NY October 7, 1879

WARD Mrs. Lewis in Caton, NY October 27, 1879

HARE John age 61y in Painted Post, NY October 25, 1879

WOOD George B. age 74y 24d in S. Dansville, NY October 10, 1879

FARWELL Hannah M. age 73y wife of Benjamin Farwell and dau of Judge John KNOX in Painted Post, NY October 24, 1879

BRADY Nettie J. age 24y dau of Robert and Mary in Cameron, NY October 31, 1879

COLE Alta age 13y dau of Barnum Cole in Prattsburgh, NY November 7, 1879

CHAPMAN Mrs. Rev. A. in Avoca, NY November 10, 1879

CRANMER George E. age 39y 6m 22d in Wheeler, NY November 11, 1879

VEEDER Mary C. age 25y wife of Byron Veeder in Cohocton, NY November 14, 1879. Born October 13, 1854 in Bath, NY

COE Fanny age 20y 3m 20d dau of William B. and Mrs. Carrie RUGGLES in Crystal Springs, NY November 23, 1879

KINNEY Michael run over by train in Hornellsville, NY November 21, 1879

VEAZIE Freddie C. age 7y son of C. H. in Coopers Plains, NY November 19, 1879

BATCHELDER Frances S. wife of John R. Batchelder of Lock Haven Pa. at Knoxville November 23, 1879

BRADLEY Zera age 83y 8m 9d in Bath, NY November 13, 1879

HATCH Mr. Marion in Cameron, NY December 1, 1879. Married 1 yr

BUTLER Lydia (STORY) age 83y in Avoca, NY November 28, 1879 (Ontario Co. papers please copy)

BROWN Mark J. in his 21st yr at Father's in Bath, NY November 27, 1879

STANTON Mrs. Mary J. from injuries in fall in Cohocton, NY December 12, 1879

HAIGHT Mrs. Daniel W. age 76y at dau in W. Urbana, NY December 17, 1879

REILLY William a brakeman run over by train December 21, 1879

COSS Catherine wife of Daniel M. Coss in Bath, NY December 23, 1879

BALLARD Fred E. in Troy, Pa. December 17, 1879

HARTY Roger age 24y in Hornellsville, NY December 21, 1879

DE WITT Sally age 80y wife of John De Witt at son's Jacob November 26, 1879. Born

DEATH NOTICES

1799 in New Brunswick, NJ, came to Tyrone, NY with parents at age 15 yrs. Married 1818 and moved to Starkey, NY

CRAWFORD Nelson R. age 74y in Lawrenceville, Pa. December 18, 1879

EARLL Mrs. Hannah age 64y at son's William in Thurston, NY December 15, 1879

HOPKINS Tannie age 84y wife of Samuel Hopkins in Bath, NY (Newspaper date January 1, 1880). Born April 14, 1795 in Putnam Co. NY. Married 1819, 10 children. Son William died 1876 age 43y

FORGUS M. in Painted Post, NY December 30, 1879

GLOVER Gilbert at Loon Lake, NY January 2, 1880

AULLS John age 54y in Corning, NY December 26, 1879

SWAIN Edward age 21y son of John Swain of Corning, NY January 5, 1880

FARWELL Alfred T. in his 24th yr son of Mrs. B. F. Farwell in Corning, NY January 6, 1880

GORTON Willie age 15y son of William and Helen in Corning, NY January 1, 1880

ROLOSON Ida age 19y dau of Lysander and Lydia in Hornby, NY January 6, 1880

BEVERLY Ella dau of Frank and Marilla in Cohocton, NY December 28, 1879

MC FARREN Mary in her 65th yr wife of A. C. in Painted Post, NY January 7, 1880

SUTTON Lottie age 2m dau of Dr. and Mrs. Orlando Sutton January 12, 1880

GLEASON Margaret age 61y 5m 4d wife of Aaron Gleason in Wayne, NY December 31, 1879. Leaves 8 children

VAUGHN Eliza in Jasper, NY January 13, 1880

DIMMICK Lydia Jane age 52y wife of Edward in Thurston, NY December 26, 1879. Born Eagle Valley, NY nee **THOMPSON**, married 1853, leaves husband and 5 children

GORDON Barlow age 53y in Gibson, NY January 19, 1880

HAUBER John age 17m 11d son of John and Ellen in Rexville, NY January 24, 1880

PETERS Ezra abt 40y formerly of Elmira, NY in Soldiers and Sailors Home in Bath, NY January 30, 1880

COOK Alice age 18y dau of Thomas Cook of E. Troupsburgh, NY funeral at Woodhull, NY January 29, 1880

GOULD Thomas P. age 65y in Woodhull, NY January 31, 1880

STEWART Col. William in his 82nd yr in Campbell, NY February 4, 1880. Born July 14, 1798 in Stillwater, NY, came to Campbell age 7y. Leaves wife and dau Mrs. COSS

WHITE David C. in his 30th yr son of Patrick White of S. Howard, NY in Detroit, Mi. February 4, 1880

LANNING Mrs. Polly age 75y at son's Henry Lanning in Woodhull, NY February 13, 1880. Also leaves son William

SMITH Edwin age 72y found dead in barn at Bath, NY February 16, 1880. Born 1808 in Rutland, Vt. son of Rev. David Smith. Came to Steuben Co. age 5y

VAN NESS Sarah in her 59th yr in Hornellsville, NY February 19, 1880

FRYE Benjamin F. in his 25th yr in Bath, NY February 23, 1880

COVERT Bell W. age 20y wife of L. H. Covert in Bath, NY February 21, 1880

FORT Isaac age 57y 6m 7d in Thurston, NY January 6, 1880. Leaves wife and 6 children

BOYER Mary age 23y dau of William Boyer in Caton, NY March 13, 1880

JOHNSON Lucius G. age 68y son of Benoni Johnson in Caton, NY March 18, 1880

BATCHELDER Charles L. age 28y at Father's in Caton, NY March 6, 1880. Married October 16, 1878 Hattie May VOSE of Merchantville, NY

LEW Mary E. wife of Henry Lew of E. Troupsburgh, NY March 3, 1880

WHITING Mary age 49y eldest dau of William H. BULL in Bath, NY March 15, 1880

NORTON Nannie wife of Thomas H. Norton of Wheeling W. Va. at Father's Gratton H. WHEELER in Hammondsport, NY February 26, 1880

SPRAGUE Joseph H. age 74y in Howard, NY February 6, 1880

PAWLING Sarah age 65y relict of Henry Pawling in Fremont, NY March 10, 1880

DUNAVON Robert Emmett age 12y 5m son of John and Elizabeth Dunavon in Hornellsville, NY March 14, 1880

SCHEIRUMANN Catherine age 65y in Hornellsville, NY March 14, 1880

DOWDELL Roger J. age 4m son of J. H. and Annie Dowdell in Hornellsville, NY March 14, 1880

BEATY Abram D. age 54y in Painted Post, NY February 27, 1880

DEATH NOTICES

VAN GORDER Sally age 81y 11m 16d (formerly of Bath, NY residing with dau Mrs. William **WALTERS**) at son's in Canandaigua, NY February 24, 1880

RICE Mrs. Placentia age 59y 5m 1d in Prattsburgh, NY March 2, 1880

BENT David in her 33rd yr of Hornellsville, NY in Cameron, NY March 6, 1880

LA BOUR Jacob age 78y in Hornellsville, NY March 20, 1880

TULLEY Newcomb T. age 81y formerly of Bath, NY bro of Mrs. James M. **EDWARDS** in Shullsburg, Wis. February 17, 1880. Went West 1855 with son N. E. Tulley and family. Son William W. died 1856, Henry B. died 1870. His wife died 1877 and youngest son Isaac B. also died

EMS Minna in Hornellsville, NY March 26, 1880

LOVEJOY Mrs. Mary age 81y in Hornellsville, NY March 24, 1880

HUNTER Maria widow of Dr. Hunter in Jasper, NY March 23, 1880

COLE Mrs. Phoebe in Hornellsville, NY March 26, 1880

PAGE Ann Elizaeth age 49y in Hornellsville, NY March 27, 1880

STILES Mrs. Anna in Young Hickory, NY March 20, 1880

WILCOX Benjamin B. in his 54th yr in Hornellsville, NY March 24, 1880

WOODARD Jacob in his 87th yr at dau Mrs. Dr. **EVERETT** in E. Campbell, NY March 21, 1880. Born Vt., married 1816 in Wardensborough Betsey **WILDER**, 5 children Mrs. Isaac **GOODSELL** of Painted Post, NY, Mrs. Dr. Everett and Nathan of E. Campbell surviving. Wife died abt 8 yrs ago

HOUGHTON Sophronia M. age 65y wife of Amory Houghton in Brooklyn, NY March 19, 1880. Leaves sons Amory Jr. and Charles F. of Corning, NY

WARD ____ infant son of Frank and Alice Ward in Canisteo, NY March 25, 1880

SMEAD Anna E. in her 25th yr wife of James B. Smead and dau of J. W. **AYLER** formerly of Bath, NY in Baltimore, Md. March 17, 1880

MARVIN Mrs. Mary Jane age 37y in Hornellsville, NY April 11, 1880

AIKEN William Fred in his 29th yr in Hornellsville, NY April 11, 1880

AYERS William S. age 50y in Boulder, Col. March 16, 1880

BAULCH William age 25y nr Avoca, NY April 15, 1880

SUNDERLIN Rev. A. W. in Wayne, NY April 1, 1880

CARTER David in his 81st yr of Knoxville, NY at dau Mrs. John **WILCOX** in Painted Post, NY April 11, 1880

GANSEVOORT Helen age 69y widow of Ten Eyck Gansevoort of Bath, NY on way home from Florida nr Wilson, NC April 21, 1880. She was youngest of 11 children of Moses **LYON** who came from Lyons Farms, NJ. Husband died September 1842 leaving 2 sons and 2 daus, youngest son Ten Eyck Jr. died early manhood, dau Mary wife of John N. **HUNGERFORD** of Corning, NY dec. 2 children living Conrad of Bath, NY and Mrs. B. F. **ANGELL** of Geneseo, NY formerly Mrs. Duncan S. **MAGEE**

SEELEY Henry T. age 56y in Bath, NY April 23, 1880

WALDO Emeline age 51y wife of L. A. Waldo in Canisteo, NY April 21, 1880

SUMNER Hattie in her 25th yr dau of A. N. Sumner in Wayne, NY April 19, 1880

ODSON Thomas in Woodhull, NY April 21, 1880

SMITH Ira M. formerly of Cohocton and Naples, NY in Jackson, Mi. April 21, 1880

CAMPBELL John age 74y in Hornellsville, NY May 1, 1880

HAVENS Mrs. Sarah age 87y in Corning, NY April 15, 1880

ROBINSON Eli age 75y in Western Ks. March 14, 1880

GARMAN Nellie age 1y dau of John and Helen Garman in Bath, NY May 11, 1880

VAUGHN Annie age 17y dau of John Vaughn in Corning, NY April 30, 1880

CROSS Reuben L. age 62y 9m 11d in Pulteney, NY May 4, 1880. Born July 23, 1817 in Pound Ridge, NY son of Lewis Cross. Came to Pulteney 1830. Married November 8, 1846 Elsie **STEWART** dau of Selden Stewart. Leaves wife, 2 sons and 2 daus

WELTY Susan O. age 35y wife of Jacob Welty at Father's Philo **BAXTER** in Woodhull, NY May 11, 1880. Leaves husband and 1 son

DAVISON Thomas age 54y in Bath, NY May 12, 1880. Came from N. Ire. Married Elizabeth **LINDSAY** dau of James Lindsay

DENNIS Mabel inf child of Boardman and Ann in Hornellsville, NY May 11, 1880

HITCHCOCK William in Canisteo, NY May 18, 1880

MORAN John suicide in Hornellsville, NY May 29, 1880

WEEKS Davis S. age 75y in Corning, NY May 25, 1880

PALMER Warren hit by falling tree in Caton, NY May 31, 1880

DEATH NOTICES

ELLISON Amanda in Hornby, NY May 18, 1880. Born January 6, 1822 in Rensselaer Co. NY, moved to Dryden, NY then to Tyrone, NY where she married 1838

TOWLE Miss Lydia E. in her 59th yr in Towlesville, NY May 24, 1880

JONES Mrs. D. D. in Avoca, NY May 26, 1880

STEVENS ____ infant son of Elias and Emily Stevens in Canisteo, NY May 30, 1880

TERBELL Dr. William age 82y at son's W. D. Terbell in Corning, NY June 3, 1880

ROWELL Mrs. Shepard age 52y in Cohocton, NY June 8, 1880. Born June 1828 in Italy Hollow, NY, buried in Italy Hollow

NILES Moses in his 80th yr in Bath, NY (Newspaper date June 18, 1880). Born June 14, 1880 in Cooperstown, NY. Leaves 1 son Jerome and 5 daus

TORRANCE Mrs. Catherine J. age 49y in Bath, NY June 11, 1880

TAYLOR Daniel L. in his 49th yr in Bath, NY May 17, 1880

STANTON Lewis of Adrian, NY run over by train at Hornellsville, NY June 19, 1880

DAVIS John William in his 40th yr in Caton, NY June 19, 1880. Born August 26, 1840 in Germany and came to US with parents 27 yrs ago. Leaves wife and 4 children. Served in Civil War

ROBINSON Mr. A. E. in Erwin Center, NY June 17, 1880

HESS Martha T. wife of Alexander Hess in Bath, NY June 25, 1880. Born December 1, 1821 in Hector Falls, NY, married age 19y. Leaves 2 children R. A. of Col. and Mrs. Agustus **DE PUYSTER** of Bath

SWART Mrs. Cornelia J. in her 76th yr formerly of Bath, NY dau of Benjamin **SMEAD** in Huntington, Oh. June 27, 1880

KOESTER Charles found dead in bed in Hornellsville, NY July 14, 1880

PETERS Mrs. David S. age 26y in Thurston, NY June 24, 1880

MURPHY Jeremiah age 71y in Bath, NY July 29, 1880

WHITE Lester S. abt 60y in Caton, NY July 29, 1880

PARKHURST K. E. age 23y killed Frances S. **HOWELL** age 22y then killed himself in Bath, NY August 14, 1880

MANLY Archibald age 75y in Tuscarora, NY July 28, 1880

AULLS William age 78y in Bath, NY August 23, 1880. Leaves 6 children

STEWART Sally abt 80y wife of Samuel Stewart in S. Howard, NY August 31, 1880

MILLER William B. age 86y in Woodhull, NY August 30, 1880

BROOKS Davie age 13m son of Levi and Helen Brooks in Bath, NY August 15, 1880

EMERSON Charles in his 45th yr in Bath, NY August 22, 1880. Born Thurston, NY, and moved to Bath with widowed Mother age 18y. Age 21y married Susan L. **BUCK** and had 4 sons, 3 living

WHITE Sarah age 27y wife of Jerome White and dau of Seymour **SANFORD** by runaway horses in W. Jasper, NY September 8, 1880. Leaves 1 dau age 7y

WELLS Benjamin age 82y at dau Emeline **WEBB** in Naples, NY September 4, 1880. Born August 24, 1801 in Syracuse, NY son of James Wells who was born September 10, 1776 at S. Ole, Long Island, NY son of James. Moved to Avoca, NY 1840, to Ind. 1867 where wife died, then moved back to Avoca

HABER William age 8y son of William H. and Nancy Haber in W. Union, NY September 8, 1880

EAVENS Adelaide age 1y dau of Welcome and Aliena Eavens in W. Union, NY September 9, 1880

KREIDLER Eliza Wood in her 39th yr wife of Fred M. Kreidler in Rogersville, NY September 23, 1880

CLISDELL William in Bath, NY September 22, 1880. Born 1822 in Caven Co. Ire. Came to US January 1846 with parents, 5 sisters, 1 bro and cousin William **DAVISON**, 1 sister died abt 8 yrs ago in Buffalo, NY and is buried Huntington, Long Island, 2 sisters in Chicago, Ill. 2 in Howard, NY and bro Edward in Corning, NY. He married sister of Hugh and Sam **MC CHESNEY** who died nr 4 yrs ago. Leaves 1 son Robert of Corning, NY

CHURCH Eunice in her 80th yr widow of Robert W. in Bath, NY October 14, 1880

WHITE James age 67y in Howard, NY October 27, 1880. Born N. Ireland

SILSBEE Clara dau of N. M. Silsbee in Haskinsville, NY November 4, 1880

PICKLE Abraham crushed by cars in Hornellsville, NY November 7, 1880

COTTON W. L. age 18y son of William G. Cotton of Fremont, NY in Albion, NY (Newspaper date November 19, 1880)

GOULD Ellen age 21y wife of H. W. Gould in Woodhull, NY October 29, 1880

DUTCHER Ruloff son of William and Mary Dutcher and bro of William A. Dutcher and Mrs. A. S. **HOWELL** of Bath, NY in Portland, Ore. November 14, 1880

DEATH NOTICES

LINDSAY Jennie dau of late John Lindsay in Bath, NY November 27, 1880

HARRISON Mrs. Myron J. in her 29th yr dau of Thomas and Sally **ELLISON** in Hornby, NY November 17, 1880. Dau Bertha died November 7, 1880 in her 10th yr and son Charlie died November 10, 1880 age 7 yrs.

SILSBEE Sarah Ann wife of A. H. Silsbee in Summit Twp. Mi. November 17, 1880. Born March 20, 1814 in NJ. Went to Mi. in 1852. Son Theodore A. of Bath, NY

COREY Mrs. Maria in Wallace, NY December 13, 1880

BROWN Ada widow of Sylvester Brown on Potter Hill, NY December 13, 1880

GUNN Clarissa B. age 64y wife of Stephen G. in Horseheads, NY December 20, 1880

GILBERT A. age 79y in Fremont, NY December 26, 1880

MERRILL Sarah in her 74th yr wife of Jacob in Cameron, NY December 27, 1880. Born August 22, 1807 in Montgomery Co. NY. Married October 14, 1826 and came to Steuben Co. 1832. Leaves husband and 3 children

MORRISON Joseph age 24y son of James Morrison in Bath, NY December 27, 1880

JACKMAN Willie age 4w son of W. J. and Kate M. Jackman January 6, 1881

WALDO M. D. relict of Aaron Waldo formerly of Prattsburgh, NY in Quincy, Ill. December 23, 1880

FIELD Agnes Fichlia age 57y wife of Rev. Field nr Buck Schoolhouse January 6, 1881. Leaves husband and 5 children

LANG Mrs. Lydia age 38y in Hornellsville, NY January 16, 1881

FAUCETT Miss Ella in Savona, NY January 25, 1881

MILLER Clara L. age 11y 3m dau of William H. Miller at Grandfather's Hiram **CLARK** in Campbell, NY (Newspaper date January 28, 1881)

BRIGGS Jonathan age 70y in Corning, NY January 22, 1881

SHULTS John age 82y in Cohocton, NY February 6, 1881

HALLETT Darius age 55y in Adrian, NY rec (Newspaper date February 25, 1881)

EASON William of Soldiers and Sailors Home in Bath, NY hit by train February 22, 1881. Res. of Buffalo, NY

SPRAGUE Lucinda in her 64th yr relict of Joseph in Howard, NY February 26, 1881

ROGERS Henry W. formerly of Bath, NY in Ann Arbor, Mi. (News rec'd March 2,

1881). Born February 14, 1806 in Unadilla, NY

HENDRICK Mrs. A. age 68y in Troupsburgh, NY March 5, 1881

PETERSON John in Cameron Mills, NY March 5, 1881

WILLIAMS J. G. age 75y in Soldiers and Sailors Home in Bath, NY March 15, 1881

WILLIAMSON Mrs. D. L. in Cameron, NY March 25, 1881

TYLER Cynthia widow of A. N. Tyler in Cohocton, NY March 29, 1881

LOOK Jennie age 14y dau of E. V. Look at brother-in-law's Abraham **SUTTON** in Bath, NY March 15, 1881

LEE Wellington age 76y formerly of Hornellsville, NY in New York City March 21, 1881. Born Sheridan, NY and lived New York abt 35 yrs

BAKER Lucretia wife of John K. Baker of Kanona, NY in Bath, NY April 5, 1881. Dau of Joseph C. **POWELL** of Towanda, Pa. Married 24 yrs

ELLIS Ida in Avoca, NY April 4, 1881

FAUCETT Miss Margaret age 45y dau of late Robert Faucett and sister of Mrs. William **LINDSAY** funeral April 2, 1881

SCRIPTER Nancy A. nr 20y dau of Amasa and Margaret **HARRIS** in Howard, NY March 29, 1881

MC ENTEE Peter age 62y shot by his nephew John Mc Entee age 16y son of his bro Hugh in Bath, NY April 19, 1881

WAGNER John J. in his 43rd yr in Avoca, NY April 19, 1881

LINDSAY Katie age 5m dau of James and Maggie in Bath, NY April 25, 1881

BRACE ___ age 4y 10m 21d child of Daniel and Phebe in Wayne, NY April 22, 1881

OATLEY Joseph L. age 23y 3m son of Almeron and Maria Oatley of Towlesville, NY drowned in Demings Pond April 27, 1881

CROUCH Ira age 32y in Cohocton, NY April 22, 1881

PRATT Samuel Lucillus age 6y son of Rev. S. W. Pratt and Lucillus **(FIELD)** in Campbell, NY May 3, 1881

SHEPARD Lawrence Church age 9y 4m 25d eldest son of William H. and Adelaide C. Shepard in Bath, NY May 8, 1881

GOFF Laney age 74y widow of P. C. Goff in Howard, NY May 2, 1881

DEATH NOTICES

JOHNSON Rosa age 22y wife of Jerome Johnson in Jasper, NY May 6, 1881

GATES Catherine age 63y wife of A. H. Gates in Savona, NY May 9, 1881

ROBIE Ira Calkins child of Helen and late Levi Robie in Bath, NY May 16, 1881

HUNTER Catherine A. age 47y wife of George Hunter and dau of late James **LITTLE** in Bath, NY May 24, 1881

WAIT Caroline age 73y in Bath, NY May 23, 1881. Born Malta, NY, married abt 1839 Marvel Wait and came to Bath 1849

HOLLIS George H. Editor of Addison Advertiser May 20, 1881. Born April 17, 1841 in Tuscarora, NY son of late William Hollis

FOGLE Nicolas age 35y in Wayland, NY June 6, 1881

HEDERMAN Bridget age 17y in Hornellsville, NY June 2, 1881

HILTON Mrs. V. R. of Hornby, NY in Corning, NY May 30, 1881

WILLIAMS William in Corning, NY June 2, 1881

GIFFORD Mary I. in Hornellsville, NY June 8, 1881

CAMPEN Mary age 60y in Hornellsville, NY June 9, 1881

MC CONNELL Francis age 67y in Horseheads, NY June 8, 1881

SAMHAMER Amanda age 27y wife of Jacob in Perkinsville, NY May 27, 1881

LANDERS Sophie age 37y wife of John Landers in Perkinsville, NY June 15, 1881

YOHAN Casper age 47y in Wayland, NY June 15, 1881

HORTON Oglesbe in His 58th yr in Savona, NY June 18, 1881

KNAPP James in his 72nd yr eldest son of Charles Knapp in Tyrone, NY June 17, 1881. Res. with dau Mrs. James **PADDOCK**. Married Mary **HALLOCK** who died December 4, 1869 leaving 5 children. Married (2) Martha **WILLOVER** who died 1878

MILLER Lizzie wife of William P. suicide by arsenic in Bath, NY June 22, 1881

MOONEY Sarah age 71y relict of Daniel Mooney at dau Mrs. J. R. **PUTNAM** in Wheeler, NY June 8, 1881

TARNEY Louisa age 50y in Woodhull, NY June 25, 1881

ALDRICH Almond D. son of Almond and Nettie in Woodhull, NY June 15, 1881

HELMER Betsey age 59y wife of Adrian Helmer in Fremont, NY June 20, 1881

BUSH Murray son of Wesley Bush in Cohocton, NY June 27, 1881

HILL Dewitt age 43y in Cohocton, NY June 29, 1881, buried S. Bradford, NY

TOBIAS Georgie age 9m 21d son of B. Tobias in Cohocton, NY June 29, 1881

VAN RIPER Mrs. Abram in Patchinville, NY July 4, 1881

SANFORD Silas age 75y in Corning, NY June 25, 1881

RUSSELL Mrs. Waldo dau of Col. James S. **MC KAY** of Campbell, NY in Concord, NH July 6, 1881

HARWOOD Mary Ann age 50y 26d wife of Francis A. Harwood in Hedgesville, NY July 8, 1881. Born June 12, 1831 in Troupsburgh, NY nee **HAYES**. Leaves husband and 1 dau

JAMES Rev. Norman B. in his 71st yr in Italy Hollow, NY July 2, 1881

TAYLOR Mrs. James at bro George **BOYD** in Pulteney, NY July 14, 1881

BURLINGAME Della in Rathbone, NY June 18, 1881. Born April 2, 1851 in Hornby, NY dau of Joseph Burlingame

MARVIN ___ dau of Knox Marvin in Cohocton, NY July 19, 1881

COCHRANE Ida dau of A. T. Cochrane in Corning, NY July 19, 1881

ALLERTON Mary A. consort of Delanson Allerton and dau of Moses and Mary **DUDLEY** of Bonny Hill, NY nr Savona, NY July 25, 1881. Born April 15, 1824 in Steuben Co. NY, married February 10, 1848. Leaves husband, 1 son and 2 daus

HICKOK Mrs. N. E. age 67y at son-in-law's Dr. L. E. **HORTON** in Avoca, NY July 27, 1881

TOWNSEND Theodore age 19y 4m 13d son of Walter and Mary Townsend in Addison, NY July 5, 1881. Born March 23, 1862 in Bath, NY

REYNOLDS James in Bath, NY August 12, 1881. Born 1822 in England

BARBER Lester E. son of J. W. Barber in Hornellsville, NY August 15, 1881

COOPER Jerusha age 53y of Corning, NY at Willard Asylum April 11, 1881

LAND Mrs. Martha age 86y at son-in-law's James A. **PARSONS** August 8, 1881

LAPP Mrs. ___ age 56y in Bath, NY August 21, 1881, buried Rochester, NY

DEATH NOTICES

CRONK Mrs. Mary age 77y in Havana, NY August 13, 1881

BONNEY Amelia **(LOOK)** age 35y wife of W. L. Bonney in Hornellsville, NY August 16, 1881

SEAMANS Ward age 11m son of Edwin and Stella in Savona, NY August 25, 1881

WOODRUFF Capitola age 11m dau of William and Caroline Woodruff in Savona, NY August 27, 1881

RICHARDSON Thomas age 80y in Howard, NY August 22, 1881

CARPENTER John age 55y in Penn Yan, NY August 20, 1881

SELLON John age 82y in Reading, NY August 19, 1881

HEDGES Seth N. atty in Dansville, NY August 27, 1881

JOHNSON J. M. age 76y in Woodhull, NY August 22/23, 1881

HEATH Hiram age 76y in Corning, NY August 24, 1881

DUNN Mrs. ____ age 65y widow of Thomas Dunn in Corning, NY August 19, 1881

CRAWFORD Lewis age 80y in Cameron Mills, NY August 18, 1881

HUFF George in Corning, NY August 22, 1881

BROTHERTON Thomas age 54y in Canisteo, NY August 20, 1881

WILLIS Henry in Hornellsville, NY September 4, 1881

MANNING Marcus age 51y in Addison, NY August 30, 1881

WARREN Mary A. age 71y widow of Phineas Warren at son's Francis in Warren Settlement, NY September 14, 1881

HARRINGTON John age 80y in Cameron Mills, NY September 10, 1881. Born May 17, 1801 in Brattleboro, Vt. Married December 26, 1825 in Chenango, Co. NY Nancy **MAR**, 5 children 3 living

CHURCH Augusta Ellen age 36y wife of Edwin L. Church and dau of Col. William H. **BULL** in Bath, NY September 21, 1881

BRAMBLE Ezra age 83y in Prattsburgh, NY October 6, 1881

BRINK Mrs. Nett at Mother's Mrs. R. R. **FARGO** in Pulteney, NY September 30, 1881

MURPHY Margaret age 17y dau of Patrick and Mary in Bath, NY October 8, 1881

WILLIAMS Adda S. age 3y 7m 21d dau of Henry L. and Mary A. Williams in Cameron, NY September 6, 1881

MOORE Le Clar in Avoca, NY October 11, 1881

RUMSEY Nathan age 68y in Campbell, NY September 24, 1881

CARR James age 55y in Corning, NY October 18, 1881

HASKINS William in his 85th yr at son's S. R. in Avoca, NY October 23, 1881

BENNETT Chauncey age 83y in Wayland, NY October 23, 1881

TRIPP Mrs. Elizabeth age 51y in Prattsburgh, NY October 19, 1881

FISHER Mrs. Rachel in her 86th yr at son-in-law's John **MC CONNELL** in Howard, NY October 13, 1881

JONES Amy age 62y wife of Israel Jones in Corning, NY October, 19, 1881

BURDICK Betsey age 84y Mother of Rev. H. P. in Hartsville, NY October 17, 1881

HUY Kittie H. R. age 32y wife of L. G. Huy of Corning, NY and dau of James **HEES** of Avoca, NY September 25, 1881

EWING Almira H. age 33y wife of Alexander Ewing and dau of Gen. J. H. **LANSING** in Corning, NY October 24, 1881

WATROUS Mrs. Nancy in her 80th yr in Cameron, NY August 26, 1881. Born March 18, 1802 in Phelps, NY, family moved to Rochester, NY where she married Samuel Watrous February 14, 1827 and moved to Cameron 1840. Husband died February 15, 1875 in his 85th yr, 8 children 3 sons and 2 dau living, 2 children died young and son Orra died 1857 age 27 yrs

BALDWIN Hannah age 91y 2m 18d relict of Israel at son's A. H. Baldwin in Howard, NY October 28, 1881. Born August 10, 1790 in Amsterdam, NY, married April 4, 1810 in Amsterdam. Husband died 1868, 8 children only 2 living

CLARK Daniel R. nr Morgan's Bridge, NY November 3, 1881

WHEELER Mrs. Barbara formerly of Avoca, NY in Buffalo, NY November 4, 1881

DENNIS Ann age 25y wife of Boardman Dennis and dau of Franklin and Rhoda **BATCHELOR** in Jasper, NY October 26, 1881

TAYLOR Sybil (**BARTLETT**) age 63y relict of Benjamin Taylor formerly of Pulteney, NY in Woodland, Ill. October 26, 1881

HOWARD Ethel age 4y 1m 15d dau of Charles E. and Louise F. Howard in Bryn Manor, Pa. November 1, 1881

DEATH NOTICES

BROWN Mary in her 66th yr wife of R. E. Brown in Cameron, NY September 29, 1881. Born October 17, 1815 in Canisteo, NY dau of Joseph **LOGHRY**

BARTON Ezra age 76y in Corning, NY November 13, 1881

ROSE Henry age 78y in Branchport, NY November 15, 1881

ELWELL Mrs. F. A. age 50y in Erwin Center, NY November 13, 1881

TRENKLER Elizabeth age 28y in Hornellsville, NY November 20, 1881

DOUGLAS Mollie (**GILBERT**) wife of Frank Douglas formerly of Painted Post, NY in Chicago, Ill. November 20, 1881

WRIGHT Hannah age 76y in Hornellsville, NY December 6, 1881

FOSS Joseph H. age 61y in Prattsburgh, NY December 5, 1881

JONES Wakefield age 64y in Wheeler, NY December 6, 1881

NEW Jacob in Cohocton, NY December 5, 1881

HARDER Mary wife of Henry Harder in Addison, NY December 12, 1881

CLARK Patrick age 78y in Addison, NY December 13, 1881

VAN VLECK Benjamin age 74y in Fremont, NY December 1, 1881

PIER Kate dau of Capt. Edward Pier in Corning, NY December 13, 1881

BULLARD Agnes age 78y wife of Joel Bullard in Howard, NY December 9, 1881

BADGER Angeline age 66y widow of John in Hornellsville, NY December 16, 1881

WOMBOUGH Maggie wife of Charles H. Wombough of Addison, NY in Hornellsville, NY December 11, 1881

MERRILL Mrs. Sarah in Neils Creek, Ny December 24, 1881

SCHWINGLE Mrs. Mary age 77y in Perkinsville, NY December 14, 1881

HARD Elizabeth age 70y widow of Rev. Amos Hard in Painted Post, NY December 20, 1881

HOFFMAN Will R. age 22y in Addison, NY December 26, 1881

KEOUGH Clarence age 6y son of John Keough in Bath, NY December 28, 1881

WIXSON Joel age 67y in Wayne, NY November 26, 1881. Born October 16, 1814 in Wayne eldest of 10 sons of Daniel Wixson. Married April 3, 1839 Lydia S. **WRIGHT**,

6 children 2 living

BOYD Robert A. age 56y of Woodhull, NY in Hornellsville, NY December 29, 1881. Born 1825 in Woodhull. Married November 22, 1859

BAILEY Eva in Hammondsport, NY December 21, 1881, buried Urbana, NY

BEDELL Elizabeth wife of Calvin C. Bedell in Eagle Valley, NY November 12, 1881. Born May 12, 1822 in Sandystone, NJ and married 1842

BRYANT Elizabeth age 83y 6m at son-in-law's C. E. **HOPKINS** in Bath, NY January 3, 1882. Born July 1798 in Co. Sligo, Ire., 2 bro late Mathew **SHANNON** of Bath, NY late Dr. Shannon of Campbell. NY and 2 sisters Mrs. John **FAUCETT** and Mrs. **LITTLE** of Bath, NY. Son James killed by lightning in Va., 3 daus Mrs. **MOWERS**, Mrs. **AULLS** and Mrs. Hopkins

GRAY Ambrose age 60y in Kanona, NY January 1, 1882. Leaves wife and 10 children

STEPHENS William H. in Canisteo, NY December 30, 1881

BARNED George age 59y in Corning, NY December 31, 1881

CONNORS Bernice in Hornellsville, NY January 5, 1882

FOSTER Mrs. Esther age 81y in Hornellsville, NY December 29, 1881

ROWLEY Josiah age 81y in Troupsburgh, NY rec (Newspaper date January 13, 1882)

METZ Adalme wife of William Metz in Troupsburgh, NY December 20, 1881

HOFFMAN Emma age 3y dau of Charles in Hornellsville, NY January 4, 1882

VAN ORSDALE James C. age 46y in Addison, NY January 2, 1882. Born July 2, 1835 in Broome Co. NY. Leaves wife and 1 son

LA GRANGE Sarah in Hornellsville, NY January 21, 1882

CLEVELAND Mrs. C. M. in Woodhull, NY January 16, 1882

BROWN Mrs. Benjamin one of the oldest res of Wayland, NY last wk (Newspaper date January 27, 1882)

MOORE James age 71y in Savona, NY December 2, 1881. Born February 24, 1810 in Savona. Leaves wife and 6 children

WOODS R. Robie son of David Woods in Chicago, Ill. (Newspaper date February 3, 1882) Born August 3 1858 in Bath, NY, buried Bath February 1, 1882

SPENCER Joshua G. age 28y in Corning, NY January 30, 1882

DEATH NOTICES

CARR Marinda age 82y of Thurston, NY at dau in Pulteney, NY January 30, 1882

RAYMOND Charlotte E. age 57y wife of T. in Corning, NY January 28, 1882

ALLEN Walter H. in the Soldiers and Sailors Home in Bath, NY February 6, 1882

SAXTON Benjamin age 85y old res of Howard, NY last wk (Newspaper date February 17, 1882)

HARRIS Mrs. Jane in her 82nd yr in Prattsburgh, NY January 29, 1882

DUNHAM David age 82y in Fremont, NY February 11, 1882

RIGBY Mrs. Ralph age 27y in Troupsburgh, NY February 7, 1882

STRONG Mrs. Isabella age 69y in Jerusalem, NY February 6, 1882

WHITE William in his 66th yr in Howard, NY February 14, 1882. Born Ireland and came to US in 1837

BATES Josephine in Hornellsville, NY February 19, 1882

CONDERMAN Sarah A. age 58y in Fremont, NY February 15, 1882

OLIVER Hiram formerly of Corning, NY in Mn. rec. (Newspaper date March 3, 1882)

COVELL Mrs. C. age 85y of Cameron, NY February 26, 1882

STONE D. H. in Arkport, NY February 23, 1882

HOLLAND Ellen in Hornellsville, NY February 25, 1882

CARRIER Mary J. wife of George W. in Hornellsville, NY February 22, 1882

SOULE Datus E. age 70y in Corning, NY March 1, 1882

ROSE O. W. in Gibson, NY March 3, 1882

SMITH Lizzie wife of Charles A. Smith on Pulteney Hill, NY last wk (Newspaper date March 17, 1882)

THORP Margaret wife of William J. Thorp in Hornellsville, NY March 11, 1882

SWARTHOUT Maria widow of Asa Swarthout in Wayne, NY February 19, 1882

PUTNAM Maria wife of Sylvester Putnam in Prattsburgh, NY March 7, 1882

MEYERS Margie (**HAMMOND**) wife of Lewis Meyers in Haskinsville, NY last wk (Newspaper date March 17, 1882)

NEWCOMB Charles abt 100y in Bradford, NY March 8, 1882. At one time he was a slave in this state

WILHELM Eugene age 27 formerly of Woohull, NY in Col. February 27, 1882

ROBIE Annie age 17y dau of Levi Robie in Bath, NY March 19, 1882

PAGE Ezekiel age 82y in Painted Post, NY March 21, 1882

FAUCETT Sandy age 27y son of Arthur and Mary Faucett in Manitoba, Can. W. November 14, 1881

MC COLLUM Hugh age 85y in Fremont, NY March 16, 1882

LOTTER M. age 53y of Bath, NY native of Landau, Bavaria, Germany March 24, 1882. Leaves wife and 3 children

DAWSON Robert B. in his 44th yr in Hornellsville, NY March 24, 1882

HALSEY Lucia wife of Peter Halsey and dau of James and Eunice **JOHNSON** one of the oldest settlers of Bath in Bath, NY March 27, 1882. Married May 31, 1838

DANIELS William H. age 46y son of Sylvanus W. Daniels while chopping wood for Eben **TOWLE** nr Towlesville, NY March 23, 1882. 1 son Sylvanus and dau Minnie by 1st wife. Married (2) Addie **WILLIS** of Towlesville, 1 infant dau

BRYAN Aseneth in her 76th yr wife of A. C. Bryan in Sonora, NY March 18, 1882. Born Jerusalem, NY, married in Monterey, NY October 11, 1831, 4 daus and 2 sons, 2 dau and 1 son dec.

PARKER Phebe relict of Lucius Parker in Rathbone, NY March 17, 1882. Born October 20, 1819 in Bath, NY. Married age 24y had 2 children, 1 died infancy and 1 dau Mrs. Thomas **ALDRICH** of Bath

SCHOFIELD ___ infant son of R. B. and Delia M. in Savona, NY March 23, 1882

GAY Frances E. age 20y 6m dau of George W. and Eleanor E. Gay in Bath, NY March 10, 1882

ADAMS Thomas J. age 59y in Prattsburgh, NY March 30, 1882

WILLIAMS Aaron age 58y in Prattsburgh, NY March 31, 1882

MILLER Fanny age 26y dau of William H. Miller threw herself into well in Greenwood, NY April 6/7, 1882

STICKNEY Tyler age 82y in Middlebury, Vt. January 31, 1882. Sons Julius and C. C. Stickney of Wheeler, NY. Married March 23, 1828 Lora **TREADWAY** of Shoreham, Vt. 10 children

DEATH NOTICES

HARDENBROOK Richard in Bath, NY April 6, 1882. Born 1809 in Hunterdon Co. NJ and came to Ovid, NY 1815. Married 1830 on his 21st birthday Catherine **SMITH** of Md. and came to Bath 1850

WRIGHT Mrs. W. W. in Woodhull, NY April 16, 1882, leaves husband and 4 children

DICKINSON Francis D. age 18y 11m 11m son of Mrs. Mary Dickinson in Bath, NY April 6, 1882

SPRAGUE Amos age 31y in Woodhull, NY April 14, 1882

MC DOWELL Georgie age 22y dau of Richard A. and Mariah Mc Dowell in Howard, NY April 22, 1882

PHELPS Hester (**MERHERTER**) widow of Capt. John Phelps in Bradford, NY April 19, 1882. Born March 17, 1794 in Lancaster, Pa. and moved to Fayette, NY age 30y to live with sister. Married March 9, 1823 and came to Bath, NY 1832

ALLISON Hannah at son's William Allison in Bath, NY April 26, 1882. Born 1818 in Bolinhurst, England and came to Bath in 1854 with 7 children, 6 living. Dr. Allison of Wayne, NY, William and Charles S. of Bath, Mrs. Carrie **WHITEHEAD** and Sarah **FRENCH** wife of Rev. J. B. French of Troy, Pa., Mrs. Elizabeth **SALT** of Canisteo, NY, eldest dau died in Iowa in 1859

WOODARD Fred W. age 22y son of late J. J. Woodard in Bath, NY April 30, 1882

HALLIDAY James Hervey in his 82nd yr in Thurston, NY May 5, 1882. Born December 2, 1800 in Bethlehem, Orange Co. NY and came to Steuben Co. 1825. Married (1) Eliza **WHITNEY** and (2) Mary Ann **LEACH**, married 41 yrs

GRAY Lydia Myrtle in her 70th yr wife of Daniel Gray formerly of Steuben Co. NY of Goodland, Ind. April 28, 1882. Born October 9, 1812 and married November 19, 1835. Arrived at Goodland April 28, 1868

ADAMS C. P. age 30y (colored) in Bath, NY May 9, 1882. Bro of R. W. of Bath and J. Q. Adams of Harrisburg, Pa.

SHEPARD Adelaide in her 41st yr wife of William H. Shepard and dau of late L. V. **CHURCH** in Bath, NY May 23, 1882. Born June 4, 1842 in Morris, Otsego Co. NY. Married September 13, 1865, husband of Albany, NY. Leaves 4 children

GUERNSEY Mrs. Alma age 94y 3m in Woodhull, NY May 12, 1882

GREEN George age 1y 2m 13d son of John and Cynthia Green at grandfather's in Woodland, Mi. May 9, 1882

SCOFIELD Sarah in her 79th yr Mother of John L. in Bath, NY May 24, 1882

SCOFIELD William A. in Corning, NY June 11, 1882

WHEELER Grace P. age 21y in Kanona, NY June 7, 1882

FORCE Levi an old res of Corning, NY June 22, 1882

WHITAKER Jonathan in Campbell, NY June 18, 1882. Born April 24, 1816 in Bath, NY nr Savona. Leaves wife and 2 sons

WHITE Robert S. son of Patrick White of Howard, NY suicide by jumping from train going from Utica Asylum to Ovid, NY (Newspaper date July 7, 1882)

ERSKINE Thomas age 40y from too much whiskey in Savona, NY July 4, 1882

SNYDER Leo age 4y son of George P. kicked by horse in Cohocton, NY July 8, 1882

SHARP Lawrence I. Sr. in Howard, NY July 7, 1882

CLARK N. G. age 67y in Bath, NY July 11, 1882. Born April 18, 1815 in Amsterdam, NY and came to Steuben Co. 1835 with Father. Married April 4, 1838 Elma **HOOSE** in Tompkins Co. NY. Leaves wife, 1 son and 4 daus

WHITING Sarah age 84y 4m relict of Maj. John W. Whiting in Howard, NY July 15, 1882. Born March 15, 1798 in Candia, NH 6th dau of Moses and Lydia **EMERSON** and came to NY 1822. Married January 1, 1821 and husband died June 15, 1871, 8 children 4 living

VAN WIE Jonas age 51y in Bath, NY July 21, 1882. Leaves wife, 1 son and 1 dau

GOULD Hannah E. in her 61st yr relict of Theodore A. Gould formerly of Bath, NY in Rochester, NY August 7, 1882

SPAULDING Catherine age 73y wife of Philo B. Spaulding in Bath, NY August 6, 1882. Born December 20, 1810 dau of late Thomas **METCALFE** of Bath 1 of 12 children, names bro George Spaulding of Buffalo, NY and siter Mrs. Ellen **GIBBS** of New York City

EMERSON Edward A. age 26y formerly of Bath, NY in Buffalo, NY August 6, 1882

HESS John P. in his 15th yr son of George P. Hess formerly of Bath, NY drowned in Iowa River August 16, 1882

LOGHRY Charles age 70y in Cameron, NY August 13, 1882. Leaves wife and 2 children

BAUTER Mrs. Clarence funeral at Towlesville, NY August 21, 1882

HORR Miss Mary in Cohocton, NY August 16, 1882

HESS George P. formerly of Bath, NY son of Hiram R. Hess in Iowa August 26, 1882. Went to Iowa age 16 yrs, married Ella **MURRAY** dau of Dr. Henry Murray, 4 children, 2 living

DEATH NOTICES

EDGETT George in Howard, NY September 5, 1882

CURTIS Rev. C. G. age 69y former Pastor in Jasper, NY at Hammondsport, NY August 19, 1882

FLETCHER Apollos abt 80y of Bath, NY in Co. Home September 1, 1882

CLARK Parmelia age 95y relict of Joshua Clark and dau of Henry **MC GONEGAL** in Avoca, NY August 25, 1882. Born August 25, 1778. 1 bro Oren Mc Gonegal

HIGGINS Frank D. age 41y in Bath, NY September 29, 1882. He was son of Dr. John D. Higgins and on Mother's side a grandson of Rev. David Higgins. Pastor of Pres. church 1813-1831

FENN Phillip C. age 81y at dau Mrs. Conrad **GANSEVOORT** in Bath, NY October 5, 1882

PURDY Mrs. W. S. an old res of Corning, NY October 9, 1882

BISHOP Jacob age 61y native of Troupsburgh, NY rec. (Newspaper date October 13, 1882)

SCHENCK Garrett age 68y formerly of Bath, NY in Jasper October 16, 1882

WHITE Margarette age 66y wife of J. L. White in Prattsburgh, NY November 4, 1882

HUNT Otis age 78y in Dixon, Ill. November 2, 1882

SULLIVAN Thomas abt 21y hit by train in Wayland, NY November 16, 1882

HOLLEY Mrs. Nancy age 68y in Hammondsport, NY rec. (Newspaper date November 24, 1882)

LARKIN William an old res of Cohocton, NY November 21, 1882

PRENTISS Fanny (**LEDYARD**) age 72y widow of William Prentiss in Pulteney, NY November 12, 1882. Native of Guilford, Ct. dau of Daniel **BENTON**, 6 bros and 3 sisters

HUBER Charles in his 43rd yr in Bath, NY December 19, 1882. Born June 8, 1839 in Germany. Served Civil War Co. G. 107th Reg. NYV

PERRY Catherine age 77y at dau Mrs. B. **TOBIAS** in Hedgesville, NY December 10, 1882

BURDEN Betsey age 74y in Fremont, NY December 30, 1882

THURBER Ella age 21y in Caton, NY January 1, 1883

COLLINS Lena age 21y in Hornellsville, NY January 16, 1883

ROE John hit by train in Canisteo, NY January 15, 1883

SOULE Mrs. Hannah in Corning, NY January 22, 1883

BRIGGS Jane age 68y in Hornellsville, NY January 26, 1883

BENTON Norman at sister's Mrs. Orson HIGGINS January 25, 1883

PATTERSON John M. age 80y in Painted Post, NY February 2, 1883. Born March 23, 1804 youngest son of Benjamin and Sarah (MC CALLA). Married March 28, 1826 Mary COOK dau of Samuel Cook of Lindley, NY, 6 children, Temperance wife of John B. MC CURG of Corning, NY, Sarah wife of J. B. FINCH of Hornellsville, NY, Harriet A. wife of Henry PATTERSON of Janesville, Wis., Robert of Chicago, Ill., Alfred D. of New York City and Samuel of Painted Post

BEARD Harriet W. age 51y 4m 9d wife of James in S. Bradford, NY February 3, 1883

MC WHORTER Mrs. ___ at res of Marvin GOFF in Arkport, NY February 26, 1883. She was 1st white child born in Howard, NY

KINNEY George in Bath, NY February 7, 1883. Born March 30, 1797 in Ct. 1 of 9 children. Came to Chenango Co. NY in 1806 and 1817 to Tyrone, NY. Returned to Ct. and married Mary FRINK and moved to Thurston, NY. Wife, son and dau dec. Married (2) Mrs. NELLIS of Campbell, NY. 1 sister living Mrs. John MOORE of Savona, NY age 74y

SMITH Amy wife of Joseph S. Smith in Bath, NY February 9, 1883. Born September 12, 1805 in Homer, NY. Married May 17, 1827 in Bath, 11 children 6 living, names 1 Rev. James Smith

HANNAN Daniel at dau in Savona, NY March 4, 1883. Born March 5, 1814, res Steuben Co. until 1878 and moved to Monroe Co. Mi.

YOUNG William age 76y in Greenwood, NY February 28, 1883, res over 40 yrs

SMITH Jane wife of Jno. J. Smith nr Morgans Bridge March 8, 1883. Born 1803 North of England dau of Edward and Elizabeth RUTHERFORD. Came to US. in 1817 and married November 1825. 6 daus Elizabeth wife of C. ELLAS of Avoca, NY, Mary A., Margaret wife of P. VAN SCOTER of Hornellsville, NY, Alice Fanny wife of F. BRUNDAGE and Harriet wife of Dr. Ira P. SMITH

RUGGLES Mary age 87y at only son's W. B. Ruggles March 7, 1883. Sister of late Mrs. Moses H. LYON

PRENTISS John Q. A. age 41y son of late John A. in Pulteney, NY March 16, 1883

STILES John in Troupsburgh, NY March 9, 1883

HURLBURT Henry M. age 57y in Arkport, NY March 14, 1883

DEATH NOTICES

CHITTICK Margaret wife of John in Corning, NY March 14, 1883

GITHLER Jacob in Corning, NY March 14, 1883

STENARIOUS Henry age 29y in Wayland, NY March 18, 1883

MILLIMAN Ezra age 86y in Wayland, NY March 19, 1883

KELLOGG Mrs. W. S. in Wayland, NY March 20, 1883

FRENCH Lizzie dau of William French in Savona, NY March 19, 1883

MORRELL Willard in the Soldiers and Sailors Home in Bath, NY March 25, 1883. Res. Oneonta, NY, mem of Co. G. 105th Reg. NYV

EIGHALTZ Theodore at Soldiers and Sailors Home in Bath, NY March 27, 1883. Member of Co. G. 105th Reg. NYV

MURPHY James at Soldiers and Sailors Home in Bath, NY March 26, 1883. Member of Co. C. 99th Reg. NYV

MOORE George of Rochester, NY at Soldiers and Sailors Home in Bath, NY April 2, 1883

ROFF Sarah A. age 40y wife of Charles R. Roff in Pulteney, NY March 13, 1883

BREWSTER Mrs. Hannah in Savona, NY March 30, 1883

DE GRAFF Jackson injured rec in fight in Howard, NY March 29, 1883

DAY Mrs. Thomas in Greenwood, NY April 7, 1883

STEPHENS J. H. M. age 76y in Adrian, NY April 6, 1883

LILLY Samuel age 89y in Hornby, NY April 9, 1883

CLOONEY Andrew of Corning, NY from drinking in Bath Jail April 13, 1883

HARE Mary A. wife of William H. Hare in Centerville, NY April 9, 1883

HUBBARD Martha in her 85th yr in Caton, NY April 9, 1883

HOES John age 82y in Prattsburgh, NY April 23, 1883

SMITH Una Maria age 30y wife of J. K. Smith in Prattsburgh, NY April 15, 1883

BAKER Mrs. Isaac in Troupsburgh, NY April 16, 1883

CAMPBELL Patrick of Auburn, NY at Soldiers and Sailors Home in Bath, NY April 19, 1883. Member of Co. E. 3rd NY AV

STEUBEN COUNTY NEWSPAPERS 181

TUITT Phillip age 73y native of Ireland at Soldiers and Sailors Home in Bath, NY April 26, 1883. Member of Co. B. 162nd NY Inf.

HESS Hiram R. in his 74th yr in Bath, NY April 23, 1883. Born 1810 in Bloomsburgh, Pa. and came to Bath 1834. Married (1) Martha **POWELL** of Philadelphia, Pa. 2 children Mary Lizzie who died 20 yrs ago and George who died abt 6 yrs ago. Married (2) Mrs. Mary **(GANSEVOORT) HOWELL**

UNDERHILL William H. nr Dunkirk, NY returning from Cal. April 20, 1883. Born July 6, 1858 eldest son of A. L. Underhill

WARD John L. in Bradford, NY April 21, 1883

GIVENS Thomas in Bradford, NY April 26, 1883

DAVISON Israel formerly of Canisteo, NY in Lawrenceville, Pa. April 18, 1883

GRANGER Mrs. Monroe age 34y in Jasper, NY April 21, 1883

SUTHERLAND John in his 41st yr in Bath, NY May 5, 1883. Born August 19, 1841 in London, England and came to US in 1848. Enl. in Co. D. 107th Reg. NYV. Married 1866 Clara **SHAUT** of Bath. Names 3 bro James of Clinton, Io., Washington and George of Bath, 2 sisters Mrs.John **PRESHO** and Miss Alice

TOWLE George D. son of John Towle of the Turnpike nr freight house in Hornellsville, NY May 3, 1883

OSBORN Benjamin in Cameron, NY April 27, 1883. Born March 14, 1809 in Dutchess Co. NY and moved to Ontario Co. NY at age 19y. Married October 3, 1831 Alta **DALY** of Fairfield Co. Ct. Leaves wife 3 sons and 1 dau

KNAPP Mrs. Sarah in her 67th yr at dau Mrs. D. **LE FEVER** in Dundee, NY April 28, 1883. Born Carmel, NY, moved to Hillsdale, Mi. age 19 where she married William A. Knapp October 13, 1839. Leaves 4 children and 1 brother

STEWART Charles of Buffalo, NY son late R. B. Stewart of Bath, NY May 12, 1883

RICE Ezekiel age 72y in Howard, NY May 18, 1883

RICE Mrs. La Cont age 30y dau of Hiram **CULVER** in Canisteo, NY May 18, 1883. 1 dau born 5 wks ago

DEXTER Mrs. Milo on Oak Hill, NY May 19, 1883

GANBY Edward in Risingville, NY May 19, 1883

KING Harriet wife of W. Nelson King in Knoxville, NY May 16, 1883

RATHBUN Mrs. Dennison age 66y nr Haskinsville, NY May 16, 1883

DEATH NOTICES

CASE Mrs. Dora in Savona, NY May 19, 1883

WHITE Mrs. Mayette in Cohocton, NY May 26, 1883

BADGER Mrs. H. C. in Painted Post, NY May 25, 1883

PROVER James age 60y of Brooklyn, NY in Soldiers and Sailors Home in Bath, NY May 31, 1883

SULLIVAN Bartholomew of Mt. Morris, NY in Soldiers and Sailors Home in Bath, NY May 31, 1883

CASE Dr. A. B. in his 80th yr in Howard, NY May 30, 1883. Born October 16, 1803 in Westford, Vt. Wife died 1873 leaving 2 children

KASSON Edwin Ruthvin in his 67th yr ex sheriff of Steuben Co. May 26, 1883. Born 1816 in Oneida Co. NY

PALMER Rev. James L. former Pastor Zion Church of Bath, NY in Eatonstown, NJ May 31, 1883

WEBER Mrs. F. J. age 77y in Hammondsport, NY May 31, 1883

JEWELL Nelson age 67y in Wayne, NY June 10, 1883

MILLER Mrs. S. A. in her 64th yr in Savona, NY June 7, 1883. Leaves 4 daus

HALL Mrs. Jane in Pulteney, NY May 17, 1883

WHITE Evangie dau of Samuel White in Hammondsport. NY May 16, 1883

STRAIGHT Asa in Bath, NY June 11, 1883. Born 1800 in Vt. moved to Tioga Co. Pa. as child and to Wheeler, NY 60 yrs ago. Married 1822 Lydia **SPAULDING**, 9 children 7 living. 4 sons Col. A. D. and C. F. of Indianapolis, Ind., J. L. of Nashville, Tn. and S. W. of Dakota, 3 daus Mrs. S. M. **TOWNSEND** of Wheeler, NY, Mrs. S. H. **IVES** and Miss Jennie of Bath. Wife died abt 12 yrs ago and he moved to Bath with dau

WOODWORTH Mrs. Samuel F. dau of Melvin H. **DAVIS** of Naples, NY in Cohocton, NY June 30, 1883. Leaves husband and 3 children

HOAGLAND C. C. wife of J. C. Hoagland in Towlesville, NY June 28, 1883

STONE Joel in Woodhull, NY June 14, 1883. Native of Pulteney, NY, his wife was sister of Judge Owen **RILEY**

LUCAS Celestine wife of Morris H. formerly of Bath, NY in Denver, Col. June 7, 1883

TURNER James at Soldiers and Sailors Home in Bath, NY July 20, 1883

DONOVAN Dennis age 58y at Soldiers and Sailors Home in Bath, NY July 23, 1883.

Member of Co. A. 7th NY Art.

SHELTZ Christopher age 74y native of NJ at Soldiers and Sailors Home in Bath, NY July 23, 1883. Member of Co. C. 5th NY Art.

MILLER Mrs. Margaret age 86y in Bath, NY July 27, 1883. Born Schuyler Co. NY, spent some yrs out west, lived last few yrs with son Hiram Miller

KLECKLER Lucy in her 51st yr wife of Elias Kleckler in Savona, NY July 29, 1883. Leaves husband and 6 children

KERR John Morris age 60y at Soldiers and Sailors Home in Bath, NY August 5, 1883. Member of Col B. 1st NY Lincoln Cav.

PARKE John age 60y at Soldiers and Sailors Home in Bath, NY August 8, 1883. Member of Co. A. 36th NY Inf.

CURTIS Daniel B. age 57y in Curtisville, NY August 6, 1883. Born March 30, 1826 in Newtown, Ct. Went to Cal. 1849 and back 1857

FITCH Olive infant dau of Maj. J. B. and M. E. Fitch of Chicago, Ill. in Savona, NY August 2, 1883

CONKLIN Van Tassell age 55y at Soldiers and Sailors Home in Bath, NY August 15, 1883. Native of New York City and member of Co. K. 173rd Reg. NYV

NELLIS Eliza of Pittsburgh, Pa. wife of Aaron J. Nellis formerly of Bath, NY at bro Grattan H. **BRUNDAGE** August 8, 1883. Born September 11, 1839 dau of Jesse and Sarah Brundage. Married October 20, 1858, 2 sons Walter W. and Monroe B.

LOCKWOOD William age 77y in Tyrone, NY August 10, 1883

SAUER Tobias age 52y in Pleasant Valley, NY August 9, 1883

HALLOCK Stephen age 26y in Gibson, NY August 16, 1883

HUBBARD Cornelia in her 43rd yr wife of E. A. in Prattsburgh, NY August 11, 1883

BLIVEN Irena wife of Rev. E. F. Bliven in Mitchellville, NY August 17, 1883. Born November 30, 1817 in Geneseo, NY, married September 1, 1838. Leaves 1 son 4 daus

HENRY Isaac age 81y at dau Mrs. J. D. **FLINT** in Cohocton, NY August 21, 1883. Res Cohocton since age 10y. 3 daus Mrs. J. D. Flint, Mrs. O. S. **WINNAGLE** and Mrs. Seth **HILL**

WHEELER Eliza K. age 38y 5m at brother-in-law's D. C. **GIBBS** in Wheeler, NY June 26, 1883. Born Almond, NY dau of Samuel P. and Orilla **FARR**

CRAMER Jeremiah age 68y in Wheeler, NY August 25, 1883

DEATH NOTICES

GREEN Ella in her 17th yr dau of William Green formerly of Prattsburgh, NY in Hammondsport, NY August 16, 1883

BECKWITH Electra age 87y at dau Mrs. Emma **HOLCOMB** wife of Sumner Holcomb in Bath, NY September 15, 1883. Born Simsbury, Ct. 2 sons John and Collins, other dau Mrs. **BABCOCK** of Ct.

NORTON Charles H. age 38y in Greenwoood, NY September 28, 1883

MILES Mrs. Samuel in her 60th yr an overdose of morphine in Rathbone, NY September 23, 1883

BRUNDAGE D'Autremont age 74y relict of Charles Brundage September 23, 1883

EDWARDS John age 40y in Wheeler, NY September 28, 1883

FRENCH Miss Elizabeth age 44y in Bath, NY October 6, 1883. Born in Bath

SMITH Oren son of late Orange Smith of Bath, NY from disability in Civel War October 11, 1883

EDWARDS John age 57y in Avoca, NY October 12, 1883

WILLIAMS P. Platt age 55y suicide at Soldiers and Sailors Home in Bath, NY October 13, 1883. Member of Co. D. 192nd Reg. NYV

BAGENSTOCK Henry native of Germany at Soldiers and Sailors Home in Bath, NY October 11, 1883. Member of Co. I 93rd Reg. NYV

PERINE Peter age 72y at Soldiers and Sailors Home in Bath, NY October 17, 1883. Member of Co. C. 16th Reg.

CURTIS Walter age 27y son of Harris Curtis in Wayland, NY October 21, 1883

THOMPSON Anna M. age 17y in Howard, NY October 11, 1883

CORYELL Mrs. Betsey age 83y formerly of Steuben Co. NY in Lansing, Mi. October 15, 1883

FRANCE Daniel H. age 84y funeral at Jasper, NY November 1, 1883

BAKER Mary E. sister of Mrs. Melvine **GRAVES** of Howard, NY at sister's Mrs. R. S. **VAN KEURAN** last Friday (from the Sioux City Journal September 30, 1883) Born April 24, 1847 in Norwich, NY

DENNISTON John C. age 79y formerly of Prattsburgh, NY in Hudson, Wis. October 29, 1883

MC MASTER Amanda wife of Guy H. Mc Master in Bath, NY November 29, 1883. Born April 16, 1831 in Hartwick, NY 2nd dau of late R. W. **CHURCH** of Bath, NY and came to Bath 1845. Married October 18, 1853, 3 children Humphrey of Salt Lake City, Ut. and Alice and Kate of Bath

THOMPSON Mrs. Phebe Minnie age 45y at Father's David **CURTIS** in Painted Post, NY November 24, 1883

HOGOBOOM Mrs. Alcey age 62y sister of Judge Asem **EDDY** of Hornby, NY in New Lebanon, Ill. November 7, 1883

NORTHRUP Warren pioneer of Woodhull, NY November 27, 1883

CHURCH Kendrick age 52y of Hornellsville, NY son of Lawrence V. Church of Bath, NY in Corning, NY November 28, 1883

PLATT Cephas F. in Painted Post, NY November 28, 1883. Married Mary **ERWIN** dau of Gen. Francis E. Erwin

CAMPBELL Clarence died December 8, 1883. Born April 6, 1851 son of late Lt. Gov. Robert Campbell

SANFORD Sarah A. in her 49th yr wife of John Sanford in Savona, NY December 6, 1883. Leaves husband, 3 sons and 3 daus

GREEN Phillip in Rogersville, NY December 16, 1883

BOYD Daniel in E. Troupsburgh, NY December 4, 1883

GRIFFIN H. Etta age 25y at Mother's in Weston, NY December 7, 1883

GOODSELL Wilson L'amoreaux in his 21st yr son of John R. Goodsell in Bath, NY December 14, 1883

KNAPP Mrs. Van Rensalaer abt 50y suicide in Wayne, NY December 24, 1883

GILLETT Alfred age 56y formerly of Caton, NY in Owasso, Mi. November 27, 1883

WYMAN Lydia age 83y in Hornellsville, NY December 18, 1883

CAMPBELL A. L. age 59y wife of C. W. Campbell at brother's Merritt **DUSENBERRY** in Cohocton, NY December 31, 1883. Married 30 yrs, husband had 2 children by 1st marriage, William of Chicago, Ill. and 1 dau dec.

CURTIS L. H. age 99y in Avoca, NY December 29, 1883

WETMORE Keyser age 69 in Rathbone, NY rec. (Newspaper date January 4, 1884)

MATHEWS Nathaniel M. age 78y in Wheeler, NY December 21, 1883

ABER Janette age 50y wife of Alva Aber in Wheeler, NY December 22, 1883

DEATH NOTICES

LYON Harriet A. wife of James Lyon in Bath, NY December 30, 1883. Born August 26, 1826 eldest child of Reuben **ROBIE**. Leaves 1 son Reuben R. and 2 daus Sarah and Harriet

HOWELL William in Bath, NY January 2, 1884. Born 1805 in Sidney, NY. Father died Unadilla, NY in 1811. Mother and 4 children moved to Bath, Mother died 1822

GRIGGS Wilson in Troupsburgh, NY January 1, 1884

ROWLEY Almon age 77y in Caton, NY December 29, 1883

SIMONS William age 56y nr Ingleside, NY December 29, 1883

STILLSON Hezekiah formerly of Caton, NY December 28, 1883

ROESSLY Mrs. Christian age 92y in Wayland, NY December 24, 1883

LANE Ives at dau Mrs. T. J. **BENNETT** in Prattsburgh, NY December 29, 1883

BOOTH Sopronia age 72y wife of Spencer Booth in Syracuse, NY December 27, 1883. She was formerly wife of John W. **HOPKINS** Pastor of 1st Pres. church in Hornellsville, NY who died 1841

SHULTS Mrs. Mary Ann age 81y in Cohocton, NY January 4, 1884

COLE Harry in Rathbone, NY January 6, 1884

GRAY Mary A. in her 34th yr wife of Willard H. Gray formerly of Hammondsport, NY in Savona, NY January 8, 1884

SMITH Ira L. in Bath, NY January 16, 1884. Born Knoxville, Pa.

JOHNSON Mrs. Laura E. age 68y in Jasper, NY January 25, 1884

PERRY Woster in Hedgesville, NY January 18, 1884

CHURCH David in Troupsburgh, NY January 19, 1884

LYKE David age 29y formerly of Kanona, NY in Minneapolis, Mn. January 18, 1884

GLEASON Michael in Hornellsville, NY January 26, 1884

BURNS J. W. in his 49th yr in Hornellsville, NY January 26, 1884

GRIEF Julia A. age 18y in Hornellsville, NY January 27, 1884

PRESTON Jacob age 22y in Hartsville, NY February 1, 1884

MC KIBBEN Henry age 74y in Howard, NY January 31, 1884

LOPER Mrs. John age 90y in Rathbone, NY January 26, 1884

MAGEE Harriet age 27y wife of Ward Magee in Howard, NY January 30, 1884

DAVIS Amasa age 59y in Avoca, NY February 8, 1884

WHEELER Mary E. in her 49th yr wife of W. H. Wheeler in Cameron, NY January 12, 1884. Born Jasper, NY nee **DRAKE**. Married March 1854

FRENCH Philmon in Wheeler, NY February 7, 1884. Born April 30, 1806 in Reading, NY

WILLIAMS Newman P. age 76y in Woodhull, NY February 3, 1884

PIERCE Frank son of Fred Pierce in Painted Post, NY February 7, 1884

MASTEN Jane age 49y wife of P. Masten in Woodhull, NY February 7, 1884

PAGE Mrs. Chester of Howard, NY formerly of Prattsburgh, NY January 30, 1884

RICE Mrs. Sarah Mother of Mrs. D. D. **JONES** in Hornellsville, NY February 6, 1884

PRESTON Jacob age 22y February 1, 1884. Married Mary **MANHART** 1 yr ago

DUTCHER Freeman age 5y son of Freeman in Hornellsville, NY February 7, 1884

HARRISON John age 66y in Hornellsville, NY February 8, 1884

HATHAWAY Mrs. Antoinette in Hornellsville, NY February 12, 1884

ROBERTS John W. age 64y in Fremont, NY February 14, 1884

LEE Richard in E. Campbell, NY February 14, 1884. Leaves daus Mrs. Ira F. **DIBBLE**, Mrs. Eugene **SMITH** and Mrs. A. W. **CUSHING** of Corning, NY and son Delos Lee of Painted Post, NY

MC KIBBEN Andrew in Howard, NY January 31, 1884. Born September 18, 1807 in Argyle, NY and came to Howard 1835. Married 1839 Chrissie Ann **WOODS**, 5 daus, 3 sons, 1 dau dec.

BOSENBARK Henry D. in Sonora, NY February 6, 1884. Born June 1833 in Sonora, NY. Leaves wife and 2 children

GAREY James killed getting wood in Bradford, NY February 21, 1884

SHOWERS A. J. in Woodhull, NY February 20, 1884

ROGERS Mathew in Troupsburgh, NY February 19, 1884

WOOLEVER Jane age 62y wife of David Woolever in Arkport, NY February 21, 1883

DEATH NOTICES

DOTY Miss Lena found dead in bed in Canisteo, NY February 23, 1884

CHITTICK John in Corning, NY February 15, 1884

KAME Heziah age 28 wife of Monroe Kame in Hornellsville, NY February 22, 1884

KILEY Cornelius son of Cornelius Kiley in Hornellsville, NY February 23, 1884

SIMMONS John J. age 55y Eng. on Erie RR in Hornellsville, NY February 26, 1884

MANNING Blanche infant dau of M. E. in Hornellsville, NY February 26, 1884

BISHOP Lola age 56y wife of William C. Bishop in Howard, NY March 3, 1884. Born Tyrone, NY dau of John **SMITH**. Leaves husband and dau

NEFF Mrs. John age 74y in Prattsburgh, NY February 24, 1884

ALDRICH Gardener age 86y formerly of Tuscarora, NY in Midland City, (?) February 14, 1884

CRUTHERS Amanda M. age 34y wife of William Cruthers and dau of William **WALTERS** in Prattsburgh, NY February 20, 1884

ROOD Mrs. G. D. in Painted Post, NY February 28, 1884

WOODARD Mrs. Ephraim in Bloods, NY March 3, 1884

WILSON Mrs. Leonard in N. Cohocton, NY March 6, 1884

HOLDEN James age 84y in Fremont, NY March 15, 1884

LOVELL Calvin age 62y in Painted Post, NY March 13, 1884

HATHAWAY Mrs. Hannah age 86y in Campbell, NY March 3, 1884

TAYLOR Mrs. Lafayette in Howard, NY March 15, 1884

HOWE H. L. age 70y in Hammondsport, NY March 15, 1884

TOWNSEND Robert age 74y 5m 24d at dau in Savona, NY March 11, 1884

KNIGHT George E. died March 27, 1884. Born September 6, 1847 nr Lodi, NY and came to Bath, NY in March 1868

BOWES Patrick in Bath, NY March 23, 1884. Born 1800 in Lisdowney, Co. Kilkenny, Ire. Married (1) Catherine **RYAN**, 8 children. Wife and 5 children died in Ire. Married (2) Ann **LANNON**, 11 children. Came to US in 1848

CURTIS Mrs. David abt 80y in Painted Post, NY March 19, 1884

HARROWER Mrs. James eldest dau of Robert **PATTERSON** in Lindley, NY March 12/17, 1884

SAXTON Aaron age 70y in Haskinsville, NY March 19, 1884

MC CARTHY John age 17y found dead nr RR track in Rathbone, NY March 30, 1884

TOMER John age 71y 9m 8d at son's nr Savona, NY March 22, 1884

MOSS Mrs. David age 25 on Oak Hill, NY March 26, 1884. Leaves husband and 4 small children

WHITE Asor an old res of Hornellsville, NY March 28, 1884

PARKER Luther age 91y in Pulteney, NY April 2, 1884

STEWART Andrew age 84y in Fremont, NY April 2, 1884

WEST Nellie age 16y dau of Clinton West in Wheeler, NY March 16, 1884

HALLENBECK Mrs. Dr. George G. age 37y in Corning, NY April 3, 1884

WALLACE Ruby R. age 10y dau of A. J. in Hornellsville, NY April 11, 1884

CLAPP Melvin H. age 71y in Kanona, NY rec (Newspaper date April 18, 1884)

HILL Mrs. Mary Ann dau of Garrett **BURNSIDE** in Addison, NY April 6, 1884

CURRY Mrs. Michael in Hornellsville, NY April 11, 1884

WEBSTER Erastus age 87y in Bradford, NY April 16, 1884

MARKHAM Mrs. Charles in Hornellsville, NY April 21, 1884

SNOW Mrs. Robert in Hammondsport, NY April 29, 1884

POWELL Mrs. Alexander in Howard, NY April 20, 1884

HARVEY William in his 52nd yr in Thurston, NY April 25, 1884

HAWKINS Harriet age 52y wife of William Hawkins in Sonora, NY April 26, 1884

HARDEN Patrick in Rexville, NY May 8, 1884

NEWSOME William age 40y in Hornellsville, NY May 12, 1884

BARROWS John age 74y in Cameron, NY May 18, 1884

SELLICK Mrs. S. D. age 60y in S. Cameron, NY rec (Newspaper date May 23, 1884)

DEATH NOTICES

HOFFMAN Louise age 12y in Perkinsville, NY May 13, 1884

INGALLS ___ infant dau of Henry Ingalls in Hornellsville, NY May 14, 1884

LANPHEAR Joseph age 66y in Hornellsville, NY May 18, 1884

CRANDALL Walter J. age 24y 10m 3d at mother's Mrs. George **HENECA** in Bath, NY May 17, 1884

WHITE Esther (**MC DOWELL**) age 62y 11m 5d in Orange, NY May 16, 1884

INSHO James T. age 23y 11m in Bradford, NY May 24, 1884

KETCHUM Mrs. Lucy age 67y in S. Dansville, NY May 22, 1884

BOWES Miss Mary age 23y in Bath, NY June 2, 1884

CHARLESWORTH Mrs. Clark H. in Wheeler, NY May 25, 1884

BROWN Emerson age 73y in Howard, NY June 2, 1884

BARTHOLOMEW Hiram S. in Savona, NY May 22, 1884. Born October 29, 1832 in Savona. Married February 4, 1864 Kate **MC GONEGAL** of Avoca, NY. Leaves wife, 2 sons and 2 daus

CAMERON Frances widow of Dugald Cameron in Bath, NY May 28, 1884. Born 1805 in White Plains, NY dau of Dr. Andrew **PURDY** who moved to Tioga Co. NY. Married January 3, 1825 at brother-in-law's Thomas **MAXWELL** in Elmira, NY. Husband died March 5, 1828 in Albany, NY at age 49y

TOMPKINS Daniel age 98y in Thurston, NY June 21, 1884

RYAN Rebecca wife of James Ryan in Hornellsville, NY June 21, 1884

CAMPBELL Ann age 47y wife of Duncan in Hornellsville, NY June 24, 1884

ROSENCRANS Mary age 72y widow of Simeon in Cohocton, NY June 20, 1884

AULLS Marinda age 72y relict of Ephraim Aulls in N. Urbana, NY June 3, 1884. Born January 26, 1812 in Herkimer Co. NY dau of Josiah **WEBSTER**. Moved to Urbana at age 4y. Became widow in 1837 with 6 small children, 4 living, Mrs. Amanda **COLE** of Belfast, NY, Mrs. Samuel **BAILEY** of Urbana, Lyman of Wayne, NY and Frank of Bradford, NY

BROTHER Henry H. son of Henry Brother cut in half with circular saw at mill in Kanona, NY (Newspaper date June 27, 1884)

SEDDEN John hit by train nr Corning, NY July 4, 1884

ROBINSON John P. age 71y in Hornellsville, NY July 4, 1884

EDGETT Mrs. George age 64y in Howard, NY July 12, 1884

BENNETT Ida age 34y wife of Sidney Bennett in Hornellsville, NY July 15, 1884, buried Canisteo, NY

CANFIELD Milo F. age 54y in Fremont, NY July 6, 1884

CARROLL Patrick age 27 in Campbell, NY July 25, 1884

BILLSON Lydia F. age 36y in Avoca, NY July 18, 1884

BORST Mrs. Julia (**SULLIVAN**) wife of J. W. Borst in Painted Post, NY July 23, 1884

FORD Carrie age 21y in Hornellsville, NY July 17, 1884

BURDETT George T. age 15y in Hornellsville, NY July 28, 1884

SCHOFIELD Jane wife of Henry Schofield in Savona, NY July 20, 1884. Born March 28, 1815 dau of Ralph **VAN HOUTEN** of Urbana, NY. Married October 4, 1838, 6 children. Alvira died March 20, 1848 just over 1 yr

COLE Rachel age 85y widow of Hiram Cole in Pulteney, NY July 21, 1884

DABOLL Julia age 72y widow of Auren Daboll in Prattsburgh, NY July 29, 1884

MORGAN Mrs. Catherine at son's James Morgan nr Prattsburgh, NY July 24, 1884

BROWN Gardner in Wallace, NY August 3, 1884

WOOLEVER Mrs. James P. in Arkport, NY August 8, 1884

CLARK Rev. Thomas R. in Cameron, NY August 4, 1884. Born Broadalbin, NY 1809

GIBSON Ira age 80y in Pulteney, NY August 19, 1884

TOWLE Richard W. of Chicago, Ill. formerly of Bath, NY from escaping gas August 14, 1884

UNDERHILL Charles A. age 50y of Bath, NY at Willard Asylum August 18, 1884

FORD Eliza (**MADISON**) in Lawrenceville, Pa. August 13, 1884. Born March 24, 1809 dau of Gen. Daniel **CRUGER**. Mother was niece of Henry A. **TOWNSEND**. Married June 17, 1830 in Syracuse, NY Charles H. L. Ford son of late James Ford of Lawrenceville. Husband died autumn of 1882, 6 children 2 living Daniel of Lawrenceville and Charles H. L. of Canisteo, NY. Dau died 10 yrs ago

HARTRUM Willie age 6y son of John Hartrum in Greenwood, NY August 20, 1884

WILBUR Griffin E. son of Frank in Bath, NY July 18, 1884. Born April 19, 1865

DE WITT William M. age 54y 9m 1d nr Bradford, NY August 19, 1884. Born Starkey, NY 4th of 10 children, 7 living. Leaves wife and 2 children

CLARK Lena in her 21st yr wife of L. H. Clark and dau of M. V. **BARTON** of Bath, NY in Avoca, NY August 26, 1884

WATROUS William B. age 55y in Cameron, NY August 15, 1884

CASTOR William age 60y in Caton, NY August 22, 1884

EDSON Daniel age 55 of sunstroke in Cohocton, NY (Newspaper date August 29, 1884)

VAN WIE Catherine widow of Henry Van Wie suicide in Jasper, NY August 26, 1884

BROWN Mrs. Marinda age 74y in Springwater, NY August 27, 1884

HEMINGWAY William age 26y in Pleasant Valley, NY September 10, 1884

THORP Mrs. William age 72y in Wayland, NY September 20, 1884

SMITH Sally widow of Sylvester Smith of Painted Post, NY in Bainbridge, NY September 22, 1884

HUY Belle age 8y dau of S. G. Huy in Corning, NY September 21, 1884

KELLY Daniel age 53y of Thurston, NY September 3, 1884

HAVENS William H. in Coopers Plains, NY September 25, 1884

DEYO ____ age 1y 10m son of A. Deyo in Caton, NY September 25, 1884

WILLIS Mrs. Isabella age 83y nr Prattsburgh, NY September 29, 1884

TALLMAN Eugene by collision on Tip Top September 27, 1884

BAUMGARTEN ____ infant dau of John and Effa in Hornellsville, NY October 3, 1884

WHITEHEAD Philander abt 35y in Bath, NY October 3, 1884

GATES A. H. in Savona, NY October 9, 1884, buried Big Flats, NY

PARTRIDGE Mrs. Carrie formerly of Fremont, NY in Pike, NY September 24, 1884

STAGE John age 85y in Corning, NY October 5, 1884

WILLIAMS Doris H. of Lindley, NY killed by cars in Corning, NY October 8, 1884

ALLEN Richard age 21y in Hornellsville, NY October 8, 1884

HANNA John age 50y in Hornellsville, NY October 6, 1884

BOWEN William H. in Fremont, NY October 7, 1884

HALEY Johanna abt 90y wife of John Haley in Prattsburgh, NY October 13, 1884

GUNN Mary wife of James Gunn in Hornellsville, NY October 14, 1884

KNAPP Barbara wife of C. J. Knapp in Hornellsville, NY October 16, 1884

STROPE Mrs. Mary E. in Hornellsville, NY October 18, 1884

TREAT Whitman in Wheeler, NY October 17, 1884

CRAWFORD Frederick in Cohocton, NY October 21, 1884

PARSONS Abram age 75y in Hornellsville, NY October 30, 1885

BARTON Alice I. in Bath, NY October 13, 1884. Born February 2, 1860 in Bath

STEPHENS Minerva P. age 70y in Fremont, NY November 4, 1884

COLE Hannah M. age 59y wife of F. S. Cole in Howard, NY November 4, 1884

PALMER Julia A. wife of J. L. Palmer in Painted Post, NY November 2, 1884

CROSS Delanson age 48y formerly of Cameron, NY and brother of Mrs. T. W. **BARBER** of Bath, NY in Colfax, Cal. October 9, 1884

LOVELACE Hattie age 21y in Knoxville/Corning, NY November 18, 1884

LEWIS Mrs. Hiram of Jasper, NY at son-in-law's W. W. **HUNTER** November 22, 1884

INGALLS Albert age 55y in Hartsville, NY November 18, 1884

HOWELL Miss Clara sister of Sidney B. Howell of Painted Post, NY in Middletown, NY November 24, 1884

MC ELWEE Samuel in Savona, NY November 22, 1884. Born April 19, 1812. Mother died 1813 and Father married (2) 1814 Sarah **FAULKNER**. Married October 21, 1838 Mary A. **FISH**, 4 children 1 died young

LINDSAY James in Bath, NY November 25, 1884. Born November 22, 1798 of Protestant parents nr Sligo Co. Sligo, Ire. son of George Lindsay. Came to US 1827. Married Maria **RICHARDSON** who died a few yrs ago, large family, names John R. of New York City, George died Civil War, Charles H. of Scranton, Pa., James of Bath, Jane died several yrs ago, Eilzabeth **DAVISON** widow of Thomas Davison of Bath and Nancy at home

DENNIS Ira age 54y 7m of Wayne, NY at Buffalo Asylum November 4, 1884. Born March 18, 1829 nr S. Bradford, NY. Married (1) Jeanette **CARR** of Bradford who died

DEATH NOTICES

February 7, 1873, 1 son. Married (2) Mary J. **LAMB** of Wayne who survives

THARP Joshua H. age 66y in Bath, NY December 3, 1884. Born August 18, 1818 in Newton, NJ and came to Bath 1839. Married 1842 Angeline **FERRIS** sister of Delanson Ferris. Leaves wife and 5 sons

PAYNE B. W. age 70y in Corning, NY December 3, 1884

SHEARMAN David age 52y of Penn Yan, NY at Soldiers and Sailors Home in Bath, NY November 27, 1884. Member of 179th Inf.

WHITE ____ age 16m son of James White in Howard, NY November 6, 1884

CRAMER Ann Eliza age 4y 10m 23d dau of Nelson and Ann Cramer in Avoca, NY November 28, 1884

VAN KEURAN Frank S. age 24y 6m in Fremont, NY December 5, 1884

ROBINSON A. E. suicide in Erwin, NY December 15, 1884

VIELE Phillip in his 81st yr brother of Mrs. James **HUNTER** in Salamanca, NY December 5, 1884, buried Hornellsville, NY

WALLBRIDGE Mary age 43y in Fremont, NY December 11, 1884

WHITE Hiram S. age 1y 7m 20d son of James L. and Ellen White in Bath, NY November 5, 1884

BIRGE Mrs. Rebecca age 84y in Prattsburgh, NY December 12, 1884

TOWSLEY Levi age 69y in Mitchellville, NY December 18, 1884

BALLOU Julia Ann age 55y in Hornby, NY December 16, 1884

AYERS Elizabeth 1st white child born in Hornellsville, NY at son's James in Arkport, NY December 20, 1884. Born 1793 dau of Elias **STEPHENS**. Married April 1812 Ezekiel Ayers of Arkport, NY. 8 children, 4 living Erastus S. of Hornellsville, Jemima wife of Samuel D. **PITTS**, John J. of Arkport and Ezekiel B. of Trenton Falls, NY

BEDIENT Curtis age 75 at Post Creek, NY December 20, 1884

Canisteo Times

October 7, 1880 - December 25, 1884

ANDRUS Maude age 1y 7m in Howard, NY September 14, 1880

BULLIS William age 30y in Hornellsville, NY October 2, 1880

MC CARTHY Michael P. age 20y in Hornellsville, NY October 1, 1880

MULLEN Archibald age 82 in Greenwood, NY September 5, 1880

DEMING Mrs. Nancy age 73y in Birdsall, NY September 16, 1880

BILLINGS Charles A. age 83y in Cameron, NY September 24, 1880

O'CONNELL John in Greenwood, NY October 7, 1880

BRUNDAGE George A. age 75y in Pleasant Valley, NY September 28, 1880

MILLER Willie age 4y 3m son of William and Jane Miller in Hornellsville, NY October 8, 1880

STOCUM Jeannette age 18y 6m in Canisteo, NY September 26, 1880

OAKS William C. age 44y 7m in Hornellsville, NY October 14, 1880

CHURCH Eunice in her 80th yr wife of Robert W. in Bath, NY October 14, 1880

HIGGINS Mrs. Daniel Jr. abt 50y in Corning, NY October 13, 1880

BENNETT Abram age 72y in Caton, NY September 25, 1880

HEDGES Cora age 19y in Canisteo, NY October 23, 1880

MULCAHEY Anna age 4y dau of Mathew and Bridget Mulcahey in Hornellsville, NY October 22, 1880

SWAIN Maggie age 6y dau of John Swain in Corning, NY October 17, 1880

FILKINS Sarah L. age 44y 2m 9d in Canisteo, NY October 20, 1880

ROBINSON James Sullivan age 70y in Corning, NY October 26, 1880

MILLS Mary L. age 2y 6m dau of William Mills in Hornellsville, NY October 28, 1880

SUTHERBY Jennie age 7m dau of E. P. and Polly Sutherby in Hornellsville, NY October 31, 1880

PIE ____ age 8y dau of Mrs. Pie in Adrian, NY October 31, 1880

FULTS Guy age 6y son of Moses Fults in Woodhull, NY November 6, 1880

DRAKE Hattie Walker age 1y 6m dau of James A. and Isabel Drake and Grand daughter of Franklin N. Drake and Charles C. B. **WALKER** in Corning, NY October 31, 1880

HODGE Edith M. age 14y 9m dau of J. E. and M. J. Hodge November 9, 1880

DEATH NOTICES

SIMONS Benoni age 80y Veteran War of 1812 in Caton, NY November 12, 1880

INSCHO Wilbur F. age 35y in Knoxville/Corning, NY November 3, 1880

PALMER Bryon age 28y in Coopers Plains, NY October 12, 1880

BATES Louisa age 70y wife of Henry Bates in E. Troupsburgh, NY November 10, 1880. Married 52 yrs

DUNN Ruth abt 55y wife of Ignatius Dunn in Troupsburgh, NY November 12, 1880

POTTER John E. age 30y in Troupsburgh, NY November 8, 1880

CARD Simeon B. age 85y in Troupsburgh, NY November 10, 1880

ROBINSON Mrs. Carrie S. age 35y dau of Melinda and late Rufus **TUTTLE** in Hornellsville, NY November 14, 1880

SILSBEE Clara dau of N. L. Silsbee in Haskinsville, NY November 3, 1880

ANDERSON Eva age 1y 7w dau of W. and Mary E. Anderson in Hornellsville, NY November 18, 1880

ANGELL Clerne age 14y in Hornellsville, NY November 18, 1880

ARWIN Charles N. age 40y in Canisteo, NY November 22, 1880

FLOHR Mrs. Anna age 37y in Canisteo, NY November 22, 1880

WELLS Norman O. age 38y in Corning, NY November 19, 1880

MC MASTER G. E. age 31y son of David in Bath, NY November 26, 1880

PRINDLE Sara age 81y wife of Charles L. in Hornellsville, NY December 5, 1880

GIBBS William at dau Mrs. William **GOFF** near Corning, NY November 23, 1880

JONES Betsey age 57y wife of L. A. Jones in Addison, NY December 4, 1880

SILL Jane A. age 48y wife of Col. A. N. Sill late of Corning, NY in Boston, Mass. December 2, 1880

WETMORE Pythagoras age 82y 8m 6d in Hornellsville, NY December 8, 1880

POWELL Ella age 15y dau of Layton Powell and Grand daughter of George **GOODSELL** in Hornby, NY December 7, 1880

BANKS Mariette age 55y wife of Daniel K. in Corning, NY December 11, 1880

WILEY Michael age 28y in Hornellsville, NY December 15, 1880

STEUBEN COUNTY NEWSPAPERS 197

GARRISON Martin age 88y in Howard, NY December 9, 1880

HILL Louisa age 18y in W. Troupsburgh, NY December 13, 1880

SHERMAN Orrin age 23y in Jasper, NY December 15, 1880, buried in Howard, NY

WHEELER Jessie M. age 7d dau of Marcus and Lavina Wheeler in Hornellsville, NY December 29, 1880

PHILLIPS Mrs. Sally J. age 33y in Troupsburgh, NY December 31, 1880

SHARP John age 71y of Canisteo, NY formerly of Jasper, NY son of late Robert and Amy Sharp, oldest and only surviving of 12 children (Newspaper date January 13, 1881

SMITH Olie age 21y son of Sidney Smith of Hornellsville, NY killed by cars at Owego, NY (Newspaper date January 27, 1881)

ROCKWELL Frank age 14y son of Edward Rockwell of Lawrenceville, Pa. killed while sledding in Thurston, NY January 13, 1881

WHITWOOD Frank age 76y kicked by horse in Canisteo, NY January 19/22, 1881

MC DOWELL Mrs. Dorcas age 78y at son-in-law's O. O. **ROE** in Rathbone, NY January 7, 1881

BENNETT Benjamin E. age 66y in Hornellsville, NY January 15, 1881

ORCUTT Priscilla age 51y wife of Lorenzo in Savona, NY November 4, 1880

SEAMANS Amella wife of C. D. Seamans in Savona, NY November 2, 1880

MERRILL Sarah age 75y wife of Jacob Merrill in Cameron, NY December 27, 1880

BROWN Willie age 6y son of Charles A. Brown in Wayland, NY December 31, 1880

FARLEY John age 86y in Canisteo, NY January 21, 1881

HILL Blanche T. age 2m 1d dau of L. F. and Phebe Hill in Cameron Mills, NY January 24, 1881

BRIGGS Jonathan abt 70y in Corning, NY January 21, 1881

HALLIDAY Mrs. Millicent A. age 69y in Pulteney, NY January 21, 1881

DICKEY Willie son of Erastus and Lydia Dickey in Cameron, NY January 8, 1881

HESS John age 70y in Wayland, NY January 10, 1881

SHUTT Dr. in Caton, NY January 21, 1881

DEATH NOTICES

KERNAN Martin age 54y in Corning, NY January 21, 1881

ST JOHN Mrs. Eliza age 31y in Bath, NY January 17, 1881

HUEY Elizabeth abt 40y found dead in snow in Howard, NY January 29, 1881

CORSON Rev. C. W. in Prattsburgh, NY January 26, 1881

MILLER Rhoda relict of Erastus Miller in Pulteney, NY January 27, 1881

HALLETT Darius abt 55y in Adrian, NY January 29, 1881

GEER ____ infant dau of Joe H. and Lila W. Geer in Corning, NY January 29, 1881

WOOD Samuel age 3m son of Thomas Wood in Fremont, NY January 26, 1881

MAHAN Mrs. William age 25y in Hornellsville, NY January 30, 1881

WAGNER Neola age 17y 11m only child of Clark Wagner in Howard, NY February 4, 1881

ORDWAY D. A. in Cameron, NY February 5, 1881

FREEBORN Ora A. age 7y 7m 2d dau of Charles and Frances Freeborn in Canisteo, NY February 19, 1881

CLARK George age 7y son of Charles and Achsah in Avoca, NY February 14, 1881

DALY John age 24y of Corning, NY in Elmira, NY February 22, 1881

MANGAN Deborah abt 55y widow of John Mangan in Corning, NY February 10, 1881

BROWN Orilla age 70y at son's Thomas D. Brown in Corning, NY February 19, 1881

CAHILL Robert age 72y in Corning, NY February 24, 1881

JONES Blanche age 6y 6m dau of L. J. Jones in Hornellsville, NY February 26, 1881

MORAN John age 26y in Hornellsville, NY February 26, 1881

CROW Thomas age 7y son of John and Margaret Crow in Hornellsville, NY February 29, 1881

SCHAUMBERG Mrs. Mary age 62y in Hornellsville, NY February 21, 1881

SAGE Lester age 21y in Hartsville, NY February 21, 1881

HAYES Mary age 58y in Hornellsville, NY February 28, 1881

QUAIN Michael age 56y in Hornellsville, NY March 2, 1881

STANDISH Hulda age 95y in Troupsburgh, NY February 28, 1881

COLLINS Ellen age 4y dau of James Collins in Hornellsville, NY March 3, 1881

DEBARBIERI Vincennes age 2y 5m child of Joseph Debarbieri in Hornellsville, NY March 3, 1881

BROWN Mrs. Sarah age 80y at dau Mrs. **ELLSWORTH** in Prattsburgh, NY March 3, 1881

GORDON James N. age 53y in Naples, NY March 7, 1881

TOBEY Mrs. Lyman age 66y in Naples, NY March 9, 1881

FREEBORN Ella C. age 9y 5m 24d in Canisteo, NY March 9, 1881

FREEBORN Ora A. age 7y 7m 10d in Canisteo, NY February 16, 1881

SWARTZ Martha A. age 27y in Hornellsville, NY March 18, 1881

HUNT Hiram T. age 40y in Knoxville/Corning, NY March 14, 1881

KINNEY George J. age 25y at brother-in-law's W. T. Bailey in Canisteo, NY March 24, 1881. Married September 14, 1876 Fanny **BAILEY**. Buried Belmont, NY

BOYD Andrew in Greenwood, NY March 21, 1881

SIMMONS Mary E. age 21y wife of Charles in Hornellsville, NY March 22, 1881

DE WOLF William Alonzo age 64y in Corning, NY March 12, 1881

KLEE Edwin age 2y 11m 4d son of Fred C. and Anna M. Klee in Canisteo, NY March 24, 1881

JOHNSON Maggie age 3y 3m dau of John and Julia Johnson in Hornellsville, NY March 31, 1881

MINARD Mrs. Mary age 60y 1m 2d in Wheeler, NY March 16, 1881

WALLACE Gratton H. age 54y in Bloods, NY March 17, 1881

STEVENS Margaret age 63y wife of Abram Stevens in Canisteo, NY April 4, 1881

DWYER Ellen J. age 18y 4m 14d in Hornellsville, NY April 3, 1881

DU BOIS Rev. G. J. age 53y in Canisteo, NY March 31, 1881. Born 1828 in N. Hudson, NY

STICKNEY Mrs. Laura of Big Rapids, Mi. dau of John **MILES** of Rathbone, NY last week (Newspaper date April 7, 1881) buried Rathbone

DEATH NOTICES

ARWIN William age 77y in Canisteo, NY April 6, 1881

HUBER Miss Ida age 25y in Corning, NY April 7, 1881

GROGAN Margaret abt 17y in Canisteo, NY April 13, 1881

HANRAHAN ___ dau of Martin Hanrahan burned to death in Rathbone, NY March 25, 1881

PHELPS Sarah wife of Mathew Phelps in Hornellsville, NY April 18, 1881

LEONARD Patrick age 34y run over by caboose in Hornellsville, NY April 17, 1881. Third brother killed at that place

WITHFORD L. W. age 86y in Hornellsville, NY April 11, 1881

RYAN George age 5y son of James Ryan in Corning, NY April 17, 1881

DRAKE Elliott A. age 26y in Jasper, NY March 26, 1881

MAPES ___ age 7w 2d son of Henry and Della Mapes in Canisteo, NY April 26, 1881

MC FARREN Andrew C. age 65y in Painted Post, NY April 19, 1881

CORBIN Charles E. age 4y in Corning, NY April 15, 1881

RAYMOND Henry T. age 20y in Corning, NY April 16, 1881

SPEARS Mrs. Margarette age 60y in Pulteney, NY April 13, 1881

STEVENS Alexander H. age 79y in Greenwood, NY April 28, 1881. His wife died 20 yrs ago

PUFFER Mrs. Rozina A. age 77y 9m 8d in Purdy Creek, NY April 14, 1881

BARRETT Charles age 60y at the Swale, NY May 5, 1881

FORD Charles Lindsay age 6m son of Charles L. and Sarah Ford in Canisteo, NY May 10, 1881

BARR Willie age 5y died April 25, 1881 and Emma Jane age 12y died April 26, 1881 children of Thomas Barr of Erwin, NY. Mother Mary Barr age 96y died April 26, 1881

FAILING Milton G. age 27y in W. Union, NY May 1, 1881

JOHNSON Mrs. Cora age 20y in Jasper, NY May 6, 1881

BERRY Mrs. Emma A. age 20y 9m dau of John Q. **STEPHENS** May 21, 1881 ? (Newspaper gave date as May 31, however the newspaper date was May 26, 1881)

HALLETT Mrs. Henry abt 70y in Adrian, NY May 23, 1881

HOLLIS George H. age 45y Editor of Addison Advertiser May 20, 1881. Born Butternuts, NY son of late William Hollis of Tuscarora, NY. Buried Nelson, Pa. Leaves wife

BALCOM Judge Lyman in Painted Post, NY May 19, 1881. Born November 19, 1800 in Norwich, NY and came to Campbell 1835 to Erwin 1852. Married July 12, 1820 Clarissa **HOLLENBECK** in Chenango Co. NY, 6 children oldest son deceased, Samuel of Bath, NY, Charles of Painted Post, NY, Susan F. wife of R. A. **SMITH** of Olean, NY and Jane E. wife of Warren **HODGEMAN** of Painted Post, NY

MURPHY Hannah age 54y 3m in Adrian, NY June 7, 1881

FITZGIBBONS Ellen M. age 33y in Hornellsville, NY June 8, 1881

BORROUGHS William nr Prattsburgh, NY June 5, 1881

FAULKNER Mrs. Frazier age 35y in Mitchellsville, NY June 5, 1881

SEFFIELD Mary E. age 42y wife of William Seffield in Greenwood, NY June 13, 1881

HURD Anna age 21y wife of Freeman Hurd in Woodhull, NY May 9, 1881

LYKE John age 86y in Howard, NY June 17, 1881

ALDRIDGE Almond G. son of Almond and Nettie in Woodhull, NY June 15, 1881

TARNEY Louisa age 50y in Woodhull, NY June 25, 1881

JOHNSON Dell in his 17th yr dau of Thomas and Samantha Johnson in Woodhull, NY May 11, 1881

SANFORD Silas abt 75y in Corning, NY June 25, 1881

MC INTOSH James C. age 33y in Corning, NY June 29, 1881

KING ____ age 2y 8d son of James King in Canisteo, NY June 30, 1881

GRINOLDS Levi age 76y in Troupsburgh, NY June 15, 1881. Came from Herkimer Co. NY age 5y

PINNEY Aaron would be 80y in August in Prattsburgh, NY June 29, 1881

BURLINGAME Della dau of Joseph Burlingame in Rathbone, NY June 18, 1881

CHARLES Louisa A. age 4y dau of A. J. Charles in Hornellsville, NY July 2, 1881

WOODARD J. J. in Bath, NY July 4, 1881

BENNETT Lillian age 15y dau of Henry and Lucinda Bennett in Augusta, Wis. June 4, 1881. Born Greenwood, NY. Mother died 4 yrs ago in Canisteo, NY since then 2 brothers died all of consumption

RIDDELL Mary at son's J. M. Riddell in Canisteo, NY July 8, 1881. Born December 9, 1800 in Mass. and came to Canisteo in 1837. Husband died 1845, 7 children names George and L. B. of Bradford, Pa.

GRAMES Voy age 14y son of Scott Grames in Canisteo, NY July 16, 1881

SILSBY ____ age 10y dau of Silas Silsby in Canisteo, NY July 18, 1881

BESS James Jr. age 24y in Andover, NY July 2, 1881

RAZEY William age 21y in Hornellsville, NY July 13, 1881

WILEY Joseph age 87y 7m in Woodhull, NY July 12, 1881. Born Albany Co. NY and moved to Cameron then Woodhull 45 yrs ago. Married 1822, 9 children 7 living. Wife died 1863

CRANCE Abram age 79y in Woodhull, NY July 16, 1881

ST CLAIR Eva May age 3m dau of W. J. St. Clair in Hornellsville, NY July 22, 1881

DAWSON ____ age 11w son of Thomas Dawson in Canisteo, NY July 31, 1881

PECK Hannah May age 4m 17d dau of M. A. and Lucinda Peck August 1, 1881

TRAVIS Sylvanus age 32y suicide near Rathbone, NY July 28, 1881. Leaves wife and 3 children, buried Fremont, NY

WILKINS Gertie L. age 3m dau of Frederick and Dora in Canisteo, NY July 18, 1881

MOORE Mrs. Mary age 45y in Jasper, NY July 28, 1881

BRAMBLE George age 51 in Prattsburgh, NY August 16, 1881. Sat in front of Post Office from 5 to 9, passers thought he had been drinking. A. D. Graves checked and found he had died. 1 yr ago he received pension, served 15th Reg. NY Eng. Leaves wife, 3 daus and 1 son

BROTHERTON Thomas age 54y in Canisteo, NY August 20, 1881

TAYLOR Eunice age 35y wife of C. S. Taylor in Canisteo, NY August 20, 1881

WHITWOOD infant child of H. L. Whitwood in Canisteo, NY August 17, 1881

CLARK infant child of Lester Clark in Canisteo, NY August 19, 1881

MACK John age 21y in Canisteo, NY August 19, 1881

WELTY George age 63y in Troupsburgh, NY August 13, 1881

TOOMEY Daniel J. age 2m son of Michael and Sarah Toomey in Hornellsville, NY July 23, 1881

REYNOLDS James in Bath, NY August 12, 1881

CRAWFORD Lewis abt 80y in Cameron Mills, NY August 18, 1881

WILSON Mina age 76y in Bath, NY August 22, 1881

MORGAN Lucy Ellen age 42y in Canisteo, NY August 31, 1881

MARLATT Frank age 22y in Troupsburgh, NY August 27, 1881

BATT Otis age 1y 3m adopted son of David **THOMPSON** in Woodhull, NY August 21, 1881

WIRT Charles age 2y son of J. A. Wirt in Canisteo, NY September 7, 1881

NICHOLS Alfred age 80y of Tuscarora, NY from accident with runaway horses in Addison, NY (Newspaper date September 15, 1881)

MILLER Louella age 3m 16d dau of Levi and Lottie Miller in Woodhull, NY September 5, 1881

WALKER Mrs. Harriet age 85y Mother of C. B. Walker in Corning, NY September 23, 1881

NORTHRUP Benedict in his 83rd yr in Woodhull, NY September 12, 1881

HAIRE Phebe age 82y at daus Mrs. J. A. **HOFFMAN** in Hornellsville, NY (Newspaper date October 6, 1881) buried Cameron, NY

CHURCH Ellen age 36y wife of Edwin L. Church in Bath, NY September 21, 1881

DYER Mrs. Thomas in Howard, NY September 23, 1881

ATCHISON Martin of Corning, NY at Willard Asylum October 1, 1881

WHITTEMORE Eddie age 2y 2m 5d son of Marshall and Fannie Whittemore in Canisteo, NY October 5, 1881

COOK Jennie age 40y in Troupsburgh, NY September 27, 1881

FOX John abt 50y unmarried in Canisteo, NY October 17, 1881

CHASE Judah age 89y in Cameron, NY September 23, 1881

PIERCE James R. age 56y 15d in Hornellsville, NY October 9, 1881

DEATH NOTICES

CAMERON Ronald age 42y of Hornellsville, NY in Salamanca, NY October 8, 1881

KANE Thomas age 29y in Hornellsville, NY October 14, 1881

HURLBURT Lelia age 6m dau of Jerry and Lizzie Hurlburt in Troupsburgh, NY October 5, 1881

BURDICK Truman in his 80th yr in Hornellsville, NY October 16, 1881

WHITMAN Eli A. age 47y in Hornellsville, NY October 23, 1881

WRIGHT Zebulon age 45y in Hornellsville, NY October 14, 1881

BENTON Col. L. D. age 78y in Hornellsville, NY October 14, 1881. Born 1813 in Benton, NY. Married Charlotte E. **HATCH** in Howard, NY

ERWIN Almira H. age 33y wife of Alexander Erwin and dau of Gen. J. H. **LANSING** in Corning, NY October 24, 1881

HIGGINS Sherman age 73 a pioneer of Howard, NY October 22, 1881

CRANE Cyrus L. age 74y 4m in Addison, NY October 2, 1881. Born Wilbraham, Mass. 12 children 9 living

DEUERLEIN Edwin infant son of George and Virginia Deuerlein in Corning, NY October 24, 1881

BOYCE Horace Wardner age 4y 11m 23d son of Cassius M. and Mary L. Boyce in Corning, NY October 24, 1881

SMITH Freddie R. age 1y 10m son of H. L. and A. F. Smith in Hornellsville, NY October 26, 1881

STEPHENS Sarah (**YAPLE**) age 80y 21d wife of John H. Stephens in Hornellsville, NY October 27, 1881

WATERMAN Fanny in her 49th yr wife of Joshua Waterman of Detroit, Mi. and dau of Ira **DAVENPORT** of Bath, NY in Bath November 6, 1881

QUIMBY Jonathan age 84y formerly of Caton, NY suicide by hanging in Spencer, NY November 4, 1881

MURPHY Patrick abt 50y in Bath, NY November 12, 1881, dau Maggie died 4 wks ago

TRANT Richard in Richburg, NY November 11, 1881, buried Hornellsville, NY

DENNIS Ann age 25y wife of Boardman Dennis and dau of Franklin and Rhoda **BATCHELOR** in Jasper, NY October 29, 1881

GARDNER Daniel age 55y in Troupsburgh, NY October 14, 1881

TRANT John age 23y in Howard, NY November 22, 1881

SMALLIDGE Jerome B. in Bath, NY November 21, 1881

MC KIBBEN George age 31y in Howard, NY December 1, 1881

STEPHENS Angeline (HINCKLEY) age 40y wife of Hiram B. Stephens in Oregon, NC November 26, 1881

WARNER Richard in his 73rd yr in Corning, NY November 19, 1881

SHOCKEY William age 71y in Addison, NY December 1, 1881

VAN ORSDALE Grace age 12y 4m dau of Henry and Jane Van Orsdale in Jasper, NY December 11, 1881

STILES Asel age 12y in E. Troupsburgh, NY December 10, 1881

STEPHENS Mrs. William H. age 33y in Canisteo, NY December 30, 1881

SCHUYLER Peter D. in Hornellsville, NY December 21, 1881. Born 1828 in Geneva, NY

COLBATH ___ infant son of W. J. Colbath in Hornellsville, NY December 24, 1881

HARRIS Rosanna age 37y in Hornellsville, NY December 24, 1881

KIMBALL Lillian age 9y in Hornellsville, NY December 11, 1881

ROBERTS Thomas age 30y in Hornellsville, NY December 19, 1881

CORCKRAN Ellen age 10y in Hornellsville, NY December 22, 1881

MORRIS Polly age 77y wife of Andrew Morris Sr. in Hornellsville, NY December 22, 1881

WALKER Robert age 81y in Hornellsville, NY December 14, 1881. Res. over 60 yrs

WHITCOMB Theresa age 6y 2m in Howard, NY December 20, 1881

GRAMES Scott age 45y in Canisteo, NY December 25, 1881

MEAD William H. age 75y in Canisteo, NY December 22, 1881

COHN Darius abt 82y in Canisteo, NY January 10, 1882

STEPHENS Mrs. Thankful age 82y 10m in Canisteo, NY January 6, 1882

EASON Mrs. Mary E. age 71y 2m 13d in Canisteo, NY January 7, 1882

DEATH NOTICES

MARTIN Willie R. age 6y 11m 4d son of J. D. and Mary Martin in Canisteo, NY December 17, 1881

ROSS Abigail age 71y in Hornellsville, NY January 4, 1882

ROWLEY Josiah age 81y in Troupsburgh, NY December 16, 1881

OWEN Georgie age 5m 3w son of Rev. and Mrs. H. J. Owen in Woodhull, NY December 23, 1881

YOUNG David age 71y in Knoxville/Corning, NY December 27, 1881

HERALD Sarah age 73y widow of John in Knoxville/Corning, NY January 3, 1882

POTTER Elsie age 91y 6m relict of Josephus in Troupsburgh, NY December 7, 1881

TAYLOR Mary Lee age 1y dau of H. S. and K. T. in Canisteo, NY January 20, 1882

ABBOTT William abt 67y suicide in Towlesville, NY January 25, 1882. Wife died 3 yrs ago and he married her niece

CHAMBERLAIN Anna S. age 14y 1m 15d dau of Dr. C. P. Chamberlain in Canisteo, NY January 25, 1882

BAKER John age 60y in Canisteo, NY January 21, 1882

ROGERS Bertie age 1y 3m son of Jasper and Eliza Rogers in Troupsburgh, NY January 11, 1882

HOAGLAND Tabitha age 82y wife of Richard in Howard, NY January 10, 1882

WHITELEY John R. in Canisteo, NY January 21, 1882

CLEVELAND Mrs. C. M. age 58y in Woodhull, NY January 16, 1882

HEERMANS John in Corning, NY January 23, 1882. Leaves wife and 9 children 3 living in South, George H., Henry C., Clinton, Mrs. Alice **FIELD** wife of Lovasso, Lena and John Jr. all of Corning

GUYON Daniel E. age 26y in Greenwood, NY January 9, 1882

WESTCOTT D. J. age 88y in Howard, NY rec. (Newspaper date February 9, 1882) Served in War of 1812

WOODS David age 52 of Chicago, Ill. formerly of Bath, NY (Newspaper date February 9, 1882) buried in Bath

RIGBY Mary E. age 27 wife of Ralph Rigby in Troupsburgh, NY February 7, 1882

POTTER Caleb age 72y in Troupsburgh, NY February 9, 1882

STURDEVANT Della abt 30y in Canisteo, NY February 20, 1882

WILEY Mabel age 5m 2w dau of Albert Wiley in Troupsburgh, NY February 16, 1882

MEAD Purdy age 45y Supervisor of Greenwood, NY during scuffle on day of advertised tax sales, hit his head on rock March 4, 1882. Leaves wife and 2 children

MASON Christina age 35y wife of R. H. Mason in Woodhull, NY March 5, 1882

MOORE Mary F. wife of William Moore in her 46th yr in Cameron, NY March 7, 1882. Leaves husband and 3 children

GRAY John F. age 36y in Howard, NY March 19, 1882

FENTON Mrs. John age 46y in Hornellsville, NY March 17, 1882

MULHOLLEN Eliza of Canisteo, NY while visiting in Decorah, Ia. February 22, 1882

MC NAIR Miss Hattie in Canisteo, NY March 19, 1882

OSBORN Eva age 4y 10m dau of George and Isadine H. Osborn and grand daughter of William and R. **ABER** of Canisteo, NY in Hornellsville, NY April 1, 1882

DEVORE Norman age 7m son of George and Lucy in Canisteo, NY April 7, 1882

ASHLEY Mrs. Joseph age 38y in Canisteo, NY April 6, 1882

BUCK J. M. age 49y in Howard, NY April 6, 1882

SARGENT Joshua in Jasper, NY March 24, 1882. Born May 5, 1791 in Dunstable, NH 5th child of 12 children of Joshua and Abigail Sargent. Married November 18, 1819 Martha **BURNHAM** who died June 9, 1876. Children James R. of Bells Run, Pa., J. Burnham, J. Sumner and Judson N. of Jasper, NY

CARTER Eli of alchohol poisoning in Canisteo, NY April 14, 1882

FRANCE Mrs. Mary E. age 54y in Canisteo, NY April 16, 1882

CRAWFORD James age 15y on the Swale, NY April 15, 1882

GOODRICH Mrs. ____ age 58y in Canisteo, NY April 8, 1882

FAULKNER Harry age 77y in Canisteo, NY April 13, 1882

FRISBEE Lucy age 65y 9m 21d on the Swale, NY April 19, 1882

ALLEN ____ age 5y dau of Phillip and Lillian Allen in Prattsburgh, NY April 8, 1882

NEWELL James K. age 61y in Painted Post, NY last wk (Newspaper date April 27, 1882)

DEATH NOTICES

KING Miss Mary age 70y unmarried in Canisteo, NY April 27, 1882

SMITH Jennett age 65y 6m at res. of David Smith in Canisteo, NY May 4, 1882

HOPPER John in Hartsville, NY May 8, 1882. Born September 16, 1800 near Patterson, NJ and came to Cayuga Co. as child, to Hartsville in 1847. 2 sons Henry and Lawrence of Hartsville, 1 dau in Missouri and 1 in Hornellsville, NY

THOMAS Cynthia age 79y 1m 16d at dau Mrs. Thomas **HALLETT** in Canisteo, NY May 1, 1882

PIERSON James of Cameron, NY white visiting dau Mrs. E. D. **PECKHAM** in Canisteo, NY May 10, 1882. Born 1804. Leaves wife, 2 sons and 3 daus

CROSS Abigail in her 34th yr wife of Asa Cross of Cameron, NY and adopted dau of Daniel **HECKMAN** of Jasper, NY in Jasper May 7, 1882. Leaves husband and 4 children

ROWE William at Soldier's and Sailors's Home in Bath, NY May 23, 1882

DIDAS ____ age 3y dau of Peter Didas ran over by bakery wagon in Perkinsville, NY May 26, 1882

CROSBY Nancy age 69y 6m 11d wife of Nathan Crosby in Adrian, NY May 31, 1882

SMITH Mrs. Sara S. age 35y in Adrian, NY May 31, 1882

HAYT Margaret (**TOWNSEND**) June 7, 1882. Married November 18, 1856 in Palmyra, NY. Sister of Mrs. C. C. B. **WALKER**

SYLVESTER Mrs. Sarah age 64y sister of James **SHOWERS** suicide by hanging in Wayland, NY June 26, 1882

SPENCER Allen age 79y 11m in Jasper, NY June 15, 1882

NUDD David age 61y in Troupsburgh, NY June 15, 1882

STROUD Mamie age 11m 16d dau of Willis and Mary in Woodhull, NY June 17, 1882

THORP Fred of Hornellsville, NY killed by cars July 1, 1882

STEDMAN Leman L. age 7m son of F. L. and Sarah (**LANGLEY**) in Hinsdale, NY July 7, 1882

ORDWAY Enoch age 79y 5m 6d in Adrian, NY July 3, 1882

HATCH William near Cohocton, NY last week (Newspaper date July 13, 1882)

VANDERHOFF Adell age 21y 1m 6d wife of C. E. Vanderhoff on Bennetts Creek, NY July 17, 1882

DIVEN Ella May 4m 22d dau of J. M. Diven in New York City July 11, 1882

CONKEY Charles age 31y in Jasper, NY July 6, 1882

ADAMS Mrs. Polly age 85y at son's H. L. **HEDGES** in Canisteo, NY July 20, 1882

LEACH Lewis age 6m 20d son of J. H. and N. E. in Troupsburgh, NY July 16, 1882

WRIGHT Albert S. age 24y of Allegany Co. NY in Ithaca, NY July 18, 1882

UPHAM Mrs. Fannie age 88y in Erwin Center, NY July 5, 1882

WARDNER Phillip age 17y 2m in Hornellsville, NY July 22, 1882

BRICK Edward age 52y in Hornellsville, NY July 26, 1882

HUNT Nellie age 12y dau of Edwin J. Hunt in Woodhull, NY July 26, 1882

CHRISCATON William age 86y in Jasper, NY July 23, 1882

COOPER Emma age 26y 8m wife of A. R. Cooper in Canisteo, NY August 7, 1882

TERRYBERRY Cora age 11y 6m 26d on Bennetts Creek, NY August 1, 1882

MILLIKEN ___ age 2m 20d dau of George Milliken in Canisteo, NY August 4, 1882

CHILDS Casper age 12y 7m 10d son of Almarion Childs in Alfred, NY August 3, 1882

STRONG Mrs. Frances C. age 75y at dau Mrs. F. C. **BARNES** in Bath, NY August 13, 1882. Another dau Mrs. E. C. **MILLER** of Canisteo, NY

COOK Edmond age 82y in Hartsville, NY August 21, 1882

FRANEY James age 29y in Howard, NY August 21, 1882

PRATT Mrs. Asa age 35y in Canisteo, NY August 29, 1882

ALGER Mrs. Catherine age 87y 7m 3d in Bennetts Creek, NY August 24, 1882

CRANE George and Clarence ages 2y and 4y sons of William and Fannie Crane in Cameron, NY August 21, and 22, 1882

STREETER Thomas in Greenwood, NY August 7, 1882. Born July 16, 1808 in Bath, NY lived in Greenwood 35 yrs. 3 sons and 1 dau, 1 son died abt 10 yrs ago

PEASE Levi D. Tax collector in Greenwood, NY suicide by hanging September 1, 1882

THOMAS Pearl age 6m dau of D. C. Thomas in Canisteo, NY September 1, 1882

DAVENPORT Henry abt 65y suicide by hanging in Caton, NY September 12, 1882.

DEATH NOTICES

Leaves wife and 2 daus Mrs. S. H. **SMITH** of Big Flats, NY and Mrs. Isaiah **JOHNSON** of Elkland, Pa.

CHAMBERLAIN Jeremiah Everts abt 60y son of Levi and Maria (**PATTON**) Chamberlain in Honolulu August 23, 1882. Born Honolulu February 5, 1831. 1st cousin of Dr. C. P. Chamberlain of Canisteo, NY

BENNETT Fanny D. age 13y 8m dau of Henry and Lucinda Bennett formerly of Canisteo, NY in Augusta, Wis. August 26, 1882

MADISON Adeline age 2y 5m 14d dau of James H. Madison in Hartsville, NY September 13, 1882

FREEBORN Harry Lamont age 7m 2d son of Charles and Frankie Freeborn in Canisteo, NY September 18, 1882

BISHOP Jacob age 61y 4m 27d in Troupsburgh, NY September 18, 1882

DAVISON Alonzo abt 54y in Canisteo, NY September 23, 1882. Wife drowned by suicide 2 yrs ago. 2 children Eva and George age 14y

BISHOP Joseph age 64y in Troupsburgh, NY September 25, 1882

COLVIN Minnie age 3m 3d dau of Delancey and Mary Colvin in Woodhull, NY October 3, 1882

BAKER Dwight E. age 9y 17d son of E. A. and Lucy Baker in Purdy Creek, NY October 14, 1882

DEVORE Ella age 16y 10m in Canisteo, NY October 15, 1882

CLARK John C. age 10y in Hartsville, NY October 17, 1882

HARRIS George age 1y 10m in Woodhull, NY September 26, 1882

STOKES Mattie age 8m 21d dau of Samuel and I. I. Stokes and grand dau of William and R. **ABER** of Canisteo, NY in Rochester, NY October 15, 1882

JOHNSON J. H. age 64y in Jasper, NY October 10, 1882

TANNER Sherman abt 70y in Troupsburgh, NY October 23, 1882

VAN SCOTER Jonas life res. of Canisteo Valley in Buffalo, NY October 18, 1882

CLARK Ruth in her 86th yr Mother of Mrs. Clark **SIMPSON** of Canisteo, NY in Southport, NY October 3, 1882

CALL Maude age 3y 3m 10d dau of Joel and Mariett Call in Hartsville, NY October 26, 1882

HALSEY Gaines age 63y in Howard, NY October 30, 1882

PURDY Harriet age 78y relict of Charles Purdy in Bath, NY October 19, 1882. Dau Mrs. D. W. **GATES**

JOSLIN Stephen N. age 65y in Hornellsville, NY October 22, 1882

HORTON Kate age 35y wife of N. M. Horton in Hornellsville, NY October 22, 1882

NEWSOM Alta E. age 29y wife of William E. in Hornellsville, NY October 29, 1882

PETTIBONE Harriet age 81y widow of John in Hartsville, NY October 22, 1882

ALLEN Joseph in S. Cameron, NY November 1, 1882

HALLETT Nancy age 82y formerly of Canisteo, NY in Kasson, Mn. October 22, 1882. Son Thomas Hallett in Canisteo

BATCHELDER Mrs. Mercy E. age 31y 9m in Canisteo, NY November 11, 1882

ANGELL John crushed by cars in Hornellsville, NY November 10, 1882

COOK Henry age 20y in saw mill accident near Corning, NY November 10, 1882

TAYLOR Clement son of William B. and Eliza Taylor November 19, 1882

NEWTON Sarah wife of Joel D. Newton in Troupsburgh, NY November 21, 1882

CALL Leonard age 1y 3m 13d son of Joel and Mariett Call in Hartsville, NY November 9, 1882

PATCHIN Cornelia age 75y 6m 4d in Canisteo, NY November 25, 1882

PAGE Mrs. Charles age 28y in Canisteo, NY December 8, 1882

CROSBY John age 74y in Adrian, NY December 10, 1882

ROGERS Mrs. Betsey S. age 65y in Adrian, NY December 10, 1882

FISHER Mrs. Cornelius age 71y in Canisteo, NY December 9, 1882

CLEMENT Orpha age 65y 10m 11d wife of Myron Clement in Canisteo, NY November 11, 1882. Born December 22, 1817 in Fairfield Co. Ct. nee **DIMON**, moved to Dutchess Co. NY age 21y. Married May 5, 1840, leaves husband, 3 sons and 2 daus

TULLER ____ oldest son of William Tuller in Hartsville, NY December 16, 1882

DEXTER John W. age 47y in Canisteo, NY January 10, 1883

SMITH Mrs. Betsey age 72y Mother of Mrs. J. H. **MAPES** of Canisteo, NY in

DEATH NOTICES

Canisteo December 31, 1882

ROE John of Canisteo, NY son of James Roe of Col. Bills Creek, NY struck by train in Canisteo Center, NY January 15, 1883

HALLETT Nelson age 67y in Adrian, NY January 20, 1883

DUTCHER Martha C. age 53y Mother of Mrs. Charles **FREEBORN** late of Canisteo, NY in Portville, NY January 18, 1883

TABER Silas W. age 48y 11m in Hornellsville, NY January 22, 1883

PATTERSON Bertie C. age 9y son of C. E. and Geraldine Patterson in Hornellsville, NY January 22, 1883

RICE Mary M. wife of L. D. Rice in Hornellsville, NY January 24, 1883

BRIGGS Jane age 68y in Hornellsville, NY January 26, 1883

DIVEN Julia age 50 in Canisteo, NY February 2, 1883, buried Greenwood, NY

CRANDALL P. H. age 67y of Howard, NY in Elmira, NY January 30, 1883. Leaves 9 children 3 sons, Lycurgis, William and Orasmus, 6 daus Elizabeth wife of W. A. **FERGUSON** of Elmira, NY, Josephine wife of James **PADDOCK** of Bath, NY, Mary wife of A. F. **VAN CAMPEN** of Corning, NY, Ensebia wife of A. F. **STEWART** of Howard, NY, Sarah wife of Isaiah **HARRIS** of Canisteo, NY and Kate of Buena Vista, NY unmarried

CURTIS F. B. age 28y of Hammondsport, NY formerly of Jasper, NY January 31, 1883. Married Lue **ANDREWS** dau of H. B. Andrews of Jasper about 6 yrs ago. Leaves wife, 1 son and 1 dau

HORTON Maj. C. H. in Hornellsville, NY February 9, 1883

ROGERS Mason age 30y suicide in Hornellsville, NY February 11, 1883

TRAVIS Henry C. age 83y in Howard, NY February 18, 1883

BULL Col. William H. age 88y in Bath, NY February 15, 1883

YOUNG Mrs. Maria age 81y in Adrian, NY February 25, 1883

SMITH ____ age 8d son of James Smith in Woodhull, NY February 26, 1883

SIMONS Lillie age 3y dau of Perry Simons in Troupsburgh, NY February 18, 1883

RUMSEY David in Bath, NY March 12, 1883. Born December 12/25, 1812 in Salem, NY. Father removed to Howard, NY in 1815 and died 1852. Married 1841 Jane E. **BROWN** dau of Antony Brown of Ogdensburg, NY. Leaves 3 children William, Lydia and Jennie

DUNNIGAN Annie C. dau of Joseph Dunnigan in Greenwood, NY February 22, 1883

FRENCH Mrs. Sally age 84y in Hornellsville, NY March 11, 1883

MERSEREAU Fida B. age 18y in Hornellsville, NY March 12, 1883

MC CHESNEY Jewett S. age 13y 3m in Fremont, NY March 9, 1883

TERRYBERRY ___ infant child of Frank Terryberry in Hartsville, NY March 1, 1883

STILES Joseph age 74y in Canisteo, NY March 10, 1883

BASSETT ___ infant son of W. C. Bassett on Bennetts Creek, NY March 1, 1883

JULIAN Jessie M. age 2y in Howard, NY March 1, 1883

SMITH Dr. William age 71y in Canisteo, NY March 17, 1883. Born England

HOLDEN Maria age 62y in Hornellsville, NY March 16, 1883

CHAPMAN Lavina age 90y in Hornellsville, NY March 16, 1883

CARRINGTON Ira age 54y in Fremont, NY March 18, 1883

PECK Mrs. Hannah M. age 28y 5m 9d in W. Cameron, NY March 25, 1883

STEPHENS Redman D. age 53y in Cedar Rapids, Iowa March 30, 1883. Born November 3, 1829 in Greenwood, NY. Married October 7, 1857 Louisa **BRIER** born January 24, 1834 in Fountain Co. Ind. Children Louise born March 31, 1871, Redman Jr. born May 30, 1874. (A family history printed in paper dated April 12, 1883)

HUNGERFORD John N. in Corning, NY (Newspaper date April 12, 1883). Born December 31, 1825 in Vernon, NY. Married 1864 sister of Duncan **MAGEE** who died a few years later. Married (2) in 1881 Mrs. George R. **FORRESTER** of Elmira, NY

HARRINGTON Louise in Hornellsville, NY April 6, 1883. 3 sisters died this year, surviving are Mrs. G. W. **ROSE** of Hornellsville, Mrs. A. W. **DURKEY** of Buffalo, NY, Mrs. M. **BROWNELL** of Bath, NY, Mrs. V. B. **WETMORE** of Canisteo, NY, Mrs. A. A. **BLISS** of Jersey City, NJ and 1 brother Dr. William B. **OLENDORF** of Red Bluffs, Cal. 1 son C. Harrington

WHITE Martin R. nr 79y in Cameron, NY April 17, 1883

CAHILL John in Greenwood, NY April 11, 1883

STEWART Edward E. age 61y in Canisteo, NY April 29, 1883

GROFF George age 21y in Canisteo, NY May 3, 1883

BENEDICT Thankful age 28y wife of William Benedict in Canisteo, NY May 7, 1883

DEATH NOTICES

CHASE ____ infant child of Sylvester Chase in Canisteo, NY May 4, 1883

HENRY Mrs. Rev. A. C. late of Hartsville, NY in Beachville, NY May 5, 1883

JILLETT Mrs. Laura funeral in Prattsburgh, NY May 3, 1883

PURDY Horace E. age 67y in Belfast, NY May 3, 1883. Born Canisteo, NY

WHITE Ella in her 38th yr wife of John White in Howard, NY May 5, 1883

ALLEN Charles son of Edward Allen on Purdy Creek, NY May 9, 1883 while playing in barn with 2 other boys who pushed the hay rigging against him and crushed his skull

WILLIAMS Charles Alfred age 8y 8m 8d in Canisteo, NY May 10, 1883

POTTER Luther age 50y in Canisteo, NY May 20, 1883, buried Troupsburgh, NY

DAVIS Wilbert infant son of Benjamin Davis in Canisteo, NY May 20, 1883

RICE Rosetta wife of S. L. Rice on her 34th birthday in Canisteo, NY May 18, 1883

GREEN Sheldon in Corning, NY May 23, 1883

TALBOT Jarvis in Hornellsville, NY May 22, 1883, buried Cameron, NY

STEPHENS Jedediah H. M. in his 77th yr in Canisteo, NY April 6, 1883 and wife Ermina Stephens age 71y 10m 2d died May 25, 1883

HOLLIS Thomas age 74y of Hornellsville, NY in Buffalo Asylum May 19, 1883

WHITE Luther age 79y in Cameron, NY April 17, 1883. Born June 24, 1804 in Addison, NY. Married abt 1830 Mary **SANTEE** dau of Isaac Santee who died 1857. 6 children 5 living, son Isaac died in army. Married (2) Mary **JACQUETT** 3 children, 1 living

CROSS Franc C. age 30y wife of Lyman Cross in Hartsville, NY May 30, 1883

CLEMENT Miss Fannie M. age 76y 6m 23d in Canisteo, NY May 31, 1883

BROWN Leland age 9m son of J. D. Brown in Canisteo, NY June 3, 1883

COLE Edward in Hornellsville, NY June 5, 1883. Took morphine instead of quinine by mistake

BENNETT Wallace W. age 62y in Canisteo, NY June 13, 1883. Born 1821 in Belfast, NY son of William Bennett who died 1840

FULTON Jane age 45y 1st wife of John D. Fulton and sister of James **SWARTHOUT** of Canisteo, NY in Iuka, Ks. May 7, 1883

HUNTER Willie J. in Jasper, NY May 30, 1883. Born November 15, 1858 in Jasper son of W. W. and T. Lavina Hunter. Married March 8, 1880 Mary A. **DU BOIS** dau of Rev. G. J. Du Bois. 1 son age 21m

COOK Mrs. Zipporah age 66y in Hartsville, NY June 18, 1883

KING Mrs. Hannah age 63y in Greenwood, NY June 9, 1883

MINOR Alden age 78y in Greenwood, NY June 30, 1883

ELLISON Franklin B. age 60y last February in Cameron, NY July 2, 1883. Leaves wife, 2 sons and 4 daus. Names Dr. M. D. Ellison of Canisteo, NY

HARRINGTON ___ infant son of B. C. Harrington of Indian Creek, Pa. in Canisteo, NY July 7, 1883

HOAGLAND Mrs. John C. in Howard, NY June 28, 1883

HENDY John age 11y in Hartsville, NY July 29, 1883

PARKHILL John R. age 77y in Howard, NY July 29, 1883. Married over 50 yrs ago Sally **MC CONNELL** sister of Benjamin Mc Connell of Canisteo, NY. 3 children M. S. Parkhill of Canisteo, NY, Mrs. James **WATERS** of Bath, NY and Mary E. wife of D. H. B. **GOFF** of Howard who died 1865

BEZENT Thomas age 53 hit by train in Buffalo, NY July 30, 1883. Son Edward Bezent of Canisteo, NY

OLMSTEAD David S. age 52y formerly of Canisteo, NY February 22, 1883

THURSTON George Edward age 9m 11d in Canisteo, NY July 31, 1883

UPSON William B. in Canisteo, NY August 14, 1883. Born January 13, 1806 and died on same place his Father bought in 1790. 4 brothers and 5 sisters, 1 brother Willis B. Upson and 1 sister Mrs. Roxy **STEPHENS** still living. Leaves 4 sons and 4 daus

PATTERSON Ann age 98y at son's in Fremont, NY September 5, 1883. Born Scotland. Several children some living out west and Dr. Patterson of Avoca, NY

ARVER James Jr. Engineer on Erie RR in Hornellsville, NY August 30/31, 1883

MESSEREAU John G. at advanced age formerly of Erwin Center, NY in Portville, NY (Newspaper date September 6, 1883)

BADGER Edward formerly of Hornellsville, NY in Jamestown, NY August 31, 1883

MC MULLEN Thomas abt 50y crushed by cars in Adrian, NY September 11, 1883

DONNELLY William crushed by cars in Cameron Mills, NY September 14, 1883

DEATH NOTICES

WILLOUR Fannie May age 3m 12d of Canisteo, NY in Bath, NY September 2, 1883

BATES Hiram age 62y in Cameron, NY September 19, 1883

CROSS Frankie L. age 3m 21d son of Lyman L. in Canisteo, NY September 2, 1883

READY Philander age 72y of Arkport, NY in Bath, NY September 21, 1883

SHARP Lucinda widow of John Sharp in N. Urbana, NY September 28, 1883. Born December 2, 1806 in Marcellus, NY dau of Phillip **BESSEE**. Married December 31, 1829, husband died December 21, 1880. 4 daus and 1 son, Phebe Susanna born August 24, 1829, Amy Ann born June 18, 1832, Clarissa Maria born August 8, 1836, Mary Cole born August 25, 1840 and John Wesley born May 21 1845

BRUNDAGE Victor age 53y formerly of Steuben Co. NY in Detroit, Mi. a few days ago (Newspaper date October 11, 1883)

SABIN John C. abt 38y in train accident near Waverly, NY October 13, 1883. Married Miss **HOFFMAN** sister of Albert and Eugene of Hornellsville, NY. No children

THOMPSON Anna E. age 17y in Howard, NY October 11, 1883

MC KENZIE Amos age 62y in Cameron, NY October 13, 1883. Wife and 6 sons

MOORE Henry suicide by hanging in Hammondsport, NY October 18, 1883

DAVIS John age 59y 2 weeks ago in Greenwood, NY October 25, 1883. Born 1824 in Dryden, NY son of Levi S. Davis

FRANCE Rev. David H. in S. Canisteo, NY October 26, 1883. Born February 22, 1803 in Sharon, NY son of Henry and Maria France. Married (1) age 21y Eliza **FARGUHARSON** of Cherry Valley, NY who died March 2, 1845, 4 children Ann Maria wife of Samuel H. **PLOSS**, James H., Hannah E. wife of Amos **BUTTON** all of Jasper, NY, Sarah Jane wife of Amasa **TRAVIS** of S. Canisteo, NY. Married (2) 1848 Mrs. Nancy **BATES** of Newport, NY who died December 28, 1874 age 70y, no children

TAYLOR Lee age 6m son of M. L. Taylor in Canisteo, NY November 7, 1883

WARNER Sabbins age 74y 9m in Woodhull, NY November 4, 1883

WHEELER Miss Louise in Buffalo Asylum November 13, 1883

MC DONNELL Daniel age 75y at dau's Mrs. Mary **O'HARGAN** in Greenwood, NY November 17, 1883. Born 1808 in Bellacastle, Ireland and came to Pa. in 1869. Married (1) in Ireland Miss **MC ALEESE** and had 1 dau. Married (2) in Scotland Isabella Mc Donnell and had 5 daus and 2 sons. Elizabeth age 9y and Jane age 7y died in Scotland, Donald age 20y died Rexville, NY. 2 sons living in Danbury, Pa. and 2 in Greenwood with Mother

BROWN Milton H. age 26y in Rush, Pa. November 23, 1883. Leaves Mother and brother Perry Brown in Canisteo, NY. Father George S. Brown age 80y 9m 23d died in Canisteo November 9, 1883

CROSBY Lorenzo age 66y 10m 22d in Jasper, NY November 11, 1883

MURPHY Mrs. L. age 38y in Howard, NY December 8, 1883

MC KAY A. S. age 50y in Addison, NY December 7, 1883. Leaves wife son and dau

MC CAIG John E. age 42y died December 31, 1883. Leaves wife and 3 daus

WATROUS John B. age 76y in Harrison Valley, Pa. December 31, 1883. Father of Mrs. H. S. **BEEBE** of Canisteo, NY, 14 children 11 living

HACKETT Abigail A. wife of Charles Hackett on the Swale, NY December 14, 1883. Born 1825 in Otsego Co. NY. 5 children

TOWNSEND Eliza in Erwin, NY December 28, 1883. Born October 15, 1801 in Easton, Pa. dau of Samuel **ERWIN**. Married November 1821 Edward Townsend son of Henry A. Townsend of Bath, NY. Infant dau died in 1823 and husband died 1825 from a kick by horse right after birth of only son Edward E. of Erwin. 3 brothers Gen. Francis E. Erwin, William and Charles

SCHOFIELD Aber age 81y in Corning, NY January 6/7, 1884

BENNETT Dr. C. H. in Co. Poor House January 5, 1884

TALLMADGE Mrs. Stephen W. of alcohol poisoning in Canisteo, NY January 5/12, 1884

HARRIS John age 73y in Canisteo, NY January 27, 1884

VANDERLIP Grace age 13m in Canisteo, NY January 13, 1884

HATHAWAY George age 73y in Tioga, Pa. January 9, 1884. Born December 31, 1811 in New Bedford, Mass. of English ancestry who came to this country abt 1700. Married 1831 Betsey R. **WASHBOURNE** of New Bedford. Settled Tompkins Co. 1836 and removed to Tioga in 1857. 5 sons and 2 daus

MAGEE Harriet age 37y wife of Ward Magee in Howard, NY January 30, 1884

SAYRE Robert S. age 55y in Painted Post, NY January 28, 1884

BRYANT Sally Ann age 68y Mother of William **MILLS** in Canisteo, NY February 12, 1884

DOUBTY Miss Azeneth age 79y 6m 13d dau of Nicolas Doubty a pioneer of Canisteo Valley who died at age 90y, at sister's Mrs. Sanuel C. **BUNN** February 23, 1884

DRAKE Allen age 72y in Jasper, NY February 27, 1884. Born November 3, 1810.

Mother died 1851 and Father died 1852. Married 1833 Priscilla **BENEWAY** who died May 27, 1847, children Sidney, Mrs. W. H. **WHEELER** rec. deceased, Mrs. Andrew **MURPHY**, Traver deceased and Mrs. W. H. **PURDY**. Married (2) Olive **SAVAGE** who died 1 yr later leaving infant dau. Married (3) Lucinda **ANDREWS** of Orange, NY who survives with children Luzerne, Mrs. Harmon **HUNTINGTON**, Mrs. H. A. **VAUGHN**, Bella, Allen deceased and Bertha

CLARK William of Howard, NY killed by train in Attica, NY March 10, 1884

DARLING Lucy M. in her 81st yr widow of Dr. Lewis Darling in Lawrenceville, Pa. March 22, 1884. Born August 1, 1803 in Springfield, Vt. dau of Capt. Luke **PARSONS**. Children Dr. Lewis Darling Jr., Lawrence, Dr. H. M. Darling of Pine City, NY and T. V. Darling of Canisteo, NY

BRASTED Rebecca in her 73rd yr formerly of Howard, NY at son's Clark Brasted in Canisteo, NY March 29, 1884

TALBOT Mark age 70y near Cameron, NY March 27, 1884

MAGEE Mrs. Edward age 35y in Canisteo, NY March 26, 1884

STEPHENS Delevan age 75y in Arkport, NY April 11, 1884. Born Canisteo, NY youngest son of John R. Stephens

PLATT Rev. Dr. J. M. in Bath, NY April 14, 1884

MANNING Merrill in Hornellsville, NY April 3, 1884. Born Greenwood, NY. Only child died 6 weeks ago

MAGEE Etta wife of Perry Magee and dau of Peter **VAN GORDER** in Howard, NY April 9, 1884

GUNN Archie in his 3rd yr son of Joe Gunn in Jasper, NY April 25, 1884

CAMPBELL Melvina abt 18y dau of Jesse and Martha in Jasper, NY April 23, 1884

ANDERSON Mrs. Matilda age 24y in Greenwood, NY April 24, 1884

GREEN Garrett in Greenwood, NY April 30, 1884

CLARK John age 82y in Troupsburgh, NY April 25, 1884

REYNOLDS H. B. age 84y in Troupsburgh, NY April 28, 1884

BIERCE Mrs. Sally age 84y in Troupsburgh, NY April 29, 1884

GRIGGS Gusta age 19y dau of W. N. and Martha Griggs in Troupsburgh, NY April 29/30, 1884

BRONG James E. age 55y in Canisteo, NY May 2, 1884. Leaves wife and 3 children

WILLIAMS Olive age 23y dau of Nathan B. Williams in Jasper, NY May 3, 1884

PLOSS Simeon H. in Jasper, NY May 8, 1884

LAWRENCE Mrs. Ruth age 74y in Cameron, NY May 9, 1884

ADSIT A. G. age 80y brother of Martin Adsit of Hornellsville, NY in Silver Creek, NY May 7, 1884

HENRY James age 62y 11m 23d in Hartsville, NY May 21, 1884

MULLIKIN Samuel Scott age 78y 8m 18d of Buena Vista, NY May 27, 1884. He was a drummer in War of 1812

HALLETT David O. age 18y in Canisteo, NY May 21, 1884

CONKEY Ervin age 15y 28d son of Erlick and Kate in Greenwood, NY June 21, 1884

KNAPP William F. age 35y 4d in Canisteo, NY July 1, 1884

CLEMENT ___ age 1m 7d son of Bloomfield Clement in Canisteo, NY June 19, 1884

NORRELL Charles H. age 23y of Georgia at res. of Mr. C. E. **LOVELL** in Canisteo, NY July 2, 1884

SMITH Sylvester age 80y burned to death at home of George **BARBER** in N. Cameron, NY June 30, 1884

FOOTE Mary B. age 68y dau of late Eli **BIDWELL** of Bath, NY in Flint, Mi. (Newspaper date July 10, 1884)

FERENBAUGH Fidelus in Painted Post, NY July 15, 1884. Born 1799 in Germany and came to US in 1824. Father opened harness shop with sons Fidelus, Valentine and John B. Married 1830 Judith **RORABAUGH** sister of Joseph of Erwin Center, NY. She died 1834 leaving son Daniel P. and dau Judith

BENNETT Ida age 34y wife of Sidney Bennett in Hornellsville, NY July 15, 1884, buried Canisteo, NY

CRULL Nellie age 4m 1d dau of Marshall and Nellie in Woodhull, NY July 19, 1884

ORDWAY Hannah age 75y widow of Daniel Ordway in Cameron, NY July 24, 1884

FORD Eliza Madison in her 76th yr in Lawrenceville, Pa. August 12, 1884 buried Lindley, NY. Born March 24, 1809 in Bath, NY dau of Gen. Daniel **CRUGER**. Mother was niece of Henry A. **TOWNSEND**. Married Charles H. L. Ford son of James Ford of Lawrenceville. Husband died 1882. 6 children, 2 living Daniel Cruger Ford of Lawrenceville and Charles L. of Canisteo, NY. Dau died 10 yrs ago.

VAN WIE Catherine widow of Henry Van Wie formerly of Howard, NY suicide by cutting throat in Jasper, NY August 19, 1884. Husband died August 16, 1883

ABER William age 65y in Canisteo, NY August 26, 1884. Born February 17, 1819 in Big Flats, NY

SWEET Nettie dau of S. C. Sweet of Hornellsville, NY formerly of Canisteo, NY August 24, 1884

TOWLE Richard W. formerly of Bath, NY from escaping gas in house while sleeping in Chicago, Ill. August 21, 1884

CUNNINGHAM Mrs. Joseph age 33y in Canisteo, NY August 30, 1884

HOLT Mrs. Nancy age 63y in Bennetts Creek, NY August 21, 1884

DAVIS Amanda Melissa wife of Benjamin Franklyn Davis Jr. and dau of Charles **CORNISH** in Jasper, NY August 29, 1884. Born June 11, 1854 and married August 31, 1873. 2 daus age 10y and 5y and 1 son age 8y

HATCH Mrs. Phebe in Jasper, NY September 3, 1884. Born June 27, 1802 in Lyndsborough, NH only dau of Timothy **ORDWAY** who had 1 dau and 3 sons, Jonathan kicked by horse and died, Enoch drowned in Canisteo river and Timothy died in NH. Married January 26, 1832 Eben Hatch who died February 26, 1863. 5 children 2 living Mrs. Homer **STEWART** Mrs. Moses F. **WHITTEMORE**

CARPENTER Charles K. age 58y formerly of Hornellsville, NY in Orion, Mi. (from Orion Review published August 28, 1884). Born January 23, 1826 in Hornellsville descendant of William C. Carpenter who came from Amesbury, England in 17th century. Married November 27, 1847 Jeannette **CORYELL**. 8 children, 6 living Prof. Rollo C. of State Agriculture College in Lansing, Mi., William L. Atty. in Detroit, Mi., E. Blanche wife of C. H. **SEELEY** of Mellett, Dakota, Louis G., Mary L. and Jenette. 2 sisters Mrs. Mary **POWELL** age 76y of Hornellsville and Mrs. Hannah **DEWEY** age 71y of Hartsville, NY.

DIVEN Harrison Lee age 1y 11m 10d in Canisteo, NY September 10, 1884

DIMMICK Grace May age 3m 15d in Hartsville, NY September 11, 1884

GRANGER Margaret (**CAMPBELL**) age 58y wife of William Granger in Canisteo, NY September 16, 1884. Married June 4, 1846 and had 15 children. Names 1 dau Mrs. Clark **SIMPSON** of Canisteo

TERRY George W. in Hornellsville, NY September 20, 1884

HALLETT ___ infant dau of Theodoric in Canisteo, NY September 23, 1884

MC KEAN Nicholas C. age 1y 2m 6d in Canisteo, NY September 25, 1884

KYSOR William Byron age 26y in Howard, NY September 26, 1884

MC GUIRE John age 10m son of John and Jessie in Hornellsville, NY October 17, 1884

BUCK ___ infant dau of Frank and Mary Buck in Hornellsville, NY October 20, 1884

PIERCE Margaret E. at son's D. C. **DAILEY** in Caneadea, NY October 17, 1884. Born October 25, 1797 dau of Rev. Thomas **MC GEORGE** of Oxford, NY. 2nd husband died 1870, lived with dau Mrs. William **BARKALOW** of Canisteo, NY. Had 8 children 7 living

HAYES Eva age 20y in Hartsville, NY October 27, 1884

WOOD Henry age 62y suicide by hanging in Cohocton, NY October 30, 1884. Born 1822 in Groton, NY. Leaves invalid wife and 4 children

COLE Hannah M. age 57y wife of F. S. Cole in Howard, NY November 4, 1884

BRASTED John age 54y son of John Brasted of Howard, NY in Alfred Center, NY October 26, 1884

INGALLS Albert age 55y hit by chain while pulling stumps in Hartsville, NY November 11, 1884

MARVIN Cynthia age 79y of Canisteo, NY in Hornellsville, NY November 25, 1884

GRANGER Jennette abt 40y wife of Leveritt in Canisteo, NY November 24, 1884

O'HARIGAN Cornelius age 81y in Greenwood, NY November 23, 1884

LEWIS Elmina age 75y wife of H. B. Lewis in Jasper, NY November 22, 1884

Corning and Blossburg Advocate

August 21, 1840 - September 6, 1843

BAILEY Charles S. age 18y son of Col. B. P. Bailey in Corning, NY August 27, 1840

ALDRICH Stephen age 68y 6m formerly of RI in Cameron, NY October 15, 1840

BISHOP Doctor William abt 36y in Corning, NY October 22, 1840

LAND Ellen age 17y dau of Robert Land in S. Corning, NY October 14, 1840

REED Sally age 36y wife of Romeo Read late of Ithaca, NY and dau of Samuel and Mary **PARCEL** near Corning, NY December 14, 1840

TERBELL Henry Stokes age 2y 7m son of W. and A. L. Terbell in Corning, NY January 25, 1841

DEATH NOTICES

BROWN Harriet wife of Nathan Brown and dau of John and Polly **WOODRUFF** formerly of Ithaca, NY in Hector, NY March 22, 1841

SHAW Robert James age 1y 13d son of Col. Daniel J. and Sarah Jane Shaw in Corning, NY March 26, 1841

MINER Maria age 43y wife of Whitman R. Miner in Campbell, NY March 24, 1841

PRATT Cerinthia B. age 16y 11m dau of Joel B. and Cerinthia Pratt in S. Corning, NY June 27, 1841

PARCEL Franklin D. age 2m 18d son of John A. and Caroline Parcel in Corning, NY August 14, 1841

FARNHAM Edward Fayette age 3y 6m son of E. J. in Bath, NY August 21, 1841

COURTWRIGHT Mrs. Mary age 66y formerly of Williamsburg, Pa. at res. of H. G. **PHELPS** in Corning, NY September 9, 1841

GRAHAM John age 34y in Corning, NY September 15, 1841

CURTIS Jane M. age 16y 7m of Campbell, NY while visiting friends in Newtown, Ct. September 11, 1841

BABCOCK Sarah age 63y in Caton, NY September 20, 1841

ROWLEY Abijah age 56y near Corning, NY August 2, 1841

KNOWLTON Sarah in her 46th yr wife of Chester in Hornby, NY October 25, 1841

ARNOLD Oliver Jr. age 8y son of Oliver Arnold in Corning, NY January 3, 1842

CLARK Theodore L. in his 21st yr son of John Clark of Lawrence, NY at res. of N. L. **SOMERS** in Corning, NY February 25, 1842

ROWLEY Miss Jane in her 20th yr dau of Abijah Rowley February 12, 1842

PRITCHARD Anna in her 47th yr consort of Calvin Pritchard in Lawrenceville, Pa. February 20, 1842

CALKINS Joseph in his 24th yr in Corning, NY April 25, 1842

BADGER Eunice age 28y consort of H. E. Badger in S. Corning, NY August 9, 1842

MUMFORD Lavina age 23y sonsort of Dr. Ores Mumford in Corning, NY August 10, 1842

PHELPS Mrs. Hannah in her 69th yr widow of Joseph D. Phelps and Mother of late Charles H. in Stonington, Ct. November 2, 1842

SHAW Sarah Elizabeth age 10m 15d dau of Col. D. J. Shaw Jr. and Sarah J. in Corning, NY March 10, 1843

MC NEIL Mary in her 73rd yr widow of John Mc Neil in Oxford, NY March 15, 1843

STEELE Stephen S. in his 45th yr at Father's June 4, 1843. Born July 1798

DUNN James age 33y in Corning, NY June 6, 1843

WELLS Relzeman in his 44th yr in Orwell, Pa. May 20, 1843

SUTLIFF Demaris M. age 30y 8m 11d wife of Milo Sutliff in Smyrna, NY July 6, 1843

PALMER Mrs. Sarah G. in her 24th yr in Corning, NY July 20, 1843

ROCKWELL Horatio age 23y in Corning, NY July 21, 1843

Corning Democrat

December 1, 1884 - December 25, 1884

DOWERS Joseph in his 91st yr at res of A. B. **FERGUSON** in Knoxville, NY December 3, 1884

BLUTE Pierre age 50y at Willard Asylum December 3, 1884

DONOVAN Patrick age 90y at dau Mrs. Henry **WIXSTED** in Corning, NY December 4, 1884

LEARY Daniel age 31y in Corning, NY December 7, 1884 and dau Mary age 7y died December 11, 1884, both died of burns

ALLEN Thomas O. age 65y nr Corning, NY December 13, 1884, buried Big Flats, NY

ROBINSON Asher E. suicide in Erwin Center, NY December 15, 1884

WICKS Hiram age 75y in Corning, NY December 16, 1884

SHAW Rose Mabel age 13y dau of Louis E. Shaw in Corning, NY December 17, 1884

GILL Patrick age 69y in Corning, NY December 17, 1884. 2 children Thomas Gill and Mrs. Kate **CONNEL**

NIXON Daniel age 85y in Corning, NY December 18, 1884

GUION H. B. fell from ladder in Corning, NY December 16, 1884

DEATH NOTICES

HEDGES Caleb in Bradford, NY December 21, 1884

AYERS Mrs. Elizabeth age 92y one of earliest settlers in Canisteo Valley in Arkport, NY December 20, 1884

FOX Joseph S. age 5y son of Alanson J. Fox in Painted Post, NY November 26, 1884

FERO Catherine age 74y wife of Abram Fero at son's Abram C. Fero in Hornby, NY November 23, 1884. Born Berk Co. Pa. dau of George and Elizabeth **ARRANCE**. Married age 19y, 10 children. Leaves husband age 92y and 5 living children

Corning Journal

July 21, 1847 - December 27, 1872

NORTHWAY Miss Elsy age 18y suicide in Campbell, NY July 18,1847

WOLLAGE Rev. Elijah in his 79th yr in Starkey, NY July 18, 1847

PERRY Dr. A. E. in his 53rd yr in W. Dresden, NY March 8, 1848

LATTIMORE Horace W. age 1m 13d son of S. Y. in Woodhull, NY March 17, 1848

WRIGHT R. S. abt 30y in Corning, NY April 17, 1848

HERRINGTON Caroline youngest dau of N. M. in Corning, NY May 11, 1848

VAN OSTRANDER Sally Ann age 45y in Corning, NY May 12, 1848

GRANGER Franklin age 17y son of Daniel in Woodhull, NY May 17, 1848

DAVIS Melchior H. in his 24th yr son of James C. Davis of Corning, NY abt May 1, 1848, killed by falling barrel on Steamship nr St. Louis, Mo.

MC KNIGHT James E. of Attica, NY son of James Mc Knight of Corning, NY drowned in Niagara River July 11, 1848

MESSENGER Rosanna Mary Theresa age 20y dau of George Messenger in Corning, NY July 20, 1848

TOMPSON Cerena abt 25y wife of John Tompson in Woodhull, NY July 14, 1848

BOUGHTON Mary Jane age 37y wife of Cornelius in Campbell, NY August 6, 1848

HALL Sarah age 21y wife of Francis Hall and dau of Miles **COVELL** in Elmira, NY August 4, 1848

GILBERT Mary P. age 32y wife of William D. in Corning, NY August 18, 1848

MILLS Charles infant son of Thomas and Jane A. **MC BURNEY** in Corning, NY August 13, 1848

REYNOLDS W. W. age 40y in Big Flats, NY October 7, 1848

KNOX Fanny in her 75th yr wife of John Knox in Campbell, NY November 5, 1848

BRIGDEN Susan Thomson age 4y dau of G. N. in Painted Post, NY December 6, 1848

MORROW Cornelia R. age 23y wife of F. W. Morrow in Hornby, NY January 3, 1849

MITCHELL John age 92y ar Revolutionary Soldier in Catherine, NY February 15, 1849

ADAMS Samuel H. age 28y 2m at Father's in Painted Post, NY February 27, 1849

PARK Emily A. consort of Henri Park and youngest dau of late George **GARDNER** of Big Flats, NY in Addison, NY April 3, 1849

MEAD Mrs. Hannah age 67y formerly of Big Flats, NY in Campbell, NY April 9, 1849

VANDERHOFF Nancy wife of Philander Vanderhoff in Campbell, NY April 7, 1849

SPENCER Ellen Julia age 4y 10m dau of G. T. and Harriet Spencer in Corning, NY April 28, 1849

ROBBINS John in his 84th yr in Campbell, NY July 25, 1849, res of Co. 34 yrs

BOSTWICK Mercy in her 62nd yr sister of H. W. in Corning, NY August 24, 1849

CLARK Jesse Jr. on way to Cal. July 12, 1849

DAVIS ____ age 10y dau of John Davis murdered by Barnard **MADDEN** in Knoxville, NY December 30, 1849

RHODES Isaac age 19y in Corning, NY February 21, 1850

POTTER Bradford A. age 58y in Corning, NY February 22, 1850

SIMONDS Juliette age 14y dau of Benona and Sally in Gibson, NY March 3, 1850

WHITE Miss Jane age 18y in Addison, NY March 5, 1850

SHERWOOD Lydia age 33y wife of Jesse D. Sherwood and dau of Rev. M. **DYER** of W. Windsor, NY in Corning, NY April 7, 1850

CUMPSTON Samuel age 60y in Corning, NY April 3, 1850

HARROWER Levi B. son of B. Harrower of Lindley, NY in Jacksonville, Fl. January

20, 1850, buried in family burying ground

STANLEY Charles Edward age 2y 13d son of Dr. S. Stanley in Corning, NY August 13, 1850

PECK Garry M. age 52y in Mansfield, Pa. August 22, 1850

HERRINGTON Daniel G. infant son of N. M. Herrington Md. in Corning, NY August 23, 1850

JONES William Baskin age 69y in Canisteo, NY September 1, 1850, res over 40 yrs

MC CUE Patrick hit by train walking tracks nr Corning, NY October 17, 1850

STEELE Edward A. son of William A. Steele of Painted Post, NY in Sacramento, Cal. October 30, 1850

SHANNON Capt. William E. age 28y son of Robert Shannon of Corning, NY in Sacramento, Cal. November 3, 1850. Native of Co. Mayo, Ire. emmigrated to US December 1830

GILLETT Emma Matilda age 11y 11m dau of J. D. in Addison, NY January 18, 1851

THOMAS Harriet in her 25th yr wife of Levi in Corning, NY February 22, 1851

ROBINSON Laban age 9y son of Sullivan and Jane in Corning, NY May 4, 1851

TURK Henrietta in her 20th yr wife of David Turk of Addison, NY at father's Richard C. **WEST** in Corning, NY June 27, 1851. Leaves infant child

PEEBLES Caherine M. in her 51st yr wife of C. Peebles Md. and dau of Judge **STEELE** in Big Flats, NY July 14, 1851

NORTHRUP Lucretia (**WATTLES**) wife of H. M. Northrup August 12, 1851

PRESTON Charles age 30y formerly of Corning, NY in Ottawa, Can. August 13, 1851

CARPENTER Isaac age 58y of Albany, NY formerly of Corning, NY in Ithaca, NY October 2, 1851

MC BURNEY Jane A. wife of Col. Thomas Mc Burney and dau of late Elisha T. **MILLS** of Fairfield Ct. in Corning, NY October 8, 1851

SANBORN Sarah E. dau of Mrs. Mary Sanborn of Corning, NY and dau of late Rev. Reuben Sanborn at New Albany, Ind. September 26, 1851

HATCH Mrs. Damon age 45y of Grand Rapids, Mi. in New York City Novemer 14, 1851

MEAD Mrs. ____ formerly of Corning, NY in Campbell, NY December 14, 1851.

Came to Steuben Co. with 1st husband Frederick **CALKINS** over 50 yrs ago

GARDNER Claeb Lewis in Elmira, NY December 7, 1851

SLY George age 87y in Knoxville, NY December 29, 1851

RIGBY Ximens age 57y wife of Daniel of Nanticoke Springs, NY January 26, 1852

HAYT Harry age 56y bro of J. C. of Corning, NY in Patterson, NY January 31, 1852

CUMPSTON C. P. age 2m 8d only son of Theodore and Margaret February 14, 1852

ASPINWALL Mrs. Eudocia age 69y 1m 29d wife of Dr. Nathaniel Aspinwall in Elmira, NY March 11, 1852

DAVISON Anna Maria in her 37th yr wife of J. R. Davison and dau of James C. and Susan H. **DAVIS** in Caton, NY March 7, 1852

JANES Joel abt 50y in Hornby, NY March 12, 1852

SORNBERGER Alfred in his 74th yr formerly of Rochester, NY in Corning, NY March 23, 1852

RUMSEY David Sr. father of David Rumsey late mem of Congress in Bath, NY March 16/17, 1852

LOVELL Henry A. in his 36th yr in Big Flats, NY February 14, 1852

WOOD Charles E. age 10m son of Willard and Maria Wood in Campbell, NY February 25, 1852

ROBINSON Mary M. age 32y wife of Charles L. Robinson in Elmira, NY April 8, 1852, buried Corning, NY

DAVIS Augusta age 6y 1m 6d dau of Rev. L. Davis in Corning, NY April 17, 1852

CUNNINGHAM William in his 56th yr in Corning, NY April 29, 1852

REED David A. in his 24th yr son of Romeo Reed in Caton, NY April 27, 1852

NORTH Lou B. wife of Theodore North and dau of James **BRADLEY** in Elmira, NY May 9, 1852

HARDENBURGH Marcia age 48y in Caton, NY May 7, 1852 (Ithaca Chronicle Please copy)

BURT Sarah Elizabeth age 18y formerly of Painted Post, NY in Orange, NY May 13, 1852

OWEN Caroline M. age 28y wife of George H. Owen in Big Flats, NY June 8, 1852

GIFFORD Benjamin age 86y of Attica, NY in Corning, NY June 15, 1852

BABCOCK Mrs. Robie age 31y wife of Henry L. Babcock and dau of late Duty **SHIPPEN** formerly of Chenango Co. NY in Caton, NY June 12, 1852. Leaves 4 children

PARCEL Samuel age 76y nr Corning, NY July 10, 1852

FERENBAUGH Mrs. Mary age 76y at son's Fidellus in Centreville, NY July 15, 1852

BRAINARD James age 1y 5m 14d son of John and Christiana Brainard formerly of Corning, NY in Poughkeepsie, NY July 14, 1852

GORTON Moses Jr. age 56y in Gibson, NY July 17, 1852

RHODES Nelson Winton abt 25y son of Silas H. in Caton, NY August 10, 1852

TODD Miss Emeline age 44y formerly of Toddsville, NY August 24, 1852

WORMLEY Sally age 54y wife of Samuel Wormley in Corning, NY August 10, 1852

ABBOTT Hiram age 45y in Corning, NY October 3, 1852

CARPENTER R. D. in his 47th yr formerly of Cayuga Co. NY in Corning, NY November 3, 1852

CALKINS Mary Ellen in her 23rd yr wife of George B. Calkins in Bethel, Oh. October 20, 1852. Married 3 yrs

PIERSON Hannah Maria in her 15th yr dau of A. T. C. Pierson formerly of Gibson, NY in St. Paul, Mn. October 23, 1852

DAVIS Mercy age 46y wife of George W. Davis in Woodhull, NY October 30, 1852

CLARKE Lester L. Engineer of NY and ERR in Wellsville, NY November 11, 1852

DAVISON Charles W. age 35y in Caton, NY November 17, 1852

REYNOLDS James De Armand age 19y in Elmira, NY December 10, 1852

BALDWIN William W. age 25y in Addison, NY December 28, 1852

GARDNER Daniel C. abt 28y in Corning, NY January 3, 1853

GREGORY John age 24y son of Burt and Hannah in Rathbone, NY January 30, 1853

FORD Phebe Ann age 20y dau of Oliver Ford in Big Flats, NY February 4, 1853

GILBERT George F. age 19y son of W. D. Gilbert formerly of Corning, NY in Corning February 17, 1853

RIGBY Mariette in her 22nd yr wife of William T. Rigby and dau of Alvah **ROWLEY** in Corning, NY February 18, 1853

VAN ETTEN Alzina age 10y dau of Robert H. and Lavina Van Etten in Gibson, NY March 7, 1853

GORTON William H. Jr. in his 25th yr in Corning, NY March 18, 1853

GREGG Henrietta J. age 30y 8m wife of Isaac B. Gregg and dau of late Mordecai **OGDEN** in Elmira, NY March 22, 1853

HILLECK O. E. age 6y 4m 9d son of Samuel and Caroline Hillick in Binghamton, NY April 9, 1853

DILLON Cornelia S. wife of William the Editor of Western Atlas March 10, 1853

SHAW Col. D. J. formerly of Corning, NY in Ithaca, NY rec (Newspaper date April 22, 1853)

WATKINS Betsey E. age 62y wife of Thomas W. in Corning, NY May 9, 1853

EDGAR Nathan in his 21st yr in Caton, NY May 24, 1853

HAMILTON Sarah in her 21st yr in Campbell, NY May 31, 1853

BARKER Imogene age 3y dau of Stillman Barker in Corning, NY June 16, 1853

LOMBARD Grace Caroline age 8m dau of Charles and Ann E. Lombard July 18, 1853

STANLEY Franke Albert son of Dr. S. and Fidelia in Corning, NY July 17, 1853

ROBINSON M. Cushman in his 23rd yr in Corning, NY June 27, 1853

COUCH Maj. Gen. Jonathan P. abt 60y in Havana, NY July 25, 1853

FULLER Frank M. age 1y 4m son of D. A. and J. E. in Corning, NY August 7, 1853

BANCROFT Catherine in her 62nd yr wife of H. D. Bancroft of Painted Post, NY and dau of George **TEEPLES** of Campbell, NY in Painted Post August 5, 1853

HYDE ___ infant dau of Dr. E. E. Hyde in Corning, NY August 24, 1853

JONES Rosalie infant dau of Israel P. Jones in Corning, NY August 27, 1853

VAN ETTEN Eliza age 4m dau of Simon Van Etten in Corning, NY September 6, 1853

BILLINGS Silas age 63y in Elmira, NY August 28, 1853

SMITH Laura Sophia age 27y dau of Nathaniel in Addison, NY September 5, 1853

DEATH NOTICES

VAN HORN Emily Ettie age 20y in Corning, NY September 10, 1853. Sister of Mrs. A. **PARKS** of Corning

GORTON Alexander A. age 6m son of Alonzo H. and Maria Gorton in Corning, NY September 15, 1853

SACKETT Margaret D. in her 27th yr in Elmira, NY September 19, 1853

LOWE Cornelius age 80y in Big Flats, NY September 16. 1853

HOLLY H. A. age 37y in Elmira, NY September 19, 1853

THOMPSON Martha C. age 20y wife of La Rue Thompson and dau of Dr. John C. **HAYT** in Corning, NY October 8, 1853

STANTON John T. age 41y in Hornby, NY October 11, 1853

FREER Cynthia Ann wife of George G. (formerly Mrs. Dr. **WATKINS**) in Watkins, NY October 1, 1853

MAYNARD George W. age 26y of Penn Yan, NY at res in Aspinwall September 3, 1853

FROST Melinda age 42y wife of E. C. Frost in Catherine, NY October 15, 1853

DAVENPORT Lewis Paysors age 6m son of L. Davenport in Corning, NY October 6, 1853

WELLMAN Selina De Ett age 8y dau of Russell and Polly M. Wellman in Hornby, September 28, 1853

DUDLEY Charles H. age 22y only son of Abram in Addison, NY October 28, 1853

FREEMAN Mrs. Elizabeth age 37y in Corning, NY October 21, 1853

PIERCE Lucien G. age 35y formerly of Otsego Co. NY in Corning, NY November 8, 1853

BEARD Mary A. age 42y wife of J. P. Beard and sis of Dr. C. **PEEBLES** of Big Flats, NY in Knoxville, NY November 7, 1853

MALLORY Mary age 44y wife of John Mallory in Knoxville, NY November 27, 1853

JONES Elijah age 67y in Elmira, NY November 30, 1853

MILLS George A. in his 21st yr son of late Charles L. Mills of Corning, NY in Brooklyn, NY December 19, 1853

FLUENT Mrs. Lucas abt 35y in Addison, NY January 5, 1854

WATKINS Thomas W. age 68y in Corning, NY January 17, 1854

WHEELOCK Paris age 57y in Corning, NY February 6, 1854

LAWRENCE Nancy Adelaide age 4y 2m dau of Whitehead and Susanna Lawrence in Gibson, NY February 8, 1854

GORTON Clinton eldest son of late Rev. J. N. in Corning, NY February 2, 1854

PALMER Rev. Abel R. age 56y in Hornellsville, NY February 16, 1854

BENNETT Abraham age 76y in Painted Post, NY March 7, 1854

DRAKE Isaac L. Md. age 27y formerly of Corning, NY in Clarksville, Oh. February 24, 1854

EVANS John E. age 76y in Erwin, NY February 27, 1854. Born England and came to US 1798 landing at Phildelphia, Pa.

WATERS Sarah L. age 26y wife of L. M. Waters of Addison, NY and dau of Otis WHITTENHALL in Howard, NY (Newspaper date March 24, 1854)

DEARMAN Mary F. L. in her 8th yr dau of George and Sally Dearman in Corning, NY March 6, 1854

HURD Mary age 26y wife of Rev. I. N. Hurd and dau of Sheldon BASSETT of Hector, NY in Madras, NY January 31, 1854

ROUSE Sophia age 60y wife of Oliver Rouse in Gibson, NY April 12, 1854

MC NEIL Deborah formerly of Poughkeepsie, NY in Corning, NY May 16, 1854

ROBINSON Catherine E. age 58y wife of Ezekiel L. Robinson in Corning, NY May 24, 1854, formerly res of Exeter, NY

KING Lewis G. age 3y 7m 20d son of Rufus and Katherine King in Elmira, NY May 21, 1854

HAYT James A. in his 34th yr in Corning, NY May 29, 1854

BUCKLEY Andrew abt 45y in Knoxville, NY May 27, 1854

PAYNE Henry Ford age 24y bro of Mrs. David BAKER of Corning, NY in Machias, NY March 29, 1854

HAWLEY Harriet S. age 34y wife of William C. Hawley and dau of late Asa NOWLEN in W. Avon, NY June 21, 1854

HAYT Dr. John C. age 67y in Corning, NY July 2, 1854

LANE Harriet age 39y wife of David Lane in Corning, NY July 13, 1854

PERKINS Caroline P. age 26y wife of S. M. in Painted Post, NY July 22, 1854

SICKEL A. Z. age 31y in Elmira, NY August 16, 1854

HELMS Frank age 1y 22d only son of E. W. in Knoxville, NY August 15, 1854

KINNEY Marian (**WILLIAMS**) wife of Charles A. Kinney of Hornellsville, NY at Father's in Yates Co. NY August 10, 1854

MALLORY William Mc Conine age 15m 13d son of William M. Mallory in Corning, NY August 26, 1854

SHARPE Orville age 39y in Painted Post, NY August 26, 1854

BALDWIN Walter in his 26th yr in Addison, NY August 24, 1854

GREEN Alexander age 21y in Addison, NY August 24, 1854

DATES ____ age 13d dau of George and Fanny Dates August 24, 1854

RHODA Eliza L. abt 56y wife of Peter Rhoda in Hornby, NY September 6, 1854

REDFIELD Hannah Mary age 36y wife of J. A. Redfield and dau of Dr. John C. **HAYT** in Corning, NY September 12, 1854

MEIGS Isaac V. L. age 33y in Addison, NY September 8, 1854

DAVIS Capt. Aaron age 58y formerly of Corning, NY at son-in-law's Harvey **COOPER** in Corning, NY September 7, 1854

JACKSON Azuba age 57y wife of Henry Jackson in Corning, NY September 15, 1854

ROBBINS Clarissa in her 39th yr wife of John in Campbell, NY September 16, 1854

WHEELOCK Mrs. Philadelphia in her 78th yr in Corning, NY September 21, 1854

BRIGGS William abt 45y in Corning, NY October 4, 1854

PHENAS Harmon of Corning, NY in Pine Valley, NY October 1, 1854

FULLER Dor K. age 28y formerly of Corning, NY in Charleston, SC September 24, 1854

ROBERTSON Timothy age 40y in Corning, NY October 17, 1854

BUNDY Philura age 56y wife of William Sr. in Horseheads, NY October 21, 1854

ROSE J. Howard age 24/25 late of Corning, NY in Rockford, Ill. October 24, 1854

WHEELOCK Lida Ademia age 8m dau of George A. and Amelia Wheelock in Corning, NY November 16, 1854 and their son Julius Lyon Wheelock age 2y 10m died November 20, 1854

MALLORY Sarah Theresa in her 27th yr wife of William M. Mallory and dau of Judge **MC CONIHE** of Troy in Corning, NY November 10, 1854

ROSE B. Franklin age 35y of Corning, NY in Williamsport, Pa. November 15, 1854

VAN ETTEN Mary age 3y 10m dau of Simon and Mary Van Etten in Corning, NY November 24, 1854

BEARD Melissa in her 23rd yr dau of William L. in Corning, NY November 28, 1854

GREENMAN Mary Ella age 1y 11m dau of E. G. and Maria H. Greenman in Corning, NY November 29, 1854

HOWELL Aseneth age 59y wife of Jeremiah in Big Flats, NY November 20, 1854

MALLORY David age 57y in Corning, NY December 3, 1854

HILL Cyrena C. age 16y dau of Noble and Jane in Caton, NY December 24, 1854

CASE William F. age 20y son of F. W. Case of Corning, NY in La Porte, Ind. December 18, 1854

WILMARTH Benjamin age 73y formerly of Newark Valley, NY in Corning, NY December 26, 1854

JONES Catherine at adv. age widow of William B. in Addison, NY December 23, 1854

BUTTOLPH Edward A. Atty. formerly of Poughkeepsie, NY at Father's Rev. M. Buttolph in Castile, NY December 27, 1854

DENNIS S. B. formerly of Corning, NY in Susquehanna, Pa. January 8, 1855

EGBERT Ralph E. son of R. Egbert in Corning, NY January 7, 1854 and son Frank E. age 6y 2m died November 27, 1854

ARNOLD Oliver age 52y 1 of the early settlers in Corning, NY January 10, 1854

MERRICK Samuel age 73y Father of Mrs. D. A. **FULLER** in Corning, NY January 17, 1855 (Madison Co. papers please copy)

JOHNS Kate Bemis age 8m 3d dau of D. L. and A. R. Johns in Corning, NY January 21, 1855

THOMAS Walter J. suicide by hanging in Caroline, NY January 22, 1855

SMITH ___ age 8y dau of Lucas Smith killed at sawmill in Painted Post, NY January

20, 1855

CORTWRIGHT Sarah L. age 26y in Waymart, Pa. February 3, 1855, niece of H. G. **PHELPS** of Corning, NY

STARK Abby K. age 27y wife of William Stark at Father's Dr. John **HATMAKER** in Torrey, NY February 7, 1855

STEWART Elizabeth age 23y 5w 26d wife of Wellington Stewart and dau of Dexter and Emily H. **DAVIS** formerly of Orange, Mass. in Corning, NY February 26, 1855

FOSTER Robert W. in his 67th yr in Corning, NY March 4, 1855

MAY Lucene age 5y 4m 10d dau of Jesse May in Corning, NY March 9, 1855

REYNOLDS Caroline Matilda dau of Nathan Reynolds in Elmira, NY March 6, 1855

STILLSON Mrs. Polly age 82y at res of J. N. **ROBINSON** in Corning, NY March 16, 1855

COLBURN Adolphus age 55y in Elmira, NY March 23, 1855

CLEEVER Miss Sarah in her 62nd yr in Elmira, NY March 28, 1855

ROBINSON Mary abt 40y wife of Joseph Robinson in Corning, NY April 3, 1855

DOWNING Benjamin age 54y at res of Robert **MERRITT** in Knoxville, NY April 11, 1855

FARR Sarahettie age 26y dau of Henry and Jane Farr in Big Flats, NY May 3, 1855

SMITH Abby age 3y 7m 2d dau of Chauncey and Mary Jane Smith in Southport, NY May 12, 1855

HAZLETON J. age 48y in Corning, NY May 28, 1855

FAY ____ age 19m dau of S. G. Fay in Corning, NY June 16, 1855

ROWLEY Asaph age 78y in Corning, NY June 27, 1855, res over 60 yrs

HOSKINS Mary E. in her 20th yr late of E. Corning, NY in Smithfield, Pa. July 15, 1855

ROWLEY Levi age 74y in Corning, NY July 27, 1855

GRAVES Mrs. Densey age 66y in Le Roy (?) August 14, 1855

CHIDESTER Lydia age 52y wife of Daniel Chidester and dau of late Enos **CALKINS** of Corning, NY in Sugar Grove, Ill. August 12, 1855

STEUBEN COUNTY NEWSPAPERS 235

ROGERS Charles son of Benjamin Rogers in Hornby, NY August 25, 1855

ROBINSON Cushman M. age 7m son of William W. and Jenny Robinson in Corning, NY September 9, 1855

BOYER Eleanor wife of Samuel Boyer in Painted Post, NY September 12, 1855

SLY Mrs. George age 50y of Southport, NY at bro Mr. **BERRY** in Tioga, Pa. September 13, 1855

HUSTON James M. in his 60th yr in Dix, NY September 9, 1855

GOODENOUGH Henry B. age 23y in Towanda, Pa. September 30, 1855

MORTON Thomas age 90y 6m at son's Rev. Charles Morton in Corning, NY October 4, 1855. Born Athol, Mass. Settled 1793 in Chautaugua Co. NY, rec living with son

PEW Bertine age 56y in Corning, NY October 16, 1855

ROOSA Rev. Egbert age 63y in Elmira, NY October 14, 1855

REDFIELD Mrs. P. age 64y Mother of J. A. Redfield of Corning, NY in Bainbridge, NY October 9, 1855

FELLOWS Milton D. age 10y 8m son of Rev. N. Fellows in Trumansburgh, NY October 9, 1855

HART Mrs. Mary Ann age 44y in Corning, NY November 10, 1855

ELWELL G. S. in his 34th yr in Big Flats, NY November 15, 1855

FARWELL Sophia Jane in her 15th yr dau of B. P. in Corning, NY November 22, 1855

ROCKWELL Electa age 64y Mother of Mrs. L. H. **ROBINSON** of Corning, NY in Lock Haven, Pa. November 22, 1855

FRY Merritt H. son of C. H. Fry formerly of Big Flats, NY in San Francisco, Cal. August 1, 1855

GILES Henry age 43y in Horseheads, NY January 7, 1856

CASS Moses age 67y in Watkins, NY February 19, 1856

RHODES John age 45y in Big Flats, NY February 23, 1856

SULLIVAN Daniel age 18y son of Daniel and Helen Sullivan in Southport, NY February 25, 1856

BROOKS Dr. Thesecs in his 68th yr in Elmira, NY March 2, 1856

DEATH NOTICES

MITCHELL Ann E. age 21y wife of William Mitchell and dau of late Dr. W. **BISHOP** in Knoxville, NY March 7, 1856. 2 children, youngest age 5m died March 8, 1856, buried with Mother

TUTHILL Thomas J. age 54y of Elmira, NY in Horicon, Wis. February 26, 1856

TOWLE Moses E. age 32y formerly of Bath, NY in New York City March 22, 1856

TOOKER Enoch formerly of Bath, NY in Elmira, NY March 21, 1856

VAN GORDON Sophia L. age 33y wife of George W. Van Grodon and dau of Hannibal **CONGDON** of Rochester, NY in Big Flats, NY March 19, 1856

CARD ____ age abt 3w dau of John P. Card in Corning, NY March 26, 1856

EGAN Margaret age 7w dau of Patrick Egan in Painted Post, NY March 25, 1856

ROBINSON James C. age 59y formerly of Penn Yan, NY in Milwaukee, Wis. rec (Newspaper date March 28, 1856)

ROBINSON Lewis Fayette age 10y son of J. Nye Robinson in Corning, NY April 2, 1856

MUNSTER Peter age 30y in Corning, NY March 31, 1856

FRASER Anna M. age 21y wife of J. Fraser in Elmira, NY April 3, 1856

MAPES William age 102y a Revolutionary Soldier at Grandson's Phillip N. Mapes in Gibson, NY April 7. 1856

MOWRY John age 46y in Knoxville, NY April 7, 1856

WOLCOTT Milo in his 12th yr died April 11, 1856 and Milner C. age 9y 2m 27d died April 13, 1856 sons of Frederick Wolcott in Corning, NY

HANNA Mrs. Fanny in her 59th yr in Kanona, NY April 5, 1856

BROWNE Thomas age 60y in Corning, NY April 20, 1856

HUBBARD Guy H. age 32y bro of C. S. Hubbard of Corning, NY in Shelbourne Falls, Mass. April 15, 1856

MILLS Silas abt 65y in Big Flats, NY April 20, 1856

RICHARDSON Susan Amelia age 44y wife of Rev. J. B. Richardson in Geneva, NY April 14, 1856

FARR George W. in his 20th yr son of Henry and Jane in Big Flats, NY April 20, 1856

SWAIN M. age 32y wife of John Swain in Corning, NY April 26, 1856

JOHNSON Mary age 1y 9m 10d dau of Seymour F. and Lucretia (**DENTON**) in Corning, NY May 6, 1856

STENETHER ___ age 10m dau of John Stenether in Corning, NY April 28, 1856

COOPER ___ age 12d son of John J. Cooper in Corning, NY May 2, 1856

MURPHY ___ infant child of Daniel Murphy in Corning, NY May 4, 1856

COVELL Caroline age 27y dau of Robert Covell in Elmira, NY May 6, 1856

OWEN ___ age 13y dau of Elijah B. Owen in Big Flats, NY May 7, 1856

HICKS William age 40y in Corning, NY May 9, 1856

KIMBLE Jenette in her 21st yr wife of David Kimble in Gibson, NY May 14, 1856

COOK Benjamin C. Atty. age 56y of Marshall, Mi. at res of Constant Cook in Bath, NY May 14, 1856

DE HAAN C. age 6m dau of G. De Haan died May 24, 1856

FORD Ann (**VAN DUSEN**) age 32y in Hoboken, NJ June 8, 1856

WILLIAMS Susan Amelia age 23y wife of Edward C. of San Francisco, Cal. and dau of Benjamin **HARROWER** of Lawrenceville, Pa. in San Francisco May 30, 1856

MILLS Sophia age 34y 1m 20d dau of Silas Mills in Big Flats, NY June 30, 1856

GORTON Moses in his 83rd yr in Amity, NY June 29, 1856. Leaves 13 children, 60 grandchildren and 25 great grandchildren

RICHTU ___ infant son of William Richtu in Corning, NY July 15, 1856

RHODES Joseph age 50y in Big Flats, NY July 22, 1856, res 28 yrs

THOMSON E. N. only bro of Mrs. James **DUNN** of Elmira, NY in New Haven, NY July 18, 1856

HOPKINS Joseph age 32y in Knoxville, NY August 3, 1856

CLARK Phineas age 27y in Wayne, NY July 27, 1856

THRALL Wesley age 6m son of Jefferson Thrall in Corning, NY August 22, 1856 (date of newspaper was August 21, 1856, date of death given was August 22)

ROWLEY Hannah age 77y wife of Asaph Rowley in Corning, NY August 21, 1856

CRETSLEY William age 63y in Gibson, NY August 28, 1856

DEATH NOTICES

HAZEN Ellen Mary age 4y 5m 16d only dau of L. H. and Frances M. Hazen in Cuba, NY August 21, 1856

EMMONS Janette M. age 24y 8m wife of T. H. Emmons and dau of Henry **SQUIRES** in Kirkwood, NY September 15, 1856

PARKS Hannah age 26y wife of Alonzo Parks in Corning, NY September 15, 1856

WOODS Van Duzer age 4y son of James L. in Elmira, NY September 11, 1856

RUMSEY Dr. W. S. abt 35y in Painted Post, NY September 7, 1856

PATCHIN Harvey age 45y killed at barn raising in Dix, NY August 30, 1856. Originally from Ct. Leaves wife and 4 children

MORSE Annette R. in her 26th yr sister of Mrs. S. F. **DENTON** of Corning, NY in Portlandville, NY September 16, 1856

BAKER Mrs. ___ wife of Dr. Andrew Baker formerly of Bath, NY in Norwich, NY September 8, 1856. Leaves 9 children

NYHART Nelson J. age 5m 1w adopted son of Thomas and Ruth Nyhart in Corning, NY September 26, 1856

SHULTS Harriet age 2m 11d dau of Frederick in Corning, NY September 26, 1856

KELLY Bridget age 2m 4d dau of John and Bridget in Corning, NY September 27, 1856

WILDER Cordelia M. age 26y in Bath, NY October 7, 1856, buried Horseheads, NY

SMITH Mrs. Catherine M. age 70y at son-in-law's James H. **GULICK** in Blossburg, Pa. October 6, 1856

WELLS Larren age 35y in Gibson, NY October 27, 1856

BARBER Rufus H. age 13m 2d son of Joseph and Polly Barber in Corning, NY October 26, 1856

BURR Sally in her 22nd yr wife of William Burr and dau of Mrs. Charles **PRESTON** of Corning, NY in Corning October 22, 1856. Born October 24, 1834 in Binghamton, NY dau of late Stephen **SEYMOUR**. Married November 5, 1854. Only child died July 25, 1856

CHAPHE Marion M. age 2m dau of Capt. F. N. Chaphe in Corning, NY November 7, 1856 (date of newspaper was November 6, 1856, date of death given in paper was November 7, 1856)

SNELL Abram H. in his 12th yr died October 15, 1856, Walter Scott in his 2nd yr died October 16, 1856, Annis Alvira in her 8th yr died October 18, 1856 and Gordon Allen in his 4th yr died October 20, 1856, children of Elias and Alvira of Lawrenceville, Pa.

PHELPS Adeline L. age 44y wife of Frederick in Milport, NY November 5, 1856

MC KINNEY John age 65y Father of Mrs. G. W. **DYER** of Corning, NY in Great Bend, Pa. October 25, 1856

RHODES Grace age 55y wife of Timothy Rhodes formerly of Corning, NY in Ottawa, Ill. rec (Newspaper date November 27, 1856)

ZIELLY Ann T. age 31y wife of Thomas Zielly of Glyde, Oh. and dau of late David **TOOKER** of Elmira, NY in Painted Post, NY November 23, 1856

MAXWELL William age 62y in Elmira, NY November 22, 1856

TURNER Emily K. age 30y wife of Horace Turner of Corning, NY and dau of late Everard **PECK** of Rochester, NY in Corning November 29, 1856

SMITH Rebecca Y. age 40y wife of Justin M. in Corning, NY December 4, 1856

SHORT Thomas J. age 2y 22d son of Ashley in Corning, NY November 27, 1856

GRAY Rev. William age 70y of New York City formerly of Seneca Falls, NY at res of Dr. H. M. Gray in San Francisco, Cal. October 22, 1856

WRIGHT Samuel T. age 43y formerly of Rochester, NY in Madison, Wis. November 10, 1856

BAILEY Elvira P. age 15y dau of Col. B. P. in Corning, NY December 11, 1856

GRANT Neverson age 59y in Corning, NY December 5, 1856

PRATT Fredrick age 2y 10m 24d son of Ransom of Elmira, NY December 20, 1856

COOPER Merritt F. age 1y 9m in Gibson, NY December 21, 1856

FULLER William D. age 9m 27d son of D. A. in Corning, NY December 26, 1856

SPENCER Helen J. age 4y 3m 5d dau of William A. and Huldah Jane Spencer in Gibson, NY December 26, 1856

CROSS Charles age 9m son of John Cross in Corning, NY December 29, 1856

PARKER William Henry age 29y 9m 20d in Geneva, NY December 20, 1856

WHITNEY Harriet Eliza age 28y wife of Edgar M. in Caton, NY December 23, 1856

PRINGLE Joseph Gilbert age 17m 12d son of John in Corning, NY January 3, 1857

ROBINSON Harriet A. age 28y 3m 13d wife of Oscar F. Robinson January 7, 1857

RIGBY Florence Ames age 4m 12d son of William and Susan Rigby in Minneapolis,

Mn. December 24, 1856

RHODES Thomas age 32y of Big Flats, NY at sea on voyage to England for health rec. (Newspaper date January 15, 1857)

MILLER Jacob age 85y 9m 2d in Southport, NY November 20, 1856

YOUNG Ann age 46y wife of Andrew Young in Corning, NY January 16, 1857

COWLEY Catherine age 23 wife of Bernard Cowley in Corning, NY January 25, 1857. Born Kilkenny, Ire. nee **KELLY**. Married abt 1 yr

LEWIS Jay M. age 3y 7m 2d son of Alexander and Rosetta Lewis in Caton, NY October 16, 1856, also son Alonzo age 7y 2m 7d died January 2, 1857

MESSEREAU Joshua age 97y 7m 12d at son's James G. Messereau in Tioga, Pa. (Newspaper date February 5, 1857) Born Staten Island son of Joshua Sr.

BEARDSLEY Clara age 71y wife of Z. Clark Beardsley in Catherine, NY February 11, 1857

PERRY Guy M. age 56y of Elmira, NY at Geneva Water Cure February 19, 1857

STOKES Margaret age 26y wife of Henry Stokes in Mile Square February 17, 1857

MARTIN John C. V. age 3y 4m son of J. P. and C. E. Martin in Hornellsville, NY February 24, 1857

WHITE Mrs. Theodocia age 77y in Caton, NY February 21, 1857

REXFORD Samuel age 81y in Lock Haven, Pa. February 24, 1857

WILKINS Phebe in her 56th yr wife of William in Caton, NY February 16, 1857

COOKE Horace Williston age 19y of Athens, Pa. son of late David M. Cooke of Elmira, NY in New York City February 25, 1857

WHITE Constant H. age 3y 3m son of C. M. White in Corning, NY March 12, 1857

HOOD Jacob age 38y late of Corning, NY in Penn Yan, NY rec (Newspaper date March 19, 1857)

JONES Rev. Simeon R. age 83y in Southport, NY March 12, 1857

SMITH Amulet abt 21y son of H. D. Smith rec of Caton, NY white visiting in Oswego, Ill. March 28, 1857

YOUNG Sarah age 68y Mother of Mrs. W. S. **LOVEJOY** of Corning, NY in Corning, NY April 8, 1857 (Poughkeepsie papers please copy)

STEUBEN COUNTY NEWSPAPERS 241

WOOD Sophia Letitia in her 6th yr dau of Lewis and Eliza Wood in Corning, NY April 8, 1857

WHITE Mrs. Sarah in her 84th yr formerly of Philadelphia, Pa. in Corning, NY April 15, 1857

DUNN Michael age 30y in Gibson, NY April 7, 1857

BULLARD Emily age 26y wife of Rev. W. Bullard in Woodhull, NY April 3, 1857

HANFORD Thomas in his 72nd yr in Elmira, NY April 21, 1857

GIFFORD Mrs. Lucy age 65y in Lawrenceville, Pa. April 24, 1857

MC HENRY William age 65y in Erwin, NY April 26, 1857

DENTON Daniel age 24y 1m 10d son of Maj. S. B. Denton of Elmira, NY in New York City May 2, 1857

HALL Mrs. Clarissa age 40y in Hornellsville, NY April 24, 1857

DOTY Christopher age 68y 9m in Hornellsville, NY April 25, 1857

HENDERSCHOTT Susan B. age 34y wife of James D. Henderschott in Hornellsville, NY April 26, 1857

TERBELL George R. infant son of Dr. W. B. Terbell in Corning, NY May 10, 1857

COVELL Mathew age 38y won of Lyman Covell in Elmira, NY May 12, 1857

GORTON Rufus age 86y formerly of Corning, NY in Le Roy, Mi. May 8, 1857. father of Samuel Gorton of Corning, 14 children, 66 grandchildren and 28 great grandchildren

SMITH Howard age 14y 7m son of John and Mary of Pa. in Corning, NY May 5, 1857

SPENCER John age 2y 4m son of George T. Spencer in Corning, NY May 21, 1857

HAWLEY Harriet J. age 30y wife of Rev. Silas Hawley Jr. formerly of Penn Yan, NY in Fon-du-lac, Wis. May 13, 1857

DAVIS Dexter age 49y in Corning, NY June 1, 1857

BROWN ___ age 3m dau of E. Brown in Corning, NY June 8, 1857

HOWE Elizabeth age 25y 8m wife of J. T. Howe in Corning, NY June 13, 1857

HORN Ellen age 9y 2m dau of Edward and Almira in Corning, NY June 14, 1857

KNICKERBOCKER Vischer age 49y in Bath, NY June 4, 1857

MONTGOMERY William age 50y in Corning, NY June 10, 1857

MARTIN Olive age 3y dau of Jacob Martin in Corning, NY June 17, 1857

OGDEN Daniel age 48y in Coopers Plains, NY June 24, 1857

BRUNDAGE Frank in his 9th yr son of R. L. in Hornellsville, NY June 14, 1857

BRUNDAGE Charity in her 70th yr wife of Benjamin in Greenwood, NY June 19, 1857

HOWE Delphine age 15m dau of James and E. Howe in Corning, NY July 9, 1857

FAIRMAN Mary Eliza age 11y dau of S. B. Fairman in Elmira, NY July 31, 1857

RATHBONE Catherine in her 67th yr wife of Gen. Ransom Rathbone in Rathbone, NY July 25, 1857

MICKS Cornelia M. wife of Dr. William G. Micks and dau of Gen. Ransom **RATHBONE** of Rathbone, NY in Clinton, NC (Newspaper date August 6, 1857)

UNDERHILL Spencer Howell age 2y 22d died July 22, 1857 and Daniel Howell age 6y 10m died July 30, 1857 sons of R. L. Underhill in Bath, NY

DE WITT Alvina infant dau of Charles and Almira M. in Corning, NY July 3, 1857

KIMBLE Jonathan age 67y in Knoxville, NY August 9, 1857

TRAVER Dr. Robert M. age 50y in Painted Post, NY August 16, 1857

BURLEY Lilly Lucella age 3m 24d dau of J. A. and Sarah Burley in Gibson, NY August 13, 1857

DAVENPORT George Wilson age 2y 6m son of Lewis Davenport formerly of Corning, NY in Madison, Wis. August 14, 1857

PAWLING Mary wife of Thomas Pawling in Bath, NY August 21, 1857

PARMALEE Mary E. age 45y wife of Rev. A. H. Parmalee in Livonia Center, NY (Newspaper date August 27, 1857)

STEVENS Ethe Ann age 2y dau of R. Stevens in Gibson, NY August 27, 1857

ROBINSON William W. in her 25th yr son of L. H. Robinson in Corning, NY August 30, 1857

HOWARD Charles W. late of Chicago, Ill. September 15, 1857

GORTON Adelia A. dau of W. H. of Corning, NY in Covington, Pa. (Newspaper date September 24, 1857)

REDFIELD Anna age 65y wife of Harvey in Hornellsville, NY September 12, 1857

PRUNER Ellen E. age 28y wife of O. C. in Hornellsville, NY September 17, 1857

WRIGHT George age 6m son of George Wright in Corning, NY Septmeber 17, 1857

BURDICK Anna wife of Edwin Burdick accidently shot by neighbor while he was shooting at chicken nr Corning, NY September 19, 1857

CORBIN Alvin age 56y formerly of Painted Post, NY in Elmira, NY September 15, 1857

METCALF John formerly of Bath, NY in Springwater, NY September 20, 1857

KING George B. in Bath, NY September 20, 1857

EGBERT Helen age 10y dau of R. R. Egbert in Corning, NY September 28, 1857

HAWLEY Abijah age 81y Father of James M. in Big Flats, NY October 3, 1857

PARKER Louisa F. age 27y wife of James M. in Corning, NY October 18, 1857

WOOLEVER John age 30y in Hornby, NY October 18, 1857

OVIATT Ada age 4y dau of L. Oviatt of Addison, NY and grand dau of Russell **HUNT** of Corning, NY in Addison October 16, 1857

STACY Samuel C. in his 31st yr formerly of Corning, NY in Syracuse, NY October 24, 1857

CHATFIELD Mary T. wife of T. I. Chatfield of Owego, NY September 18, 1857. Leaves husband and Mother Mrs. **BUNDY**

HOLBROOK Dr. George W. age 38y in Elmira, NY November 15, 1857

PURDY Margareeche age 107y Mother of Dr. J. Purdy of Elmira, NY in Spencer, NY November 9, 1857. Born June 10, 1750 in Westchester Co. NY. Married October 23, 1773 Jotham Purdy who died October 5, 1777. She came to Tioga Co. NY with late son Andrew 40 yrs ago

SEWARD A. H. age 43y in Corning, NY December 14, 1857

RINESS John J. age 17y 3m 11d son of George and Jane Riness in Corning, NY December 28, 1857

ATWATER Jane M. age 34y wife of Dwight Atwater in Corning, NY January 4, 1858

HALE Jane T. age 49y 2m wife of J. K. in Hornellsville, NY December 22, 1857

GARDNER Susan M. age 55y wife of Dr. N. D. Gardner in Horseheads, NY December

29, 1857

COOLEY Susan A. age 55y 3m wife of L. J. Cooley and dau of late Guy **MAXWELL** in Elmira, NY January 4, 1858

LLOYD John age 35y res of Elmira, NY in Caton, NY December 31, 1857

WESTCOTT D. Clinton abt 30y in Caton, NY January 1, 1858

HOLLENBECK John age 66y in Corning, NY January 6, 1858

NEYHART Ada Margaret age 4m 9d dau of Thomas and Ruth Nayhart in Corning, NY January 8, 1858

BURLEY Sarah age 22y wife of Ithiel Burley in Corning, NY January 12, 1858

OWEN Joel age 28y bro of Blake Owen in Knoxville, NY January 27, 1858

CHAPMAN Miss Harriet age 22y in Gibson, NY January 27, 1858

GILBERT Samuel L. age 41y in Hornellsville, NY January 27, 1858

CLEAVELAND James age 27y in Knoxville, NY January 27, 1858

JOHNSON Mrs. Esther age 37y in Gibson, NY January 27, 1858

LARROWE Albertus age 82y Father of Judge Larrowe in Wheeler, NY (Newspaper date February 4, 1858)

WRIGHT Erastus in his 71st yr formerly of Bath, NY at son's Rev. A Wright in Cleveland, Oh. (Newspaper date February 4, 1858)

BROWN Miss Betsey A. age 31y in Corning, NY March 5, 1858

PEAK Helen age 3y dau of Oliver Peak in Gibson, NY March 15, 1858

MC BANE James Henry age 5y son of Jerome Mc Bane in Gibson, NY March 11, 1858

CLARK William Arthur age 3y 6m son of William B. in Knoxville, NY March 28, 1858

HARRISON William age 25y son of Jesse Harrison in Caton, NY March 27, 1858

HOLLY Mary Francis age 4y 7m dau of David and Ann in Knoxville, NY April 2, 1858

MALLORY Sarah Kate age 8y 5m dau of William M. in Corning, NY April 13, 1858

WHITMARSH Elisha age 7y 5m son of Ezra in Knoxville, NY April 22, 1858

MILES Ira J. in his 17th yr in Elmira, NY April 25, 1858

STEUBEN COUNTY NEWSPAPERS 245

ELEANDER Rhoda age 28y 7m died March 25, 1858 and husband John Eleander age 37y died April 9, 1858 in Pulteney, NY

STONE Sarah age 24y 2d in Pulteney, NY April 23, 1858

BARBER Helen age 6m dau of Joseph Barber in Corning, NY May 13, 1858

BELL Austin M. in his 45th yr in Elmira, NY May 11, 1858

SCOVILLE Hattie dau of Thadeus S. Scoville in Buffalo, NY May 14, 1858

CALKINS George W. age 38y in Knoxville, NY May 22, 1858

ROBINSON Jennie V. age 23y wife of William W. Robinson of Corning, NY in Kinderhook, NY June 6, 1858

WEDGE Lyman age 72y in Corning, NY June 2, 1858

GARDNER Nial in his 27th yr in Hornby, NY June 2, 1858

FAY Sarah age 19y dau of Dr. Fay in Painted Post, NY June 14, 1858

MITCHELL William P. age 30y in Ithaca, NY June 12, 1858

HAVENS Clarissa L. age 1y 5m dau of James H. and A. in Gibson, NY June 16, 1858

DRUMMOND Mary Weeks age 23y wife of William H. in Corning, NY June 28, 1858

BREES ___ age 2y 2m 27d dau of A. B. and N. H. Brees in Caton, NY June 23, 1858

OLCOTT Lucy M. age 10m 14d dau of Theodore Olcott in Corning, NY July 15, 1858

PLATT Charles age 28y in Knoxville, NY July 1, 1858, buried Owego, NY

HOAG Oscar Woodbury age 6m son of Charles H. and Addie J. H. **(CLARKE)** in Minneapolis, Mn. July 5, 1858

GREEN Kate age 10m dau of James Green August 2, 1858

AUSTIN Gertrude age 34y 5m wife of Richard Austin in Corning, NY July 29, 1858

SLY John age 71y in Knoxville, NY July 25, 1858

PATTERSON Mary wife of Robertson Patterson in Painted Post, NY July 31, 1858

LATTIMORE John age 65y in Woodhull, NY August 14, 1858

JONES Mary age 1y 6m dau of Edward Jones in Gibson, NY August 18, 1858

SANDFORD Ezra age 20y youngest son of Ira Sandford late of Dix, NY in Hartwood,

Va. July 29, 1858

HUGHSON James in his 70th yr in Big Flats, NY August 26, 1858

MORSE Dr. Floyd abt 35y in Painted Post, NY September 19, 1858

INGHAM Miss Mary E. age 20y in Middletown, Ct. September 14, 1858

STEVENS Martin in Deep River, Ct. September 26, 1858

CLARK Sarah Eliza age 23y 2m 28d wife of Erastus L. Clark and dau of W. T. **JOHNSON** formerly of Owego, NY in Owego October 5, 1858

DODGE Lorain age 65y 3m formerly of Sullivan, Pa. Father of Orrin Dodge in Knoxville, NY October 21, 1858

ABRAMS Nelson abt 60y in Caton, NY October 27, 1858

CHASE Mrs. Sophia age 47y in Elkland, Pa. November 11, 1858

BRIGDEN Charles L. in his 15th yr son of G. W. Brigden in Painted Post, NY (Newspaper date November 18, 1858)

WOLCOTT Capt. Charles age 90y one of the 1st settlers in Corning, NY November 18, 1858

CLEAVER M. A. age 31y wife of P. P. in Painted Post, NY December 15, 1858

THURBER Hezekiah age 65y in Corning, NY December 20, 1858

BAKER Harrison H. abt 40y in Painted Post, NY December 24, 1858

PALMER Rufus R. age 59y in Howard, NY December 30, 1858. Native of Otsego Co. NY and came to Howard 1835

MC CLENNAN Joseph D. age 35y 9m 17d in Hornellsville, NY January 10, 1859

TOWNSEND Sidney S. age 33y of Palmyra, NY at res of Father-in law David **CLARK** in Trenton, NJ January 9, 1859. He was bro of Mrs. C. C. B. **WALKER** and Mrs. S. T. **HAYT** of Corning, NY

CASS Mary E. age 21y in Watkins, NY January 18, 1859

RANDALL Hiram A. age 3m son of Charles E. in Gibson, NY January 14, 1859

GILDERSLEEVE Sarah L. age 5w 5d dau of B. Gildersleeve in Corning, NY January 27, 1859

HAIGHT Hester Ann age 38y wife of Silas Haight in Elmira, NY February 8, 1859

BEARD Mrs. S. M. in his 86th yr Mother of W. L. Beard of Corning, NY in Big Flats, NY February 13, 1859

HOPKINSON William age 50y in Gibson, NY February 21, 1859

LEAVENWORTH Anna Maria age 4y 6m dau of A. E. and M. R. Leavenworth in Hinesburgh, Vt. February 6, 1859

SPAULDING Sarah C. in her 31st yr wife of T. S. in Elmira, NY February 26, 1859

CHAPMAN Fannie age 28y wife of James H. Chapman of Reading, NY at Father's Maj. A. B. **DENTON** in Elmira, NY February 26, 1859

ROBINSON Joseph age 50y in Corning, NY March 3, 1859

ALLEN Charlotte age 34y wife of Oscar Allen in Corning, NY March 11, 1859

WOODARD Iris H. formerly with Newark Tioga Co. in Erwin, NY March 19, 1859

PRESTON Amanda R. age 30y wife of George W. Preston and dau of late Richard C. **WEST** in Corning, NY April 5, 1859

POTTER John A. age 32y son of Hiram Potter formerly of Elmira, NY in Weston, Wis. March 27, 1859

HODSKINS Jonas age 70y formerly of Corning, NY in Lisle, NY April 12, 1859

SWAN Amos S. Md. in his 49th yr in Hornby, NY April 7, 1859

BARNARD George age 4y son of Charles Barnard in Corning, NY April 7, 1859

BARNARD Martha Louisa age 2y 10m dau of George in Corning, NY April 7. 1859

BANKS Rev. Joseph age 52y bro of Dr. John Banks of Painted Post, NY in Cool Springs, Pa. April 8, 1859

SMITH Clarence W. age 9m 15d son of Thomas and Anna Smith in Corning, NY April 14, 1859

ELLIOTT Isabella age 15y in Hornellsville, NY May 12, 1859

OLCOTT Maj. Robert age 34y son of Thomas W. Olcott of Albany, NY in Corning, NY May 10, 1859

DURAND Nancy age 23y wife of D. D. Durand formerly of Westfield, NY in Addison, NY April 30, 1859

BAILEY John age 47y in Addison, NY May 29, 1859

HAVILAND J. Ward age 59y in Elmira, NY May 30, 1859

DEATH NOTICES

HOOD Frank Wellington age 9y 4m 7d son of William and Catherine Wood in Corning, NY June 7, 1859

ROSA Letitia C. age 28y wife of Rev. E. D. Rosa and dau of Phillip and Sarah **COKE** in Wellsville, NY May 27, 1859

BEEMAN Perry age 36y formerly of Lawrenceville, Pa. in Mendocino, Cal. April 26, 1859

BREES Nelson Le Grand abt 24y son of A. B. Brees in Caton, NY July 1, 1859

GORTON Silas age 78y Father of Mrs. Charles **PAGE** in Corning, NY July 1, 1859

PRATT Vernon Phelps age 5m son of Claudius B. in New York City June 27, 1859

DYER Polly age 72y wife of Rev. Moses Dyer and Mother of George W. of Corning, NY in W. Windsor, NY July 12, 1859

WHEELER Mrs. Fannie age 54y in Corning, NY July 23, 1859

MC INTYRE James W. age 10m 8d son of James in Corning, NY August 4, 1859

SCOTT Llewellyn age 11y son of Leonard Scott in Corning, NY August 10, 1859

PECK Ida Helen age 5m dau of Nelson W. Peck in Gibson, NY August 16, 1859

THRALL Maria age 2m dau of F. Thrall in Corning, NY August 12, 1859

WEEKS Nicholas age 71y 8m in Corning, NY August 13, 1859

PARK Anna Maria in her 16th yr dau of Rev. Charles C. Park in S. Pulteney, NY August 10, 1859

GLUR Ida age 2y 4m dau of Frederick Glur in Corning, NY August 25, 1859

FORD James age 76y 3m in Lawrenceville, Pa. August 18, 1859

BISHOP Jane age 1y 2m dau of Hoyt C. and Amelia in Corning, NY August 29, 1859

SAWYER Nathan of Bath, NY in Alton, Ill. August 24, 1859

BROWN Lucy age 8y 7m dau of Jonathan Brown in Corning, NY September 4, 1859

BANES David abt 80y in Corning, NY September 6, 1859

BABCOCK Ralph age 85y formerly of Corning, NY in Townsend, Oh. July 15, 1859

ERNEST Magdelina age 10m dau of Henry Ernest in Corning, NY September 18, 1859

TUPPER Virgil age 35y of Buffalo, NY formerly of Corning, NY in Corning September

25, 1859

SIMMONS Charles Martin age 1y 9m 17d son of M. B. and C. Simmons in Rochester, NY September 20, 1859

METCALF Levi age 38y formerly of Bath, NY in Canton, Ill. September 29, 1859

DINNIN Catherine (BRADLEY) age 45y wife of F. in Corning, NY October 9, 1859

VAN METER Sarah C. age 16y 7m wife of Joseph W. Van Meter and dau of George W. **WILLIAMS** formerly of Corning, NY in Oneco, Ill. November 5, 1859

BROWN James age 72y in Corning, NY November 7, 1859

PERRY Clement E. age 14y son of Everett W. Perry formerly of Dresden, NY at Cherokee Nation October 5, 1859

CORNELLSON Amanda M. age 29y wife of James in Elmira, NY November 15, 1859

BLAKESLEE Julia age 55y wife of Nathaniel in Addison, NY November 23, 1859

HATCH M. W. son of Dorus of Elmira, NY in New York City November 16, 1859

GILBERT Eunice D. age 21y wife of Dr. Horace E. in Caton, NY November 20, 1859

POTTER Byron age 3m 15d son of Roderick Potter in Corning, NY November 30, 1859

ADAMS Hugh age 5y son of Thomas W. Adams in Olean, NY December 4, 1859 and dau Lilly age 3y 8m 26d died December 13, 1859

CUNNINGHAM Martha age 25y wife of Claude in Corning, NY December 23, 1859

MAXWELL Guy in his 40th yr in Horseheads, NY December 7, 1859

MAYNARD John in his 3rd yr son of John in Corning, NY January 16, 1860

KIMBALL Moses age 71y in Monterey, NY January 8, 1860

TERBELL Eddie Douglas age 14m son of Dr. W. D. in Corning, NY January 29, 1860

COON William age 47y in Gibson, NY January 26, 1860

STURDEVANT Flora L. age 10y dau of Darius and Mary Sturdevant in Addison, NY January 27, 1860

CLUTE Derrick G. age 72y in Corning, NY February 3, 1860

BENJAMIN Sarah age 63y wife of Simeon Benjamin in Elmira, NY February 2, 1860

PRATT Mary age 80y Mother of D. and R. Pratt in Elmira, NY February 3, 1860

DEATH NOTICES

MERSEREAU Charles age 8y 3m in Corning, NY February 11, 1860

HOWARD Seth C. age 38y of New York City bro of H. A. Howard of Hornellsville, NY in Hornellsville February 11, 1860

STEVENSON Henry age 5m 15d son of Alma in Corning, NY February 28, 1860

BRINK Almira age 31y wife of Stephen Brink in Knoxville, NY (Newspaper date March 1, 1860)

PEW Adelia age 1y 23d died November 28, 1859 and Ida J. age 6y 2m died February 4, 1860 only children of Franklin and Sarah E. Pew formerly of Corning, NY in St. Louis, Mo.

BADGER Warren age 42y formerly of Corning, NY in Binghamton, Ill. February 26, 1860 and dau Nellie Maria age 2y 5m died February 22, 1860

CHIDESTER Martha age 46y wife of Samuel in Corning, NY March 17, 1860

PACKER Elizabeth B. age 16y dau of Charles Packer in Corning, NY March 26, 1860

GARDNER Mercy Ann age 61y wife of Caleb S. Gardner in Friendship, NY January 27, 1860. Born May 26, 1829 in Peru, NY. Married 1856

MATTERN Jacob age 5y 2m son of William and Mina in Corning, NY March 26, 1860

GOODWIN Julia H. age 43y wife of Sylvester Goodwin and dau of late Jeremiah **HALL** at bro Samuel Goodwin in Elmira, NY March 31, 1860

WILKES Mary age 1y dau of William Wilkes in Corning, NY March 26, 1860

WHITNEY Abraham in his 80th yr 1 of oldest settlers in Hornby, NY March 25, 1860

STEPHENS Rebecca T. age 28y wife of William W. Stephens March 29, 1860

FARRINGTON James Henry age 2y 7m 27d son of P. J. Farrington in Corning, NY April 9, 1860

TOBEY Pashall age 39y in Caton, NY March 31, 1860

BONHAM Harriet abt 55y wife of Amos Bonham in Caton, NY April 17, 1860

HAVENS Esther age 75y Mother of Jabez Havens in Corning, NY April 22, 1860

ROGERS Ruth Elizabeth in her 33rd yr wife of Dr. W. E. Rogers and dau of John and Eliza **LEE** (now Mrs. Jesse **CLARK** of Corning, NY). Born Wayne Co. Pa. in early life lived with Grandmother Mrs. Polly Lee

GILBERT Bertha age 26y 4m 6d wife of Dr. Rufus H. Gilbert of New York City and sister of John **MAYNARD** of Corning, NY in New York May 14, 1860

MC CORMICK George W. age 26y son of Edward Mc Cormick of Corning, NY at brother-in-law's Wilson **DEAN** in Catlin, NY May 18, 1860

HOOD Ella age 6y 4m dau of U. D. and Olive Hood in Corning, NY May 23, 1860

COMSTOCK Harriet wife of D. D. Comstock and sister of Col. H. W. **BOSTWICK** in Corning, NY May 26, 1860

DYER George W. age 38y in Corning, NY June 8, 1860

BARBER George age 13m son of Joseph and Polly in Corning, NY June 23, 1860

MANN Samuel age 48y in Erwin, NY June 24, 1860

LYON Deborah age 45y wife of Eli B. of Geneva, NY in Gibson, NY June 26, 1860

FULLER Jennie E. age 1y 11m 6d dau of D. A. and J. E. Fuller in Corning, NY July 22, 1860

MC KEAN W. H. H. age 45y in Erwin, NY July 23, 1860

LEONARD ____ age 10y son of Lewis Leonard drowned while fishing in Ithaca, NY (Newspaper date July 26, 1860)

CONROY Timothy age 13y son of Michael of Corning, NY drowned July 23, 1860

DAVIS Susan M. dau of John **HARDENBURGH** of Caton, NY in Ulster Co. NY July 13, 1860

WESTCOTT Leonora V. age 34y wife of Daniel P. Westcott and dau of J. B. **PRATT** of Corning, NY in Corning August 3, 1860, Leaves husband and 4 children, 1 only a few days old

EDWARDS A. age 70y Father of H. D. Edwards in Painted Post, NY August 16, 1860

DODGE Willie O. age 6y son of L. D. and Delia E. in Corning, NY August 10, 1860

MOORE James age 8m son of Joseph and Adele in Corning, NY August 22, 1860

DE WITT Charles age 35y in Corning, NY August 19, 1860

DEMING Elizabeth J. age 31y wife of E. F. in Corning, NY August 25, 1860

TROWBRIDGE William age 45y formerly of Corning, NY in Vicksburg, Miss. July 25, 1860

VAN ETTEN Peter age 28y in Gibson, NY August 28, 1860

ERWIN Rachel (**HECKMAN**) relict of Capt. Samuel Erwin in Painted Post, NY August 26, 1860. Born May 1, 1783 in Easton, Pa. and came to Painted Post in 1803. Named

DEATH NOTICES

1 dau Mrs. E. E. **TOWNSEND** of Painted Post

STEPHENS Miss Clara H. in Athens, Pa. August 10, 1860

JEFFREY John Edwin Lee age 11w son of E. A. in Corning, NY September 13, 1860

WEALE Elizabeth age 14y 2m 11d dau of William in Corning, NY September 1, 1860

WHITING William in his 18th yr son of W. B. Whiting of Corning, NY in Laurens, NY September 10, 1860

CALKINS Sarah age 23y dau of Ira M. Calkins in Bath, NY September 17, 1860

BURGESS Mrs. M. age 35y in Gibson, NY September 26, 1860

WOLCOTT Solomon B. formerly of Utica, NY in Addison, NY September 14, 1860

TIFFT Christiana in her 22nd yr wife of Charles B. Tifft and dau of A. H. **JOHNSON** in Corning, NY September 15, 1860

THOMSON Horatio age 57y father of C. H. Thomson of Corning, NY in Belchertown, Mass. October 5, 1860

EATON William age 17m son of John and Martha in Corning, NY October 24, 1860

BEEBE Edward age 2y 6m son of George Beebe in Corning, NY November 19, 1860

MC GAMMON Fanny May age 14m 10d dau of Charles and Martha Mc Gammon in Corning, NY November 14, 1860

CURTIS William Edward age 5y son of William in Corning, NY November 27, 1860

ROUSE Urana A. dau of Oliver of Gibson, NY in New York City November 23, 1860

ADAMS Sally age 67y wife of Capt. Samuel Adams of Painted Post, NY at son-in-law's John **FERENBAUGH** in Corning, Ny December 10, 1860

FARR Esther Anna age 8y 1w died November 23, 1860, Mary Ella age 9y 4m 25d died November 27, 1860 and Martha F. age 5y 11m died December 6, 1860, children of Valentine and Mary Farr of Big Flats, NY

DUTTON Deodatus age 83y formerly of Munson, Mass. in Brookfield, Mo. December 2, 1860

ENGLISH Sarah age 88y Mother of Rev. A. English of Caton, NY in Minooky, Ill. January 6, 1861

CUTLER Mary in her 63rd yr wife of Dr. J. Cutler of Knoxville, NY in Lyndon, Mi. December 17, 1860

HEATH Nellie Adelia age 2y 10m dau of John and Catherine Heath in Corning, NY January 24, 1861

COCHRANE Mary E. age 34y wife of A. T. Cochrane in Corning, NY January 26, 1861

BRADLEY Harriet E. age 3y 9m 14d only dau of George B. Bradley in Corning, NY February 12, 1861

HAYT Amelia E. age 21y 10m at Stephen T. Hayt's in Corning, NY February 20, 1861

SPENCER Frances Mary age 1y 6m dau of William in Corning, NY February 16, 1861

FERENBAUGH Charles M. age 6y 2m son of John in Corning, NY February 7, 1861

AMEY Lucy age 66y wife of Frederick Amey in Corning, NY February 18, 1861

ROBINSON Oscar F. age 30y formerly of Corning and Howard, NY in Handsboro, Miss. rec (Newspaper date February 21, 1861)

STEELE Theodore J. age 50y in Elmira, NY February 28, 1861. Born 1810 in NJ, son of Judge Steele of Corning, NY. Came to Painted Post 1813

BROWN Arnold age 24y 3m 4d son of Jonathan and Eliza Brown in Corning, NY February 27, 1861

CRITTENDEN Mrs. Caroline E. age 34y in Gibson, NY February 28, 1861

ORTON Nellie C. age 3y 2m 26d dau of William in Corning, NY February 25, 1861

REDFIELD D. Irene age 21y dau of J. A. Redfield in Elmira, NY March 7, 1861

GAYLORD Marcus age 82 in Hornby, NY March 13, 1861, native of Ct.

LAUNY Mrs. ___ Mother of Dr. N. B. Launy of Corning, NY in New York City March 16, 1861

PAYNE Stephen Henry in his 20th yr son of B. W. Payne of Corning, NY in Brooklyn, NY March 22, 1861, buried Corning

BELDING Chloe in her 58th yr wife of E. Belding and Mother of W. J. Belding of Corning, NY in Corning March 27, 1861

SWEET Lucy in her 8th yr dau of E. A. Sweet in Corning, NY March 24, 1861

YOUNG Mary (**ANDERSON**) in her 69th yr wife of John Young (she formerly of Morris Run, Pa.) March 14, 1861. Born Ruglen, Scotland, came to US 1827, 8 children

RHODA Wandle age 82y 9m Father of Peter Rhoda in Hornby, NY March 28, 1861

DURHAM John W. in his 65th yr in Big Flats, NY April 17, 1861

FRIDLEY Mary Jane age 19y dau of A. M. Fridley of St. Anthony, Mn. formerly of Gibson, NY at Elmira Female College April 20, 1861, buried Corning, NY

JACOBS Lorinda age 6y 8m 4d dau of V. R. Jacobs in Corning, NY May 4, 1861

WARNER Charlotte in her 65th yr wife of Lucius Warner and Mother of Mrs. George **THOMPSON** nr Geneva, NY May 4, 1861

ROBINSON Agnes age 18y of Geneseo, NY sister of Mrs. J. F. **TOMLINSON** of Corning, NY in Corning May 26, 1861

STEWART John age 19y bro of C. and E. S. Stewart in Corning, NY May 28, 1861

STURDEVANT Estes age 50y formerly of Corning, NY in Hornellsville, NY May 2, 1861

GORTON Sarah Ann age 52y wife of Samuel Gorton in Corning, NY May 24, 1861

MALLORY Laurin age 73y in Corning, NY June 13, 1861

TERBELL Eliza Ann age 50y sister of E. C. and Walter **ADAMS** of Corning, NY in Horseheads, NY June 29, 1861

EVERTS Stephen age 23y in Kalamazoo, Mi. June 20, 1861. Native of Elbridge, NY, married 5 wks before he died Alevilda **WILKERSON** of Kalamazoo. Bro of Mrs. Nelson **PEAK** of Corning, NY

RATHBONE Gen. Nelson age 81y in Rathbone, NY July 17, 1861

YOUNG Mrs. Ophelia in her 71st yr in Hornellsville, NY July 24, 1861, buried in Painted Post, NY with husband

VEAZIE Clara E. age 13y 6m 17d dau of Laban and Lucy in Caton, NY July 9, 1861

POTTER Hiram age 62y 8m formerly of Elmira, NY in Janesville, Wis. (Newspaper date August 8, 1861)

MILLS Penelope age 68y wife of M. Mills in Le Roy (?) August 16, 1861

REYNOLDS Mrs. Benjamin age 78y of Corning, NY in Gibson, NY August 25, 1861

HAVENS Myron F. age 27y 8m 5d formerly of Corning, NY bro of Charles W. Havens in Three Rivers, Mi. August 8, 1861

FOX Jane age 61y wife of Rev. Dana Fox late of Elmira, NY in Highland, Ks. (Newspaper date September 5, 1861)

JACOBS Ira M. age 15m son of Richard Jacobs in Gibson, NY August 28, 1861

ROBINSON J. Nye age 36y in Corning, NY September 12, 1861

WALKER Alvah age 6y 9m son of C. C. B. Walker and wife in Corning, NY September 12, 1861

FINK Francis age 44y in Bath, NY August 29, 1861

DUNNING Lucy age 5y 2m 28d dau of Rev. A. and Mary E. (NILES) in Corning, NY September 15, 1861

HAWLEY James M. age 43y in Corning, NY September 25, 1861

THORN Henry age 6y son of George W. Thorn of Lock Haven, Pa. at Grandfather's B. P. BAILEY in Corning, NY September 22, 1861

JACOBS Ferrin W. age 15y 4m 9d son of Jesse H. Jacobs at Grandfather's W. H. GORTON in Corning, NY September 29, 1861

GILDERSLEEVE Delos age 2m 23d adopted son of Benjamin September 30, 1861

TALLMADGE Mary D. age 14y dau of Mrs. Newton at res of George W. NEWTON in Corning, NY September 27, 1861

HUNT Anna age 5w 4d dau of T. E. and Elizabeth in Corning, NY October 1, 1861

KENYON Charlotte E. in her 11th yr dau of Mrs. Harriet Kenyon in Corning, NY October 7, 1861

STEVENS Samuel age 8y 8m son of Saul Stevens in Corning, NY October 4, 1861

ROSE Samuel Hopkins in his 17th yr son of E. S. Rose in Rockford, Ill. September 22, 1861

GRAY Robert C. age 21y 10m eldest son of Hiram in Elmira, NY October 10, 1861

HOLLENBECK Martha age 28y wife of Joseph Hollenbeck October 16, 1861

SAWDY Ida age 5y dau of Hiram and Catherine in Caton, NY September 15, 1861

BALDWIN Elizabeth age 36y wife of J. Davis Baldwin and dau of Samuel H. MAXWELL in Elmira, NY October 20, 1861

MAYNARD Benjamin age 8m son of John Maynard in Corning, NY October 28, 1861

HAYT Maria T. age 3y 10m 7d dau of Stephen T. in Corning, NY October 30, 1861

STEVENSON Sarah Jane age 4y 2m dau of Elmer in Corning, NY November 4, 1861

THRALL Charles F. age 14y and Harriet E. age 3y children of Jefferson Thrall in Corning, NY November 9, 1861

DEATH NOTICES

HUNT Benjamin J. age 12y 1m 13d son of Nathaniel Hunt November 11, 1861

TAYLORSON William age 14y 9m 14d son of Thomas and Ann Taylorson in Corning, NY November 14, 1861

BLANCHARD Eliza E. age 7y 15d dau of Philander Blanchard in Corning, NY November 14, 1861

PAYNE William H. age 6y 4m son of William and Eliza Payne in Corning, NY November 18, 1861

EDGAR Andrew abt 14y son of Robert Edgar in Corning, Ny November 17, 1861

MC INTYRE Elvira T. age 29y wife of Henry E. Mc Intyre and dau of William B. **HATCH** formerly of Corning, NY in New York City December 2, 1861

GORTON William E. age 11y 7m 24d son of Orley and Eliza Gorton in Corning, NY December 4, 1861

WALLER Harriet A. eldest dau of William L. Waller formerly of Corning, NY in Washington, DC November 21, 1861

DOWNS Lela age 8y 6m dau of E. H. Downs in Havana, NY December 2, 1861

GILBERT Henry E. age 18y son of William J. Gilbert of Erwin, NY at Falls Church, Va. December 1, 1861. Member of Co. D. 23rd Reg. NYV

ROBINSON Spencer F. age 72y 10m 14d in Jasper, NY November 22, 1861. Leaves wife and 6 children, 5 brothers and 2 sisters

FOLWELL Jane age 85y 2m 12d widow of William W. Folwell at son-in-law's Rev. S. M. **BAINBRIDGE** in Painted Post, NY November 21, 1861. Born Bucks Co. Pa., moved to Romulus with husband. 9 children 7 living

DUTCHER J. of Hornellsville, NY fell from top of cars December 10, 1861

LAUNY Dr. N. B. age 51y in Corning, NY December 14, 1861

HILL Esther age 57y wife of George J. Hill in Caton, NY December 16, 1861

MC GIVEN Charles P. age 44y in Corning, NY January 5, 1862

CLARK Henry G. infant son of George M. Clark in Corning, NY January 9, 1862

MONTOREY John W. age 26y of Elmira, NY member of band 33rd Reg. NYV at brother-in-law's John **MC INTOSH** in Corning, NY January 7, 1862

BROWN Joseph abt 50y formerly of Corning, NY in Caton, NY January 5, 1862

WILLIAMS Emily age 40y wife of H. N. Williams January 13, 1862

STEUBEN COUNTY NEWSPAPERS 257

HIGGINS Justin in Howard, NY January 4, 1862

DEARMAN Fanny dau of Nathan **REYNOLDS** of Elmira, NY January 21, 1862

MUNDY Reuben M. age 68y in Big Flats, NY January 21, 1862

STEERE Mary E. in her 8th yr dau of Elisha B. and Frances H. Steere in Laurens, NY January 9, 1862

FERENBAUGH Margaret age 2y 11m dau of John in Corning, NY January 26, 1862

CRAWFORD John B. in his 74th yr in Dix, NY January 31, 1862

BOYD Theron hit by falling tree in Gaines, Pa. February 10, 1862. Leaves wife and 5 children

MC COWLEY Margaret wife of John Mc Cowley and sister of Patrick **DWYER** of Corning, NY, run over by train in Blossburg, NY February 26, 1862

PIER Emerson D. age 17y son of Edwin and Jane Pier of Corning, NY at Brigade Hospital in Hancock, Md. February 21, 1862. Member of Co. I 19th Reg. NYV

GARDNER Sophronia abt 33y wife of Lewis Gardner and dau of George W. **NEWTON** in Corning, NY March 5, 1862

ROTHSUSS William Fred age 2y 8m son of William Fred Rothsuss in Corning, NY February 28, 1862

GORTON Mrs. Miles formerly of Hornby, NY nr Gibson, NY March 6, 1862. Married abt 1 yr. 1st husband was Lewis **BRONG**

CAMPBELL Jane age 56y wife of Solomon A. in Painted Post, NY March 12, 1862

PIFFER Willoughby H. age 19y 11m son of Frederick Piffer of Corning, NY at Camp Good Hope nr Washington DC March 18, 1862. Member of Co. C. 86th Reg. NYV

AMBLER Thomas age 70y in Knoxville, NY March 16, 1862. Came from Oswego, NY 9 yrs ago

LEE John age 21y son of William Lee of Corning, NY, a brakeman fell between cars in Livonia, NY March 20, 1862

WELLMAN Lucy A. age 35y wife of Darius L. in Hornby, NY March 15, 1862

HANWELL Stephen age 80y in Corning, NY March 26, 1862

CONKIE Govina age 9y 11m dau of Stephen Conkie in Corning, NY March 29, 1862

SMITH Margaret dau of John Smith in Gibson, NY March 27, 1862

DEATH NOTICES

BENTLEY Charles W. age 1y 8m son of George W. in New York City April 3, 1862

FASSETT Lawrence age 58y in Knoxville, NY April 4, 1862

SMITH Mary Amelia age 10m 28d in Gibson, NY April 7, 1862

PHELPS Mary L. age 38y consort of Charles H. in Corning, NY March 30, 1862

KEYES Mary Age 24y wife of Emerson W. Keyes and dau of Minos **MC GOWAN** of Ithaca, NY in Albany, NY April 23, 1862

LAMPHIRE Mr. Adel age 82y in Corning, NY May 13, 1862

WOLCOTT Margaret age 17y dau of late Nelson in Caton, NY June 2, 1862

WOLCOTT Isabel age 20y wife of Charles N. Wolcott and dau of John **VAN ARSDALE** in Caton, NY June 7, 1862

EVANS John E. age 32y 6m in Painted Post, NY May 27, 1862

BONHAM Charles abt 25y son of William Bonham in the Jefferson Barracks in St. Louis, Mo. rec (Nwewspaper date June 26, 1862)

WILLIAMS George D. age 46y 11m formerly of Corning, NY in St. Louis, Mo. June 10, 1862

LAW Mrs. William age 23y in Gibson, NY June 11, 1862

FANNING Jerusha age 95y mother of Mrs. G. W. **HERRICK** formerly of Preston, NY in Corning, NY June 23, 1862

LASON James age 18y of Canisteo, NY at battle of Hanover Court House, Va. May 27, 1862. Member of Co. I 5th Reg. NY Cav.

DUTTON Floyd P. age 6y 5m son of William **LAW** in Gibson, NY June 25, 1862

SALMON Mrs. Jane L. age 32y in Corning, NY July 1, 1862

PARCEL Mariam A. age 23y wife of William T. Parcel of Curtisville, NY at res of Joel Parcel in Oreapolis, Neb. June 21, 1862

BROWN Leona age 3y 4m dau of William H. Brown and Granddau of Rev. H. **PATTENGILL** of Susquehanna, Pa. in Corning, NY July 8, 1862

WOLCOTT Charles N. abt 25y in Caton, NY July 11, 1862

GORTON Eleanor age 42y wife of S. D. Gorton in Corning, NY July 14, 1862

SPENCER Richard age 11m 21d son of George T. in Corning, NY July 18, 1862

HUNT Grace Annette age 10m 23d dau of Thadeus E. and Elizabeth Hunt in Corning, NY July 16, 1862

MORRISON Richard A. age 7m 25d son of William in Gibson, NY July 17, 1862

SCHERMER Julius age 37y 11m 21d in Corning, NY July 29, 1862

BAKER George P. abt 28y son of David Baker at Hospital nr Washington DC August 4, 1862. Member of Co. C. 86th Reg. NYV

DAVENPORT James age 71y 10m in Corning, NY July 29, 1862

ROBINSON Lemuel H. age 67y 10m in Corning, NY August 5, 1862

PACKER ____ age 4w dau of Charles Packer in Corning, NY Agust 3, 1862

COBURN Harriet age 54y in Corning, NY August 2, 1862

WEALIE Nelson age 7y 6m 20d died July 4, 1862, Thomas age 2y 10m 14d died July 22, 1862 and Samuel age 5y 7m 20d died July 26, 1862 children of William and Mary Wealie in Caton, NY

DAVIS Cyrene age 51y wife of G. L. Davis formerly of Knoxville, NY in Elmira, NY August 14, 1862

ROWLEY Ruth age 76y widow of Abijah Rowley in Corning, NY August 19, 1862

FAIRMAN C. G. Sr. age 77y late of Lewiston, NY in Elmira, NY August 25, 1862

WEST Sarah age 65y widow of C. F. of Corning, NY in Elmira, NY August 22, 1862

CLISDELL Grace age 1y 8m dau of Edward and Mary A. Clisdell of Corning, NY August 30, 1862

GAYLORD Willis H. in his 59th yr thrown from wagon in Hornby, NY September 3, 1862. Born Ct. son of late Marcus Gaylord and came to Hornby age 17 yrs. Leaves bro Alonzo of Monterey, NY, wife and 9 children

GOLDY William W. abt 32y formerly of Elmira, NY in Shirland, Ill. August 19, 1862

SHOEMAKER John age 79y 5m in E. Painted Post, NY (Newspaper date September 11, 1862)

RHODES Silas B. abt 65y in Caton, NY September 14, 1862

FOWLER Albert E. age 2y son of Abram and Louisa Fowler in Corning, NY September 15, 1862

ROBERTSON Clark M. age 17y son of Samuel C. in Corning, NY September 19, 1862

DEATH NOTICES

DAVIS Leroy abt 19y son of George Q. Davis of Troupsburgh, NY in Baltimore Hospital rec (Newspaper date October 2, 1862)

FITZPATRICK Daniel age 18m son of John in Corning, NY September 24, 1862

CLARK Julia age 6m 10d dau of Charles and Eunice S. (**VAN NAME**) of Corning, NY in Chenango, NY October 2, 1862

DODGE Orrin age 41y 6m in Knoxville/Corning, NY October 11, 1862

SMITH Henry P. age 19y son of Dr. S. H. Smith of Caton, NY at Harper's Ferry October 18, 1862. Member of Co. A. 107th Reg. NYV

WOOD Phidelia A. age 8y 4m 19d dau of Lewis M. and Lavina C. Wood in Caton, NY October 9, 1862

BARBER Polly age 39y wife of Joseph Barber in Corning, NY October 15, 1862

JAYNES Cardelia Ann age 21y in Caton, NY October 8, 1862

SMITH Lucy age 19y died October 14, 1862, Mary age 9y died October 19, 1862, Scott age 6y died October 19, 1862, Robert age 17y died October 26, 1862 and Martha age 15y died October 29, 1862 all children of Richard H. and Polly Smith of Caton, NY

GRIDLEY Alice age 5y died October 25, 1862, Viola age 9y died October 31, 1862 and Elsie age 11y died November 7, 1862 daus of Lewis Gridley of Caton, NY

VAN NORMAN George W. abt 21y son of Isaac Van Norman of White Creek, Wis. formerly of Corning, NY at the battle of Antietam September 17, 1862. Member 3rd Wis. Reg.

LINDSAY Hannah Ann in her 17th yr dau of Allen of Corning, NY November 23, 1862

BEECHER Harry age 2y 11m son of C. F. and R. A. **WEST** in Elmira, NY December 2, 1862

ETHERIDGE William H. in Corning, NY December 4, 1862

CASTLE Louisa M. age 27y 4m 10d wife of P. H. Castle in W. Addison, NY December 9, 1862

WHITE Almira S. in her 26th yr dau of Mrs. E. L. **ROBINSON** December 19, 1862

VAN ETTEN Eleanor age 85y at son's John in Corning, NY December 24, 1862

HUNGERFORD Jerome B. age 13y 8m son of E. B. Hungerford in Corning, NY December 26, 1862

CARR Mrs. ___ wife of Rev. C. C. Carr in Burdett, NY January 1, 1863

MC MULLEN John in his 86th yr in Centerville, NY January 11, 1863

HARING Chaumcey G. Atty. age 35y in Corning, NY January 7, 1863

WILCOX Gershom age 80y at son's in Caton, NY January 14, 1863

PHILLIPS Albert W. age 24y son of Andrew B. in Jasper, NY January 13, 1863

DAVIS Adelaide wife of Nelson D. Davis and dau of Horace **WESTCOTT** of Caton, NY in Caton January 23, 1863

SEELY M. H. abt 45y at Seely's Hotel in Erwin, Ny January 28, 1863

CLARK Dr. Jacob F. age 57y of Saugatuck, Mi. formerly of Corning, NY at son's Caleb Clark in Corning (Newspaper date February 12, 1863)

SMITH Mrs. Rhoda dau of Horatio N. **GORTON** of Caton, NY in Southport, NY February 9, 1863

HOWELL Margaret age 86y 4m Mother of Mrs. J. **EMMONS** in Corning, NY February 8, 1863

AUSTIN John age 1y 7m 21d son of Richard Austin in Corning, NY February 11, 1863

THAYER Myrtie Lauraetta age 4y 4m dau of William M. Thayer in Elmira, NY February 15, 1863

NICHOLS Priscilla (**SIDNEY**) in her 71st yr wife of James Nichols formerly of Corning, NY in Albany, NY February 4, 1863

PARCEL Mariam age 9m dau of William T. Parcel in Oreapolis, Neb. January 18, 1863. Mr. Parcel enlisted in Cav. of Ky. Wife died a few months ago

REED Romeo abt 60y in Caton, NY February 22, 1863

WARD Charlotte age 14y dau of Col. P. C. in Hornellsville, NY February 19, 1863

HOVEY John abt 40y of Maine, NY trying to cross tracks at Union, NY rec (Newspaper date March 5, 1863)

WICKHAM Johnson age 45y in Corning, NY February 24, 1863

NICHOLS Alonzo D. age 36y son of James Nichols in Albany, NY February 25, 1863

PARK Frederick W. age 17y 4m son of William Park in Corning, March 1, 1863. Born Conklin, NY and came to Corning April 1861

CUMPSTON David B. age 39y formerly of Corning, NY in Washington DC February 27, 1863

DEATH NOTICES

LOVELL James W. in camp nr Hope Landing, Va. March 7, 1863. Member of Co. G. 107th Reg. NYV

WOLCOTT Carrie Estelle age 3y 3m 9d dau of J. E. and P. E. Wolcott in Caton, NY March 13, 1863

PEW Andrew J. abt 35y in Caton, NY March 2, 1863

WITTER Frances age 10y dau of Lester Witter in Caton, NY March 21, 1863

WEST Anna age 87y Mother of late Dr. Silas West of Binghamton, NY in Corning, NY April 1, 1863

BARBER Naomi age 1y dau of David Barber in Corning, NY March 26, 1863

KING Catherine wife of Dr. Rufus King in Beloit, Wis. March 19, 1863. Sister of Dr. N. D. **GARDNER** of Elmira, NY

GENUNG Samuel S. bro of Mrs. Dr. **HERRINGTON** at St. Louis, Mo. April 1, 1863 from wounds received at Vicksburg. Member of 13th Ill. Vol., buried Almond, NY

DARRIN Charles age 2y son of Charles Darrin in Gibson, NY April 1, 1863

HUBBARD Wilbur F. of Caton, NY bro of W. Martin Hubbard of Caton, NY at Arlington Heights, Va. March 27, 1863. Member of Co. D. 141st Reg. NYV

OLDFIELD Harriet H. age 2y dau of Thomas Oldfield in Hornby, NY April 9, 1863

KELLY Alice M. in her 8th yr dau of Charles and Esther Kelly in Caton, NY February 21, 1863

LYON Moses H. age 73y in Corning, NY April 22, 1863, res over 50 yrs

HENDRICK Sophia L. age 34y wife of Orva Hendrick and dau of Willis H. **GAYLORD** of Hornby, NY in Hornby April 14, 1863

MOORE Willis R. age 5y 5m son of Joseph F. and Adelia D. Moore April 24, 1863

EMPIE Mrs. John age 26y formerly of Corning, NY in Middleport, Ill. March 23, 1863

BARNED Susan Maria age 5y 3m 11d dau of George Barned formerly of Corning, NY in Medina, NY May 5, 1863

THOMPSON Hattie B. age 9m 18d dau of Larue P. and Harriet B. Thompson in Corning, NY May 8, 1863

HAINES William in his 72nd yr in Gibson, NY June 3, 1863. Vet War of 1812

JONES Elmer Ellsworth age 1y 7m 9d son of I. P. in Corning, NY June 3, 1863

FARRAR Frances E. age 32y wife of Prof. Charles S. in Elmira, NY May 27, 1863

JONES Oscar T. age 21y at Father's I. P. Jones in Corning, NY May 29, 1863. Member of Co. C. 86th Reg. NYV

GILLINS Cpl. Timothy of E. Painted Post, NY May 29, 1863. Mem. of Co. F. 23rd Reg. NYV

SHERWOOD Sarah age 58y wife of James at son's Delos in Corning, NY June 8, 1863

BUNT John R. age 3y 6m 6d died May 2, 1863, Mary E. age 1y 2m 5d died May 8, 1863 and James E. age 6y 8m 1d died May 9, 1863 all children of Simon T. and Sarah Bunt of Colesville, NY

DUDLEY Martha age 51y wife of Abram Dudley in Addison, NY May 30, 1863

HOWE Corbitt age 22y in Caton, NY June 13, 1863

CHADWICK John W. age 24y in Hornellsville, NY June 9, 1863

GOODRICH William Henry age 6y 11m 25d son of John M. and Harriet Goodrich nr Tioga, NY June 8, 1863

BELL Jennie S. in her 26th yr wife of Rev. John D. in Wellsboro, Pa. June 7, 1863

MULFORD Mulford age 12y son of E. P. Mulford in Lindley, NY June 19, 1863

DAVISON Susan age 13y dau of C. M. Davison in Caton, NY June 15, 1863

WOLF Carl age 42y in Bath, NY June 16, 1863

ROUSE William age 2y 4m son of Charles Rouse in Corning, NY June 25, 1863

SMITH Mary age 70y wife of David Smith in Hornby, NY June 27, 1863

UNDERWOOD Jesse abt 73y in Hornby, NY May 30, 1863, res over 50 yrs

TAYLOR Nate W. age 3y 11m son of William E. Taylor drowned in Canal in Gibson, NY June 29, 1863

TOBEY Jane abt 25y wife of Ransford Tobey in Caton, NY June 30, 1863

GILBERT Dr. Horace E. age 26y 5m son of William Gilbert of Caton, NY at Craney Is. 8 miles from Fortress Monroe July 3, 1863

LUMBARD H. J. age 36y formerly of Corning, NY in Elmira, NY July 4, 1863

RICHARDS Bertha M. age 2y 1m 11d dau of George and Lucinda Richards in Caton, NY June 30, 1863

DEATH NOTICES

WOODARD Whitney P. age 9y 4m son of Nathaniel M. and Fanny A. Woodard in Corning, NY July 4, 1863

LANDEN Carrie age 1y 3m dau of John and Anna Landen July 1, 1863

ELY Martin W. age 23y at Father's Caleb Ely in Hornby, NY July 21, 1863. Member of Co. I. 107th Reg. NYV

SMITH Elizabeth age 23y wife of William Smith while visiting at Father's I. **TIFFANY** in Jamestown, NY July 15, 1863

HART Horace W. age 26y at Haranden Hospital nr Fortress Monroe July 14, 1863. Member of Co. A. 141st Reg. NYV

ERWIN Arthur H. age 60y in Erwin, NY August 1, 1863

BISHOP Araminda age 57y wife of John Bishop in Corning, NY August 3, 1863

HOLDEN Jane A. age 49y wife of Patrick Holden in Corning, NY August 9, 1863

GIBSON Otis L. Md. age 56y in Wellsboro, Pa. July 31, 1863. Born June 8, 1807 in Vt. and came to Wellsboro 1830

PHILLIPS Mary in her 83rd yr in Corning, NY August 19, 1863. Born N. Woodstock, Ct. Came to Exeter, NY with husband 61 yrs ago. Later moved to Corning to live with son-in-law late L. H. **ROBINSON**

DEYO Lewis age 24y in Caton, NY (Newspaper date August 20, 1863)

GRIDLEY Elizabeth H. age 21y dau of Lewis Gridley in Caton, NY August 11, 1863

GRANT Mary Helen infant dau of Charles L. Grant in Corning, NY July 16, 1863

GIFFORD Thomas age 78y in Corning, NY August 25, 1863

FANTON Louise age 27y 8m 9d wife of Hull Fanton and dau of Peter **TRACY** in Havana, NY August 24, 1863

MURDOCH John P. age 4m son of John Murdoch in Elmira, NY August 19, 1863

PECKMAN Isaiah age 67y formerly of Binghamton in Rathbone, NY August 18, 1863

TUTHILL Herbert Monroe age 2y 3m son of Lt. Col. H. G. Tuthill in Corning, NY August 26, 1863

GILLETT Mary Elizabeth age 1y 5m dau of Joseph H. Gillett in Corning, NY August 21, 1863

ELLISON Richard F. age 1y in Corning, NY August 23, 1863

COOPER James age 69y in Corning, NY September 9, 1863

DEYO James L. age 25y in Caton, NY August 12, 1863

TOBEY Manley B. age 5y 10m son of William in Caton, NY September 13, 1863

PHELPS Oliver H. age 76y Father of G. J. Phelps of Corning, NY in Mansfield, Pa. September 19, 1863

GIFFORD Ida age 8y in Corning, NY September 17, 1863

ROBINSON E. Lee age 72y in Corning, NY October 2, 1863

SANDERS Nellie Tousey age 6y dau of George A. Sanders in Dansville, NY September 25, 1863

FOX Rev. Norman in his 72nd yr in Painted Post, NY October 3, 1863

DE WOLF Sarah E. age 8y 6m 26d dau of William Alonzo De Wolf in Corning, NY October 19, 1863

WHITING Rev. Francis Lane in his 87th yr at son-in-law's A. G. **OWEN** in Big Flats, NY (Newspaper date October 22, 1863)

HARADON Cpl. Charles A. age 24y son of Parnach Haradon of Hornby, NY at Bridgeport nr Chattanooga, Tn. October 20, 1863. Member of Co. D. 141st Reg. NYV

BUTCHER Mrs. Philetus age 82y at son-in-law's M. F. **LUCAS** in Corning, NY October 22, 1863. Born a slave in Md.

COOPER Dr. John age 65y in Coopers Plains, NY October 23, 1863

PRATT Joel age 13y son of William B. Pratt in Prattsburgh, NY October 19, 1863

GORTON Daniel age 64y of Ovid, NY at bro Rufus in Corning, NY November 9, 1863

HUKE Lt. George D. age 29y 7m of Geneva, NY son-in-law of J. **HAVENS** of Corning, NY at Balfour Hospital in Portsmouth, Va. November 5, 1863 Member of 148th Reg. NYV

MARSHALL Jesse age 75y father-in-law of Simon **VAN ETTEN** in Gibson, NY November 8, 1863

CHIDESTER Samuel age 56y formerly of Corning, NY in Dunkirk, NY November 11, 1863

OWEN George H. age 36y 6m in Knoxville/Corning, NY November 18, 1863

BIRDSALL Henry James age 15y 1m 19d of Erwin, NY on board Steamer Dakotah October 31, 1863

DEATH NOTICES

STRANG Malvina in her 43rd yr wife of Samuel S. in Elmira, NY November 27, 1863

LEONARD Mrs. Deborah age 75y sister of Mrs. Ambrose **POND** in Hornby, NY December 5, 1863

VEAZIE J. B. age 24y in Caton, NY December 7, 1863

MALLORY Katie E. age 20m dau of Edward J. of Knoxville, NY December 16, 1863

LAND Robert age 71y in Corning, NY December 20, 1863

REVILLE Nicolas age 48y of Caton, NY in Nashville, Tn. November 22, 1863. Member of Co. D. 141st Reg. NYV

HORTON Charles D. age 6y 10m son of S. D. Horton in Coopers Plains, NY December 31, 1863

SWARTHOUT Alexander H. late of 104th NY Cav. in Hornby, NY December 24, 1863

LEWIS Alonzo D. in sawmill accident in Hornellsville, NY December 24, 1863

HILTON V. R. abt 50y in Corning, NY January 14, 1864

HATHAWAY Laura age 56y of Rochester, NY wife of George W. Hathaway formerly of Corning, NY in Corning January 12, 1864

BERRY Samuel F. age 77y in Caton, NY January 16, 1864. Came from RI 1828

NICHOLS Clarissa age 41y wife of William M. Nichols formerly of Bath, NY and dau of John **ST JOHN** of Hornby, NY in Manitowee, Wis. (Newspaper date January 21, 1864)

STEWART Claude D. age 7y son of Anthony Stewart and grandson of Mrs. J. **SHERWOOD** in Corning, NY January 21, 1864

STEARNS Mary A. wife of A. C. in Corning, NY January 20, 1864, buried Mass.

MC KEAN Samuel abt 40y in Painted Post, NY rec (Newspaper date February 18, 1864)

STANTON John Freeman age 45y formerly of Hornby, NY at Shippen, Pa. February 14, 1864

CAPRON Rebecca M. C. age 39y wife of E. W. Capron in Williamsport, Pa. February 16, 1864

ENGLISH Nancy Adelia eldest dau of Amzi English in Caton, NY February 21, 1864

HEGGIE Archibald age 59y formerly of Elmira in Ithaca, NY February 17, 1864

QUACKENBUSH Mary age 44y wife of William Quackenbush and sister of Mrs. Hiram **GORTON** of Corning, NY at Mitchell's Station February 20, 1864

JACOBS Eloise M. age 5y 2m dau of David Jacobs in Big Flats, NY February 29, 1864

WARD Robert age 57y in Painted Post, NY February 26, 1864

TAYLOR Richard age 29y son of George Taylor formerly of Corning, NY in Trenton, NJ January 3, 1864. Member of NJ Cav. Reg.

KING Henrietta age 30y 4m wife of Martin King in Mansfield, Pa. March 10, 1864

SHEARDOWN A. M. Md. age 25y in Troy, Pa. January 13, 1864

WATROUS Harriet in her 27th yr wife of Charles B. Watrous in Gaines, Pa. February 22, 1864. Born Caton, NY

CROSBY Ransom age 64y formerly of Corning, NY in Newark, NJ February 28, 1864

CHATFIELD C. J. abt 45y in Painted Post, NY March 23, 1864

ROWLEY Anna age 82y at son's Almon Rowley in Caton, NY March 9, 1864

SOUTHWORTH Schuyler in his 62nd yr Father of Mrs. A. J. **OWEN** of Corning, NY in Canisteo, NY March 20, 1864. Born Burlington NY. Leaves wife and 2 daus

GREGORY David abt 50y late of US Army in Hornby, NY March 30, 1864

MC INTOSH Bell age 3m 4d dau of John and Rachel in Corning, NY March 31, 1864

SLY Betsey age 75y wife of John Sly and dau of late John **JENNINGS** in Knoxville, NY April 11, 1864, res 50 yrs

WHITING W. B. age 63y 10m in Corning, NY April 7, 1864, res 20 yrs

STANTON Emma age 17y dau of Mrs. Mary Stanton in Hornby, NY April 9, 1864

SWEET Ellen age 11y died April 6, 1864 and Louise age 5y died April 8, 1864 daus of Dennis Sweet in Catlin, NY

GLUE Frederick abt 38y of Corning, NY abt April 15, 1864. Member of Co. D. 141st Reg. NYV. Leaves son age 9 yrs

TUTTLE William A. age 53y in Big Flats, NY April 4, 1864

SMITH Mortimer J. age 46y son of Dr. Norman Smith of Elmira, NY in Sacramento, Cal. February 20, 1864

WARD Gython age 23y son of Jonas Ward in Hornby, NY April 16, 1864

DEATH NOTICES

SCHUYLER Harriet age 24y wife of Daniel Schuyler and dau of A. D. **EASLING** in Hornby, NY April 18, 1864

PLATT Rufus age 63y Father of C. S. Platt of Painted Post, NY in Campbell, NY April 14, 1864

SKELTON Mott age 14y son of Dr. J. N. Skelton in Caton, NY April 7, 1864

CHRISTIAN Isabella age 14y dau of Thomas Christian in Corning, NY April 21, 1864

BAKER Jennie Leona age 14y 28d dau of Lt. Arthur S. and Leona P. Baker and grand dau of Rev. H. **PATTENGILL** in Washington DC Arpil 23, 1864

PRESTON Sally age 73y wife of Charles Preston in Corning, NY May 2, 1864. Married May 2, 1829

WOLCOTT John age 84y 3m at son's E. J. Wolcott in Corning, NY April 28, 1864, res since 1793

HAMLIN Amos age 65y in Caton, NY May 7, 1864

SMITH Henry D. age 60y in Sugar Grove, Ill. April 26, 1864, one of 1st settlers of Caton, NY and moved to Ill. 6/7 yrs ago

REED George P. infant son of B. B. Reed in Caton, NY May 7, 1864

WHEELER Wilbur age 6y son of William Wheeler, member of 107th Reg. NYV in Corning, NY May 18, 1864

GIBSON Luke D. age 78y in Corning, NY May 13, 1864

PIESTER Levi age 6y son of Mrs. Hiram **FRANCISCO** in Corning, NY March 21, 1864

BROWN Marion W. age 21y 1m 17d dau of Rev. Ira in Corning, NY May 24, 1864

CURRAN Chauncey T. age 17y 10m 24d died May 24, 1864, Sarah Ann age 21y 3m 16d died June 7, 1864, Captain Leroy age 14y 2m 24d died June 15, 1864, Anna May age 7y 2m 20d died June 20, 1864 children of S. M. and S. A. in Coopers Plains, NY

BARNEY George age 21y in Corning, NY May 5, 1864

MOREHOUSE Mrs. Anna age 78y in Corning, NY May 9, 1864

STEWART Anna age 3y 3m dau of Anthony Stewart in Corning, NY May 15, 1864

RAMBLES Jack age 64y in Corning, NY May 23, 1864

BARNARD Delos W. age 2y 8m son of George A. and Mary Barnard in Caton, NY May 2, 1864

FREEMAN Edward age 49y in Corning, NY May 30, 1864. Native of Gloucester, Eng. and came to US in 1840

BIXBY John C. age 29y hit by falling tree June 8, 1864. Leaves wife and 3 children

HOOD Benjamin F. of Geneva, NY bro of U. D. and William Hood of Corning, NY in Hospital at Point Lookout Md. June 8, 1864. Member of Co. I. 148th Reg. NYV

SHUTTS Harriet M. age 6y 1m 17d dau of John R. and Clarissa Shutts in Corning, NY July 13, 1864

LOOK Ada age 6y 10m dau of J. B. Look in Havana, NY June 27, 1864

WILLIAMS Rhoda age 78y Mother of Edwin Williams in Corning, NY July 14, 1864

HILL Monroe E. abt 23y son of Noble Hill in Caton, NY July 17, 1864

HARRIS Elizabeth Allen age 18y dau of late Mrs. P. **HOLDEN** suicide by shooting herself July 19, 1864

HALLETT Samuel age 37y formerly of Steuben Co. NY shot in Wyandotte, Ks. July 27, 1864

GRANT Mary Ann age 56y widow of Neverson Grant in Corning, NY August 7, 1864

COOPER Samuel Erwin in his 24th yr son of late Dr. Cooper in Coopers Plains, NY August 3, 1864

GILDERSLEEVE Benjamin G. nr Atlanta, Ga. (Newspaper date August 18, 1864). Member of Co. E. 141st Reg. NYV

COLBY Mary E. age 29y of Corning, NY wife of Lt. Col. N. T. Colby of Vet. Res. August 15, 1864. Dau Mary E. age 3y died August 13, 1864

ROOF Fanny age 20y 2m dau of John Roof in Orange, NY August 21, 1864

MANN William son of late Samuel Mann of Erwin, NY in New Orleans July 31, 1864. Member of the US Colored Inf.

MANN Fred age 17y bro of William Mann in Erwin, NY August 24, 1864

CRIDDLE Edward J. age 4y 15d son of William and Anna Criddle August 15, 1864

GENUNG Leroy D. age 21y of Almond, NY bro of Mrs. Dr. **HERRINGTON** of Corning, NY in Rockford, Ill. August 24, 1864

THORP Henry of Caton, NY nr Atlanta, Ga. July 20, 1864, mem. of Co. D. 141st Reg.

HAYT Edward age 3y 6m son of S. T. Hayt in Corning, NY September 14, 1864

MC BURNEY Thomas age 2y 10m son of James and Lucy A. Mc Burney in Corning, NY September 23, 1864

ADDISON Georgiana age 16y of Wellsville, NY in Corning, NY October 3, 1864

HERRICK M. A. age 22y 24d wife of Hugh T. Herrick and dau of G. W. **BUCK** of Chemung, NY in Waverly, NY September 26, 1864

WHITENACK John abt 54y in Centerville, NY October 5, 1864. Native of NJ, res here 30 yrs. Leaves wife and 7 children

SHERWOOD John B. abt 22y of Vet. Res. at Carver Hospital Washington DC September 25, 1864

CARR May age 7m dau of John P. Carr in Corning, NY October 8, 1864

CUMMINS Clarence age 25y of Caton, NY in City Pt., Va. September 28, 1864. Member of Co. H. 50th Reg.

COX W. L. age 38y of Caton, NY in Washington DC October 5, 1864. Member of Co. A. 50th Reg.

OLDFIELD Mary M. age 5y 6m dau of Thomas and Phebe M. Oldfield in Hornby, NY October 5, 1864

MUMFORD Dr. Ores age 49y in Corning, NY October 20, 1864

MORSE Lizzie E. age 7y 6m dau of Willard C. and Mary E. Morse in Coopers Plains, NY October 21, 1864

FREEMAN Josephine age 12y 7m 7d dau of William H. Freeman in Corning, NY October 17, 1864

GREGORY Seely D. age 22y 11m 16d son of Orlando and Eleanor Gregory in Caton, NY October 11, 1864. Member of Co. H. 50th Eng. Reg.

POTTER Sarah J. age 33y wife of J. T. Potter in Corning, NY October 26, 1864

WICKHAM William in his 80th yr last of the pioneers of Hector, NY October 20, 1864

HAYT Col. William W. nr 40y in City Pt, Va. November 1/8, 1864, mem. 189th Reg.

WEBB Lewis H. age 18y son of Z. Webb of Auburn, NY formerly of Corning, NY in Newburn, NC October 27, 1864. Member of Bat. I 3rd NY Art.

ELLISON Lilly Ann age 3y 6m dau of Robert and Ellen Ellison in Corning, NY August 12, 1864

OWEN Mary J. age 40y wife of Blake Owen in Corning, NY November 2, 1864

BURNAP George funeral at Hornby, NY November 13, 1864, mem. of 50th Eng. Reg.

WELLS Orren of Tuscarora, NY hit by fallen log November 23, 1864

HOWE George B. age 5m son of William and Lydia Howe in Centerville, NY November 29, 1864

PHELPS Fleda Elma age 1y 7m 11d dau of L. D. and M. A. Phelps in Titusville, Pa. November 26, 1864

VAN NAME Robert M. age 11m 2d son of Charles H. and Eunice H. Van Name in Corning, NY December 2, 1864

SMITH Polly age 53y wife of Elias H. Smith in Corning, NY November 27, 1864

TARBOX Mrs. Submit abt 70y in Co. Home November 5, 1864, husband William died Co. Home November 8, 1864

JOLLY James D. age 18y 22d son of Dexter S. Jolly of Corning, NY in Rebel Prison in Andersonville, Ga. August 25, 1864

MC CREA William S. stepson of Uri **SCOFIELD** of Painted Post, NY and half bro of Neville E. **WAITE** of Corning, NY in Hospital in Chattanooga September 21, 1864

BILLINGHURST Elizabeth age 21y dau of L. Billinghurst in Knoxville, NY December 5, 1864

FITZPATRICK Frank bro of Thomas and John Fitzpatrick of Corning, NY in Andersonville, Ga. November 21, 1864

THOMPSON George age 48y formerly of Corning, NY in Oil City, Pa. December 20, 1864. Native of Broadalbin, NY and came to Corning 1847. Married dau of Lucius **WARNER** of Geneva, NY, buried Corning

COWAN Jennie age 20y wife of T. A. Cowan and dau of S. F. **DENTON** in Elmira, NY December 21, 1864

HARE Lydia A. age 24y 10m wife of William Hare and adopted dau of Blake **OWEN** of Knoxville, NY in Centerville, NY December 25, 1864

SMITH Toya Bell age 1y 10m dau of Lewis B. and Electa R. Smith in Caton, NY December 21, 1864

THOMPSON Lt. John nephew of La Rue P. Thompson and only bro of late Lt. George E. Thompson in Rebel Prison rec (Newspaper date January 5, 1865)

SMITH Joseph age 68y in Corning, NY January 3, 1865

THURBER Mary age 11y 11m 11d dau of Alfred in Caton, NY December 11, 1864

DEATH NOTICES

MILLER Isaac in his 72nd yr in Lawrenceville, Pa. December 6, 1864

OSBORNE Margaret age 48y wife of Charles E. in Corning, NY January 10, 1865

GRIDLEY Olive age 62y wife of Levi Gridley in Caton, NY January 4, 1865. Born Hartford Co. Ct. 1802. Married 1822 and moved to Caton 1826

SHULER Phillip crushed by log nr Mithchellville, NY January 3, 1864

WELTS William age 23y eldest son of late Phillip Welts of Corning, NY in Nashville, Tn. January 6, 1865. Father was killed by guerillas abt November 1, 1867

BROOKS Henry S. age 52y in Elmira, NY February 1, 1865

WAY Mary Jane age 33y 19d wife of W. T. Way in New York City January 26, 1865

MORGAN Col. A. C. age 60y in Lindley, NY February 18, 1865

UPSON George Morris age 5y 1m 8d son of Archibald M. and Sarah A. Upson in Corning, NY February 16, 1865

HATHAWAY Franklin K. age 22y 8m son of Mahlon D. Hathaway in Woodhull, NY February 16, 1865

DICKINSON Jennie A. age 24y wife of A. B. Dickinson 2nd in Hornby, NY February 2, 1865

WHITMORE Lemuel age 11m son of Calvin and Sarah Whitmore in Caton, NY February 19, 1865

JOHNSON Polly A. in her 58th yr wife of Thomas in Corning, NY February 11, 1865

BAKER Lizzie wife of Gilbert Baker and dau of Z. **WILDER** of Painted Post, NY in Milo, NY March 9, 1865

PIERCE Sylva age 71y wife of Alson Pierce in Coopers Plains, NY March 18, 1865

MC BURNEY Antha age 2y 2m dau of John Jr. in Knoxville, NY February 27, 1865

WEBB Dorcas age 85y at son's David H. **FULLER** in Corning, NY March 20, 1865

SOMERS James age 85y Father of Nelson L. Somers in Corning, NY March 16, 1865

NEYHART Thomas age 36y formerly of Corning, NY in Seneca Falls, NY March 24, 1865

ADAMS Eliza A. age 53y wife of Capt. Samuel in Painted Post, NY March 30, 1865

HYDE Henry M. of New York City formerly of Corning, NY in Savannah, Ga. March 25, 1865

BEMENT Sarah wife of Rev. William Bement in Elmira, NY April 9, 1865

BROWN Dayton F. in his 21st yr son of D. F. Brown in Corning, NY April 7. 1865

YOUNG George H. infant son of Hugh and L. A. in Wellsboro, Pa. April 8. 1865

MC NEIL Thomas E. age 21y only son of Peter Mc Neil in Hospital in Alexandria, Va. April 15, 1865, buried Corning, NY

COLE William on Hospital Boat in Cape Fear River March 17, 1865, Sgt. in 141st Reg. NYV 1st Brigade, 1st Div.

THOMPSON John eldest son of Henry Thompson of Corning, NY nr Petersburg March 29, 1865. Mem. of 189th Reg. NYV

VAN SCOTER Benson F. an Engineer of Corning, NY run over by train April 23, 1865. Married dau of Rufus **GORTON**, 1 dau

DENTON Jane age 61y wife of Maj. S. B. Denton in Elmira, NY April 29, 1865

UPSON Ira Martin age 7y 3m 19d son of Archibald and Sarah A. May 13, 1865

HODSKINS Fanny in her 71st yr relict of Jonas in Lisle, NY May 17, 1865

CROSBY Thomas R. in his 34th yr only surviving son of Ransom Crosby formerly of Corning, NY in Newark, NJ May 8, 1865. Bro Ransom died in Army some months ago

HULL Nathaniel age 70y Father-in-law of S. M. **CURRAN** of Coopers Plains, NY in Campbell, NY May 30, 1865

EDWARDS Frankie W. age 16y dau of Milton Edwards and niece of Mrs. La Rue P. **THOMPSON** in Hinsdale, NY May 27, 1865

CAMPBELL Emeline age 39y wife of James Campbell in Corning, NY June 21, 1865

SAGAR Miss Nattie J. age 28y in Corning, NY July 5, 1865

ANDERSON Douglass age 25y 3m son of T. K. and Catherine Anderson of Hornellsville, NY in Alexandria, Va. June 23, 1865

GORTON Josephine age 25y wife of Jackson Gorton and dau of Norris **DAVIS** in Phillipsburg, Pa. July 23, 1865

BROWN Hattie A. age 32y 11m wife of J. Lewis Brown in Corning, NY August 8, 1865

TEEPLES Solomon J. age 47y in Campbell, NY August 12, 1865

MAYNARD John age 38y son of John of Seneca Co. in Corning, NY August 17, 1865

DEATH NOTICES

RICHARDS Amanda age 35y wife of Robert W. Richards in Caton, NY July 30, 1865

GILLETT Luther M. formerly of Corning, NY in Elmira, NY September 6, 1865

CAMPBELL Minor in his 86th yr at dau Mrs. Albert **DUVALL** in Hornby, NY September 7, 1865. Born 1780 in Ct. of Scotch Irish Descent, moved to Stillwater, NY 1784 and to Hornby 1800. Sister Mrs. George **TEEPLE** of Campbell, NY

COLE Harriet T. age 35y dau of H. H. and Isabella **MATHEWS** in Elmira, NY September 8, 1865

HUNTER Dr. William age 66y in Jasper, NY September 5, 1865

CROMBIE Emma age 4m dau of Humphrey and Louise Crombie in Corning, NY September 10, 1865

BOYD Rebecca A. age 48y wife of Tompkins W. in Pulteney, NY September 3, 1865

PRATT Catherine T. in her 33rd yr 2nd dau of Rev. B. Foster Pratt formerly of Campbell, NY in Oberlin, Oh. July 27, 1865

DELAMATER Louisa age 20y dau of I. C. and Harriet Delamater in Minneapolis, Mn. August 31, 1865. Born Corning, NY

QUACKENBUSH J. D. abt 60y late of Corning, NY in Ill. October 2, 1865

SMITH Titus age 64y in Caton, NY October 22, 1865, native of Bainbridge, NY

TIFFT John G. age 58y of Corning, NY nr Gibson, NY October 28, 1865. Born Washington Co. NY and married in Dutchess Co. Came here 1843

BORST Ira late of 107th Reg. in Painted Post, NY November 1, 1865. Leaves wife and 4 children

WEEKS Adeline age 53y wife of David S. in Corning, NY October 30, 1865

DEVORE Abagail age 62y Mother of Ezra Devore in Corning, NY November 4, 1865, buried Baldwin, NY, her former home

BISHOP Thomas age 77y at nephew's J. A. **PARSONS** in Corning, NY November 3, 1865

WHEAT Elizay age 2y 2m 27d dau of John L. and Mary E. Wheat in Louisville, Ky. November 9, 1865

REED Mrs. Mercy abt 85y in Caton, NY November 13, 1865

CARTER Eva only child of Reuben and Leurancy Carter October 13, 1865. Father Reuben formerly of Corning, NY died in Ceres, Pa. November 20, 1865

RATHBONE John F. son of late Gen. Rathbone of Rathbone, NY in Woodbridge, Cal. October 28, 1865

BROWN Willie age 6m son of Thomas D. and Phoebe Brown in Curtis Sta., NY November 21, 1865

HOFFMAN Sally age 79y 10m wife of William in Elmira, NY December 7, 1865

BROWN Eliza Jane age 42y wife of Daniel F. Brown in Corning, NY December 12, 1865. Married 22 yrs

missing issues

REARDON Dr. Patrick age 61y in Corning, NY March 19, 1868

MELONEY Margaret age 17y 3m 11d dau of John in Corning, NY March 8, 1865

SHERWOOD Johnie age 7y 9m son of De Los Sherwood in Corning, NY April 5, 1868

FRENCH Albert G. abt 46y in Corning, NY April 4, 1868

SPENCER Delilah at advanced age in Caton, NY April 10, 1868

COOPER Ruth age 66y wife of James Cooper in Corning, NY April 11, 1868

GORTON William H. age 78y in Corning, NY April 19, 1868

MUNDY Hannah age 76y widow of Reuben M. Mundy at son's N. S. in Big Flats, NY April 26, 1868

HOWARD Dora age 12y in Corning, NY April 30, 1868

HOOD Nellie age 5m died May 11, 1868 and Ruth May age 3y 20d died May 13, 1868 daus of U. D. Hood in Corning, NY

THOMPSON Richard in his 46th yr in Milport, NY May 9, 1868

LAUER Katie age 3y in Corning, NY May 14, 1868

BAKER William H. age 25y son of James in Williamsport, Pa. May 20, 1868

HOOD Anna Eudora age 7y 3m dau of Uriah D. and Olive C. Hood in Corning, NY May 22, 1868

DAVIS Eleanor age 63y wife of Charles T. Davis in Corning, NY June 3, 1868

MILLER Charles age 63y in Southport, NY May 26, 1868

BROWN Ira age 62y in Corning, NY June 2, 1868. Born Groton, NY. Leaves widow and 4 children

DEATH NOTICES

LOWER Eliza age 58y wife of James B. Lower in Corning, NY June 7, 1868, buried Philadelphia, Pa.

HAVENS Sabrina age 54y wife of W. P. Havens in Corning, NY June 6, 1868

RYNESS Mary Jane age 3y 18d dau of Henry and Mary in Corning, NY June 18, 1868

HOOD Joseph age 82y Father of Uriah D. and William Hood of Corning, NY at son's John D. Hood in Campbell, NY, June 19, 1868, buried Bellona, NY

MURRAY Hetty age 95y in Wellsboro, Pa. July 4, 1868. Grand dau of a chief on Guinea Coast of Africa, slave of William **WELLS** who settled in Wellsboro in 1804 and freed her

THACHER Byron age 41y in Hornellsville, NY June 27, 1868

TOWNLEY Benjamin age 67y 11m Father of William F. and Thomas L. Townley in Corning, NY July 18, 1868

WAGNER Frederick age 91y father of Dr. F. R. Wagner of Corning, NY in Addison, NY July 17, 1868

READ Charles M. age 8y in Corning, NY July 14, 1868

DAVIS Nellie Florence age 5m 25d dau of Henry G. and Louise Davis and Grand dau of William **CASTOR** of Caton, NY in Williamsport, Pa. July 25, 1868

OLDFIELD Samuel age 69y in Hornby, NY August 3, 1868

LOVELL John S. abt 60y late of Corning, NY in Watkins, NY August 5, 1868, buried in Caton, NY

KNAPP Sally Ann age 72y wife of William T. in Southport, NY August 17, 1868

CURTIS Parthena age 38y wife of W. T. Curtis in Corning, NY August 30, 1868, buried Tioga Co. Pa.

BARNES Olcott age 8y son of George Barnes in Corning, NY September 15, 1868

ROWLEY Freddie age 1y 6m 21d only son of Henry and Hattie Rowley and Grand son of William **WILLIAMS** of Corning, NY in Aleona, Mi. September 1, 1868

TOWLE Percy Ann wife of F. M. and dau of Rev. E. B. **ROLLINS** of Corning, NY in Stratford, Vt. September 12, 1868

RORABAUGH Mrs. Elizabeth in Erwin Center, NY September 21, 1868

STICKLER William age 35y late of Corning, NY in Chemung, NY September 30, 1868

LOVELL Lucinda P. age 54y widow of John P. Lovell and sister of Orlando

GREGORY of Caton, NY in Syracuse, NY September 16, 1868

LEONARD Ariel age 1y 4m only child of C. P. and Nellie Leonard in Lawrenceville, Pa. (Newspaper date October 22, 1868)

MIDDLEBROCK Louise age 14y dau of J. H. and M. L. Middlebrock in Lindley, NY October 13, 1868

PHELPS Elizabeth age 95y widow of Alexander Phelps and Mother of H. G. of Corning, NY in Simsbury, Ct. October 12, 1868. Born 1773, had 9 children 8 living

FENTON Adelaide S. wife of William M. Fenton and sister of Henry H. **BIRDSALL** of Erwin, NY in Flint, Mi. November 9, 1868

CUNNINGHAM Edwin W. age 11m 20d son of Mc Leod and Catherine Cunningham of Corning, NY November 19, 1868

BENNETT Wilson L. age 25y son of Ira P. in Painted Post, NY December 1, 1868

THROOP Chauncey W. age 63y 5m in Painted Post, NY November 27, 1868

SAVORY Mary age 31y dau of Willis J. in Big Flats, NY December 12, 1868

RELIHAN John in sawmill accident nr Painted Post, NY December 10, 1868

BARNES Clifford age 11m 4d son of James and Morelus Barnes in Painted Post, NY January 7, 1869

GILBERT Mary Packer age 25y dau of W. D. Gilbert and niece of Charles **PACKER** of Corning, NY drowned January 9, 1869

KNOX Catherine age 47y wife of F. W. Knox and sister of Mrs. K. F. **REYNOLDS** of Corning, NY in Coudersport, Pa. January 9, 1869

MILLS Eliza in her 30th yr wife of Ellsworth D. Mills and dau of late Samuel B. and Amelia **WELLINGTON** in Corning, NY January 16, 1869

MARTIN E. T. age 25y 2m formerly of Broome Co. NY in Gibson, NY January 18, 1869, nephew of Jacob Martin of Corning, NY. Lost a leg in Civil War

CALKINS Sarah abt 30y wife of William in Painted Post, NY January 23, 1869

RUSSELL Ruth in her 83rd yr Mother of Mrs. Moses P. **LITTLE** formerly of Corning, NY in Joliet, Ill. January 13, 1869

HAWLEY Judge William M. in Hornellsville, NY February 8, 1869

BIGELOW William age 9y 1m 21d died February 15, 1869 and Charles Thompson Bigelow age 6y 7m 26d died February 19, 1869 children of William L. Bigelow formerly of Corning, NY in Stapleton, NY

DEATH NOTICES

FINN Florence age 25y wife of E. J. Finn in Ceres, Pa. February 14, 1869

SIMONS Hannah age 9y dau of Simon in Hornellsville, NY February 23, 1869

WOLCOTT Amanda age 27y 8m wife of George Wolcott and dau of Joseph **FERENBAUGH** in Corning, NY February 22, 1869

FITCH Rev. Octavius age 67y native of Oxford, NY in Lawrenceville, Pa. February 24, 1869

LOVELESS Thomas J. age 22y at Father's Daniel Loveless in Knoxville, NY March 5, 1869

EDWARDS Mrs. A. age 75y Mother of H. D. Edwards of Painted Post, NY at dau Mrs. B. F. **FARWELL** in Corning, NY March 10, 1869

SPENCER Elizabeth age 77y at dau Mrs. **EASTERBROOKS** in Corning, NY March 16, 1869

CLARK Jahiel age 4y son of Henry Clark in Corning, NY April 12, 1869

OWEN Stephen Hagaman age 13m son of Stephen T. in Big Flats, NY April 17, 1869

HUDSON Freddie age 4y son of Charles and Augusta in Corning, NY April 17, 1869

TODD Martha Hebrietta age 35y dau of Jerah Todd in Corning, NY May 5, 1869

TOWLE Lilly M. in her 13th yr dau of F. M. Towle of S. Strafford, Vt. at Aunt's Mrs. O. R. **JENNESS** in Corning, NY May 3, 1869

HAVENS Fannie E. in her 16th yr twin dau of Jabez and Fannie E. Havens formerly of Corning, NY in Binghamton, NY April 30, 1869

CLAUHARTY Kate age 33y wife of Oscar M. Clauharty in Havana, NY April 24, 1869

FULLER Marie D. age 23y dau of late Capt. H. Fuller of Corning, NY in Howard, NY May 2, 1869

WELDEN Sybil age 28y 10m 17d wife of Daniel Welden in Corning, NY May 8, 1869

DAVIS Anne age 73y Mother of Mrs. H. **COOPER** of Hornellsville, NY in Woodhull, NY May 6, 1869

POND Ambrose age 77y in Hornby, NY May 9, 1869. Native of Ct. came here 1825

SEXTON Eliza age 63y wife of John L. Sexton in Big Flats, NY May 25, 1869

THURBER James B. in his 17th yr son of Frederick in Corning, NY May 20, 1869

RUNDELL Amos age 78y at son's A. B. Rundell in Corning, NY May 23, 1869

BROWN Melissa A. in her 27th yr wife of Frank A. in Corning, NY May 20, 1869

GILLETT Sylvester in his 70th yr east of Corning, NY May 26, 1869

HERRICK Georgiana age 12y 9m dau of Franklin in Corning, NY June 8, 1869

MARTIN Jacob age 55y in Corning, NY June 15, 1869

COON Mathew age 45y late of 141st Reg. in Caton, NY June 11, 1869

HONNESS Conrad abt 60y in Corning, NY June 20, 1869

CARVER Sarah age 63y wife of John Carver in Caton, NY June 20, 1869

SMITH Florilla in her 18th yr dau of Samuel Smith in Corning, NY June 30, 1869

SMITH Olive age 70y wife of Col. A. C. Smith in Erwin Center, NY June 17, 1869 (Delaware Co. papers please copy)

SPENCER William Henry age 1y 6m son of William G. and Jerusha Spencer in Corning, NY June 27,1869

WHITE Mary D. age 22y wife of W. D. White in Prattsburgh, NY July 5, 1869

RICHARDSON Thomas nr 70y in Almond, NY (Newspaper date July 15, 1869)

CAPRON Rev. Benjamin W. age 75y in Milport, NY July 13, 1869

BAKER Samuel age 45y in Hornellsville, NY July 25, 1869, buried Campbell, NY

WILCOX Harry age 6m son of William R. and Hattie in Philadelphia, Pa. July 22, 1869

SEDGEWICK Mary A. age 51y 8m wife of William Sedgewick in Painted Post, NY July 25, 1869. Leaves daus Mrs. A. D. **DUDLEY** and Mrs. George **HEERMANS** of Corning, NY

JEFFREY Thomas age 28y late of Co. D. 141st Reg. in Corning, NY July 23, 1869

PORTER Jane age 77y wife of Judge Porter of Dansville, NY at son-in-law's Lewis **WOOD** in Hammondsport, NY August 24, 1869, mother of late Mrs. William **SEDGEWICK** of Painted Post, NY

TOWNSEND Edwin D. age 48y in Corning, NY August 28, 1869. Sisters Mrs. S. T. **HAYT** and Mrs. C. C. B. **WALKER** and son Lt. J. G. Townsend of 139th Reg. NYV. Buried in Palmyra, NY

MILLER Myrtie dau of George and Alice Miller in Corning, NY September 6, 1869

CRAMPTON Mary **(BOGARDUS)** age 22y 5m wife of Alexander Crampton in Candor, NY September 6, 1869. Funeral at Mother's in Corning, NY

GARDNER Susan nr 73y widow of William T. Gardner and sister of Jeffrey **SMITH** of Woodhull, NY in Corning, NY September 2, 1869. Born Southport, NY

WALKER Fred Leach age 3y 8m son of William and Helen E. Walker in Corning, NY September 11, 1869

GILBERT Julius H. age 60y in Gibson, NY September 4, 1869

TOWNSEND Eliza E. age 9y dau of Edward and Nancy L. Townsend in Erwin, NY September 16, 1869

WHEELER Mrs. E. K. age 67y formerly of Corning, NY Mother of Mrs. M. M. **POMEROY** in Milwaukee, Wis. September 7, 1869, buried Union, NY

DE WOLF Mary Ophelia age 18y dau of William A. and Adeline De Wolf in Corning, NY September 26, 1869

PRUTZMAN Caroline abt 35y wife of John A. Prutzman late of Waverly, NY and dau of Wendell **VAN OSTRAND** of Corning, NY in Van Etten, NY October 3, 1869

COLE Charles Erastus age 2y 11m son of H. H. and E. J. Cole in Knoxville, NY September 28, 1869

WING Thomas age 75y in Caton, NY October 11, 1869

FOX Julia (**MC KNIGHT**) age 21y wife of Rev. Norman Fox in St. Louis Mo. October 8, 1869

MALLORY Mary age 78y 11m 16d widow of Laurin Mallory and dau of Eldad **MEAD** in Corning, NY October 16, 1869

WILCOX Annie age 31y wife of B. B. Wilcox and dau of Richard **BROWER** in Hornellsville, NY November 2, 1869

PALMER Isaac C. age 64y 5m 5d in Corning, NY November 8, 1869

BUTLER Abigail age 59y wife of William in Blossburg, Pa. November 12, 1869

HULL Susan E. age 77y in Coopers Plains, NY November 25, 1869

ATWATER Lucy sister of Dwight Atwater of Elmira, NY formerly of Corning, NY in Corning November 27, 1869

LATHROP Daniel of Corning, NY at Father's in Lawrenceville, Pa. December 2, 1869. Born Lawrenceville 1843

WAY Harry age 6y 11m 26d son of John and Augusta Way December 3, 1869

TAYLOR George M. age 4y 8m 14d in Corning, NY December 7, 1869

ROBINSON Carlos age 35y in Corning, NY December 26, 1869

HAYES Mrs. John age 35y in Horseheads, NY December 20, 1869

MALLORY Nancy age 71y 10m 18d widow of David Mallory of Corning, NY at son-in-law's David HODGEKIN in Skaneateles, NY December 30, 1869, funeral at son-in-law's Pliny A. ROUSE in Corning

BISHOP Frank A. age 2y 2m son of Hoyt and Emelie in Corning, NY January 11, 1870

GREEN John age 26y in Lawrenceville, Pa. January 1, 1870 (Dundee, NY papers please copy)

HOLLENBECK Eve age 76y 5m Mother of Joseph of Corning, NY January 20, 1870

BAKER Genevieve Lucy age 1y 4m 26d dau of Arthur S. and Leona P. Baker in Saratoga Springs, NY January 30, 1870

QUACKENBUSH Robert age 2y 1m 13d son of William Quackenbush in Corning, NY February 13, 1870

COMFORT David age 73y in Caton, NY February 11, 1870

PHELPS Horace G. age 73y in Corning, NY February 21, 1870 native of Simsbury, Ct.

JENKS Helen A. in her 27th yr wife of William H. Jenks and dau of Erastus LEE in Campbell, NY February 10, 1870

SAYLES Minnie Bell age 1y 3m 14d dau of Martin and Mary Sayles and Grand dau of Hiram PRITCHARD in Corning, NY March 2, 1870

BURT Susan age 28y 4m wife of S. W. Burt in Corning, NY January 6, 1870

NOYES Hannah age 76y 1m 5d widow of Thomas Noyes at son's Henry B. in Corning, NY March 5, 1870

MC GEORGE Rebecca age 73y in Canterbury, NY February 27, 1870, funeral at Athens, Pa.

OWEN Stephen W. age 74y in Orange, NY March 5, 1870

REESE Helen Frances age 8m 10d dau of Frank Reese in Gibson, NY March 12, 1870

KIMBALL Elvira age 35y in Painted Post, NY March 3, 1870

BERRY Lewis Oliver age 12y 4m 28d son of V. O. and Mary A. Berry in Phillipsburg, Pa. February 22, 1870

RICHER Lovina Eliza only child of Charles Richer in Corning, NY March 26, 1870. Mother died 9 days ago

DEATH NOTICES

AKINS Augusta age 27y wife of John M. Akins and dau of Alonzo **PARKS** of Corning, NY in Varna, NY April 7, 1870

MC INTYRE Mrs. Sarah in her 40th yr in Knoxville, NY April 7, 1870

FROST Mrs. J. age 41y in Painted Post, NY April 12, 1870

DAVIS Addie age 8y 6m died April 8, 1870 and Jennie age 6y 5m died April 11, 1870 children of Erastus and Mary Davis in Phillipsburg, Pa.

PAGE Martha Jane age 30y wife of George W. Page in Williamsport, Pa. May 3, 1870

GORTON Warner age 36y 11m 3d son of Orley and Eliza Gorton (Newspaper date May 26, 1870). Leaves wife and 6 children

PAGE Martha Jane age 30y wife of George W. in Williamsport, Pa. May 3, 1870

BROWN Frank P. age 2y son of Charles J. Brown in Corning, NY June 22, 1870

COLE Charles C. in his 23rd yr in Knoxville, NY July 12, 1870

GORTON Rufus age 73y 3m 7d in E. Corning, NY July 15, 1870

LYON Mary J. age 27y 2m 15d dau of A. K. Lyon in Gibson, NY August 1, 1870

GORTON Mary E. age 4m 22d dau of Jerome Gorton in Corning, NY August 10, 1870

GENUNG Hannah in her 64th yr wife of Moses Genung in Caton, NY August 9, 1870

STEEN Hugh age 68y in Painted Post, NY August 12, 1870

TYLER Polly Ann **(CARTER)** age 41y wife of Chauncey Tyler in Chippawa, Mi. August 4, 1870

ERWIN Amelia age 42y wife of Samuel S. Erwin in Corning, NY August 23, 1870

POTTER Louie Albert son of Cranston T. and Louise in Elmira, NY August 29, 1870

BUNDY Maria age 60y formerly of Otsego Co. NY at son-in-law's E. P. **BARNARD** in Corning, NY September 8, 1870

BURNS William age 72y Father of H. Burns of Corning, NY in Moreland, NY September 15, 1870

DODGE Harry age 76y formerly of Corning, NY in Otego, NY September 10, 1870

ROSE Jonas age 78y in Watkins, NY September 18, 1870

TERBELL Celina N. age 46y wife of Dr. William D. Terbell and dau of L. H. **ROBINSON** in Corning, NY September 21, 1870

KETCHUM William abt 35y murdered in Corning, NY September 27, 1870

KELSEY L. Cornelia age 39y wife of George E. Kelsey and dau of late Willis H. **GAYLORD** of Hornby, NY in Lyndon, Ill. September 9, 1870, infant child age 23d died September 20, 1870

TERBELL Abbie L. **(DOUGLAS)** age 72y wife of Dr. William Terbell of Corning, NY on her birthday October 20, 1870

PRESTON Oliver W. Jr. age 11y in Corning, NY October 23, 1870

CHATMAN Mary E. age 27y dau of Daniel and Sarah Chatman and Grand dau of late Chester **KNOWLTON** in Monterey, NY September 14, 1870

GIBSON John age 76y formerly of Gibson, NY in Albany, NY September 19, 1870

FOSTER Mary E. age 54y wife of A. H. Foster and dau of Jonathan **CARD** formerly of Corning, NY in Oshkosh, Wis. November 9, 1870

SMITH Sarah age 65y widow of Henry D. at son's Henry D. Smith Jr. in Corning, NY November 17, 1870. Born Harrisburg, Pa. nee **BUCHER**. Married 1825 and moved to Ill. where husband and dau died

KUHL Richard H. age 43y in Lindley, NY November 13, 1870

PFIEFFER Frederick G. age 77y in Corning, NY November 18, 1870. Soldier in French Army under Napoleon, res here 21y

ROSE John N. age 70y in Esperanza, Yates Co. NY November 7, 1870

EVELETH Atwood age 67y in Orange, NY November 6, 1870

SHULTS Mrs. Eve age 73y in Avoca, NY December 2, 1870

BUMP Benona F. age 52y in Corning, NY December 2, 1870

HOGUE Mary age 49y in Painted Post, NY January 1, 1871

ARGUE Charles E. son of Thomas Argue in Corning, NY January 1, 1871

SMITH William C. age 4y 4m 16d son of Welcome and Hannah V. Smith in Pt. Byron, NY December 16, 1870

SEAMANS Parley abt 90y in Savona, NY November 25, 1870, born RI res here 50 yrs

FULLER Lewis T. age 57y in Corning, NY January 15, 1871

SHARPSTEEN Benjamin age 66y bro of Richard Sharpsteen of Corning, NY in Rome, NY January 3, 1871

DEATH NOTICES

STODDARD L. P. age 60y in Corning, NY January 24, 1871

VEITH Frank in Corning, NY January 20, 1871. Born Baden, Germany and came here 1837. Leaves wife and 3 children

DAVIS Charles L. age 68y 6m in Corning, NY January 31, 1871

MILLER E. age 68y 10m in Elmira, NY January 26, 1871, funeral at Caton, NY

HOWELL Edward in his 79th yr in Bath, NY January 30, 1871. Born October 16, 1792 in Newburgh, NY and came to Bath in 1811

JOHNSON Lucy age 1y 9m 29d dau of Augustus and Jane Johnson in Corning, NY January 28, 1871

BOGART Louise age 37y wife of Samuel D. Bogart and sister of Mrs. Henry R. MAY of Corning, NY in Fayette, Io. February 13, 1871

FOSTER Polly age 85y at son's Henry P. Foster in Corning, NY February 28, 1871

STEVENS Lizzie Jane age 8y 2m 12d dau of Harrison and Martha J. Stevens in E. Corning, NY March 2, 1871

BABCOCK Marilla age 72y in Knoxville, NY March 6, 1871

DEUERLEIN Willie age 3d son of John M. and Lovica Deuerlein in Centerville, NY March 13, 1871

PRESTON Elmira L. age 34y wife of Oliver Preston in Corning, NY April 2, 1871

HOWE Rufus in his 81st yr in Caton, NY March 26, 1871. Born 1790 in Brattleboro, Vt. and came to Caton 1824. Wife died March 17, 1871

WENTZ Rhoda age 70y wife of Justus Wentz in Union, NY March 1, 1871, resided Dix, NY 17 yrs and moved to Union last August

SKINNER Thomas age 63y in Corning, NY May 2, 1871

SEELEY Mary Donna age 9y 9m 2d dau of Dr. N. R. and Mary C. Seeley in Elmira, NY May 4, 1871

LYON Cornelius abt 45y in Corning, NY May 10, 1871

FERRY Charles H. age 45y Native of New York St. in San Francisco May 2, 1871

BUTLER Ella May age 3y 11m dau of William M. and Eliza A. Butler in Blossburg, Pa. May 2, 1871

RATHBONE Hattie age 7m 8d dau of Capt. John B. Rathbone in Caton, NY May 12, 1871

STEUBEN COUNTY NEWSPAPERS 285

TOWNLEY Hannah age 64y Mother of William F. and Thomas L. Townley in Corning, NY May 13, 1871

LEE Susan J. age 46y wife of Harvey Lee and dau of Nathan **FELLOWS** in Farmington, Pa. May 5, 1871

MILLER William abt 45y in Corning, NY May 24, 1871

YOUNG Mrs. Joseph W. age 44y in Lindley, NY May 23, 1871 buried Horseheads, NY

TUPPER Dr. Archelaus age 86y in Corning, NY May 28, 1871

BLIVEN Mrs. Hannah in her 47th yr in Bath, NY May 26, 1871

COLE Jacob age 76y in Rathbone, NY May 25, 1871

BARRETT Mary A. age 47y wife of Walter S. Barrett in Elmira, NY June 11, 1871

BAXTER Jane age 58y wife of Duncan Baxter in Corning, NY June 9, 1871. Leaves 4 sons and 4 daus, oldest son John died Civil War November 1863

O'SHAUGHNESSY Joseph B. age 56y in Corning, NY June 19, 1871

LINDSLEY Eliza age 36y wife of C. S. Lindsley at bro Caleb **CLARK** in Corning, NY (Newspaper date June 22, 1871)

EDMINSTER Levi B. in his 38th yr in Catlin, NY June 13, 1871

KENMORE Rev. Charles of Tallahasse, Fl. in Hornellsville, NY June 22, 1871

COBB Samuel age 62y in Hornellsville, NY June 14, 1871

TOBEY Louise age 30y wife of Edwin Tobey in Caton, NY June 25, 1871

SKIFF Lottie in her 35th yr wife of Myron Skiff and dau of Rev. R. **SHERMAN** in Tyrone, NY July 2, 1871

RILEY Rhoda age 86y at son's Owen Riley in Pulteney, NY July 1, 1871

GILLETT Mary P. (PAUL) wife of Joseph Gillett formerly of Corning, NY in Jay Co. Ind. May 2, 1871

WHEAT Lucy H. widow of Rev. Benjamin Wheat and sister of Aaron H. **GILLETT** of Corning, NY in Dresden, Mo. June 16, 1871. 6 children dec. 2 sons 1 dau living

DOUGLAS Mary R. age 25y wife of Charles G. Douglas and dau of Daniel F. **BROWN** in Corning, NY July 26, 1871

GILLETT Charlotte age 89y at son's William P. **HILL** in Caton, NY August 22, 1871. She and 1st husband Ephraim Hill were one of 1st settlers of Caton. He died and she

DEATH NOTICES

Married (2) Joseph Gillett

KIMBALL Luzelle P. age 33y son-in-law of William P. **HILL** of Caton, NY in Wellsboro, Pa. August 20, 1871

WOLCOTT Adelia L. wife of Timothy S. Wolcott and dau of Amaziah **TOBEY** of Caton, NY in Missouri Valley, Io. August 26, 1871

QUACKENBUSH Matilda J. age 20y dau of David in Big Flats, NY August 22, 1871

TOBEY Clarissa age 65y wife of Stephen Tobey in Caton, NY September 8, 1871

GRAVES Charles M. Md. age 30y in Corning, NY September 9, 1871

GOODSELL Ann Eliza age 25y late of Cleveland, Oh. wife of Byron W. Goodsell and dau of William **DICKINSON** in Hornby, NY September 9, 1871

BUNKER Sybil age 80y Mother of Samuel W. **BURT** of Corning, NY and sister of late Dr. Eli **HILL** of Geneseo, NY in Tuscarora, NY August 23, 1871. Married (1) Samuel Burt and (2) Nathaniel Bunker of Newfield, NY

MAY Henry age 6y son of Mrs. Charles **VAN NAME** formerly of Corning, NY in Binghamton, NY October 26, 1871

BROWN Hiram age 71y late of Lindley, NY at son's William C. Brown in Corning, NY November 5, 1871

SMITH Nelson W. age 11m son of Henry D. in Corning, NY November 21, 1871

MILLS Laura P. wife of Rev. Sidney Mills in Lawrenceville, Pa. (Newspaper date November 23, 1871)

ERWIN William age 16y son of Edward E. Erwin in Erwin, NY December 10, 1871

WEALE Mary abt 45y wife of William Weale and dau of late Nelson **WOLCOTT** in Caton, NY December 12, 1871

STANTON Sherman age 65y formerly of Prattsburgh, NY in Hornby, NY December 15, 1871

SPENCER Clarissa wife of Richard P. Spencer formerly of Corning, NY in Chester, Ct. December 16, 1871

THOMAS Hattie N. age 20y dau of Levi S. Thomas formerly of Corning, NY in Washington DC, buried Corning, NY December 23, 1871

WARNER Ira age 46y formerly of Scoharie Co. in Corning, NY December 23, 1871

WILSON James R. age 66y nr Mansfield, Pa. December 24, 1871

ROBERTS Mary age 90y Mother of Henry and Peter **COVENHOVEN** at Grand son's Thomas Covenhoven in Hornby, December 16, 1871

BRIDGEMAN Orlando age 79y in Jasper, NY January 1, 1872

TAYLOR J. Wesley age 44y in Prattsburgh, NY January 1, 1872

WHEELER Mrs. Seth age 72y in Wheeler, NY January 6, 1872

PRESTON Charles age 80y late of Corning, NY in Caton, NY January 18, 1872

LINDSAY Allen age 96y in Caton, NY January 29, 1872. Vet. of War of 1812, had 24 children

FRYMIRE Rogenia L. age 28y wife of Samuel Frymire and dau of late Dr. **MUMFORD** in Knoxville, NY February 4, 1872

COOPER Betsey age 53y widow of Anson Cooper and dau of late Enos **CALKINS** of Corning, NY in Caton, NY February 20, 1872

REDFIELD Chloe A. age 58y wife of Jared A. in Elmira, NY February 24, 1872

RECE Mrs. Edward formerly Mrs. **ELLIS** of Corning, NY in Hornby, NY February 17, 1872

HARADON Delana in her 72nd yr wife of Parnach in Hornby, NY February 7, 1872

HONNESS William age 67y in Caton, NY March 1, 1872

GRAVES Joshua Bascom age 5m son of George E. and Carrie P. Graves in Corning, NY February 29, 1872

BROWN Sally abt 65y at son's George Brown in Caton, NY March 4, 1872

KIRKENDALL Florence Adell age 6y 7m 25d dau of Erastus Kirkendall in Corning, NY February 24, 1872

LINDSAY Horace age 33y in Caton, NY February 23, 1872, wife and 3 children

REYNOLDS Fanny (**STEWART**) in her 32nd yr wife of Theodore Reynolds formerly of Corning, NY in St. Joseph, Mo. February 25, 1872. Born nr Ithaca, NY

DARRIN William Henry age 21y in RR accident kn Knoxville, NY February 27, 1872. Leaves wife and 5 children

RUNNELL Lando age 3w son of Uri Runnell in Corning, NY March 9, 1872

WOLCOTT George in his 6th yr son of Z. Jones Wolcott in Corning, NY March 7, 1871

DEATH NOTICES

SINCLAIR Fanny A. age 38y wife of H. P. Sinclair in Corning, NY March 9, 1872

WOOD Claude P. age 10y 6m son of Harvey and Violetta Wood in Phillipsburg, Pa. February 12, 1872

HEWLETT Ellsworth S. age 8y son of James Hewlett in Corning, NY March 15, 1872

HASELBAUER Augustin W. age 2y son of Augustin in Corning, NY March 16, 1872

GIACOMO Barlozi age 21y of Switzerland in Corning, NY March 17, 1872

PUGH Sarah age 22y dau of late A. Jackson Pugh of Caton, NY in Phillipsburg, Pa. rec (Newspaper date March 21, 1872)

MURPHY Harry Sarsfield infant son of Harry S. and Emma R. Murphy in Elmira, NY March 19, 1872

REED Martha E. age 5y 8m dau of Charles M. and Fannie E. Reed in Corning, NY March 20, 1872

COE Almeda age 65y wife of Horace Coe and Mother of Mrs. T. B. **FIELD** of Corning, NY in Lima, NY March 25, 1872

HOLDEN Samuel E. age 8y 9m son of John and Sarah in Corning, NY March 23, 1872

WHITE W. Elmer age 23y son of Benjamin White late of Caton, NY in Scio, NY March 17, 1872

HOLMES Mary age 40y wife of James Holmes and dau of Amos **BONHAM** in Caton, NY March 21, 1872

DOW Nancy age 14y dau of I. C. Dow in Corning, NY April 2, 1872

SMITH Mrs. Maria age 55y in Hornellsville, NY March 23, 1872

SWITZER Sarah age 86y in Bradford, NY March 27, 1872

KNAPP George W. age 18y only son of Erastus Knapp in Gibson, NY April 7. 1872

HAVENS Ambrose W. age 18y 4m son of late James H. in Gibson, NY March 19, 1872

POTTER William abt 20y son of James T. Potter of Fall Brook formerly of Corning, NY in Corning, April 6, 1872

JOHNSON Lucius age 18y son of Jonas and Mary Johnson in Caton, NY April 11, 1872

PARKS Mary Luella age 14y dau of A. Parks in Corning, NY May 6, 1872

CLARK Henry E. age 33y in Corning, NY May 5, 1872

GIBSON Adeline age 35y wife of Luke Gibson and dau of late Isaac G. **PALMER** of Corning, NY in Erwin, NY May 6, 1872. Leaves 4 children

MACK Mary Jane dau of late Ebenezer Mack in Ithaca, NY May 14, 1872

TOBEY Fidelia age 85y widow of Christopher Tobey in Caton, NY April 20, 1872

MURRAY Willie age 3y son of William and Ellen in Corning, NY May 11, 1872

WILSON Amanda age 27y wife of John Wilson and dau of William **QUACKENBUSH** of Corning, NY in Catlin, NY May 9, 1872

BROWN Jennie age 8m 18d dau of Charles and Roby in Corning, NY March 19, 1872

HUY Jane C. age 34y wife of L. Grant Huy in Corning, NY May 25, 1872

CLARK Lillis Ophelia age 18y dau of Robert Clark in Corning, NY June 2, 1872

RUTHERFORD Ada age 16y sister of E. D. of Corning, NY in Corning May 25, 1872

MOSHER Mrs. Sarah age 23y in Corning, NY June 11, 1872

GARDNER William age 77y in Corning, NY June 9, 1872

DANIELS Addie age 3m 20d dau of Horace L. in Lawrenceville, Pa. June 8, 1872

GRAVES Maria A. age 59y wife of Dr. Joshua B. in Corning, NY June 19, 1872

PRESTON James Edward age 12y son of late Oliver W. Preston Jr. at Grandfather's O. W. Preston in Corning, NY June 22, 1872

WILDER Zatter F. abt 70y in Painted Post, NY June 22, 1872

DAVIS Norris age 61y in Caton, NY July 1, 1872

KIRKENDALL Myron B. formerly of the 86th NYV in Campbell, NY June 24, 1872

HUNT Mary age 64y widow of George Hunt of Caton, NY and Mother of William Hunt of Corning, NY and Mrs. Joseph **HOLLENBECK** in Caton, NY June 10, 1872

FRYMIRE Albert E. age 1y son of Samuel Frymire in Corning, NY July 15, 1872

HEALY Catherine in her 44th yr wife of John Healy and dau of John **HARRINGTON** of Shandrum nr Bantrum, Co. Cork Ire. in Corning, NY July 10, 1872

WINFIELD Elizabeth age 86y at son's Justus Winfield in Corning, NY July 13, 1872, buried Big Flats, NY

SHARPSTEEN Seneca age 33y son of Richard B. Sharpsteen of Corning, NY in Elmira, NY July 21, 1872

DEATH NOTICES

WOODWARD Florence Eugenia age 2y 6m dau of William E. and Sarah Eliza Woodward of Watkins, NY in Big Flats, NY July 20, 1872

WHEELOCK Charlotte L. age 42y 9m 2d wife of Ezekiel F. Wheelock in Knoxville, NY July 16, 1872

CLARK Emmett age 9m son of I. P. Clark in Corning, NY July 17, 1872

CALKINS George B. age 48y son of late James Calkins of Corning, NY in Dwight, Ill. July 31, 1872. Leaves wife and 7 children

CALKINS Sarah age 77y widow of James Calkins in Clyde, NY August 17, 1872, buried Corning, NY

LAND Benjamin D. in his 44th yr of Jersey City, NJ son of late Robert Land of Corning, NY in Corning August 22, 1872

SMITH Martha A. age 23y dau of Thomas Smith in Corning, NY August 22, 1872

TEXIDO Arthur Hunt age 3y 28d son of Frank and Bell Texido in Corning, NY August 12, 1872

BRINK George W. age 53y formerly of Elmira, NY in Ithaca, NY August 24, 1872

BARTLETT Eva age 19y dau of Collins Bartlett of Moreland, NY August 20, 1872, last of 4 children

SPENCER John C. age 11y son of William Spencer in Gibson, NY August 22, 1872

WOODWARD Charles age 11m son of William E. and Sarah Eliza Woodward in Watkins, NY August 20, 1872

MOORE David age 94y in Corning, NY September 23, 1872

WELLINGTON Edward age 33y bro of G. W. of Corning, NY September 19, 1872. Buried Tioga, Pa.

GORTON Betsey age 84y widow of Silas Gorton and Mother of William and S. D. Gorton in Corning, NY September 24, 1872

BEARDSLEY J. Seymour in Ithaca, NY September 18, 1872

BALCOM Henry Horace age 10m son of Prof. Henry A. and Lulie C. Balcom in Corning, NY September 27, 1872

KNAPP Carrie Bell age 6m dau of George W. Knapp in Corning, NY October 6, 1872

RICHARDS Nellie age 30y wife of Robert Richards in Caton, NY October 20, 1872

MORRILL Bertie age 2m son of Frank P. and Jennie A. Morrill and Grandson of Dr.

J. D. **GILBERT** in Corning, NY October 17, 1872

PFIEFFER Josephine in her 25th yr in Corning, NY October 19, 1872

PACKER Juliett age 23y dau of Charles and Sarah in Corning, NY October 24, 1872

TUPPER John age 36y 18d in Corning, NY October 29, 1872

DENNISON Eunice age 80y Mother of Charles G. Dennison of Corning, NY at son-in-law's R. T. **STEPHENS** in Great Bend, Pa. October 8, 1872

HOWELL Emily age 45y wife of W. N. Howell and dau of late William **BONHAM** of Corning, NY in Marion, NY November 6, 1872

ECTANOCKER George in his 70th yr in Corning, NY November 8, 1872

WADSWORTH Abner J. age 24y formerly of Corning, NY in Council Bluffs, Io. November 22, 1872

TIFF Charles B. age 40y in Corning, NY December 2, 1872

JOHNSON Thomas A. age 68y in Corning, NY November 30, 1872

AGETT James age 83y Father of Mrs. Dr. H. C. **MAY** of Corning, NY in Lyons, NY December 6, 1872

COBB Roby age 26y wife of Henry Cobb and dau of W. M. **SHERWOOD** of Woodhull, NY in Woodhull December 10, 1872

BOWERS Lizzie wife of William Bowers in Campbell, NY December 11, 1872

VAIL Mrs. Phebe age 75y at son-in-law's Dr. A. J. **INGERSOLL** in Corning, NY December 13, 1872

EMMONS Frankie age 10y 11m son of Theodore H. and Nancy A. Emmons in Towanda, Pa. December 13, 1872

Hammondsport Herald

May 7, 1874 - December 31, 1884

CHAMPLAIN Lucy age 72y in Hammondsport, NY June 21, 1874. Born Spencerport, Columbia Co. NY 1 of 8 children. Leaves bro Ira **DAVENPORT** of Bath, NY, Charles of Hammondsport and 1 sister Mrs. **HODGEKIN** of Franklin, NY. 4 children 2 living Charles D. of Pleasant Valley, NY and dau Mrs. Lucinda **WILCOX** of Stamford, NY

YOUNGLOVE Hannah in her 45th yr dau of Aaron Younglove at stepfather's S. H.

DEATH NOTICES

PALMER in Avoca, NY June 25, 1874

SEAMAN Mrs. A. N. age 38y in N. Urbana, NY July 15, 1874

LONGWELL Mrs. Ira in her 43rd yr dau of Samuel **HAWLEY** who came from NJ to Wayne, NY when she was 4y old, nr Hammondsport, NY July 24, 1874. Married 1858

SHEPARD Ransom G. age 69y in Hammondsport, NY August 9, 1874

ERWIN Samuel age 55y in Calvert, Tx. July 24, 1874. Left Painted Post, NY in 1872. Leaves widow and 2 sons

GARDNER Mary age 8m dau of Maj. H. and Eliza Gardner in Hammondsport, NY August 24, 1874

FREY Delbert age 2y 2m son of Charles and Susannah Frey in Mt. Washington, NY August 11, 1874

WATROUS William Henry age 39y son of Samuel and Elizabeth Watrous at Father's in Hammondsport, NY August 25, 1874

CONDERMAN Eliza age 84y at son-in-law's Mathew **HEFFERMAN** in Hammondsport, NY September 10, 1874

DE PUY Dr. J. N. age 31y in Wayne, NY September 11, 1874

LOCKWOOD Bradley R. age 29y son of John and Nancy Lockwood of Mt. Washington, NY in RR disaster in Moberly, Mo. August 17, 1874. Wife died nr 2 yrs ago and son nr 3 yrs

WATROUS Elizabeth age 78y wife of Samuel Watrous September 21, 1874

LAWRENCE James in Cameron, NY October 6, 1874. Born June 6, 1801 in Greenfield, NH and in 1823 walked from Greenfield to Cameron

LOVERIDGE Ruth Carolina age 1y 2m 1d dau of Orren and Louise Loveridge in Hammondsport, NY November 16, 1874

DE PEW Hester age 44y wife of William De Pew and dau of late Benjamin **EGGLESTON** in Pulteney, NY (Newspaper date December 9, 1874)

FULSOM Robbie age 1y 3m son of F. L. and Martha Fulsom in N. Urbana, NY November 8, 1874

CHAMPLIN Charles Davenport age 47y of Pleasant Valley, NY in New York City January 8, 1875. Born August 31, 1828 in Delaware Co. eldest of 4 children. Mother was sister of late Ira and Col. Charles **DAVENPORT** of Hammondsport, NY

DREW Samuel in Urbana, NY January 27, 1875. Born January 25, 1795 in Warwick, NY and came to Steuben Co. 1817. 12 children

GASS Mrs. Margaret age 50y in New York City February 25, 1875. Sister of Mrs. Jules **MASSON** and Mrs. J. D. Masson of Pulteney, NY

DUNNING Frank age 27y son of L. O. and Loretta S. in Penn Yan, NY March 1, 1875

LOCKWOOD Hannah age 79y widow of Joseph Lockwood of Mt. Washington, NY at son-in-law's William **SMITH** in Pleasant Valley, NY February 21, 1875. Several children, names Jonathan and John of Mt. Washington, Joseph of Penn Yan, NY, Mrs. William and Mrs. Ameron **SMITH** of Pleasant Valley. Husband died 1845

HARRIS Sarah Adell age 7m in Hammondsport, NY March 21, 1875

COVERT Edward age 20y formerly of Hammondsport, NY RR accident April 1, 1875

PRENTISS William in Pulteney, NY March 18, 1875. Born May 10, 1801 in Lancaster, Mass.

MC DOWELL William age 84y in Barrington, NY March 24, 1875

RHINEHART Christopher nr Hammondsport, NY April 18, 1875

SPRAGUE Sarah in her 91st yr in Bradford, NY April 11, 1875. Came from NJ 31 yrs ago. 8 children 7 living, names oldest Mrs. Jane **CARR** age 66y and youngest Mrs. Margaret **CARMAN** age 50y. Lived with son William

BENNITT Ida age 25y wife of Depew Bennitt and dau of Lineus **FRENCH** May 9, 1875. Leaves 2 children 1 age 3y and 1 a few days old

NICHOLS Sarah C. age 73y at Mrs. Eleanor **DE PEW** in Hammondsport, NY May 13, 1875. Married 28 yrs ago George Nichols of Milo, NY who died 14 yrs ago

YORK Lizzie age 12y dau of Patrick York in Hammondsport, NY May 31, 1875

BRUNDAGE Capt. Monroe age 38y nr Bath, NY May 26, 1875, single with 2 bro Grattan H. and Frank and 1 sister Mrs. Aaron J. **NELLIS** of Pittsburgh, Pa.

GIBSON William age 68 in Wayne, NY May 27, 1875

HOAGLAND Mary (**FAUCETT**) wife of Martin in Mt. Washington, NY May 6, 1875

VAN DYKE Mrs. Davis in her 73rd yr Mother of Mrs. Lewis P **WYGANT** of Mitchellville, NY in Canton, Pa. July 4, 1875

BRUNDAGE Emily age 69y of N. Urbana, NY (res 50 yrs) at son-in-law's M. V. **BARTON** in Bath, NY July 10, 1875. Names dau Mrs. Henry **BIRDSALL** of Bath

WATROUS Samuel in his 75th yr in Hammondsport, NY July 19, 1875. Born 1800 in Avon, NY and came to Hammondsport 1836. Wife and 1 son died in past yr, dau died abt 12 yrs ago, 1 son John Watrous living

DEATH NOTICES

COVELL Minerva age 61y in Pulteney, NY August 13, 1875

BRUNDAGE Abraham age 80y Vet. of War of 1812 nr Bath, NY August 19, 1875. Born October 10, 1794 nr Mifflin, Pa. son of James Brundage. Came to Elmira at age 5y and in 1803 to Pleasant Valley, NY. Married December 14, 1820 Elizabeth **CONGER** of Wheeler, NY who died April 9, 1872. 3 bros and 2 sisters living Benjamin and Mrs. Sally **READ** of Seneca Co. Oh. and Mrs. Jacob **ACKERMAN** Of Waterloo, NY. Living children Mrs. J. W. **TAGGART** of Cold Springs, NY, C. Y. Brundage of Seneca Co. Oh and A. C. and S. B. Brundage of Hammondsport

NICHOLS Clarissa age 44y wife of George W. Nichols and dau of William **HASTINGS** in Hammondsport, NY September 26, 1875

CASE Dr. George F. age 45y of Pulteney, NY At Father's in Howard, NY September 8, 1875

PALMER William age 74y in Pleasant Valley, NY August 30, 1875

LAUGHLIN Nancy age 53y in Hammondsport, NY September 30, 1875, 3 sons 1 dau

DAMOTH Freddie age 3y son of Alvin and Carrie Damoth in Hammondsport, NY November 13, 1875

WOOD Lewis age 66y in Hammondsport, NY November 17, 1875. 6 bros, names 2 David of Ohio and Henry of Penn Yan, NY. Leaves wife, 3 sons and 1 dau, Edward in Ill. William in Iowa, Mrs **SANFORD** in Tyrone, NY and Charles at home

SWEET Martha age 67y wife of Edward A. Sweet, dau of James **GREGORY** and grand dau of Capt. **STONE** in Pleasant Valley, NY November 26, 1875. Leaves husband and 1 dau

MARGESON Miss Hannah age 69y in Wayne, NY December 15, 1875

MC INTYRE John in Wayne, NY December 19, 1875

SPRAGUE Margaret age 52y wife of Thomas in Pleasant Valley, NY January 6, 1876

CHICHESTER Rev. Darwin age 58y in Hammondsport, NY January 6, 1875. Married 1850 dau of Judge **CHAPIN** of Rochester, NY, buried Mt. Hope cem. in Rochester

CINCEBOX Harvey in his 52nd yr nr Hammondsport, NY January 11, 1876. Born Dutchess Co. NY and formerly resided in Cayuga Co. NY

MARGESON Deborah age 81y at son-in-law's Daniel **GARLINGHOUSE** in N. Urbana, NY January 19, 1876. Large family 3 dec. some out west, Ira, Cyrus, Bradley and Mrs. Garlinghouse in N. Urbana

BAKER John H. in his 50th yr in Cleveland, Oh. February 27, 1876. Born 1826 in Urbana, NY son of late Samuel Baker and Catherine (**HAMMOND**) of Pleasant Valley, NY and Grand son of Judge Baker and of Judge Lazarus Hammond. Married Roxina

KINGSLEY dau of F. J. Kingsley of Hammondsport, NY. Leaves 1 son and 1 dau

SIMMONS Randolph abt 53y in Mt. Washington, NY March 5, 1876. Leaves wife and 2 children

LAYTON ___ wife of Lewis Layton in Hammondsport, NY March 12, 1876

TAYLOR Phebe age 60y wife of Henry Taylor and dau of late James **LONGWELL** in S. Bradford, NY March 10, 1876. Leaves husband, 2 daus and 1 son

GOBLE Mills Hila E. age 21y in Bradford, NY March 17, 1876

BELL Philander F. in his 68th yr formerly of Hammondsport, NY in Courtland, NY March 21, 1876. Born March 4, 1809 in Jefferson Co. NY. Married Miss **JONES** and came to Hammondsport abt 1840, later moved to Courtland. 5 daus and 2 sons

DICKESON Charles A. age 23y in Wayne, NY March 10, 1876

CHISSOM Lucetta age 23y in Pleasant Valley, NY April 6, 1876

STEWART Ella **(HALLETT)** at Mother's in Wayne, NY April 16, 1876

SANFORD Rosanna age 30y wife of Thomas Sanford formerly of Pleasant Valley, NY in Mt. Washington, NY April 6, 1876. Leaves husband and young children

HORACE Minnie age 21y formerly of Hammondsport, NY in Buffalo, NY May 30, 1876

WHITE Moore C. in Chicago, Ill. June 5, 1876

SOULE James R. Md. formerly of Hammondsport, NY in Belvidere, Oh. May 2, 1876. Born March 4, 1824 in Otsego Co. NY

TILLOTSON Don L. in saw mill accident nr Bath, NY July 28, 1876. Father died 2 wks ago, funeral at Mother's in Canisteo, NY

VAN GELDER Margaret wife of James Van Gelder in Hammondsport, NY July 28, 1876. Leaves dau age 15 yrs

ROSENCRANS Hannah age 77y wife of Aaron in Hammondsport, NY September 1, 1876. Born and married in NJ. 7 children 4 living, Ann Eliza and George of Hammondsport, S. B. of Webster City, Io. and Mrs. A. **MORRISON** of Ft Dodge, Io.

SMITH James an old res of Tyrone, NY September 8, 1876

BROWN Theodore M. age 39y son of Morris Brown in Penn Yan, NY October 2, 1876. Younger bro Morris killed at Gettysburg, older bro Smith served Rebellion and died after returning home. Married in St. Louis, Mo. Miss **WEBER**. Leaves wife and 1 son

LONGWELL Elizabeth in her 79th yr at res of Jeptha **RETAN** in Pulteney, NY October

1, 1876. Born Sussex Co. NJ. Married 1816 William Longwell who died 1843, married 6 yrs later James Longwell who died April 10, 1871, 11 children 8 living.

LAYTON Elmer age 11y son of Lewis Layton in Urbana, NY October 3, 1876

RAYMOND Tryphena age 70y at sister's Mrs. Jacob **THOMPSON** in Wheeler, NY October 26, 1876

HAMMELL Frank only rem. son of Kate in Hammondsport, NY December 9, 1876

MOORE Adelia wife of Walter Moore of Hammondsport, NY in RR. disaster at Ashtabula, Oh. December 29, 1876. Born April 29, 1822 in New Lisbon, NY. Leaves husband and 4 children, Mrs. Anna **MC MINN** of Chicago, Ill. Trevor, Hobart and Clara of Hammondsport. Bro Charles **FAIRCHILD** of Bath, NY and sister Mrs. Eunice **MYRICK** of Quaquago, NY

WRIGHT ____ age 1m 2d child of B. J. and Rena Wright in Woodhull, NY January 6, 1877

PURDY Charles age 72y in Bath, NY January 12, 1877. Born Lower Canada, res here 44y. Son W. H. Purdy and dau Mrs. **GATES**

RICE Seth of Howard nr Towlesville, NY March 1, 1877

WALTERS Charles age 34y in Hammondsport, NY March 10, 1877. Native of Switzerland. Leaves wife, 2 children and aged Mother

SUNDERLAND Mary Ann in her 70th yr wife of A. W. Sunderland in Wayne, NY February 6, 1877

CHAPMAN Charlotte age 53y wife of Richard L. in Tyrone, NY February 22, 1877

WILLIAMS Ezra B. age 41y son of Ira C. Williams of Prattsburgh, NY in Campbell, NY March 4, 1877

DILDINE Frank age 25y at Father's nr Hammondsport, NY March 30, 1877

SEXTON Elmer age 15y of Woodhull, NY at res of T. M. **YOUNGLOVE** in Pleasant Valley, NY April 21, 1877

HILL Priscilla age 77y 9m at dau Mrs. Lathrop **DREW** in Pulteney, NY May 4, 1877

BOMBARD Sarah M. age 40y dau of late Samuel **DREW** of Hammondsport, NY at Alden, Ill. March 28, 1877. Leaves husband and 3 children

ELLIS Phebe in her 90th yr at son's Addison F. Ellis in Bath, NY May 1, 1877

WRIGHT Charles W. killed by Mr. **WHITE** in Bath, NY May 24, 1877

BRUNDAGE Samuel age 33y in Urbana, NY May 25, 1877. 2 bro A. C. of Urbana and Cornelius of Oh.

MAXWELL James age 59y nr Bath, NY April 19, 1877. Father of Mrs. Hiram **MORRISON** of Hammondsport, NY

COVELL Jane C. age 44y 5m 2d wife of M. D. Covell formerly of Hammondsport, NY and dau of Francis and Elizabeth **SHERMAN** in Dundee, NY May 27, 1877. Born Reading, NY 1 of 12 children, 7 living. Married October 14, 1854. Leaves husband and 3 children Eva A. age 21y, Fred F. age 16y and Jennie M. age 10y. Buried Hillside

BUTLER Louie age 6y dau of John H. Butler formerly of Cohocton, NY in Penn Yan, NY June 9, 1877

ROBERTS Mrs. Betsey half sister of Peter **COVENHOVEN** of Painted Post, NY, oldest part of house fell on her in Hornby, NY June 23, 1877

DUNNING Mary P. wife of L. O. in Prattsburgh, NY June 23, 1877. Born May 25, 1818 in Prattsburgh dau of Henry and Charlotte **ALLIS**. Married February 1848

NOBLE Edward age 46y 21d nr Hammondsport, NY June 27, 1877

MILLS Guitta age 66y wife of Jabez Mills in Hammondsport, NY August 4, 1877. Leaves husband and 8 children

BAILEY Samuel L. age 78y in Urbana, NY August 13, 1877. Wife died 12 yrs ago, 11 children 8 living Samuel Jr. and Lewis of Storey Co. Io., Daniel and Andrew J. of Rock Rapids, Io., Mrs. Ferris **MARGESON** and Erastus of Allegany Co. NY, Stephen and Mrs. Warren **WEBSTER** of Hammondsport, NY

LAUGHLIN Mrs. Catherine age 86y in Hammondsport, NY August 15, 1877

CARR Lottie age 10m dau of Alfred and Mary in Hammondsport, NY August 18, 1877

DECKER Nettie age 2y dau of Sylvester and Margaret Decker in Hammondsport, NY August 19, 1877

RAPLEE Caroline age 66y in Penn Yan, NY August 13, 1877. Born April 18, 1811 in Barrington, NY, she was 2nd wife of Mr. Raplee. His 1st wife was her sister Polly who died 1846 the mother of his children. They were daus of Uriah **SMITH**

CLARK Nelson age 2y 7m son of Peter and Nancy Clark in Pleasant Valley, NY August 30, 1877

WILSON Laura age 10m only child of Stanley and Dora Wilson in Pleasant Valley, NY September 2, 1877

CLARK Ann age 27y wife of Martin Clark in Mitchellville, NY August 30, 1877. Leaves husband and 4 children

GRANNIS Sally G. in her 80th yr wife of Samuel Crannis in Hammondsport, NY

August 19, 1877. Married over 61 yrs

FAIRCHILD Charles Henry age 1y 3m 17d son of H. O. Fairchild in Hammondsport, NY October 13, 1877

SAYRE Del age 29y wife of Mortimer Sayre in Denison, Io. September 28, 1877. Born Allegany Co. NY nee **GENUNG**. Married 5 yrs, 2 children

WOOD Sarah O. in her 33rd yr wife of Ira M. Wood and dau of William and Hannah **FULLER** in N. Urbana, NY October 21, 1877. 2 children ages 8y and 4y

STONE Amos in his 61st yr in Cohocton, NY November 25, 1877. Born June 5, 1817 in Pleasant Valley, NY, married February 30, 1836 (possibly the 20th) Jane **MILLS** of Bath, NY

BRUNDAGE Edward funeral in Pleasant Valley, NY December 28, 1877. Born March 23, 1816 in Pleasant Valley. Leaves wife and 2 sons, 1 bro Henry and 2 sisters mrs. K. **LONGWELL** and Mrs. D. **CAMERON**

DYKERMAN Mrs. Dorcas age 85y formerly of Hammondsport, NY in Penn Yan, NY January 12, 1878

CALKINS Dr. Alonzo at sister's Mrs. Henry **BONHAM** in Hammondsport, NY March 3, 1878. Born Waterford, Ct.

COTTON Phebe Ann in her 54th yr wife of Edward W. in Hammondsport, NY March 10, 1878. Born Cohocton, NY dau of Almon **EGGLESTON**. 3 children died young

LARROWE Jacob in Hammondsport, NY March 21, 1878. Born December 19, 1807 son of Albertus Larrowe in Wheeler, NY 1 of 13 children, Jonathan of Oh., Franklin of Io., Albertus now of Wheeler, NY, Charlotte wife of S. B. **ROSENCRANS** of Webster City, Io. surviving. Married Janet **VAN WORMER** of Cohocton, NY. Leaves wife and 3 children, Capt. E. B. of Urbana, NY, L. A. of Herkimer Co. NY and Mrs. Emily **CHASE** of Avon, NY

MILLER Mary (**HENDERSON**) age 27y wife of Wilber Miller in Pleasant Valley, NY March 18, 1878. Leaves husband and son nor yet 1 yr

TAYLOR Daniel formerly of Hornellsville, NY in Prattsburgh, NY March 20, 1878

KING Amy in her 76th yr at dau Mrs. **SNOW** March 24, 1878. Born April 21, 1802 in Genoa, NY, lived in New York until 1868, now of Hammondsport, NY. 3 daus Mrs. Snow, Mrs. **VAN GELDER** and Mrs. **ROCKWELL**

WHITE John Jr. in his 65th yr in Cohocton, NY April 19, 1878. Born September 5, 1813 in Groveland, NY

DE PEW Roswell age 56y in Hammondsport, NY June 4, 1878. Born 1822 4th son of late Abram De Pew of Pulteney, NY. 1 bro Samuel died May 3, 1878. Married Emeline **WIXON** dau of Stephen Wixon of Urbana, NY. Leaves wife and 1 dau

STEUBEN COUNTY NEWSPAPERS 299

GIFFIN Rachel in her 84th yr at son's James Giffin in Catawba, NY July 8, 1878. Born New Brunswick, NJ, lived there 40 yrs.

BEACH Obadiah in his 75th yr in Tyrone, NY June 24, 1878. Father of Daniel of Watkins, NY and Lewis of Tyrone

DAMOTH Addison age 37y in Hammondsport, NY July 21, 1878. Born 1841 son of late Marcus Damoth of Bradford, NY. Married Sarah **JEWELL** dau of Nelson Jewell now of Wayne, NY. 2 children Nettie age 10y and Lena age 5y

DAVENPORT Col. Charles in his 79th yr, unmarried, in Hammondsport, NY August 27, 1878. Born June 5, 1800 in Spencertown, Columbia Co. NY. Father died 1840

LA RUE Fred B. age 24y 3m 13d in Wheeler, NY September 27, 1878

DOLSON Mary Ella age 19y dau of Dr. Dolson in Bath, NY October 19, 1878

BAKER Maria age 33y wife of Isaac Baker and dau of George **LONGWELL** of Bath, NY in Stillwater, Mn. December 2, 1878, buried in Bath

SHULTS Ella age 32y wife of Arnold Shults and dau of Daniel **GRAY** nr Bath, NY December 21, 1878

HENDERSON Dryden in Hammmondsport, NY January 29, 1879. Born October 15, 1805 in Norway, NY. Married age 24y Maria **COE** of Norway and moved to Hammondsport in 1830. Children born Hammondsport, Frances wife of Judge **GOODSPEED** of Joliet, Ill., Minerva **BENHAM** widow of George R. late of 161st Reg. and Nathaniel of St. Louis, Mo.

CHISM David age 54y in Hammondsport, NY January 31, 1879. Born Cameron, NY. Leaves 2 sons and 4 daus

WOOD John in his 61st yr in W. Urbana, NY February 20, 1879. Born Chester Co. nr Manchester, England and came to US 1849. Leaves wife and 6 children, 2 bro and 1 sister, Joseph and Mrs. Jonathan **WOODHOUSE** of Mt. Washington, NY and Thomas of Anoka, Wis., 3 bro and 1 sister in England

ZIMMERMAN Frantz age 61y from Vienna March 5, 1879. Leaves 3 daus Henrietta, Emma and Mrs. Caroline **HELSKER** of Hornellsville, NY

MILLER Charles in Penn Yan, NY March 4, 1879. Born Mt. Washington, NY

WOOD Jonathan in N. Urbana, NY March 15, 1879. Born in Urbana son of Israel Wood, 1 of 13 children, only 3 bros and 2 sisters living, Israel, Joel, Andrew, Mrs. Henry **BRUNDAGE** and Mrs. Jonas **WHEELER**. Age 21y married Rebecca **HOLLY** dau of late Timothy of N. Urbana, no children. Had 40th anniversary March 13

SPRAGUE Elizabeth age 63y 2m wife of William Sprague in Urbana, NY March 15, 1879. Born February 24, 1816 in Vernon, NJ dau of Tobias and Olive **VAN GELDER**. Married September 22, 1832 in Vernon and moved to Urbana 1842. Leaves 7 bro, 3

sisters, 10 children 8 living

GELDER Harriet age 64y in Prattsburgh, NY March 2, 1879. Leaes husband and 11 children

LOUNSBERRY Mrs. Arminda A. wife of Nathan in Hammondsport, NY March 19, 1879. Born November 6, 1823 in Pulteney, NY. Married April 16, 1848

DE PEW Riley at res of Mrs. John **BAILEY** in Hammondsport, NY March 28, 1879. Son of late Abram De Pew. Leaves bros Ferris, William and late Peter, Samuel and Roswell, wife and 2 children in Ill.

CLARK Jarvis P. age 73y nr Arkport, NY rec (Newspaper date April 2, 1879)

SAYRE John B. formerly of Hammondsport, NY funeral in Crawford Co. Io. April 3, 1879. Sisters Mrs. G. H. **WHEELER**, Mrs. Sarah **CRANSTON** the former Mrs. Capt. **KING**

MC DOWELL Maria at dau Mrs. Samuel **HALLETT** in Wayne, NY April 11, 1879. Sons George and Francis Mc Dowell

GILMORE Maria wife of Richard Gilmore one of oldest res of Wixon Hill April 11, 1879. Leaves husband and 2 daus Mrs. S. C. **HAIGHT** and Mrs. David **CORYELL**

SMITH Emeline wife of Charles G. Smith and dau of George S. **BRUNDAGE** of Pleasant Valley, NY in Elk Run, Pa. April 7, 1879. Born September 9, 1827

AXTELL Joseph abt 76y in Pulteney, NY April 15, 1879

VAN NESS Ira age 69y in Hammondsport, NY April 26, 1879. Born 1810 in Sussex Co. NJ son of late Peter Van Ness. Married Angelina **ROBINSON** dau of Dr. Robinson of Howard, NY. Children, Foster, Henry, Helen and Abbie. Sister Mrs. Lydia **COGSWELL** of Hammondsport. Mem. Co. I 34th Reg in Civil War

ZUBLER Jacob in his 88th yr at dau Mrs. Jacob **FREY** April 29, 1879. Born Argan, Switzerland 2nd son of Jacob Zubler. Age 17y joined army under Napoleon's staff. Married in Switzerland Frances **SOUTER**. Came to US 1850 and settled in Rochester, NY. Moved to Ovid, NY 1827 and Hammondsport in 1863. 1 son and 1 dau

CHASE Emily wife of Rev. L. D. Chase and dau of late Judge **LARROWE** of Hammondsport, NY in Avon, NY April 16, 1879, buried Hammondsport

ATWILL Rev. William in his 81st yr formerly of Bradford, NY in San Antonio, Tx. April 19, 1879 on 33rd wedding anniversary

KEELER J. H. in his 58th yr formerly of Penn Yan, NY in Hammondsport, NY May 16, 1879. Born January 1, 1822 in Pa. Leaves wife and 2 sons William and George

GARLINGHOUSE Daniel B. in his 62nd yr funeral May 24, 1879. Born NJ and came to NY age 8y. Married Mary **MARGESON** dau of Thomas of Hammondsport, NY, 2

sons and 1 dau. Married (2) Sarah Margeson, sister of his 1st wife, 5 children 3 living, names 1 Dr. J. A. of Cleveland, Oh. 3 bros and 3 sisters John and David of Mi. Thomas of Oh. and widow **READ** of Pleasant Valley, NY, Mrs. Gurdon **WEBSTER** of Bath, NY and Mrs. **FRENCH** of Tecumseh, Mi. Buried Mt. Washington

TOMLINSON Minerva widow of Horace Tomlinson in N. Urbana, NY June 11, 1879. Born March 24, 1800 in Vt. dau of Lockwood and Mercy **MEAD**. Married 1825, husband died 1844. Res. Essex Co. and Clinton Co. NY where 3 children were born. Mary died age 3y. Moved to Wayne, NY 1837. Oldest son Wilbur Fisk enl. 34th Reg. for 2 yrs and 22nd Reg. NY Cav. and died at Andersonville nr end of war.

HAWLEY Richard formerly of Pulteney, NY in Branchport, NY August 15, 1879

WRIGHT John an old res of Hammondsport, NY August 28, 1879. Born July 27, 1813 in Co. Carberay, Kildan, Ire. Came to Canada 1846, to Albany, NY 1848 and to Steuben Co. 1850. Married 1842 Lucy **STRONG** of West May Co. Ire. 13 children 4 living, William W., Benjamin and Mrs. **HOLLIS** all of Woodhull, NY and Mary at home. 1 son John Jr. died in Peninsular Campaign under Gen. Mc Clelland in 1851

BOYD Tompkin W. age 72y of Pulteney, NY at dau Mrs. James **TAYLOR** in Branchport, NY September 17, 1879. Leaves 5 sons and 2 daus

CHURCH Katherine in her 71st yr dau of Hezekiah **RIPLEY** in Hammondsport, NY September 22, 1879. Married (1) Mr. **WILMERDING** who died 1 mo after marriage. Married (2) Dr. Amasa Church who died 1852. 3 children Mrs. John **DIMON**, Amasa E. Jr. and Miss Mary Church, 2 sisters Mrs. **GARDNER** and Miss Harriet Ripley

SHERWOOD Betsey in Hammondsport, NY October 1, 1879. Born October 16, 1784, married (1) 1811 Nathan **TAYLOR**, married (2) in 1850 John H. Sherwood who died 1858 age 83y

MUNSON Jesse in his 80th yr formerly of Bradford, NY in Williamsport, Pa. last wk. Funeral at Bradford October 25, 1879. Born August 21, 1792 in Vt.

DREW Julia age 15y dau of B. F. Drew in Hammondsport, NY November 18, 1879

BENNER Ann in her 74th yr widow of Timothy Benner in Hammondsport, NY November 14, 1879. Born June 23, 1816 in Tralee Co. Kerry, Ire. and came to Hammondsport 1855. 8 children Henry of Wis., Mrs. Catherine **LEARY**, Jane and William in Hammondsport, Mrs. Helen **DONNELLY** in Hornellsville, NY, Mrs. Ann **HARRINGTON** in Greenwood, NY, Mary wife of Hesro **JEWELL** in Savona, NY and Eliza wife of Marion Jewell in Wayne, NY

PORTER William H. age 25y in Urbana, NY November 14, 1879, buried Dundee, NY

BENHAM Julia wife of James Benham formerly of Hammondsport, NY in Angelica, NY November 13, 1879

LEE David B. age 87y 5m formerly of Hammondsport, NY in Detroit, Mi. November 15, 1879

DECKER Mrs. ___ widow of Simeon Decker at son-in-law's William **BROWN** in Pulteney, NY December 12, 1879

DALRYMPLE Elizabeth age 63y wife of Samuel Dalrymple at son-in-law's A. **BALLARD** in Pleasant Valley, NY January 5, 1880. Born March 4, 1817 in Trenton, NY. At age 17 married Henry **LARROWE** who died July 29, 1854, 10 children 7 living, 3 in Iowa, 1 in Yates Co. NY and 3 in Steuben Co. Married 5 yrs later Samuel Dalrymple

WOOD ___ age 18m dau of Adelbert Wood in N. Urbana, NY January 24, 1880

CROOKSTON Moses only son of M. W. Crookston of Wayne, NY February 15, 1880

ROBBINS Samuel abt 55y in Pulteney, NY February 11, 1880

REYNOLDS Jesse age 82y in Milo, NY February 7, 1880

NORTON Nannie age 28y wife of Maj. Thomas H. Norton at Father's Grattan H. **WHEELER** in Hammondsport, NY February 26, 1880. Oldest son Redington died abt 4 yrs ago

MORRISON Mary (MC CONNELL) wife of William E. Morrison in Hammondsport, NY February 17, 1880. Born June 11, 1824 in Starkey, NY, married July 9, 1843

BRUNDAGE Daniel abt 70y at bro George in Pleasant Valley, NY February 27, 1880

ROFF Julia A. (BALL) wife of David Roff in Pulteney, NY February 28, 1880. Born November 17, 1859. Married abt 1 yr

GLEASON Clayton youngest of 3 sons of James R. and Mary Gleason of Wayne, NY in Starkey, NY March 14, 1880

GARLINGHOUSE Sarah abt 50y in N. Urbana, NY March 21, 1880. Born Urbana dau of Thomas and Deborah **MARGESON**. Married abt 20 yrs ago D. B. who was husband of her sister. 5 children 2 living, Grant age 11y and Alice age 13y

WHEATON John M. age 85y in Hammondsport, NY April 8, 1880. Born May 19, 1795 in Hebron, NY, family moved to Westfield, Mass. Age 22y moved to Salem, NY and married August 22, 1820 Susan **BELLOWS**, 1 son and 6 daus, son lives in Ohio, 2 daus in Hammondsport, 1 in Prattsburgh, NY, 1 in Corning, NY and 1 in Bath, NY

WARREN Julia Ann wife of George Warren and dau of late Jonathan **EATON** in Wayne, NY April 16, 1880. Born Hammondsport, NY. 2 children both dec.

COTTON Edward W. age 58y in Hammondsport, NY April 26, 1880

HORTON Amanda E. age 27y wife of John Horton Jr. and dau of Stephen and Eunice **BAILEY** in Wayne, NY April 12, 1880, buried in N. Urbana, NY. Married abt 7 yrs, 3 children

BRUNDAGE James abt 82y in N. Urbana, NY April 11, 1880. 4 sons 4 daus, James and Zebulon in Rochelle, Ill., Hiram and Lewis in N. Urbana, Mrs. Nathaniel **CRAWFORD** dec., Mrs. **BARTON** and Mrs. **STRATTON** in Bath, NY, and an invalid dau at home

TOMER Albert William age 36y in Hammondsport, NY May 23, 1880. Born August 21, 1843 in Cambridge, Mi. Family moved to Branchport, NY when he was 10. Married 1869 Alida **ORTON**, 4 children

DUNN James age 76y in Pulteney, NY May 28, 1880. Born Greene Co. NY. Leaves wife and 8 children

LONGWELL Nathan age 59y in Starkey, NY June 1, 1880. Married (1) Sarah **DE PEW** who died 1870 and married (2) Mrs. Mary **SAWYER**. 2 sons John M. and Norton N.

FRENCH Linus H. nr Hammondsport, NY July 30, 1880. Born January 17, 1812

KRANZ Mrs. William set fire to house then hanged herself July 29, 1880

SILVERNAIL Seymour possibly poisoned in Bradford, NY July 23, 1880. Frank **ANGELL** arrested

FAUCETT Eleanor nr 77y at dau Mrs. David **CASTERLINE** in Hammondsport, NY August 12, 1880. Born Ovid, NY nee **JAYNES**. Married (1) Horace **ATWELL** and settled in Mt. Washington, NY. He died and she married (2) George Faucett. Dau married (1) Drew **GLANN** and (2) David **CASTERLINE**

BARRETT Seth W. age 72y in Hammondsport, NY September 4, 1880. Born September 1808 in Putnam Co. NY. Married Amanda **BOYD** of Putnam Co. 2 daus Mrs. Emily **EGGLESTON** and Lovisa who died abt 12 yrs ago

AULLS Ephraim age 72y in Wheeler, NY August 31, 1880

SMITH George in Wayne, NY September 18, 1880

STRAWAY Mrs. S. V. in Wayne, NY September 21, 1880

CULVER Amy age 98y 4m 19d at son's Solomon **FERGUSON** in Hammondsport, NY September 12, 1880. Born April 24, 1782 nee **LAY** in Chatham, NY, parents from Ct. Abt age 20y married David Ferguson, married 25 yrs when he died. Married (2) at age 63y William Culver who died 2 yrs later. 2 sons Lewis of Fishkill, NY and Solomon

BRUNDAGE George S. age 75y in Pleasant Valley, NY September 29, 1880. Born 1805 in Hammondsport, NY son of James Brundage 1 of 14 children 3 living, James M. on homestead, Mrs. Sally **REED** of Reedtown, Oh., Mrs. Anna **ACKERMAN** of Waterloo, NY. Married Maria **BLACK** who died 1874, 5 daus 4 living

CONNELLY Katie age 13y dau of John and Jane at Pine Pt. NY October 9, 1880

DEATH NOTICES

HAASE Fred age 16y son of Margaret Haase in Pleasant Valley, NY October 10, 1880

CONNON Callie (**MOODY**) age 40y formerly of Hammondsport, NY in Webster Grove, Mo. October 14, 1880. Leaves husband and 5 children

FLYNN Edwin of Wayne, NY thrown from wagon November 19, 1880. Leaves wife and 4 children

MC MASTER George Edward at father's Judge David Mc Master in Bath, NY November 26, 1880. Half bro Judge Guy Mc Master

CLARK Mrs. Sarah age 63y in Mitchellville, NY November 28, 1880. Sister of Ewing and Bradley **BAILEY** and Mrs. **BROOKHART**

ROSENCRANS Aaron age 79y in Hammondsport, NY December 7, 1880. Born December 15, 1802 in NJ and moved in early life to Pulteney, NY. 1 son and 1 dau

GRANNIS Samuel in his 88th yr in Hammondsport, NY December 8, 1880. Born April 5, 1793 in New Haven, Ct. Married 64 yrs ago Sally **BARNARD** of Geneva who died September 1877. 3 sons living, 1 at Gowanda, 1 in Hornellsville, NY and 1 a popular ballad singer

BAKER Aaron Y. age 53y formerly of Pleasant Valley, NY son of William Baker and Grand son of Judge Samuel Baker in Colistoga, Cal. December 12, 1880. Married Eunice **CONGER**. Sister married Angus **CAMERON** in Elmira, NY. Leaves wife and 4 children in Chilicothe, Mo.

BRUNDAGE Lewis P. age 39y son of Charles nr Bath, NY November 22, 1880

WASHBURN ___ age 5w son of Addison and Susan in Pulteney, NY February 2, 1881

STONE Betsey age 86y at son's James D. Stone in Pulteney, NY February 1, 1881. Had 9 children 6 living

BEATON Donald age 65y in Hammondsport, NY February 3, 1881. Born Isle of Mull, N. Scotland. Wife died young, came to US 1849 and to Steuben Co. 1856. Leaves son James in Col.

CLARK Freeman age 29y son of Charles in Hammondsport, NY February 4, 1881

RANDALL John in Hammondsport, NY February 14, 1881. Born March 12, 1801 in New York City. Married age 20y Charlotte **PARSELLO** who died 7 yrs ago. 1 son and 3 daus, moved to Hammondsport 1832/33

BENNITT George S. age 57y son of Abraham Sayre Bennitt in Pulteney, NY February 24, 1881. Married Sarah **FULLER**, 4 daus Mrs. John **GIFFIN**, Mrs. Eugene **RILEY** of Pulteney, Lily and Josephine at home

DAVIS Jonas age 19y 3rd son of Darius and Sarah Davis of Catlin, NY at res of John **COMSTOCK** in N. Urbana, NY February 20, 1881

JAYNES Alice age 23y dau of George M. and Hester Jaynes in Barrington, NY February 18, 1881, buried Wayne, NY

RICHARDS Jennie age 3y dau of George and Mary Richards February 25, 1881

BRADLEY Jennie age 2y died March 14, 1881 and Joseph abt 17y died March 21, 1881 children of Thomas and Bell Bradley in Hammondsport, NY

WIXOM Avery age 81y in Hammondsport, NY March 9, 1881

BOYD Mrs. Mary (colored) in her 27th yr oldest child of George and Maria **JAMES** in Hammondsport, NY March 11, 1881. Leaves 3 children

HAUGHEY Charlie age 10y son of John in Hammondsport, NY March 9, 1881

ELLIS Mrs. Elizabeth in her 71st yr in Hammondsport, NY March 12, 1881

WHEELER Addison in his 53rd yr youngest son of Grattan H. Wheeler in Wheeler, NY March 23, 1881. Married dau of late George **SHEPARD**, 3 children, son died early manhood, 1 dau died last fall and Mrs. **WOOD** on homestead with Mother

SMITH Louise age 20y dau of David Smith in Mt. Washington, NY April 7, 1881

SMITH Helen (**PALMER**) age 23y wife of John in Hammondsport, NY April 9, 1881

SMITH William age 63y in Urbana, NY March 29, 1881. Born February 22, 1818 in Hector, NY 1 of 7 children, moved to Urbana age 11y. Married Julia **LOCKWOOD** dau of Joseph Lockwood, 1 child Mrs. John L. **WARD** of Bradford, NY

HOAGLAND Columbus of Mt. Washington, NY in Bath, NY April 23, 1881

COGSWELL Lydia age 82y dau of Peter **VAN NESS** in Hammondsport, NY April 23, 1881. At age 50y married Anson Cogswell who died a few yrs ago

GLEASON Lois age 20y dau of James R. and Mary Gleason April 25, 1881

WEBSTER Mrs. Byron in her 31st yr in N. Urbana, NY May 5, 1881, only surviving dau of George and Hester **JAYNES**

SPRAGUE Charlotte in her 39th yr wife of John L. Sprague and dau of Solomon **CHASE** of Cameron, NY in Urbana, NY May 27, 1881

MARROW Mrs. John of Tyrone, NY Mother of Mrs. William **NICHOLS** of Bath, NY in Tyrone June 24, 1881

BRUNDAGE Charles age 78y at Bonney Hill nr Bath, NY June 9, 1881. Born April 1803 in Painted Post, NY. Married 52 yrs, 3 sons and 7 daus, son Lewis died last November, dau Cornelia wife of Frazier **FAULKNER** died June 15, 1881

FREY Jacob age 80y of Mt. Washington, NY in Sonora, NY July 3, 1881. 4 sons and

2 daus, George of Mn., Charles and Eliza of Bath, NY, John of Barrington, NY, Mrs. John **LOCKWOOD** of Mt. Washington and Mrs. Aaron **BROWN** of Savona, NY

GILMORE Richard in his 74th yr in Urbana, NY July 30, 1881

SLAGHT Matilda age 69y of N. Hector, NY at dau Mrs. George **SMITH** in Hammondsport, NY September 20, 1881. 4 sons, 2 in N. Hector, 1 in Mi. and 1 in Waterloo, NY. Husband died 1851, buried in Hector

DILDINE Uriah in his 53rd yr nr Hammondsport, NY September 21, 1881

BRINK Mrs. Nettie in Pulteney, NY September 30, 1881

WATERMAN Fanny in her 49th yr wife of J. W. Waterman of Detroit, Mi. at bro John **DAVENPORT** in Bath, NY November 6, 1881

SHAW Mrs. Orren age 74y Mother of Charles B. in Penn Yan, NY November 9, 1881

HULTS Fred age 17y son of Thompson Hults in Pulteney, NY October 23, 1881

BENHAM Jennie dau of George K. Banham who died in Civil War in Hammondsport, NY November 17, 1881

BAILEY Eva W. in her 24th yr youngest and last of 4 children of Stephen and Eunice Bailey in Urbana, NY December 29, 1881. Sister Mrs. Amanda C. **HORTON** died April 12, 1880

CARR Alfred in Hammondsport, NY January 2, 1882. Born November 6, 1825 in Orange Co. NY. Leaves wife and several small children

BAKER Eunice G. abt 87y relict of William Baker 1 of the early settlers of Pleasant Valley, NY, rec of Washington DC with dau Mrs. Angus **CAMERON**, buried nr Hammondsport, NY November 29, 1881

MITCHELL Elizabeth age 71y of Wayne, NY relict of John Mitchell (Newspaper date January 11, 1882). Born 1810 nr Bath, NY dau of H. A. **TOWNSEND**. Leaves 3 sons 4 daus living, 1 son died Civil War

GRAY Ambrose killed by cow horns bet. Avoca and Kanona, NY January 8, 1882

KNAPP William K. age 66y in N. Urbana, NY February 9, 1882. Born 1816 in Barrington, NY

SCHMOKER Ulrich in Hammondsport, NY March 17, 1882. Born 1822 in Switzerland and came to US in 1848. Lived Rochester, NY until 1868

NETTH Martha age 25y wife of Henry Netth in Hammondsport, NY March 16, 1882

MASSON Apolonia widow of J. D. Masson in Pulteney, NY March 15, 1882. Born May 18, 1831 in town on Rhine river, Germany. Came to US with brothers and sisters in 1852. Married 1855, 2 sons and 2 daus

WEBSTER Isaac age 61y at brother-in-law's D. J. **ROYCE** In Wayne, NY March 20, 1882

HANNABERGER George age 51y in Hammondsport, NY April 4, 1882. Born May 25, 1830 in Lemenbach, Germany. Served 13th Reg. NY Inf.

LONGWELL James M. in Mt. Washington, NY June 8, 1882. Born 1828 in NJ son of late James Longwell 1 of 11 children, 4 bro and 3 sis living. Married 1852 Mary **WOODRUFF**

DREW Benjamin F. age 51y in Hammondsport, NY June 25, 1882. Born 1830 in Urbana, NY son of John Drew 1 of several children 6 living, Schuyler, Bolivar, Mary, J. Milton, Jeanette wife of M. H. **DILDINE** and Eliza wife of Jeptha Dildine. 1st 3 in Mn. an others in Hammondsport. Married Susan Mandaville **GAREY** of Hammondsport

SCHMATZ Nellie age 3y dau of David Schmatz June 20, 1882

WHEELER Edify age 43y wife of J. W. Wheeler and dau of William **BROWN** in N. Urbana, NY July 11, 1882

WILLSON Dora E. in her 31st yr wife of Stanley Willson and dau of Hankerson **DILDINE** of Hammondsport, NY in Pleasant Valley, NY July 20, 1882

CURTIS Rev. C. G. age 69y in Hammondsport, NY August 18, 1882. Leaves wife, 2 sons and 1 sister

KIMBALL Stephen suicide nr Dundee, NY September 1, 1882

NETTH Harry infant son of Henry Netth at Grandmother's Mrs. **CHISSOM** in Pleasant Valley, NY September 2, 1882

CLARK Elizabeth (**GILMORE**) age 76y wife of Solomon Clark in Hammondsport, NY September 28, 1882. Born Lodi, NY, married 54 yrs and had 4 children

MYRTLE Mrs. Benjamin in Hammondsport, NY September 25, 1882. Born 1817 in Carmel, NY. 1 son Van Buren Myrtle of Corning, NY 2 daus Mrs. Dr. **STODDARD** of Lacrosse, Wis. and Mrs. Hoyt **YOUNGLOVE** of Hammondsport

WHEELER Carrie L. dau of Charles G. in Hammondsport, NY November 4, 1882

HOLLEY Mrs. Nancy in her 68th yr of N. Urbana, NY at son's Judson Holly in Hammondsport, NY November 7, 1882

FAIRCHILD Stanley Bostwick in his 73rd yr in Hammondspart, NY December 19, 1882. Born January 10, 1810 in New Lisbon, NY and came to Bath at age 17y with cousin Lay **NOBLE**. Married February 1836 Maria **SMITH** who died February 1865, 4 children S. S. and E. B. of Hammondsport, H. N. of Denver, Col. and dau who died young. Married (2) Mary **HAMMOND**

DEATH NOTICES

SMITH Seneca of Savona, NY at Father-in-law's D. **CAMERON** in Hammondsport, NY January 21, 1883

GILLETTE Lewis H. age 32y in Hammondsport, NY January 21, 1883

MC CAIQUE Mary sister of Joseph in Hammondsport, NY January 24, 1883

DE GRAW John in his 86th yr on 57th wedding anniversary in Wayne, NY February 2, 1883. Born June 6, 1797 in NJ and came to Seneca Co. NY age 7y, to Wayne 1822. Married February 2, 1826 Catherine **HALL** dau of David Hall. 8 bro 1 living

HOWELL Robert of Bath, NY May 3, 1883. Born 1859

FAIRCHILD Charles Stone age 71y at dau Mrs. Edward **NOBLE** nr Bath, NY March 25, 1883. 3 sons H. O. of Hammondsport, NY, Benajah of Abilene, Tx. and Charles L. of Savona, NY

VAN AUKEN Miss Jennie of Hammondsport, NY in New York City April 24, 1883

BOWES Miss Julia in her 29th yr of Bath, NY at sisters Mrs. F. J. **RICHARDS** in Hammondsport, NY May 1, 1883

BRONSON Lucy in her 73rd yr widow of Jesse Bronson at dau Mrs. James W. **BRUNDAGE** in Cold Springs, NY May 3, 1883. Children Isaac and George of this Valley, Clark of Severne, NY, Sarah wife of James W. Brundage and Mrs. Harriet **GRANT** of Pharsalla, NY

HUTCHES ___ age 3m dau of Marion and Harriet Hutches June 1, 1883

WEBER Mrs. F. J. in her 78th yr in Hammondsport, NY May 24, 1883. 3 sons George and Richard of Cal. and Frank at home

JEWELL Nelson in his 68th yr in Wayne, NY June 10, 1883. Born Phelps, NY, married October 5, 1836 Hannah **HOUGHTON**, 3 sons and 3 daus, 1 son died age 8y

HALL Mrs. Jane in Pulteney, NY June 17, 1883

WHITE Evangie age 16y dau of Samuel White in Hammondsport, NY June 17, 1883

LE BARR Susan in her 89th yr wife of A. W. Le Barr in Pulteney, NY July 18, 1883. Born NJ, came early to Tompkins Co. NY, buried Hammondsport, NY

PLOOF Eva V. in her 14th yr in Hammondsport, NY July 24, 1883

BENHAM James in his 77th yr bro of H. Benham of Hammondsport, NY in Oakland, Cal. July 21, 1883

ALLCOCK Mrs. ___ age 75y formerly of Hammondsport, NY at dau Mrs. D. E. **LOVERIDGE** in Unadilla, NY August 11, 1883, buried Hammondsport

SAUER Tobias age 53y in Pleasant Valley, NY August 10, 1883

CARR Mattie age 9y dau of George Carr in Hammondsport, NY August 23, 1883

GREES Ella age 16y 3m dau of William Grees in Hammondsport, NY August 16, 1883

GILBERT Mary Angeline (**ADAMS**) age 48y wife of Timothy Gelbert in Pleasant Valley, NY September 19, 1883. Born Canandaigua, NY and married in Penn Yan, NY, Leaves husband and 3 children

COMSTOCK Ida age 2y dau of John C. and Louise Comstock in N. Urbana, NY September 28, 1883

QUINN Maria in her 84th yr mother of E. C. of Pulteney, NY November 18, 1883

MARGESON Israel in Wayne, NY November 21, 1883

MEEKER Mrs. ___ nr 80y in Hammondsport, NY January 1, 1884. Came from Germany. Husband died abt 14 yrs ago

ELLIS William an old res of Wayne, NY January 17, 1884, buried Dundee, NY

ELLIS Laura in her 23rd yr wife of Harry formerly of N. Urbana, NY and dau of Hiram **FINCH** of Bath, NY in Wyoming Terr, December 30, 1883. Married last March

MARGESON Ira nr 66y in N. Urbana, NY January 24, 1884. Born N. Urbana. Leaves wife and 7 children

HALSEY William a native of Wayne, NY adopted son of late Peter Halsey in Rochester, NY February 5, 1884. Married 12 yrs ago dau of late George **MUMFORD** of Bath, NY

BABCOCK Mrs. Phoebe mother of Dr. O. and M. T. Babcock of Hammondsport, NY in Middlesex, NY February 2, 1884

BAILEY Elsie at son's Jefferson Bailey in Mt. Washington, NY February 7, 1884. Born Orange Co. NY dau of Abram **DE PEW**. Married age 16y John Bailey, bro of late David and Samuel. Large family 4 living, Samuel, Jefferson and Samantha of Hammondsport, NY and Mrs. Leonard **CRAWFORD** of Tyrone, NY

RETAN Rachel wife of John Retan who died 14 yrs ago in Pulteney, NY February 17, 1884. Born 1811 in Vernon, NJ and moved to Hector, NY age 9y. 5 sons 2 daus, Nelson, Jeptha, Olney and Cynthia of Pulteney, Sylvester and Mrs. John **SPRAGUE** of Hammondsport, NY and Anson who died in South during Civil War

BEATON Eliza (**READ**) age 44y wife of James Beaton in Pleasant Valley, NY March 12, 1884. Married April 14, 1880

HADDEN Absolum age 87y of Cold Springs, NY at dau Miss Georgie **GRANT** in Bath, NY March 19, 1884. Large family, names G. P. of Pulteney, NY, A. of Corning, NY and Mrs. William **GOFF** of Urbana, NY

DEATH NOTICES

ROWLETT Rev. James at res of dau Mrs. Frank **AULLS** in Bradford, NY March 29, 1884. Born March 12, 1830 in Sligo, Ire. Other dau Mrs. J. P. **KENMUIR** of Kansas City, Mo.

NICHOLS George W. would be 60 yrs old in June in Hammondsport, NY April 4, 1884. Came from Milo, NY 40 yrs ago. Married 1850 Clarissa **HASTINGS** dau of William Hastings, 2 children Kate and William H. Wife died 1875 and he married (2) 1877 Elizabeth **CLARK** dau of Solomon Clark

MARGESON Martha J. age 43y dau of late Ira in N. Urbana, NY April 2, 1884

BRADLEY Anna in her 19th yr dau of Thomas in Hammondsport, NY April 7, 1884

GARRISON John I. in Mitchellville, NY April 7, 1884. Born February 28, 1835 in Sussex Co. NJ. Married dau of William **SPRAGUE**

DOTY Mrs. William H. an aged lady of Wayne, NY April 19, 1884

SNOW Mrs. R. G. age 48y in Hammondsport, NY April 29, 1884, 6 children 5 living

HAWKINS Harriet age 52y wife of William Hawkins in Sonora, NY April 26, 1885. Leaves husband, 1 child, bro and sisters. Names 1 bro H. L. **LEWIS** of Hammondsport, NY

NORTHRUP E. D. age 53y in Pulteney, NY May 2, 1884

MC MINN Anna wife of E. B. Mc Minn and dau of Walter L. **MOORE** of Hammondsport, NY in Chicago, Ill. May 12, 1884

VAN GELDER Mathew in his 82nd yr at son's Wesley Van Gelder in Bradford, NY May 28, 1884. 14 children 4 living, William of Hammondsport, NY, John and Wesley of Bradford and Mrs. Jane **HALL** of Lowell, Mi. Married 60 yrs, wife died 6 wks ago

WILLIAMS Mary age 29y 7m wife of Henry in Hammondsport, NY June 14, 1884. Leaves husband and 3 children, 1 an infant a few weeks old

VOGT Nicholas age 63y formerly of Hammondsport, NY in Rheins, NY June 20, 1884

MILLER A. age 40y at sister's Josephine in Hammondsport, NY July 7, 1884

COLE E. C. age 28y son of Andrew Cole of Pleasant Valley, NY in Waverly, NY August 10, 1884. Leaves wife and 2 children

DALRYMPLE Samuel age 78y at res of Mrs. A. **BALLARD** in Hammondsport, NY August 16, 1884

JAYCOX Emily age 38y wife of George and dau of Harriet and late Otis **FOLSOM** of Hammondsport, NY in Pleasant Valley, NY August 26, 1884. Married 1871, leaves husband and 3 young children

SCHOFIELD John L. age 61y formerly of Hammondsport, NY in Bath, NY September 7, 1884. Born February 22, 1823 in Pound Ridge, NY. Leaves wife and 2 children

BROWN Mrs. Ann age 81y in Mitchellville, NY September 12, 1884

BROWN Richard Lynn age 3m son of Cornelius and Adda Brown of Clarksville, NY at Grandfather's R. F. **HORTON** in Pulteney, NY (Newspaper date September 24, 1884)

TAYLOR Mary A. wife of William Taylor in Hammondsport, NY (Newspaper date September 24, 1884). Born 1826 in New Rodnorshire, Wales nee **OWEN**. Married (1) age 22y Richard **DAVIS** and with infant dau Levia (now wife of Rev. C. **TOWNSEND**) came to US on ship Zion's Hope. Moved to Bethel, NY then Italy Hill, NY, 3 children born here William, Martha and Mary twin daus. Mary lived only few wks. Husband died 1866, married (2) 1867 William Taylor of Branchport, NY. children Fanny and Milford dec.

MILLER Erastus in S. Pulteney, NY September 24, 1884. Leaves wife, 1 son 2 daus

SCHOLL George a German res in Pleasant Valley, NY October 7, 1884

KNAPP George C. in his 32nd yr son of Rev. John and Aurelia Knapp in Hammondsport, NY October 28, 1884. Born May 10, 1858 in Prattsburgh, NY and buried Prattsburgh

HIGBEE Mrs. M. A. age 59y formerly of Tioga Ctr. in Pleasant Valley, NY October 30, 1884. 2 daus, 1 in Hornellsville, NY and Hope at home

VROOM Miss Sincha age 80y nr Hammondsport, NY November 11, 1884

GARDNER Mary age 73y at son's Maj. H. Gardner in Pleasant Valley, NY November 28, 1884. Born Bridgeport, Ct. After marriage moved to Belvidere, Ill. where husband later died. Sister of late Mrs. **CHURCH** and Miss Harriet **RIPLEY**

DE PEW Mrs. Ferris dau of late Sherman **STANTON** in Hammondsport, NY December 12, 1884. Leaves 3 sons and 1 dau

WINTERS George N. in S. Pulteney, NY December 18, 1884

TOWSLEY Isaac age 79y of Mitchellville, NY father of Mrs. Frank **DECKER** of Hammondsport, NY, buried December 21, 1884

HEDGES Caleb S. age 80y in Bradford, NY December 20, 1884

DEATH NOTICES

Steuben Signal (Hornellsville, NY)

April 4, 1883 - January 23, 1884

OAKS Ernest of Hornellsville, NY run over by switch engine in Elmira, NY March 30, 1883

HARRINGTON Louise age 60y in Hornellsville, NY April 6, 1883. Sisters Mrs. W. G. **ROSE**, one sister died rec Mrs. William **WILLARD** of Hornellsville, Mrs. **BURLINGHAM** of Hartwick, NY and Mrs. Charles **STRAWN** died 4 yrs ago. Leaves 1 son Charles Harrington

HAWLEY Mary L. age 81y widow of Judge Hawley (who died 14 yrs ago) in Hornellsville, NY April 3, 1883. Native of Delaware Co. NY. 9 children 4 living, C. L., Miles W., Lester D. Hawley and Mrs. Homer **HOLLIDAY**

OSBORN Lewis M. age 36y in Fremont, NY April 5, 1883

DANIELS Nathan R. age 80y in Almond, NY April 2, 1883

DARLING Jonathan age 69y in Arkport, NY April 15, 1883

HART Michael age 10y in Almond, NY April 9, 1883

WALLACE Dr. William age 69y in Avoca, NY April 7. 1883

FRENCH Miss Persis age 73y in Bath, NY April 10, 1883

KURTZ Mrs. Mary age 83y at son's nr Rogersville, NY April 11, 1883

DERENBECKER Mrs. Mary L. age 82y in S. Dansville, NY April 10, 1883

TERRY Nathan age 87y in Prattsburgh, NY March 26, 1883

ZELIFF Adam age 68y in Arkport, NY April 20, 1883

GLAZIER Margaret wife of James T. Glazier in Hornellsville, NY April 22, 1883

WILLOR Mrs. Louisa age 59y in Hornellsville, NY April 26, 1883

SHERMAN Henry age 22y in Hornellsville, NY April 26, 1883

GEORGE Benjamin age 74y in Troupsburgh, NY April 12, 1883

OLMSTEAD Lorena M. age 9y dau of Samuel and Abigail D. Olmstead in Troupsburgh, NY April 19, 1883

MESSEREAU Pansy age 8w dau of Ward L. in Hornellsville, NY April 30, 1883

LAUTENSCHLAGER John age 63y in Hornellsville, NY May 3, 1883

BRODERICK Julia dau of Patrick Broderick in Hornellsville, NY May 3, 1883

HOGAN John age 71y in Hornellsville, NY May 4, 1883

DONLON Catherine age 79y in Hornellsville, NY May 4, 1883

DOORLEY Thomas age 82y in Hornellsville, NY May 8, 1883

TALBOT Jarvis abt 42y accident in Erie Yards in Hornellsville, NY May 22, 1883

MC FARLAND Mrs. O. L. age 60y in Troupsburgh, NY May 21, 1883

DENNIS Rodney in Hornellsville, NY May 16, 1883. Born 1835 in Jasper, NY. Married 1865 his 2nd wife Frances M. **BENNETT** of Harpersfield, NY, 5 children

LARIMER Louisa at dau Mrs. William **O'CONNOR** in Hornellsville, NY May 16, 1883

STEBBINS Charlotte in her 58th yr in Wileyville, NY May 14, 1883

FOSTER John abt 60y in Hornellsville, NY May 25, 1883

MERSEREAU Charles F. son of Theodore and Caroline Mersereau in Hornellsville, NY June 4, 1883

STEPHENS Mrs. Ermina age 71y 10m 2d in Canisteo, NY May 25, 1883

BUCK Nellie age 21y dau of L. W. Buck in Hornellsville, NY May 30, 1883

PRESTON Gilbert H. age 63y in Hornellsville, NY June 1, 1883

NORTON William age 58y in Hornellsville, NY May 29, 1883

SWEET Noble formerly of Prattsburgh, NY in Painted Post, NY May 29, 1883

HAWLEY Mrs. J. B. abt 60y in Hornellsville, NY June 6, 1883

SHERWOOD George W. age 45y in Hornellsville, NY June 8, 1883

EDGAR Mrs. Martin age 42y in Hornellsville, NY June 12, 1883

BAKER Jeremiah age 92y in Canisteo, NY June 17, 1883. Born April 18, 1791 in Canisteo son of Jeremiah Baker who was Rev. Soldier and born in New England. Age 19y married Eunice **POWERS** of Addison, NY who died 1829 leaving 7 children. Married (2) 1829 Hilda **STEPHENS** dau of Rev. Jedidiah Stephens and widow of Phineas Stephens, 3 children Jedediah, Orlando and Mrs. James F. **O'CONNOR**. 2nd Wife died 1871

DEATH NOTICES

VAN SCOTER William in his 9th yr son of Amariah M. and Isadora Van Scoter in Hornellsville, NY June 13, 1883

HATHAWAY Charles G. age 19y 9m in Hornellsville, NY June 14, 1883

MUNNING Charles age 47y in Buffalo, NY June 24, 1883

LISMAN John age 83y in Arkport, NY June 29, 1883

VAN NESS Milton in his 66th yr in Hornellsville, NY July 1, 1883

SCHERER John P. age 76y 10m in Dansville, NY July 1, 1883. Leaves dau Mrs. W. W. **WHITE** of Hornellsville, NY

PETERSON Martha N. wife of Stephen Peterson in Canaseraga, NY July 2, 1883. Lived early life in Howard, NY

MOORE James age 77y 8m in Hornellsville, NY July 11, 1883

SWARTZ Thurza in her 59th yr wife of Ross H. in Hornellsville, NY July 15, 1883

KINGSBURY S. N. abt 64y in Bound Brook, NJ July 13, 1883

LOGHRY Ebenezer age 42y 6m in Bath, NY July 8, 1883. He enlisted in 23rd Reg. April 30, 1861

WALLACE Joseph age 79y in Hornellsville, NY July 25, 1883

HORTON Mrs. Cordelia age 61y in Hornellsville, NY July 22, 1883

OSTRANDER Harry age 3m son of H. E. and Carrie Ostrander in Hornellsville, NY July 25, 1883

STILLMAN ___ age 8m son of R. B. and Lydia L. in Hornellsville, NY July 27, 1883

LEACH ___ infant son of Horace D. and Mary in Hornellsville, NY July 30, 1883

DAVENPORT Mrs. George age 61y of Arkport, NY at dau Mrs. J. A. **RIDER** in Wellsville, NY July 30, 1883. Leaves husband, 3 sons and 3 daus, Will in Mi., Stephen and Henry at home, Mrs. C. D. **ALLEY** of Whitehall, Mi. and Mrs. David **CURRY** of North Valley

TROWBRIDGE Jennie age 19y wife of Hiram in Fremont, NY July 31, 1883

CHAPMAN Christina age 66y widow of Joshua S. Chapman of Greenwood, NY at son-in-law's D. C. **AMEY** in Hornellsville, NY August 3, 1883

STRANG James age 20y of Dundee, Scotland in Hornellsville, NY August __, 1883

ROBERTS Marion C. age 30y in Hornellsville, NY August 11, 1883

CROSS S. B. age 35y wife of James B. Cross and dau of Charles **MARKHAM** in Hornellsville, NY August 12, 1883

LOONEY Mary dau of Dennis Looney in Hornellsville, NY August 13, 1883

HART Catherine age 14m dau of John and Mary in Hornellsville, NY August 1, 1883

UPSON William B. age 77y 7m 1d in Canisteo, NY August 14, 1883. 12 children 2 living Mrs. Roxy **STEPHENS** of Canisteo and Willis of Almond, NY who was 80 yrs old on July 17. 1st 2 children half bro and sister were Hiram and Elizabeth **BISHOP**. Other 10 children were Wyllis, Cynthia, William B., Erastus, Roxy, Sylvia, Calvin, Daniel, Phebe and Helen. His bro Eraustus died July 10, 1883 in Ishua, NY

SIMMONS William H. age 63y in Hornellsville, NY August 16, 1883

JONES H. Ross old res of Addison, NY August 17, 1883

CUTLER Ira age 63y in Almond, NY August 17, 1883

CORN Ada age 53y 3m wife of Jacob Corn in Hornellsville, NY August 21, 1883

GREEN Arthur Eugene age 8m 15d son of Frank L. and Clara (**RUDIGER**) in Hornellsville, NY August 21, 1883

WOODRUFF Laura E. age 4m dau of Charles G. and Laura Woodruff in Hornellsville, NY August 9, 1883

PIERCE Sarah wife of H. C. Pierce and dau of James P. **CLARK** in Cohocton, NY August 25, 1883. Leaves husband and 8 small children

HENRY Isaac age 81 res of Cohocton, NY at dau Mrs. Jerome **FLINT** August 21, 1883

HURLBUT Emeline age 64y wife of Syrenus Hurlbut in Fremont, NY August 23, 1883

BROWN Mrs. Ann L. age 73y in Almond, NY August 24, 1883

KILDAY Katie in Hornellsville, NY September 4, 1883

AMEY Sarah J. age 43y 8m wife of Charles in Hornellsville, NY September 1, 1883

BLIVEN Irene wife of Rev. E. F. Bliven in Mitchellville, NY August 17, 1883. Born November 30, 1817 in Geneseo, NY. Married September 1, 1838, 4 daus and 1 son

BADGER Edward H. formerly of Hornellsville, NY in Jamestown, NY August 31, 1883. Came from New Milford, Pa. with father John. Buried Hornellsville

KING John age 6y son of Patrick and Bridget in Hornellsville, NY September 10, 1883

SWARTWOOD Willie J. age 6m son of J. A. and Mary Swartwood in Hornellsville, NY September 10, 1883

DEATH NOTICES

BENJAMIN ____ infant son of Ledran and Phebe in Fremont, NY September 9, 1883

WHEELER Mrs. Eliza K. age 38y 5m at res of D. C. **GIBBS** in Wheeler, NY June 26, 1883. Born Almond, NY dau of Samuel P. and Serilla **KARR**, buried Almond

GIBBS Col. Jesse B. in his 74th yr in Almond, NY September 11, 1883. Children, Wesley and Jesse of Almond, Samuel of Denver, Col. Will in NM, dau Libbie of Beatrice, Neb. and Mrs. John **OSTRANDER** of Hornellsville, NY

PITTS Sybil (**DORR**) age 95y 5m widow of John in Arkport, NY September 12, 1883

HORTON Jeanette age 56y 10m widow of Charles Horton at res of J. Cotton **SMITH** in Wellsville, NY September 12, 1883

COVERT Cornelia age 25y wife of William in Painted Post, NY September 18, 1883

PARKHURST Ophelia age 46y wife of P. D. Parkhurst and dau of Col. F. E. **YOUNG** in Painted Post, NY September 17, 1883

FORRESTER Julia C. age 50y 6m wife of Charles Forrester and dau of Dr. A. B. **CASE** of Howard, NY in Scranton, Pa. September 16, 1883

WHITFORD Chester G. age 76y formerly of Hornellsville, NY in Union, NY September 18, 1883. Leaves wife, dau Julia and brother-in-law Dwight **HARRISON** of Hornellsville

CORYELL Samuel S. age 50y formerly of Hornby, NY in Bay City, Mi. September 7, 1883

SAULSBERRY Zenie age 80y in Hornellsville, NY September 30, 1883

POLAND Clara age 35y wife of William in Hornellsville, NY October 1, 1883

BECKWITH Electa B. age 87y at dau Mrs. Emma **HOLCOMB** in Bath, NY September 15, 1883

FORD Fannie wife of G. T. Ford formerly of Bath, NY and dau of Ira M. **CALKINS** of Bath in Toledo, Oh. September 19, 1883

READY Philander age 72y of Arkport, NY in Bath jail September 21, 1883

FAIRBANKS Frank E. age 30y in Friendship, NY September 27, 1883

GLOAD John age 80y in Pulteney, NY September 29, 1883

CLARK Almira age 37y wife of F. L. Clark in Ingleside, NY September 29, 1883

KELLOGG Calvin age 75y in Rushford, NY September 30, 1883

ZIRKLEBACH Andrew age 58y in Hornellsville, NY October 6, 1883

BARBER Gardiner age 71y in Almond, NY October 6, 1883

SEILER Willie S. age 26y son of John in Hornellsville, NY October 8, 1883

GROSS Ellis age 88y shot himself in N. Almond Valley, NY October 14, 1883. Names 1 son Freeman

HAYES Hiram age 70y in Jasper, NY October 12, 1883

HOAGLAND Elizabeth dau of Richard Hoagland at sister's Mrs. P. G. **WILLIS** in Howard, NY October 6, 1883

THACHER Mowry in his 82nd yr in Hornellsville, NY October 17, 1883. Born June 15, 1802 in Gloucester, RI son of Nathaniel who came to Hornellsville 1810

CUTLER Martha age 31y wife of John Cutler in Hornellsville, NY October 16, 1883

HAYES Amy age 82y at res of John **HEALY** in Troupsburgh, NY October 17, 1883

FISHER Elizabeth age 64y 3d widow of Asa M. Fisher (who died October 24, 1881) in Denmark, Io. October 13, 1883. Born October 10, 1819 in Hancock, NH eldest child of Samuel **DENNIS** late of Jasper, NY. Bro and sisters Sarah **LAMSON** of Jasper, Alice **KENT** of Jasper, Samuel of Hornellsville, NY, Rodney died last May, Abigail died 1841 age 2y. Married April 24, 1846, 1 child Emily E.

BEATTIE Thomas age 68y in Hornellsville, NY October 27, 1883

JONES Eveline age 63y in Burns, NY October 30, 1883

CHEESBROUGH Charles in his 24th yr in Addison, NY October 26, 1883

COOPER Charles abt 60y in Erwin, NY November 4, 1883

MUNN ___ infant dau of Frank Munn in Hornellsville, NY November 5, 1883

DILDINE John R. age 77y in Hornellsville, NY November 1, 1883

WARNER Stebbins age 75y in Woodhull, NY November 4, 1883

WOOLEVER John S. age 16y in Hornellsville, NY November 13, 1883

CHAPMAN Edward abt 45y in Hornellsville, NY November 16, 1883

RUSSELL Mary Z. age 43y wife of F. M. in Hornellsville, NY November 17, 1883

WALTON Mrs. Amanda age 35y in Cameron, NY November 8, 1883

CLARK Joseph age 3y son of Thomas Clark in Hornellsville, NY November 18, 1883

STEPHENS Sarah E. age 40y 10m wife of J. D. Stephens in Fremont, NY November

23, 1883. Sister of A. T. **ALLIS** of Hornellsville, NY

HEALY Harriet I. age 59y wife of W. W. Healy in Dansville, NY November 23, 1883

EGAN Joanna age 91y in Hornellsville, NY November 21, 1883

WALBRIDGE Albert D. age 32y son of James in Hornellsville, NY November 30, 1883

THACHER Agnes only dau of William **GOODWIN** of Mi. in Hornellsville, NY December 1, 1883. Niece of Henry **GRANGER** of Hornellsville

MOORE Mrs. A. H. former wife of Gen. P. **HARTSHORN** of Hornellsville, NY who died 1856 and dau of Judge **HORNELL** in Hastings, Mn. November 28, 1883. Born April 28, 1806 in Hornellsville and married March 12, 1827. Moved to Hastings 1855 where husband died October 31, 1865. Married (2) Maj. Alpheus Moore who died January 18, 1882

HOWARD Frank B. age 37y son of Mrs. Mary Howard in Hornellsville, NY December 2, 1883

COON George age 83y in Hornellsville, NY December 2, 1883, old German res.

SWEET Prudence in her 77th yr in Hornellsville, NY December 5, 1883

BURDICK Susan age 7m dau of B. F. and Nellie in Almond, NY December 5, 1883

MC CARTY Mary Agnes age 33y wife of Timothy Mc Carty in Hornellsville, NY December 9, 1883

BENNETT Hiram in his 69th yr son of late Maj. Thomas Bennett in Hornellsville, NY December 9, 1883. Wife was dau of late Christopher **DOTY**, 1 son Frank and adopted dau Estella surviving

BOYD David in E. Troupsburgh, NY December 4, 1883

WALKER Mrs. Harriet in her 86th yr buried in Ashley Cem. in Springwater, NY December 7, 1883

KNIPPER Polly age 61y 9m wife of John Knipper in Fremont, NY December 14, 1883

HARTSHORN Mrs. Mary in her 91st yr sister of Nathaniel **CHADWICK** of Hornellsville, NY in Angelica, NY December 13, 1883

PERRY Rhoda age 56y wife of Nelson Perry in Rathbone, NY December 8, 1883

WARREN Mrs. Isaac age 78y in Troupsburgh, NY December 3, 1883

UPDYKE Jonathan age 93y Vet. of War of 1812 in Jasper, NY December 14, 1883

WHITE William J. from overdose of chloral in Corning, NY December 15, 1883

SHULTS William H. age 37y in Kanona, NY December 16, 1883

GREGG Elizabeth H. in her 29th yr wife of Thomas Gregg in Thurston, NY December 10, 1883

GILLETT Albert age 56y formerly of Caton, NY in Owasso, Mi. November 27, 1883

WILCOX Philander age 76y in E. Troupsburgh, NY December 18, 1883

O'CONNOR Michael drowned in well in Hornellsville, NY December 18, 1883

MATHEWS N. M. in Wheeler, NY December 22, 1883. Born February 1805 in Dutchess Co. NY. Married February 1828 Anna **CROSSMAN** of Wheeler

ABER Mrs. Alva age 50y in Wheeler, NY December 23, 1883

CAMERON Mrs. John nr 60y in Hornellsville, NY December 30, 1884, 15 children

BOOTH Sophrona age 72y in Syracuse, NY December 27, 1883. Leaves dau Mrs. B. **MC CONNELL** of Hornellsville, NY

WETMORE Vernon B. age 59y of Canisteo, NY in Lovelton, Pa. January 3, 1884. Leaves wife, 1 son and sister Mrs. W. G. **ROSE** of Hornelsville, NY

OWEN Sherman W. age 51y in Hornellsville, NY January 11, 1884

HORN E. H. age 71y in Addison, NY January 19, 1884

Hornell Daily Times

January 2, 1879 - June 30, 1881

MULHOLLEN William age 80y in Canisteo, NY January 1, 1879. Born 1799 in Painted Post, NY and came to Canisteo with bro Samuel in 1806. Married 1832 Elizabeth A. **CULBERTSON** of Dansville, NY

WARD Burr age 30y accident at ice house in Hornellsville, NY January 6, 1879. Leaves wife and 3 children

TOWLE Archie age 2y son of Richard and Lucinda Towle in Hornellsville, NY January 4, 1879

LAUDER Ada Bertha age 11y 5m dau of Walter and Margaret D. Lauder in Oregon Hill, NC December 29, 1878

GRISWOLD John age 75y in Southport, NY January 9, 1879

DEATH NOTICES

HANKS Mrs. Hannah age 97y in Wheeler, NY January 5, 1879. Came to Steuben Co. 1794. Married 1806 Elijah Hanks of Bath, NY. In 1874 dau Mahala married Ira P. **BARNEY** of Wheeler, NY

KLINE Margaret age 71y in Almond, NY January 11, 1879

REED James age 82y Father of George T. Reed of Hornellsville, NY in Harleton, Pa. January 12, 1879

HOWARD Phoebe age 76y Mother of M. Howard of Hornellsville, NY in Dunkirk, NY December 27, 1878

WILCOX Mrs. Mary J. age 45y in Canaseraga, NY January 11, 1879

VORHEES Isaac age 50y in Canisteo, NY January 12, 1879

BURRELL Samuel age 83y in Canisteo, NY January 20, 1879. Born Binghamton, NY, leaves 2 sons Alphonso and A. M. Burrell

DUNNING Robert age 1y son of Eli and Lucinda in Hornellsville, NY January 11, 1879

NILES Nathaniel age 87y 6m in Dansville, NY January 15, 1879. Born July 8, 1791 in Groton, Ct. and came to Burlington, NY 1800. Served War of 1812

BRUNDAGE Alma age 20y wife of Frank in Greenwood, NY January 13, 1879

LINDSAY John age 60y in Bath, NY January 19, 1879

MIER Joseph abt 55y in Hornellsville, NY January 24, 1879

DE WITT Thomas abt 28y in Hornellsville, NY January 26, 1879

UTTER Susan age 79y in Ward, NY January 19, 1879

TAYLOR George A. age 23y in Hornellsville, NY January 31, 1879

GARDNER Willard age 46y 8m in Hornellsville, NY February 3, 1879

STEPHENS Robert L. age 3y son of Christopher and Alice Stephens in Hornellsville, NY February 2, 1879

DE WITT Theodore age 36y of Hornellsville, NY January 26, 1879, served Civil War

DYGERT James S. age 67y in Kanona, NY January 29, 1879

CARPENTER Benjamin age 77y in Wayne, NY rec (Newspaper date February 8, 1879)

MANVILLE Burrell age 73y in Hornellsville, NY February 8, 1879

CORY Orlando age 37y 3m in S. Dansville, NY January 21, 1879

GIBBS Betsey age 75y in Hornby, NY February 3, 1879

PAGE Matilda age 58y 11m wife of Charles in Hornellsville, NY February 18, 1879

HITE John age 81y in Independence, NY February 13, 1879

STEPHENS Gracie age 8m dau of Eugene and Ella Stephens in Hornellsville, NY February 13, 1879

CULLINAN Patrick age 84y in Hornellsville, NY February 16, 1879

DUNCAN J. C. age 94y in Angelica, NY February 8, 1879

KENNEDY Mrs. Polly W. age 78y in Hartsville, NY February 7, 1879

KENNEDY Francis age 75y in Hartsville, NY February 18, 1879

BARNES Nelson age 64y in Jasper, NY February 13, 1879

SULLIVAN Dennis age 64y in Hornellsville, NY February 22, 1879

TERRELL William O. formerly of Ithaca, NY in Soldiers and Sailors Home in Bath, NY February 14, 1879. Late of Co. I 32nd Reg. NY Inf.

LAKE Vinton age 8m son of Martin and Ann in Hornellsville, NY February 25, 1879

BECHTOL Clarissa age 67y wife of Evan Bechtol in Caton, NY February 23, 1879

HILL John age 81y in Independence, NY February 13, 1879

PORTER Capt. David a Vet of War of 1812 in Dansville, NY February 24, 1879. Born February 14, 1789 in Trenton, NJ

MOORE Huldah wife of Joseph (who is now 73y) in Canisteo, NY February 24, 1879. Born May 2, 1806 in Cameron, NY. Married April 26, 1829, 5 sons and 3 daus

LYON Mary dau of James A. and Ellen Lyon in Hornellsville, NY March 4, 1879

HARRIS Sadie age 7y dau of John and Annie Harris in N. Almond, NY March 3, 1879

TORPY Nellie age 2y 10m in Hornellsville, NY March 1, 1879

WHITTAKER Mrs. Susan age 81y in Almond, NY March 1, 1879

LAKE Annie in her 10th yr dau of Martin and Melissa Lake nr Hornellsville, NY March 5, 1879

KRINER Anthony age 70y in Corning, NY March 1, 1879

HAMMOND Mason age 65y in Erwin Ctr., NY March 2, 1879

DEATH NOTICES

BATES James abt 50y in Corning, NY March 4, 1879

CROW Regina age 6m 9d dau of Patrick and Margaret Crow in Hornellsville, NY March 6, 1879

BOYNTON Joshua age 60y in Hornellsville, NY March 10, 1879

THARP Ray age 4y son of C. G. and Anna Tharp in Hornellsville, NY March 8, 1879

DOLOHERY Patrick age 2y in Hornellsville, NY March 10, 1879

SHANIHAN James age 92y 2m in Hornellsville, NY March 12, 1879

DAVIS Elias in Greenwood, NY March 10, 1879

BALLOU Hosea age 73y in Hornellsville, NY March 15, 1879

DENNIS ___ infant son of Daniel and Mary Dennis in Jasper, NY March 6, 1879

SPENCER John in his 88th yr in Bath, NY March 6, 1879. Born August 1791 in Philadelphia, Pa. Children, James of Branchport, NY, Mrs. George **DRAKE**, Mrs. James P. **HAND** and Mrs. O. W. **HAND** of Bath

STEPHENS Christopher age 35y in Hornellsville, NY March 16, 1879

BROWN Lowell age 2y son of A. R. and Sophia in Hornellsville, NY March 16, 1879

SWEENEY Patrick age 94y in Willing, NY March 13, 1879

MADISON Mrs. Charles age 45y in Wellsville, NY March 12, 1879

KELLY Patrick age 28y in Hornellsville, NY March 18, 1879

SIDMAN Susan age 60y widow of George Sidman in Fremont, NY March 16, 1879

DRAKE Lettice age 64y wife of Peter H. Drake and dau of Isaac **SANTEE** an early settler in Cameron, NY March 4, 1879. Married 1831

GOODRICH Flavilla L. age 52y wife of John M. Goodrich in Hornellsville, NY March 18, 1879. Leaves husband, 1 son and 2 daus, names 1 Mrs. Cass **RICHARDSON**

MONROE Joseph L. C. in his 59th yr in Alfred, NY February 22, 1879

STEWART John in his 63rd yr in W. Almond, NY March 13, 1879

CASE Jarvis P. age 73y in Arkport, NY March 21, 1879. Born June 9, 1805 in N. Canton, Ct. Only son killed by accidental discharge of gun in 1857

EICH George age 9m son of George and Mary in Hornellsville, NY March 21, 1879

SNOOK Jacob formerly of Steuben Co. in Jasper, Mi. March 4, 1879

VUNK Mrs. Lydia age 83y formerly of Avoca, NY in Belmont, NY March 12, 1879

KIRKHAM Nancy age 84y widow of Seth Kirkham a Vet. of War of 1812 in Cameron, NY March 16, 1879

VAN KEURAN Mary age 87y in Sonora, NY March 12, 1879

KEEFE Mathew in Hornellsville, NY March 20, 1879

LOCKWOOD Sarah age 97y 9m 18d in Horseheads, NY March 20, 1879. Born 1798 in Dutchess Co. Married 1798 Angevine Lockwood who died 8 yrs ago age 93y, 2 sons and 12 daus, oldest age 80y still living

MC COLLOUGH John age 85y in Bath, NY February 15, 1879

LOGHRY Mrs. Wilson abt 35y in Cameron, NY March 20, 1879

MATHEWS Mrs. Sarah age 78y in Hornellsville, NY March 21, 1879

HICKEY Miss Sarah age 19y in Hornellsville, NY March 27, 1879

THOMAS William L. age 4y 10m in Hornellsville, NY March 29, 1879

STEVENS Amanda age 47y wife of James H. in Hornellsville, NY April 4, 1879

STEVENS Mabel L. age 4y 8m dau of I. M. and Diantha Stevens in Hornellsville, NY April 7, 1879

MONAHAN Mathew age 5y son of Edward in Hornellsville, NY April 7. 1879

FITZGERALD Michael age 51y in Hornellsville, NY April 4, 1879

PECKHAM Minnie age 11y dau of Stephen and Sarah in Almond, NY April 3, 1879

BODINE Sylvanus age 72y in Prattsburgh, NY March 23, 1879

MACK Elisha age 85y in Bath, NY March 31, 1879

MATHEWS Samuel age 73y in Arkport, NY April 10, 1879. Leaves sons Hubbard and William Mathews

BULLOCK Frank M. age 37y in Hornellsville, NY April 12, 1879

MAJOR Lena age 3m 2w dau of Newton J. and Emma in Almond, NY April 13, 1879

MORGAN Olive in her 43rd yr widow of William Morgan in Bath, NY March 14, 1879

DOUGHERTY James age 28y of Hornellsville, NY crushed by cars in Bradford, Pa.

April 15, 1879. Leaves wife and 4 children

TRUESDALE Rebecca E. in her 51st yr wife of Dr. J. B. Truesdale in Hornellsville, NY April 17, 1879. Born September 1828 in New Berlin, NY. Married 1848 and leaves husband and 2 daus

LANPHEAR Nathan age 87y in Andover, NY April 8. 1879

YOST Mrs. Catherine age 86y in Thurston, NY April 4, 1879

GATES Sallie Ann age 57y in S. Dansville, NY April 17. 1879

STONE T. P. age 65y in Woodhull, NY April 6, 1879

HILGERS John Joseph age 53y in Soldiers and Sailors Home in Bath, NY April 12, 1879. Member of Co. A. 46th Inf.

WALKER James E. age 57y bro of C. C. B. Walker of Corning, NY in Albany, NY April 11, 1879

WELDON William age 40y in Hornellsville, NY April 14, 1879

CARTER Mrs. Almira age 74y in Bath, NY April 15, 1879

SMITH Platt Perlee age 86y in Bath, NY March 13, 1879

BRIGGS George age 71y in Corning, NY April 10, 1879

COON Elvira **(STILLMAN)** age 54y 8m 24d wife of Prof. H. C. Coon of Alfred University in Alfred, NY April 20, 1879

JOHNSON Miss Rose in her 20th yr formerly of Hornellsville, NY in Flint, Mi. April 16, 1879

GRAY James age 78y at son-in-law's John R. **BENNETT** in Bath, NY April 10, 1879

NIENDORF Clara Louisa in her 6th yr dau of Lew and Josephine Niendorf in Hornellsville, NY April 25, 1879

DELANCY Michael age 63y a native of Ireland in Soldiers and Sailors Home in Bath, NY April 20, 1879. Member of Co. G. 97th Inf.

DAWSON Charles in his 32nd yr of Hornellsville, NY in Wellsville, NY April 25, 1879

SHARP Mrs. Robert in her 90th yr in Jasper, NY April 2, 1879. Born 1790 in Canisteo, NY dau of Dr. **HALLETT**. Married 1808. Leaves husband age 96y and 7 children living

TOLAN Mrs. Mary in her 48th yr in Hornellsville, NY April 30, 1879

STEUBEN COUNTY NEWSPAPERS 325

NIENDORF Louis age 2y 11m son of Louis in Hornellsville, NY May 1, 1879

LEE Lucinda D. in her 63rd yr wife of Alonzo B. in Andover, NY April 25, 1879

WATSON Joseph B. in his 55th yr in W. Almond, NY April 19, 1879

BARNEY Henriette in her 74th yr wife of Dr. Anthony Barney in Independence, NY May 1, 1879

BOUGHTON Nattie in his 6th yr son of Chauncey Boughton in Hornellsville, NY (Newspaper date May 6, 1879)

PLACE Ella in her 26th yr wife of Elbert Place former teacher in Hornellsville, NY in Marathon, NY April 23, 1879

COYLE Margaret age 7y dau of John and Catherine in Hornellsville, NY May 7, 1879

BRYANT Mrs. Ellen in her 102nd yr in Fremont, NY May 7, 1879

WEAVER Charles J. age 11y 2m in Bishopsville, NY May 9, 1879

GALPIN V. O. age 71y in Burns, NY May 8, 1879

DEMERY Lena Mary age 5w dau of James J. and Carisey in Fremont, NY May 9, 1879

KENNEDY Eddie E. age 4y in Hornellsville, NY May 10, 1879

MAYNARD Richard in his 71st yr in Fremont, NY May 11, 1879

TAYLOR Elizabeth age 45y wife of Reuben in Hornellsville, NY May 11, 1879

KELTY Michael age 48y in Hornellsville, NY May 17, 1879

BRADY Mrs. B. B. age 28y in Hornellsville, NY May 16, 1879

BOUGHTON Bertie age 6y 2m son of Chauncey and Sarah Boughton in Hornellsville, NY May 19, 1879

VAN ORDER Lewis age 71y in Howard, NY May 6, 1879

CARRINGTON Patience age 91y at son's Eli in Bath, NY (Newspaper date May 20, 1879)

CAMPBELL Julia Ann age 52y wife of Daniel in Jasper, NY April 25, 1879

STREETER Mrs. Betsey age 65y in Greenwood, NY April 28, 1879

BRONSON E. E. late of Hornellsville, NY in Florence, SC May 14, 1879

GILCHRIST Freddie age 2y 4m son of Alexander and Mary Gilchrist in Hornellsville,

DEATH NOTICES

NY May 26, 1879

SUTTON Daniel in his 82nd yr nr Hornellsville, NY May 30, 1879

DODGE Miss Cornelia abt 60y burned to death in home of Lemuel **BUMP** in Troupsbrugh, NY May 28, 1879

MAGNUSON Ellen age 10y dau of Johann Magnuson a Swedish emigrant on train Corning/Hornellsville, NY May 27, 1879

LANE Abram age 42y in Almond, NY May 31, 1879

RILEY Peter age 78y in Birdsall, NY May 23, 1879

GILCHRIST James age 5y son of Alexander and Mary Gilchrist in Hornellsville, NY June 4, 1879

PERRY Ida abt 13y dau of Martin Perry in Birdsall, NY May 2, 1879

SMITH Amy age 54y widow of William N. Smith formerly of Cameron, NY and dau of John **HALLETT** of Cameron 1 of 13 children in Bath, NY June 1, 1879. Married 1834

WASHBURN Lillian Ione age 6y and Frankie age 4y children of Abraham and Anna Washburn in Almond, NY May 27, 1879

WELLS Mary E. age 57y wife of M. S. Wells in Addison, NY May 22, 1879

BURT ____ age 5w son of William H. and Della in Hornellsville, NY June 9, 1879

RATHBUN Susan in her 29th yr dau of Hiram and Louisa Rathbun in Jasper, NY June 9, 1879. Born Howard, NY

COLLAR Frances age 17y dau of Mrs. Jane Collar in Hornellsville, NY June 12, 1879

ROBSON John age 68y in Prattsburgh, NY May 22, 1879

MORAN Willie age 2m son of T. F. and Annie in Hornellsville, NY June 16, 1879

GALLAGHER Michael age 26y 9m in Hornellsville, NY June 18, 1879

GOODMAN Minerva age 83y 4d in Hornellsville, NY June 15, 1879

WELSH Warren age 5y son of Hendrick Welsh hit by falling tree in Cameron Mills, NY June 26, 1879

PRENTISS Capt. John age 42y in Hornellsville, NY June 27, 1879. Born Altay, NY, served in Co. G. 23rd Reg.

FORD Nancy age 73y 9m wife of Isaac Ford in Canisteo, NY June 20, 1879

BURRIS Michael age 39y in Hornellsville, NY June 29, 1879

KELLER Nancy age 64y wife of Henry Keller in Alfred, NY June 2, 1879

BURDICK Almira in her 43rd yr wife of Daniel in Alfred, NY July 4, 1879

WOOLEVER Mrs. Hiram W. nr Hartsville, NY July 8, 1879

BAXTER Charles F. suicide at bro P. A. Baxter in Woodhull, NY July 2, 1879

BIXBY Silas of Clarendon, NY in Hornellsville, NY July 10, 1879

HICKEY Mrs. ____ age 91y in Hornellsville, NY July 11, 1879

ANNABEL May age 4y 8d dau of Albert C. Annabel in Cameron, NY July 4, 1879

ASHLEY Charles E. age 27y in Hornellsville, NY July 15, 1879

WEEKS Mrs. Jane age 74y in Hornellsville, NY July 27, 1879

HAYES George age 33y suicide by morphine in Hornellsville, NY July 27, 1879

HERRICK Albert age 55y in Hornellsville, NY July 26, 1879

DAVIS William E. infant son of J. L. and C. M. in Hornellsville, NY July 27, 1879

KINNEY Lavina abt 30y wife of Barney Kinney and dau of Joseph and Nancy **WOODRUFF** of Andover, NY in Woodhull, NY July 25, 1879. Married March 20, 1870, 1 son age 6y

ROUNDS Sophrone age 26y in Hornellsville, NY July 29, 1879

COLE Robert U. age 74y at dau Mrs. John **MC DOUGAL** in Hornellsville, NY July 31, 1879

SPARKS John age 73y in Corning, NY July 26, 1879

WILLOUR Jacob age 82y in Bath, NY July 24, 1879

DAVIS ____ age 7m son of R. and Mary Davis in Howard, NY July 31, 1879

BROWN Mrs. George in Hornellsville, NY August 12, 1879

KNAPP Simeon age 71y in N. Cameron, NY August 9, 1879

KETCHUM Grattan E. age 2y 13d son of Edmond F. and Maria Ketchum in Hornellsville, NY August 14, 1879

BROWN Henry age 43y kicked by horse in Troupsburgh, NY August 15, 1879. Leaves wife and 6 children

WALDO D. D. Atty. formerly of Caniseto, NY In Prattsburgh, NY August 17, 1879

PETTIBONE John age 47y in Hornellsville, NY August 27, 1879

VINCENT George age 5w son of J. and H. in Hornellsville, NY August 22, 1879

RATHBUN Riley age 7y in Fremont, NY August 29, 1879

DOLOHERY Michael age 28y in Hornellsville, NY August 31, 1879

GATES Rena age 2y 8m dau of Sinhorne and Mary in Fremont, NY August 19, 1879

JEFFERSON Benjamin in his 80th yr in Wellsville, NY August 21, 1879

MALONEY Michael age 27y in Hornellsville, NY August 31, 1879, son Michael J. age 6m died August 30, 1879

HADLEY J. M. age 58y formerly of Canisteo, NY in Tidioute, Pa. August 23, 1879

EASLING Abraham D. age 65y formerly of Hornby, NY in Knoxville August 28, 1879

GOODRICH Theron age 45y in Canaseraga, NY August 20, 1879

CONDERMAN Nancy in her 88th yr widow of Jacob Conderman who was Vet. of War of 1812 in Fremont, NY September 8, 1879. Res. of Fremont 60 yrs

HOLLY Emma B. in her 75th yr in Hornellsville, NY September 14, 1879

GROSS Wilbur E. in his 13th yr in N. Almond Valley, NY September 9, 1879

CARPENTER Mrs. Emma S. age 82y in Erwin, NY September 6, 1879

KRIEGER Dena age 48y wife of Jacob Krieger in Corning, NY September 17, 1879

PIERCE Levi H. age 62y nr Hornellsville, NY September 20, 1879

GOFF Pliny age 74y in Howard, NY September 14, 1879

DAVIS Euradide age 87y in Avoca, NY September 15, 1879

WILLIAMS T. Wayland age 24y in Hornellsville, NY September 15, 1879

HURD Mrs. Jemima in her 73rd yr in W. Almond, NY September 15, 1879

COON Jared in his 82nd yr in Alfred, NY September 19, 1879

JOLLY D. D. age 6m son of Philo D. and Libbie Jolly in Haskinsville, NY September 24, 1879

EMERY Sarah E. age 22y in Hornellsville, NY October 2, 1879

PHINNEY Frank age 3m son of A. S. and Louise in Hornellsville, NY October 1, 1879

GORTON Mrs. Polly age 75y in Gibson, NY September 25, 1879

FORD Charles B. age 25y in Campbell, NY September 22, 1879

BUTLER Henry formerly of Hornellsville, NY killed by bro Robert in drunken quarrel nr Bradford, NY October 6, 1879

STEVENS Lucy age 80y relict of William Stevens in Addison, NY October 6, 1879

HULSE Anna age 73y wife of Benjamin Hulse in Jasper, NY September 21, 1879

WOODARD Ephraim age 87y a Vet. of War of 1812 in Jasper, NY September 23, 1879

DEXTER Dauphine in Whitesville, NY September 28, 1879

NAST Sidney age 4y son of Phillip M. Nast October 9, 1879

STUDDERT John B. age 4y son of Thomas in Hornellsville, NY October 10, 1879

STILLMAN Abby in her 70th yr widow of Silas in Alfred, NY October 9, 1879

OWENS Frederick of Hawley, Pa. by train while attempting to board in Canisteo, NY October 16, 1879

PRIOR Charles H. age 6y son of Charles in Hornellsville, NY October 16, 1879

MORRIS Lucretia age 81y in Hornellsville, NY October 16, 1879. 2 sisters Lydia and Sally Morris and bro Andrew Morris. Came from Branford, Ct. to Canisteo, NY 1812

GORHAM Michael age 7y 7m in Hornellsville, NY October 15, 1879

COOLEY Fanny age 93y in Hornellsville, NY October 16, 1879

COULTRY Ellie age 4y dau of Dominick in Hornellsville, NY October 17, 1879

ROSS Joshua C. in his 46th yr in Hornellsville, NY October 17, 1879

PRESTON Willie age 2y 10m 16d son of George and Allie Preston in Hornellsville, NY October 18, 1879

LEE Frank L. age 16m son of Merritt A. and Kate Lee in Hornellsville, NY October 25, 1879

O'CONNOR Vena J. age 19m 7d dau of George W. and Jennie O'Connor in Hornellsville, NY October 24, 1879

GRANGE John age 46y in Hornellsville, NY October 28, 1879. Wife and 7 children

DEATH NOTICES

QUIGLEY John age 28y in Corning, NY October 27, 1879

KNISELY John age 62y in Corning, NY October 27, 1879

REDFIELD Harvey B. in his 84th yr in Hornellsville, NY November 1, 1879

KLEIN Peter abt 80y in Hornellsville, NY November 6, 1879

DANIELS Frank E. age 29y in Belmont, NY November 3, 1879

GORHAM James age 12y son of Ellen in Hornellsville, NY November 5, 1879

KILEY John J. age 3y son of Cornelius in Hornellsville, NY November 6, 1879

BOSTON Maria N. in her 6th yr dau of Thomas and Mary Ann Boston in Hornellsville, NY November 3, 1879

WOOD George B. age 74y in S. Dansville, NY October 10, 1879

WOOD Mrs. Lewis age 47y in Caton, NY October 27, 1879

SHINEBARGER Archie B. age 3y and May children of Stewart and Rosetta Shinebarger November 8, 1879

COYE J. Morris in his 71st yr in Hornellsville, NY November 14, 1879

WHITE Eliza age 27y in Canisteo, NY November 5, 1879

THACHER Henry Hart age 2y 3m son of Scott and Medelia Thacher in Hornellsville, NY November 19, 1879

KINNEY Michael age 16y 7m hit by train in Hornellsville, NY November 21, 1879

SMITH Capt. Ashbel in his 86th yr in Alfred, NY November 10, 1879

HUTCHINS John R. age 51y in Corning, NY November 14, 1879

BURLEY W. W. age 45y 9m in Hornellsville, NY November 28, 1879

EVANS James K. age 60y in Arkport, NY November 28, 1879

CORNELIUS Elmer J. in his 16th yr son of John in Alfred, NY November 22, 1879

SEWELL Elmer J. in his 16th yr son of A. A. and M. P. Sewell in Howard, NY November 22, 1879

SHINEBARGER John age 9y son of Stewart and Rosetta Shinebarger in Hornellsville, NY November 28, 1879

SULLIVAN Jennie age 15y in Hornellsville, NY November 28, 1879

RUGGLES Fannie Coe age 20y in Crystal Springs, NY November 23, 1879

HATHAWAY Van Wort age 15y son of H. D. and C. G. Hathaway in Hornellsville, NY November 30, 1879

TAYLOR George H. age 1y 6m in Hornellsville, NY December 8, 1879

BEST Joseph age 4y 3m 20d son of H. D. and M. Best in Hornellsville, NY Decembr 7, 1879

MORENCE Kittie F. age 10y 8m dau of Joseph and Jane Morence in Hornellsville, NY December 15, 1879

VAN LOON John age 72y in Bath, NY November 22, 1879

DECATUR James abt 56y in Hornellsville, NY December 16, 1879

SMITH Mrs. Alexander age 59y in Wellsville, NY December 8, 1879

MORAN Peter age 65y in Hornellsville, NY December 10, 1879

BAKER Mrs. Eliza age 26y 7m in Hornellsville, NY December 12, 1879

KINNEY Mary W. age 2y 7m dau of W. M. and Carrie Kinney in Hornellsville, NY December 11, 1879

COON Julia (**BABCOCK**) age 68y 9m 21d wife of Aaron Coon in Alfred, NY December 3, 1879

HARTY Roger in his 24th yr in Hornellsville, NY December 21, 1879

PINCH Lotta age 16y dau of John and Lavina in Hornellsville, NY December 21, 1879

DOTY Philander an aged res of Jasper, NY December 14, 1879

STEARNS Mrs. Henry age 63y in Jasper, NY December 20, 1879

missing issues

WILCOX Whitman age 22y son of Fred in E. Troupsburgh, NY December 18, 1880

DONLON John age 78y on Honey Run January 4, 1881

KNISKERN Eliza age 64y in Howard, NY January 7, 1881. Sister of James Kniskern of Almond, NY and half sister of Mrs. D. W. **FORD** of Hornellsville, NY. Step father Martin **GARRISON** died abt 4 wks ago

RILEY Cornelius age 61y in Hornellsville, NY January 9, 1881

SMITH William age 56y in Arkport, NY January 7, 1881

DEATH NOTICES

FINCH John age 71y 2m 22d at only son's Orman B. Finch in Tecumseh, Mi. December 23, 1880. Born NJ and came to Yates Co. at age 8 yrs. Married at age 23y Ann **GARLINGHOUSE**, 48th anniversary 1 wk ago. Moved to Tecumseh 1865. Uncle of Alexander **PATTON** and Mrs. E. J. **COYKENDALL** of Hornellsville, NY

BURROWS Clarence age 59y in Arkport, NY January 7, 1881

HENESSEY Mary age 27y in Hornellsville, NY January 12, 1881

SHARP Joseph P. age 86y in Oak Park, Ill. January 4, 1881. Born Staten Island son of William who came to Arkport, NY 1812. Later years spent with sons George and Perine Sharp of Chicago, Ill. Buried Dansville, NY

LANG Mrs. Lydia age 33y in Hornellsville, NY January 13, 1881

FULTS Mrs. Henry in Woodhull, NY January 10, 1881

HIBBARD Mrs. Isaac age 58y in Addison, NY January 20, 1881

SMITH Olin age 21y of Hornellsville, NY in Owego, NY January 18, 1881

FANROTE Byron age 2m 17d son of Thomas W. in Fremont, NY January 21, 1881

MORRIS Jane abt 50y wife of James Morris formerly of Easton, Md. and dau of Maj. Thomas J. **REYNOLDS** January 24, 1881

GOODNO Jonas age 64y in Hartsville, NY January 8, 1881. Son of Isaiah Goodno eldest of 7 bros. Married 1838 Anna J. **TITSWORTH** who died April 26, 1846. Married (2) in 1848 Polly **WHITFORD** and moved to Hartsville, NY 1850

MARKHAM Elizabeth age 22y in Hornellsville, NY January 27, 1881

DICKEY Willie son of Erastus and Lydia Dickey in Cameron, NY January 8, 1881

MAHAN Mrs. William abt 28y in Hornellsville, NY January 30, 1881

SWAIN Minnie age 3y 4m dau of Albert S. and Alice D. Swain in Hornellsville, NY February 4, 1881

NEPHEW ___ infant son of John and Olie Nephew in Arkport, NY February 7, 1881

DAVISON Gracie age 3y dau of Wesley and Phoebe in Birdsall, NY February 6, 1881

KNAPP Eva M. age 16m dau of Ernest and Grace Knapp in Hornellsville, NY February 9, 1881

BLACKWEDE ___ infant dau of Charles in Hornellsville, NY February 9, 1881

BARBER ___ infant dau of Samuel and Margarette Barber in Hornellsville, NY February 9, 1881

DUNHAM Nettie age 23y in W. Almond, NY February 12, 1881

CABLE Rote age 55y in Kaw Valley February 16, 1881

SHAFFER Katie age 3y dau of Joseph and Catherine Shaffer in Hornellsville, NY February 15, 1881

WARD Martie age 6m son of Aaron and Sarah in Hornellsville, NY February 15, 1881

SOUTHERBY Mrs. E. R. P. age 35y in Hornellsville, NY February 15, 1881

MORAN John in his 27th yr run over by cars in Hornellsville, NY February 26, 1881

SEELEY Ann Eliza age 41y 9m wife of J. E. in Hornellsville, NY February 19, 1881

MEAD Bridget age 55y in Hornellsville, NY March 2, 1881

TEED ___ age 1y son of Harry Teed in Hornellsville, NY March 9, 1881

BENDRICK Mrs. A. age 65y in Troupsburgh, NY March 5, 1881

CALLAHAN Thomas age 44y in Hornellsville, NY March 12, 1881

SPRAGUE Lucinda in her 64th yr relict of Joseph in Howard, NY February 26, 1881

EDWARDS John age 78y in Co. Home March 13, 1881

SAUSMAN William D. age 54y in Hornellsville, NY March 22, 1881. Born 1826 in Ithaca, NY. Came to W. Almond, NY in 1865 and later to Hornellsville

BURDICK Amos age 96y 6m in Alfred, NY March 16, 1881

BEEBE Polly age 81y wife of Seth Beebe in Alfred, NY March 14, 1881

BARBER Alta D. age 23y 9m dau of A. D. and S. L. in Almond, NY March 16, 1881

ROSS ___ infant child of Edward Ross in Hornellsville, NY March 26, 1881

SNELL Ann Louisa wife of Thomas Snell in Hornellsville, NY April 2, 1881

ROOT Jennie age 17y dau of Erastus Root in North Valley, NY March 25, 1881

COLEGROVE Andrew age 86y in Woodhull, NY March 28, 1881. Wife died 11 yrs ago, 17 children 11 living

BAKER Clarine age 36y in Fremont, NY April 5, 1881

BROWN Marcus E. age 55y formerly of Hornellsville, NY now of Grand Rapids, Mi. in Hornellsville while visiting at brother-in-law's Peter P. **HOUCK** April 7, 1881. Leaves wife and 3 children

ALLEN Jemima age 72y 2m in Hornellsville, NY April 11, 1881

FOSTER Clarey M. age 7m dau of C. D. and Josephine Foster in Hornellsville, NY April 5, 1881

BENNETT Martha age 74y in Hornellsville, NY April 10, 1881

TRENKLER Katie M. age 4y dau of John G. and Elizabeth Trenkler in Hornellsville, NY April 12, 1881

BRIGGS Charles W. in his 42nd yr in Hornellsville, NY April 14, 1881

MANNING Lucinda (**MARTIN**) in her 59th ry at her son-in-law's F. M. **BASSETT** in Greenwood, NY April 18, 1881. Born October 23, 1822 in Washington Co. NY, and came to Hornellsville, NY 1825. Married December 25, 1845 Daniel Manning who died October 15, 1865. Moved to Greenwood 1876. 2 sons 2 daus, 1 dau dec

MANDEVILLE J. Bradley age 35y formerly of Hornellsville, NY in Bradford, NY April 20, 1881

ECCLES John age 52y in Campbell, NY April 8, 1881. Served Co. E. 141st Reg.

BURDICK Asa in his 82nd yr in Andover, NY March 30, 1881

SCHELL John in his 85th yr at Job's Corners, NY April 23, 1881

RYMER Mrs. Alzina age 77y in Andover, NY April 18, 1881

GORHAM Alice E. age 24y in Hornellsville, NY May 4, 1881

PHELPS Mathew L. age 58y in Hornellsville, NY May 7, 1881

JOHNSON Rosa age 22y wife of Jerome Johnson in Jasper, NY May 6, 1881
GRIEF Mary in her 22nd yr in Hornellsville, NY May 13, 1881

ROBIE Sophia age 9y 2m 2d died April 27, 1881 and Ira C. age 11y 2m 3d died May 1, 1881 children of Helen C. and late Levi Robie in Bath, NY

CRANDALL Cynthia (**POTTER**) in her 85th yr wife of Amos Crandall in Alfred Ctr. NY May 21, 1881

HASKINS J. S. age 67y in Hornellsville, NY May 30, 1881. Leaves wife and 1 child Mrs. Floyd **MC CONNELL**

CANFIELD Orlando S. age 23y in Fremont, NY May 23, 1881

HEATHERMAN Bridget age 18y in Hornellsville, NY June 2, 1881

BARNES Z. C. age 42y in Hornellsville, NY June 4, 1881. Leaves wife and 4 children

WIRKS M. E. abt 38y in Bradford, NY June 16, 1881

GRAY Maria A. abt 6y in Burns, NY June 15, 1881, buried Arkport, NY

SHEFFIELD Mary E. **(WYCKOFF)** in her 42nd yr in Greenwood, NY June 13, 1881. Born June 3, 1840 in Monmouth Co. NJ. Married May 6, 1863 William Sheffield at Shrewsbury, NJ

MILLER Mrs. William suicide with arsenic in Bath, NY June 21, 1881

MC INTEE Mrs. Hugh whose son was arrested for killing his uncle, in Bath, NY June 25, 1881

COLLIER John D. age 80y formerly of Hornellsville, NY in Castile, NY June 27, 1881. Born April 4, 1801 in Greene Co. NY and came to Steuben Co. 1811 and res in Howard, NY then to Hornellsville for 16 yrs, to Castile 1870

Painted Post Times

October 5, 1870 - September 27, 1871

WOLCOTT Pantha age 21y dau of Fred W. of Corning, NY in Winchester, Oh. October 11, 1870

BROWN Jonathan age 73y in Corning, NY December 19, 1870. Born RI and married December 1828 Eliza **FRIDLEY**

WHITFORD Joseph abt 60y by falling tree in Caton, NY December 23, 1870

DAY Abby W. age 44y wife of John Day formerly of Painted Post, NY in Emporium, Pa. rec. (Newspaper date January 11, 1871). Leaves 6 children eldest under 12y

DAVENPORT Scott at 40y in Elmira, NY March 7, 1871

FOX Abbie L. age 35y wife of Alanson J. Fox in Painted Post, NY June 21, 1871

YOUNG George of Hornellsville, NY formerly of Painted Post, NY July 11, 1871

Prattsburgh News

December 12, 1872 - December 25, 1884

MOONEY Daniel age 62y in Prattsburgh, NY December 12, 1872

WALDO Elizabeth E. age 68y wife of Charles in Prattsburgh, NY January 16, 1873

DEATH NOTICES

MINER Egert age 21y son of Ira B. Miner in Bath, NY January 15, 1873

BENNETT Jennie age 16y dau of T. J. and Adelia in Pulteney, NY February 14, 1873

JUDSON Charles L. age 17y February 16, 1873

BALDWIN Curtis C. age 74y at son's D. W. Baldwin in Prattsburgh, NY March 3, 1873. Born April 8, 1798 in Durham, NY. Wife Vanessa (**SMALLEY**) age 67y at same place died March 8, 1873. She was born January 1, 1808 dau of Judge Smalley of Lenox, NY. Married July 4, 1828, 7 children 5 living

SKINNER Erastus age 83y in Prattsburgh, NY March 10, 1873. Born July 8, 1789 in Caanan, NY and came to Prattsburgh December 1823. 8 sons and 1 dau, 1 son dec.

FARGO Mrs. Polly age 96y 1m 13d in Benton, NY March 9, 1873

STRATTON Harriet age 69y at dau Mrs. Allen **SMITH** in Prattsburgh, NY March 17, 1873

WILCOX Philanda F. age 48y wife of Lewis Wilcox in Prattsburgh, NY March 14, 1873. Leaves husband and 4 children

HOPKINS Asa age 73y of Prattsburgh, NY at son-in-law's Harrison **SPEARS** in Jerusalem, NY March 21, 1873

CHITTICK Thomas son of Christopher drowned nr Kanona, NY March 29, 1873

WARREN Jeremiah age 45y in Prattsburgh, NY March 26, 1873. Born Westchester Co. NY

LEWIS Grandus age 71y in Prattsburgh, NY April 11, 1873. Born Perth, NY and came to Prattsburgh 1823. Married 1822 Cornelia **SWART**, 11 children 1 in Mi.

HORTON Cynthia Ann age 35y wife of Ira H. Horton in Pulteney, NY April 14, 1873

WANAMAKER Mrs. M. age 83y at son-in-law's B. F. **AUSTIN** in Pulteney, NY April 18, 1873

HAYES Chauncey age 51y in Prattsburgh, NY April 23, 1873. Leaves wife and 5 children

WOOD Carolina wife of Rev. A. T. Wood and dau of late Decon **JUDSON** of Prattsburgh, NY in Falls City, Neb. April 15, 1873

LEE Alice Swenson age 14y 5m dau of Orvis and Sarah Lee whie returning home to Prattsburgh, NY in Naples, NY (Newspaper date July 3, 1873)

TRACY John age 2y 3m son of John J. and Hannah in Prattsburgh, NY July 31, 1873

CRAFT Elijah age 87y in Riker Hollow, NY August 12, 1873

ROBINSON Mary age 29y wife of Sherman in Prattsburgh, NY August 16, 1873

PARSONS Simeon Lewis age 67y in Prattsburgh, NY August 27, 1873. Came to Prattsburgh at age 15 yrs. Married 1827 Catherine **BEAMAN**, 2 sons names 1 Dr. R. L. of Blackwell Is.

CARR Olive age 82y at res of James B. **COLEGROVE** in Prattsburgh, NY October 1, 1873

FLYNN Thomas age 87y at son's Michael Flynn October 3, 1873

RANDALL Alida Bell age 7y 2m dau of Albert P. and Emeline Randall in Prattsburgh, NY October 8, 1873

WELD Harvey age 65y 7m 10d in Naples, NY September 22, 1873. Born February 12, 1808 in Patterson Co. son of David Weld. Came from Delaware Co. NY to Riker Hollow in 1830. Married September 8, 1831 Mary **DE GOLIA**. Moved to Naples 1865

CLARK Huldah age 81y wife of Gaius Clark at res of U. T. **CARPENTER** in Prattsburgh, NY October 14, 1873. Native of Geneva, NY

HAYES Dr. Chauncey formerly of Prattsburgh, NY at son-in-law's Rev. W. D. **TAYLOR** in Havana, NY October 14, 1873. Came to Prattsburgh 1806, married 1832 Cynthie **EDWARDS** of Skineatelas, NY

READY John age 22y at Mother's in Prattsburgh, NY October 26, 1873

LEWIS Margaret A. age 6y 7m 22d dau of Charles and Amanda J. Lewis in Prattsburgh, NY October 25, 1873

BENTON Col. Jared T. age 68y formerly of Pulteney, NY in Auburn, NY October 28, 1873

SMITH James S. age 88y at res of Agnes **COOK** November 5, 1873. Vet War of 1812

MILLER May age 23y dau of Granger and Rhoda **GATES** at Grandfather's A. R. **COWING** (Newspaper date November 20, 1873)

BONNEY Truman H. age 57y at dau Mrs. A. **BORDEN** in Wheeler, NY December 3, 1873

ALLIS Florence Fay age 5y 6m dau of Elijah and Emily Allis in Prattsburgh, NY December 21, 1873

COOK Mrs. Amos age 53y in Prattsburgh, NY January 2, 1874

EARLEY Susan age 73y wife of Thomas Earley in Prattsburgh, NY January 1, 1874. Born Putnam Co. NY, married September 1822

ROSENCRANS Ella age 2y 4m 10d dau of Isaac and Eliza Rosencrans in Pulteney, NY

DEATH NOTICES

January 11, 1874

WARFIELD Anna D. age 2y 7m 10d dau of M. F. and Frances Warfield in Prattsburgh, NY January 21, 1874

MIDDLETON Abigail Maria age 54y wife of James Middleton January 23, 1874, native of Pulteney, NY

WILCOX William Halsey age 53y in Prattsburgh, NY January 24, 1874

TRANT Mrs. Mary age 65y in Prattsburgh, NY January 25, 1874

PARSONS Anna age 61y wife of William Parsons of Woodhull, NY at res of Joel **TOMER** in Prattsburgh, NY January 30, 1874. Born Kings Co. Ireland, married in Troy, NY 8 children 7 living

HULTZ Charles Thompson age 57y in Pulteney, NY January 31, 1874

DERRICK Inez wife of George E. Derrick and eldest dau of Willett **SEARLES** at res of P. F. **MYRTLE** January 29, 1874

WHEELER Harriet in her 31st yr wife of Horace B. Wheeler and dau of John B. and Abigail **HARRIS** of Jerusalem, NY in Oswayo, Pa. January 19, 1874. Leaves husband and 1 son age 6y 9m

TALL Anna age 28y wife of William Tall in Prattsburgh, NY February 17, 1874

MARSHALL Sarah age 11y 7m in Prattsburgh, NY February 17, 1874. Born Remsey, Huntingshire, England. Here 2 yrs

HIGBY John C. in Prattsburgh, NY March 23, 1874. Born December 6, 1796 in Cooperstown, NY and came to Prattsburgh 1819

EMERSON John in Prattsburgh, NY March 20, 1874. Born 1796 in Candia, NH and came to Prattsburgh 1818

SMITH ____ age 5m son of Myron and Mary in Prattsburgh, NY March 22, 1874

DRAKE Satie age 17y dau of Aaron and Caroline Drake in Riker Hollow, NY March 14, 1874

EDSON Daniel in Prattsburgh, NY April 6, 1874. Born April 1, 1785 in Chester, Vt. and came to Prattsburgh 1806. Married January 11, 1811 Esther **CARTER** who died over 2 yrs ago

MC CONNELL Peter age 73y in Pulteney, NY April 11, 1874

WATERS Mrs. Abigail age 60y 9m 21d in Pulteney, NY April 8, 1874

CLARK Ella age 1y 8m dau of Nathaniel and Emily in Prattsburgh, NY April 21, 1874

BROWNELL Frances age 27 at Father's Oliver Brownell in Prattsburgh, NY April 10, 1874. Elizabeth age 52 wife of Oliver died April 13, 1874

COOK Charles T. age 41y nr Prattsburgh, NY April 12, 1874

BARNEY Ada wife of Frank Barney and dau of Dr. G. E. **WATERS** of Fenton, Mi. in Avoca, NY April 21, 1874

BARTLETT Martha age 30y wife of James Bartlett nr Prattsburgh, NY April 25, 1874. Leaves 5 children youngest 10 days old

WILLIAMS Orvey age 21y nr Prattsburgh, NY April 21, 1874

SINCEBOX Alonzo age 4y 10m adopted son of Franklin and Maria **PATCH** in Prattsburgh, NY May 31, 1874

SULLIVAN Margarette age 66y in Pulteney, NY June 7, 1874

EDSON Hattie A. age 14y 8m dau of Edmund Edson in Pulteney, NY June 28, 1874

PRENTISS Frankie A. age 5y 5m son of J. Q. A. and Ella Prentiss in Pulteney, NY July 27, 1874

BARDEEN Catherine J. age 25y 6d wife of J. W. Bardeen and dau of Eber and Matilda **HILL** in Riker Hollow, NY August 4, 1874

BARTLETT George W. age 59y of Italy, NY at res of James Bartlett in Wheeler, NY July 30, 1874

LANE Nattile age 10m dau of Frank and Sarah Lane in Pulteney, NY August 10, 1874

SMITH Jacob D. age 45y in Urbana, NY (Newspaper date August 27, 1874)

LANE Floy Adell age 11m dau of Frank and Sarah in Pulteney, NY September 12, 1874

MILLER Jane age 2y 1m 4d dau of George M. and Harriet P. Miller and Grand dau of Franklin and Jane **HOLDEN** in Pulteney, NY September 15, 1874

MILLER Erastus age 65y formerly of Prattsburgh, NY in Milo, NY October 1, 1874

SMITH Mariah age 70y wife of William R. Smith at res of Joel Smith in Pulteney, NY October 14, 1874

GRAVES Elnora A. age 15y 26d dau of Charles D. and Zardilla Graves in Prattsburgh, NY October 15, 1874

HAYES Stella age 2y dau of George E. and Mary R. in Rockford, Ill. October 22, 1874

PIERCE Herbert age 1y 10m adopted son of William C. and Flora Pierce in Pulteney, NY October 9, 1874

COOK Lucy (**HOPKINS**) age 72y relict of Quartus Cook formerly of Prattsburgh, NY at son's Henry H. in White Lake Center, Mi. (Newspaper date November 5, 1874)

BROWN May age 10y in Prattsburgh, NY November 29, 1874

PICKETT Marilla age 27y wife of Milton in Pulteney, NY November 12, 1874

DE PEW Hester age 45y wife of William De Pew in Urbana, NY November 27, 1874

PUTNAM Lydia age 39y of Lakeport, Mi. at res of John **BORDEN** in Wheeler, NY November 30, 1874

MITCHELL George age 63 at res of Aaron **BLOOMER** in Prattsburgh, NY December 27, 1874

GOULD Hannah M. wife of Appleton M. Gould in Owego, NY January 21, 1875. Born Wantage, NY dau of James **MC CARRICK**

TYLER Daniel H. in his 52nd yr of injuries from a falling tree in Prattsburgh, NY January 22, 1875. Leaves wife and 5 children, youngest age 4m

WADSWORTH Mrs. ____ in her 70th yr in Clay, NY January 4, 1875. Born Russia, NY. Leaves husband and 3 children, names 1 Mrs. R. **HANSON** of Prattsburgh, NY

HIGBY John L. in his 72nd yr unmarried at bro C. G. Higby February 2, 1875. Born Brutus, NY and came to Prattsburgh, NY 1818

BROWNELL Oliver in his 67th yr nr Lyons Hollow, NY February 2, 1875. Born January 9, 1809 in Barrington, NY. 8 children

COLEGROVE Josephine L. age 31y wife of James B. Colegrove at parents in Branchport, NY March 1, 1875. Married February 9, 1870. 2 sons, oldest age 3y and Edward E. age 1y 5m buried 6 days ago

PULVER Henry age 78y formerly of Milo, NY in Prattsburgh, NY March 7, 1875

HUBBARD Maria M. age 26y dau of M. A. and Laura Hubbard in Prattsburgh, NY March 7, 1875

BALL Experience (**HEMPSTEAD**) in Pulteney, NY March 10, 1875. Born 1816 in Guilford, Ct.

PRENTISS William in his 74th yr in Pulteney, NY March 18, 1875. Born May 10, 1801 in Lancaster, Mass. and came to Pulteney 1813. Married December 31, 1829 Fanny L. **BENTON**, 8 children all living except 2nd dau

MILLER Warren age 84y in S. Pulteney, NY March 24, 1875

STICKNEY Eliza M. age 39y 6m wife of Julius Stickney and dau of Ephraim **AULLS** in Wheeler, NY April 7. 1875. 13 children 11 living, youngest age 5 days

MC CANN Annie E. age 20y wife of Henry Mc Cann and dau of Moses and Rhoda M. **THOMAS** in Pulteney, NY April 16, 1875

WILLIAMS Jennie age 13y dau of Aaron and Mary Jane Williams in Prattsburgh, NY May 9, 1875

SEARLES Harriet age 26y wife of C. W. Searles and dau of Benjamin **GULICK** in Pulteney, NY May 19, 1875

SMOKE David E. age 40y 9m at nieces's Mary E. **SITTS** in Prattsburgh, NY April 27, 1875. Born Enfield, NY

BROCKWAY Dolly H. age 62y wife of Walter Brockway June 2, 1875. Leaves husband, 1 son and 4 daus

MURPHY George W. age 19y son of Robert and Mary Murphy June 19, 1875

HALL Mathew in his 41st yr in Pulteney, NY June 28,1875

WYGANT Chauncey age 67y formerly of Prattsburgh, NY in Marlborough, NY July 28, 1875. Bro H. Wygant of Cohocton, NY

OSTRANDER James age 30y in Urbana, NY August 6, 1875

COVELL Minerva age 61y wife of William Covell in Pulteney, NY August 13, 1875

LOUNSBERRY John age 92y in Pulteney, NY August 30, 1875

CARPENTER Mrs. Minerva in her 59th yr in Pulteney, NY August 27, 1875

KETCH Hiram in his 83rd yr at Lent Hill, NY August 31, 1875

STANTON Dr. Elijah age 95y at son's Robert Stanton at Lent Hill, NY August 27, 1875. Born Quemona, NY, married twice, 10 children. Buried Lyons Hollow, NY

CHENEY Mary J. age 31y 9m 1d widow of Dr. Walter S. Cheney of Prattsburgh, NY at Father's Robert **FRENCH** August 27, 1875

WATKINS Maria L. age 55y wife of E. T. Watkins in Prattsburgh, NY September 4, 1875. Native of Tioga Co. NY. A few months ago oldest dau Mrs. W. H. **LEWIS** lost 3 children. Dau Mrs. **MERRITT** buried only child

WAGENER David S. age 51y 10m 22d son of Melchior one of the 1st settlers in Pulteney, NY September 9, 1875. Married Mary Ann **MC ARTHUR** of Lapeer Co. Mi.

STOWE Freddie age 6y son of Benjamin and Melissa Stowe September 15, 1875

PULVER Peter age 57y in Italy, NY September 14, 1875

DEATH NOTICES

HOES Mrs. John age 71y at dau Mrs. George **SHULTS** October 6, 1875

MATTISON Lizzie age 17y dau of Helen **BELLIS** of Prattsburgh, NY at res of D. F. **WOODWARD** in Jasper, NY November 9, 1875

ANDERSON Jane relict of John Anderson (who died 16 yrs ago) in Prattsburgh, NY December 18, 1875. Born August 1813 in Ontario Co. NY. Married June 1835

DOWNS David G. age 75y formerly of Prattsburgh, NY in Walker, Io. January 26, 1876. Born W. Bloomfield, NY. Married (1) dau of Aaron **COOKE** 5 sons, married (2) Ann **HILLS** dau of Bohan Hills who survives

SMITH Benjamin abt 75y formerly of Prattsburgh, NY in Tyrone, NY February 9, 1876

ELY Emma N. age 35y wife of Edward Ely and dau of Harvey **CURTIS** formerly of Prattsburgh, NY in Chicago, Ill. February 17, 1876

FULLER Alva age 80y nr Prattsburgh, NY March 9, 1876

WYGANT Sarah B. age 67y wife of Elias Wygant in Prattsburgh, NY March 18, 1876. Born September 7, 1808 in Norfolk, Ct. nee **MINER**. Married September 30, 1837

CAPEL Mary E. age 47y wife of Sanford Capel in Italy Hollow, NY January 6, 1876. Born October 23, 1828 in Milo, NY dau of William and Eliza **KLICE**. Married December 19, 1843, 4 children

TAYLOR M. Janette age 43y wife of J. W. Taylor in Prattsburgh, NY April 21, 1876. Born April 28, 1833 in Seneca, NY. Married September 13, 1849

WHEELER George Shepard age 15y son of Addison and Olive Wheeler in Wheeler, NY April 30, 1876

LANE Miss Abigail age 82y at res of Benjamin F. **AUSTIN** in Pulteney, NY May 6, 1876. Born NJ and came here 15 yrs ago

RICE Anna in Prattsburgh, NY May 11, 1876. Born May 13, 1785 in Spencertown, NY dau of Capt. Joel **PRATT** who came here 1802. Married 1806 Burrage Rice then of Marcellus, NY who died 1841

GRAY Nancy age 77y formerly of Bath, NY in Prattsburgh, NY June 5, 1876

STRONG Mark age 13y son of David Strong in Prattsburgh, NY June 5, 1876

STURDEVANT Milton G. age 36 at bro in Prattsburgh, NY June 11, 1876

WELD James Albert age 34y 6m 11d formerly of Prattsburgh, NY in Penn Yan, NY May 25, 1876. Born December 5, 1841 in Prattsburgh son of Harvey and Mary. Married January 13, 1864 and moved to Penn Yan 1872. Eva Matilda age 1y 10m 11d died May 20, 1876 and Hannmah Maud age 9y 8m 3d died May 26, 1876 daus of James A. and Matilda Weld. All buried in one grave

BURCHFIELD Robbie age 2y 3m 2d son of Robert L. and Hellen W. Burchfield in Wheeler, NY July 2, 1876

HAVENS Mrs. Eliza age 56y in Prattsburgh, NY July 17, 1876

CARHART Hackaliah age 66y in Prattsburgh, NY July 15, 1876. Leaves wife and 3 married daus

LEE William in Prattsburgh, NY July 31, 1876. Born Janury 4, 1791 in E. Haddam, Ct. Married (1) Rosanna **ORVIS** and (2) Phebe **ORVIS**. 7 children 5 living

LEWIS John age 84y at son-in-law's H. A. **JOHNSON** in Prattsburgh, NY August 4, 1876. Born January 24, 1792 in Montgomery Co. NY. Married December 24, 1816 Clarissa **VROOMAN** and came to Prattsburgh 1819. 6 sons and 3 daus

FOSS Joseph Sr. age 85y at son's Joseph Foss Jr. September 15, 1876

HUNT Thomas age 73y in Italy, NY September 15, 1876. Native of England and came here 1837

EARLEY Charlie E. age 2y 3m died August 20, 1876 and Joey age 3y 11m died September 1, 1876, sons of Henry F. and Catherine Earley in Prattsburgh, NY

DEUER Mrs. Janette age 57y in Prattsburgh, NY September 25, 1876

HORTON Daniel T. age 41y in Tyrone, NY October 13, 1876

YOUNG Martin age 52y nr Prattsburgh, NY October 30, 1876

PUTNAM Nelson age 7y son of Richard and Anna in Wheeler, NY December 7, 1876

BOSS Zephaniah age 70y in Pulteney, NY December 18, 1876

HUBBARD E. T. age 64y bro of E. A. in Prattsburgh, NY December 21, 1876

POTTER Susan A. age 34y wife of John Potter in Prattsburgh, NY January 3, 1877

CLARK Arnold age 61y in Pulteney, NY January 8, 1877

SMITH William R. age 81y at son's in Pulteney, NY December 27, 1876

CASTOR William age 84y in Prattsburgh, NY February 12, 1877

PHELPS Hannah age 76y in Prattsburgh, NY February 20, 1877. 1 son and 2 daus

NILES George age 77y in Prattsburgh, NY February 22, 1877. Came here with father Rev. John Niles in 1802

MC LEAN George age 54y in Prattsburgh, NY February 24, 1877. Born December 14, 1822 in Pulteney, NY. Married 1845 Catherine **RILEY**, 3 children Mrs. Rosa

DEATH NOTICES

SKINNER wife of Frank and Mrs. Rena **WRIGHT**. Wife died May 1845 and he married (2) in 1855 Mrs. Anna Maria **WYGANT** of Prattsburgh, 1 dau Katie

DOUD Mathew age 60y in Prattsburgh, NY March 12, 1877. Born Co. Kern, Ireland and came to US 1847

CAWARD Willie H. age 20y 9m at father's in Prattsburgh, NY (Newspaper date March 15, 1877)

TURNER David age 85y 10m in Prattsburgh, NY March 23, 1877

HILL Priscilla age 79y 2m mother of Daniel and Cyrus Hill in Pulteney, May 4, 1877

TERRY William H. age 55y in Prattsburgh, NY May 4, 1877

HORTON Theron age 20y in Pulteney, NY May 15, 1877

VAN WINKLE Mrs. Mary Jane age 50y dau of Dr. S. **LOOK** formerly of Prattsburgh, NY in Hornellsville, NY June 10, 1877

BLOOD Luther B. age 11m son of M. L. and Ella in Italy Hill, NY June 13, 1877

SQUIRES Nathaniel age 76y in Italy Hill, NY June 19, 1877

MIDDLETON Hannah E. age 5m 15d dau of James A. and Hannah Middleton in Mt. Pleasant, Mi. July 15, 1877

PELTON Ezra age 96y 3m 18d an early settler of Pulteney, NY in N. Urbana, NY August 15, 1877. Only surviving son Clinton Pelton

STONE Bradley age 8m 13d son of Lafayette and Belle Stone in Pulteney, NY September 15, 1877

WHEELER Seth age 81y 5m 12d at res of Jonas Wheeler in Prattsburgh, NY October 7, 1877. Born April 19, 1796 in New Ipswich, NH and came to Wheeler 1815

HOPKINS Hattie formerly of Prattsburgh, NY at uncle's James **HOLMES** in Tecumseh, Mi. October 15, 1877

MC GRADA Lois age 47y wife of Samuel in Prattsburgh, NY November 2, 1877

SELOVER Mary Frances age 44y wife of Dr. John R. in Bath, NY November 9, 1877

STEVENS Dennis P. age 76y 7m 9d in Seneca Castle, NY November 14, 1877. Came to Prattsburgh, NY 1820 and to Seneca Castle 1849

GLOAD John A. age 38y son of John Gload of Pulteney, NY in Lebanon, Mo. January 7, 1878

HOTCHKIN Elizabeth A. wife of B. B. Hotchkin formerly of Prattsburgh, NY in

Marple, Pa. January 22, 1878

CAWARD George age 77y in Hopeton, NY February 5, 1878. Wife died July 16, 1877 in Dresden, NY

LEWIS Elijah T. age 2y 1m son of William and Jennie Lewis in S. Pulteney, NY February 7, 1878

HORTON Ann Eliza age 75y wife of William Horton in Pulteney, NY March 18, 1878. Born 1803 in Whitestown, NY 1 of 15 children of Joseph and Lydia **STEWART**. Married 1821, 6 sons and 1 dau

LAZELLE Miss Cynthia age 56y formerly of Prattsburgh, NY at Willard Asylum March 1, 1878

TAYLOR Daniel formerly of Hornellsville, NY in Prattsburgh, NY March 20, 1878. Leaves wife, 2 sons and 2 daus

FULLER Miss Almira age 58y at bro D. A. in Prattsburgh, NY March 25, 1878

AUSTIN Joanna E. A. in Prattsburgh, NY March 30, 1878. Born March 16, 1826 in Pulteney, NY dau of Alexander and Jane **PARKER**

BURTON Athea in Prattsburgh, NY May 3, 1878. Born May 7, 1803 in Otisco, NY nee **AINSWORTH**. Married 1864 Gilbert Burton of Corning, NY. Names 1 bro Isaac

PRENTISS John A. age 80y (birthday on May 7, 1878) and died May 8, 1878. Native of Lancaster, Mass. Leaves wife, 4 sons and 5 daus

RINGROSE Esther wife of John Ringrose in Prattsburgh, NY May 6, 1878. Born May 2, 1807 in Onieda Co. NY. Married March 1837 in Gorham, NY, 2 sons and 2 daus

DE PEW Samuel age 67y in Pulteney, NY May 4, 1878. Leaves wife and 1 dau

STODDARD Benjamin age 82y in Jerusalem, NY June 4, 1878. Born 1796 in Cherry Valley, NY and came to Jerusalem age 21 yrs. Married 1818 Hannah **KELLY** of Cherry Valley

HORTON Lewis in Pulteney, NY June 15, 1878. Born July 8, 1829 in Pulteney son of William and Eliza Horton

ALLEN Rebecca relict of R. P. Allen and mother of Mrs. Rev. E. F. **OWEN** of Prattsburgh, NY in Rochester, NY June 12, 1878

GRAVES Rebecca in her 78th yr in Prattsburgh, NY August 3, 1878. Born October 16, 1800 in Norfolk, Ct. dau of James **STURDEVANT** Sr. Married 1844 Luther Graves

MC LEAN Frank L. age 11m 8d son of F. E. and L. C. Mc Lean in Union City, Pa. August 15, 1878

DEATH NOTICES

HARE George age 82y in Rikers Hollow, NY August 9, 1878. Native of Yorkshire, England. Married Janet **PRINGLE** who died abt 9 yrs ago. Married (2) Louisa **COOK**, 2 daus Mrs. B. L. **LYON** and Mrs. H. **GRAVES** of Riker Hollow. 1 bro Charles Hare of Castile, NY

CLARK Jane R. in Clifton Springs, NY October 8, 1878. Born August 1825 in Geneva, NY. Married 1848 John Clark of Prattsburgh, NY

STODDARD Chester in Italy, NY October 5, 1878. Born November 16, 1817 eldest of 4 sons of Benjamin. Married February 6. 1840 Catherine **VAN TUYL**, 3 daus 1 died infancy, Mrs. E. E. **SMITH** and Mrs. W. **AINSLEY** both of Jerusalem, NY

HUTCHINSON Smith age 42y 9m 3d in Bradford, NY October 10, 1878. Sister Mrs. A. E. **BRAMBLE** of Prattsburgh, NY

STEWART Experience age 77y relict of Joseph Stewart formerly of Prattsburgh, NY at son's J. K. Stewart in Woodhull, NY October 30, 1878. Born Pulteney, NY 1800, married age 16 yrs, 2 sons and 3 daus

CHAPPELL Lyman age 75y found dead in field nr home in Prattsburgh, NY October 31, 1878. Born 1803 in eastern New York State and came to Prattsburgh 1814. Married 1824 Elma **SWEET**, 5 sons and 2 daus

PARSONS Addie R. wife of Charles Parsons in Rochester, NY November 4, 1878. Born 1839 in Wheeler, NY, married January 10, 1858. Leaves 1 dau age 18 yrs

STONE Frankie age 6m 10d son of Lafayette and Belle Stone in Pulteney, NY October 21, 1878

ARNOLD E. C. in Pulteney, NY November 19, 1878. Born June 6, 1810 in Carmel, NY, res of Pulteney 40 yrs

HUBBARD Laura C. in Prattsburgh, NY December 12, 1878. Born April 15, 1819 in Prattsburgh, NY dau of Ezra **CHAPIN**. Married October 1838 E. Austin Hubbard, 1 son and 2 daus

WEAVER Stephen G. age 35y formerly of Prattsburgh, NY in Williamson, NY December 26, 1878. Married Caroline **COOK** dau of Aaron Cook and moved to Wayne Co. NY 1845

GREGORY Sarah Elizabeth in her 16th yr dau of Elizabeth and late Rev. David D. Gregory in Binghamton, NY December 27, 1878

PRATT Sarah (**BRIGHAM**) age 47y wife of Harvey E. Pratt formerly of Prattsburgh, NY in Spencerport, NY January 21, 1879

CURTIS William B. in his 79th yr at bro William B. Curtis in Prattsburgh, NY January 27, 1879. Came to Prattsburgh 1805

VAN VLEET Isaac in Prattsburgh, NY February 3, 1879. Born October 18, 1817 in

Vt., moved to Angelica as child and to Prattsburgh 1840. Married September 1842 Emily **PHELPS**, 2 sons and 2 daus

BARKER Laura (**PURDEE**) wife of Levi S. Barker in Ann Arbor, Mi. January 8, 1879. Born December 1, 1813 in Prattsburgh, NY. Married February 21, 1833 and moved to Batavia, NY and to Mi. in 1850

AINSWORTH Sarah S. age 30y dau of Addison and Sarah Ainsworth in Prattsburgh, NY February 20, 1879. Born August 25, 1848 in Prattsburgh

DENNISTON Goldsmith of Prattsburgh, NY at son's Maj. H. G. Denniston in Naugatuck, NY February 15, 1879. Born August 3, 1801 in Blooming Grove, NY and came to Prattsburgh 1848

GELDER Harriet wife of Thomas Gelder in Prattsburgh, NY March 2, 1879. Born January 20, 1815 in River Bridge, Yorkshire, England and came to Canada 1836, to Waterloo, NY 1837 and 1854 to Prattsburgh. 15 children 11 living

BABCOCK Joseph Stanton of Prattsburgh, NY in Naples, NY February 24, 1879. Born September 11, 1792 in Bridgeport, Ct. Married 1820 Phebe **HONEYWELL**

SCOTT John V. age 41y in Prattsburgh, NY March 9, 1879. Born April 7, 1838 in Crawford Co. Pa. Married October 3, 1859 Helen **BANTA**, 2 sons, 1 dau age 2 yrs

MILLER Edwin age 54y in St. Joseph, Mi. March 7, 1879. Born March 24, 1825 in Hartland, Ct. only son of Giles H. and Lucy Miller. Married June 16, 1852 Fanny **GRAHAM** of Broome Co. NY. Moved to Kansas 1857 and after war to St. Joseph. Leaves wife and 3 sons. Mother lives in Stratford, Ct. with dau Mrs. George E. **WHEELER** and other dau Mrs. Rev. J. W. **SIMPSON** of Long Island

MERRITT Jesse in Wheeler, NY May 30, 1879. Born June 20, 1820 in Albany Co. NY and came to Steuben Co. at age 7 yrs

ROBSON John age 68y in Prattsburgh, NY May 22, 1879. Native of England and came to Prattsburgh 1842. Leaves wife and 2 children

HORTON Rachel age 77y wife of Thomas Horton in Weston, NY June 18, 1879. Born November 17, 1802 in Kent, NY dau of David **LEE**. Married February 27, 1822

NOXON James age 43y hit by lightning in Wheeler, NY June 26, 1879. Born Prince Edward Co. Ontario, Canada, lived Orange Co. NY and came to Wheeler 3 yrs ago. Leaves wife and 4 children

VAN HOUSEN John nr Prattsburgh, NY July 11, 1879. Born August 2, 1802 in Kingsbury, NY son of Henry and Betsey (**BENEDICT**). Married September 1829 Ann **HOFFMAN** and moved to Howard, NY with wife and 2 children Charles H. and Catherine both dec. 2 children born Howard, Edward H. and Israel A. Wife died October 1841 and he married (2) Adeline **HOTCHKIN** dau of Beriah, 1 dau Mrs. Dr. Warren **STEWART** of Savona, NY. Second wife died May 12 1846 and he married (3) Mrs. P. W. **ANDREWS** dau of Joseph H. **WILLIAMS** of Rushville, NY

DEATH NOTICES

DUGAN Jennie age 26y wife of John Dugan and dau of Mrs. H. B. **EDDY** in Dixon, Cal. July 6, 1879. Born October 1853 in Prattsburgh, NY

WIXOM Charlotte age 81y in Prattsburgh, NY August 7, 1879. Born February 10, 1797 in Vernon, NJ dau of William and Charlotte **DE KAY**. Moved to Cayuga Co. NY and married abt 1816 Shubel Wixom and moved to Pulteney, NY. Husband died December 4, 1862, 1 dau Jennie at home

BRADLEY George F. son of Frank W. Bradley in Kanona, NY August 1, 1879

WALDO Daniel D. in Prattsburgh, NY August 17, 1879. Born May 8, 1837 in Edmeston, NY son of Erastus and Hannah D. Waldo. Married 1857 Mary **DAVIS** who died January 1, 1860. Married (2) September 1860 Mrs. Hannah E. **HOTCHKIN**, 2 sons Harvey and Lucius A. and dau Mary

DUNNING Charlotte Elizabeth age 22y dau of L. O. Dunning of Prattsburgh, NY in South River, NJ August 25, 1879

LAMPORT Erastus in Prattsburgh, NY August 27, 1879. Born March 29, 1812 in Renssalaer Co. NY. Moved to Benton, NY age 6 wks and to Prattsburgh April 1879. Married Lucelia J. **WEIR** of Ohio. 3 children Charles who died infancy, Grace L. and Franz W.

CLARK Aurelia age 48y wife of Joseph R. Clark in Prattsburgh, NY September 12, 1879. Born Woodhull, NY dau of Stephen **KENT**. Married October 26, 1848. 1 son Darwin and 2 daus Ellen and Carrie

BOHANAN Miss Mary C. age 69y at res of A. Y **ROSA** September 14, 1879

MILLS Frank E. in Arnot, Pa. October 5, 1879. Born September 23, 1856, married January 15, 1879 Clara **FOSTER** at Lawrenceville, Pa. 5 bro and 3 sisters

CHAPMAN Anna L. age 7y 9m 16d died December 23, 1879, Harry age 4y 7m 17d died December 29, 1879 and Freddie age 10y 9d died December 30, 1879, children of William and Emily Chapman in Breesport, NY

WILLIAMS Mary H. in her 84th yr of Wheeler, NY at son-in-law's Emmett **TAYLOR** in Starkey, NY December 28, 1879. Born 1796 in Middletown, Ct. dau of Eber **BLAKESLEE** and Sally **(WARD)**. 7 bro and 3 sisters, 2 bro living, William of Kanona, NY and George of Nashua, NH. Married 1822 Orva Williams now dec. 4 children Seabury killed at Antietam, Eliza A. of Starkey, NY and John C. of Macosta Co. Mi. and Thomas who died at Mother's home in Wheeler, NY 1861

EARLEY John age 9y son of John S. and Harriet in Prattsburgh, NY February 1, 1880

MC CORMICK Clarissa age 43y wife of Harrison Mc Cormick in Pulteney, NY February 12, 1880. Born June 28, 1838 dau of James **PIERCE** formerly of Prattsburgh, NY. Married May 27, 1855, 5 children

GILBERT Harmon M. age 56y in Italy, NY February 29, 1880. Born March 5, 1824

in Prattsburgh, NY. Married March 5, 1850 Laura **INGRAHAM** of Wayland, NY, 1 son and 1 dau living, oldest dau died 14 yrs ago

OLNEY Benjamin of Wayland, NY found dead by son L. B. Olney February 27, 1880

ENGLISH Mrs. Elizabeth age 84y in Pulteney, NY March 3, 1880. Born April 27, 1795 in Ct. Married in Ct. December 1, 1816 Jonathan **CRABB** who died April 28, 1822, 4 children Elisha, Richard, Jonathan and 1 son died infancy. Richard only survivor. Returned to Ct. and married William English, 1 son Isaac born October 10, 1833. Came to Pulteney 1836

ALLEN John son of William and Sarah Allen in Pulteney, NY February 16, 1880. Born March 17, 1858 in Prattsburgh, NY. Names bro Charles

CAIG Ann Eliza age 39y March 19, 1880. Leaves husband and 2 young children

RICE Placentia in Prattsburgh, NY March 2, 1880. Born October 1, 1820 in Jerusalem, NY dau of William and Eunice **GENUNG**. Married 1814 Richard **VAN LOON** of Jerusalem who died 1859. Married Clark Rice a few years later who died 1872 in Seneca Co. NY. Came to Prattsburgh with dau Mrs. B. F. **NORTHRUP**

RINGROSE John Sr. in his 85th yr in Prattsburgh, NY March 30, 1880. Born January 30, 1796 in Yorkshire, England. Came to US 1830 and married 1836 Esther **HERRICK** in Gorham, NY, moved to Prattsburgh next May. 2 sons and 2 daus Thomas D. and John Jr., Esther Victorie and Lucy Ann who died in autumn of 1864

STEVER Susan V. age 51y wife of George W. Stever in Pulteney, NY March 28, 1880. Born February 13, 1829 in Pulteney dau of Joel and Sarah **TOMER**. Married January 13, 1849

WILCOX Charlotte relict of William H. Wilcox in Prattsburgh, NY April 6, 1880. Born March 17, 1822 in Johnson, Vt. dau of Joseph and Elizabeth **FOSTER** who came to Warren Co. NY 1826. 3 bro and 5 sisters. Married October 30, 1843 in Warren Co. and in November moved to Prattsburgh. 8 children 6 living, names dau Mrs. B. S. **CARPENTER** of Pittstown, NY

COREY Mary Whitman relict of Christopher Corey late of Penn Yan, NY at res of Leman Corey in Italy, NY April 19, 1880. Born 1805 in Norflok, Ct. nee **COTTON**. Married April 27, 1837, Christopher Corey who was born 1799 in RI and had 3 children by his 1st wife. Names Francis Monroe 1839 - 1863

WHEATON John M. age 85y in Hammondsport, NY (Newspaper date April 22, 1880). Born May 19, 1795 in Hebron, NY and family moved to Mass. At age 22 yrs he moved to Salem, NY and married August 22, 1820 Susan **BELLOWS**. 1 son and 6 daus

CARTER David in his 81st yr in Painted Post, NY April 11, 1880

HILL Matilda W. age 70y in Riker Hollow, NY April 22, 1880. Born January 26, 1810 in Delaware Co. NY dau of David and Hannah **WELD**. Married 1830 Eber Hill and had 11 children

DEATH NOTICES

BLODGETT Mrs. Nancy G. age 68y in Beatrice, Neb. March 21, 1880. Born Prattsbugh, NY

SMITH Asa C. at son's in Penn Yan, NY April 29, 1880. Born October 2, 1807 in Galway, NY. Married January 1, 1830 Elizabeth **HARMON** of Ballston, NY and moved to Prattsburgh, NY. Last year moved in with son in Penn Yan

VAN HOUSEN Edward H. in his 44th yr son of late John Van Housen of Howard, NY in Prattsburgh, NY May 14, 1880

CARPENTER Harry S. age 13m son of Sheldon and Augusta (**WILCOX**) in Pittstown, NY June 1, 1880

ENGLISH William died June 11, 1880. Born July 2, 1798 in Ct. and married September 9, 1832 Elizabeth **CRABB** and moved to Pulteney, NY 45 yrs ago. Wife died March 2, 1880. 1 son Isaac

LOOK Jennie Maude dau of Dr. W. G. and Jane Look in Prattsburgh, NMY July 25, 1876

CARR Charlotte age 37y in Lake Mills, Wis. June 10, 1880. Born Huron, NY eldest child of Rev. E. F. **WALDO**

BRUSH Malvira age 44y wife of James Brush in Pulteney, NY June 27, 1880

DABOLL Auren age 87y in Prattsburgh, NY July 14, 1880

BRUCE Andrew S. age 4m 3d son of L. D. and Julia in Pulteney, NY August 1, 1880

STEVER Bertie age 4y dau of Rupert and Sarah in Pulteney, NY August 9, 1880

KLICE William Sr. age 84y in Italy, NY August 7, 1880

BELLIS Mary Ann age 85y wife of Isaac in Prattsburgh, NY August 21, 1880

TYLER Emily age 58y 9m 11d wife of Ira L. in Prattsburgh, NY August 31, 1880

CURTIS Julia E. wife of Silliman B. Curtis September 4, 1880. Born 1835 in Savannah, NY nee **MERRITT**. Leaves 2 bro, 3 sisters, husband and 1 son

HIBBARD N. B. age 74y in Branchport, NY September 17, 1880

FERGUSON Amy age 98y at son's Solomon L. in Pulteney, NY September 12, 1880

WHEELER Della M. in Wheeler, NY September 6, 1880. Born August 29, 1856 2nd dau of Addison and Olive Wheeler

PARKS Parmela age 84y in Pulteney, NY October 8, 1880

CLARK Jeremiah age 82y in Prattsburgh, NY October 8, 1880

STANTON Mrs. John T. in Oxford, Mi. October 21, 1880. Born October 25, 1822 in Prattsburgh, NY and married December 21, 1842, 1 dau

HARRIS Thomas age 68y in Prattsburgh, NY November 16, 1880

SNYDER Mrs. Anthony in Prattsburgh, NY November 17, 1880

BURGER Benjamin age 34y in Riker Hollow, NY November 21, 1880

CLARK Degolia abt 54y wife of Stephen Clark in Prattsburgh, NY November 22, 1880. Born April 4, 1826 in Prattsburgh

GARRISON Martin at one time a res of Prattsburgh, NY in Howard, NY December 9, 1880. Names dau Mrs. John A. **BROWN**

WALDO Mary D. age 77y relict of Aaron Waldo formerly of Prattsburgh, NY at son's John D. Waldo in Quincy, Ill. December 23, 1880. Born Ct. nee **DAVENPORT** a lineal descendant of Rev. John Davenport

BELLIS Isaac age 84y at son's in Prattsburgh, NY December 31, 1880

SMITH Artemus in Prattsburgh, NY January 14, 1881. Born April 5, 1806 in Sempronius, NY and moved to Prattsburgh at age 5 yrs. Married 1849 sarah **WILLIAMS**. Leaves wife and son Artemus Jr. and 1 dau

STANTON Charlotte A. wife of Abel Stanton on Lent Hill, NY January 19, 1881. Born 1827 in Allen, NY dau of Daniel and Sally **STURDEVANT** who moved to Prattsburgh, NY when she was 6 yrs old. Married August 10, 1846, 9 children Louis dec., Mrs. Brainard **WING** and Charles A. of Cohocton, NY, Daniel dec., Edward B. of Wheeler, NY, Lizzie dec., Mrs. Lottie A. **EARNEST** and Augustus of Cohocton

MILLER Rhoda relict of Erastus H. Miller formerly of Prattsburgh, NY at res of Joel **SMITH** in Pulteney, NY January 27, 1881

CORSON Rev. Charles Wesley (Newspaper date February 3, 1881). Born September 19, 1838 in Besley's Pt. NJ son of Joseph and Harriet Corson. Married September 1860 Marietta **BABCOCK**, 5 daus Clara age 19y, Emma age 15y, Etta May age 8y, Frankie age 6y and Hattie age 5y. Served 25th Reg. NJV, buried Penfield, NY

HARRIS Thomas died November 18, 1880. Born April 30, 1817 in Scotland and came to US 1839. Married 1852 Jane **HUFFTALEN** of Dundee, NY who died 3 yrs later. Moved to Prattsburgh, NY 1855 and married (2) 1856 Ann **SANFORD** of Naples, NY. 1 son and 1 dau

MILLER Henrietta age 8y dau of Norman W. and Abigail Miller in Pulteney, NY February 18, 1881

ALLEN Sally C. in Prattsburgh, NY February 18, 1881. Born June 29, 1811 in NH and came to Middlesex, NY 1820. Married December 23, 1830 Caleb Allen. Moved to Prattsburgh 1865. 9 children 6 living

DEATH NOTICES

COLLINS Genevieve age 32y 14d wife of A. F. Collins and dau of Spencer T. and Lemira F. **HOLTON** in Fon Du Lac, Wis. February 21, 1881

CLAYSON Hiram age 26y 2m 8d in Bloods Depot, NY February 16, 1881

BROWN Sarah age 80y at dau Mrs. Henry **ELLSWORTH** in Prattsburgh, NY March 3, 1881

MATTICE Anna age 60y wife of John W. Mattice in Cohocton, NY March 17, 1881

O'FLAHERTY Mary age 64y in Wheeler, NY April 1, 1881

WHITNEY Mrs. Joan age 65y in Waterford, Pa. March 28, 1881. Sister of late George **MC LEAN** of Prattsburgh, NY

BANTA John in Prattsburgh, NY April 13, 1881. Born June 4, 1806 in Broadalbin, Montgomery Co. NY. Married June 16, 1834 Jane E. **LA DUE**, 2 sons and 4 daus. 1 son died at Battle of Wilderness

PIERCE Miss Addie age 23y in Springwater, NY April 25, 1881

STRONG Ezra age 65y in Wheeler, NY April 19, 1881

ACKERSON Marilda died May 10, 1881. Born September 12, 1825 dau of Phillip **MYRTLE**. Married January 1, 1846 Henry Ackerson

LAFLER Ida age 25y wife of Frank Lafler and dau of William and Ophelia **HILER** in Italy Hollow, NY May 4, 1881

ARNOLD Esther D. age 40y 4d wife of Austin J. in Crookston, Mn. May 22, 1881

WILLIAMS Ernest Clark age 1y 7m son of Thoedore B. and Clara C. Williams in Unadilla, Mi. May 28, 1881

SMITH Parmela age 84y relict of Jay Smith late of Prattsburgh, NY in Washington, DC June 25, 1881

LEWIS Sebastian age 72y in Prattsburgh, NY June 29, 1881. Born May 14, 1809 in Broadalbin, NY. Married age 22 yrs Marion **CHALMERS** of Galway, NY and moved to Prattsburgh, NY 1849. 9 children 8 living. Celebrated 50th anniversary on March 24, 1881 at dau Mrs. D. W. **BALDWIN**

FORD George age 10m son of Elisha B. and Mary in Pulteney, NY July 10, 1881

FLYNN Thomas age 38y in Prattsburgh, NY August 8, 1881. Native of Ireland, came to US 1868, res of Prattsburgh 10 yrs. Leaves wife and 7 children

HOTCHKIN Leman age 35y in Prattsburgh, NY August 31, 1881

WINTERMUTE Miss Hannah in her 67th yr at Father's H. B. Wintermute in Pulteney,

NY September 6, 1881. Born September 1, 1815 in Stillwater, NJ. dau of Henry B. and Sarah Wintermute

WILLOUGHBY Maria B. age 87y in Prattsburgh, NY September 29, 1881. Born 1794 in Danbury, Ct. dau of Nathan and Ruth **BABCOCK** who moved to Montgomery Co. NY 1795. Married 1815 Horace **ST JOHN** of Galway, NY who died 1825, 1 son and 2 daus, Charles R. or Prattsburgh only survivor. Married (2) in 1839 Prof. Westel Willoughby

BRINK Mrs. Nett at mother's Mrs. R. R. **FARGO** in Pulteney, NY September 30, 1881

HOLLEY Ebenezer age 45y in S. Pulteney, NY (Newspaper date October 20, 1881)

CRABB Susan (**CLARK**) age 65y wife of Richard Crabb in Prattsburgh, NY October 21, 1881. Born September 18, 1816 in Westchester Co. NY and came to Pulteney 1819. Married 1836

DEAN Darius funeral October 18, 1881. Born March 18, 1828 son of William N. and Polly Dean of Pulteney, NY both dec. Married September 1858 Mary E. **STEWART**, 9 children

CARPENTER U. T. formerly of Prattsburgh, NY at son's H. K. C. Carpenter in Clifton Springs, NY November 7, 1881. Born June 12, 1804. Moved to Hilsdale, Mi. 1834 and back to Geneva, NY 1837. Married 1839 Caroline **CLARK**. Moved to Prattsburgh 1857

HULTS Fred C. age 17y in Pulteney, NY October 23, 1881

NIMS Ernest age 9y son of Charles Nims in Wheeler, NY December 3, 1881

BAKER Maria age 60y relict of Daniel Baker and dau of Henry **PULVER** of Milo, NY in Prattsburgh, NY December 9, 1881

POTTER Alanson C. age 30y in Barrington, NY November 19, 1881

KAPLE Polly age 87y 4m in Prattsburgh, NY December 18, 1881

VORHEES Andrew Md. formerly of Prattsburgh, NY in Vanceburg, Ky. December 14, 1881. Born Pulteney, NY, married Harriet M. **JACKSON** dau of Dr. Jackson of Prattsburgh

TOMER Joel A. age 40y in Prattsburgh, NY January 1, 1882

WELCH Laura age 64y relict of Solomon Welch at son-in-law's David **DREW** in Urbana, NY January 10, 1882. 2 daus Mrs. Drew of Urbana and Mrs. Mary J. **SALTSMAN** of Avoca, NY and 1 bro Samuel B. **NILES** of Prattsburgh, NY

HAIGHT Lewis age 63y in Prattsburgh, NY February 9, 1882. Born Westchester Co. NY, formerly lived in Jerusalem, NY. Married 1872 Katie **CASTOR**. 2 sons Charles dec and Adelbert of Penn Yan, NY

OLNEY Nathaniel age 67y in Avoca, NY February 24, 1882. Born Scipio, NY oldest son of Nathan Olney. Married 1836 Mary **MILLS**. Leaves wife and 5 children, R. E. of Mansfield, Pa., H. C. of Naples, NY, Mrs. W. E. **WELD** of Prattsburgh, NY, Mrs. A. G. **FOWLER** of Avoca and Adelaide at home

HARE Mrs. Louisa nr 82y in Rikers Hollow, NY March 13, 1882

GELDER Barney age 72y formerly of Prattsburgh, NY at son's in Bristol, NY March 11, 1882

CONINE Leila age 1y 8m dau of G. T. Conine in Dundee, NY March 4, 1882

COLE Mrs. Lydia in her 78th yr in Benton, NY March 12, 1882. Born November 17, 1804 nee **WILKINSON**. Married October 1829 Richard **FRANCIS** Jr. of Sodus, NY who died August 1830. Married (2) November 6, 1836 Asa Cole of Penn Yan, NY who died 1860

BELL Mrs. Philow in Rikers Hollow, NY March 25, 1882

DREW Catherine age 38y wife of David Drew in Urbana, NY March 14, 1882

NORRIS Squire son of Shadrick Norris in S. Pulteney, NY March 26, 1882

HUBBARD Selina age 39y wife of Henry Hubbard and dau of Charles **SHULTS** in Lyons Hollow, NY March 25, 1882

HORTON Lewis A. age 78y formerly of Pulteney, NY in Commerce, Mi. February 24, 1882. Leaves bro Thomas Horton of Prattsburgh, NY

FOSTER Nancy age 65y sister of W. S. Foster of Prattsburgh, NY in N. Lansingburg, NY March 22, 1882

ALLEN Ella age 5y 3m 10d dau of Phillip W. and Lillian M. Allen April 8, 1882

CHAPPELL Julia Elma age 80y relict of Lyman at son's O. N. April 17, 1882. Born March 31, 1802. 5 sons and 2 daus, Francis of Cameron, NY, Norman of Eureka, Wis., Mrs. Thomas **DONALDSON** nr Branchport, NY, O. N. of Prattsburgh, 1 dau dec, Isaac died 1863, Edwin served at Battle of Wilderness and was never heard from

WILLIAMS Jacob age 60y in Prattsburgh, NY April 23, 1882

HILL Eber age 72y at dau Mrs. Henry **OLNEY** in Naples, NY April 24, 1882

HAYES Julia in Prattsburgh, NY May 4, 1882. Born October 26, 1803 in Clinton, NY dau of William P. and Abba A. **CURTIS** who came to Prattsburgh 1805. Married November 6, 1821 Samuel Hayes, 8 children 4 died infancy. Emma Jane died age 16 yrs, oldest dau Adeline Christina of Milwaukee, Wis., Mary Eliza of Alexandria, Mn. and Sarah Lucretia at home

HORTON Hannah age 52y wife of William Horton in Pulteney, NY May 21, 1882.

Born Pulteney dau of late Jacob and Harriet **BEDELL**, 4 bro and 3 sisters. Married May 1851

GRAVES Zama age 91y relict of Israel Graves formerly of Prattsburgh, NY at dau Mrs. Joseph H. **AVERY** in Cohocton, NY May 25, 1882

WHEELER Silas P. age 54y in Wheeler, NY June 11, 1882. Born October 27, 1827 son of Seth and Maria Wheeler who came from Ct. Married January 1, 1860 Mary M. **FULLER** of Avoca, NY, 7 children 5 living

VORHEES Lena Estell age 1w 1d dau of Z. T. in W. Urbana, NY June 13, 1882

HORTON William in Pulteney, NY August 9, 1882. Born November 4, 1795 in Dutchess Co. NY. After war Father moved to Seneca Co. NY and to Pulteney 1841. Married May 1820 Ann Eliza **STEWART** who died March 1878, 9 children eldest died 1842 and youngest died 1848, 6 sons and 1 dau living

CHISSOM Jessie Blanche age 1y dau of John and Flora **(BLOOMER)** at Kinneys Corners, NY August 12, 1882

BUSH Alfred H. age 26y at sister's in Bellona, NY August 17, 1882

MC CORMICK Isaac T. age 35y in Pulteney, NY August 20, 1882

KLICE Eliza age 76y relict of William Klice at res of Henry Klice in Italy, NY October 11, 1882

LOCKWOOD Anna age 55y wife of Lewis in Wheeler, NY October 6, 1882

DOUBLEDAY Gavin E. in his 57th yr in Italy, NY October 19, 1882. Born September 17, 1825 oldest and last surviving son of Dr. Elisha and Sally Doulbeday. Married in his 22nd yr Almira J. **GLOAD** of Pulteney, NY. 5 children, Livonia A. born 1851 and died 1854, Florence E. born 1856 and died 1863, Evert M. born 1857 and died 1863, S. Estella born 1864 and Myra F. born 1871 surviving. 2 sisters Mrs. Dr. **WIXOM** of Italy and Mrs. E. **GULICK** of Starkey, NY

FAIRFIELD Charles age 17y died October 17, 1882 and Maud age 11y died October 18, 1882 children of Baker Fairfield formerly of Pulteney, NY in Cohocton, NY. Another child died in March

WHEELER Mary Elizabeth age 61y wife of Luther Wheeler in Prattsburgh, NY November 6, 1882. Born October 30, 1821 in Lancaster Co. Pa. dau of Abraham **WAUGH** of Cohocton, NY. Married July 10, 1853, 3 sons and 2 daus and 4 children of husband's by former marriage

TOMER Louisa in Prattsburgh, NY December 16, 1882. Born October 23, 1808 in Westchester Co. NY. Married January 26, 1825 Ira Hyatt of Pulteney, NY. 2 children Mrs. E. T. Watkins of Prattsburgh and N. R. **HYATT** of Pulteney, NY. Husband died May 19, 1868 and she married (2) in 1871 Webster Tomer who died July 24, 1882

DEATH NOTICES

ACKERSON Mary in Prattsburgh, NY January 13, 1883. Born July 17, 1805 in Colebrook, Ct. Married early James **HOTCHKISS** and moved to Norfolk, Ct. Husband died 1841, 7 children. Moved to Prattsburgh 1842 and married (2) June 1855 Henry Ackerson who died 11 yrs later. 2 bro Martin **MINER** of Prattsburgh and Augustus Miner of Canisteo, NY. 3 children Miss Maryette Hotchkiss of Prattsburgh, Mrs. George **MC LEAN** now of Nunda, NY and 1 sister in north west Mi.

DINEHART William C. nr Prattsburgh, NY November 9, 1882. Born May 10, 1821 in Columbia Co. NY. Married September 9, 1843 Lucinda **COOPER**. Resided in Yates Co. NY until 1866

MC KALLOR George age 67y in Victor, NY January 12, 1883. Married 1852 Delia **HAMLIN** of Naples, NY

GRAVES Luther age 89y in Prattsburgh, NY February 16, 1883. Born January 16, 1794 in Whately, Mass. Moved to Steuben Co. age 21y. Married October 20, 1819 Hannah **BURTON** of Prattsburgh. 2 children Mrs. Sidney **LUCE** of Brighton, NY dec and Mrs. Francis **BRIGLIN** of Prattsburgh. Wife died May 17, 1824 and he married (2) October 28, 1824 Charlotte **COOPER** of Prattsburgh, 2 sons Martin Luther and Asher (dec) and 1 dau Jemima Elizabeth died young. Wife died March 17, 1843 and he married (3) Rebecca **STURDEVANT**. She died August 1878 age 78y

BROCKWAY B. F. formerly of Prattsburgh, NY in Lakeview, Mi. January 28, 1883. Leaves wife and 2 children

BRIDGES Edmond Elijah in Prattsburgh, NY February 27, 1883. Born July 3, 1813 only child of Elam and Almira (**ALLIS**) Bridges. Married Sarah Alida **GONSOLUS**, 1 son Elam Allis. Wife died abt 1858 and he later moved to Fenton, Mi. and married Millie **VAN AUKEN**. 1 dau Ella M. now age 18 yrs

MORGAN A. B. formerly of Prattsburgh, NY in Hornellsville, NY February 24, 1883. Served in 107th Reg. NYV. Leaves wife and 2 daus Emma and Mary

WILSON Sarah A. age 64y wife of Edwin in Prattsburgh, NY February 27, 1883. Native of Geddis, NY and came to Prattsburgh age abt 16 yrs. Married September 1842. Leaves husband, 1 son and 3 daus

KIRKPATRICK Elizabeth age 39y wife of James Kirkpatrick and dau of William and Hannah **BRIGLIN** at parent's in Prattsburgh, NY March 5, 1883

TOWNER James Edward age 44y in Prattsburgh, NY March 4, 1883. Born May 18, 1838 in Avoca, NY. Married January 23, 1866 Mrs. Delia **ALLEN**, 3 children

SCOTT Willie R. age 23y at Mother's Mrs. Jane Scott in Bath, NY March 2, 1883

CURTIS Miss Sarah age 48y dau of William B. in Prattsburgh, NY March 14, 1883

RUMSEY Hon. David age 72y in Bath, NY March 12, 1883

PRENTISS John Q. A. age 40y in Pulteney, NY March 16, 1883

TRENCHARD Jane age 40y wife of Frank Trenchard and dau of J. B. **GREEN** of Prattsburgh, NY in Wheeler, NY March 14, 1883. Leaves husband and 5 small children

TERRY Nathan age 87y south of Prattsburgh, NY March 27, 1883. Native of Chester, NJ 1 of 6 children

DOUBLEDAY Estella age 19y 2d at Mother's Mrs. Gavin Doubleday in Italy Hill, NY April 3, 1883

VORHEES Elisha age 38y at parent's in Prattsburgh, NY March 25, 1883

DRAPER Mary age 77y wife of George Draper in Prattsburgh, NY April 10, 1883

WHEELER Fidelia age 62y relict of Silas Wheeler (who died October 1856) at son's C. D. Wheeler in Wheeler, NY April 15, 1883. 4 sons and 1 dau

CURTIS Mrs. Lucy M. age 80y in Prattsburgh, NY May 10, 1883

TINKLEPAW Anna age 83y wife of John Tinklepaw (now age 86y) at dau Mrs. Ezra **BRAMBLE** in Prattsburgh, NY June 2, 1883. Born and married in Otsego, Co. NY and moved to Yates Co. 1850. 5 children 3 living, Mrs. Bramble, Mrs. Martin **SCUTT** and Mrs. John **ROAT** of Jerusalem, NY

WILLIAMS Mandavilla wife of John F. Williams in Prattsburgh, NY June 30, 1883. Born June 15, 1808 nr Auburn, NY nee **BEAMAN**. Married January 15, 1832 in Cayuga Co. and removed to Prattsburgh. Children, H. B. and John W. of Corning, NY, S. Worcester, Chauncey, Mrs. Henry **HORTON** and Charles of Prattsburgh

MIDDLETON Nettie J. dau of J. A. Middleton in Prattsburgh, NY July 22, 1883

MC LEAN George H. age 18y 9m 6d son of Lewis and Eliza Mc Lean in Union City, Pa. July 21, 1883

BROWN David age 87y formerly of Prattsburgh, NY at dau Mrs. J. J. **CHAMPLIN** nr Italy Hill, NY August 3, 1883

NIMS Pomeroy age 74y in Prattsburgh, NY August 8, 1883. Res over 40 yrs

OLMSTEAD James F. age 85y in Wheeler, NY August 22, 1883. Leaves wife, 1 son and 4 daus

ALLEN William S. in Pulteney, NY September 6, 1883. Born September 4, 1824 in Madison Co. NY. Married twice, 1st wife died many years ago. Married (2) September 4, 1854. 1 son and 1 dau living, 1 son died young

HALSEY Peter an old res in Bath, NY September 24, 1883

STRONG Daniel H. age 74y in Prattsburgh, NY October 1, 1883. 1 dau Mrs. J. W. **DE GOLIA** of Grass Valley, Cal.

DEATH NOTICES

SCOTT Robert of Prattsburgh, NY at sister's Mrs. Janette **READ** nr Geneva, NY November 2, 1883. Born 1805 in Rockford, Scotland. Leaves 2 sons and 1 dau

FOSTER Ella L. age 31y wife of Myrvin Foster in Prattsburgh, NY November 7, 1883

PALMER A. D. age 75y at son's Horace Palmer in Wheeler, NY November 24, 1883

MATHEWS H. N. in Wheeler, NY December 22, 1883. Born February 1805 in Dutchess Co. NY and moved to Hector, NY age 1 yr. Age 21y moved to Wheeler and married February 1828 Anna **CROSMON** of Wheeler, 5 children 1 living

GARDNER Elizabeth age 85y at son's William Gardner in Wheeler, NY December 22, 1883. Born 1799 in Pa. oldest child of Phillip and Margaret **MYRTLE**. Married June 17, 1817 Freeman Gardner. 5 sons and 3 daus, eldest son Silas died in Mi. abt 12 yrs ago, Addison, Rebecca and Hattie in Mi., Henry, William, Thomas and Sally of Prattsburgh, NY

PERRY Eva age 75y relict of Solomon Perry at dau Mrs. William **JOHNSON** January 22, 1884. Born Pa. and lived here 54 yrs. 3 sons and 7 daus, 1 son and 4 daus dec. Husband died 1862

OLMSTEAD Harriet (**GONSOLUS**) age 79y of Wheeler, NY at dau Mrs. Daniel **MORGAN** in Howard, NY February 9, 1884. Married March 1822 James Olmstead who died last summer. Leaves 1 son and 4 daus

GALIVAN Joanna wife of Patrick Galivan February 21, 1884. Leaves husband, children, James of Cleveland, Oh., Mrs. Mary **CLAUDIUS** and Daniel of Auburn, NY

TUTHILL Elizabeth age 91y wife of Tyrus Tuthill in Pulteney, NY March 15, 1884

DOWNS Rev. E. C. age 55y 8m 11d in Alexandria, Dakota Terr. March 15, 1884. Born July 4, 1829 in Prattsburgh, NY, moved to Newton Falls, Oh. and married Eliza **REED**. Leaves wife, 5 sons and 1 dau

PARKER Ozias in Pulteney, NY April 3, 1884. Born November 13, 1800 in Whitestown, NY and moved to Pulteney age 12 yrs. Married in his 23rd yr Elizabeth **FRANCIS**, 3 children, R. T., J. S. and Mary E. Wife died October 23, 1832 and he married (2) May 23, 1833 Cynthia **BUTLER**. Their children, Louisa A. (dec) George O. and J. A.

CURTIS Harriet Ann wife of William B. Curtis in Prattsburgh, NY April 7, 1884. Born December 19, 1811 in Ira, NY. Married March 1834, children Sarah who died March 1882, Silliman B., James F. and Mary A.

PARMALEE Rufus age 62y formerly of Prattsburgh, NY in Huron, Oh. April 12, 1884

FRIES William T. from accident while cutting trees May 19, 1884. Born November 20, 1840 in Jerusalem, NY. Enl. Co. I 148th Reg. NYV

CLARK John in Prattsburgh, NY June 6, 1884. Born July 10, 1809 on farm where he died son of John Clark, 2nd of 6 children. Morris died yrs ago, Stephen , Albert, Mrs. Samantha **UPTHEGROVE**, Mrs. Lydia **MERRITT** all living this area. Married March 21, 1833 Phebe Ann **UPTHEGROVE** who died 1844. 2 children Anna wife of William **FISHER** died Rushville, NY 1861, John Jay at home. Married (2) 1858 Jane Black **CLARK** of Geneva, NY who died 1878

HIBBARD Mary age 76y relict of Nathaniel Hibbard in Jerusalem, NY July 19, 1884. Husband died September 1880

MIDDLETON Miss Ida A. age 26y 9m 18d in Prattsburgh, NY August 1, 1884. Born October 23, 1857 in Yates Co. NY

PUTNAM M. A. age 84y relict of Aaron Putnam at son's A. H. August 12, 1884

NEFF Henry age 60y in Prattsburgh, NY August 30, 1884

HAYES Samuel age 92y 2m 10d in Prattsburgh, NY September 8, 1884. Born Hartford Co. Ct. and came to Prattsburgh 1806. Married November 1821 Julia **CURTIS** dau of William P. Curtis, 4 daus, Emma Jane the youngest died age 17 yrs

SQUIRES Phoebe age 82y died September 5, 1884 at son-in-law's Leman **COREY** in Italy Hill, NY

WARFIELD Frances G. in her 40th yr at bro-in-law's Ephraim **MOWERS** in Rushville, NY September 15, 1884. Born March 4, 1845 in Rushville dau of Robert **GREEN**. Married autumn of 1866 Capt. M. F. Warfield

NEALY Mathew age 57y at sister's Mrs. F. E. **TOWLE** in Prattsburgh, NY September 13, 1884

HORTON Thomas age 81y in Prattsburgh, NY September 11, 1884. Born March 1803 in Hector, NY and moved to Pulteney age 3 yrs. Married February 27, 1822 Rachel **LEE** dau of David Lee . She died Tyrone, NY June 18, 1879. Married (2) 1881 Mrs. Rhoda J. **PURINGTON** of Prattsburgh

MORGAN Effie E. age 25y in Prattsburgh, NY October 4, 1884, buried Austinville, Pa.

BRIGLIN Robert age 71y 6m in Ingleside, NY September 24, 1884. Born England and came to US age 4 yrs. Married January 1835 Hannah **COOK** dau of George Cook. Leaves wife and 4 children, George of Prattsburgh, Harrison of Bloods, NY, Mrs. George **SMITH** and Mrs. Alvin **JOHNSON**

SHADER James age 52y 11m 27d in Wheeler, NY October 18, 1884. Born October 21, 1831 in Dutchess Co. NY and came to Wheeler 1851. Leaves wife and 2 children

DENSE Mrs. Urvilla in Durand, Mi. October 16, 1884. Born Pulteney, NY dau of late Luther **PARKER** of Pulteney and widow of James **HORTON** bro of Thomas Horton of Prattsburgh, NY

SURNAME INDEX

ABBEY 93
ABBOTT 38, 206, 228
ABEL 100, 109, 131
ABER 84, 126, 127, 149, 185, 207, 210, 220, 319
ABLE 92
ABRAMS 151, 246
ACKERMAN 294, 303
ACKERSON 136, 352, 356
ACKLEY 31
ADAMS 8, 13, 35, 66, 77, 103, 175, 176, 209, 225, 249, 252, 254, 272, 309
ADDISON 270
ADSHEAD 2
ADSIT 73, 84, 127, 131, 219
AGETT 291
AHERN 157
AIKEN 162
AINSLEY 346
AINSWORTH 32, 45, 53, 78, 81, 98, 129, 136, 147, 345, 347
AKINS 282
ALBEE 32, 33
ALBRO 124
ALDEN 39, 134
ALDERMAN 69, 111, 118
ALDRICH 30, 31, 33, 99, 138, 151, 168, 175, 188, 221
ALDRIDGE 201
ALEXANDER 46
ALGER 209
ALLCOCK 308
ALLEN 16, 18, 21, 32, 72, 79, 90, 91, 111, 118, 125, 133, 134, 146, 148, 151, 174, 192, 207, 211, 214, 223, 247, 334, 345, 349, 351, 354, 356, 357
ALLERTON 115, 132, 169
ALLEY 314
ALLINGTON 17
ALLIS 65, 297, 318, 337, 356
ALLISON 176
ALVORD 120
AMBLER 257
AMES 7, 30, 46
AMEY 253, 314, 315
AMIDON 66
ANDERSON 98, 196, 218, 253, 273, 342
ANDREWS 7, 54, 118, 129, 132, 212, 218, 347
ANDRUS 92, 194
ANGELL 16, 92, 163, 196, 211, 303
ANNABEL 14, 55, 327
ANTHONY 65
ARGUE 283
ARLINGTON 10
ARMSTRONG 122, 130, 157
ARNOLD 32, 75, 103, 131, 222, 233, 346, 352
ARRANCE 224
ARVER 215
ARWIN 196, 200
ASHLEY 207, 327
ASPINWALL 227
ATCHISON 203
ATWATER 97, 243, 280
ATWELL 303
ATWILL 112, 300
ATWOOD 8, 22, 132

AULLS 44, 89, 137, 160, 164, 173, 190, 303, 310, 340
AUSTIN 6, 113, 245, 261, 336, 342, 345
AVERILL 114
AVERY 355
AXTELL 300
AYERS 96, 162, 194, 224
AYLER 162
BABCOCK 10, 20, 53, 57, 73, 81, 108, 184, 222, 228, 248, 284, 309, 331, 347, 351, 353
BACHMAN 8, 49, 77, 97, 102, 108
BACON 44
BADEAU 130
BADGER 3, 172, 182, 215, 222, 250, 315
BAGENSTOCK 184
BAILEY 15, 67, 72, 83, 98, 104, 117, 124, 147, 158, 173, 190, 199, 221, 239, 247, 255, 297, 300, 302, 304, 306, 309
BAIN 84
BAINBRIDGE 256
BAKER 29, 38, 50, 99, 119, 122, 151, 152, 154, 167, 180, 184, 206, 210, 231, 238, 246, 259, 268, 272, 275, 279, 281, 294, 299, 304, 306, 313, 331, 333, 353
BALCH 31
BALCOM 10, 201, 290
BALDWIN 4, 5, 16, 24, 35, 72, 122, 141, 144, 153, 171, 228, 232, 255, 336, 352
BALL 131, 302, 340
BALLARD 159, 302, 310
BALLOU 194, 322
BANCROFT 229
BANES 248
BANKS 196, 247
BANTA 347, 352
BARBER 16, 24, 169, 193, 219, 238, 245, 251, 260, 262, 317, 332, 333
BARDEEN 339
BARDEN 76, 133
BARKALOW 221
BARKER 33, 131, 229, 347
BARNARD 3, 75, 247, 268, 282, 304
BARNED 173, 262
BARNES 97, 141, 152, 209, 276, 277, 321, 334
BARNEY 31, 42, 58, 69, 85, 103, 138, 142, 157, 268, 320, 325, 339
BARNUM 59, 154
BARR 200
BARREN 7
BARRETT 12, 39, 200, 285, 303
BARROWS 189
BARRY 33
BARSE 14
BARTHOLOMEW 61, 190
BARTLETT 84, 171, 290, 339
BARTO 87
BARTON 36, 37, 56, 70, 94, 135, 146, 157, 172, 192, 193, 293, 303
BASSETT 134, 213, 231, 334
BATCHELDER 45, 159, 161, 211
BATCHELOR 171, 204
BATES 4, 120, 174, 196, 216, 322
BATT 203
BATY 138

BAUDER 145
BAULCH 162
BAUMGARTEN 192
BAUTER 177
BAXTER 3, 157, 163, 285, 327
BAYMAN 94
BEACH 3, 299
BEAMAN 50, 337, 357
BEAN 38
BEARD 19, 179, 230, 233, 247
BEARDSLEY 10, 240, 290
BEATON 304, 309
BEATTIE 317
BEATY 161
BECHTOL 2, 24, 321
BECKWITH 47, 49, 124, 143, 184, 316
BEDELL 173, 355
BEDIENT 194
BEEBE 217, 252, 333
BEECHER 77, 260
BEEMAN 2, 20, 119, 248
BEERS 14, 121
BEGOLE 72
BELDEN 22, 87
BELDING 253
BELL 57, 63, 116, 138, 156, 245, 263, 295, 354
BELLIS 342, 350, 351
BELLOWS 57, 302, 349
BELYEA 17
BEMENT 273
BEMIS 7
BENDRICK 333
BENEDICT 18, 213, 347
BENEWAY 218
BENHAM 111, 299, 301, 306, 308
BENJAMIN 69, 73, 82, 109, 249, 316
BENNER 301
BENNETT 50, 51, 141, 155, 171, 186, 191, 195, 197, 202, 210, 214, 217, 219, 231, 277, 313, 318, 324, 334, 336
BENNITT 293, 304
BENT 162
BENTLEY 94, 258
BENTON 57, 70, 77, 144, 178, 179, 204, 337, 340
BERNS 137
BERRY 200, 235, 266, 281
BERTINE 58
BESLEY 70
BESS 202
BESSEE 29, 216
BESSIL 158
BEST 331
BEULL 86
BEVERLY 160
BEYER 156
BEZENT 215
BIDWELL 40, 54, 62, 64, 72, 79, 81, 83, 88, 101, 102, 142, 219
BIERCE 218
BIERLY 16
BIGELOW 277
BILES 56, 79, 120
BILLINGHURST 271
BILLINGS 50, 195, 229
BILLINGTON 97
BILLSON 151, 191
BIRDSALL 9, 32, 43, 265, 277, 293

SURNAME INDEX

BIRDSEYE 135
BIRGE 194
BISHOP 9, 43, 178, 188, 210, 221, 236, 248, 264, 274, 281, 315
BIXBY 22, 80, 109, 269, 327
BLACK 53, 57, 100, 121, 135, 142, 303
BLACKWEDE 332
BLAIR 49
BLAKE 132
BLAKESLEE 34, 35, 110, 154, 249, 348
BLANCHARD 256
BLISS 7, 19, 213
BLIVEN 183, 285, 315
BLODGETT 350
BLOOD 38, 41, 52, 59, 67, 68, 83, 101, 344
BLOOMER 340, 355
BLUTE 223
BLY 26
BLYN 118
BODINE 67, 156, 323
BOGARDUS 92, 112, 279
BOGART 22, 284
BOHANAN 348
BOMBARD 296
BOND 116
BONHAM 19, 38, 78, 87, 97, 98, 151, 250, 258, 288, 291, 298
BONIFIELD 17
BONNETT 15
BONNEY 170, 337
BOOM 25
BOOTH 31, 186, 319
BORDEN 14, 20, 56, 86, 105, 337, 340
BORROUGHS 201
BORST 191, 274
BOSARD 21
BOSENBARK 187
BOSS 343
BOSTON 330
BOSTWICK 7, 23, 66, 79, 81, 225, 251
BOUGHTON 152, 224, 325
BOUTEN 116
BOWEN 29, 76, 156, 193
BOWERS 291
BOWES 188, 190, 308
BOWLBY 63, 86, 104, 154
BOYCE 204
BOYD 12, 42, 75, 132, 169, 173, 185, 199, 257, 274, 301, 303, 305, 318
BOYER 161, 235
BOYNTON 322
BOZZARD 123
BRACE 29, 57, 88, 167
BRADLEY 56, 83, 143, 159, 227, 249, 253, 305, 310, 348
BRADY 14, 31, 135, 159, 325
BRAINARD 228
BRAMBLE 170, 202, 346, 357
BRANNON 110
BRASTED 111, 218, 221
BRECK 65, 84, 99, 104, 153
BREES 27, 245, 248
BREWSTER 27, 144, 180
BRICK 209
BRIDGEMAN 50, 287
BRIDGES 77, 82, 94, 356

BRIER 213
BRIGDEN 225, 246
BRIGGS 166, 179, 197, 212, 232, 324, 334
BRIGHAM 126, 133, 346
BRIGLIN 356, 359
BRINK 62, 117, 124, 136, 146, 170, 250, 290, 306, 353
BRINKERHOFF 43
BRISCOE 141
BROADHEAD 113
BROCKWAY 341, 356
BRODERICK 313
BRONG 218, 257
BRONSON 29, 88, 100, 308, 325
BROOKHART 304
BROOKS 1, 5, 20, 65, 117, 136, 165, 235, 272
BROTHER 82, 116, 190
BROTHERTON 170, 202
BROTZMAN 19
BROWER 129, 280
BROWN 4, 6, 7, 17, 19, 23, 25, 26, 30, 34, 36, 38, 39, 58, 74, 94, 96, 108, 111, 113, 114, 121, 139, 147, 148, 157, 159, 166, 172, 173, 190-192, 197-199, 212, 214, 216, 222, 241, 244, 248, 249, 253, 256, 258, 268, 273, 275, 279, 282, 285-287, 289, 295, 302, 306, 307, 311, 315, 322, 327, 333, 335, 340, 351, 352, 357
BROWNE 236
BROWNELL 101, 141, 213, 339, 340
BRUCE 75, 350
BRUNDAGE 42, 102, 123, 129, 135, 136, 138, 140, 143, 144, 179, 183, 184, 195, 216, 242, 293, 294, 296, 298-300, 302-305, 308, 320
BRUSH 350
BRUSS 85
BRYAN 49, 101, 175
BRYANT 24, 97, 104, 157, 173, 217, 325
BUCHER 283
BUCK 27, 165, 207, 221, 270, 313
BUCKLEY 23, 231
BULL 48, 76, 89, 90, 107, 114, 120, 139, 161, 170, 212
BULLARD 87, 172, 241
BULLIS 194
BULLOCK 11, 323
BUMP 12, 283, 326
BUNDY 83, 88, 232, 243, 282
BUNKER 286
BUNN 217
BUNT 263
BURCH 107
BURCHFIELD 343
BURDEN 178
BURDETT 191
BURDICK 31, 152, 171, 204, 243, 318, 327, 333, 334
BURGER 351
BURGESS 119, 252
BURGHER 42
BURKE 35, 80, 143
BURKET 62
BURLEY 61, 242, 244, 330
BURLINGAME 169, 201
BURLINGHAM 312

BURNAP 271
BURNHAM 22, 69, 207
BURNS 150, 186, 282
BURNSIDE 20, 32, 43, 53, 189
BURR 51, 238
BURRELL 154, 320
BURRIS 327
BURROWS 98, 332
BURT 227, 281, 286, 326
BURTON 103, 345, 356
BUSH 43, 51, 151, 169, 355
BUSHNELL 120, 126, 128, 137
BUTCHER 265
BUTLER 50, 51, 116, 117, 124, 125, 134, 156, 159, 280, 284, 297, 329, 358
BUTTOLPH 233
BUTTON 216
BUTTS 148
BYNDERS 132
CABLE 333
CAHILL 198, 213
CAIG 349
CALKINS 41, 81, 85, 105, 110, 118, 146, 222, 227, 228, 234, 245, 252, 277, 287, 290, 298, 316
CALL 210, 211
CALLAHAN 158, 333
CALLANAN 146
CAMERON 44, 48, 49, 55, 58, 126, 143, 190, 204, 298, 304, 306, 308, 319
CAMPBELL 23, 58, 60-62, 69, 88, 110, 127, 140-142, 146, 147, 155, 163, 180, 185, 190, 218, 220, 257, 273, 274, 325
CAMPEN 168
CANFIELD 191, 334
CAPEL 342
CAPRON 266, 279
CARD 196, 236, 283
CARHART 343
CARLEY 155
CARMAN 293
CARPENTER 20, 22, 25, 31, 71, 103, 112, 123, 125, 145, 170, 220, 226, 228, 320, 328, 337, 341, 349, 350, 353
CARR 6, 12, 16, 144, 171, 174, 193, 260, 270, 293, 297, 306, 309, 337, 350
CARRIER 174
CARRINGTON 117, 125, 213, 325
CARROLL 191
CARTER 62, 78, 94, 135, 144, 156, 158, 163, 207, 274, 282, 324, 338, 349
CARUTHERS 63
CARVER 279
CASE 95, 182, 233, 294, 316, 322
CASS 23, 235, 246
CASSON 30
CASTERLINE 303
CASTLE 31, 260
CASTOR 192, 276, 343, 353
CAULKINS 156
CAVENER 93
CAWARD 344, 345
CHADWICK 61, 263, 318
CHALMERS 352
CHAMBERLAIN 40, 54, 61, 62, 70,

113, 141, 206, 210
CHAMPLAIN 291
CHAMPLIN 117, 157, 292, 357
CHAPHE 238
CHAPIN 51, 69, 76, 80, 84, 125, 126, 294, 346
CHAPMAN 27, 67, 72, 159, 213, 244, 247, 296, 314, 317, 348
CHAPPELL 346, 354
CHARLES 201
CHARLESWORTH 99, 190
CHASE 18, 83, 102, 128, 130, 134, 141, 203, 214, 246, 298, 300, 305
CHATFIELD 20, 243, 267
CHATMAN 283
CHEESBROUGH 317
CHENEY 78, 113, 119, 127, 136, 138, 341
CHICHESTER 72, 101, 139, 294
CHIDESTER 234, 250, 265
CHILDON 46
CHILDS 46, 209
CHISM 299
CHISSOM 157, 295, 307, 355
CHITTICK 180, 188, 336
CHRISCATON 209
CHRISTIAN 31, 150, 156, 268
CHURCH 34, 87, 91-93, 101, 165, 170, 176, 184-186, 195, 203, 301, 311
CINCEBOX 294
CLAPP 189
CLARK 11, 20, 25, 48, 49, 54, 59, 63, 74, 78, 79, 83, 102, 104, 110, 119, 122, 125, 133, 149, 158, 166, 171, 172, 177, 178, 191, 192, 198, 202, 210, 218, 222, 225, 237, 244, 246, 250, 256, 260, 261, 278, 285, 288-290, 297, 300, 304, 307, 310, 315, 316, 317, 337, 338, 343, 346, 348, 350, 351, 353, 358, 359
CLARKE 67, 228, 245
CLAUDIUS 358
CLAUHARTY 278
CLAWSON 91
CLAYSON 352
CLEAVELAND 244
CLEAVER 246
CLEEVER 234
CLEMENT 90, 91, 211, 214, 219
CLEMMONS 29
CLEVELAND 59, 64, 173, 206
CLINTON 8, 31
CLISBE 49
CLISDELL 165, 259
CLIZBE 39, 66
CLOONEY 180
CLUTE 30, 249
COATS 86
COBB 285, 291
COBURN 4, 8, 26, 124, 259
COCHRANE 169, 253
COE 159, 288, 299
COFFMAN 46
COGSWELL 300, 305
COHN 31, 205
COKE 248
COLBATH 205
COLBERT 25
COLBURN 19, 234
COLBY 269

COLCORD 58
COLE 33, 41, 43, 60, 90, 92, 124, 152, 159, 162, 186, 190, 191, 193, 214, 221, 273, 274, 280, 282, 285, 310, 327, 354
COLEGROVE 333, 337, 340
COLGAN 126
COLLAR 326
COLLIER 68, 89, 100, 110, 115, 130, 141, 142, 335
COLLINS 64, 147, 155, 178, 199, 352
COLLYER 52
COLVIN 7, 17, 28, 210
COLWELL 4
COMFORT 281
COMPTON 56, 109, 129, 142
COMSTOCK 40, 95, 109, 251, 304, 309
CONDERMAN 111, 138, 174, 292, 328
CONE 113
CONGDON 7, 236
CONGER 294, 304
CONINE 354
CONKEY 209, 219
CONKIE 257
CONKLIN 115, 183
CONNEL 223
CONNELLY 10, 303
CONNER 126
CONNON 304
CONNOR 36, 56
CONNORS 173
CONROY 251
CONTARANAN 40
CONWAY 94
COOK 5, 26, 37, 40, 56, 61, 71, 80, 81, 83, 106, 109, 112, 115, 142, 152, 153, 160, 179, 203, 209, 211, 215, 237, 337, 339, 340, 346, 359
COOKE 240, 342
COOLEY 12, 30, 244, 329
COON 17, 24, 249, 279, 318, 324, 328, 331
COOPER 3, 63, 64, 66, 70, 85, 89, 96, 105, 127, 158, 169, 209, 232, 237, 239, 265, 269, 275, 278, 287, 317, 356
CORBIN 200, 243
CORBITT 92, 95
CORCKRAN 205
COREY 166, 349, 359
CORKINS 30
CORN 315
CORNELIUS 330
CORNELL 27, 50, 77, 81, 120, 154
CORNELLSON 249
CORNISH 220
CORNWELL 23, 154
CORSON 198, 351
CORTWRIGHT 234
CORY 155, 320
CORYELL 149, 184, 220, 300, 316
COSO 20
COSS 6, 71, 159, 161
COTTON 39, 48, 66, 88, 133, 165, 298, 302, 349
COUCH 229
COULTRY 329
COUNTRYMAN 20
COURTNEY 115

COURTWRIGHT 222
COVELL 29, 80, 174, 224, 237, 241, 294, 297, 341
COVENHOVEN 107, 287, 297
COVERT 80, 158, 161, 293, 316
COWAN 271
COWEN 14
COWING 337
COWLEY 10, 22, 240
COX 270
COYE 330
COYKENDALL 332
COYLE 325
CRABB 349, 350, 353
CRAFT 5, 336
CRAGAN 142
CRAIKS 123
CRAM 18, 28
CRAMER 183, 194
CRAMPTON 279
CRANCE 30, 202
CRANDALL 30, 73, 104, 190, 212, 334
CRANE 13, 20, 21, 33, 104, 131, 204, 209
CRANMER 159
CRANSTON 300
CRAWFORD 28, 32, 46, 127, 160, 170, 193, 203, 207, 257, 303, 309
CRETSLEY 237
CRIDDLE 269
CRITTENDEN 143, 253
CROCKER 68, 86, 96
CROFT 24
CROMBIE 274
CRONAN 117
CRONK 170
CROOKS 138
CROOKSTON 123, 302
CROSBY 88, 96, 130, 208, 211, 217, 267, 273
CROSMON 358
CROSS 134, 163, 193, 208, 214, 216, 239, 315
CROSSMAN 319
CROUCH 43, 60, 167
CROW 198, 322
CRUGER 47, 191, 219
CRULL 219
CRUTHERS 188
CULBERTSON 319
CULLINAN 321
CULVER 129, 181, 303
CUMMINGS 102, 146
CUMMINS 270
CUMPSTON 225, 227, 261
CUNNINGHAM 220, 227, 249, 277
CURRAN 121, 268, 273
CURRY 189, 314
CURTIS 4, 16, 20, 26, 28, 52, 64, 95, 96, 113, 123, 152, 178, 183-185, 188, 212, 222, 252, 276, 307, 342, 346, 350, 354, 356, 357, 358, 359
CUSHING 187
CUTLER 9, 252, 315, 317
DABOLL 57, 91, 191, 350
DAGGETT 46
DAILEY 96, 221
DALRYMPLE 302, 310
DALY 181, 198
DAMOTH 294, 299

SURNAME INDEX

DANFORTH 15
DANIELS 14, 38, 55, 90, 93, 96, 145, 146, 175, 289, 312, 330
DANNALS 132
DARLING 8, 218, 312
DARRIN 28, 53, 152, 262, 287
DARROW 90
DATES 12, 232
DAVENPORT 23, 58, 89, 121, 131, 204, 209, 230, 242, 259, 291, 292, 299, 306, 314, 335, 351
DAVIDSON 11, 21, 67
DAVIS 12, 25, 41, 89, 99, 128, 131, 144, 164, 182, 187, 214, 216, 220, 224, 225, 227, 228, 232, 234, 241, 251, 259-261, 273, 275, 276, 278, 282, 284, 289, 304, 311, 322, 327, 328, 348
DAVISON 107, 118, 145, 149, 163, 165, 181, 193, 210, 227, 228, 263, 332
DAWSON 21, 28, 61, 70, 72, 90, 118, 148, 175, 202, 324
DAY 59, 180, 335
DE CAY 117
DE FOREST 93
DE GOLIA 337, 357
DE GRAFF 180
DE GRAW 17, 308
DE HAAN 237
DE HUNTER 19
DE KAY 348
DE PEW 292, 293, 298, 300, 303, 309, 311, 340, 345
DE PUY 121, 143, 144, 292
DE PUYSTER 164
DE WITT 71, 159, 192, 242, 251, 320
DE WOLF 199, 265, 280
DE WOLFE 141
DEAN 108, 251, 353
DEARMAN 231, 257
DEBARBIERI 199
DECATUR 331
DECK 6
DECKER 61, 66, 134, 153, 297, 302, 311
DELAMATER 11, 274
DELANCY 324
DELEVAN 52, 131
DEMAREST 144, 147
DEMERY 325
DEMING 195, 251
DENNIS 13, 34, 79, 163, 171, 193, 204, 233, 313, 317, 322
DENNISON 291
DENNISTON 106, 115, 184, 347
DENSE 109, 359
DENTON 80, 120, 237, 238, 241, 247, 271, 273
DERENBECKER 312
DERRICK 338
DEUEL 130
DEUER 343
DEUERLEIN 204, 284
DEVORE 207, 210, 274
DEWEY 220
DEXTER 181, 211, 329
DEY 52
DEYO 192, 264, 265
DIBBLE 187
DICKERSON 1

DICKESON 295
DICKEY 116, 129, 197, 332
DICKINSON 15, 24, 40, 44, 67, 81, 114, 140, 176, 272, 286
DIDAS 208
DILDINE 72, 296, 306, 307, 317
DILLAYE 32
DILLENBACK 124
DILLON 229
DIMMICK 130, 160, 220
DIMON 211, 301
DINEHART 356
DINGMAN 26
DINNIN 249
DIVEN 139, 209, 212, 220
DIVINE 52
DOBBS 62
DODGE 66, 97, 110, 246, 251, 260, 282, 326
DOLBY 70
DOLLY 66
DOLOHERY 322, 328
DOLPH 20, 87
DOLSON 299
DONAHE 34, 37, 77, 104, 146
DONALDSON 354
DONLON 313, 331
DONNELLY 215, 301
DONOVAN 182, 223
DOOLITTLE 47
DOORLEY 313
DORR 65, 72, 316
DORSEY 59, 136
DOTY 37, 138, 188, 241, 310, 318, 331
DOUBLEDAY 106, 355, 357
DOUBTY 217
DOUD 2, 344
DOUGHERTY 323
DOUGHTY 102, 121
DOUGLAS 172, 283, 285
DOW 19, 288
DOWDELL 161
DOWERS 223
DOWNEY 68
DOWNING 234
DOWNS 256, 342, 358
DRAKE 8, 11, 68, 74, 82, 90, 97, 141, 187, 195, 200, 217, 231, 322, 338
DRAPER 157, 357
DREW 16, 292, 296, 301, 307, 353, 354
DRISCOLL 25
DRUMMOND 245
DRYER 85
DU BOIS 199, 215
DUDLEY 1, 16, 35, 41, 55, 76, 78, 79, 85, 86, 102, 119, 132, 135, 138, 139, 145, 146, 169, 230, 263, 279
DUGAN 348
DUNAVON 161
DUNCAN 321
DUNHAM 24, 174, 333
DUNN 4, 25, 30, 94, 170, 196, 223, 237, 241, 303
DUNNIGAN 213
DUNNING 76, 255, 293, 297, 320, 348
DUNTON 126
DURAND 10, 247
DURFY 112, 117
DURHAM 105, 149, 254

DURKEY 213
DUSENBERRY 185
DUTCHER 90, 165, 187, 212, 256
DUTTON 252, 258
DUVALL 274
DWYER 199, 257
DYER 203, 225, 239, 248, 251
DYGERT 37, 155, 320
DYKE 131
DYKEMAN 42
DYKERMAN 298
EARLEY 337, 343, 348
EARLL 160
EARLY 33, 122
EARNEST 125, 151, 351
EASLING 268, 328
EASON 11, 64, 166, 205
EASTERBROOKS 278
EATON 10, 32, 64, 65, 252, 302
EAVENS 165
ECCLES 334
ECTANOCKER 291
EDDY 49, 152, 185, 348
EDGAR 229, 256, 313
EDGER 157
EDGETT 29, 158, 178, 191
EDMINSTER 15, 285
EDMONDS 142
EDSALL 73
EDSON 152, 192, 338, 339
EDWARDS 19, 37, 40, 47, 54, 58, 75, 86, 98, 117, 118, 145, 162, 184, 251, 273, 278, 333, 337
EGAN 236, 318
EGBERT 34, 233, 243
EGGLESTON 148, 292, 298, 303
EICH 322
EIGHALTZ 180
ELDRED 46
ELDRIDGE 7, 8
ELEANDER 245
ELLAS 47, 50, 74, 84, 104, 115, 120, 145, 149, 179
ELLIOTT 247
ELLIS 45, 66, 95, 136, 137, 142, 167, 287, 296, 305, 309
ELLISON 164, 166, 215, 264, 270
ELLSWORTH 139, 199, 352
ELMENDORPH 101
ELMER 18, 31
ELWELL 172, 235
ELY 264, 342
EMERSON 29, 51, 64, 66, 112, 129, 135, 137, 142, 165, 177, 338
EMERY 137, 328
EMMONS 238, 261, 291
EMPIE 262
EMS 162
ENGLISH 252, 266, 349, 350
ENSIGN 31
ERNEST 248
ERSKINE 177
ERWAY 40
ERWIN 36, 42, 51, 55, 93, 105, 143, 185, 204, 217, 251, 264, 282, 286, 292
ETHERIDGE 260
EVANS 39, 69, 107, 231, 258, 330
EVELETH 283
EVERETT 162
EVERSON 14, 143

EVERT 27
EVERTS 27, 254
EWING 171
FAILING 200
FAIRBANKS 7, 154, 316
FAIRCHILD 137, 296, 298, 307, 308
FAIRFIELD 355
FAIRMAN 24, 242, 259
FALLS 127
FANNING 258
FANROTE 332
FANTON 264
FARGO 124, 132, 139, 170, 336, 353
FARGUHARSON 216
FARLEY 197
FARNHAM 10, 42, 60, 222
FARR 140, 183, 234, 236, 252
FARRAR 263
FARRINGTON 13, 250
FARRON 104
FARWELL 9, 159, 160, 235, 278
FASSETT 8, 258
FAUCETT 110, 135, 147, 150, 166, 167, 173, 175, 293, 303
FAULKNER 38, 51, 71, 72, 85, 94, 103, 108, 115, 122, 130, 150, 193, 201, 207, 305
FAWCETT 95
FAY 36, 94, 120, 128, 141, 234, 245
FELLOWS 139, 150, 235, 285
FENN 178
FENTON 9, 207, 277
FERENBAUGH 33, 219, 228, 252, 253, 257, 278
FERGUSON 212, 223, 303, 350
FERO 224
FERRIS 69, 99, 194
FERROW 16
FERRY 284
FIELD 10, 166, 167, 206, 288
FILKINS 195
FINCH 13, 116, 118, 120, 179, 309, 332
FINK 255
FINN 278
FINNICAN 22
FISH 193
FISHER 9, 64, 171, 211, 317, 359
FISK 29, 69, 112
FITCH 144, 183, 278
FITZGERALD 323
FITZGIBBONS 201
FITZHUGH 71
FITZPATRICK 260, 271
FLEET 42
FLEMING 108
FLETCHER 112, 127, 178
FLINT 183, 315
FLOHR 196
FLUENT 43, 65, 230
FLYNN 9, 118, 125, 149, 150, 304, 337, 352
FOGLE 168
FOLSOM 140, 310
FOLWELL 256
FONDA 34
FOOTE 219
FORBES 42
FORCE 177
FORD 30, 64, 66, 76, 110, 146, 191, 200, 219, 228, 237, 248, 316, 326,

329, 331, 352
FORGUS 160
FORRESTER 152, 213, 316
FORT 161
FORTNER 157
FOSS 83, 172, 343
FOSTER 173, 234, 283, 284, 313, 334, 348, 349, 354, 358
FOWLER 53, 55, 85, 90, 106, 117, 259, 354
FOX 203, 224, 254, 265, 280, 335
FRACE 84
FRANCE 184, 207, 216
FRANCIS 61, 354, 358
FRANCISCO 268
FRANEY 209
FRANKLIN 39, 53, 66, 67
FRASER 236
FRASHER 113
FREEBORN 198, 199, 210, 212
FREEMAN 61, 125, 133, 138, 230, 269, 270
FREER 230
FRENCH 47, 74, 83, 87, 105, 111, 116, 176, 180, 184, 187, 213, 275, 293, 301, 303, 312, 341
FREY 292, 300, 305
FRIDLEY 254, 335
FRIES 358
FRINK 64, 149, 179
FRISBEE 207
FRONK 152
FROST 67, 158, 230, 282
FRY 99, 101, 122, 235
FRYE 161
FRYMIRE 10, 287, 289
FULFORD 2
FULKERSON 23
FULLER 85, 229, 232, 233, 239, 251, 272, 278, 283, 298, 304, 342, 345, 355
FULSOM 136, 292
FULTON 214
FULTS 195, 332
FULTZ 26
GALIVAN 358
GALLAGHER 326
GALPIN 325
GAMBLE 79, 142
GANBY 181
GANSEVOORT 14, 36, 49, 60, 81, 83, 121, 135, 163, 178, 181
GANTROP 158
GARDNER 37, 69, 73, 80, 91, 98, 108, 204, 225, 227, 228, 243, 245, 250, 257, 262, 280, 289, 292, 301, 311, 320, 358
GAREY 187, 307
GARLINGHOUSE 132, 294, 300, 302, 332
GARMAN 163
GARRETT 33
GARRISON 130, 197, 310, 331, 351
GARROW 55
GASS 293
GATES 156, 168, 192, 211, 296, 324, 328, 337
GAY 56, 175
GAYLORD 3, 73, 253, 259, 262, 283
GEER 198
GELDER 300, 347, 354

GENUNG 32, 150, 262, 269, 282, 298, 349
GEORGE 312
GERMAN 51
GERRY 137
GIACOMO 288
GIBBONS 27
GIBBS 33, 80, 177, 183, 196, 316, 321
GIBSON 13, 20, 191, 264, 268, 283, 289, 293
GIFFIN 299, 304
GIFFORD 168, 228, 241, 264, 265
GILBERT 60, 110, 143, 166, 172, 225, 228, 244, 249, 250, 256, 263, 277, 280, 291, 309, 348
GILCHRIST 81, 91, 325, 326
GILDERSLEEVE 137, 246, 255, 269
GILES 1, 74, 235
GILL 223
GILLETT 9, 25, 38, 139, 140, 185, 226, 264, 274, 279, 285, 319
GILLETTE 308
GILLINS 263
GILMORE 52, 114, 139, 300, 306, 307
GILSTON 62
GITHLER 180
GIVENS 181
GLANN 303
GLASS 41, 50, 55, 58, 64
GLAZIER 312
GLEASON 160, 186, 302, 305
GLEN 46
GLENN 61, 62
GLOAD 64, 316, 344, 355
GLOVER 160
GLUE 267
GLUR 248
GOBLE 35, 150, 295
GOFF 48, 167, 179, 196, 215, 309, 328
GOLDY 259
GONSOLUS 79, 356, 358
GOODENOUGH 235
GOODMAN 326
GOODNO 332
GOODRICH 57, 63, 68, 207, 263, 322, 328
GOODSELL 56, 90, 91, 95, 119, 120, 162, 185, 196, 286
GOODSPEED 299
GOODWIN 28, 75, 250, 318
GORDON 79, 100, 124, 160, 199
GORHAM 329, 330, 334
GORMAN 26
GORTON 11, 21, 150, 160, 228-231, 237, 241, 242, 248, 254-258, 261, 265, 267, 273, 275, 282, 290, 329
GOSS 25
GOULD 23, 41, 52, 65, 92, 103, 130, 161, 165, 177, 340
GRACE 40
GRAHAM 13, 24, 26, 43, 44, 77, 102, 134, 138, 140, 157, 222, 347
GRAMES 202, 205
GRANGE 329
GRANGER 153, 181, 220, 221, 224, 318
GRANNIS 297, 304
GRANT 86, 111, 117, 120, 239, 264,

SURNAME INDEX

269, 308, 309
GRAVES 33, 39, 47, 66, 84, 91, 106, 120, 132, 155, 184, 234, 286, 287, 289, 339, 345, 346, 355, 356
GRAY 12, 139, 173, 176, 186, 207, 239, 255, 299, 306, 324, 335, 342
GREEK 17, 18, 28
GREEN 9, 119, 127, 176, 184, 185, 214, 218, 232, 245, 281, 315, 357, 359
GREENHOW 29
GREENMAN 233
GREES 309
GREGG 57, 100, 136, 144, 229, 319
GREGORY 10, 46, 49, 228, 267, 270, 277, 294, 346
GRENELL 22
GRIDLEY 3, 260, 264, 272
GRIEF 186, 334
GRIFFIN 185
GRIFFITH 81, 124, 127
GRIFFITHS 8, 24
GRIGGS 186, 218
GRINOLDS 46, 201
GRISWOLD 4, 11, 18, 319
GROFF 213
GROGAN 200
GROSS 317, 328
GUERNSEY 176
GUEST 80
GUILE 120
GUINNIP 16, 17, 126
GUION 223
GULICK 238, 341, 355
GULLIVER 153
GULWITE 109
GUNN 166, 193, 218
GUNSOLUS 55
GUSTIN 89, 90, 104, 119
GUYON 60, 206
HAASE 304
HABER 165
HACKETT 217
HADDEN 121, 148, 309
HADLEY 59, 328
HAGADORN 107
HAHN 112
HAIGHT 141, 159, 246, 300, 353
HAINES 262
HAIRE 20, 28, 203
HALE 243
HALEY 193
HALL 27, 44, 46, 51, 54, 60, 61, 140, 150, 182, 224, 241, 250, 308, 310, 341
HALLENBECK 189
HALLETT 14, 33, 123, 146, 152, 166, 198, 201, 208, 211, 212, 219, 220, 269, 295, 300, 324, 326
HALLIDAY 44, 79, 176, 197
HALLOCK 70-72, 121, 141, 153, 168, 183
HALSEY 76, 108, 120, 175, 211, 309, 357
HAMILTON 10, 61, 66, 81, 229
HAMLIN 268, 356
HAMMELL 296
HAMMOND 55, 153, 174, 294, 307, 321
HAMPTON 50
HAND 146, 147, 322

HANDEE 11
HANFORD 94, 145, 241
HANKS 42, 45, 50, 60, 61, 71, 320
HANNA 48, 192, 236
HANNABERGER 307
HANNAN 179
HANRAHAN 200
HANSON 340
HANWELL 257
HARADON 265, 287
HARD 172
HARDEN 30, 189
HARDENBROOK 123, 176
HARDENBURGH 227, 251
HARDER 21, 172
HARDING 40
HARE 159, 180, 271, 346, 354
HARFORD 4, 12
HARING 72, 261
HARKINSON 38
HARMON 350
HARRADAN 140
HARRINGTON 170, 213, 215, 289, 301, 312
HARRIS 11, 65, 114, 167, 174, 205, 210, 212, 217, 269, 293, 321, 338, 351
HARRISON 14, 37, 48, 166, 187, 244, 316
HARROWER 44, 63, 67, 78, 79, 84, 87, 91, 92, 101, 126, 189, 225, 237
HART 39, 110, 235, 264, 312, 315
HARTRUM 191
HARTSHORN 34, 67, 318
HARTWELL 61
HARTY 159, 331
HARVEY 33, 189
HARWOOD 169
HASELBAUER 288
HASKINS 171, 334
HASTINGS 41, 75, 94, 153, 294, 310
HATCH 15, 159, 204, 208, 220, 226, 249, 256
HATHAWAY 15, 32, 57, 187, 188, 217, 266, 272, 314, 331
HATMAKER 234
HATTER 117
HAUBER 160
HAUGHEY 305
HAUSE 53
HAVENS 13, 94, 148, 163, 192, 245, 250, 254, 265, 276, 278, 288, 343
HAVERLING 45, 49, 98, 150
HAVILAND 247
HAWKINS 13, 130, 189, 310
HAWLEY 231, 241, 243, 255, 277, 292, 301, 312, 313
HAYES 45, 72, 86, 97, 107, 169, 198, 221, 281, 317, 327, 336, 337, 339, 354, 359
HAYNES 28
HAYT 65, 98, 208, 227, 230-232, 246, 253, 255, 269, 270, 279
HAZEN 238
HAZLETON 234
HEAD 32, 149
HEALY 289, 317, 318
HEATH 170, 253
HEATHERMAN 334
HECKMAN 14, 133, 208, 251
HEDERMAN 168

HEDGES 170, 195, 209, 224, 311
HEERMANS 206, 279
HEES 109, 134, 135, 141, 171
HEFFERMAN 292
HEGGIE 266
HELLER 12
HELM 68, 71
HELMER 24, 38, 169
HELMS 232
HELSKER 299
HEMINGWAY 12, 192
HEMLEY 18
HEMMENWAY 3, 50
HEMPSTEAD 340
HEMPSTED 44, 46, 55, 148
HENDERSCHOTT 151, 241
HENDERSON 3, 19, 155, 298, 299
HENDRICK 167, 262
HENDRYX 83
HENDY 215
HENECA 190
HENESSEY 332
HENRY 42, 109, 118, 183, 214, 219, 315
HENSLEY 43
HERALD 206
HERKIMER 61
HERRICK 46, 48, 72, 157, 158, 258, 270, 279, 327, 349
HERRINGTON 31, 224, 226, 262, 269
HERRON 99
HESS 36, 79, 85, 87, 90, 92, 103, 123, 131, 134, 139, 164, 177, 181, 197
HEWLETT 288
HEYSHAM 32
HIBBARD 332, 350, 359
HICKEY 323, 327
HICKOK 28, 114, 115, 169
HICKS 101, 237
HIGBEE 311
HIGBY 338, 340
HIGGINS 11, 35, 54, 59, 74, 80, 93, 100, 155, 178, 179, 195, 204, 257
HIGLEY 1
HIGMAN 151
HILER 352
HILGERS 156, 324
HILL 7, 12, 20, 23, 34, 71, 111, 120, 125, 129, 143, 150, 155, 169, 183, 189, 197, 233, 256, 269, 285, 286, 296, 321, 339, 344, 349, 354
HILLECK 229
HILLS 342
HILTON 97, 168, 266
HINCKLEY 21, 205
HINES 321
HITCHCOCK 163
HITE 321
HOAG 245
HOAGLAND 86, 140, 153, 182, 206, 215, 293, 305, 317
HOAGUE 27
HOAR 151
HOBER 13
HODGE 71, 195
HODGEKIN 281, 291
HODGEMAN 86, 119, 129, 201
HODSKINS 247, 273
HOES 180, 342

SURNAME INDEX

HOFFMAN 2, 22, 28, 29, 65, 172, 173, 190, 203, 216, 275, 347
HOGAN 313
HOGENCAMP 24
HOGOBOOM 130, 185
HOGUE 283
HOLBROOK 243
HOLCOMB 184, 316
HOLDEN 122, 143, 153, 188, 213, 264, 269, 288, 339
HOLLADAY 50
HOLLAND 174
HOLLENBECK 133, 153, 201, 244, 255, 281, 289
HOLLETT 111
HOLLEY 178, 307, 353
HOLLIDAY 151, 312
HOLLIS 1, 4, 22, 25, 149, 168, 201, 214, 301
HOLLY 230, 244, 299, 328
HOLMES 12, 95, 141, 288, 344
HOLT 220
HOLTON 352
HONEYWELL 347
HONNESS 279, 287
HOOD 240, 248, 251, 269, 275, 276
HOOSE 177
HOPKINS 38, 44, 47, 75, 97, 103, 110, 126, 151, 160, 173, 186, 237, 336, 340, 344
HOPKINSON 247
HOPPER 70, 157, 208
HORACE 295
HORN 4, 12, 19, 25, 33, 241, 319
HORNELL 318
HORR 177
HORTON 149, 168, 169, 211, 212, 266, 302, 306, 311, 314, 316, 336, 343-345, 347, 354, 355, 357, 359
HOSFORD 114
HOSKINS 234
HOTCHKIN 36, 77, 79-81, 87, 94, 111, 153, 344, 347, 348, 352
HOTCHKISS 356
HOUCK 140, 141, 333
HOUGHTALING 31
HOUGHTON 162, 308
HOVEY 62, 261
HOWARD 76, 98, 171, 242, 250, 275, 318, 320
HOWE 47, 188, 241, 242, 263, 271, 284
HOWELL 6, 38, 48, 60, 69, 89, 105, 119, 125, 147, 164, 165, 181, 186, 193, 233, 261, 284, 291, 308
HOWLETT 128
HOYT 35, 48, 72, 77, 88, 91, 95, 110, 128
HUBBARD 74, 113, 180, 183, 236, 262, 340, 343, 346, 354
HUBBELL 47, 50, 59, 88, 89, 141
HUBER 178, 200
HUDSON 138, 278
HUEY 198
HUFF 170
HUFFTALEN 351
HUGGINS 32
HUGHES 108, 150
HUGHSON 246
HUKE 265
HULBURT 47

HULETT 101
HULL 31, 114, 273, 280
HULSE 158, 329
HULTS 306, 353
HULTZ 338
HUMPHREYS 15, 57, 123
HUNGERFORD 14, 163, 213, 260
HUNT 18, 39, 48, 122, 178, 199, 209, 243, 255, 256, 259, 289, 343
HUNTER 41, 58, 62, 65, 66, 90, 99, 120, 149, 162, 168, 193, 194, 215, 274
HUNTINGTON 148, 218
HUNTLY 21
HURD 201, 231, 328
HURLBURT 179, 204
HURLBUT 78, 315
HURLEY 105
HUSTED 14
HUSTON 155, 235
HUTCHES 308
HUTCHINS 330
HUTCHINSON 21, 346
HUY 92, 171, 192, 289
HYATT 131, 355
HYDE 229, 272
INGALLS 24, 190, 193, 221
INGERSOLL 117, 291
INGHAM 246
INGRAHAM 349
INSCHO 196
INSHO 190
IRVING 148
IRWIN 20, 60
IVES 90, 182
JACKMAN 166
JACKSON 48, 114, 232, 353
JACOBS 33, 63, 146, 254, 255, 267
JACOBUS 104, 117
JACQUETT 214
JAMES 139, 169, 305
JAMIESON 42
JAMISON 60
JANES 227
JAYCOX 310
JAYNES 2, 3, 15, 260, 303, 305
JEFFERSON 328
JEFFREY 252, 279
JENKS 156, 281
JENNESS 278
JENNINGS 26, 129, 267
JEWELL 182, 299, 301, 308
JEWETT 112
JILLETT 214
JOHNS 233
JOHNSON 23, 27, 35, 39, 45, 55, 59, 64, 67, 80, 81, 84, 85, 94, 97, 116, 118, 126, 133, 141, 161, 168, 170, 175, 186, 199, 200, 201, 210, 237, 244, 246, 252, 272, 284, 288, 291, 324, 334, 343, 358, 359
JOLLY 271, 328
JONES 3, 11-14, 16, 19, 21, 26, 27, 30, 49, 60, 66, 76, 121, 129, 132, 136, 141, 143, 156, 164, 171, 172, 187, 196, 198, 226, 229, 230, 233, 240, 245, 262, 263, 295, 315, 317
JOSLIN 12, 211
JUDSON 155, 336
JULIAN 213
JUNE 18, 28

KAME 188
KANE 204
KAPLE 353
KARR 316
KASSON 92, 182
KATHAN 4
KATNER 43
KEEFE 323
KEELER 300
KELLER 327
KELLEY 25
KELLOGG 11, 59, 102, 109, 127, 148, 180, 316
KELLY 41, 123, 192, 238, 240, 262, 322, 345
KELSEY 283
KELTY 325
KENMORE 285
KENMUIR 310
KENNARD 88
KENNEDY 49, 51, 65, 74, 82, 321, 325
KENT 53, 317, 348
KENYON 255
KEOUGH 142, 145, 172
KERNAN 198
KERR 78, 183
KETCH 341
KETCHUM 190, 283, 327
KEYES 5, 258
KEYSER 120
KILDAY 315
KILEY 188, 330
KIMBALL 25, 128, 205, 249, 281, 286, 307
KIMBLE 237, 242
KING 62, 129, 154, 181, 201, 208, 215, 231, 243, 262, 267, 298, 300, 315
KINGKADE 71
KINGSBURY 314
KINGSLEY 118, 295
KINNE 11
KINNER 113
KINNEY 2, 41, 59, 150, 159, 179, 199, 232, 327, 330, 331
KIRKENDALL 287, 289
KIRKHAM 323
KIRKPATRICK 356
KLECKLER 183
KLEE 199
KLEIN 330
KLICE 342, 350, 355
KLINE 28, 320
KLOCK 143
KNAPP 5, 12, 23, 106, 114, 168, 181, 185, 193, 219, 276, 288, 290, 306, 311, 327, 332
KNICKERBOCKER 46, 149, 241
KNIGHT 25, 82, 91, 112, 122, 126, 188
KNIPPER 318
KNISELY 330
KNISKERN 331
KNOWLES 135
KNOWLTON 58, 222, 283
KNOX 39, 91, 150, 159, 225, 277
KOESTER 164
KRANZ 303
KREIDLER 165
KRIEGER 328

KRINER 321
KUHL 283
KURTZ 312
KYSER 87
KYSOR 220
LA BAR 24
LA BOUR 162
LA DUE 352
LA FORGE 88
LA GRANGE 173
LA RUE 299
LAFFERTY 121
LAFLER 352
LAKE 18, 92, 321
LAMB 154, 194
LAMPHEARE 7
LAMPHIRE 258
LAMPORT 348
LAMSON 137, 317
LAND 169, 221, 266, 290
LANDEN 264
LANDERS 22, 156, 168
LANE 6, 18, 55, 148, 186, 232, 326, 339, 342
LANG 77, 145, 166, 332
LANGLEY 208
LANNING 152, 161
LANNON 188
LANPHEAR 190, 324
LANSING 8, 46, 171, 204
LAPP 169
LARIMER 313
LARKIN 178
LARROWE 89, 244, 298, 300, 302
LASON 258
LATHROP 280
LATTIMORE 224, 245
LAUDER 319
LAUDERBEAU 112
LAUER 275
LAUGHLIN 294, 297
LAUNY 253, 256
LAUTENSCHLAGER 313
LAW 258
LAWRENCE 42, 74, 219, 231, 292
LAWTON 58
LAY 303
LAYTON 98, 111, 295, 296
LAZELLE 345
LE BARR 308
LE FEVER 181
LE MUNYAN 29
LEACH 176, 209, 314
LEARY 223, 301
LEAVENWORTH 247
LEDYARD 178
LEE 99, 152, 167, 187, 250, 257, 281, 285, 301, 325, 329, 336, 343, 347, 359
LEGGETT 61, 142
LEGRO 60
LEIGHTON 93
LELAND 44, 56, 58, 92
LEMM 48
LEMON 64
LENHART 36, 110
LEONARD 158, 200, 251, 266, 277
LETTS 151
LEW 161
LEWIS 31, 42, 43, 51, 53, 88, 90, 99, 100, 140, 147, 193, 221, 240, 266,

310, 336, 337, 341, 343, 345, 352
LILLY 74, 180
LINDLEY 75, 121
LINDSAY 101, 154, 163, 166, 167, 193, 260, 287, 320
LINDSLEY 41, 47, 64, 285
LINNELL 18
LINZA 26
LISMAN 314
LITTLE 44, 64, 69, 140, 145, 149, 168, 173, 277
LIVERMORE 46
LIVINGSTON 51, 54
LLOYD 244
LOCKWOOD 36, 183, 292, 293, 305, 306, 323, 355
LOGAN 5, 46, 94
LOGHRY 53, 172, 177, 314, 323
LOMBARD 229
LONGWELL 141, 144, 145, 155, 292, 295, 298, 299, 303, 307
LOOK 128, 133, 148, 158, 167, 170, 269, 344, 350
LOOMIS 39, 45, 68, 90, 135
LOONEY 315
LOOP 2
LOPER 13, 21, 33, 187
LORD 9, 121
LORIN 56
LOSEY 107
LOTTER 175
LOUCKS 104, 106, 117
LOUNSBERRY 93, 112, 151, 300, 341
LOVEJOY 162, 240
LOVELACE 193
LOVELESS 104, 158, 278
LOVELL 188, 219, 227, 262, 276
LOVERIDGE 292, 308
LOWE 230
LOWER 276
LOZIER 13, 80, 89, 102, 143
LUCAS 61, 182, 265
LUCE 356
LUDLOW 42
LUGG 16
LUMBARD 263
LYKE 119, 186, 201
LYNCH 4, 5, 10, 30, 68, 104
LYON 9, 18, 33, 49, 75, 90, 91, 94, 100, 147, 163, 179, 186, 251, 262, 282, 284, 321, 346
LYONS 132
MACK 31, 88, 202, 289, 323
MACKEY 132, 134
MACKIE 135
MACOMBS 56
MADDEN 225
MADISON 191, 210, 322
MADOLE 39
MAGEE 7, 38, 44, 52, 68, 90, 108, 139, 163, 187, 213, 217, 218
MAGNUSON 326
MAHAN 198, 332
MAJOR 323
MALLORY 13, 18, 27, 43, 80, 124, 230, 232, 233, 244, 254, 266, 280, 281
MALONEY 328
MANDEVILLE 4, 334
MANGAN 198
MANHART 187

MANLEY 16, 24, 27
MANLY 164
MANN 251, 269
MANNERS 2, 9, 17
MANNING 28, 170, 188, 218, 334
MANSON 86
MANTOR 97
MANVILLE 320
MAPES 82, 200, 211, 236
MAR 170
MARCH 103
MARCY 111
MARGESON 133, 154, 294, 297, 300, 302, 309, 310
MARIM 105
MARION 1
MARK 25
MARKHAM 58, 189, 315, 332
MARLATT 24, 203
MARROW 305
MARSELL 96
MARSH 126
MARSHALL 47, 96, 129, 265, 338
MARTHER 46
MARTIN 21, 32, 68, 147, 206, 240, 242, 277, 279, 334
MARVIN 162, 169, 221
MASON 36, 68, 73, 115, 121, 207
MASSON 134, 293, 306
MASTEN 18, 51, 187
MATHER 30, 87, 140, 145
MATHEWS 28, 45, 51, 63, 156, 185, 274, 319, 323, 358
MATHEWSON 118
MATTERN 250
MATTESON 6, 148
MATTICE 352
MATTISON 79, 342
MAXWELL 34, 190, 239, 244, 249, 255, 297
MAY 41, 44, 55, 88, 93, 120, 132, 139, 148, 234, 284, 286, 291
MAYNARD 157, 230, 249, 250, 255, 273, 325
MC ALEESE 216
MC ANDREW 108
MC ARTHUR 341
MC BANE 244
MC BEATH 45, 82
MC BURNEY 48, 51, 120, 128, 225, 226, 270, 272
MC CAIG 11, 14, 217
MC CAIQUE 308
MC CALL 36, 70, 89, 93, 95, 141, 151
MC CALLA 84, 127, 179
MC CANN 10, 341
MC CARRICK 340
MC CARTHY 189, 195
MC CARTY 21, 318
MC CAY 62, 88, 89, 109
MC CHESNEY 21, 165, 213
MC CLARY 70, 88
MC CLENNAN 246
MC CLURE 42, 65, 80, 90, 141
MC COLLOUGH 14, 72, 155, 323
MC COLLUM 175
MC CONIHE 233
MC CONNELL 20, 168, 171, 215, 302, 319, 334, 338
MC CORMICK 251, 348, 355

SURNAME INDEX

MC COWLEY 257
MC CREA 271
MC CUE 226
MC CURG 179
MC DANIELS 133
MC DONNELL 216
MC DOUGAL 327
MC DOWELL 111, 124, 176, 190, 197, 293, 300
MC ELWAIN 67
MC ELWEE 67, 70, 73, 96, 121, 193
MC ENTEE 167
MC FARLAND 313
MC FARREN 160, 200
MC GAMMON 252
MC GEORGE 17, 221, 281
MC GIVEN 256
MC GONEGAL 146, 178, 190
MC GONNEGAL 121
MC GOWAN 9, 258
MC GRADA 344
MC GUIRE 221
MC HENRY 46, 56, 75, 241
MC INTEE 335
MC INTOSH 201, 256, 267
MC INTYRE 248, 256, 282, 294
MC KALLOR 356
MC KAY 23, 141, 169, 217
MC KEAN 220, 251, 266
MC KENSIE 82, 87
MC KENZIE 5, 14, 113, 216
MC KIBBEN 60, 186, 187, 205
MC KIBBIN 205
MC KINNEY 239
MC KNIGHT 224, 280
MC LEAN 343, 345, 352, 356, 357
MC MASTER 57, 85, 123, 184, 196, 304
MC MINN 296, 310
MC MULLEN 134, 215, 261
MC MURRAY 19
MC NAIR 207
MC NAMARA 146
MC NEIL 118, 223, 231, 273
MC NORTON 50
MC PHEE 22
MC QUAHAE 66
MC WHORTER 91, 179
MEAD 30, 205, 207, 225, 226, 280, 301, 333
MEADE 127
MEDBURY 54
MEDDICK 145
MEEKER 309
MEEKS 90, 146
MEGRADY 64
MEIGS 232
MELONEY 275
MERHERTER 176
MERIARD 121
MERRICK 233
MERRILL 39, 66, 148, 166, 172, 197
MERRIMAN 81
MERRITT 106, 108, 116, 234, 341, 347, 350, 359
MERSEREAU 213, 250, 313
MESICK 69
MESSENGER 38, 55, 224
MESSEREAU 215, 240, 312
METCALF 53, 92, 243, 249
METCALFE 63, 67, 71, 78, 177

METZ 173
MEWYER 7
MEYERS 174
MICKS 242
MIDDLEBROCK 277
MIDDLETON 338, 344, 357, 359
MIER 320
MILES 30, 75, 100, 106, 110, 184, 199, 244
MILLARD 11, 31, 52
MILLER 8, 14, 16, 17, 19, 27-29, 75, 82, 85, 107, 117, 135, 143, 148, 154, 158, 165, 166, 168, 175, 182, 183, 195, 198, 203, 209, 240, 272, 275, 279, 284, 285, 298, 299, 310, 311, 335, 337, 339, 340, 347, 351
MILLIKEN 209
MILLIMAN 180
MILLS 13, 37, 63, 78, 85, 100, 110, 113, 119, 135, 195, 217, 225, 226, 230, 236, 237, 254, 277, 286, 297, 298, 348, 354
MINARD 34, 199
MINDRINK 128
MINER 12, 83, 140, 222, 336, 342, 356
MINOR 56, 215
MITCAELL 75
MITCHELL 2, 41, 46, 47, 95, 114, 123, 125, 138, 225, 236, 245, 306, 340
MOFFATT 138
MOLSON 34
MONAHAN 323
MONELL 75, 117
MONROE 322
MONTANYA 12
MONTGOMERY 49, 242
MONTOREY 256
MOODY 304
MOONEY 168, 335
MOORE 40, 78, 89, 106, 113, 147, 150, 152, 171, 173, 179, 180, 202, 207, 216, 251, 262, 290, 296, 310, 314, 318, 321
MORAN 163, 198, 326, 331, 333
MOREHOUSE 133, 268
MORENCE 331
MOREY 97
MORGAN 8, 50, 124, 191, 203, 272, 323, 356, 358, 359
MORRELL 139, 180
MORRILL 290
MORRIS 63, 124, 130, 205, 329, 332
MORRISON 46, 150, 166, 259, 295, 297, 302
MORROW 136, 225
MORSE 117, 118, 238, 246, 270
MORTON 235
MOSER 27
MOSHER 289
MOSS 189
MOURHESS 24
MOWERS 173, 359
MOWRY 236
MUDGE 150
MULCAHEY 195
MULFORD 32, 263
MULHOLLEN 66, 72, 154, 207, 319
MULLEN 35, 195
MULLIKIN 219

MUMFORD 158, 222, 270, 287, 309
MUNDY 257, 275
MUNN 317
MUNNING 314
MUNSON 95, 119, 131, 301
MUNSTER 236
MURDOCH 264
MURPHY 116, 156, 164, 170, 180, 201, 204, 217, 218, 237, 288, 341
MURRAY 6, 19, 23, 30, 78, 97, 177, 276, 289
MYRICK 296
MYRTLE 67, 307, 338, 352, 358
NAST 329
NEALLY 42, 45, 55-57, 143
NEALY 359
NEAR 110, 152
NEFF 188, 359
NELLIS 116, 134, 179, 183, 293
NEPHEW 332
NETTH 306, 307
NEW 172
NEWCOMB 37, 175
NEWELL 207
NEWHALL 5
NEWMAN 28
NEWSOM 32, 211
NEWSOME 189
NEWTON 111, 147, 211, 255, 257
NEYHART 244, 272
NICHOLS 32, 101, 140, 203, 261, 266, 293, 294, 305, 310
NICHOLSON 5, 64
NICKERSON 26
NIENDORF 324, 325
NILES 42, 54, 73, 77, 150, 164, 255, 320, 343, 353
NIMS 353, 357
NIVER 152
NIXON 70, 223
NOBLE 2, 82, 85, 89, 95, 119, 134, 297, 307, 308
NORRELL 219
NORRIS 13, 154, 354
NORTH 227
NORTHRUP 8, 19, 30, 31, 33, 143, 185, 203, 226, 310, 349
NORTHWAY 224
NORTON 32, 76, 87, 161, 184, 302, 313
NOWLEN 231
NOXON 347
NOYES 281
NUDD 208
NUTE 46
NYCE 69
NYHART 238
O'BRIEN 28, 138
O'CONNELL 195
O'CONNOR 313, 319, 329
O'DELL 81
O'FLAHERTY 352
O'HARGAN 216
O'HARIGAN 221
O'NEIL 136
O'SHAUGHNESSY 285
OAKDEN 22, 25
OAKLEY 135
OAKS 195, 312
OATLEY 167
ODSON 163

SURNAME INDEX

OGDEN 90, 98, 229, 242
OGLEY 60
OLCOTT 245, 247
OLDFIELD 262, 270, 276
OLENDORF 213
OLIVER 174
OLMSTEAD 19, 21, 39, 87, 89, 92, 125, 137, 139, 149, 215, 312, 357, 358
OLNEY 132, 349, 354
ORCUTT 150, 197
ORDWAY 15, 198, 208, 219, 220
ORR 3, 6, 30, 33
ORSER 29
ORTON 99, 253, 303
ORVIS 15, 99, 343
OSBORN 47, 63, 75, 181, 207, 312
OSBORNE 9, 121, 272
OSGOOD 149
OSMUN 137, 140
OSTRANDER 28, 116, 314, 316, 341
OTIS 1, 103, 130, 133
OTTS 27
OVENSHIRE 148
OVIATT 243
OWEN 15, 99, 206, 227, 237, 244, 265, 267, 270, 271, 278, 281, 311, 319, 345
OWENS 329
OXX 154
PACKER 250, 259, 277, 291
PADDOCK 168, 212
PAGE 65, 162, 175, 187, 211, 248, 282, 321
PALMER 53, 87, 93, 105, 110, 139, 163, 182, 193, 196, 223, 231, 246, 280, 289, 292, 294, 305, 358
PARCEL 221, 222, 228, 258, 261
PARK 8, 225, 248, 261
PARKE 26, 183
PARKER 175, 189, 239, 243, 345, 358, 359
PARKHILL 215
PARKHURST 164, 316
PARKS 10, 230, 238, 282, 288, 350
PARMALEE 242, 358
PARMETHER 112
PARSELLO 304
PARSON 87
PARSONS 149, 169, 193, 218, 274, 337, 338, 346
PARTRIDGE 109, 192
PATCH 339
PATCHIN 91, 134, 156, 211, 238
PATTENGILL 258, 268
PATTENT 64
PATTERSON 54, 71, 83, 151, 179, 189, 212, 215, 245
PATTON 210, 332
PAUL 23, 154, 285
PAULDING 102
PAWLING 65, 80, 87, 104, 126, 161, 242
PAYNE 13, 194, 231, 253, 256
PEAK 53, 244, 254
PEARSALL 181
PEASE 24, 209
PECK 2, 10, 89, 202, 213, 226, 239, 248
PECKHAM 208, 323
PECKMAN 264

PEEBLES 226, 230
PEEK 13, 43
PELTON 104, 344
PENCE 17
PERINE 39, 73, 78, 98, 135, 143, 184
PERKINS 23, 65, 67, 110, 113, 120, 146, 232
PERRIGE 94
PERRY 34, 39, 60, 178, 186, 224, 240, 249, 318, 326, 358
PERSOS 37
PETERS 39, 100, 160, 164
PETERSON 127, 167, 314
PETRIKIN 69
PETTIBONE 94, 211, 328
PEW 235, 250, 262
PFIEFFER 283, 291
PHALING 59
PHELPS 22, 42, 153, 176, 200, 222, 234, 239, 258, 265, 271, 277, 281, 334, 343, 347
PHENAS 232
PHILLIPS 2, 5, 30, 129, 197, 261, 264
PHINNEY 4, 329
PIATT 128
PICKETT 340
PICKLE 165
PIE 195
PIER 25, 71, 172, 257
PIERCE 21, 26, 158, 187, 203, 221, 230, 272, 315, 328, 339, 348, 352
PIERSON 26, 208, 228
PIESTER 268
PIFFER 257
PINCH 77, 331
PINNEY 201
PITTS 194, 316
PLACE 325
PLANK 32
PLATT 13, 54, 74, 96, 137, 154, 185, 218, 245, 268
PLOOF 308
PLOSS 216, 219
PLUMB 144
POLAND 316
POLMITER 29
POMEROY 130, 135, 280
POND 266, 278
POOLE 118
PORTER 50, 53, 57, 58, 83, 92, 95, 122, 126, 279, 301, 321
POTTER 17, 22, 36, 57, 72, 93, 95, 134, 148, 196, 206, 214, 225, 247, 249, 254, 270, 282, 288, 334, 343, 353
POWELL 19, 63, 167, 181, 189, 196, 220
POWERS 23, 81, 96, 106, 153, 313
PRATT 1, 7, 25, 41, 44, 52, 73, 87, 92, 97, 107, 118, 124, 132, 134, 142, 167, 209, 222, 239, 248, 249, 251, 265, 274, 342, 346
PRENTICE 49, 94
PRENTISS 44, 94, 106, 145, 178, 179, 293, 326, 339, 340, 345, 356
PRESHO 181
PRESTON 41, 186, 187, 226, 238, 247, 268, 283, 284, 287, 289, 313, 329
PRICE 18
PRINDLE 138, 196

PRINGLE 239, 346
PRIOR 329
PRITCHARD 8, 80, 222, 281
PROTZMAN 8
PROVER 182
PRUNER 243
PRUTZMAN 280
PUFFER 200
PUGH 288
PULLING 60, 61, 76, 118
PULVER 340, 341, 353
PUNCHES 30
PURDEE 347
PURDY 14, 16, 38, 50, 52, 58, 63, 97, 178, 190, 211, 214, 218, 243, 296
PURINGTON 359
PURSONS 11
PUTNAM 47, 168, 174, 340, 343, 359
QUACKENBUSH 267, 274, 281, 286, 289
QUAIN 198
QUICK 97
QUIGLEY 330
QUILL 154
QUIMBY 124, 204
QUINN 309
RAGAN 28
RAMBLES 268
RANDALL 98, 246, 304, 337
RANDLE 38
RANNEY 52
RAPLEE 125, 297
RATHBONE 1, 64, 70, 136, 242, 254, 275, 284
RATHBUN 181, 326, 328
RAYMOND 57, 82, 174, 200, 296
RAZEY 202
READ 51, 60, 62, 72, 73, 85, 91, 103, 111, 131, 276, 294, 301, 309, 358
READY 216, 316, 337
REARDON 275
REASON 42
RECE 287
REDFIELD 92, 232, 235, 243, 253, 287, 330
REDINGTON 111
REED 221, 227, 261, 268, 274, 288, 303, 320, 358
REEDER 140
REESE 281
REILLY 159
RELIHAN 277
RETAN 128, 130, 295, 309
REVILLE 266
REXFORD 240
REYNOLDS 6, 17, 27, 33, 98, 108, 127, 137, 151, 169, 203, 218, 225, 228, 234, 254, 257, 277, 287, 302, 332
REZNOR 127
RHINEHART 293
RHINEVAULT 131
RHODA 232, 253
RHODES 35, 69, 225, 228, 235, 237, 239, 240, 259
RICE 5, 9, 13, 38, 44, 58, 63, 80, 82, 87, 95, 116, 117, 122, 125, 126, 148, 151, 162, 181, 187, 212, 214, 296, 342, 349
RICHARDS 24, 263, 274, 290, 305,

SURNAME INDEX

308
RICHARDSON 49, 54, 69, 70, 74, 78, 92, 95-97, 100, 107, 110, 119, 124, 130, 135-138, 149, 170, 193, 236, 279, 322
RICHER 281
RICHTMYER 149
RICHTU 237
RICKEY 18, 31
RIDDELL 202
RIDDLE 7, 62
RIDER 25, 156, 314
RIGBY 174, 206, 227, 229, 239
RILEY 124, 182, 285, 304, 326, 331, 343
RINEHART 156
RINESS 243
RINGROSE 345, 349
RIPLEY 51, 301, 311
RISING 102
ROAT 357
ROBARDS 63
ROBBINS 3, 44, 55, 81, 225, 232, 302
ROBERTS 64, 68, 187, 205, 287, 297, 314
ROBERTSON 15, 30, 232, 259
ROBIE 33, 38, 65, 71, 86, 106, 120, 122, 133, 136, 146, 168, 175, 186, 334
ROBINSON 5, 42, 53, 71, 76, 90, 113, 144, 163, 164, 190, 194-196, 223, 226, 227, 229, 231, 234-236, 239, 242, 245, 247, 253, 254-256, 259, 260, 264, 265, 281, 282, 300, 337
ROBSON 326, 347
ROCHESTER 45
ROCKWELL 8, 83, 197, 223, 235, 298
ROE 179, 197, 212
ROESSLY 186
ROFF 180, 302
ROGERS 9, 15, 85, 146, 166, 187, 206, 211, 212, 235, 250
ROLFE 118
ROLLINS 276
ROLLS 20
ROLOSON 160
ROOD 188
ROOF 269
ROOKS 107
ROOSA 235
ROOT 5, 43, 76, 155, 333
RORABAUGH 219, 276
ROSA 248, 348
ROSE 9, 48, 49, 58, 61, 70, 77, 78, 107, 125, 130, 158, 172, 174, 213, 232, 233, 255, 282, 283, 312, 319
ROSEBOOM 119, 134
ROSENCRANS 45, 71, 89, 114, 118, 127, 141, 190, 295, 298, 304, 337
ROSS 158, 206, 329, 333
ROTHSUSS 257
ROUNDS 327
ROUSE 23, 231, 252, 263, 281
ROW 170
ROWE 44, 56, 58, 71, 86, 107, 125, 130, 208
ROWELL 164
ROWLAND 69
ROWLETT 310
ROWLEY 20, 35, 48, 71, 173, 186, 206, 222, 229, 234, 237, 259, 267, 276
ROYCE 127, 307
ROYER 100
RUDIGER 315
RUGGLES 20, 150, 159, 179, 331
RUMSEY 38, 48, 78, 99, 113, 118, 171, 212, 227, 238, 356
RUNDELL 278
RUNNELL 287
RUNYAN 110, 142
RUSS 80
RUSSELL 16, 75, 169, 277, 317
RUTHERFORD 6, 9, 34, 49, 58, 59, 64, 67, 89, 92, 179, 289
RYAN 22, 188, 190, 200
RYERSS 42
RYMER 334
RYNESS 276
RYNIKER 139
RYNOE 52
SABIN 216
SACKETT 230
SAGAR 148, 273
SAGE 198
SALISBURY 48, 67
SALMON 83, 258
SALT 107, 176
SALTSMAN 113, 353
SAMHAMER 168
SAMPLE 122
SANBORN 16, 226
SANDERS 113, 265
SANDERSON 145
SANDFORD 245
SANFORD 58, 105, 111, 165, 169, 185, 201, 294, 295, 351
SANTEE 54, 214, 322
SARGENT 207
SAUER 183, 309
SAULSBERRY 316
SAUSMAN 333
SAVAGE 30, 218
SAVORY 277
SAWDY 255
SAWYER 248, 303
SAXBURY 26
SAXTON 19, 174, 189
SAYER 115
SAYLES 88, 281
SAYRE 78, 109, 154, 217, 298, 300
SCHANK 117
SCHAUMBERG 198
SCHEIRUMANN 161
SCHELL 334
SCHENCK 139, 178
SCHERER 314
SCHERMER 259
SCHERMERHORN 42
SCHMATZ 307
SCHMOKER 306
SCHOFIELD 175, 191, 217, 311
SCHOLL 311
SCHOONOVER 29
SCHOTTS 16
SCHUE 7
SCHUYLER 205, 268
SCHWINGLE 172
SCOFIELD 176, 271
SCOTT 74, 124, 248, 347, 356, 358
SCOVEL 71
SCOVILLE 245
SCRAFFORD 155
SCRIPTER 167
SCUTT 137, 357
SEAGER 101
SEAMAN 26, 32, 83, 292
SEAMANS 113, 123, 170, 197, 283
SEARLES 1, 17, 22, 51, 338, 341
SEARS 58
SECOR 101, 151
SEDDEN 190
SEDGEWICK 47, 123, 139, 279
SEELEY 97, 105, 122, 128, 163, 220, 284, 333
SEELY 261
SEFFIELD 201
SEILER 317
SELLICK 189
SELLON 170
SELOVER 344
SERGEANT 9
SEVERANCE 29, 33
SEWARD 2, 158, 243
SEWELL 330
SEXTON 10, 17, 105, 107, 108, 278, 296
SEYMOUR 18, 78, 116, 128, 137, 144, 238
SHADER 146, 359
SHAFFER 333
SHANIHAN 322
SHANNON 37, 82, 88, 93, 95, 103, 134, 151, 173, 226
SHARP 6, 9, 73, 177, 197, 216, 324, 332
SHARPE 232
SHARPSTEEN 283, 289
SHATTUCK 60, 82
SHAUGER 152
SHAUT 43, 181
SHAVER 134, 135
SHAW 222, 223, 229, 306
SHEARDOWN 267
SHEARMAN 194
SHEFFIELD 98, 335
SHELDON 41, 127, 143
SHELTZ 183
SHEPARD 1, 4, 5, 13, 15, 63, 101, 103, 113, 140, 167, 176, 292, 305
SHEPPARD 154
SHERMAN 79, 197, 285, 297, 312
SHERWOOD 4, 8, 14, 19, 54, 59, 102, 158, 225, 263, 266, 270, 275, 291, 301, 313
SHINEBARGER 330
SHIPMAN 21, 45
SHIPPEN 228
SHOCKEY 57, 205
SHOEMAKER 98, 111, 259
SHORT 239
SHOWERS 187, 208
SHUART 126
SHULER 272
SHULTS 6, 89, 102, 116, 136-138, 157, 166, 186, 238, 283, 299, 319, 342, 354
SHUMWAY 20, 43
SHURBIN 5, 119
SHUTT 197
SHUTTS 269
SIBLEY 36

SURNAME INDEX

SICKEL 232
SICKELS 114
SIDMAN 156, 322
SIDNEY 261
SILL 154, 196
SILSBE 73, 85
SILSBEE 49, 57, 106, 165, 166, 196
SILSBY 27, 202
SILVERNAIL 104, 120, 303
SIMERSON 90
SIMMONS 6, 19, 25, 68, 188, 199, 249, 295, 315
SIMONDS 225
SIMONS 77, 108, 110, 186, 196, 212, 278
SIMPSON 62, 210, 220, 347
SINCEBOX 339
SINCLAIR 133, 137, 288
SITTS 341
SIZER 17
SKELTON 268
SKIFF 285
SKINNER 39, 114, 115, 126, 157, 284, 336, 344
SLAGHT 306
SLAIGHT 124
SLATER 131
SLINEY 102, 142
SLY 9, 227, 235, 245, 267
SMALL 38
SMALLEY 336
SMALLIDGE 116, 148, 205
SMEAD 49, 56, 103, 106, 120, 162, 164
SMITH 2, 5, 6, 10, 11, 16-18, 23, 27, 31, 32, 35-37, 43, 48, 50-53, 55, 56, 58, 59, 62, 68, 70, 75, 76, 85, 86, 91, 95, 97, 102, 104, 107, 111, 112, 114, 116, 123, 125, 128, 129, 133, 136, 139, 142-145, 147, 150, 151, 155-157, 161, 163, 174, 176, 179, 180, 184, 186-188, 192, 197, 201, 204, 208, 210-213, 219, 229, 233, 234, 238-241, 247, 257, 258, 260, 261, 263, 264, 267, 268, 271, 274, 279, 280, 283, 286, 288, 290, 293, 295, 297, 300, 303, 305-308, 316, 324, 326, 330-332, 336-339, 342, 343, 346, 350-352, 359
SMOKE 341
SNELL 105, 116, 155, 238, 333
SNOOK 54, 114, 323
SNOW 189, 298, 310
SNYDER 110, 177, 351
SOBER 57
SOMERS 222, 272
SORNBERGER 227
SOULE 174, 179, 295
SOUTER 300
SOUTHARD 152
SOUTHERBY 333
SOUTHERLAND 53
SOUTHWORTH 267
SPAFFORD 105
SPALDING 100, 108
SPARKS 327
SPAULDING 119, 177, 182, 247
SPEARS 200, 336
SPENCE 117
SPENCER 80, 91, 127, 173, 208, 225, 239, 241, 253, 258, 275, 278, 279,
286, 290, 322
SPICER 3, 123
SPORE 66
SPRAGUE 24, 30, 67, 111, 161, 166, 176, 293, 294, 299, 305, 309, 310, 333
SPRING 84
SQUIRES 59, 94, 238, 344, 359
ST CLAIR 202
ST JOHN 5, 149, 198, 266, 353
ST PETERS 140
STACY 243
STAGE 192
STANDISH 199
STANIFORD 37, 127
STANLEY 96, 226, 229
STANTON 87, 150, 159, 164, 230, 266, 267, 286, 311, 341, 351
STARK 234
STARKWEATHER 84
STARR 20, 43, 98
STEARNS 2, 266, 331
STEBBINS 3, 19, 313
STEDMAN 208
STEEL 52
STEELE 86, 223, 226, 253
STEEN 282
STEERE 91, 257
STENARIOUS 180
STENETHER 237
STEPHENS 35, 43, 52, 62, 75, 82, 84, 150, 155, 173, 180, 193, 194, 200, 204, 205, 213-215, 218, 250, 252, 291, 313, 315, 317, 320-322
STEVENS 5, 15, 31, 34, 39, 40, 82, 96, 130, 164, 199, 200, 242, 246, 255, 284, 323, 329, 344
STEVENSON 54, 81, 134, 250, 255
STEVER 349, 350
STEWARD 17
STEWART 23, 52, 56, 63, 65, 67, 77, 86-88, 102, 103, 123, 125, 131, 143, 146, 161, 163, 165, 181, 189, 212, 213, 220, 234, 254, 266, 268, 287, 295, 322, 345-347, 353, 355
STICKLER 276
STICKNEY 12, 175, 199, 340
STILES 162, 179, 205, 213
STILLMAN 314, 324, 329
STILLSON 186, 234
STITSON 132
STOCKING 41, 98
STOCUM 104, 195
STODDARD 91, 112, 122, 284, 307, 345, 346
STOKES 210, 240
STONE 44, 47, 73, 174, 182, 245, 294, 298, 304, 324, 344, 346
STORY 18, 114, 156, 159
STOUT 5
STOWE 341
STRAIGHT 65, 182
STRAIT 14, 24, 157
STRANG 266, 314
STRATTON 77, 303, 336
STRAWAY 303
STRAWN 312
STREETER 209, 325
STRICKLAND 51
STROCK 21
STRONG 47, 108, 115, 144, 174, 209,
301, 342, 352, 357
STRONGATHRAM 22
STROPE 193
STROUD 208
STRYKER 21, 135
STUDDERT 329
STURDEVANT 3, 207, 249, 254, 342, 345, 351, 356
SULLIVAN 131, 178, 182, 191, 235, 321, 330, 339
SUMNER 163
SUNDERLAND 296
SUNDERLIN 162
SUTHERBY 195
SUTHERLAND 132, 155, 181
SUTLIFF 223
SUTTON 121, 133, 139, 160, 167, 326
SWAIN 160, 195, 236, 332
SWAN 32, 247
SWART 53, 62, 115, 122, 164, 336
SWARTHOUT 47, 54, 99, 174, 214, 266
SWARTWOOD 27, 315
SWARTZ 199, 314
SWEENEY 322
SWEET 44, 220, 253, 267, 294, 313, 318, 346
SWENSON 136
SWEZEY 43
SWICK 58, 67
SWITZER 50, 63, 79, 100, 103, 288
SYLVESTER 208
SYTEZ 35
TABER 212
TAGGART 4, 294
TALBOT 214, 218, 313
TALERDAY 1
TALL 338
TALLMADGE 86, 115, 117, 121, 217, 255
TALLMAN 192
TANNER 210
TARBOX 271
TARNEY 168, 201
TAYLOR 42, 57, 84, 89, 95, 96, 99, 101, 112, 128, 129, 133, 154, 164, 169, 171, 188, 202, 206, 211, 216, 263, 267, 280, 287, 295, 298, 301, 311, 320, 325, 331, 337, 342, 345, 348
TAYLORSON 256
TEACHMAN 132
TEED 21, 26, 333
TEEPLE 274
TEEPLES 229, 273
TEFFT 13
TERBELL 140, 164, 221, 241, 249, 254, 282, 283
TERRELL 60, 155, 321
TERRY 120, 220, 312, 344, 357
TERRYBERRY 209, 213
TEXIDO 290
THACHER 276, 317, 318, 330
THARP 136, 153, 194, 322
THAYER 131, 261
THOMAS 26, 40, 46, 75, 81, 144, 149, 208, 209, 226, 233, 286, 323, 341
THOMPSON 18, 67, 72, 75, 86, 128, 160, 184, 185, 203, 216, 230, 254,

SURNAME INDEX

262, 271, 273, 275, 296
THOMSON 237, 252
THORN 255
THORP 174, 192, 208, 269
THRALL 237, 248, 255
THROOP 277
THURBER 11, 50, 63, 79, 116, 178, 246, 271, 278
THURMAN 150
THURSTON 215
TICHENOR 76
TICKNER 60, 146
TIFF 291
TIFFANY 55, 98, 119, 264
TIFFT 252, 274
TILLOTSON 295
TILTON 52, 127, 133
TINKLEPAW 357
TINSLEY 20
TITSWORTH 332
TITUS 31
TOBEY 30-32, 199, 250, 263, 265, 285, 286, 289
TOBIAS 169, 178
TOBINS 20
TODD 228, 278
TOLAN 324
TOLBERT 49
TOLLIVER 45, 71
TOMER 111, 149, 189, 303, 338, 349, 353, 355
TOMLINSON 254, 301
TOMPKINS 190
TOMPSON 55, 224
TOOKER 73, 236, 239
TOOMEY 203
TOPPING 88, 149
TORPY 321
TORRANCE 164
TOUCEY 101
TOWLE 36, 48, 73, 87, 107, 128, 139, 141, 147, 149, 158, 164, 175, 181, 191, 220, 236, 276, 278, 319, 359
TOWNER 147, 356
TOWNLEY 276, 285
TOWNSEND 10, 15, 20, 40, 50, 53, 73, 106, 107, 112, 114, 136, 153, 169, 182, 188, 191, 208, 217, 219, 246, 252, 279, 280, 306, 311
TOWSLEY 194, 311
TRACY 264, 336
TRANT 204, 205, 338
TRAVER 242
TRAVIS 202, 212, 216
TREADWAY 175
TREAT 193
TREMAIN 136
TRENCHARD 152, 257
TRENKLER 172, 334
TRIMBLE 37, 100
TRIPP 171
TROUP 47
TROWBRIDGE 251, 314
TRUE 7
TRUESDALE 324
TUBBS 15, 125
TUITT 181
TULLER 211
TULLEY 93, 162
TUPPER 248, 285, 291
TURK 7, 226

TURN 129
TURNER 15, 22, 88, 107, 182, 239, 344
TUTHILL 82, 84, 236, 264, 358
TUTTLE 196, 267
TUTTON 5
TWOGOOD 2
TYLER 102, 115, 167, 282, 340, 350
UNDERHILL 45, 68, 124, 181, 191, 242
UNDERWOOD 263
UPDYKE 32, 318
UPHAM 209
UPSON 137, 215, 272, 273, 315
UPTHEGROVE 106, 359
UTTER 320
VAIL 72, 291
VAN ARSDALE 258
VAN AUKEN 97, 308, 356
VAN BINDER 10
VAN BUSKIRK 85, 93
VAN CAMPEN 67, 212
VAN DUSEN 72, 237
VAN DYKE 293
VAN ETTEN 11, 229, 233, 251, 260, 265
VAN GELDER 61, 74, 108, 110, 112, 115, 128, 295, 298, 299, 310
VAN GORDER 162, 218
VAN GORDON 29, 31
VAN HEUSEN 156
VAN HORN 230
VAN HOUSEN 79, 80, 84, 94, 97, 109, 153, 347, 350
VAN HOUTEN 123, 191
VAN KEURAN 184, 194, 323
VAN LOON 36, 331, 349
VAN METER 249
VAN NAME 260, 271, 286
VAN NESS 39, 161, 300, 305, 314
VAN NORMAN 260
VAN ORDER 325
VAN ORSDALE 4, 21, 173, 205
VAN OSTRAND 280
VAN OSTRANDER 224
VAN PELT 117
VAN RIPER 169
VAN SCOTER 179, 210, 273, 314
VAN SICKLE 38, 39
VAN SKIVER 74
VAN TUYL 19, 346
VAN TUYLE 138
VAN VALKENBURGH 3, 43, 104, 131, 144, 155
VAN VLECK 172
VAN VLEET 346
VAN WIE 177, 192, 219
VAN WINKLE 344
VAN WORMER 298
VANDERHOFF 208, 225
VANDERHOVEN 66
VANDERLIP 217
VANN 32
VAUGHN 160, 163, 218
VEAZIE 159, 254, 266
VEDDER 45
VEEDER 159
VEITH 97, 128, 284
VERMILYEA 23
VIELE 194
VINCENT 328

VOGT 310
VORHEES 320, 353, 355, 357
VOSE 161
VROOM 311
VROOMAN 74, 343
VUNK 323
WADDELL 8
WADE 10
WADSWORTH 117, 291, 340
WAGENER 341
WAGGONER 59
WAGNER 3, 22, 26, 130, 167, 198, 276
WAIT 110, 133, 168
WAITE 271
WAKELEY 16
WAKEMAN 51
WALBRIDGE 318
WALDO 75, 77, 83, 100, 103, 128, 144, 155, 163, 166, 328, 335, 348, 350, 351
WALDON 13
WALKER 18, 32, 41, 47, 56, 61, 62, 73, 85, 129, 131, 195, 203, 205, 208, 246, 255, 279, 280, 318, 324
WALLACE 34, 100, 118, 189, 199, 312, 314
WALLBRIDGE 194
WALLER 256
WALLING 93, 103
WALRATH 27
WALTERS 162, 188, 296
WALTON 11, 317
WANAMAKER 336
WARD 15, 35, 68, 92, 142, 145, 155, 158, 162, 181, 261, 267, 305, 319, 333, 348
WARDEN 57, 91
WARDNER 209
WARFIELD 338, 359
WARNER 31, 95, 147, 205, 216, 254, 271, 286, 317
WARREN 40, 45, 47, 56-59, 82, 85, 99, 118, 119, 134, 147, 170, 302, 318, 336
WASHBOURNE 217
WASHBURN 304, 326
WASS 23, 53
WATERMAN 121, 204, 306
WATERS 215, 231, 338, 339
WATKINS 19, 68, 83, 126, 129, 138, 229-231, 341
WATROUS 35, 68, 171, 192, 217, 267, 292, 293
WATSON 32, 63, 98, 325
WATTLES 62, 226
WAUGH 94, 355
WAY 132, 272, 280
WEALE 252, 286
WEALIE 259
WEATHERBY 1
WEAVER 124, 325, 346
WEBB 9, 70, 114, 165, 270, 272
WEBER 182, 295, 308
WEBSTER 6, 64, 68, 69, 189, 190, 297, 301, 305, 307
WEDGE 245
WEED 2
WEEKS 163, 248, 274, 327
WEIR 348
WELCH 102, 353

SURNAME INDEX

WELD 137, 337, 342, 349, 354
WELDEN 278
WELDON 324
WELLES 95, 96, 101, 114, 119
WELLINGTON 277, 290
WELLMAN 12, 230, 257
WELLS 6, 100, 165, 196, 223, 238, 271, 276, 326
WELSH 326
WELTS 272
WELTY 163, 203
WENTWORTH 50, 63
WENTZ 284
WEST 42, 48, 52, 189, 226, 247, 259, 260, 262
WESTCOTT 8, 10, 26, 29, 122, 154, 206, 244, 251, 261
WESTLAKE 14, 15, 17, 18, 23
WETMORE 185, 196, 213, 319
WHEAT 3, 33, 274, 285
WHEATON 123, 302, 349
WHEELER 56, 68, 69, 88, 109, 114, 129, 130, 143, 158, 161, 171, 177, 183, 187, 197, 216, 218, 248, 268, 280, 287, 299, 300, 302, 305, 307, 316, 338, 342, 344, 347, 350, 355, 357
WHEELOCK 8, 77, 78, 231-233, 290
WHIPPLE 76, 90, 130, 142
WHITAKER 62, 177
WHITCOMB 205
WHITE 41, 109, 112, 133, 142, 155, 157, 161, 164, 165, 174, 177, 178, 182, 189, 190, 194, 213, 214, 225, 240, 241, 260, 279, 288, 295, 296, 298, 308, 314, 318, 330
WHITEHEAD 20, 109, 124, 176, 192
WHITEHORN 96
WHITELEY 206
WHITENACK 270
WHITFORD 316, 332, 335
WHITING 22, 69, 70, 74, 82, 88, 98, 101, 131, 133, 146, 151, 161, 177, 252, 265, 267
WHITMAN 73, 204
WHITMARSH 244
WHITMATH 121
WHITMORE 28, 33, 272
WHITNEY 40, 76, 99, 115, 176, 239, 250, 352
WHITTAKER 86, 124, 321
WHITTEMORE 85, 105, 122, 123, 203, 220
WHITTENHALL 2, 5, 7, 28, 29, 231
WHITWOOD 98, 197, 202
WICKHAM 261, 270
WICKS 223
WIGHTMAN 54
WILBER 8, 53, 66, 99, 100, 113, 119, 137, 148
WILBUR 63, 95, 132, 145, 191
WILCOX 10, 15, 52, 75, 80, 110, 113, 134, 139, 142, 145, 147, 162, 163, 261, 279, 280, 291, 319, 320, 331, 336, 338, 349, 350
WILDER 126, 162, 238, 272, 289
WILDRICK 27
WILEY 11, 77, 196, 202, 207
WILHELM 17, 29, 69, 175
WILKERSON 254
WILKES 40, 127, 250

WILKINS 202, 240
WILKINSON 354
WILLAGE 1
WILLARD 6, 312
WILLIAMS 6, 12, 45, 59, 75, 98, 101, 103, 104, 106, 109, 121, 122, 147, 157, 167, 168, 171, 175, 184, 187, 192, 214, 219, 232, 237, 249, 256, 258, 269, 276, 296, 310, 328, 339, 341, 347, 348, 351, 352, 354, 357
WILLIAMSON 6, 153, 167
WILLIS 125, 170, 175, 192, 317
WILLISTON 93, 146, 150
WILLOR 312
WILLOUGHBY 26, 353
WILLOUR 58, 67, 68, 84, 156, 216, 327
WILLOVER 168
WILLSON 307
WILLYS 56
WILMARTH 233
WILMERDING 301
WILSON 10, 16, 136, 188, 203, 286, 289, 297, 356
WILTSIE 52
WINCHELL 2
WINFIELD 289
WING 280, 351
WINNAGLE 183
WINSHIP 157
WINSOR 4, 73
WINTERMUTE 158, 352
WINTERS 311
WIRKS 335
WIRT 203
WISE 114
WISNER 71, 100
WISWALL 110
WITHFORD 200
WITTER 262
WIXOM 13, 57, 70, 94, 96, 121, 130, 148, 305, 348, 355
WIXON 298
WIXSON 172
WIXSTED 223
WOHLGEMUTH 109
WOLCOTT 12, 28, 48, 86, 99, 153, 236, 246, 252, 258, 262, 268, 278, 286, 287, 335
WOLF 153, 263
WOLLAGE 224
WOMBOUGH 1, 5, 7, 9, 29, 89, 172
WOOD 9, 76, 79, 91, 108, 109, 123, 137, 159, 198, 221, 227, 241, 260, 279, 288, 294, 298, 299, 302, 305, 330, 336
WOODARD 55, 65, 99, 138, 147, 162, 176, 188, 201, 247, 264, 329
WOODHOUSE 299
WOODRUFF 62, 106, 126, 170, 222, 307, 315, 327
WOODS 46, 48, 82, 133, 136, 173, 187, 206, 238
WOODWARD 63, 68, 87, 113, 290, 342
WOODWORTH 156, 182
WOOLEVER 187, 191, 243, 317, 327
WOOSTER 27
WORMLEY 31, 153, 228
WRIGHT 35, 115, 172, 176, 204, 209, 224, 239, 243, 244, 296, 301, 344

WYCKOFF 335
WYGANT 83, 86, 125, 293, 341, 342, 344
WYLLYS 37
WYMAN 185
YAPLE 204
YEISLEY 108
YOHAN 168
YORK 293
YOST 39, 118, 133, 148, 155, 324
YOUMANS 84, 85, 105
YOUNG 14, 54, 102, 116, 127, 141, 179, 206, 212, 240, 253, 254, 273, 285, 316, 335, 343
YOUNGLOVE 291, 296, 307
YOUNGS 115
ZELIFF 312
ZIELIE 59
ZIELLY 153, 239
ZIMMERMAN 299
ZIRKLEBACH 316
ZUBLER 300

Other Heritage Books by Mary S. Jackson and Edward F. Jackson:

1850 Census for the Town of Howard, Steuben County, New York, and Genealogical Data on the Families Who Lived There

Death Notices from Steuben County, New York Newspapers, 1797-1884

Death Notices from Washington County, New York Newspapers, 1799-1880

Marriage and Death Notices from Schuyler County, New York Newspapers

Marriage and Death Notices from Seneca County, New York Newspapers, 1817-1885

Marriage Notices from Steuben County, New York Newspapers, 1797-1884

Marriage Notices from Washington County, New York Newspapers, 1799-1880

Other Heritage Books by Mary S. Jackson:

Marriages and Deaths from Tompkins County, New York Newspapers

www.ingramcontent.com/pod-product-compliance
Lightning Source LLC
Chambersburg PA
CBHW071950220426
43662CB00009B/1074